Happy Birthday To You all
from
" Janie "

INSIDE ASIA

The Japanese Empire:

1. Japan proper, with 70,000,000 people jammed into an area less than that of California, is bursting outward. Country of discipline, conformity, *Shinto*, imperial ambitions, earthquakes, no humor, a wonderful sense of mimicry, and raw fish. Observe its growing empire, Korea (**2**), where the farmers wear white, Formosa (**3**), which the Japanese call Taiwan, and the southern half of Sakhalin (**4**). Recently Japan took Hainan (**5**), and the Spratly Islands (**6**) far in the south.
7. Manchukuo. This state, as big as pre-Munich Germany and France combined, is Japan's great foothold on the mainland. Ruled by the Kwantung army under the puppet Emperor Henry Pu-yi. Economic experiments in progress. Carved out from China in 1931–32. The opium province of Jehol (**8**) annexed in 1933.
9. Inner Mongolia, above the Great Wall, still being fought over in 1939. Part of it may soon become a new puppet state. "Ruler" is Prince Teh.

Russia in Asia:

10. From the Urals to the Pacific the Soviets are busy: prodigious timber and coal development, new steel towns, Arctic fisheries, gold. Across the Amur river frontier they watch the Japanese balefully. At Vladivostok and Khabarovsk their military machine stands defensively ready. The Japanese, if they attack, will try to push the frontier back to Lake Baikal (**11**), thus free Tokyo from threat of air bombardment. Along the Soviet fringes are a dozen autonomous republics, populated by Mongoloid folk and Buryats, Turkomans, Uzbeks (near Golden Samarkand—**12**). One which has its own postage stamps, and colorful they are, is Tannu Tuva (**13**).
14. Outer Mongolia. Perhaps technically this vast area, over a million square miles, belongs to China. But the Mongolian Peoples Republic rules it in fact, which is to say that it is a Soviet sphere of influence. Bound to the U. S. S. R. by a military pact. The people are nomads, try to sell hides, die of thirst in the Gobi desert.
15. The great, little-known province of Sinkiang (Chinese Turkestan) is in theory under Chinese sovereignty, but China's writ here is pale. Sinkiang is not quite a Russian "sphere of influence," but almost.

The Chinese Republic:

16. Colossal China, the most durable of nations, one of the most finely civilized, resists the "Dwarf Monkeys," which is what the Chinese—when they are impolite—call the Japanese. China stands for charm, intelligence, poise, and a fierce new national spirit to overcome the past few generations of corruption and decay. Methodist Chiang Kai-shek and the great Soong family are its leaders. Population between 400 and 450 million—the biggest in the world. Land of anarchic rivers, ethical religion, famine, the family system, and western imperialism at its most predatory.
17. These are the five northern provinces, those above the Yellow River—Shantung, Chahar, Hopei, Shansi, Suiyuan—which the Japanese are trying to nip off. Scene of heavy fighting, heavier intrigue. Here the Chinese Red Army and its guerrillas have been active.
18. Chungking, in Szechwan, is the present (April, 1939) headquarters of the Generalissimo. He lost Hankow (**19**) and Canton (**20**) last October, but the Japanese have not yet consolidated their gains. The country has risen *behind* Japan's front line. The Chinese have lost most of the coast served by railroads, as well as the Yangtze valley (**21**) draining to Shanghai. Chinese supplies come chiefly from the Soviet Union via Lanchow (**22**), or from French Indo-China and Burma to Yunnanfu (**23**).
24. Tibet. This is technically part of China, but is in essence a British sphere. Rival imperialisms find their greatest activity in China. A theocratic state, Tibet is complexly ruled by priests.

ASIA
Scale of Miles
0   250   500   750   1000

British Possessions
Under British Influence
Native States in India
Japanese Empire
Under Japanese Influence

EUROPE
EGYPT
AFRICA
Nile R.
Damascus
Amman
Jerusalem
Bagdad
Basra
Mecca   Riad
SAUDI
ARABIA
Aden
BR. SOM.
KENYA

54
57
56
52
55
51
50
45
48
49
47
46

NEW YORK STATE
DRAWN TO SAME SCALE

INSIDE

ASIA

By JOHN GUNTHER
Author of INSIDE EUROPE

HARPER & BROTHERS

NEW YORK AND LONDON 1939

INSIDE ASIA

6-9

SIXTEENTH EDITION

F-O

This Book Is For

JOHNNY

Who Suggested It

TABLE OF CONTENTS

Note

THIS book is an obvious companion, a twin to *Inside Europe*. I wanted to call it *Outside Asia* instead of *Inside Asia*, but my publishers politely overruled me. I hope they are right. My attitude was that in Asia I was "outside" looking in. But this book is, I believe, just as closely written as *Inside Europe*, just as intimately detailed and comprehensive. My approach is the same, and so is my point of view. And I "looked in" under particularly fruitful circumstances.

In 1937-38 I visited every important place I have written about, except Saudi Arabia and the Mongolias. This book has been over two years in the making and is both a reporter's job and a kind of political guide. I traveled around the world, about 30,000 miles, by steamship, railway, airplane, and motor car. In each country I saw most of the leading political personalities. Previously I had been to the Near East four times, as a correspondent for the *Chicago Daily News*.

Inside Europe was built up on a thread of personality, and so is this book. There are full chapters on The Emperor of Japan, Generalissimo Chiang Kai-shek, the Soong Sisters, Manuel Quezon, Mr. Gandhi, Jawaharlal Nehru, the Shah of Persia, King Ibn Saud, and Dr. Weizmann, as well as a multitude of passages on less eminent figures. Some critics thought I put too much emphasis on personality in *Inside Europe*. I never intended to minimize the influence of political or economic factors. I wanted simply to draw attention to personality too. Politics in Asia, are, by and large, more concerned with mass populations than individuals—despite the importance of the individuals—and in this book the reader will find a considerably closer balance between politics, economics, religion, and personality.

Japan, a powerful and dangerous nation, the third country in the great trinity of so-called Have-Nots, is waging war in China. This war, in its origins, its course of events, its possible future, is of the greatest consequence to us in the West. In April 1939 it seemed that Europe too would be defaced by warfare. *It is the same war.* Japan, Germany, Italy, are allies. If a general conflagration comes, we cannot neglect or ignore any sector.

Asia, indeed, the most complex of continents, is inextricably dovetailed with the rest of the world. Problems of the Pacific involve the United States acutely. The Soviet Union is closely associated with

Asiatic problems, and so is France. What is happening in China concerns everyone in Europe, just as what is happening in Albania and Poland concerns Japan. And Great Britain, as everyone knows, is the greatest Asiatic power.

To a certain extent *Inside Europe* was a study of nationalism and the internecine nationalisms of Europe. *Inside Asia* is analogously a study of that development of nationalism known as Imperialism. For years Asia was devoured by imperialist western powers. And now the Japanese, who are wonderful imitators, have borrowed and developed the technique of imperialism, and have turned imperialist themselves. This book is a sketch of both the old and new imperialisms in Asia: the Dutch in the East Indies, the French in Indo-China, the Americans in the Philippines, the Japanese in Manchukuo and China, and the British almost everywhere.

Inside Europe began with Hitler, then traced a ring around Germany, seeking to explore ramifications of German policy everywhere in Europe. Similarly *Inside Asia* begins with Japan and then, for at least half its course, follows the path of Japanese policy. After Japan we visit Manchukuo, that strange state of 30,000,000 guinea pigs; touch on Asiatic Russia briefly, proceed to China with its inundation of peoples and problems; progress downward to the Philippines, Malaya, and Siam; turn westward to the gigantic complex of India, its peoples, rulers, and frontiers; inspect Iran, Iraq and the Middle East; and conclude in the Near East and Palestine.

J. G.

INSIDE ASIA

Chapter 1
The Emperor of Japan

The King's leavings are better than the Lord's bounty.

—CERVANTES

EVEN the Emperor of Japan is a human being. He eats, sleeps, and has an individual life like the rest of us. He was born; he begat children; he will die. But his human characteristics, interesting as they may be, are overwhelmingly outweighed by the factor of divinity. The Emperor of Japan was "born": but assuredly not to a tradition shared by merely mortal men. The Emperor of Japan will "die": but his death, like his birth, will be no more than an episode in a cosmic, eternal process. He is human, but also he is virtually a god.

The Japanese Emperor, being divine, is more than the head of the state. He *is* the state. Sovereignty is believed by the orthodox to reside actually *in* the person of the Emperor, not in any organ of government. The Emperor and the people are one. All Japanese, not merely the Emperor, consider themselves to be of divine or semi-divine origin; the Emperor is the ruling deity, a kind of father, uniting the entire population in his august, impersonal, and radiant being.

The godlike qualities of the Emperor of Japan are difficult concepts to describe. First, we plunge at once into mysticism. But no understanding of Japan is possible until the position of the Throne is made reasonably clear, which is quite above and beyond that of any throne in the West, largely because of the religious factor. Second, we risk offending the Japanese, to whom the person of the Emperor is not a fit subject for description.

The veneration, the indubitable awe, with which loyal and patriotic Japanese—which means a very considerable proportion indeed of the Japanese nation—hold the Emperor is a phenomenon unique in contemporary politics. To westerners it may be a baffling phenomenon. But most westerners, who inherit the tradition of Aristotle and Newton, who believe in the validity of scientific inquiry, in the free play of the free mind, in the rational characteristics of experience, will find a very great deal that is baffling in the mysticism of Japan.

By mysticism I do not mean self-delusion. I mean merely the instinct of a people to accept freely phenomena which cannot be accounted for by purely intellectual processes.

. . . .

The bulk of the Japanese people have great reverence for their Emperor, but very few have ever seen him. This is because they are supposed to cast down their eyes when, in some ceremonial procession, he approaches. They are not, strictly speaking, permitted to *look* at him—though doubtless some bold spirits peek. The origin of this practice is the mythological belief that direct view of the Son of Heaven will cause blindness.

Portraits of the Emperor are comparatively rare. By common custom the face is covered with tissue or cellophane.

When the Emperor travels, even if it is for hundreds of miles across Japan, every window shade along the entire route must be drawn—which necessitates a good deal of work by the assiduous police.

No one must look *down* on the Emperor. The tower of the new police building in Tokyo has never been completed, because it was discovered that windows therein might give a view of the imperial gardens. (On the other hand, modern exigencies have compelled modifications of this rule; for instance, when the Emperor opens the Diet, journalists in the gallery do look down on him.)

In February 1939 the Japanese police forbade a production of Hamlet, because its "dangerous thoughts are likely to cause disrespect for royalty."

Time magazine published a front-cover portrait of the Emperor in 1936. The editors were asked to appeal to their readers not to handle the magazine upside down, or to place any object on it. The cartoonist William Gropper once caricatured the Emperor in *Vanity Fair*—not very savagely. The Japanese Embassy in Washington immediately lodged an official protest. The Japanese issue of *Fortune*, an admirable job, was suppressed in Japan not so much for its contents, but because on the cover it printed the imperial chrysanthemum, a precious Japanese symbol. (Curiously *Fortune* gave the chrysanthemum fifteen petals instead of the correct sixteen. Or perhaps this was a clever—but unsuccessful—dodge to avoid offense, by means of deliberate inaccuracy.)

When a member of the imperial family visits the Yamato Hotel in

Mukden, he occupies the entire third floor, which is the most comfortable. The fourth floor is then cleared of other guests.

A distinguished foreign ambassador asked his Japanese secretary his opinion of the Emperor's appearance (which was quite good and normal) after both had attended an imperial garden party. The secretary refused to reply on the grounds that a reply would be blasphemy.

Once a traffic policeman misdirected the imperial procession during a village ceremony. He killed himself in shame. (It is not true, however, that the Emperor's chauffeur or locomotive driver must commit *hara-kiri* if their conveyances are late.)

Doctors were not allowed to touch the bodies of the Emperor's father and grandfather, except with silk gloves. The legend is that even the court tailor had to measure the late Emperor's clothes from a respectful distance—which made a good fit somewhat difficult.

A very well known jurist and professor, Dr. Minobe, who had held the chair in government at Tokyo Imperial University for thirty years, lost his job and narrowly escaped assassination because it was discovered that in a book published twenty years before he had referred to the Throne as merely an "organ" of the state.

Details like these, which are chosen from among dozens available, are sufficient preliminary indication of both the brightness and the impenetrable opacity of the aura that surrounds the Emperor. We must try to define this aura, to circumscribe it. One hesitates to affront Japanese susceptibilities; what follows in this chapter is written with proper deference. The Emperor is the living symbol, the emblem, the personification, of Japanese destiny, which may be the destiny of much of Asia, and which demands complete and impartial investigation.

So, with the Emperor of Japan, we begin this circumnavigation of a continent.

Son of the Sun

His Imperial Majesty Hirohito, one hundred twenty-fourth emperor of Japan in an unbroken dynasty, was born on April 29, 1901, in Tokyo at 10:10 P.M. He was educated by tutors, in the Peers' School, and on a trip to Europe. He became regent in 1922, when his father was overcome by illness. In 1924 he married Princess Nagako Kuni, by whom he has six children. On Christmas Day, 1926, Hirohito ascended the throne, and in 1928 was formally enthroned.

First let us tackle the name. Japan has had only one dynasty in 2,599 years, according to Japanese mythologists and historians; thus no family or dynastic name is necessary. Literally Hirohito, the given name of the Emperor, which is written in two ideographs (symbols) in Japanese, means "magnanimous" and "exalted." The second ideograph in the name, "hito" (exalted), appears in the names of most emperors. Only the first ideograph (in English each ideograph is a pair of syllables) varies. No one else in Japan may use the syllables "hito" in his name; the law does not forbid it, but implacable custom does. Rumor is that a peasant in a remote district once named his son "Hirohito"; when he discovered that this was the Emperor's name, he killed his family and committed *hara-kiri*.

Immediately an emperor begins his reign, he chooses another name. This is the name of the reign, while he lives; when he dies, *he* becomes known by this name. Thus the last emperor, Hirohito's father, was named (at birth) Yoshihito; now he is called "Taisho," the name he adopted for his reign. The present emperor calls his reign "Showa," which means—quaintly enough!—"Radiant Peace." After his death his reign will be called the Showa period, and he himself will be known, not as Hirohito, but as Showa. Years in Japan are calculated in these periods; 1939 is Showa 13.

Japanese never refer to the Emperor by his name. To do so is to commit sacrilege. They never, in fact, even mention him, if they can avoid doing so; when they must, they refer simply to the Throne, or say *Heika Denka* (Sublime Majesty), or *Tenshi-Sama* (Son of Heaven). After an emperor is dead he is called the "Tenno," a posthumous title. Of course, Japanese continue to venerate and indeed worship him, as they do all ancestors, after death as well as before.

The term "Mikado" is never used in Japan to identify the Emperor. Such usage of "Mikado" is purely foreign. Literally "Mikado" means "gate" with an honorific prefix; hence "Gate of Heaven," which is analogous to terminology in our experience, like Sublime Porte. Japanese sometimes use "Mikado" as an indirect way of referring to the Emperor impersonally, as some one in London might say "the Court" to indicate George VI. But he is *never* called "the" Mikado.

Emperors seldom even write their own names; names were not, in fact, used on official proclamations until 1868. Now the Emperor signs some papers, using "Hirohito" in Japanese ideographs, but as a rule a seal is used, not a signature. When a law is promulgated in the official gazette, two characters meaning simply "Honorable Name" are printed to indicate the seal. Once or twice in bestowing decorations to foreigners the Emperor has signed his name in English.

There have been three emperors in the modern period, i.e., since the "Meiji Restoration" in 1868, when Japan reëntered the world with such a rush and push as the world has seldom seen before. The Emperor who was "restored," that is, liberated from control by the Shoguns (dictators), was Mutsuhito, known now as Meiji. He was the present Emperor's grandfather, and one of the great men of Asia; he ruled from 1868 to 1912—forty-four tremendous years. His son, Yoshihito or Taisho, the present Emperor's father, was a lesser man.

But the family of Hirohito, the present Emperor, goes back considerably more than these two generations. Indeed, it goes back in uninterrupted succession for 2,599 years, all the way to 660 B.C. when the first Emperor Jimmu[1] founded the dynasty! It goes back even further than that, for Jimmu himself was a fifth-generation descendant of the Sun Goddess, the chief Japanese deity, who was herself a descendant of other deities. The picturesque legend is that the Sun Goddess sent Jimmu to Japan to found "her" dynasty of chosen people there; it is, of course, pure mythology, since written records of Japanese history do not exist before the fifth century A.D. But a Japanese historian would lose his job for saying this. The point to make is that the orthodox Japanese like to believe that the mythology, even if it is mythology, is true. For instance the actual *date* (February 11 by our reckoning) of Jimmu's accession is celebrated as one of the great Japanese national holidays. The Japanese are a thorough and methodical people, with considerable sense of detail.

The dynasty has never died out. It has survived 2,599 years. One reason is a fertility natural to the Japanese. Another is that in Japan adoption is legally the equivalent of actual kinship. Another is that, until recent times, a considerable number of Japanese emperors had concubines; monogamy was not established till 1889. At any rate there are to-day no less than fifteen different branches of the royal house. Women may not inherit the throne, but there is no danger that the males will give out. The remarkable thing is not so much that the imperial line survived naturally, but that it was never over-

[1] One of Jimmu's female successors, presciently enough, had the nice name "Jingo."

thrown. During many centuries the emperors were shadows, utterly
without temporal power, but no Japanese tyrant, Shogun, or mayor-
of-the-palace ever dared to change the dynasty.

Japanese emperors are not crowned. They simply accede to the
succession. There is no crown. At once the new emperor issues his
first imperial rescript. That of Hirohito, following time-honored
phraseology, began as follows:

Having succeeded, through the benign influence of Our Imperial
Ancestors, to the Throne of a lineal succession unbroken for ages
eternal, and having assumed the power to reign over and govern the
Empire, We have now performed the solemnity of the accession to the
Throne. It is Our resolve to observe the fundamental rules of the State,
to cultivate the inherited virtues, and to maintain intact the glorious
tradition set by Our Ancestors.

The equivalent of coronation is the great festival of enthronement
(*Go-Tairei*) and the food festival (*Daijo-sai*), held in Kyoto, the
old capital, after the accession. These are a combination of secular
and religious rites—just as is a coronation in Westminster Abbey—
but the religious element is more pronounced. In the eloquent words
of Hugh Byas (Enthronement Number, *Japan Advertiser*), "We
see him [the Emperor] as a Priest-King entering into mystic communion with the spirit of the race. This mystic and religious element
runs like a nerve through the ceremonies and explains their power
to awaken the deepest national instincts in the Japanese people. They
are a living link between past and present and not merely a picturesque survival."

First in circumstances of great ceremony the Emperor approaches a
small, simple Shinto shrine and "informs the spirits of his ancestors
that he has ascended the throne." Second, appearing in dull orange
robes ("the earliest color of the rising sun"), he listens to the official
communication from the prime minister announcing the accession.
The scene is tremendous; nothing in Europe or even Asia can
rival it. "The living world is informed of what previously had been
announced to the world of spirits." Finally, quite alone, the Emperor
celebrates a kind of harvest rite, by giving food to the gods, and
communing in a lonely hut with his heavenly kin.

Three paramount symbols of kingship and divinity play their rôle
in these rites, the Mirror, the Necklace, and the Sword, which the
Sun Goddess "gave" Jimmu as symbols of sovereignty. Of these the

mirror is the most sacrosanct, because in it one sees the soul of the sun; even the Emperor is supposed never actually to look at it; in a black box, bound with white silk, it reposes in the great shrine at Ise. A replica of the mirror, however, is kept in that room of the Tokyo palace known as the Kashkidokoro, or Place of Awe. According to legend the mirror was the supreme instrument of warfare in the early days; its reflection caught the august and terrible eye of the sun, and blinded all adversaries.

The necklace or chaplet, composed of stones—rather like our wampum—is kept in Tokyo. The sword exists only in replica, since the original was "lost" in battle in feudal times. When a new emperor accedes to the throne, his first privilege is to accept custody of the sword-replica, the mirror-replica, and the necklace. All three, the supreme holinesses of Japan, go with him to Kyoto for the enthronement; but the *original* mirror never leaves the shrine at Ise, near Nagoya, which is the most hallowed place in Japan. It was put there by an emperor in the year A.D. 3.

The shrine of Ise, that of the Sun Goddess herself, is visited by the Emperor on great occasions. He goes there ceremoniously to inform the Sun Goddess, to report to her as it were, of imposing events. He went after his father's death; both before and after his trip to Europe; after his marriage, and so on; if Japan should *declare* a war, he would go again. All cabinet ministers or other high officials must at once go to Ise, pray there, and *notify* the Sun Goddess of their appointment. This is their first duty. Some years ago a cabinet minister named Mori, visiting the shrine, inadvertently committed the sacrilege of lifting its curtain with his walking stick. He was assassinated, and his murderer exalted as a hero.

I quote once more from the Enthronement Edition of the *Japan Advertiser*:

Not only is the Shrine of Ise a holy spot in the religious sense, but it is the visible symbol of the nation's whole being. The Japanese attitude toward it is one of *makoto*, a word which can not be accurately rendered into English. Patriotism, nationalism, Emperor worship, the attitude toward the throne, are words or phrases used for *makoto*, but each of them is very inexact. Loyalty, filial piety, the emphasis on the family rather than on the individual, are still other attempts to put *makoto* in English. *Makoto* embraces all of these, but no one of them has the exact connotation to the Japanese consciousness that it has to the American or European. Foreign thought does not comprehend the reverence, loving loyalty, respectful *kinship* of the Japanese toward his Emperor, and therefore toward the nation, and therefore toward himself as a part of the nation.

A few months ago I stood near the entrance of the great Meiji shrine in Tokyo. Few things can be more interesting than to watch Japanese prayer. It was a rainy afternoon, but ladies in kimonos, old gentlemen in frock coats walked along the shiningly neat grass, up the combed gravel path, and stood there, briefly, in the rain. It is all done outdoors. The devotee approaches, bows, then sharply claps his hands. This is to summon the spirit of the ancestor with whom he wishes to confer. A few moments then of conversation with the ancestor—in a quick, urgent, audible whisper. Then another bow, copper pennies tossed across the straw mat, a final bow, and departure backward.

When I arrived in Japan I distinguished myself for naïveté by asking what I thought was a simple question: "If the Emperor is himself a god, to whom does *he* pray?"

He prays, of course, to his forbears. But inadvertently I had raised a complex theological point. Is the Emperor himself actually a god? Of course he is divine, but is he "a god"? Authorities vary. By some orthodox Japanese he is considered definitely to be, in his own person, "an actual, living Deity."[2] Others say merely that he is to the Japanese mind "the supreme Being in the Cosmos of Japan as God is in the universe to a pantheistic philosopher."

Shinto, the national religion, is a difficult concept to define. Recently a government commission spent three years trying to do so, and then gave up. In essence it is simply worship of Japan—the nation itself. It exists in two forms, secular and theological; all Japanese patriots are believers in Shinto, but they may be Buddhists—or even Christians—at the same time. Its distinguishing mark is a combination of ancestor worship and patriotism; all Japanese have a common descent from the Sun Goddess, and they venerate their ancestors; all may derivatively be said to be members of the same great family, with the Emperor at its head. There are eighty *million* gods in the Japanese Pantheon. Every soldier killed in battle is enshrined, revered

---

[2] See W. H. Chamberlin's admirable *Japan Over Asia*, p. 275, the best book on contemporary Japan.

by his descendants, and becomes, if not an actual god, at least a definite figure in the general religious structure.

In his beautiful and indispensable book, *Japan: A Short Cultural History,* Sir George Sansom says:

At the core of all Shinto ceremonial is the idea of purity, and at the core of all Shinto belief is the idea of fertility. . . . In its earliest days the religion which, much later, came to be known as Shinto, the Way of the Gods, seems to have been a polytheism of a crude and exuberant type. . . . To say that primitive Japanese conceived of all natural objects as harbouring a spirit, or that their religion was an animistic nature worship, is to apply exact terms to things which are too vague and various for simple definition.

The chief point to make about Shinto is its comparatively recent *revival* as a political as well as a religious force. Like the temporal power of the Emperor himself, Shinto was in eclipse until the Meiji Restoration in 1868. Gradually the architects of the Restoration[3] discovered the extreme practical use of such religio-patriotic symbolism. The Emperor, as head of the nation, was also head of a vast single *family*, if Shinto doctrine was to be believed; thus—to put it crudely —Shinto could be made to serve an extremely pertinent political aim, namely, the conception of indissoluble unity of the people. Japanese worship of the Emperor has existed since the earliest times, but it is extraordinarily significant that this worship has been latterly much reinforced and reëmphasized. For instance, the Emperor Meiji was the first *recent* emperor to pray on his accession at the Ise shrine.

When you ask an intelligent, modern-minded Japanese, a research student in biology for instance, or a political journalist who went abroad to school, if he believes the Emperor of Japan to be divine, he will probably reply—if the door is shut—that he does not. The official story of the Emperor's descent from the Sun Goddess is too difficult to accept. But most Japanese, even the minority with highly modern minds, believe it to be a good and valuable thing that the bulk of Japanese *do* believe in imperial sanctity. Thus even the skeptics encourage the mythology. And they serve their purpose best by behaving as if they believed in the mythology too.

Thus we reach a cardinal point. The divinity of the Emperor is a political weapon of great potency in the hands of those who rule Japan.

[3] In the next chapter I discuss this event.

Personal Life of the Emperor

The Emperor lives to-day in the inner, hidden halls of Kyujo palace in the center of Tokyo, one of the most formidably picturesque buildings in the world. For centuries it was the fortress and castle of the Shoguns; the imperial family took it over on being restored to temporal power in 1868. With great pictorial impact it symbolizes the austere and magnificent phenomenon it houses. A broad outer moat (once there were three separate moats), with water of iridescent green, reflecting the gnarled pines alongside, bounds a tremendous granite wall. The bulwark of this irregularly circular wall, some miles in length, is interrupted by forty gates, and by a series of commanding towers. The wall is built of very large square gray bowlders, set against a bank of earth without mortar or plaster, so that it is earthquake proof. Inside the wall are the green lawns, the gardens, the villas, the palace, and the various subsidiary paraphernalia of the imperial establishment. Entrance, except to specially invited guests, is forbidden.

In summer Hirohito and his family go as a rule to Hayama, a watering place near Kamakura, about thirty miles from Tokyo. Here the Emperor swims (he is an excellent swimmer) and otherwise relaxes. Often he collects specimens of marine biology for laboratory work. His beach is, of course, private, but in the adjacent area other male bathers must wear tops to their suits, which is not obligatory elsewhere in Japan. The imperial family has other villas scattered through eastern Japan—perhaps fifty in all. The Emperor seldom visits them.

His routine of work, his official occupations, are determined by ancient custom and are severely circumscribed. Twenty-one times each year there are ceremonies of worship to conduct. Once a year the Emperor attends services at the Yasakuni shrine, where the Japanese military dead are enshrined; once a year he attends the graduation exercises of the military and naval academies; he attends the opening of the Diet and similar ceremonies; he is consulted by the prime minister and the army chieftains. He receives newly accredited foreign ambassadors, and occasionally gives audiences to other distinguished foreigners.

The presentation of letters of credence by a new ambassador is an extremely formal ceremony. The new ambassador is received quite alone. None of his staff enters. He advances, bows three times, and reads his letter. The Emperor then reads his reply. After this there may be a few moments of conversation. The Emperor speaks through an interpreter, who must keep his eyes on the ground, and who *whispers*. The new ambassador then bows again three times, and departs backward.

When the Vice-President of the United States, Mr. Garner, visited Tokyo en route to the Philippines, he told friends in his jovial way that, when he was received by the Emperor, he was going to take an American dollar watch from his pocket, and say, "Your Majesty, here is *one* thing you folks can't imitate and undersell!" Horrified, the Americans in Japan told Mr. Garner that he must under no circumstances do this, since, if he did, the Emperor's aides in the room would consider that the Emperor had been insulted and would have to commit suicide. In any case Garner gave up the idea—after finding several Japanese watches that *were* imitation Ingersolls selling for thirty cents.

Three times in his reign the Emperor has received foreign journalists.[4] One, however, Jules Sauerwein, was received not as a newspaper man but merely as a distinguished French visitor; the other two, Ward Price of the *Daily Mail* and Roy W. Howard of the Scripps-Howard newspapers, got some moments of amiable conversation but not much news. American editors offer a standing $100 bonus to any Tokyo correspondent who interviews the Emperor. None ever has.

Twice a year, however, the Emperor gives a large garden party—a cherry blossom party in April and a chrysanthemum party in November—to which journalists are invited, among the 7,000 other guests. This is at variance with the tradition of other royal courts, where newspaper men are as a rule excluded. The invitation contains no R.S.V.P.: it is a command. Guests assemble in formal afternoon dress, and the Emperor and Empress walk slowly through the garden from the imperial pavilion. Hats may be worn by gentlemen (of course they are doffed as the Emperor passes), but not overcoats, no matter how cold the weather. Until recently the old-style frock coat was *de rigueur*, because it covered more of a person than a cutaway, and hence was considered to be more modest. The garden parties were

[4] Isaac Marcosson of the *Saturday Evening Post* also saw him, but when he was Crown Prince, not Emperor.

canceled in 1937 and 1938 on account of the China war, or, as the Japanese say, "incident."

Very occasionally the Emperor gives a dinner party, for instance if a visitor like a British royal prince is in Tokyo. At a big banquet, the Emperor sits alone on a small dais, higher than his guests. If the party is small, his chair is at the normal level. The Emperor knows a little English and French, but he converses in Japanese through an interpreter. Guests at an imperial party, by universal Japanese custom, must take food away with them. In the old days they were supposed to carry away fruit or rice, as symbol of the Emperor's hospitality; now a small box of cake is given each guest. This should be carefully preserved. Food, any food, is precious in Japan; historically it is a hungry country, and the custom derives from this. Ministers and ambassadors, once a year, receive small teacups as gifts; you can tell how long any diplomat has been in Tokyo by the number of these cups carefully and conspicuously placed in his dining-room.

The Emperor plays tennis and golf—persistent rumors describe a nine-hole golf course inside the palace wall, but no one has ever seen it—but his chief hobby is marine biology. (His golf score, by the way, is a zealously guarded secret.) Visiting biologists of distinction see him fairly regularly, though the visits are never officially announced. Several rooms of the palace serve as a laboratory, and the Emperor is happiest when he is working with his microscope, inspecting minute growths and organisms, which he likes to collect himself. Photography is another hobby, as it is of almost all Japanese. He likes to ride occasionally, and his white stallion, *Shirayuki* (White Snow), is famous.

He is up at six as a rule, and retires early. He neither drinks nor smokes. His health is stated to be good, though he was frail as a boy. He is, as everyone knows, shortsighted. One curious item is that he is said never to wear any clothes twice, not even underwear. The used clothing is given to minor officials, provincial administrators and the like, and is a precious gift. When he must leave the palace for some ceremony, he is driven in a maroon limousine, a color reserved for the imperial family; no other maroon automobiles are allowed in Japan. Extreme precautions are taken to guard him. Streets are shut off; every building on the route is rigidly inspected.

The Emperor had several tutors as a child, one of whom, General Nogi, who captured Port Arthur in the Russo-Japanese war, committed suicide with his wife as a mark of devotion when the Emperor Meiji died. Thus when still a child the Emperor was brought in contact with a striking Japanese tradition. A subsequent tutor was Admiral Togo, the greatest Japanese hero of the age. The Emperor, it is recorded, showed marked talent as a schoolboy; one of his early enthusiasms was Æsop, and before he was ten he was composing fables in the Æsop manner. At eleven he began keeping a diary, and has kept it methodically ever since. When, at thirteen or fourteen, he was asked what person in Japanese history impressed him most, he nominated the Emperor Kameyama, who prayed that his life be sacrificed to spare Japan from the Mongol invasion. Asked for his favorite poem, he quoted one which says: "The light of the sun and moon withholds no favors; they shine equally upon all."

In 1921, when heir apparent, he went abroad—something that no Japanese royal prince had done for 2581 years. When his departure was announced, one hundred Tokyo boys offered to commit *hara-kiri* jointly, if he would give up the trip. He went. Presumably the boys are still alive.

Most of the existing anecdotes about the Emperor—there are not many—derive from this period of travel. Aboard a warship a pet monkey put a screw in his mouth. No one could make him disgorge it—until Hirohito had the bright idea of giving him a piece of sugar instead. In the London underground Hirohito, who is not allowed to touch money, had no ticket, and replied to the rebuke of the conductor with "exemplary sang-froid." And so on. In Gibraltar the Prince bet on the races. He won. "With rare presence of mind and exquisite tact," wrote a Japanese witness quoted by *Time*, "His Imperial Highness took the bundle of notes, handing it at once to Admiral Oguri so that it might be properly dealt with."

Earnest and conscientious—courage and tranquillity are adduced by Japanese as his other outstanding characteristics—the Emperor continues with his studies even to-day. Lecturers on various subjects, specialists in their fields, which may include art, economics, zoölogy, foreign literature, come to the palace at regular intervals for what are in effect regular courses of instruction. The names of the professors and details of their teaching are a strict secret.

Cautiously—very cautiously—attempts are being made to "humanize" the Emperor. He has never spoken on the radio, and has never been photographed inspecting workers' dwellings or even greeting winners at athletic meets, but gradually—very gradually—he is being presented to the Japanese people as a human as well as a divine being. For instance, statements were recently issued by the Imperial Household, an unprecedented occurrence, mentioning the arduousness of His Majesty's inspection of troops, his assiduous work in politics, and describing in "warm, human, and intimate" terms his daily routine and régime.

Emperor as Poet

Every New Year's Day the poetry bureau of the Imperial Household announces the results of the annual poetry competition, and the winning poems are read aloud with time-honored pageantry. All subjects of the Empire of Japan, without regard to rank or station, may submit a poem of the *tanka* variety, which means that it must consist of thirty-one syllables, on a given subject, every year. The Emperor and members of the imperial family always write poems in association with the competition, though they do not take prizes, being *hors concours*; the Emperor's poem is read first, and then the efforts of the ten prize winners. Normally about 17,000 poems are submitted each year. But last year 30,000 poems came in, partly, it was thought, because of the number of soldiers in the field, who have the ear of His Majesty through the circumstances of this event, and by no other.

The Emperor's poem in 1936 was:

> As I
> was visiting
> the Shino Point in Kii
> clouds were drifting far
> over the Sea.

In 1938 he wrote:

> Peaceful
> is morning in the shrine garden;
> World conditions it is hoped
> will also be
> peaceful.

And like a subterranean hiss the word went through Japan, quite without other basis: the Emperor is unhappy because there is a war; the Emperor wants the soldiers to come home; the Emperor wants peace.

Richer Than Crœsus?

From one point of view, even though traditionally he never handles money, the Emperor of Japan is beyond doubt the richest individual in the world. This is because he owns Japan. The entire country is his. The statement may seem astounding, but Japanese authorities bear it out. For instance, the words of a cabinet minister named Uyehara, author of *Political Development of Japan*: "From the Emperor everything emanates; in him everything subsists; there is nothing on the soil of Japan existent independent of him. He is the sole *owner* of the Empire."

This conception, even though acknowledged by Japanese law, is not strictly adhered to; much of the forest land of Japan is the actual property of the Imperial House, and is exploited as such; the agricultural land—though theoretically belonging to the Emperor—is in practice the property of individual landowners. In the old days the emperors allotted agricultural land to the feudal lords, who in turn let it to peasant occupants. These peasants still hold it. Japan is the country par excellence of small peasant landholders. There are few big farms, few big estates.

The actual civil list is not abnormally high—4,500,000 yen ($1,350,-000) per year. But of course the imperial family has its private investments. When Prince Ito went to Berlin to get Bismarck's advice about the Japanese Constitution, the old Prussian is supposed to have said that the monarch must be independently rich if the monarchy was to work on a constitutional pattern. The exact extent, variety, and amount of imperial investments are not authentically known. But good authorities agree that the House is the third or fourth greatest capital enterprise in the kingdom, and owns shares in a great number of private industries.

Commonly it is said that the House owns the Imperial Hotel where almost all visitors to Tokyo reside. This is denied in Japan, however. It is also assumed that imperial investments are very heavy in such companies as the South Manchuria railway, the great N. Y. K. shipping line, and so on. But no one in Tokyo will say a word. Late in 1938 the Emperor gave the Bank of Japan seventy solid gold articles, to encourage others to do likewise. But his advisers must have cautious minds financially, since it was stated that the gold, after two years, might be "redeemed."

Imperial Family

Hirohito is almost unique among emperors; his marriage was a love match. A love match, moreover, in the teeth of a convention established thirteen centuries ago.

At a reception in Tokyo the youthful Crown Prince met Princess Nagako, eldest daughter of Prince Kuniyoshi Kuni. The young Princess was certainly of excellent blood; her mother, for instance, was a member of the Satsuma clan, one of the two clans that made the Meiji restoration. But—the Princess Nagako was *not* directly a member of the great and distinguished Fujiwara family, which, by tradition 1,300 years old, was the sole family group in Japan from which empresses might be chosen. Nevertheless young Hirohito fell in love with her, and the marriage was arranged. There was very serious opposition among the orthodox; wounded feelings were salved, however, by the fact that the Princess Nagako, though not directly a member of one of five eligible lines of Fujiwaras, did have remote Fujiwara blood, which is indeed shared by most of the aristocracy of Japan.

The Empress is an exceptionally pretty woman. Between her betrothal and marriage she made a good many public appearances; for instance, at such functions as art exhibitions, teas at the Tokyo Woman's Club, and so on. In those days she usually wore native-style kimono; since the enthronement she appears almost always in western dress. But her public appearances nowadays are very rare. The Empress was born in 1903, and thus is two years younger than His Majesty. She is an accomplished musician. Following the Russo-Japanese border incident in 1938 she wrote a poem, and presented it with a box of candy to the families of each of the Japanese dead.

Six children have been born to the throne. The first three, one of whom died, were daughters. Vast pleasure surged through Japan with the birth of a boy, the Crown Prince Tsugu, on December 23, 1933. Since then another boy, Prince Yoshi, has been born. The eldest daughter, Princess Teru, now thirteen, is a student at the Peeresses' School, a long-legged youngster who is seen occasionally in middy uniform. Recently—enormous concession—she was permitted to take a street car ride alone. (But no one else was allowed in the street car!)

The Crown Prince has his own household. By ancient custom he left the palace of the Emperor and Empress at the age of three, and moved into his own establishment, which is in the grounds of another Tokyo royal residence, the Omiya "detached" palace. He visits his parents constantly, but does not live with them. He is to enter the kindergarten of the Peers' School next year.

A very remarkable member of the imperial family is the Empress Dowager Sadako, widow of the Emperor Taisho and mother of Hirohito. It was she, by common consent, who supported her son when he insisted on marrying the lady of his choice; it was she who fought off the great court nobles, like Prince Yamagata, who bitterly opposed the marriage. The Empress Dowager, an accomplished old lady with keen political sense, is still a power, though she is no longer conspicuous publicly. She has received few foreigners since Taisho died. It is in her palace that the present Crown Prince lives, though technically the boy has an independent house.[5]

The Emperor's first brother, H. I. H. Prince Chichibu, a lively personage is fond of sports and travel, democratic by instinct, informal, and very popular with the army. His wife, Princess Setsuko, was daughter of Tsuneo Matsudaira, then Japanese Ambassador to Washington and now Minister of the Imperial Household. Matsudaira is a commoner, though a member of one of the greatest families of Japan; the daughter, before her marriage, was adopted by a titled cousin in the same family in order to give her a fitting rank. The Chichibus have no children; it would, of course, have been considered unfortunate if the brother had had a son before the Emperor. Prince Chichibu visited Europe in 1937, and was a guest of Adolf Hitler at the Nuremberg party congress—a perhaps significant development. Recently it was announced that he returned from the southern front in China "well-tanned." Others there got a tanning of a different kind.

Two younger brothers of the Emperor, Prince Takamatsu, born in 1905, and Prince Mikasa, born in 1915, have so far been inconspicuous. Prince Takamatsu was married in 1930, into the family of the last Shoguns, but like Chichibu has no children. Prince Mikasa

---

[5] The Empress Dowager was a member of the Kujo line and a proper Fujiwara. By Fujiwara tradition she, like other Kujo princesses, was taken from her parents at the age of seven *days,* and put in charge for five years of peasant farmers near Tokyo, who treated her exactly as one of their own children. She was carried on the back of the peasant foster-mother, who worked in the rice fields.

became a sub-lieutenant of cavalry in 1938. The titular chiefs of both army and navy are imperial princes; it was considered a striking innovation when both received their appointments in 1932. They have ranks equivalent to Field Marshals, though their duties are largely nominal. Prince Haruhito Kanin, the chief of the army general staff, was the sixteenth son of old Prince Kunii Fushimi, and is an uncle of the Empress. He was educated in France, and has strong French leanings. The chief of the navy general staff, Prince Hiroyasu Fushimi, born in 1875, comes of a family founded by the ninety-third emperor, and is a distant cousin of the ruler.

The Imperial Household maintains a large secretarial staff; in fact 5,000 employees work in the palace, and eleven pages of the official handbook are necessary to name the chief officials, whereas the Foreign Office fills only ten. One group of functionaries is in charge of the imperial forests, another of the orchestra which plays old court music. There are 121 imperial mausoleums in Japan, all of which have keepers; the tomb of one emperor, incidentally, has never been found. Another odd point is that whereas Hirohito is one hundred twenty-fourth emperor, his father Taisho was officially the one hundred twenty-second. The explanation is that, in 1926, it was decided to include in the imperial line an obscure emperor of the fourteenth century who abdicated after a brief reign.

If one asks if the present Emperor, despite the comprehensiveness of his establishment and the great number of his imperial relations, has any really close and intimate friends, the answer is No.

"L'Etat, C'est Moi!"

By terms of the Japanese Constitution promulgated in 1889, the Emperor has legal powers far exceeding those of a normal "constitutional" monarch. He has (like most heads of states) supreme command of army and navy and is empowered to declare war and make peace; but also he may "determine the organization and peace standing of the army and navy," he may convoke or prorogue the parliament, he may initiate and veto legislation, and in time of crisis he may suspend the Constitution.

But the point is also severely established in Japan that the Emperor is outside politics. He may not, by the rule of unchallengeable precedent, participate actively in political affairs. When, for instance, the military coup d'état in February, 1936, threatened the existence of the state, many people thought that the Emperor should step in; had he faced the mutineers on his white horse, they might have instantly dispersed. But he did not do so. His advisers presumably prevailed upon him not to do so. Even at such a moment, it was inconceivable that he himself should do something.

Thus a paradox. Japan is ruled, not "by" the Emperor, but in the name of the Emperor. The Emperor is a man, as we have seen; he is a god, as we have seen; he is a symbol, as we have seen; he is an embodiment, a projection, of a conglomerate mass of theories and traditions and influences; but is *not* a dictator. He is no Peter the Great, no Stalin, no Cromwell, no Mussolini.

As *Fortune* says, the object of political struggle in Japan is "control of the means of access to the Imperial Person." In blunter terms, "Since the year 536 the sole political question of any realistic significance in Japan has been the question, 'Who is using the Emperor now?'" The Constitution would make it easy for any strong and ambitious emperor to become a legal dictator; but it hasn't happened yet. The Emperor is the state; but other people run it in his name.

Who Are "They"?

I had not been in Japan twenty minutes before I heard a strange use of the word "they." "They," I was told, had decided thus-and-so; "they" had determined to fight the war to a finish. "They" had suggested recent changes in policy; "they" had decided that the country should do this and not that. "They" had arranged the appointment of Prince Konoye, head of the Fujiwara family, as prime minister; "they" were reasonably well satisfied with him.

A recent premier, General Hayashi, went to the palace to obtain the seal of His Imperial Majesty on a routine matter. He came back to tell his cabinet that the cabinet, including himself, was out. "They" had been to Hirohito.

Who are "they"?

This is the most difficult question in Japan. Beside it comparatively stiff questions like, for instance, how Fascist Japan is, are simple. No one knows precisely who "they" are, because "they" themselves do not precisely know. The ruling clique is fluid and elastic; yet its policy retains a constant quality. "They" may be unknown, but what they do is predictable, like a ball rolling slightly from side to side, but returning always to equilibrium. "They" are, in a rough sense, like the College of Cardinals—if Cardinals changed more often.

The Japanese have, of course, an almost fiercely perverse love of indirect government. From 1185 to 1868 the country was ruled by mostly hereditary Shoguns (tyrants or dictators) *behind* the hereditary emperor. This passion for indirection reached excessive and acute forms. Sir George Sansom, for instance, writes of a period in the thirteenth century: "We have thus the astonishing spectacle of a state at the head of which stands a titular emperor whose vestigial functions are usurped by an abdicated emperor, and whose real power is nominally delegated to an hereditary military dictator but actually wielded by an hereditary adviser of that dictator."

As everyone knows, the dominating factor of the "they" of contemporary Japan is the Japanese *army*. This remarkable and indeed unique army I shall consider in Chapter III.

But it is not correct to assume that the Japanese army even now influences the Emperor exclusively. The army is overwhelmingly the most important single factor. But it is not the only factor.

Close to the Emperor there is—still—a group of civilian officials and advisers, who, it goes without saying, often see eye to eye with the army, so that no conflict between them need arise, but who are still a check on unmitigatedly exclusive army domination of policy. They are, in a sense, "referees" between the Throne, the army, and the people.

Let us briefly deal with this palace group, of whom two men at least are of exceptional importance.

The Palace Group

The veteran elder statesman, the last of the Genro (pronounced with a hard "g"), Prince Kimmochi Saionji, comes incontestably first. This old gentleman—he was born in 1849—became a chamberlain of the pre-restoration emperor at the age of six; in 1868 he fought to oust the Shoguns, wearing green armor and carrying a crimson banner; he has been three times prime minister; he spent ten years in France, and knew and admired Gambetta; he is a profound liberal and democrat, at least by Japanese definition; he was ambassador to several European countries, and signed the Versailles treaty; five times he has escaped assassination.

The span of Saionji's long career is peculiarly remarkable in that, as Hugh Byas says, "it telescopes the feudal age and the twentieth century in one lifetime." One of Saionji's earliest public acts was to advocate the training of troops with guns instead of bows and arrows!

Once a well-known foreign journalist arrived in Tokyo and asked if he might see three persons: the Emperor, the Emperor of Manchukuo, and Prince Saionji. The foreign office spokesman listened politely, and said that of the three the hardest to see would be Saionji.

The Genro was the original council of elder statesmen who helped make the Restoration and who thereafter became an unofficial advisory council to the Emperor. The group is not mentioned in the Constitution, and has no legal status; it was a sort of super-shadow cabinet, with the privilege of recommending the choice of prime minister. As members died, successors were *not* appointed. The army wanted the Genro to die out. In the original Genro were the great chieftains and Japan-makers Prince Ito, Prince Inouye, Prince Yamagata, Prince Matsukata. Saionji was the last man to be taken in, and is the only survivor.

At eighty-nine Prince Saionji is too old to take active part in politics. He is sound in health, and lives in a simple cottage in Okitsu, a fishermen's village; but he has not been to Tokyo for some years. He is consulted still—for instance, he approved the appointment of Konoye as prime minister in 1937—but he no longer is in a position to influence affairs directly. Like many Japanese statesmen of the last generation, he knows French perfectly and got most of his political ideas from France. Once he said: "Nothing is worth learning unless it can be learned in Paris." A few years ago he began to read Karl Marx's "Capital" in a French translation. (*Asia,* May, 1936.)

Another Elder Statesman, not quite so historic a figure as Prince Saionji, but who has more contemporary influence, is Count Nobuski Makino, born in 1861 of noble blood (his father was leader of the Satsuma clan), who as Imperial Household Minister for some years gained a very close knowledge of the workings of the palace, and where his influence was profound. Makino and Saionji in effect "ruled" Japan during the illness of the Emperor Taisho and the first period of Hirohito's regency.

Makino is a liberal. The army hates him. There have been several attempts on his life, and like Saionji, he barely escaped assassination in the army Putsch of 1936. Until he joined the Household—he has also been Lord Keeper of the Privy Seal—Makino was a civil servant,

provincial governor, and diplomat. He would have been a member of
the Genro, if "they" had decided that the Genro should survive. He
has been called the Elihu Root of Japan. When Saionji has anything
to say these days, he says it "through" Makino.

I have mentioned the addiction of Japanese to the process of adoption. Both Saionji and Makino were *adopted* into the great families
which they head. According to Miss Utley (*Japan's Feet of Clay,*
p. 265) Saionji belongs to an illustrious group, the Kuge line, which
was traditionally pledged to celibacy, and always adopted its heirs.
Count Makino was likewise adopted; his brother is Count Okubo,
head of one of the greatest Japanese banks, the Yokohama Specie
Bank.

Tsuneo Matsudaira, at present the Imperial Household Minister,
and the father-in-law of Prince Chichibu, is another key man, and he
holds a key position. He has been ambassador both to Washington and
London. He is tall, stoutish, and rather Chinese in appearance. A son
of one of the old Shogunate families (the wives of Shoguns were taken
from five special families, exactly like the empresses, but the families
were different), he chose as a youth to remain a commoner, and he is
a commoner still. Matsudaira was born in Tokyo in 1877, and went to
the Tokyo Imperial University. His career as a diplomat was distinguished. He is a good golfer. He has always called himself a liberal,
and is supposed to be the chief present liberal influence at the palace.

Count Kurahei Yuasa, born in 1874, the Lord Keeper of the Privy
Seal, is supposed to be closer to the Emperor at present than any man
in Japan. No one knows him well. No one knows with great certainty
what he stands for. Yuasa was born a commoner, went to the Imperial University in Tokyo, and entered the civil service. For a long
time he served in the home office, and he was president of the Metropolitan Police Board in Tokyo at the time of the 1923 earthquake. In
1924 came an attempt to assassinate the Emperor; Yuasa, though of
course he had no personal responsibility, had to resign his post. He was
later civil governor of Korea, head of the Imperial Bureau of Audits,
and finally Lord Privy Seal. His chief duty is to be day-to-day political
adviser to the Emperor.

Finally, there is Baron Kiichiro Hiranuma, the former president of
the Privy Council, who represents a somewhat different point of view.
Baron Hiranuma, the son of a knight, born in 1867, a law student,
judge, minister of justice, and president of the supreme court before

he reached his present post, is an extreme nationalist. For some years he was head of the Kokuhon-Sha, one of the most powerful chauvinist organizations. Baron Hiranuma is the reactionary among the intimate palace advisers, and is a close friend of the army group. Openly he has been called a Fascist. He became prime minister early in 1939.

Imperial Headquarters

In January, 1938, when the Chinese refused to sue for peace even though Nanking had fallen, the Emperor summoned the first Imperial Conference that had been held in Japan since 1914, and the fifth in all Japanese history. At this conference decision was taken to "withdraw" recognition from Chiang Kai-shek, presumably because he was not gentleman enough to call off the war.

At about the same time an institution known as "Imperial Headquarters" was set up as a permanent advisory council to the Emperor during this period of crisis. The last time such an "Imperial Headquarters" existed was during the Russo-Japanese war early in the century. It may be said to be the ultimate crystallization of the "they" who rule Japan. Every really important decision nowadays comes from this small group.

Obviously the key military and naval authorities are included in "Imperial Headquarters," and doubtless the most important civilian ministers and court officials. The point is significant that no one, even now, knows specifically who all the members are. But what they do is what is important. And we know what they do—too well.

Chapter II
First Course in Japanese

∼∼∼∼∼∼∼∼∼∼∼∼∼∼∼∼∼∼∼∼∼∼

*Nations have their black or their white periods as well as
their black or white individuals and groups.*

—H. VERE REDMAN

THE word "Japan," like so many things Japanese, comes from
China. Literally the Chinese ideographs (日本) for Japan mean
"sun-origin"; the Chinese pronounce the word as Jihpen, the Japanese as Nihon, from which comes Nippon. The Japanese add a
suffix (*kuo* meaning "country" or "land") and call Japan the "land
of rising sun." This name is obviously of great emotional significance.
But the Japanese have other names too for their puzzling country.
One is Yamato, which is the aboriginal name, predating Chinese influence. Some names are exceedingly flowery; for instance Toyo-ashi-
wara-no-chi-aki-no-naga-i-ho-aki-no-mizu-hono-kuni, which means
"Land of Luxuriant Reed Plains, Land of Fresh Rice Ears, of a
Thousand Autumns, of Long Five Hundred Autumns."[1] The rising
sun, in this connection, seems to connote autumnal shortening of the
days.

What is Japan? The answer exists in several spheres. Japan is an
archipelago of 4,072 volcanic islands, extraordinarily susceptible to
seismic disturbances; for instance no fewer than 600 earthquake
shocks—all minor of course—were recorded in the single month of
December, 1938. Japan is a country containing 72,000,000 crowded
people; the birthrate, 31.63, is the highest in the world, and the population increases by 1,000,000 every year. Japan is an empire with
considerable continental territory in Korea, Manchukuo, Mongolia,
and China, a territory which it aspires to augment. Japan is a contemporary political force of great magnitude, a force which derives
strength from an ideal of divine, imperial destiny. And Japan is many
other things.

We must attempt to concentrate something of Japanese historical

[1] See *Things Japanese*, by Basil Hall Chamberlain, a remarkable book first
issued half a century ago, and still very up-to-date.

24

background in a paragraph or two. Nothing authentic is known about Japan before roughly the 3rd century A.D., when the name first appears in Chinese records. The Japanese did not come out of barbarism till perhaps the fifth century. Some Japanese aborigines, the Hairy Ainus, still exist in remote outer islands—tribute to Japanese adhesiveness. The issue is disputed by scholars, but the original Japanese appear to have been largely of Mongol stock, with strong Pacific and Malayan admixtures. The first Japanese were a combination of Asiatic mainland and oceanic peoples; Japanese policy to this day reflects this double push; Japan is possessed by a double atavism, desire to expand on the Asiatic continent, and to expand in the Pacific.

In the sixth century A.D. came the Chinese. Invasion by China was basically a cultural phenomenon, not military. (But already the Japanese had shown a certain tendency to militant expansionism; the Empress Jingo attacked Korea in 200 A.D.) The Chinese transformed the life of Japan. They brought the first enticing whisper to Japan of what we call civilization. They brought, first of all, a written language, an alphabet—which the Japanese still use. They brought religion to Japan in the form of Buddhism, which still survives strongly; most Japanese today are Buddhists, though they may be devotees of Shinto too. China gave to Japan—I quote from an impressive list drawn up by Dr. Lin Yutang—the following:

Pottery	Painting
Silk	Lacquer
Printing and Writing	Copper coins
Paper windows	Lanterns
Firecrackers	Confucianism
Tang poetry	Tea drinking
Flowers and rock gardens	Several national holidays

The tremendous debt in culture and religion, in art and handicrafts, in language and philosophy, which Japan indisputably owes to China, is almost certainly a dominant psychological reason for the discord between the two countries today. The Japanese resent violently their obligation to the Chinese. They are jealous of superior Chinese culture. They despise China partly because their debt is so big. Their wars against China are the expression of a subconscious desire to prove to the Chinese that, despite the fact that they owe them so much, they are better men.

Until the 16th century Japanese history is a confused and gloomy business—as, for that matter, is much European history of the same period. The record is largely an account of the growth of great feudal families and the implacable quarrels between them. Civil war was virtually continuous. The emperor became a puppet, with merely nominal authority, and from 1185 A.D. power resided with the Shoguns (literally "generals") who ruled on a *hereditary* basis. Their power was that of the sword, plus the wealth they drew out of the land. Under the Shogun were various competing feudal lords, known as the "Daimyo"; their retainers, knights—the men who did the actual fighting—were called "Samurai" (literally "one who serves"). A complicated chivalric code developed, known as "Bushido" (the way of the warrior) which held the Samurai to certain rules, and emphasized such virtues as obedience, conformity, loyalty. The Samurai could at sight cut off the heads of peasants or commoners who showed them disrespect. The ingrained tradition in Japan that privileged individuals may inflict punishment on offenders, with virtual impunity, has its consequences in modern Japanese history, as we shall see.

In 1542 came the first impingement of the west, when some Portuguese ships were wrecked in Japanese waters, and westerners began to come in, especially traders and missionaries. Firearms and Christianity came to Japan in the same year. St. Francis Xavier, a Spanish missionary, started to proselytize. Some Japanese turned Christian, but others resented invasion by a western faith, and bitter religious rivalry led to bloodshed. The Japanese ruling lords noted with apprehension the tide of conquest that followed religious impenetration; they saw the Philippines subjugated by Spain. Then missionaries of various Christian sects began in Japan to quarrel among themselves. The Japanese decided suddenly that the world of the west was a nuisance. They decided to get rid of it bag and barrel. So in 1637 came the amazing series of edicts that ejected all foreigners from Japan,[2] and hermetically sealed it from any hint of intercourse with the western world for 216 years. No Japanese was permitted to leave the country; no foreigner was allowed to enter it; the penalty for building a ship that might reach a neighboring shore was death.

But in 1853 came an American naval officer, Commodore Perry,

[2] Except an infinitesimal colony of Dutch—protestant—traders marooned on an island near Nagasaki.

knocking on the sealed door. His original mission was to ask better treatment of American sailors shipwrecked on Japanese islands; behind it was desire for trade. Perry's orders forbade him to use force, but the tottering Shogun of the day capitulated. The British presently followed the United States in demanding entry for its citizens. In 1863 an allied fleet bombed Japanese coastal towns—ostensibly because some pioneer westerners had been murdered—and Japan was compelled to open itself up. So, somewhat annoyed, Japan rejoined the world, and entered the sphere of western politics. Soon Japan learned to attack the west with its own imperialist medicine.

Ruling Japan at the time was the debilitated Tokugawa Shogunate. It had been in power since 1598. It was corrupt and decadent. The blast of air forced into Japan from the west blew it apart. It collapsed, because obviously it was in no position to meet its new historical responsibilities. Two great families or clans, the Satsumas and Choshus, which had long been rivals of the Tokugawas, combined to establish a new order. They needed a symbol, a figurehead, and they chose a good one—the neglected and almost forgotten emperor. They abolished the Shogunate, and resurrected the emperor as the supreme embodiment of power. Conveniently, a new emperor had just acceded to the throne, and he was a boy, Mutsuhito; in 1868 he was reinstated to authority and signed a Charter Oath. This event—Mutsuhito became known as Meiji—was the great "Meiji Restoration," a cardinal event in history.

Now the Japanese leaped forward with almost inconceivable rapidity, efficiency, and success. The west had forced open their secret doors; the Japanese set out—in revenge?—to beat the west. A case might be made out for Japan as a Pandora's box. Before the Restoration, the country was a medieval wilderness; ten years after, it was fast becoming a modern state. "Never in all history," says H. G. Wells, "did a nation make such a stride as Japan then did. . . . She completely dispelled the persuasion that Asia was in some irrevocable way hopelessly behind Europe. She made all European progress seem sluggish and tentative by comparison." Japan skipped centuries of trial and error by Europe; she jumped full-dressed, full-grown, from feudal times to the modern mechanism of industrial civilization.

This unprecedented overgrowth, this climbing leap from national childhood to maturity without the intervening experience of adolescence, is the root cause of most of Japan's difficulties to-day. The shock of psychological adjustment to sudden maturity with no preparatory pangs and ardors of puberty has been profoundly disturbing. Japan has never been sweet sixteen.

Japanese and Chinese

I have said that Japan took a great deal from China; but it would be an error to assume that nowadays the Japanese and Chinese much resemble one another. We are apt to think that the two peoples are intimately alike; in reality a Chinese differs from a Japanese at least as much as an Englishman differs from a Russian. Chinese and Japanese dislike each other, and are conscious of their differentiation; intermarriage between Chinese and Japanese is extremely rare, almost as rare as intermarriage between a white American and a negro.

Both Chinese and Japanese are Asiatics; both have yellowish skins, Mongol origins, great regard for the family system, a sense of frugality, and veneration for their ancestors. They share some aspects of the same religions, and the Japanese use the Chinese alphabet. A Japanese can often read simple Chinese, but a Chinese cannot as a rule read Japanese. Both Chinese and Japanese like to take their children to the theater and spend the day there; both eat large amounts of rice with chopsticks (but the chopsticks are shaped differently); both like the company of their own kind; but at these points the resemblance begins to taper off.

Most Japanese are short and squat; some Chinese are six feet tall or bigger. Many Japanese have thick pouting lips (the legend is that Japanese mothers, to economize on milk, suckle their children so long that their teeth are malformed) and thick ankles and short legs caused by years of squatting on straw mats, without furniture; most Chinese lack these stigmata. Japanese suck in breath sharply when they talk to superiors and foreigners, a kind of hiss, which is intended to demonstrate respect; Chinese do not.

The Japanese love to drink, and get drunk easily, especially on beer; many Chinese love to drink, but have good heads and stomachs. Japanese wear "digitated" socks, in order to give space for a strap next to the big toe; Chinese do not. The Japanese love color in clothes; Chinese clothes on the whole are drab. The Japanese are very good at sports, like baseball and tennis; the Chinese think that exercise is nonsense. Chinese often westernize their names; Japanese never do. Chinese use pidgin English; Japanese don't. The Japanese buy goods 90 percent made in Japan; Chinese buy goods 90 percent made outside China. The Japanese love Chinese food; Chinese are horrified at Japanese food, though it is beautiful to look at. The Japanese do not mean much when they smile; the Chinese smile because they are friendly folk, who enjoy laughter. I was told on arrival in Japan never to smile at a Japanese sentry or soldier; the friendly gesture will be misconstrued as a sneer. But you can buy any Chinese sentry with a smile.

The Japanese are more stubborn than the Chinese, and less logical. The Chinese are infinitely less efficient than the Japanese, and more disillusioned. In China your visiting card is more important than your passport; in Japan your passport is considerably more important than your visiting card. The Japanese possess those virtues which a cynic might consider rather dull: industriousness and an exaggerated tendency to hygiene, for instance. The Chinese on the other hand have all the charming vices. They love to flirt, to waste time in amiable conversation, to meditate, to gamble. The Japanese never smoke opium. But they make money selling it to the Chinese. The Japanese are men in armor, carrying a machine gun; the Chinese are men in undershirts, wondering when it is going to rain. If you ask a Japanese to choose between spending the rest of his life on an island with either a Chinese or an Englishman, he will pick the Chinese, who would presumably become his slave; the Chinese, confronted with a similar choice, would almost certainly pick the Englishman, who he assumes might be educated to become his equal. The Japanese are fanatics. The Chinese are almost indescribably reasonable.

It would be hard to tell whether the Japanese despise the Chinese more than the Chinese despise the Japanese. The Japanese call the Chinese contemptuously the "half-dead" men. I have heard a Japanese dismiss the entire 450,000,000 people of China with a disgusted wave of his hand on the ground that all have venereal disease! The Chinese do not waste time in argument. They simply describe the Japanese as "dwarf thieves," or sometimes "monkey thieves." In her official communications, the Chinese Empress Dowager (circa 1900) called the Japanese the "Island Monkey People." This is in line with the old legend (apocryphal) with which Chinese regale themselves as to the origin of the Japanese people. It is that the Emperor Shih Huang Ti in the third century B.C., the greatest emperor in Chinese history, sent a shipload of beautiful youths and maidens to Japan to find an elixer of youth, since Japan, the source of the sun, might reasonably provide it. But the shipload never came back. The youths and maidens intermarried with monkeys to found the Japanese race.

A Chinese proverb says, "A rat which gnaws at a tiger's tail invites destruction." The rat is presumably Japan.

Things Japanese quotes a remarkable letter from a young Japanese expressing his attitude to China:

Here is an old man whose body is very large; he is about four thousand years of age and China is his name. His autobiography tells me that he was born in early times in Eastern Asia. He was a simple baby smiling with amiable face, and as a young man he progressed hopefully. When he was full grown he accomplished many bright acts; he married a sweet lady who conceived the beautiful children of the arts and sciences. But by and by he became old, lame, blind, and decrepit. I must feel sorry for the sad fate of an old teacher and neighbor of mine.

This sentiment is to some extent echoed by a recent statement by Yosuke Matsuoka, president of the South Manchuria Railway:

China and Japan are two brothers who have inherited a great mansion called East Asia . . . The ne'erdowell elder brother turned into a dope fiend and a rogue, but the younger—lean, rugged, ambitious—dreams of bringing back past glories to the old House. The younger brother, Japan, sold newspapers on the streets to support the family. The elder brother flimflammed the younger out of his meager savings, sold him out to a common enemy. So the younger brother, in a towering rage, is beating up the elder, trying to beat him into some sense of shame.

When, according to Sansom, the Japanese in A.D. 607 sent their first envoy to the Chinese court, the opening phrase of the letter of credential was "The Emperor of the Sunrise country writes to the Emperor of the Sunset country." Which the Japanese will say is an exceedingly prescient remark to have been made 1,372 years ago. And indeed it has a disconcertingly contemporary sound.

Traits and Characteristics

The Japanese are a prickly and difficult people. Japanese character is full of paradox. One can mention any number of startling juxtapositions. Generalizations about national character are always risky, but one may at least attempt to outline a few distinctive Japanese traits.

I have mentioned several of the good qualities of the Japanese, and there are many others. Take patriotism, for instance. Japanese patriotism is to a certain extent a function of Shinto, which teaches that the country is a single family, a unit. Take Japanese efficiency and industry, which are enormous. One need only point out the manner in which Tokyo and Yokohama were rebuilt after the great earthquake. Japanese sense of detail includes the smallest items: for instance soldiers in China are given printed postcards to send home, which say simply: "I am well. The war is splendid. I will be home soon." The soldier needs merely to write the address and sign his name. Again, the Japanese have an almost unique sense of national discipline, an inheritance from the Samurai tradition, which emphasized conformity and solidarity; to a great extent they are creatures of convention. Most of them never dream of disobeying rules; no police are ever necessary to keep Japanese in line. Hugh Byas tells a wonderful little story of the death of a former Empress, who died suddenly in a country villa. But the rule was that all Empresses should die in Tokyo. So her body, fully and imperially dressed, was inserted dutifully in a special railway carriage and moved to the Tokyo palace. Then the corpse was put to bed and the death was announced in the proper manner.

The Japanese cannot endure demonstrations of lack of discipline. A whole essay on Japan might be written from the fact that in Japan the film "Mutiny on the Bounty" was called "Heroes of the South Seas"—and was only shown after drastic cuts.

Another essay might be written on Japanese inventiveness and ingeniousness, which are considerable. The Japanese are not only good mimics, as is notorious; they have a very direct and original practicality. For instance, they solved the street cleaning problem in Mukden—where the rikshas are drawn by horses—by the simple expedient of putting a small pail under the tail of every horse in town. To watch the pails dancing down the street is an entrancing experience.

Many Japanese lack grace; many seem to lack poise, charm, tolerance, and a sense of humor—all of which are notable Chinese characteristics. But it is impossible to deny the Japanese stoicism and courage. The episode of the three "human bombs" is familiar: three Japanese privates blew themselves up deliberately in order to make a passage through Chinese barbed wire. I have seen Japanese troops entrain for the front, while at the same station a second train was unloading a cargo of little white boxes—the ashes of soldiers killed. Women saying good-by to their husbands and sons betrayed small apprehension or emotion. No one wept.

Sansom has written: "In the history of Japanese thought little part is played by the personal sense of sin, which in western man has engineered puritanical complexes and driven him to extremes of restless enquiry and despair. The Japanese have cared little for abstract ideas of Good and Evil, but they have always been concerned with problems of behavior, as questions of a man's duty not so much to himself as to the society of which he is a member."

The question of Japanese puritanism is indeed complex. The visitor to Tokyo may be impressed by the night club sign, WINE WOMEN SONG AND WHATNOT; but he will also be impressed by the fact that dancing is not permitted in hotels frequented by foreigners, that beerhalls close at midnight, that no alcohol is allowed in dance halls, that gambling—even shaking dice for drinks—is forbidden. There is a law, the "anti-necking" law, which makes it obligatory to light up the inside of taxis and closed automobiles after 9 P.M. Japanese puritanism seems insane and monstrous. Yet Japanese brothels are the most extensive in the world; thousands upon thousands of young girls—even children—are sold into prostitution by their parents every year; and the kind of professional hostess known as the Geisha is a distinctive feature of Japanese life. There is little odium attached to prostitution in Japan. If she is lucky, a prostitute may eventually save enough money for a dowry, in which case she will return to her village and marry. Japanese prostitutes, like workers in a Russian factory, have their "culture corner," and take lessons in ethics once a week. Alcohol, gambling, and music are forbidden in Japanese brothels; they may detract from the efficiency of the performance. Prostitution is simply a business—a serious business—from which the government derives revenue.

An American photographer in Tokyo, searching for material for a documentary film, confessed to a Japanese friend that he could get nothing to photograph of the lighter side of Japanese life. He asked what on earth he could use as picture material to illustrate, for instance, what the Japanese did on Saturday nights at home. The Japanese friend replied, "I should advise you to consult our vital statistics."

Another Japanese paradox has to do with the national trait of sensitiveness. The Japanese are incredibly touchy, which may be partly a result of diet; they eat too much iodine in the shape of raw fish, and their thyroids are overdeveloped. Yet, with all their sensitiveness, they continually enact policies which open them to rebuff. Like adolescents, they fear and resent snubs, while at the same time they make snubs inevitable by their course of action.

Still another paradox is the matter of discipline. It is extreme, especially in the army; but the Japanese army is unique in that a youthful colonel may sometimes overrule his superiors. Again there is the Japanese instinct to democracy, which, even in these times, is very considerable. Japan was a feudal kingdom until 1868 and it is now a military oligarchy; yet all Japanese consider themselves equal—a most challenging and important point—and more than one statesman has risen to eminence from extremely humble origins.

The Japanese have a great sense of team play. When workmen dig up a road, they wield their picks in unison, as if they were practicing calisthenics. The story is that no one in the world is so unintelligent as a single Japanese, and no one so bright as two. They love to pool effort. This instinct for team play, which derives from the basic desire to conform, is one reason why the Japanese—despite their bad eyesight —are good aviators in formation flying, though as individual pilots they lack initiative.

Almost all educated Japanese wear eyeglasses, and one is apparently justified in the assumption that the fantastically difficult Japanese language is more responsible for their bad eyesight than any basic optical defect. Children wear out their eyes trying to learn to read. A child should learn about 3,000 different characters by the time he is ten or twelve; he must know about 5,000 to read a newspaper intelligently. These characters are Chinese, but the *language* is different. To simplify interpretation of the Chinese characters, the Japanese have invented two explanatory alphabets, called *kana*, which—rather like an elaborate system of punctuation—are printed parallel to the Chinese text. The combination makes Japanese by all odds the most formidable tongue in the world. I have asked a young attaché of the Tokyo foreign office, who went to Oxford, to translate some street signs in a Japanese village; he could not do so—could not read his own language—because the explanatory *kana* were omitted.

Japanese interest in education is intense and admirable; Japan has a record in education that no Oriental country can remotely match. Very nearly every Japanese child goes to school. Education in theory at least is free and compulsory. We are proud of our record in the Philippines, where we have lifted literacy to perhaps 60 percent, but Japanese literacy—even if some street signs are puzzling—is 95 percent. Compare with India, where literacy is only about 15 percent, with China where it is 10 percent or even less.

One curious Japanese characteristic is lack of tact. For instance an American officer, who had been badly wounded in the attack on the *Panay*, visited Japan subsequently, and called on some Japanese naval men. They insisted on inspecting his wounds—which they had inflicted on him! Another American, seriously shaken up on the *Panay*, avoided Japanese company afterwards. His Japanese friends persuaded him to come to dinner on the understanding that the whole *Panay* episode be buried and forgotten. But the Geisha girls invited for the occasion said nothing to the American all evening except *"Panay! Panay!* So sorry! So sorry!"

Japanese literal-mindedness is considerable. An American correspondent was traveling through Manchuria. He happened to say to a Japanese companion, the editor of an English-language newspaper in Dairen, "I hope it will be a nice day. Fair and warmer." And he knocked on wood. The Japanese asked him to explain the significance of knocking on wood. The next day the weather report of the newspaper read *Fair and Warmer Knock on Wood*.

And Japanese lack of humor is, as everyone knows, famous. When Archibald MacLeish, the American poet, spoke at a luncheon in Tokyo, he mentioned the difficulty of gathering material for *Fortune's* Japanese number. He said it reminded him of the New Yorker visiting Vermont, who said, "There are so many rocks here. Where did they come from? Do you grow rocks in Vermont?" The Vermont farmer replied, "The rocks were brought here by the great glacier." The New Yorker said, "What became of the glacier?" The Vermonter said, "It went back to get more rocks." The Americans in the audience howled with laughter. But none of the Japanese got the point.

One famous story describes the American newspaper correspondent who wrote to a friend, "I don't know if this letter will ever arrive, because the Japanese censor may open it." A week later he received a note from the Japanese post office saying, "The statement in your letter is not correct. We do not open letters."

Closely associated with literal-mindedness, with lack of humor and imagination, is the extraordinary Japanese habit of disingenuousness—the combination of naïveté and self-deception which calls a war an "incident," which makes the Japanese say that they wage war only because they are "friends of the Chinese people." Examples may be culled from any Japanese newspaper. A recent one from the *Japan Times*: "What is termed guerrilla warfare by Chiang Kai-shek amounts to disturbing Japan's efforts to maintain peace in China." The Japanese call their daylight saving time, now established in North China, "friendship time." As one friend put it in Tokyo, "The Japanese are forever committing acts of peace."

Here is an example from no less a personage than the new Japanese prime minister, Baron Hiranuma. Prepare to blink:

The peaceful policy of Japan has been evident in all the major problems that have beset our country. The Sino-Japanese war, the Russo-Japanese war, and the recent conflicts in Manchuria furnish examples of the desire of our nation to maintain peace (*sic!*) and stability in the Far East.

But—it is important to remember—such statements are not so much examples of hypocrisy or duplicity as of a peculiar and intense Japanese tendency to self-delusion.

The Japanese have—like most people—an occasional tendency to bloodthirstiness. An American official is witness for an occasion when Japanese sailors, half-insane with nervousness, opened fire on a group of Chinese playing with—firecrackers. Recently in a Tokyo newspaper I saw an account of a 22-year-old murderer who had run amok and killed twenty-eight people. The story almost gloated over the accomplishments of this mass murderer; he was portrayed as a hero, if a monstrosity. In a recent *Japan Times* I saw an editorial note to the effect that 300,000 Chinese troops were surrounded. "It is the intention of the Japanese forces," the story said, "to kill all the trapped Chinese." With my own eyes I have seen irritated Japanese soldiers—men in uniform, presumably disciplined—slap Chinese women, kick old men, and slam coolies on the head with bamboo poles. When the Japanese took Nanking, forty *thousand* Chinese—many of them civilians—are said to have been executed, and several thousand women raped.

Another Japanese trait is suspiciousness. The country is ridden with spies, and with spy mania. You cannot, in Tokyo to-day, buy a map of Japan or a plan of Tokyo; recently the police visited the art shops to confiscate some 18th century prints because they portrayed Nagasaki harbor! A few years ago the National City Bank of New York narrowly escaped serious trouble, because, in order to assemble some perfectly innocent publicity material, it took photographs from an Osaka roof. Spies—most of them highly polite—investigate travelers on all the trains; detectives—who become very friendly and useful as guides—are stationed throughout Manchukuo and Korea. Hardly a week passes without some new bizarre case of "espionage." Recently a Danish citizen was arrested. He had some suspicious photographs. They turned out to be X-rays of a broken rib!

Japan seals itself against infection from the great world outside. Short wave radios, capable of getting Philippine or Chinese stations, are rigorously forbidden.[3] The Japanese police go in for what they call "thought control," and thousands of men and women have been arrested for possessing—not firearms or illicit political literature— but "dangerous thoughts." The Japanese instinct to secrecy, to suspicion, clearly derives from the long period when intercourse with foreigners was forbidden. It also has direct roots in a contemporary political situation, in that the essence of the Japanese naval program is secret building.

Finally one may mention another Japanese trait, which might be called patriotic masochism. It is a trait which—among several others —Japan shares with Germany. The Japanese seem actually to enjoy suffering, if suffering is for the sake of Emperor and country. The Japanese pull in their belts, and say—almost literally—"Thank God! We are hungry to-day! We suffer gladly for the motherland!"

What a lot Commodore Perry did uncork that gray morning in Yokohama Bay 86 years ago!

Hara-Kiri

The other day I read the following news note in the *China Weekly Review:*

A Japanese soldier, wearing his uniform, fell from a truckload of

[3] But no *law* forbids them. The Japanese have considerable capacity for indirection. The constitution guarantees certain civil liberties; but the police have wide discriminatory powers under the "Peace Preservation Law." A regulation was enacted licensing radios. And licenses are simply not given for sets capable of getting distant stations.

soldiers, which was passing along Kiangwan Road [Shanghai]. A foreign resident passing along the street was amazed to see the Japanese soldier sit up, reach in his pocket, and proceed to cut his jugular vein. The foreigner hurried up but was too late to prevent the man from killing himself.

This is an excellent contemporary example of *hara-kiri*, or ceremonial suicide. The soldier killed himself in shame at having fallen off the truck. It is not, however, a classic example, because correctly the person committing suicide should slice open his abdomen, not his throat. *Hara-kiri* dates back at least five hundred years. Its origin was partly the feeling that death by suicide was preferable to death by torture, in case of capture by the enemy, partly the Samurai code which taught that suicide was the better alternative to any kind of dishonor or disgrace. Nowadays *hara-kiri* is becoming less fashionable, though it is an iron-clad tradition of the Japanese army that any officer taken prisoner must kill himself.

The Japanese do not as a rule call *hara-kiri* by this name; they say "seppuku," which is a transliteration of the same characters, but in Chinese form. It is of some psychological interest that most Japanese prefer a Chinese rendering of the name for this national ceremonial. It is also of interest to point out that a deeply rooted characteristic like *hara-kiri* may, conceivably, express itself some day in national as well as individual terms. I do not mean that the Japanese are at the moment committing suicide in China. But I have heard several Japanese say that, rather than suffer defeat by China, they would deliberately attack a stronger foe—Russia for example—and perish in a really first class conflagration.

Japanese Factory

The most interesting question in Japan is this. How has Japan managed to undersell so cardinally its great industrial competitors; how does she manage to sell silk, toys, electric light bulbs, cameras, cotton goods and rayon, ceramics, canned food, and so on, in foreign markets, at prices cheaper than foreign countries can produce such goods themselves? How is it possible for Japan to sell a fountain pen in New York City for ten cents?

The Japanese, like the British—another island people—live by importing raw materials, manufacturing finished products, and selling these products abroad. Let us take one example. Japan buys raw cotton somewhere in India, and pays its transportation to an Indian port, Bombay. From Bombay Japan pays freight on this raw cotton to the mills of Nagoya or Yokohama. Japan processes the cotton into shirts, ships the shirts all the way back to India, pays a stiff discriminatory duty in Bombay again on Japanese imports, and then proceeds to sell the shirts in India two or three cents cheaper than Indian shirts made in India. Not merely cheaper than Lancashire shirts or Egyptian shirts. But cheaper than *Indian* shirts.

How can Japanese manage this? One reason is, of course, low Japanese wages. But that is not the whole story: because Indian wages are lower even than Japanese. The answer is more complex. One reason—for a time at least—was the depreciation of the Japanese yen, which made her exports cheaper abroad; now, however, this is working the other way to damage Japanese economy, since the cheap yen makes it more expensive for Japan to import foreign raw materials. Another reason is efficiency. The country has practically a new industrial plant, spick, span, and shiny; the Japanese use every modern technological device, and one girl, working on the new Toyada looms, can do the work of twenty Indians. Another reason is a centralized purchasing agency for raw materials, and a subsidized merchant marine. Still another is honesty in industrial organization; there is no corruption in a Japanese factory, no graft, no "jobber" or middle man to pay off. Finally, most important of all, there is the national solidarity of most Japanese, which makes efficient work not merely an exercise in getting wages, but in patriotism. The country is extraordinarily homogenous (rather like France) racially, socially, economically. Most Japanese consider themselves cogs in a single giant machine.

Abstractions such as these come to life in a Japanese factory, and a Japanese factory is one of the most extraordinary phenomena on earth.

We visited a silk finishing plant near Tokyo. Most new factories in Japan are suburban. There is an attempt to get out of the cities, and build industries on green lawns; the plant we saw, with manorial walls inclosing trees and shrubbery, looked like an English country house. It was a "model" factory of course; that was why we were permitted to visit it. Other industrial undertakings are not so elegant. (But most of them, it goes without saying, are neat. I have never seen anything to rival Japanese tidiness and passion for sweeping. On every road, the very twigs are collected and packed neatly into bundles.) There are what might be called "depressed" areas in Japanese cities, but few real slums. Japan, by industrializing herself overnight, escaped the worst evils of the industrial system. Nothing in Japan is comparable to the unspeakable slums of Shanghai or Bombay.

We are inside the factory. 900 girls are employed, 100 men. This means that it is a big factory; most of Japan's 95,000 factories employ only a handful of workers. The girls catch our eye at once. They stand in rows of thirty before the softly oscillating looms. They wear black smocks, a sort of uniform; they are not permitted to sit down. At the end of each tier of looms is either a large birdcage, filled with parrots, or an aquarium splashing with goldfish—apparently to give color and the illusion of the great outdoors. But the analogy that these animals are also captives comes instantly to mind.

The girls work ten hours a day, from 6 A.M. to 5 P.M. for a daily wage of 85 sen, about 24¢. There is half an hour for lunch, and two rest periods of fifteen minutes each—which are devoted to compulsory gymnastics! The girls get every other Sunday off, but only rarely are they permitted to leave the compound to visit Tokyo. At 5 P.M., free until lights-out at 9, they may don their bright kimonos and flash colorfully through the great gardens; but they may not go outside the walls. The food is simple but apparently ample: the girls looked healthy. They sleep in dormitories, on shelves, six or eight to a room. Everything is spotlessly clean. Culture lessons are provided before bedtime—lectures from the supervisor on flower arrangement, the tea ceremony, ethics, and the like.

The girls are employed on a uniquely Japanese system. The great majority come from country villages; a contractor hires them from their parents, usually for a year, and their wages go in part to pay the parents' debt. The girls cannot leave the factory until the contract has expired; usually it is extended to cover several years. In the factory I visited the girls, beginning at 16, worked till they were twenty or twenty-one, by which time they might save perhaps 300 yen or $81.00.[4] Then they were free in theory to return to their villages, and to use their capital as dowry. Most of them marry, and promptly set about producing children to repeat the process.

The system has its overtones of horror. Yet one should point out

[4] Exchange rate as of April 1, 1939, when the yen in New York was worth 27¢.

that, as a result of the continual labor turnover, there is no permanent industrial proletariat among women in Japan. The girls rotate to and from the villages. One gasps at the evils of temporary slavery; yet, as Redman points out, "to deprive a young woman of her free will in the matter of selling her labour is obviously an outrage only in a community where the enjoyment of free will is relatively general." We are shocked and horrified at the system. But so will a youthful Japanese be horrified when he learns that, in America or Europe, he or she may grow up willing to work and be unable to find a job. Unemployment in the west seems to him as intolerable as the Japanese system seems to us. There is virtually no unemployment in Japan.

* * * * * * *

Japanese industrial wages are low, but so are managerial and other salaries, as well as prices. In Chapter V we shall inspect the great Japanese financial houses, and the princely share of Japanese national income they absorb; underneath these great structures, the bulk of the Japanese people lead frugal and meager lives. The 1938-39 income tax returns show that only seventy people in Japan get more than $500,000 annually. The average industrial wage for a skilled worker is about 80 sen (21.6¢) per day. According to W. H. Chamberlin, only ten per cent of the people earn more than 100 yen ($27.00) per month; according to *Fortune*, only two and one-half per cent of the Japanese population earn more than $3,000 per year.

The Japanese prime minister gets 9,600 yen ($2,592) per year; other ministers get 6,800 yen. A university professor gets from 175 to 280 yen per month; a local bank manager may get 200. A young man, fresh from college and starting work in an industrial enterprise, is lucky if his first wages are 60 yen per month; a civil servant may get even less. A policeman gets from 45 to 80 yen a month. A good cook is happy with 10 yen ($2.70!) a month, and a gardener gets about the same.

But prices, too, are very low—though the war has lifted them. A pleasant five room house may be rented for 30-60 yen a month, and food for a family of four is calculated to cost only about 75 sen (20¢) per day. Carfare is 7 sen (8/10 of 1¢); lunch in a restaurant is 20 sen; a first class movie is 50 sen (13½¢). One yen (27¢) will buy twenty apples or twenty-five eggs; a haircut, shampoo, shave, and manicure will total 50 sen (13½¢) together. You can buy a pair of wooden clogs for 15 sen, and a mechanical pencil (I am still using an excellent one I bought in Tokyo last summer) for 30 (8¢). A good pair of leather shoes will cost 12 yen, a suit of clothes containing 40% wool from 20 to 40 yen. Kimonos run from 10 yen up.

A youthful Japanese journalist went to his employer recently. He wanted to get married. The negotiations provided a curious insight into Japanese domestic finance. In order to marry, the young man needed a total of 450 yen ($121.50) divided as follows: betrothal gifts, 100 yen; remuneration for go-between, photographs, and ring, 160 yen; dinner party for bride, 70 yen; honeymoon expenses, 60 yen; furniture 60 yen. But the bride was giving him a dowry of 50 yen ($13.50) which cut his needs to a net 400. But the young man's capital was only 20 yen ($5.40) and his salary only 80 yen a month. So his employer collected a staff fund of 30 yen, gave him a wedding present of 50 yen, and lent him the remainder necessary—300 yen—on the understanding that it would be paid back, out of salary, ten yen a month.

. . . .

Japan, like France, possesses in theory an economy almost perfectly balanced between industry and agriculture. The country is 55 per cent industrial and 45 per cent agricultural. But agriculture in Japan presents serious and pressing problems. Japan is densely populated, but only 15.6 per cent of the land is arable; there is only ½ acre of arable land per head of population, the lowest ratio of any country in the world. Most of the land is held by small tenant farmers, who till every square millimeter of cultivable soil. There are very few big estates. The staple crop is rice and, it has been said that the history of Japan is the history of its rice production. Almost one-third of the rice crop, incidentally, goes to produce *sake*, which is rice wine.

Agrarian Japan suffered severely as industrialization proceeded apace. Of Japan's 95,000 factories, not less than 30,000 have been built since 1919. The farmer pays high taxes to subsidize industry; the islands are being transformed into a prodigious factory, and the farmers suffer in consequence. Another difficulty is that, worried by the possibility of food shortage, the Japanese have sought to plant more and more rice, at the expense of other crops; as a result the price of rice sagged catastrophically, all but ruining the rice farmers. Rice culture is no longer profitable.

Japan has, however, achieved virtual self-sufficiency in food. If rice fails, the Japanese may dip into the sea, eat more raw fish. It will not be easy to blockade Japan, starve Japan out.

Tokyo To-day

One's first impression is apt to be of the spaciousness, modernity, and dignity of Tokyo, in contrast to the noisy squalor of most Oriental cities—broad boulevards, blunt skyscrapers, neon lights (now dimmed by war economy), a subway, glittering shopwindows. Then one may have luncheon with a Japanese friend and turn back ten centuries. Tokyo seems very western; you see Japanese playing baseball in corner lots! Then you hear a Japanese lady describe the dagger her father gave her as a wedding gift, so that she may kill herself if she should dishonor her husband.

One discovers soon that Tokyo, for all its modernity, is the hardest of the great eastern capitals to get around in. This is largely because a recent Home Minister, in an excess of nationalist spirit, abolished foreign language street signs. In most eastern cities, signs on streets and in railway stations are in English or French; in Japan, they are in Japanese. (Later, when tourists became hopelessly confused, some English signs were permitted to reappear in railway stations.) The authorities frowned even on such picturesque semi-English expressions among Japanese as "Papa-San," which children used for father.[5] Foreign amusements, too, came to be discouraged. A recent dispatch from Amagasaki announced the formation of a committee "for the extermination of dance halls and western dancing."

Tokyo feels severely, but not yet critically, the strain of war. Streets are crowded; shops are full and animated, and one feels a curious kind of artificial excitement produced by the first stimulus of war economy. Underneath this is a stubborn drabness, a sense that the war is going to last a long time, that it must cause gigantic sacrifices, that it must be won. Tokyo has an undercoating of bleakness, but not of defeatism. Recently a government department, in coöperation with the "East Asia Costume Designing Committee," announced plans for a compulsory semi-uniform of gray to be worn by all male civilians. The Japanese cannot like this, because they love color. But they

[5] "San" is an honorific in Japanese, meaning something between "honorable" and "mister"; it is added to both names and things. Japanese usually call their sacred mountain Fuji-San, not Fujiyama.

submit to it dutifully, because wartime contingencies override any other sentiment.

The drain of war is tremendous in the entire field of non-essentials, that is, civilian luxuries. There is no steel or copper available for private building; no leather or cotton for boxing gloves or baseballs; very little foreign exchange for books or magazines. One gallon of gasoline per day is the ration for private automobiles, and all matches (!) have been shortened .029 inches, which saves $300,000 a year in timber. The government controls absolutely the distribution of such products as coal, Oregon pine, lead, zinc, tin, and nickel. Ersatz materials are being developed as fast as the scientists can invent them; whalehide is being used for leather, and 15,000 Tokyo policemen, it was announced recently, would henceforth be equipped with "substitute footgear." Twenty-two rubber articles are henceforth forbidden manufacture, except for military use, including shoes, gloves, garden hose, rubber bands, sporting goods, and (sic) chewing gum. No cotton—a serious blow to Japanese—may be used in domestic textiles, which are to be made of staple fiber (with certain exceptions), which comes from wood pulp.

Yet it would be grossly inaccurate to assume that Japan is in any imminent danger of collapse. One may ask how long the Japanese ruling classes can depress the standard of living of their people without causing surreptitious resentment to become overt revolution, but the question stated so baldly is almost meaningless; one must take into account the peculiar qualities of the Japanese people, their sense of national solidarity and discipline, their patriotism. The average Japanese may not like war. But he feels that he has got to finish the job, now that it is under way; the mouthful he has bitten off is tremendous, but he must swallow it, else it will poison him.

Japanese financial statistics—those that are available—are appalling. The war to date is believed to have cost two and a half billion dollars, which is more than three times the cost of the Russo-Japanese war; at present the war is costing not less than 500,000,000 yen a month, or roughly $4,500,000 per day. This seems a gigantic sum, but after all the national income of Japan is calculated at sixteen billion yen per year, which means that the nation can go on spending 500,000,000 per month for a considerable time. The budgeted cost of war, April 1938 to April 1939, was 4,850,000,000 yen, of which all but 400,000,000 yen was raised by loans; this budgetary expense is in addition to the *normal* budget of 2,800,000,000 yen, the deficit of which was estimated at 690,000,000 yen. The budget for 1939-40 is the highest in history, with ordinary expenditure estimated at 3,694,-000,000 yen, military expenditure at 5,000,000,000 more. At least 6,000,000,000 yen of this 8,694,000,000 total must be raised by loans. No wonder Japanese bonds are written in red ink.

The national debt of Japan has risen from roughly six billion yen in 1931, before the Manchurian adventure, to roughly 10,500,000,000 yen in 1937, at the beginning of the China war. Now it is somewhere above 16 billion yen; in other words it has increased 250 percent in eight years. These too are appalling figures. Yet we know from the experience of Germany what complex financial juggleries may be performed by totalitarian states; we know from our own experience that a huge rise in national debt may mean little. The most ominous figures about Japan relate to its export trade, which by early 1939 had shriveled twenty percent, though the trade balance as a whole is still favorable. Domestic debt means comparatively little, but a fall in exports is a highly serious matter, because, with its gold supply drastically depleted, Japan can pay for essential raw materials and implements of war only by selling goods abroad. The rising sun is not setting—at least not yet. If it does start to set, falling exports will be one reason.

And now we turn to the fighting services, which manage to expend such a fantastically great amount of cash and credit.

Chapter III
Army Bearing Pamphlets

〜〜〜〜〜〜〜〜〜〜〜〜〜〜〜〜〜〜〜〜〜

To die for the sake of the Emperor is to live forever.
—JAPANESE ARMY PAMPHLET

L IKE many institutions in Japan the army is unique, differing from
all other armies in a number of important particulars. For one
thing, it bears an extremely special relation to the Emperor; for another, it represents a curious combination of feudal tradition and
modern technique; for another it plays a political rôle unapproached
by any other military force; again, it has extraordinarily strong *social*
impulses and ambitions. Then there is the religious factor. When a
soldier goes to battle, he tells his comrades, "I will meet you at the
Yasakuni shrine"—the place in Tokyo where, if he is killed, his ashes
are deified.

A correspondent of the Paris *Excelsior* was recently permitted to
ask nine Japanese soldiers why they were fighting in China. (How
the correspondent managed to do this is beyond me; to ask direct
questions of the Japanese military is like trying to pry open a tin
can with cardboard.) The answers:

1. It is the Emperor's wish.
2. The Chinese have broken a treaty with us.
3. My regiment was ordered here.
4. Japan is overpopulated.
5. No idea.
6. Because the Chinese attacked us.
7. The Emperor ordered us to fight.
8. The honor of Japan is at stake.
9. We wish to restore order in China.

(Quoted in Stephen King Hall's News Letter,
February 23, 1938.)

In the feudal era, until 1868, Japanese soldiers were peasant retainers of the Daimyo, the lords of the land; each great Daimyo had
his own fighting force. The "officers" were an outgrowth of the
Samurai class, and in 1868, be it remembered, there were no less than

45

300,000 Samurai families in Japan. Then in 1872 the army was na-
tionalized and compulsory military service introduced—only 67 years
ago!—and the clan armies were absorbed into a national force. The
new conscripts cut across the old clan affiliations, and gradually the
Samurai were displaced by a new generation of professional officers.
But the Samurai spirit remained strong. Result: the Japanese army
is a double growth. It is like a medieval sword manufactured by a
modern assembly line.

Japan has been a military state for at least a thousand years;
in most countries the army is the servant of the state, in theory at
least; in Japan, in practice if not in theory, the army is, and always
has been, the state itself. But roughly from 1922 to 1931, from the
Washington Treaty to the Mukden incident, government by civilians
on a liberal basis—that best of all importations from the west—did
attempt successfully to compete against military influence. Those were
golden years. Civilian ministers, though they did not displace military
authority entirely, bossed the show. Japan seemed bent on a course
of peace. Then came 1931 and the invasion of Manchuria; the army
has controlled Japanese policy ever since.

Nowadays the rank and file of the Japanese army—like that of all
conscript armies—necessarily reflects the rank and file of population.
It is not a special caste like the old German army. The bulk of recruits comes from the farms and from small villages, representing the
chief reservoirs of population. One hundred and fifty thousand boys
of twenty go into the army each year, and they serve two years. The
army is considered a school for the man power of the nation; as in the
Red Army in the Soviet Union—the Japanese would be shocked at
the comparison—service is considered part of education. In fact, the
army itself says that "Seishin Kyoiku," spiritual education, is the
motive of army training. Two years in the army give the Japanese
the rough equivalent of our B.A. or Ph.B.

At twenty, every male in Japan is given a severe physical examination. The system is comprehensive and ruthless; no one is favored,
no one escapes. The 150,000 men called up each year are chosen by
lot from the group found to be "absolutely fit." This giant game of
chance is likewise sternly administered. Every town, every district
in the country has its quota; farmers from the rice fields, clerks from
the towns, sons of diplomats or hereditary princes, all submit equally

to choice. There are no distinctions of class, party, or privilege. Only health and the law of lot determine who will serve.

As to officers, they no longer—a highly important point—represent a special caste. There is no "officer class" in Japan; the great majority of Japanese officers come from humble families, who rise by merit. Samurai spirit may still be evident—with its good as well as evil accretions—but Samurai blood no longer dominates the army. Hardly ten percent of Japanese officers to-day are of noble or Samurai origin. The army is a people's army, representing the mass of the nation; the officers are people's officers. Japanese officers, in general, do not remotely resemble the chic young men who adorn the Coldstream guards. Many of them don't shave more than once a week. Nor are Japanese officers well-paid. A full general gets 6,600 yen per year, or $1,782.

Officers are selected by an interesting process. There are three categories of entrants for the training schools which comprise the Japanese West Point. First, any boy of 14, having completed his compulsory primary education, may enter the junior academy at once. This academy is free, so that poor boys may enter; selection is based on competitive examination. Second, a group of "candidates at large" may similarly enter the academy at 16 to 18, having finished secondary school. Third, conscripted privates may enter the academy until they are 22, provided they pass a stiff examination. This opportunity offered to rank-and-file privates to become officers is unique among modern armies. Before *any* officer is commissioned, he must spend eight months in the ranks.

Promotion of officers depends on merit more than on seniority, another unique item. Advance may be very rapid; there are Japanese colonels of unbelievable youth, and a man may be a general at 46 or 47. One interesting point is that no officer may reach the rank of lieutenant-general until he has served abroad as a military attaché.

The army is a law unto itself—as more than one unlucky politician has discovered. There are two reasons for this. First, the minister of war (of the navy also) has the inestimably important privilege of immediate and direct access to the Emperor, a right not shared by the civilian ministers. This privilege is not included in the Japanese constitution, but it is sanctioned by custom deriving from the fact that the Emperor, personally, is head of army and navy. The army and navy chiefs of staff have similar direct access to the imperial person. And, of course, the oath of the Japanese officer is not to the government, but to the Emperor alone.

Second, the minister of war (and navy) is by ironclad rule an officer on the *active* list—another uniquely Japanese phenomenon. Since most Japanese officers are ambitious to reach the top, and since they know the top is necessarily a political post, they develop political interests and ambitions early. The minister of war has immense power, since he can short-circuit any negotiation by civilian ministers by his right of direct access to the Emperor. No politician can form a cabinet without a war minister. The army can overthrow any cabinet by withdrawing him, and can prevent any new ministry being formed by refusing to nominate a new war minister.

Another point is that the Japanese army and navy have never lost a war—and therefore assume to themselves immunity from criticism— and that the army at least quite frankly conceives of itself in terms of its mission, its divine and imperial mission, which is to conquer East Asia. The Japanese army has what might be called a "Yellow Man's burden" to control the East.

Now we turn to the social and economic policy of the Japanese fighting force, which demands a section to itself.

The Army Pamphlets

Japan's army not only fights but writes. It shoots guns at the Chinese, and ideas at the rest of us. It utilizes not only tanks and fighting aircraft, but the linotype machine and ink.

Beginning in 1934 the press department of the imperial war ministry began to issue a series of remarkable pamphlets, distributed free or at nominal cost, which flooded the nation. They have appeared intermittently ever since. At first the pamphlets were domestic propaganda setting forth the aims of the fighting forces, and showing the need for bigger military budgets; they developed into what amounts to official army statements on a great variety of matters. The first pamphlet discussed Japanese expansionism; one of the last, issued in 1938, vigorously attacks the United States. Titles of some pamphlets:

National Defense in Asia
The U.S.S.R. Viewed from the Point of View of National Defense
British and French Activity in Yunnan
Modern National Defense and Economic Warfare

The Disturbed Political State of Europe
Conditions in the South Sea Islands
Progressive Japan and Heavy Pressure of Foreign Powers
National Defense in the Air
Third Anniversary of the Mukden Incident.

So far as I know, complete translations of these pamphlets do not exist in English. But Domei, the official Japanese news agency, makes summaries which are printed in the *Japan Advertiser*, Tokyo's excellent American daily, from time to time. Also I have had the privilege of seeing private translations of several.

The most interesting thing about the pamphlets as a whole is their appeal for a new type of economic order in Japan. The Japanese army believes very definitely in social planning, as has been proved by the example of Manchukuo. The pamphleteers have sacked the world for material, and have borrowed ideas all the way from Plato to Stuart Chase. The terminology is often bewilderingly reminiscent of the Moscow *Pravda*—though communism in Japan is a crime—and it borrows heavily from the totalitarian doctrine of the Fascist states. The prevailing spirit is of vigorous dislike of communism and capitalism both. The pamphleteers attack orthodox capitalism very severely. What they want seems to be a type of state capitalism with some socialist admixtures.

It may shock and offend good liberals who believe that the Japanese are purely Fascist-capitalists to read quotations from the pamphlets like the following:

Japan is now at the crossroads of her destiny. It is impossible to get sufficient armaments from the present system. The attempt would bring about national bankruptcy and dissolve the unity of the nation. We must set up a new economic system . . .

Again:

Uneven distribution of wealth has led to poverty and unemployment for many people . . . Egotism, individualism, and materialism—these are the evils of modern capitalist society. The time has come when we must liquidate the modern civilization based on individualism . . .

Who wrote that? Comrade Stalin? No. Again:

So long as economic profits, and especially unearned incomes, are enjoyed by one section of the nation alone, the majority of the people will be left in the utmost misery and distress . . . The situation is such that prompt measures must be taken . . . to readjust fundamentally our policies on finance and economics . . . It is necessary to set our house in order by complete social and economic stabilization.

This paragraph and others like it produced serious alarm in 1934 in Tokyo financial circles. There was a sharp break on the stock exchange, and the big industrialists feared an army coup d'etat to put the reforms into effect at once. Several newspapers dared to criticize the pamphlet with some asperity, and the minister of war had to allay alarm by discounting its implications.

In a pamphlet which formally proposes the establishment of a totalitarian state:

The principles of freedom which previously pervaded the entire world are dying out. The world war was caused by conflicts in imperialism which were the ultimate growth of this period of free enterprise . . . A clash now seems inevitable between free enterprise and government control, between individualism and collectivism.

(Totalitarianism, incidentally, is a complex word in Japanese. It is *Zentai shugi-teki-kokka*, literally total-state-structure-ism.)

The pamphlets are full of that wonderful Japanese capacity for self-delusion I have already noted. The writers dip the blade in honey. An example:

It is absolutely necessary for Japan to have a powerful navy sufficient to defeat any state which will attempt to frustrate Japan's noble effort of making the Far East a paradise of peace (*sic!*) and prosperity.

One pamphlet mentions the "pitiable bigotry" of Chiang Kai-shek, who refuses to understand Japan's "true intentions." There is much talk of Japan's "holy task" of achieving "world peace," and of rejuvenating China in the interests of "peace." Also:

If the Japanese nation should lose its zeal for consummation of its three great policies, coöperation between Japan and China, development of Manchukuo as an independent state, and building up of military strength, she will be unable to maintain [now guess what] peace in the Far East.

And, as usual, we have the messianic note, on an ominously cosmic basis:

The rational distribution of territory, national resources, and population—this should be the keynote of international peace. The establishment of world peace is Japan's aim. *No country in the world has so high a mission as Japan to save the world.*

Why should the Japanese army have adopted such semi-Fascist, semi-socialist, and definitely anti-capitalist ideas? There are several reasons.

First, the Japanese army reflects to a certain extent the tradition of Samurai days, when the merchant or trader was a despised underling. It views orthodox capitalism as a comparatively new growth, not indigenous to Japan. And the army hates and fears communism, which, an interesting point, it believes to have been caused by capitalist abuses. Japan blames capitalism for communism, and hence attacks them both.

Second, the majority of Japanese soldiers and officers were poor farm boys. The peasants think they have been sacrificed to the business men of the towns, and army personnel reflects this attitude.

Third, the officers dislike the "international" aspects of Japanese finance capital. They know that the great financial houses, which make money on shipping, on insurance, on banking and trade, prefer peace to war, and therefore have tended to oppose steep military budgets, and to support the civilians in the ministries.

Fourth, the army thinks that the industrialists, who believe in profits, are not as efficient as they might be in supplying the needs of a great war machine. Obviously the capitalists make money. The radical officers think that munitions will be more economically produced and Japan will hence be stronger—if profits are turned back to the state.

In any case it is a remarkable phenomenon that an army, which is usually the repository of conservatism in a nation, should have grasped so eagerly at such "radical" ideas. On the other hand, one should point out that the army, no matter how anti-capitalist it is, has not yet attacked the fundamental principles of capitalism, namely the right to own land, to own production, and to make profit out of labor.

The leftist tendencies of the army have naturally produced a bitter subsurface conflict with the great Japanese financial houses, Mitsui and Mitsubishi. This we shall discuss in a later chapter. Radicalism in the army also contributed to one of the most extraordinary mutinies in history, the abortive coup d'etat of February 1936. This too we shall deal with soon.

General Itagaki and the Kwantung Clique

The Japanese minister of war, who next to the Emperor is probably the most important personage in Japan, is Lieutenant-General Seishiro Itagaki, born in 1885 in the north of Japan of a poor peasant family. He was commissioned in 1904, and became a general in 1932, at the age of 47. For a time he was chief of staff of the Kwantung army. It is a remarkable fact that, when he became minister of war in 1938, Itagaki was not even listed in the Japanese *Who's Who*, which contains 25,000 names. A man may rise from complete obscurity to overwhelming power almost overnight.

General Itagaki's great importance derives more from the position he holds than from his personality. The Japanese army has no single hero or leader. Itagaki may be replaced to-morrow; his successor will not differ from him much, and policy remains continuous. A group of officers rotate in power; there is no Japanese Moltke or Kitchener, not even a Japanese Schlieffen. Instead there are half a dozen sub-Moltkes, sub-Schlieffens, who work together, each contributing his own specialty to the ensemble. In Japan leadership is usually a composite phenomenon.

Like all armies the Japanese army has cliques. The most important is the group, headed by Itagaki, of staff officers of the Kwantung army, which is the army of occupation in Manchukuo. These Kwantung officers are the "Young Turks" of the Japanese military establishment. They are a corps d'elite. Kwantung[1] is the name of the tip of the Liaotung peninsula, a part of Manchukuo, which Japan has garrisoned for 34 years, since the conclusion of the Russo-Japanese war in 1905. Thus the Kwantung officers became the spearhead of Japanese penetration into Manchuria and China. The Kwantung army is not an autonomous force; regular Japanese divisions comprise it, just as regular English divisions serve in India, but it has a

---

[1] To be carefully distinguished from Kwangtung—note the unpleasantly semi-invisible "g"—which is the southern Chinese province of which Canton is the capital. The characters for Kwantung mean "east of the pass." Kwangtung is a geographical expression; a literal translation would be "Extensive border of the ancient Chinese feudal kingdom."

very special tradition and cohesive quality. Kwantung officers stick together. Since 1931 it has not been merely the Japanese army that has ruled Japan, but the Kwantung clique inside the Japanese army that has ruled Japan. It is not merely the army as a whole which is dominant, but the officers of this very special *Kwantung* army. Of the five full generals in Japan, three are Kwantung men.

In essence this is because General Itagaki and his Kwantung group were the authors of the Mukden incident of 1931, which led to the invasion of Manchuria and thus opened the modern phase of Japanese history. Manchuria, now called Manchukuo, has been their baby ever since. They invented Manchukuo. They created it. The officers were only colonels then. They were the force behind the general staff. Itagaki was the leader. Among his companions were Colonel Doihara and Colonel Ishihara, who have had great careers since, as we shall see. The Kwantung army, another point, is the repository of much of the radicalism of the Japanese fighting forces. It is the young Kwantung officers who are behind the pamphlets, who are most notable for radical ideas.

It is said that the commander-in-chief of the Kwantung army considers himself not responsible to the imperial general staff or to the minister of war, but only to the Emperor himself. This is because he is not only commander-in-chief, but also Japanese Ambassador to Manchukuo; in other words he is supreme boss of the country, which is Japan's most precious preserve. Whether or not the Kwantung commander actually has such a close connection to the Emperor, it is certainly true that his army behaves as if it did. The Kwantung army works like a separate organism, a separate and supreme military entity.

General Itagaki is popular. He is what the Japanese like in a soldier: a man who talks little, who does his job, a simple man of the people. He is an officer of broad policy, well rounded and grounded, not quite so specialized as Ishihara, who is a Russian expert, or Doihara, who is a "China man." Itagaki has been called the most intelligent soldier in Japan. His greatest accomplishment is, it goes without saying, the creation of Manchukuo; he was also the inventor of the Autonomous East Hopei Regime, which cost the Chinese millions upon millions in customs revenue; this we shall discuss in Chapter VII. Itagaki has a fairly strong Leftist slant. In September 1938, he stated, "The Japanese government must undertake planning and control. It must turn from light industries to heavy, from capitalism to the control principle." He is the man behind the Kwantung army's planning board, which has transformed Manchukuo into a kind of totalitarian experimental station.

Next to Itagaki the most important officer in Japan is probably Major General Kanji Ishihara, formerly vice chief of staff of the Kwantung army, then head of the military operations board of the general staff, and now commander of Maizuru fortress (which is across the sea from Soviet territory). Ishihara was born in Yamagata-ken in 1889, and became a general at 47. He is said to be a very religious man, and is almost worshiped by the younger officers; an Ishihara "cult" exists. Ishihara is the author of the war plan against the Soviet Union. He believes that Japan's primary military orientation should be northward and he disapproved strongly of the extension of the China conflict beyond North China. He thought—for a time at least—that it was unsafe to go further. He had a great deal to do with Japanese penetration of Inner Mongolia, which aims to cut China off from the U.S.S.R.

Another Kwantung officer of great importance is General Kuniaki Koiso, born in 1880. He was chief of the bureau of military affairs at the time of the Mukden incident, and worked closely with Itagaki. For a time he was chief of staff of the Kwantung army, and then became commander-in-chief in Korea. Koiso, like Itagaki, is strongly "social-minded," and is part author of the economic experiments in Manchukuo. Aside from being a Kwantung man, Koiso is a member of another group, that known as the "Twelfth Year Class." Officers in the same academy class tend to stick together—as at West Point— and Koiso had some remarkable classmates: General Araki, former war minister, General Sugiyama, another war minister, and General Hata, recently commander-in-chief in central China. Recently Koiso became a cabinet minister.

Then there is General Jiro Minami, an older officer, now on the retired list; he has been commander-in-chief of the Kwantung army, governor-general of Korea, and minister of war. A squat, solid officer with a bullet head, General Minami came from a remote village in Kyushu; he was a poor boy, and tramped to Tokyo when he was 14, vowing that some day he would be a general. Once during the march he fainted from hunger, but he had taken the precaution to tie a placard on his neck, giving the name of a Tokyo friend who might help him. A strong-willed man, the Japanese say that he likes *sake* (rice wine) and laughter. The American publicist James A. B. Scherer, in his *Japan Defies the World*, compared Minami to Hitler and Mussolini, saying that he was the hidden but actual dictator of Japan, the real ruler of the country. When Minami saw the book, his friends say that he was stupefied.[2]

In 1939 the commander-in-chief of the Kwantung army, and as such Japanese ambassador to Manchukuo, was General Kenkichi Ueda. He once lost an eye when a Korean terrorist attempted to assassinate him. Ueda is usually considered less important than the officers under him, like Lieutenant-General Eiki Tojo, who was his chief of staff until Itagaki made him vice minister of war. In December 1938 General Tojo forecast probable war with the Soviet Union, and said that Japan must be able to fight China and Russia at the same time.

The Legendary Doihara

Outside Japan the best known Japanese soldier is Lieutenant-General Kenji Doihara, known as the "Lawrence of Manchuria," who for years controlled Japan's military secret service, whose exploits in undercover Chinese negotiation made him almost a mythical character. Doihara was born, a poor boy, in Okayama in 1883. He stood first in his class at the military academy, and became a specialist in Chinese, which he learned to speak expertly. He is sociable, a pleasant chunky man with confident manners and a liking for negotiation. He became a general at 49.

Doihara's special job has been mainly to make trouble, then to smooth it over to Japanese advantage. He is a "fixer." His technique is to go into a disordered area, where the political situation is fluid, meet important people there, get their confidence, and arrange a settlement. He has a gift for getting to the right people, and making them like him. He has a practical mind, and enjoys practical solutions to difficult problems. He has very strong "Pan-Asia" feelings—though whether Pan-Asia is a practicable ideal remains to be seen.

---

[2] The Japanese dislike extremely to expel a foreign journalist or writer on formal grounds. But they disliked Scherer's book extremely too. One day, the story goes, Scherer was called to the telephone, and told that he had better leave Japan at once, since his daughter in America was ill. Scherer has no daughter in America. But he took the hint. A typical example of Japanese indirection.

Doihara spent some years in China, learning several Chinese dialects, becoming friendly with Chinese politicians. An early job was support of the Anfu group of Chinese leaders who, with Japan's connivance, ruled Peking and at outrageous prices sold concessions to Japanese. When the Anfu clique broke up, Doihara smuggled the leader to safety—in a laundry basket. Doihara flirted with warlords, purchased generals. Just before the Mukden incident (1931) he went to Japan to report to the war office; the day after, he became mayor of Mukden. A few months later, he appeared in Harbin as chief of the special Japanese military mission there. Promptly rival Chinese began to "fight," and Doihara found it "necessary" to occupy Harbin with troops—Japanese troops. A little later, almost the same thing happened in Chinchow, near the Great Wall, after riots had conveniently "started" in Tientsin.

These riots, which occurred immediately after Doihara arrived in November 1931, were important. Because of them, Mr. Henry Pu-yi, the former Emperor of China, who had been living quietly in the Japanese concession, was "forced" to flee. Doihara and Henry Pu-yi were good friends, since it had been Doihara who, seven years before, had smuggled him out of Peking when he was threatened by the Christian General, Feng Yu-hsiang. Doihara and Henry Pu-yi "disappeared" from Tientsin the same night, November 10; they showed up again, having been spirited away on a Japanese launch, at a seaside resort near Dairen, on Japanese territory. There Doihara held the young emperor until it was time to make him puppet ruler of Manchukuo.

Occasionally Doihara has been outwitted. Once he sought to wean a northern general, Shang Chen, from allegiance to Chiang Kai-shek. But the general refused to be seduced; he failed to keep an important rendezvous with Doihara, on the grounds of illness. The illness, he said, was "stove-poisoning"; he had sat too near an overheated stove. China rocked with laughter; Doihara was not amused. At another time he opened secret negotiations with Han Fu-chu, the late warlord of Shantung, to tie him to Japan. Han came to Doihara's secret headquarters in Tsinan, but he refused to accept Doihara's offer. Doihara, in angry mood, said that Han would not leave the house alive, unless he acceded to the Japanese demands. Han took out his watch, and said, "How interesting. It is now 11:25. Before coming here I instructed my troops to massacre every

Japanese in the city if I did not return to my headquarters by midnight. Good evening." Doihara could do nothing. Han went.

Doihara's greatest accomplishment, next to the installation of Henry Pu-yi in Manchukuo, was the progressive disintegration of North China. His dream was to detach the Five Northern Provinces[3] from suzerainty to Chiang Kai-shek and set them up as a Japanese puppet area *without warfare*. He almost—not quite—succeeded. He did succeed, with Itagaki, in establishing the East Hopei Autonomous region; he did succeed in setting up the Hopei-Chahar political council, which weakened the Chinese hold on these two important provinces. His method was intrigue plus purchase. But he could not do the whole job. When war began, however, Doihara's work still had value, because it had undermined Chinese ability to resist—at least in the north.

During the war Doihara was transferred to command of a division in the field. It was severely mauled in fighting in Shansi. Doihara is much better known out of Japan than at home. In Tokyo his importance is usually minimized, but we shall hear much of him in this book.

Other Military Men

At the moment of writing, April 1939, four Japanese armies are in China. First is the Kwantung army, above the Great Wall and in Mongolia. Then comes the North China army, with headquarters in Peking and Tientsin; then the central army, fighting along the Yangtze and headquartered at Hankow; finally the small force which is in occupation of Canton in the extreme south. These armies do not coalesce, and there is no unified command. Each army is autonomous, and takes orders only from Tokyo, where Itagaki holds the strings. Rivalry between the four is considerable.

The commander in the north is General Hajime Sugiyama, born in 1880, who was inspector general of military education and later war minister in the first Konoye cabinet. He succeeded one of the few Japanese generals who is of noble birth, General Count Terauchi. The first commander in central China was General Iwane Matsui, who had retired from the army and was president of the "Great Asia" society, a chauvinist organization. Matsui, a small man—he weighs 99 pounds—was subsequently recalled because the younger officers

[3] These are described briefly in Chapters VII and X.

didn't like him, and after he was accused of losing too many men. None of these officers are—or were—Kwantung men.

General Matsui has certain mild eminence as a poet. A recent work:

> Where arises the Yangtze river I fail to see,
> But all the mountains of China in dream I see;
> How noisy is the League of Nations?
> We have fine roads for kings to follow.
>
> —*Asia,* April 1938

Another officer, and one of great consequence, though at the moment he is obscured by Itagaki, is Lieutenant-General Yoshijiro Umedzu. He is known as the "business-man" officer, and does not like the social theories of the left-wing Kwantung men. He was several times vice minister of war, and he negotiated the Ho-Umedzu agreement; yet he is not in the Japanese *Who's Who.* Like top-flight civil servants in England, Umedzu is a man of shadow, who retains great power over the permanent organization of his department. He has been called "the strongest man in the army," and was given the thankless job of cleaning up after the 1936 mutiny. He is an exceptionally cautious man. People quote the proverb that "he will knock stone on a stone bridge before crossing it," to see that it is safe.

Japanese Navy

The navy in Japan is quite a different kettle of metal. The army is radical, by and large; the navy is conservative. The bulk of army officers were peasant boys; the bulk of naval officers are sons of tradesmen and aristocrats. Rivalry between army and navy is strongly marked.

There are several reasons why army and navy should be so differentiated. For one thing, the imperial naval academy takes boys only at 17, whereas youngsters can begin army training at 13; this means that a boy entering the navy must come of a family able to afford four years of private schooling. Again, the navy grew out of the shipping interests which rose after the Meiji restoration, particularly the Mitsubishi concern which had a tremendous maritime business; thus the navy personnel is associated with ideas of foreign trade. Again, the army was at the beginning dominated by Choshu clansmen, whereas the navy represented—more or less—the Satsuma clan. Again, the army is an expansionist force, which in Manchukuo was forced to undertake economic experiments; the navy is predominantly defensive. Together these factors have produced the situation: an agrarian, anti-capitalist army versus a conservative, commerce-minded, semi-aristocratic navy.

Naval limitation as established by the treaties of London and Washington has lapsed, and the Japanese are building as fast as they can to the Anglo-American level. Early in 1939 it was said that Japan was constructing four battleships over 40,000 tons, armed with sixteen inch guns, which may be the most powerful fighting craft in the world. Japan wants a navy strong enough in the Pacific to defeat any rival force. When it became clear that Japan was ignoring treaty restrictions, the United States, Great Britain, and France invoked the "escalator clause" of the London treaty, and raised the upper limit for battleships to 45,000 tons.

One cannot in this space go into the complex issue of naval ratios and limitation. There should, however, be room for a word about Japanese policy at the 1935 London conference because it throws such sharp light on Japanese character. The conference collapsed because the Japanese, as a matter of prestige, demanded abolition of the Washington ratio, Japan's 3 to 5 for America and England. Japan wanted parity, i.e., the *right* of equal tonnage with both Great Britain and the United States, even if it did not choose to avail itself of this right. The Japanese, however, did not call parity by the name "parity"; they invented the locution "common upper limit." The British and Americans refused to grant parity to Japan, which would have ended the idea of limitation. The British suggested the interchange of information, so that each country would at least be informed of the building programs of the others, since actual limitation seemed impossible. The Japanese refused this, on the ground that they could find out about British and American building, but that the British and Americans could not find out what they were building. Japan traded on its ability to conceal its naval activity. As a price for exchange of information, the Japanese demanded parity. They said in effect, "If you want to know what we are building, our price is the common upper limit." And the conference—with little credit to either side—broke up.

The most notable "political" naval officer to-day is Admiral Nobumasa Suetsugu, who was home minister in the Konoye cabinet. As such he was the most Fascist-inclined man in Japan; it was he who created the "ideological squads" to rout out "dangerous thinkers." Suetsugu, born in 1881, is a distinguished tactician and submarine commander, but his fame rests on his outspokenness and political extremism. He wants the navy to expand southward; he was the father of the campaign to take Canton; he once provoked a sensation by saying that the white race must be turned out of Asia. At one time he was accused of seeking to establish a private army in Japan; once, while commander-in-chief of the fleet, he called Colonel Lindbergh "a spy."

The Admiral has the common Japanese trait of seeing only what he wants to see. On January 17, 1934, he was quoted in the *Japan Advertiser* as follows:

Let me be frank. A great country like the United States, which is self-sufficient, does not need the largest navy in the world, which it has at present. Without a big navy, it would feel no inconvenience. Its possession of a large navy simply menaces other countries. How happy the world would be if the United States did not have so big a navy!

Other important naval officers are Admiral Baron Osumi, a member of the supreme war council, twice navy minister, and a cultured and traveled man; Admiral Osami Nagano, also a war council member and former navy minister, who represented Japan at the London Naval Conference, and who is a picturesque and attractive character; and Admiral Mitsumasa Yonai, the present minister of navy, who lately said that if the United States fortifies Guam it will be "too bad."

Chapter IV
How Fascist Is Japan?

〜〜〜〜〜〜〜〜〜〜〜〜〜〜〜〜〜〜〜〜〜〜〜〜〜〜〜〜〜〜〜

Japan's mission is to lead the world spiritually and intel-
lectually. . . . Japan will be the cradle of the new Messiah.
— Yosuke Matsuoka

ARON KIICHIRO HIRANUMA, former president of the privy council
B who became prime minister in January, 1939, is a lawyer by
training, a bureaucrat by profession, a typical enough nationalist in
aspiration. He is 73. For a time he was public prosecutor in Tokyo,
then a department head in the justice ministry, then minister of
justice. Politically ambitious, he became head of a patriotic society,
the Kokuhon-sha, which was a sort of combination of Ku Klux Klan
and American Legion, with 40,000 service members. The society
stood for "the Emperor, Nipponism, and all the advantages of nationalism, Fascism and communism."

In 1936, when he became president of the privy council—a key
post—Hiranuma resigned from the Kokuhon-sha. It is said that for
years Prince Saionji, the last of the Elder Statesmen, blocked Hiranuma's path to this job; the old prince, a genuine liberal, distrusted
Hiranuma's Fascist views. But in January, 1937, Saionji suggested
Hiranuma as prime minister—perhaps to squeeze him out of the privy
council post, and push him upstairs to the hurlyburly of active politics. Count Yuasa, another of the palace group, went to Saionji's
country house to discuss the choice, "on the instructions of the Emperor." This is the way it is "done." Yuasa then called on Hiranuma,
offering him the job, but Hiranuma declined it on the ground that
it was too heavy a responsibility. . . . Then, two years later, Hiranuma was again picked out to be prime minister, and this time could
not refuse.

Baron Hiranuma exemplifies some typical Japanese virtues; he is
frugal, industrious, laconic. He has been called the "Hitler of Japan";
this is nonsense. No one could resemble Hitler less than the infinitely
cautious and taciturn Hiranuma, who is a dry man, not a demagogue,
juridically-minded, and a facade behind which the army works. He

61

sleeps only four hours a night, whereas Hitler seldoms gets up till noon. Once during a 90-minute conference, he uttered exactly one word, and it was "No!" He likes such exercise as archery and fencing; Hitler takes no exercise whatever. However, like Hitler, he is a bachelor, a teetotaler, and a vegetarian.

The prime minister lives in an extraordinary house, said to be "assassination-proof" and "earthquake-proof." Like Frank Lloyd Wright's Imperial Hotel, which withstood the 1923 earthquake, it is built on a kind of floating foundation to resist seismic shocks, and is full of bewildering passage-ways, interior bridges, and rooms within rooms. It contains, too, various devices to impede assassins, including secret exits and bombproof doors; one legend—the Japanese scoff at it but not very convincingly—is that the prime minister, if he is in danger at night, can push a button, whereupon, bed and all, he disappears into a steel vault. When one prime minister, General Hayashi, moved into the house, he announced that even his wife would not know exactly where he slept. This was soon after the 1936 mutiny when cabinet ministers were still somewhat nervous. Prince Konoye, Baron Hiranuma's predecessor as prime minister, loathed the house, and used it only as an office.

I have given one example of Baron Hiranuma's somewhat remarkable prose style. Let it be spoken from their own mouths. Here is another:

Rumors to the effect that the national policy of Japan is imperialistic and aggressive should be deplored. It is ignorance of the true motives of Japan that leads to such unfounded rumors . . . Any student of Japanese history will recall that, since the foundation of the nation, our goal has been peace and security . . . The national policy of Japan is benevolence directed toward *the good development of all.* We wish to extend this spirit first to our nationals, secondly to the Far East, and third to the *rest of the world.*[1]

The italics are mine. They ought to be.

Hiranuma knows well that the function of a prime minister in Japan is to be an arbiter—if he is strong enough—between the radical army and the conservative industrialists. He has not found it an easy job. But, cautiously, he seeks a middle path. Recently he said that capitalism was not "necessarily evil," but that it should benefit society

[1] Quotations in this chapter are from the *Japan Advertiser*, the admirable American owned and edited Tokyo daily.

as a whole, not be the instrument of private gain. Hiranuma, like so many Japanese, likes to think of building a new society without daring to risk casting off the old.

Fascism in Japan

Hiranuma has been called a Fascist, and at this point we must examine critically the position of Japan in regard to Fascism. Is Japan a Fascist state? We know, of course, that Germany and Italy are its allies in the anti-Comintern pact. We know that Japan, even if it has borrowed some socialist ideas, is bitterly anti-communist, as are the other Fascist countries. What else? What other characteristics of Fascism have the Japanese, those assiduous mimics, acquired?

Fascism is an extraordinarily difficult and elusive concept to define. Perhaps one might list some Fascist characteristics, and see in what measure Japan shares them. First, Fascism is distinguished by the *Führer Prinzip*, by the totalitarian rule of a single man, a Hitler or Mussolini. There is no such man in Japan. The Emperor is a symbol, not a leader. Second, a Fascist state is ruled by an exclusive mass party, like the Nazis. There is no such mass party in Japan. Third, Fascism is served by totalitarian private armies, like the Blackshirts in Italy. But there are no shirted organizations in Japan—except the khaki of the army.

The conventional Marxist definition of Fascism is that it is the last stand of private monopoly capitalism against social revolution. I do not find this definition very satisfactory, since it ignores the considerable revolutionary element in Fascism. It ignores the fact that Fascism borrows heavily from Marxism, and makes a pretense at least of establishing a social order in which some of the extravagances of capitalism are curtailed. Under Fascism both capital and labor are at the mercy of the state, which is the supreme embodiment of economic as well as political authority. From this point of view Japan is certainly a Fascist state, though the capitalists are still wriggling.

Again, Fascism stands for race. In this Japan is Fascist, since it believes in Japanese racial integrity. Fascism is nationalist, it is aggressive, and it is militant. Japanese policy fills the Fascist bill in these particulars. Fascism makes war, and Japan makes war. Fascism suppresses civil liberties; so does Japan, but it should in all fairness be stated that the Japanese government is not nearly so repressive as the governments of Hitler and Mussolini. Japanese politicians still argue with some freedom; Japanese trade unions still exist on the old model, and strikes are still legal, though frowned upon; the Japanese press still has a voice, even if it whispers more than it shouts.

Fascism is anti-Semitic. And herewith a pretty story. The Japanese saw that anti-Semitism in Germany served a useful purpose (the same purpose served by persecution of the kulaks in the U.S.S.R.); the government needed some one to attack, since attack on a helpless minority was an excellent device for releasing internal pressure, for promoting domestic enthusiasm. So the Japanese began to encourage anti-Semitic speeches and exhibits. They wanted some one, not merely the Chinese, to whack at; they chose the inevitable scapegoat, the Jews. (Indeed it was difficult for them to whack at the Chinese, since the official yarn is that Japan is "liberating" its "friends," the Chinese people.) But the anti-Semitic campaign failed ignominiously. Reason: there are no Jews in the country, and the Japanese did not understand what anti-Semitism was.[2] Of course, if the Japanese wish to name what they really consider the enemy, they can do so easily enough: the white race. This produces a nice paradox. We whites, whom Hitler calls Aryans, are Jews to Japan.

Finally, Fascism is distinguished by what might be called the totalitarian instinct, that is, submission to national unity and solidarity under an authoritative régime. This instinct certainly exists in Japan. It exists so strongly, in fact, that one might suggest that there is no need for the Japanese to adopt supplementary Fascist ideas. A totalitarian system is unnecessary; everyone is obedient anyway. The enormous disciplinary machine of Fascism is useless, since conformity is ingrained in Japanese nature. Army and emperor are enough.

There are, however, several extremist politicians in Japan who think in overt Fascist terms. Take Toshio Shiratori, for instance, who was spokesman in the Foreign Office for a time, who is now ambassador to Rome, and who may some day be a rightist foreign minister. Mr. Shiratori told Jane Howard, a recent interviewer for the United Press: "I welcome the term Fascism as I do the term totalitarianism. There has been enough Anglo-Saxon influence in this country. It is time we allied ourselves with Italy and Germany. The

[2] But in January 1939 it was announced that no Jewish refugees from Germany would be allowed entry to the Japanese areas of China.

'glass house' democracy of the United States and the communism of soviet Russia go hand in hand."

. . . .

In theory Japan is a constitutional monarchy (of a peculiar kind) operating through the mechanism of parliamentary democracy. The paraphernalia is still intact: universal manhood suffrage (since 1925); a bicameral legislature; cabinet and privy council; a party system. But the Diet meets only a few months a year, and may be prorogued at the Emperor's will, i.e., the will of those nearest him; and the cabinet can do almost anything it wants, without regard to responsibility to parliament. The two great political parties, the Seiyukai and Minseito, are in decay; there are only two party men in the present cabinet. And if the army dislikes the result of an election— as in May, 1937—it has its own methods of counterbalancing it. That election was in a way a rebuke to the military. So promptly the military initiated the war in China.

A movement to abolish the parliamentary façade and to inaugurate a single Fascist-totalitarian party replacing the old parties began several years ago. Among the politicians behind it were Baron Hiranuma and Admiral Suetsugu; its leadership was to go to Prince Konoye, who later became prime minister. The machinery was to have been an organization with the fancy name of Central League for National Spiritual Mobilization. But the plan collapsed. Konoye became shy of the idea, and other leaders were coy. Apparently they feared that Japan was not ready for such a formally totalitarian step. Then came national preoccupation with the China war, which made it in a way unnecessary.

One of the fathers of the single party idea was a remarkably explosive young officer, Colonel Kingoro Hashimoto, who was retired from active service after the 1936 mutiny, and whose name was connected later with the *Panay* incident. Hashimoto, presumably with the backing of the army—which was finding the political situation irksome—organized a group known as the Japanese Youth Party. The international ideas of Colonel Hashimoto and his group deserve a word. Only by incessant quotation can I hope to make clear the extremity of view of prominent Japanese:

Britain, the United States, and France are the sinking sun at dusk . . . National Socialists and Fascists are the crescent moon against the evening sky. The Soviets are a bright star of early night . . . but adequate only to illuminate a corner of the sky. Things can revive only in the morning sunlight of great Japan . . . I am looking far and wide for pure hearted youths to work for the cause of the imperial nation, whose policy is to write itself in letters of fire in the eight corners of the universe.

The chief present manifestation of Fascism in Japan is the National Mobilization Law, passed on March 3, 1938, despite vigorous opposition by those members of the Diet still with courage to oppose it. The bill is a kind of Enabling Act, insisted upon by the army, which gives the government complete control of the resources and productive capacity of the nation. It was drafted by the Government Planning Board; it empowers the government to

    Determine wages and labor conditions
    Control exports and imports
    Expropriate goods, plants, land, house, mines, water rights
    Fix transportation charges
    Store raw materials
    Make vocational censuses
    Subsidize industry
    Censor publications

This is certainly totalitarianism of a very complete kind, but almost all governments adopt totalitarian measures in time of war. Britain and the United States did so in the Great War. Not all the provisions of the Mobilization Law have yet been invoked. There was a fierce dispute in November, 1938, when the industrialists and civilians, fearful at last that they were being socialized, summoned strength for a last ditch fight against application of Article XI of the law, which provides for government control of private profits and dividends. The army fought back, and a compromise was reached, limiting profits of any business enterprise to ten percent for the duration of the war. (Ten percent? Not bad!)

Another totalitarian creation is the newly organized "China Affairs Board," which will control exploitation and development of the areas occupied in China by the Japanese. This follows the example of Manchukuo, which we shall soon inspect.

*   *   *   *   *

A word about the traditional political parties. In a vague sense the

Minseito (179 seats) is "liberal," and the Seiyukai (175 seats) "conservative," but there is little serious difference between them. The Minseito tended to represent commerce, trade, and the urban communities, and for a time was more or less allied to the Mitsubishi financial interests. The Seiyukai was the party, by and large, of the aristocrats and landlords; the Mitsui interests supported it, though Mitsui was never so unintelligent—in the days when Japan was more of a democracy—as to put all its eggs in one basket.

The leader of the Minseito is 75-year-old Chuji Machida, an old line parliamentarian. He was the son of a Samurai; he had a distinguished career as a private banker, and then went into politics. The man behind him, the chief secretary of the Minseito, is Sachio Sakurauchi, whose origins are humble; he began life as a *tofu* (bean curd) peddler. The Minseito has traditionally stood for peace with China and a pacific foreign policy, but nowadays it adjusts itself—what remains of it—to the prevailing winds. In January 1939 it came out for establishment of an "East Asiatic League" comprising Japan, Manchukuo, and China.

The Seiyukai is at present in a state of disorganization. It has had no single leader since the retirement of aged Dr. Kisaburo Suzuki in 1936, and is managed by a board of four men; of the four the most interesting is Chikuhei Nakijama, the minister of railways and former head of a prosperous aviation company. Though a civilian, he might be called a triple-threat man from a military point of view: he served in the army, went to the naval engineering school, and traveled abroad, to study aviation. He was the first Japanese to get a pilot's license in the United States. Nakijama became minister of railways partly because he is independently rich and honest. At the time of his appointment no fewer than three railway ex-ministers were in jail, all having been charged with corruption.

Early in 1939 it was said that General Koiso, former chief of staff of the Kwantung army, would become head of the Seiyukai. His choice would confirm the current trend.

Prince Fumimaro Konoye

"I was a gloomy youth in my student days, with an inclination to read extremist literature from the west."

—Prince Konoye

One of the most interesting men in Asia is the subtle, complex, diffident and difficult Prince Fumimaro Konoye, prime minister of

Japan—though he never wanted the job and disliked it considerably —from May 1937 to January 1939, and thereafter minister without portfolio. Last summer I talked with him in his modest country house in Ogikubo, near Tokyo. His windows show a rolling valley that might be Surrey or Connecticut, except for the pond full of lotus petals.

Prince Konoye is tall for a Japanese, just under six feet. Because he is so tall, he hates to travel; Japanese railway berths do not hold him comfortably. Sleek, handsome, clean shaven, with close cropped hair (he goes to the barber every five days), Konoye seems younger than his age. He became prime minister at forty-six, the youngest (with one exception) in Japanese history; and forty-six is practically infanthood in Japan, where venerability counts as it does in England. A Japanese, like an Englishman, can be a rising young parliamentarian at fifty-five.

Konoye is a patrician. His aristocratic fingers seem eight inches long. His manner is reserved; the head is held high and tilted; the glance, underneath long lashes, is almost supercilious. He is rather Balfouresque; he gives the impression of political dilettantism. He seems to lack energy—or perhaps he is bored; after each sentence comes a sigh and a pause for breath. His subtlety of mind is considerable, and so is his humility. He is one of the very few Japanese ever to have refused the premiership; when in 1937 he finally did take the job, he announced that he was not capable of holding it. His sense of humor is considered odd.

His friends say that he makes a cult of languor. When, visiting America in 1934, he played golf in Washington, he would break off the game after two or three holes. He seldom makes appointments before 11 A.M., and his unpunctuality is the despair of secretaries. Once he could not bear to face the Diet—the discussion concerned the National Mobilization Law—and he simply went to bed for a week, pleading ill health; the journalists in Tokyo called it a "lie-down" strike. To make sure that he would be on time for a recent radio address, he stayed overnight in town, not caring to risk a journey from the country (the drive takes twenty minutes) at 10 A.M., which seemed to him the grisly equivalent of dawn.

He belongs to one of the great families of Japan: his blood is so special that, literally, a Japanese scientist recently suggested medical tests for civil servants, to favor men with a peculiar "O type" of

blood which Konoye has. He comes from one of the five families of
court nobles, all of them offshoots of the Fujiwaras, from which
traditionally the Empress must be chosen. The Konoye branch dates
from A.D. 1202. But the Konoyes trace their descent far behind that;
they say that, like the Emperor, they are of divine origin, descendants
of the god Amenokoyane who welcomed Amaterasu, another deity,
when she came to earth.

Konoye was born in Tokyo in October, 1891. He was the eldest
son of Prince Atsumaro Konoye, who was president of the House of
Peers—a position corresponding to that of Lord Chancellor in England. The father was an intimate associate of Prince Saionji, the last
Genro, and Saionji, then Ambassador to Vienna, took him there.
Thirty-five years later Saionji similarly took young Konoye, the present prince, abroad; he was one of Saionji's secretaries at the Paris
Peace Conference. Thus—another example—does old Prince Saionji
span the generations.

Konoye's mother died eight days after his birth. The father composed two poems, one of them a dirge for his wife, the other a lament
for his baby son, "who thereafter must be reared by nurses." The
father died at 41. From 1904 on, young Prince Konoye was an orphan.
He was a lonely, unhappy child. He had little money. It is recorded
that the young prince became "melancholy and bitter, brooding over
social injustice and absorbing Marxist philosophy."

Indeed Konoye left the University of Tokyo, where he first
matriculated, to attend lectures by Professor Kawakami, a radical
economist and student of Marx, at the University of Kyoto. He came
under the influence of Tolstoy, and wrote a youthful pamphlet on
social justice. He decided to renounce his titles and emigrate to the
United States. He records: "I began to feel interest in the social
sciences . . . Dr. Kawakami gave me two books, the *Life of Karl
Marx* by John Spargo, and *Contemporary Social Problems* by Professor Achille Loria, of Trieste, Italy." When I saw Prince Konoye
I asked him about this Marxist "period." He smiled, but his secretary
blushed furiously that I should bring up such a gruesome topic.

Then came a dominating event. Young Konoye went to pay respects
to his father's old friend, Prince Saionji. "My first impression was
not good," Konoye records, "because Saionji (who was at least forty
years his senior) treated me like a superior, using the expression
'Your Excellency,' whereas I was only a humble student. I thought

he was making a fool of me. So I didn't call on him again." After graduation Konoye chanced to meet him. This time the old man talked "in a full and very frank manner." He saw the struggle in the youth's mind, and sought to give him comfort and advice. "Prince Saionji said that I should become a provincial governor. He thought everyone could be a provincial governor, since he himself had been one at 18. When told that to become a governor was not easy, the Prince advised me to enter the service of some political party. I, however, did not have the courage to enter a political party." More and more interested in this strange young man, Saionji persuaded him to come to Paris with him.

Konoye returned to Japan, forgot his Marxist leanings, took his hereditary seat in the House of Peers, and in 1933 became its president, the same position his father had held. Aside from occupying this post, he took no active rôle in politics until he became prime minister.

His strength in the premiership came, first, because he was favorably regarded by the Emperor, second because the army respected him, third because he was an independent in politics, with no clique controlling him, and no ax to grind. He had no enemies, and very little personal ambition. But he didn't like the job, since he was in the uncomfortable position of having to accept responsibility without real power. He several times attempted to resign, but the war came, and he could not leave office without causing loss of face to the nation.

Twice he had to reshuffle his cabinet, as army demands for political control became more pressing. He got rid of Koki Hirota as foreign minister, and in May 1938 acceded to the appointment of General Itagaki as minister of war. A few months later occurred the Mobilization Bill crisis. His civilian ministers came to open conflict with the military; his foreign minister, General Ugaki, who opposed the creation of the China Board and who was willing to make some concession to the British in regard to opening the Yangtze and otherwise reducing Japanese military pressure in China, had to go. The army demanded the final word in everything. So, after an interval, Konoye went too. But it is doubtful if he disagreed *basically* with army sentiment.

Konoye married the second daughter of Viscount Takanori Mori, of a distinguished family. He has two brothers, one of them a poet, the other a competent musician who is conductor of a Tokyo orchestra devoted to occidental music. He has two sons. One promises to be a lively lad. As a student at Princeton, he was a champion golfer, and was voted the boy in his class most likely to succed; then he failed to get his degree. When, in October 1937 President Roosevelt made his Chicago speech denouncing the aggressor nations, young Konoye said, "The speech was nothing much—or at least I hope not." When his father made his first speech to the Diet as prime minister, he announced, "It may be impolite to say so, but Father's speech did not impress me." The young man is now in Tokyo, preparing for a career in journalism. His father's great friend Yukichi Iwanaga, head of the Domei news service, gave him his first job.

During his premiership, despite great pressure, Prince Konoye tried to take a moderate line. His main idea was to win the war as quickly as possible; and though recognition had been withdrawn from the Nanking government, he wanted to find a formula for negotiation with Chiang Kai-shek, if he would prove himself "sincere." Konoye was asked once if the growing coalescence between England and France did not weaken Japan's faith in the power of the German-Italian combination and hence in the value to Japan of the Anti-Comintern Pact. He paused long before replying. "Ah!" he exclaimed. "But we would like England to join the Anti-Comintern Pact too!"

When Hitler took the Sudetenland in October, 1938, Konoye's hearty congratulations were among the first received.

Nobles and Peers

The composition of the upper house of the Diet is peculiar. First come hereditary princes and marquesses; incidentally the number of these is limited, since Japanese are commoners until the titled father dies; sons do not, as in England, take on lesser titles while awaiting inheritance. Lower categories of nobility come next; they choose from among themselves members for seven year periods. Then there are peers appointed to the Diet by the throne: distinguished educators, scientists, and the like, some of whom serve for life, some for seven years. Finally the fifteen richest taxpayers in each prefecture elect one of themselves for a seven year term.

Nobility in Japan is in three categories. First come members of the Imperial House, who are outside politics. Next are great court nobles, like the Fujiwaras and Konoyes, who have had titles for centuries.

The third group comprises those whose titles were created after the Meiji Restoration, when—roughly on the English model—a peerage ranging from viscount to prince was set up. Roughly 600 peers have been named in seventy years; one reason for creating the system was to break the power of the old feudal barons.[3]

The most eminent of present day nobles is probably Prince Iyesato Tokugawa. He is an adopted son of the last Shogun; if there had been no Meiji Restoration, Tokugawa—he is seventy-seven—would be Shogun now, ruler of Japan. The old man is married to a Konoye princess. He was for twenty-four years president of the House of Peers—between two Konoyes—and was chief Japanese delegate at the Washington Disarmament Conference. He is head of the Japanese Red Cross and was chairman of the Japan Olympic Committee; when the army canceled the 1940 Olympic games scheduled for Tokyo, the news was at first withheld from Tokugawa because his family feared it would break his heart.

Foreign Office

A squat, decisive, red-faced, bullet-headed little man. Not more than five foot four, and seemingly as broad. The vigor of a man of thirty. The hiss of Japanese politeness increased almost to a whistle. Punch and clarity in the conversation. This is General Kasunari Ugaki, until late in 1938 the foreign minister of Japan.[4]

Ugaki was—and is—a moderate. Konoye chose him as foreign minister hoping that he would be a bridge between the civil administration and the military. But the army hated him, though he was one of its own. This was because, when minister of war in 1924, he cut the Japanese army by two divisions (perhaps 50,000 men), and reduced military expenditure by 20,000,000 yen per year, pursuant to the Shidehara policy of peace. In 1937 Ugaki was named prime minister, but he could not form a cabinet; the army radicals refused to

[3] Titles are by no means universally popular in Japan. My friend Frank Hedges tells me that the great financier Dr. Dan, who was murdered when he was head of the House of Mitsui, refused a title twice. Finally he consented to be named a Baron, partly because, a democrat of democrats, he was fatigued even by his innocuous title Doctor (he was a Ph.D. from the Massachusetts Institute of Technology); the ruse did not work, because promptly he was dubbed "Baron Dr. Dan."

[4] The given name is sometimes romanized to Kasashigi instead of Kasunari. Kasunari means literally "To Become First." Ugaki adopted it when he entered military academy. And he became first in his class.

give him a minister of war. They pushed him out of the foreign office the next year.

Ugaki is a picturesque and attractive character, who may conceivably come back. He was born in Okayama prefecture in 1868; he belongs, like Baron Hiranuma, to what is called the "Okayama circle." His origins were humble; as a youth he taught school for 6 yen per month. He managed to get into the military academy, and had an excellent career; for seven years he was governor-general of Korea. He is widely read, and intellectually more curious than most Japanese. He likes to drink.

General Ugaki was succeeded in the foreign office by a career diplomat, a much less striking man, and one who is assumed to be more pliable in the hands of the military—Hachiro Arita, a former Ambassador to China. As a professional diplomat he has never expressed views on politics; as a China specialist he is competent. He was born in 1884, and has served in Manchuria, Siam, China, Washington, and Brussels. When his appointment was announced the Japanese press said that it "lacked vitality," though in a former term as foreign minister he signed the Anti-Comintern Pact.

A favorite game in Tokyo is to try to determine what the rank and file of foreign office men think of the policies the army makes them adopt. A safe guess is that most approve of army design, and dislike army tactics. Most of their work is finding ex post facto excuses for what the army does.

The old school foreign office men are, however, severely ignored in Tokyo these days. In 1938 fourteen active ambassadors and ministers were cooling their heels in the outer corridors, awaiting new posts. Military influence in Japan has another odd characteristic; it seems to infect the foreigners assigned to duty there. Actually five members of the diplomatic corps to-day are former military attachés, including the German Ambassador General Ott and the Mexican Minister General Aguilar.

The Amiable Hirota

Mr. Koki ("Cocky") Hirota, a bright and forceful man, was General Ugaki's immediate predecessor at the Foreign Office. Previously he had been a prime minister: and specialists in protocol say that he erred in accepting a lesser post after having been on top. To which Mr. Hirota's friends would say that he was self-sacrificing, that he

would take any job to serve his country; and to which his enemies
assert that he takes what crumbs he can get, because he is tremendously ambitious—a "subtle equilibrist in careerism," I heard it said.

Hirota was born in 1878. He was a poor boy,[5] whose father was a
stone cutter. Hirota has no noble or Samurai blood. He struggled to
get an education, and came under the influence of the nationalist
philosopher Toyama, in whose neighborhood he lived. He entered the
diplomatic service in 1906, and has served widely abroad. In Washington he was very popular. He is called a "deadly earnest" man,
whose only avocation is the collection of tulip bulbs.

An important item in Hirota's career is his membership in the
Black Dragon society, the most potent and militant of the 200-odd
semi-secret societies which infest Japan. The Black Dragon, a collection of young men devoted to active pan-Asia policy, reached great
importance after the Great War, though its roots are older; originally
it derives from the *soshi*—unemployed Samurai who had no place
in society after the Meiji Restoration. In the Black Dragon are hooli-
gans, army officers, chauvinistic politicians, avowed terrorists, quite
respectable cabinet ministers, and secret agents who worked closely
with the Military Intelligence in continental Asia. Japanese ideographs for "Black Dragon" are identical with those of "Amur River,"
which is an interesting coincidence, if coincidence it be—since the
Amur River is the frontier between Manchukuo and the Soviet Union,
where Japanese imperialist ambitions are high.

Hirota's policy was frankly "positive." It was he, as foreign minister, who announced that Generalissimo Chiang Kai-shek would be
beheaded when—or if—the Japanese got him. Recently he said:

The United States should keep her hands off Far Eastern Affairs
and place implicit confidence in Japan's efforts to maintain peace
[again!] and order in Asia. The world should be divided into three
parts, under the influence of American, European, and Asiatic Monroe doctrines.

The Japanese often seek to justify their conquest of China by
adducing the "analogy" of the Monroe Doctrine. This is nonsense,
of course. The United States never invaded the South American continent by force of arms in order to preserve the Monroe or any other
doctrine.

[5] Once he asked for a job as translator to General Pershing, then American
military attaché in Japan.

The Extremist Fringe

One cannot but begin with the incredible Araki. General Baron Sadao Araki, born in 1877 in Tokyo of a Samurai family, former minister of war and present minister of education, is the extreme type of military chauvinist. He is the most pronouncedly anti-Russian man in Japan. Also he is a good deal of a mystic, and something of a philosopher.

The old general has a hot temper and a quick tongue, and his indiscretions, particularly in regard to the U.S.S.R., have once or twice caused embarrassment. Once he was quoted by an interviewer for the *Japan Advertiser* as hinting that Japan, in signing the Anti-Comintern Pact, was influenced by opportunist motives. A storm of protest came from Japanese officials. Negotiations began between the *Advertiser* and the General. Finally the *Advertiser* printed a brief statement, "General Baron Araki has asked the *Japan Advertiser* to amplify an interpretation conveyed to an interviewer last week. In addition to sharing a common antipathy toward the Comintern, Japan entered the Pact, says Araki, because of certain natural and spiritual affinities between the Fascist countries, and there was in no sense a feeling of 'expediency' which might suggest 'sacrifice of moral principles for the sake of an end.'"

Soon afterwards Araki gave an interview to the Tokyo correspondent of the Associated Press, in which he asserted that a war between Japan and Russia was inevitable and necessary—an opinion which, indeed, most Japanese officers would support, though it was maladroit to state it openly. The Russians raised pained eyebrows, and asked the A.P. if the interview were authorized. The General said, "Let the Russians protest to me!"

Sometimes Araki is misquoted because his language is so difficult. He likes oriental imagery and abstractions. He talks in metaphor and allegory. Once, in fact, a distinguished American newspaper executive saw him, and never understood a word he said, though an expert interpreter was present. When he talks—a storm of eloquent words— he scribbles on a piece of paper, then ceremoniously signs the paper, gives it to the interviewer. Sometimes he scrawls pictures of tigers, sometimes maps of Manchukuo, sometimes indecipherable designs.

His house is full of tiger heads and skins. He was born in the month devoted to the tiger by the Japanese zodiac. He also preserves carefully a stuffed crane and a stuffed tortoise, which are symbols of old age. Other decorations are suits of medieval armor and chain mail. These ornaments aside, he is a frugal man. He disproves of *sake,* and cultivates the Spartan virtues. He saw to it that his son entered the army as a common conscript. He fences—against a robot—every morning.

Araki, though of Samurai descent, lived as a youth in extreme poverty. At the age of 14 he was an apprentice in a soya bean factory. He entered the army, fought in the Russo-Japanese war, and during the World War was attached to the Japanese military mission in Moscow; he learned Russian, and ever since has been more interested in Russia than in any country—except Japan. As minister of war, it was his custom to visit relatives of dead soldiers incognito; they would be informed simply that an "officer" would come to see them.

He once told a friend that he disliked Napoleon, whom he called a professional warmaker. He said:

Napoleon could do nothing except kill his enemies. Viewed from my point of view, which is that of the Japanese Imperial Army, a messenger of world peace, [again!] Napoleon was a hateful being with vicious attributes. The armies of Europe are organs for the executions of militarism . . . The imperial army of Japan is ever peaceful in its message.

Once communists broke up an Araki meeting. A 19-year-old boy was arrested as the ringleader. The boy's father went to the General to apologize, and Araki summoned the boy. The *Japan Advertiser* says:

In the interview that followed between the General and the somewhat frightened student, the General patiently listened to the youth's views on communism and why he believed in it. The General then engaged his visitor in philosophic discussion and in the end convinced the young man that his conception of radicalism was in substance identical with the national imperialism of Japan.

Araki, it is said, wept when the Lytton Commission refused to believe his testimony that the occupation of Manchuria was "peaceful." When army mutineers attempted to kill off the civilian cabinet in 1936, Araki was minister of war. He resigned, but was prevailed upon to withdraw his resignation.

.   .   .   .

Another Japanese rightist with mystical overtones is the redoubtable 85-year-old Mitsura Toyama, likewise an apostle of pan-Asian
nationalism, who has been called Japan's "superman." For a time
he ate only grass and leaves. Once, competing in endurance with
a Zen priest, he sat motionless, sleepless, foodless, waterless, and
silent, for five days and five nights. Even in midwinter, he refuses
to heat his house, and sits in a kimono on a bearskin. Once he was
arrested after a political opponent had been bombed and injured. No
damaging evidence was found among his effects—except a lot of love
letters.

Toyama is a native of Fukuoka province, like his protégé Hirota.
For a time his activity was spiritual and literary; he was a kind of
Japanese Tagore, and "aspired to transcend human nature as far as
possible." Then he became interested in Asiatic nationalist movements; he was a close friend and associate of the Chinese revolutionary leader Dr. Sun Yat-sen, and for eight years he contrived
to keep hidden an exiled Indian agitator, Rash Behari Bose, who fled
to Japan in 1915, though the British tried to extradite him. He
wanted to liberate the Philippines from their "oppressors." Then
Toyama turned to nationalism more exclusively Japanese, and reached
great fame and influence as head of the Black Dragon Society.

Too old now to take active part in politics, Toyama is a waning
influence. But few men in Japan are more revered. It is said that
he is the only man in the country who can collect a crowd of 50,000
on two hours' notice.

.   .   .   .

Another Fukuoka man, Seigo Nakano, is the leader of the only
outright Fascist party in Japan. A youthful nationalist of extreme
views, he became a journalist, then visited Europe and saw Hitler
and Mussolini; returning to Japan he founded the Tohokai group
in the Diet, which admits to being Fascist. Nakano is a highly articu-
late young man. He wants vigorous prosecution of the war in China,
and a reformed industrial and social structure in Japan. Recently
his group absorbed the Social Mass or "labor" party.

A semi-Fascist party is the Kokumin Domei (People's League),
led by the former minister of communications, Kenzo Adachi, born in
1864 and nicknamed "God of Elections." He has sat in the Diet thirteen times in a row. Like so many Japanese "patriots" he is a direct

actionist, with a tendency to justify direct action by appeals to mysticism. Adachi was one of the bright young men who prepared for the annexation of Korea by political intrigue there; he was accused of complicity in the murder of the Korean queen, and served a term in jail. Later he built an "Eight Saints' Hall" for pilgrims, where his eight heroes are enshrined: Christ, Buddha, Confucius, Socrates, Mohammed, Lao Tse, and two Japanese saints, Kobo Daishi and Nichiren.

Matsuoka in Mid-Career

"To wait for political parties to improve is like waiting for pigs to fly."
—YOSUKE MATSUOKA

In a class by himself among Japanese politicians is Yosuke Matsuoka, who was once a bus-boy in a Seattle hotel, who is now president of the South Manchuria Railway, probably the biggest enterprise in the Japanese empire. Matsuoka came of good family; he is a prominent member of the Choshu clan. He was born in 1880, and went to America at 12, where he worked his way through the University of Oregon. He entered the diplomatic service, and was the slippery and unquenchable Japanese delegate at Geneva during the occupation of Manchuria. He is easier to talk to than most Japanese; at Geneva he was as hard to grasp as an eel, but normally he is exceptionally concrete in conversation, a practical man, a realist:

Listen to him on the China war:

At last Japan is in for the final, the knockout decision . . . The task calls for heroic surgery . . . Japan will permit no foreign interference whatever . . . A historic fact dominates Asia like Mt. Fuji—without Japan, there can be no China . . . We are free to admit that Japan has been exceedingly annoying to her neighbor China. And what expanding country ever failed to be trying to its neighbors? Ask the American Indian or Mexican how excruciatingly trying the young U. S. A. was once upon a time . . . Japan's expansion, like that of America, is as natural as the growth of a child. Only one thing can stop the growth of a child—death.

What is Japan fighting for? For the fulfillment of her mission in Asia. That is the whole answer.

This is candor of a type extremely rare in Japan.

Returning from Geneva Matsuoka entered politics, and became a deputy. In 1933, fed up, he resigned his seat, and also his position in the Seiyukai party. He announced that he no longer believed in political parties, and set up an organization for their extinction. "If there is to be a rebirth to the nation," he said, "the parliamentary system must be abolished. I believe the future of Japan lies in . . . the establishment of government by the Emperor." Then he became a "Showa Restorationist," i.e., one who sought to "redeem" Japan by stronger service to the ruler.

Matsuoka's movement was a failure. Few deputies imitated his resignation, and soon the "Showa Restoration" group became severely unpopular, because the 1936 army mutineers used the phrase. Matsuoka spent several years in the wilderness, trying to organize a single political party. "Neo-Nipponism" (whatever that may mean) became his creed. Then he was appointed suddenly to the presidency of the South Manchuria Railway, one of the biggest jobs in Japan. It was called the greatest "come-back" in Japanese political history.

In 1939 it was reported that Matsuoka was resigning his railway job. He is exceptionally ambitious, and is probably feeling the itch for politics again; he was said to be scheduled for an important post directing the new agencies "developing" the China conquests.

Opposition—If Any

Until recently the Japanese equivalent to His Majesty's Loyal Opposition was the Social Mass party, with thirty-six deputies, led by the venerable professor Iso Abe. This was theoretically a party devoted to Fabian socialism of a very mild variety; during the war it decided to support the government, and thus lost practical significance. Then, astonishingly enough—almost anything can happen in Japan—it merged in February 1939 with the Fascist party of Seigo Nakano.

Professor Abe, 73 years old, is a mild-mannered and respectable socialist. His ideas are in the main those held by British Fabians thirty years ago; he says that his ideal is "Marxism minus revolution." He is an academician with a long record at Waseda University and his ambition was to make the Diet "a schoolroom for gentlemen." He was badly beaten up by nationalist rowdies early in 1938, apparently because he opposed the National Mobilization Bill.

There should be a line at least for the grand old men of Japan, the old-line liberals, who are on the shelf to-day, who play no rôle in politics, but whose past careers are admirably distinguished. Old Yukio Ozaki, "the Elihu Root of Japan," is eighty; he has sat in the

Diet without interruption since its foundation, a unique record. He was once mayor of Tokyo; he befriended Sun Yat-sen; he advocates romanization of the Japanese language—an unpopular idea nowadays . . . Another veteran liberal is Viscount Kikujiro Ishii, born in 1866, foreign minister during the Great War and for many years chief Japanese delegate at Geneva.

Baron Kijuri Shidehara, born in 1872, and Baron Reijiro Wakatsuki, born in 1866, are the only conspicuous survivors of those civilian ministries which in the 1920's stood for conciliation and peace—without quotation marks—in international affairs. Their colleagues have passed into complete obscurity, or have been assassinated by "patriots." Baron Shidehara, one of the ablest living foreign ministers, must be guarded by police wherever he goes, for fear that some fanatic may attack him. Shidehara and Wakatsuki are called "traitors" by the inflamed radicals, whereas no Japanese alive have finer records of public service.

In a special category is the Christian salvationist, Toyahiko Kagawa, who for a time bade fair to be a Japanese Gandhi, but whose importance was obliterated by the war. Kagawa is a poet, an evangelist, and a social reformer. He was a well-to-do boy, of Samurai descent; a German missionary converted him to Christianity, and he turned to social work. He opposed violence, like Gandhi, but led strikes in the rice fields; he organized the Japanese federation of labor, and was the father of Japanese coöperatives, which now have 25,000,000 members. For a time the authorities considered Kagawa a dangerous radical, but his work organizing relief after the 1923 earthquake made him "respectable."

Kagawa is a strong nationalist. One of his poems:

> A new day has come
> A new day;
> The buds are swelling,
> Fresh leaves are bursting,
> And from the brown clay
> Green plants are sprouting.
>
> The day of God is come;
> The day of God
> That none expected
> Is now at hand.

On that great day
The League of Nations
And the Anti-War Pact
Both lose their luster;
For only love's eternal truth
Can crowned be
With God's glory.

The ablest genuine left-winger in Japan is probably Kanju Kato. He is in his early forties, and gained prominence as the most radical deputy in the Diet, and the leader of the All-Japan Council of Trade Unions. He is not a communist, but is in sympathy with communist ideas. There are very few communists in Japan; and any man who is a communist would be foolish to admit it. Kato was arrested late in 1938, when Admiral Suetsugu, the home minister, rounded up between three and four hundred liberals and radicals who had somehow escaped the police until then, and jailed the lot.

Between 1933 and 1936, according to the semi-official *Japan Times*, the police arrested no fewer than 59,013 persons charged with "dangerous thoughts," i.e., political dissidence. Of these, however, only about 5,000 were indicted and tried; the rest were presumably freed after police examination which in some cases was brief, in some cases prolonged. Of the 5,000-odd who were tried, about 2,500 went to prison. The Japanese assert that every man arrested is given a public trial, but he may have to wait in jail months or years before the trial occurs. Formally, there are no concentration camps.

Prospects of social revolution in Japan are not bright. Radical ferment exists, and is probably more extensive than the Japanese like to admit, but it is not a major phenomenon, and it is ruthlessly extirpated when it appears. There are several obvious reasons for the slow development of radical opposition to Japanese institutions. For one thing, there is no proletariat in our sense of the term, and, although the standard of living is very low, unemployment scarcely exists. Again, one must remember the unique solidarity of Japan under the Emperor; discontent is the equivalent of treason to one's own family. Finally, there is the Japanese tradition of conformity and discipline.

If Japan should suddenly and disastrously lose the China war, if there should be a complete debacle in the field, or overwhelming defeat at the hands of some other power, then revolution might conceivably occur.

Chapter V
Men of Yen

~~~~~~

JAPANESE are small men. But Japan is a land of giants from the point of view of finance and industry. We come now to the mammoth "Five" of Japanese economy—the Houses of Mitsui, Mitsubishi, Sumitomo, Yasuda, and Okura—which embody a concentration of financial power unparalleled in the world, and which are a unique and extraordinary factor in the life, private and public, of Japan. These five houses control not less than sixty-two percent of the *total* wealth of Japan. Seventy percent of Japanese textiles, forty percent of Japanese bank deposits, are in their hands. The three biggest of them, Mitsui, Mitsubishi, and Sumitomo, control about one-quarter of all Japanese trade and industry, and 16.54 percent of Tokyo's capital investment is held by Mitsui alone. In no country in the world does a single giant concern account for such a share of the national economy. Mitsui is a colossus beside which organizations like Du Pont, Standard Oil, Imperial Chemicals, seem like children.

Statistics tell the story briefly. According to the admirable analysis in the Japanese number of *Fortune*, Mitsui and its subsidiaries control fourteen percent of *all* Japanese cotton business, fifteen percent of rayon, seventy-eight percent of paper, seventeen percent of cement, seventeen percent of mining, five percent of engineering, eleven percent in coal and shipping, five percent in electro-chemicals. Mitsubishi controls 4.6 percent of *all* Japanese banking, ten percent of trust business, thirty-nine percent of marine and fire insurance, thirty-seven percent of shipping, twenty-two percent of warehousing, six percent of life insurance, forty-seven percent in glass, nineteen percent in sugar, seventeen percent of beer, forty-seven percent in wheat. Sumitomo controls twenty percent in warehousing, thirty-two percent in wires and cables, ten percent in trust business. Monopolies of such grandiose longitudinal direction are unique.

Searching for explanation we must again turn to feudalism. Japanese industry was not fragmented by generations of competition and free development. The industrial revolution came overnight. A handful of families controlled wealth and the opportunities for production

82

when the machine age came, and they expanded throughout industry assiduously. The nation voraciously needed—almost without warning —a vast industrial equipment, and only those rare merchants and traders who already had some hold on economic resources were able to supply the spectacular demand. They seized this opportunity; they proliferated; they entrenched.

The House of Mitsui

Mitsui history goes back a long way. Like almost everything else in Japan, it has medieval roots, a modern surface. The legend is that the Mitsuis were originally Fujiwaras (of course it is convenient to talk about relationship to such noble blood), but that a young man Kanpaku Michinaga, who lived from 967 to 1028 A.D., disliked the Fujiwara connection, and assumed the name Mitsui from the village where he lived. Apparently he walked out of the court circle in Kyoto to discover himself and explore his soul among humble surroundings. Generations later, in the 16th century, the Mitsui family found itself without an heir. So it adopted a successor named Takahisa, who came from the exalted Minamoto family. From that date to this all Mitsuis have the syllable "taka" in their names. "Mitsui" itself means literally "three wells."

At about the time the original Mitsuis became Takahisas, the head of the family in some unaccountable way decided that the life of a Samurai was a bore—or perhaps the rice crop failed or perhaps he didn't want to earn a living by pillage—and unprecedentedly he entered trade. This was an iconoclastic step. Trade was little respected in those days. But his business, largely of handicraft textiles, grew handsomely. By the late 17th century the Mitsuis owned warehouses for cloth in Kyoto, had a kind of embryo department store in Yedo (the old name for Tokyo), and did a flourishing trade in cotton in Osaka. The family then necessarily became bankers. They had to deal in money as well as goods. In fact, to make business easier, they *invented* money, substituting tokens of metal instead of the unwieldy bags of rice that hitherto served as cash. Then, a natural progression, they developed credit too.

A member of the family named Takatoshi had eleven sons. This was still in the 17th century. He took eight of them, and set them up as heads of eight parallel family groups. (Why the other three sons were eliminated we do not know; perhaps they were too young, perhaps they were ne'er-do-wells . . .) The eldest son was selected as the leader of the eight. These eight Mitsui families persist to this day. They are bound by a family law, which was written more than two hundred years ago, which is amended from time to time, and which in theory at least is followed in every particular by contemporary Mitsuis. Some of its provisions:

1. The members of the House shall deal with one another in close friendship and with kindness. A single stick may be easily broken. Do not forget this fact; make the family fortune more secure by mutual harmony.
2. Do not endlessly increase the number of families in the House. Everything has its limits. Know that over-expansion, which you may covet, will beget confusion.
3. A certain part of the income earned by all branches of the family shall be set aside as a reserve, and only after this is accomplished shall each family receive its individual share.
4. Thrift enriches a House, while luxury ruins a man.
5. In making marriage, incurring debts, or underwriting the debts of others, act always with the advice of the family council.
6. Each family shall select one man to be known as the Elder. He shall direct all acts of the family.
7. Quarrels between the families are forbidden, as is extravagance.
8. The head of each family must know everything, great and small, about his family.
9. Weak soldiers do not exist under a strong general. See that able men are selected for important tasks, so that there shall be no grumbling among the workers.
10. All Mitsui sons shall work for a certain time in the company, under identical conditions with other employees.
11. The life work of a man lasts as long as he lives. Therefore, do not, without reason, seek the luxury and ease of retirement. The most important thing in business is to know when to retire.
12. The essential of a business enterprise is to employ men of great ability and take advantage of their special talents. Replace those who are old and decrepit with young men of promise.
13. You who have been born in the land of the gods, worship your gods, revere your Emperor, love your country, and do your duty as subjects.

When a Mitsui son comes of age he swears allegiance to these family laws at a semi-religious ceremony. This is the oath, in the form it has been prescribed for more than a hundred years:

In obedience to the precepts of our forefathers, and in order to strengthen the everlasting ancestral foundation of the families of our House and to expand our enterprises bequeathed by our forefathers, I solemnly vow in the presence of the August Spirits of our ancestors that, as a member of the House of Mitsui, I will observe and follow the regulations handed down in the Constitution of our House, and that I will not wantonly seek to alter them. In witness whereof, I take the oath and affix my signature thereto in the presence of the August Spirits of our ancestors.

Note well the extraordinary resemblance between the Mitsuis and the European Rothschilds. Both grew to eminence at about the same time; both were merchants who became dealers in exchange; both had a strong family sense, grew up in parallel families, and obeyed a family constitution. The Mitsuis simplified greatly the technique of domestic credit; similarly the Rothschilds invented the technique of international money transfer and exchange. Both made great fortunes by an industrial revolution. Both played politics. Mitsui consolidated its power by becoming financial agent for a government, which is exactly what the Rothschilds did with several governments. That two such financial families should have pursued almost precisely the same development, at approximately the same time, while separated from each other by many thousands of miles, and with no conceivable opportunity for exchange of information until 1868 or later, is an extraordinary example of parallelism in economic affairs, of an essential likeness in financial problems, and of the insatiable activism of finance capital whether white or yellow.

Came the Restoration in 1868. Before that the Mitsuis were merely a big business. Afterward they became a dominating national institution. They had helped to finance the tottering Daimyos; they helped now to finance the new imperial government. The government needed cash quickly, in part to crush a rising of Shogunate troops; Mitsui provided it, and helped win the civil war. For generations, when the Emperor was a puppet, Mitsui had managed and collected the imperial revenue; with the Emperor restored, this duty and privilege was retained and amplified. The new government set up two organizations, the Office of Specie and Currency, the Office of Commercial Law; Mitsui men ran both. Mitsui became the fiscal agent of the government. For a time, so indispensable was the House in this connection, that it was permitted to use funds of the national treasury without security or interest.

For thirty years after the Restoration Mitsui history is so remarkably like Rothschild history that one blinks. As exclusive treasury agents the Mitsuis became incredibly wealthy, and they began to invest their profits in industry, which grew apace. They became manufacturers and traders as well as merchant-bankers. In 1874 the new paper money began to wilt; Mitsui alone had the cash to make it good, and thus saved the government; after which Mitsui was shrewd enough not to ask too many favors—at the beginning. Like the Rothschilds, the Mitsuis flirted with various political groups, obliterated competitors by adroit purchase, backed promising statesmen, and financed wars. The old Marquis Inouye, one of the Genro, became a "Mitsui man." And wealth tumbled into the Mitsui basket like golden rain.

Another point is a very Japanese point. Throughout this entire period of inordinate expansion the House of Mitsui was not actually operated by Mitsui men. This is true to-day. "Like the English kings, the Mitsuis reign but do not rule," I heard it said. The executive head of the enormous conglomerate organization is, by invariable rule, *not* a member of the family but some one imported from outside as a director-specialist. He is known as the "Banto," literally "watchman." The Mitsuis own the business exclusively (no outside capital is permitted), but it is operated by a hired employee. This system of control by a subordinate is, of course, strikingly analogous to the way Japan itself is operated, until 1868 by a Shogun behind the Emperor, and nowadays by an army behind a constitution.

We have no space to describe the complex organization of the Mitsui domain at present. Even a simplified chart of the family enterprises fills a large page; one virtually needs a slide rule and a pair of dividers to understand it. Suffice it to say that a gigantic holding company, the Mitsui Gomei Kaisha, is on top. The head of each Mitsui branch has unlimited liability in this company, which is the fountain-head of the organization. It controls directly six great subsidiaries (shipping, insurance, banking, trust business, mining, warehousing), and eleven indirect subsidiaries; the structure then ramifies down to ninety-six different "main enterprises" or "relationship companies." One subsidiary, the Mitsui Bussan Kaisha, the largest trading company in the world, handles nineteen percent of

Japan's *total* exports, fourteen percent of its *total* imports. The authorized capital of all Mitsui enterprises is 2,146,409,000 yen.[1] No one knows what the aggregate wealth of the family is.

The head of the House of Mitsui until 1933 was the Honorable Takamine Mitsui. He had been created a baron in 1896—he was an obvious choice for a Restoration peerage—but subsequently, like so many Japanese, he gave up his title. He was succeeded in nominal control of the House by Baron Takakimi (the consonants change slightly) Mitsui, his second son, who was born in 1895. This Mitsui was educated in political science at the University of Tokyo, came into the Mitsui house as a young man, and has had no other career. His wife is a Matsudaira.

Actually the "Banto" who ran Mitsui for many years is Seihin Ikeda, who was also Prince Konoye's minister of finance. Ikeda, one of the most cultivated of modern Japanese, a charming old gentleman, went to Harvard.[2] After a year of newspaper work he entered Mitsui service in 1895—the word in those days was that the best brains of the country went either to the army general staff or the Mitsui board of directors—and eventually he succeeded Baron Dan as Banto. For a time he was governor of the Bank of Japan, and was called—rather inappropriately—the "Tiger of the Money Market." He has a great reputation for value in a crisis. In the eloquent and somewhat Americanized language of the Tokyo *Nichi Nichi*, "Ikeda is a de-luxe pinch hitter. It is up to him to knock a home run with the bases loaded." But the army didn't approve of him in the finance ministry, and out he went.

Relation to the Army

The present situation is peculiar. For the first time in generations the Mitsui house is tucking its heels in, confronted with a power

[1] If any specialist in investment should be interested in how Mitsui Gomei Kasha distributes its holdings, the list is as follows:

Banking and Insurance	10.86%	Trade	11.33%
Textiles	12.67%	Steel	1.75%
Foods and Beverages	6.61%	Machinery	5.73%
Chemicals	19.31%	Transport	3.03%
Mines	16.72%	Light and Power	0.62%
Warehousing	1.74%	Miscellaneous	2.64%

[2] It is interesting that for a time the financial brains on each side in the China War were Harvard men. China's T. V. Soong is Harvard 1915. Ikeda, incidentally, is a widely traveled man in Europe and America, but has never once been in Manchuria or China. This is rather typical of prominent Japanese.

stronger than itself. Obviously Mitsui still pulls enormous and cohesive weight, and obviously it is all but unassailable in its special sphere. The army needs Mitsui, because only through the great industrial houses can it get munitions. But this does not much modify the fact that the army, particularly the young radicals, dislike Mitsui and all it stands for, and have hinted at the necessity to nationalize it. The army's point of view is quite simple. Why should Mitsui continue to make enormous profits, if the army itself can utilize them, absorb them, to make more munitions, to make a stronger Japan? Thus the quarrel—and compromise—on Article 11 of the National Mobilization Law, which curtailed if it did not abolish Mitsui—and other—profits.

The Mitsuis and their allies are as a result in a fine state of apprehension. They customarily influenced affairs by partial control of the political parties; their influence has naturally suffered as that of political parties waned. And now the army subtly but implacably attacks the capitalist system itself. Mitsui has replied by several maneuvers. First, it has attempted to make itself popular by huge charities for "national service"; recently the House created a 30,-000,000 yen "national welfare fund." Second, the Mitsuis are performing patriotic service by buying up the government's "red-ink" bonds, which so far have scarcely begun to reach the public at large. Third, they are assiduously cultivating friendships among army officers, particularly those of a conservative trend. (The army does not repay in kind. Recently a company of rookies, en route to the front, was quartered in the Mitsui residence. This is as if the American general staff in 1917 billeted doughboys at the New York home of J. P. Morgan.) Fourth, the Mitsuis seek to make their wealth as inconspicuous as possible. For instance, the present heir, a boy of twelve, goes to an ordinary school, and wears the cheapest clothes. The Mitsuis are terrified of spending money—which is an odd situation to say the least. The Baroness Mitsui—whose husband is probably worth $100,000,000—hardly dares have a dinner party for more than eight, or appear in the street in a new costume.

That the army is a "puppet" of the House of Mitsui is, it goes without saying, nonsense. It is as much nonsense as it would be to say that Hitler is a puppet of Dr. Schacht, whom he recently fired. Nor is the House of Mitsui a puppet of the army—at least not yet. The two, despite jealousy and friction, still manage to work together.

But the tension between them is slowly, steadily, mounting. The more it mounts, the weaker Mitsui becomes, what with the present distribution of power in Japan.

House of Mitsubishi

Mitsubishi is not a family name. It is a trademark meaning "three lozenges." The family which owns the huge Mitsubishi concern, junior only to Mitsui, is the Iwasaki family, and it is of comparatively recent origin. The Iwasakis are not of feudal or Samurai blood. The basis of the fortune, rather like the great American fortunes of the last century, was accumulated in a generation. Much of it was amassed in the lifetime of the founder of the family, the late Yataro Iwasaki, who died in 1885.

Mitsubishi differs from Mitsui not only because it has shallower roots but in its special type of business. It is organized like Mitsui, with a gigantic holding company at the top (capitalized at 120,000,000 yen as against 300,000,000 yen for Mitsui), but its activity is different. Mitsui is par excellence the company of cotton, metals, rayon, mining—basic industries. Mitsubishi is more particularly a finance and trading company; its specialties are banking, shipping, insurance. It controls the great N. Y. K. shipping line, and founded the Japanese merchant marine. This division of interest between Mitsui and Mitsubishi has its advantages. They split the field.

Yataro Iwasaki, the founder of the house, was entirely a self-made man. His father was a Ronin—a Samurai without master or employment. One of Iwasaki's first feats was an attempt to rescue his father from jail, where he was incarcerated after a quarrel with a friend; the adventure ended with Iwasaki going to jail himself. He was a violent young man, and he grew up to be "ruthless, calculating, and utterly selfish," in the words of one of his biographers. From the beginning he was interested in ships; he discovered and explored several remote islands. Then, still a youngster, he managed to organize a coastwise shipping service, and at the time of the Meiji Restoration his ships became highly important in transporting government troops who fought the Shogun. By 1880 he was expanding in other lines of business, and had become extremely rich. He was a buccaneer in finance. Like that of the late John D. Rockefeller, his general policy was to buy up competitors when he could not destroy them otherwise. He died in 1885, aged only fifty-two.

This Iwasaki was succeeded by his younger brother, named Yano-suke, who had educated himself in the United States; the saying was that his only baggage as he worked his way through American schools was a dictionary. Yanosuke performed incredible speculations in Tokyo real estate; he bought most of the business district of Tokyo for 1,500,000 yen. In 1896 he was created a baron, but at first refused the title. His successor was Yataro's son, Hisaya, who is still head of the house, though active operation is in the hands of two younger Iwasakis and their Banto.

The Mitsubishi house played politics exactly as the Mitsuis did. Its "man" was the murdered Marquis Okuma, one of the first great Japanese nation-builders. For years it more or less controlled the Minseito party, which believed in overseas trade and hence deplored warlike adventures. The army radicals have not forgotten this, and to-day probably dislike Mitsubishi even more than Mitsui. But Mitsubishi, like Mitsui, is useful to them, and it seeks to buy favor by proper deference.

. . . .

Of the other great houses we cannot write in detail. Sumitomo, which is older than Mitsui, has a fascinating history. It is a single family, with no collateral branches; its activities center in Osaka rather than Tokyo, and emphasize engineering and heavy industry; it is known for convervatism and "aristocratic" methods. The Sumitomo line goes back to the Emperor Kwammu (782-805 A.D.), whose younger son founded the house. Nineteen generations later it adopted the Sumitomo name. But at the moment—Japanese paradox again—the house contains not a drop of Sumitomo blood, since the present family derives from a court noble named Kichizaemon, who was adopted by the Sumitomos—apparently their own blood had given out—as recently as 1892.

The foundation of the Sumitomo fortune was a copper and silver mine discovered in 1691. A shrewd series of Bantos preserved it in Restoration times, when several wealthy families were wiped out because they lent money to the various Daimyo, whom the Restoration ruined. The Sumitomos, like the Mitsuis, quickly dropped the Shogun, and supported the new government. One article in the house law is "Secrets are secrets." Sumitomo has a close connection with old Prince Saionji, who was a relative of Baron Kichizaemon.

The House of Yasuda is as new as Sumitomo is old. Its origin was a money-lending business which began in the 1860's, and its leader, Baron Yasuda, was assassinated in 1921 at the age of eighty-four. The Yasuda bank is the biggest in Japan—bigger even than Mitsui. . . . The House of Okura is the smallest of the Big Five. It is of comparatively recent origin, it specializes in trade and engineering, and it has a strong "East Asia" policy, seeking expansion on the mainland.

Among old-line financiers must be mentioned Baron Seinosuke Goh, 73 years old, stout, independent, and a liberal. Goh came of a noble family, and studied abroad in Germany and Belgium; he is a Ph.D. from Heidelberg. He has never had a government job, but his importance as president of the Japan Federation of Commerce and Industry is considerable. He has been called the "Andrew Mellon of Japan."

The Upstart Generation

A different type of financier altogether is Yoshisuke Aikawa. This resourceful promoter and organizer compares to the Mitsuis as, say, the young automobile men of Detroit compared twenty years ago to J. P. Morgan. Born in 1880 of a trading family, Aikawa came to the United States to study the steel business, and for a time worked as a laborer in a Pittsburgh mill. His importance has notes of iconoclasm. For one thing, he opened his companies to the public, and thousands upon thousands of small shareholders invested in them, whereas Mitsui and Mitsubishi are owned in private, with the public frozen out. For another, the army likes him, thinks he understands "modern conditions," and backs him against other interests. Finally, he is concentrating in Manchukuo.

Aikawa is president of an enormous company, capitalized at 450,-000,000 yen, called the Manchuria Industrial Development Corporation. Its subsidiary and associated companies are occupied in mining, glass, fisheries, iron and steel, phonographs, soya beans, automobiles, matches, animal fats, rubber. In 1927 Aikawa was hardly known. Ten years later he was a tremendous force, because he invaded Manchuria in competition with the historically entrenched South Manchuria Railway. But the railway was, as we shall see, engaged in covert conflict with the Kwantung army, which is the real boss of Manchuria, and the Kwantung officers threw their support to the rising Aikawa. He picked up pieces of the South Manchuria Empire as a kind of agent for the army, which wanted to break the railway's hold on Manchurian economy.

If he does not overreach himself, Aikawa may become a dominant figure in Japanese finance. He is certainly its most conspicuous contemporary star. Recently he visited the United States drumming up capital—not very successfully—for his Manchurian enterprises. He wants to be the economic viceroy of the new Manchukuoan state. Mitsui and Mitsubishi are jealous of him, but in a way he serves their inmost design: he keeps the army off.

Chapter VI

The Story of Two Twenty-Six

~~~~~~

FEBRUARY 26, 1936, was a cold morning in Tokyo. Snow glistened on the streets, and people shivered on the way to work. Then they noticed an unwonted concentration of troops, and they began to shiver with more than cold. Hours passed before anyone had certain knowledge of what was going on, whereupon it became clear—military rebellion. The army had cut loose! For eighty-one hours, under martial law, Tokyo waited in suspense. Then the mutineers quietly surrendered. The story of the attempted coup d'état contains picturesque as well as tragic features. Its importance was that, in these eighty-one crowded hours, the triple struggle I have adumbrated in these chapters, the confused and shifting grasp for power by army, politicians, and financiers—with the life of Japan at supreme stake—came to abortive climax.

The mutineers murdered three eminent Japanese: Admiral Viscount Saito, 77-year-old Lord Privy Seal and former prime minister; General Jotaro Watanabe, inspector general of military education, aged seventy-one; and the veteran finance minister Korekiyo Takahashi, who was eighty-three and probably the most popular man in Japan. They gravely wounded the Grand Chamberlain to the Emperor, Admiral Suzuki; and the prime minister, Admiral Keisuke Okada, escaped with his life only because his brother-in-law was killed in his stead—an almost Hollywoodian episode. Several other escapes were almost as remarkable, including that of Count Makino of the inner palace circle. At least twenty-four eminent Japanese were to have been killed in all—Prince Saionji, the last Elder Statesman; the heads of the Houses of Mitsui, Mitsubishi, and Okura; Baron Shidehara, Baron Goh, Seihin Ikeda, and several cabinet ministers. It was probably the most comprehensive murder plot in modern history.[1]

The mutiny failed, though several of the assassinations were successful. Let us tell the story briefly.

· · · · · · ·

For several months radical officers in the army had been restive.

---

[1] Some of the financiers—who had their spies in the army—got out of town just in time. And some stayed out of town for a considerable period after.

The finance minister was resisting their budget demands, and the Manchurian campaign was dying down. A group of young extremists, officers and civilians both, became converted to the idea of what they called the "Showa Restoration," whereby Japan was to be "purified" in the name of the Emperor, for the sake of the "Kingly Way." They of course did not dare to attack the Emperor himself, but sought to gain the imperial authority to effect their ends. A book called *Plans for the Reconstruction of Japan*, by a young socialist Ikki Kita, was their guide to politico-economic reformation. The "Showa Restorationists" were united by a general dissidence. They were against the privileged classes and aristocrats, against the exploiters of national wealth, against the high army command, even against those closest to the Throne, whom they accused of frustrating their aims. Then, a torch in a pool of oil, came the Aizawa-Mazaki-Nagata incident.

A serious quarrel was proceeding in army circles over military education. General Watanabe, one of the officers killed, was on the conservative side. His predecessor as Inspector General of Military Education had been General Mazaki. He was a zealot, a schemer, a politically minded officer rather like General Schleicher, but a radical—and dangerous. Mazaki was dismissed from his post; he was too extreme. So a friend of Mazaki's, Colonel Aizawa, went to another of the conservative group, General Nagata, an important man in the War Office, to complain. Aizawa demanded that Nagata change his methods. Contemptuously Nagata dismissed him—an insolent underling daring to insult a superior. Whereupon Aizawa took up his sword, and slashed Nagata to death.

This was in August 1935. On January 28, 1936—just before the February outbreak—Aizawa was brought to court-martial. The trial stirred public opinion deeply. Aizawa was presented as a patriot and hero. Mazaki testified in his behalf, and a strong wing of the army backed him. Aizawa told the judges that he had no regrets for his action, that he had taken it only after prayer at the Meiji shrine. He said:

The Emperor is the incarnation of the God who reigns over the universe. The aim of life is to develop according to His Majesty's wishes . . . The world is deadlocked by capitalism, communism, anarchism, atheism . . . I came to realize that the elder statesmen, those close to the throne, the powerful financiers and bureaucrats, were attempting . . . to corrupt the Government and Army . . . In-

ternal conditions are becoming deplorable . . . Mah-jong and cafes
are becoming a fad in the country. . . . When I observed these conditions, the teaching on which I was educated—to give up everything
for the Emperor in an emergency—burst out and encouraged me.

Aizawa's court-martial was still proceeding amid an explosive atmosphere when the February 26 mutiny (the Japanese usually call it
the "2.26 incident") occurred.

. . . .

The conspirators were carefully but inadequately organized. Their
roots were in the Third Guards Regiment, and in the First and Third
Infantry regiments of the First Division, which—unpleasant indication
—was the Imperial Guard. These detachments were en route to Manchukuo, and had just got arms, provisions, and ammunition for active
service. The fact that they had been marching around Tokyo for
several days diminished suspicion when, at dawn on February 26,
they began to dispose their forces for rebellion. No leader was of
higher rank than captain. But they looked to eminent military figures
like Mazaki (who was court-martialed after the mutiny) as friends.
They also looked for financial support to certain radical industrialists,
including one Fukunosuke Kuhara, who had flirted with army "ideas."
Kuhara was tried later for complicity in the affair, but acquitted.

Various conspirators were selected for the concrete jobs of assassination which were the kernel of the plan. One group went to the house
of Viscount Saito. They burst in at 5:30 A.M. The old Viscount had
been a dinner guest of the American Ambassador, Joseph C. Grew,
the night before. The admiral's wife, Viscountess Saito, threw herself
at the assassins, shouting: "My husband's life belongs to the state. If
you have to shoot, shoot me." They did, but only wounded her. The
admiral was killed. Previously there had been no fewer than six attempts on his life.

Another group "called on" General Watanabe, who grabbed his
pistol and tried to repel the murderers; his ammunition gave out, and
he was machine-gunned to death with his wife and daughter looking
on. Madame Watanabe tried to save him. . . . A third group went
to the house of the aged finance minister Takahashi.[2] He was asleep

---

[2] Old Korekiyo Takahashi was one of the most remarkable men of modern
Japan. He was illegitimate, born of a 15-year-old mother. He went to the
U. S. A. as a boy, worked in a Peru silver mine, became an English teacher,
and then had a tremendous career in politics, finance, and industry.

on an upper floor. His maid woke him, hearing noise outside. To reassure her, he said, "It's probably snow falling on the roof." But he knew better. The mutineers shot him as he was lying there. In his hand was a copy of the London *Times*. . . . Admiral Suzuki was similarly attacked early in the morning. He looked incredulously at the uniforms of his assailants, demanded to see their commanding officer, and was promptly shot. Miraculously, he recovered.

Another group left Tokyo to find Prince Saionji and kill him—he got away—and still another went to Yugawara, a hot-spring resort where Count Makino was vacationing. Makino's escape was dramatic. His personal guard saw the soldiers approaching, and killed three of them before he himself was shot. Makino (who is 78), heard the shots; he aroused his wife, granddaughter, two maids, and a sick nurse, and climbed with them out of a back window. The cavalcade, all in night dress, streamed over a brick wall toward escape in the hills, while the mutineers burned down the house, on the chance that it might not have been Makino himself who escaped. This was the third time Makino escaped death in ten years.

But the most remarkable adventure was that of the prime minister, Admiral Okada, probably the only statesman in history to attend his own funeral alive.

At 5 A.M. the mutineers, shivering with cold and the burden of their job, arrived at Okada's official residence. They shot the four policemen guarding it, and forced their way in. A system of alarm bells had recently been installed; these began to ring, and the prime minister's brother-in-law and secretary, Colonel Matsuo, woke up. With two maids he rushed to warn Okada, who was a character noted for stolidity, occasional bibulous indulgence, and a sense of humor. Okada groaned in his sleep, refused to wake up, and said, "Well, if it's all up with us, there's no use getting excited."

Colonel Matsuo forced Okada out of bed, and pushed him into the curious kind of large steel vault which, in most important buildings in Japan, is an earthquake shelter. Matsuo slammed the vault door, and at that precise moment the mutineers burst in. They mistook Matsuo for Okada—the facial resemblance between the two was striking—shot him dutifully, and took command of the establishment. Dying, Matsuo cried out, "*Banzai* (a cheer meaning literally 10,000 years) for *Dai* (great) Nippon. *Banzai* for the Emperor!"

The mutineers assumed that their job was done, and grew careless. Two servants had seen Matsuo hide the prime minister in the vault. They waited patiently for their chance, rescued him (he had nearly suffocated) and smuggled him into the kitchen where he disguised himself in rude clothes. There he waited in tense secrecy while the announcement went around the world—issued in terms of great solemnity and mourning from the imperial palace itself—that he was dead.

The problem of getting him out was solved ingeniously. The funeral, by Buddhist canon, had to take place at once, and the mutineers politely allowed relatives to call for the body next day. A loyal gendarme, who had somehow escaped being killed and who had learned that Okada was alive, managed to insert himself next to the representative of the family who arrived. He had time only to whisper, "Show no surprise." The relative looked at the dead man's face, saw that it was not Okada, and almost perished of shock. He recovered quickly, and escorted the body out. Other relatives asked to see the face. He said smartly, "The head has been too much damaged by bullet wounds."

Among the mourners who departed with the body was—Admiral Okada himself! He could no longer risk discovery by the rebels of their mistake. Dressed inconspicuously, his head bowed, he slipped out with the funeral cortège, and spent long hours mourning publicly at his "own" bier. A day later the bewildering announcement came to Tokyo—and to the mutineers who thought they had murdered him and still held his residence—that he was very much alive. This contretemps brought typically Japanese difficulties. One might think that the Admiral would have been greeted as a hero, or at least as a remarkable apparition. Not so. He was bitterly abused—because, by being still alive, he was embarrassing to the Emperor, who believed him to be dead!—and had to resign office as prime minister at once. There were even indignant suggestions that he commit *hara-kiri*, presumably so that he might attend another funeral dead.

One should note that among the conspicuous victims or would be victims of the mutiny were three admirals. Two other admirals were on the death list. The mutiny was made by the army; and the navy has not forgotten this.

．　．　．　．　．　．

Meantime 1,400 troops had occupied the central district of Tokyo.

Snow was still falling; the mutineers whistled on their fingers, shuffled in the mud. They took over the metropolitan Police Office, the War Office, the bureau of the General Staff, and the Home Office. They fortified themselves, set up machine guns in the streets, and surrounded the imperial palace. Then they prepared to see—what would happen.

But nothing happened. It became clear that, having made a start toward seizing power, the insurgents did not know what to do with it. They waited: which was fatal. They summoned the war minister and General Mazaki, and offered them command of the rebellion; both refused. And loyal troops began to converge on the circle held by the rebels; there were in effect two circles around the palace, with the inner rebels gradually being surrounded by government forces. The rebels did not dare go into the palace itself.

Young insurgents continued to picket the street corners, and with rather touching innocence handed civilian passers-by the mimeographed pronunciamento they had prepared. This deserves quotation in part:

The essence of the nation of Japan, as a land of the Gods, exists in the fact that the Emperor reigns with undiminished power. . . . The present time is a favorable moment for Japan to bring about a greater expansion of national power and prestige. In recent years, however, there have appeared many persons whose chief aim and purpose have been to amass personal material wealth, disregarding the general welfare and prosperity of the Japanese population. . . .

The Genro, senior statesmen, military cliques, plutocrats, bureaucrats and political parties are all traitors who are destroying national polity. They infringed on the Imperial right of Supreme Command when they concluded the London Naval Treaty of 1930 and changed the Inspector-General of Military Education in 1935. . . . Japan's relations with Russia, China, Great Britain and the United States are so strained at present that a single misstep will cast the Divine Land of Japan into ruin. The Imperial work will fail unless we take proper steps to safeguard the Fatherland by killing all those responsible for impeding the Showa Restoration and slurring Imperial prestige. . . .

It is our duty to remove the evil retainers from around the Throne and to smash the group of senior statesmen. It is our duty as subjects of His Majesty the Emperor. . . .

What happened, after eighty-one hours, was that this army revolt was put down by the army itself. But careful and discriminating negotiation was required. The authorities were sure that, if they invoked the name of the Emperor, the mutineers would disperse, but they disliked having to put the imperial prestige to this stringent test. So they had to work delicately. One peculiarly Japanese touch: large balloons customarily used for commercial advertising were sent overhead, festooned with patriotic appeals to surrender. The mutineers were also attacked with pamphlets, instead of bombs, which urged them to give up peaceably, rather than subject Tokyo to street fighting. Finally the rebels did surrender. Not a shot was fired.

Cleverly the army command rebuked the underlings of the conspiracy as lightly as possible. Only a very few privates were punished, and it was announced piously that they were a minority with misguided notions of their duty to the throne. The government announced its "awe and regret," and in effect told the boys to go home and behave better the next time. It was continually stressed that the rank and file mutineers were dupes of the ringleaders, which indeed they were.

One insurgent officer committed *hara-kiri*. Only one. Other officers were arrested, and after a long trial were given severe sentences. Fourteen officers and three civilians were sentenced to death, and of these, fifteen were duly executed—the first time in twenty-eight years any Japanese met the death penalty for a "patriotic" murder. Five officers were condemned to life imprisonment, and forty-four others received shorter sentences. Colonel Aizawa, incidentally, the murderer of General Nagata, was duly found guilty when his trial was resumed, and to everyone's surprise was executed.[3] One youthful lieutenant on active service—who had nothing to do with the plot—was so shamed and horrified that, with his wife, he committed ceremonial *hara-kiri* when the bulk of the mutineers did not do so. "I must atone for their disgrace," he said. A Buddhist priest likewise killed himself at the Meiji shrine.

The Emperor, the core of the whole story, was, it was announced, profoundly disturbed by the episode. For thirteen days he took no exercise, and "almost forgot to eat and sleep." As to the army, it might be said to have gained from the incident. It became "a trustee for fundamental reform," and has in fact adopted much of the program of the mutineers.

[3] He had boasted at the trial that soon he would be on active service again.

"I Come Fairly to Kill Him Honestly!"

Of the sixteen Japanese prime ministers since the Great War, five have been assassinated—Hara, Takahashi, Hamaguchi, Inukai, Saito. A sixth, Admiral Okada, only narrowly escaped assassination, and at least two others have been in danger. This is not merely a post-war phenomenon; Japanese statesmen were murdered wholesale in pre-war days, for instance such great Japan-builders as Ito and Okubo. Assassins usually got off with light sentences; at least one murderer of a premier is now free after having served a short term. The situation developed that any politician tending to be liberal or conciliatory, especially in foreign affairs, was liable to murder. Among modern peoples only the Arabs have such an instinct to consider assassination as an acceptable political weapon.

In 1921 Prime Minister Hara was stabbed at the Tokyo railway station. He was the first commoner to become premier of Japan. He had opened the way to the Washington naval treaty, and thus was damned.

In 1930 Prime Minister "Lion" Hamaguchi was shot, to die later of his wounds. He was a liberal, who believed in retrenchment, and who insured the ratification of the London naval treaty. This cost him his life.

In February, 1932, a former finance minister, Inouye, was murdered by members of a "Blood Brotherhood League," who were inspired by fanatic Buddhist priests.

In March, 1932, Baron Dan of the House of Mitsui was murdered by a young naval officer. He was one of the best liked—as well as the most powerful—men in Japan; but neither his popularity nor power counted with the radicals who hated him.

In May, 1932, Prime Minister Inukai was killed by soldiers. He believed in a peaceful policy toward China; he had been a friend of Sun Yat-sen's. He was seventy-seven. On this occasion, too, attempts were made to bomb the Mitsubishi bank, the police headquarters, and Count Makino.

Four years later came the carnival of Two Twenty-Six. Since then there have been no important political murders.

Japanese Miscellany

In Japan a belch is a compliment. In Japan the monstrous professional wrestlers wear their hair up, women were for generations forbidden to climb Mt. Fujiyama, and manicurists stand at work. When a Japanese politician gets drunk it may be prominently reported in the papers, since little stigma attaches to drunkenness in Japan.

In Japan the northwest corner of a garden is protected by shrubbery, because this is the direction from which evil spirits may enter; in Japan no one will have 4 or 49 as a house number, because these numbers are considered unlucky like our 13 (the ideograph for 4 is pronounced similarly to the one for death, and 9 means sadness); in Japan an officer sentenced to death is shot through a curtain, since it is inconceivable that a private should actually see that he is shooting a man of higher rank.

In Japan a person's age is counted from the date of conception, not from birth; nouns have no inflection or number and verbs no person; a cup of tea should properly be drunk in exactly three and one-half gulps; and pillows are made of wood.

In Japan the traffic policemen and school children wear nose guards to keep out the dust and influenza germs; the color and shape of the *Obe* (a kind of sash) gives evidence of a woman's age and social station; newspaper extras are announced by bells; waitresses in cafés are called, more or less, "Mister Girl"; and snake soup is a great delicacy.

Chapter VII

Japan Makes War

~~~~~~

JAPAN's foreign policy, which is the expression of its urgent will to expand, is based on a trinity of factors. First, economic shortages at home. Second, population pressure. Third, political considerations, which include ethnic and semi-religious items.

The position in regard to shortage of raw materials is not quite so serious as is generally assumed. From several points of view it is rather difficult to call Japan a "Have-Not" nation—if only because a country which has swallowed Manchuria and a considerable part of China is suffering from a glut of unassimilated hinterland, rather than a lack of it. Japan is the first nation in the world in exports of textiles, and first in rayon manufacture and export, the first in silk, the first in manufacture of plate glass. It is the third country in cotton spindling, the third in shipping, the fourth in hydro-electric development, the fourth in chemicals. Japan is self-sufficient in food, as I have already noted, and it produces ninety-five percent of its own coal. It is very nearly self-sufficient in graphite, sulphur, and some minor metals.

Conversely Japan has drastic weaknesses in other important raw materials. It must import very nearly all its raw cotton, the basis of its great export trade. It must import one hundred percent of its nickel and mercury and—of critical significance—ninety percent of its petroleum, sixty-five percent of its iron and steel. It is seriously deficient in lead, zinc, aluminum, copper.

Of course the fact that a country lacks raw materials does not necessarily justify aggression to secure them. Switzerland and Sweden are Have-Not powers; but they do not make wars. The Japanese could normally purchase raw materials quite freely. No one objected to selling them rubber or cotton or anything else. The United States is at this moment contributing a large part of the material—especially scrap iron and oil—with which they make war. The difficulty is not that the Japanese cannot buy raw materials, but that they don't have enough cash to buy all they need. Another difficulty—and justification for the expansionist program, from the Japanese point of view—

is that in the event of a general conflict, a *world* war, sources of supply might be cut off.

As to population pressure the Japanese are beyond doubt in a unique position. The density of population, 2,750 per square mile of *arable* land, is the highest in the world.[1] The area of Japan is 148,000 square miles, which is less than that of California. Yet in that area, of which less than one-fifth is arable, Japan must support a population approximately half of that of the entire United States. One is tempted in regard to Germany and Italy, the other so-called "Have-Not" states, to minimize the claim for expansion on population grounds, since it has notes of sophistry: the Germans and Italians demand room *because* their population is expanding, while at the same time they do everything possible to encourage more babies. In Japan this is not quite the case; birth control is legal—though no one seems to pay much attention to it. Four Japanese babies are born every minute, and by 1960 the population of Japan will be 90,000,000 people if the present birthrate and deathrate are maintained.

Despite the fact that they are so unbelievably congested the Japanese are indifferent colonizers. The average Japanese hates to leave his own country, unless to go to some warm place with a much higher standard of living. They dislike cold. Hokkaido, the northern island, part of Japan itself, is only half occupied. Many Japanese have gone to Brazil, and until the American Exclusion Act of 1924—which greatly irritated Japan and which was a contributory cause to the "active" China policy—they liked California. But it has been almost impossible to persuade Japanese to emigrate to the colonies which they now possess, a point which makes it doubtful if population pressure *per se* is full justification for the expansionist program. Japan has had Formosa since 1895, and Korea since 1905, but very few Japanese have settled in either place; in Formosa the Japanese have had actually to import Chinese labor. Japan has had Manchukuo since 1931, but only about ten thousand Japanese colonists have emigrated there—an infinitesimal number—although it is both rich and underpopulated, though Chinese went there by the millions, and though the Japanese authorities have made every effort to encourage and indeed subsidize emigration.

[1] Figures for England are 2,170, Italy 819, Germany 806, France 467, U. S. A. 229. The island of Java has a greater density of population, but only if all land is taken into account, not arable land.

Above and beyond the economic and demographic factors is consideration of politics. Japan wants to expand because it considers itself a world power invested with an imperial mission to dominate East Asia. This mission has racial and religious overtones—as the quotations in the preceding chapters have, I hope, indicated—but the main motive is political. Japan wants to expand in order to be stronger vis-à-vis the Soviet Union, in order to squeeze Great Britain out of China, in order to extend its nationalist influence southward into Asia and the Pacific. It has never precisely defined what it means by "East Asia," but it regards large sections of Asia as we regarded the land west of the Mississippi in our own expansionist days. Questions of ultimate *power* move Japan. It wants political hegemony over what it calls its hinterland.

Now let us point out that Japan was by no means the only country which bit off chunks of Asia in recent times. By no means. Prostrate China was loot for all. The French successively nipped pieces off Indo-China, quite as unconscionably as Japan snapped up Manchuria. France seized Cochin-China and Cambodia, which were then integral parts of China, in 1863, without bothering to ask anybody's permission, and later took Annam. In the 1860's Czarist Russia calmly stole the Amur River region and the Maritime Provinces of Siberia. The British have swashbuckled through China for almost a century. They grabbed Hong Kong, pinched off Burma (which no one remembers was once part of China), and "absorbed" some subordinate Chinese provinces, like Bhutan and Nepal, just as Japan "absorbed" Jehol. Pre-war Germany took the Kiaochow region in Shantung.

Japan was late to the imperialist feast, and perhaps her methods were more brusque, more brutal and direct. *But in essence Japan did nothing that the other powers had not done.* No European hands are clean. The Japanese are, we have noted, excellent mimics; and the technique of modern imperialism was something they were very quick to copy—and augment. The fact, of course, that they imitated and amplified the European system of seizure and exploitation does not make the system any pleasanter, or the exploitation more justifiable.

So much for general aspects of Japanese foreign policy. We have already in Chapter II indicated something of Japan's particular attitude to China. Let us proceed.

Japanese Expansion: First Phase

In a sense Japan for some years looked at the China seaboard much as Great Britain looked at the low countries, Holland and Belgium, a century ago. In another sense Japan versus China resembled Germany versus pre-Nazi Austria: a new, powerful, and ambitious state attempting to seize an older, mellower state with which it shared a common origin. A highly placed Japanese statesman told me, "You must never forget that China is the woman, and we are a man. She must be punished." I asked what would happen if the woman continued to resist. "Ah," my friend replied, "we cut off her arms and legs."

Then there is trade. Eighty percent of all Japanese overseas investments are in China, amounting to roughly $600,000,000; the great mills in Shanghai—with their hideous slums—are twenty-four percent Japanese owned. In normal times China took ten percent at least of Japan's total exports, which amounted to sixteen percent of China's total imports. Of China's total export trade, 15.7 percent went to Japan in 1933, 14.5 percent in 1936. This trade was of great value to Japan. It has been disastrously crippled by Chinese boycott and war. But one must assume that Japan hopes to revive it, hopes to resume exploitation of the China market, which potentially is the greatest in the world. Thus the double aspect of Japan's policy. Crush China—in order that it may be forced to buy. Make war on China—but don't kill it altogether. Cut off the arms and legs—but leave the profitable body.

For a long time it was as impossible to get a Japanese to define precisely what Japan's *ultimate* policy toward China was as to get an inclusive definition of "East Asia." (Are the Philippines part of "East Asia"? Are the Dutch East Indies part of "East Asia"? We do not know—though we may have a pretty good guess.) For a long time no one—in Japan itself as well as outside—knew if Japan would be satisfied with the Five Northern Provinces of China, or would attempt conquest southward. We did not know if Japan wanted to establish a colony, or a puppet state, or a military protectorate, or all three together—which is what is happening now. We still do not know how far Japan intends to go militarily—or how far Japan *can* go. But late in 1938 Japanese designs at least were officially made concrete, with the announcement that Japan, Manchukuo, and "China" were to become a single political and economic bloc.

We cannot presume to include a history of Sino-Japanese relations in this brief space. We can only barely mention such events as the first Sino-Japanese war (1894-95), as a result of which China was forced to surrender Formosa to Japan and to give up her claims to Korea, or the Russo-Japanese war (1904-5), which established Japan as a world power. Both these wars were fought basically over Korea, which Japan needed as a preliminary toehold on the mainland. Korea has been a Japanese colony since 1910. Politically it is a land of 20 million slaves. Beyond Korea—China.

In 1915 came the famous Twenty-One Demands, which were forced on China during the Great War, when China was helpless and when Japan's then allies—Great Britain, Russia, France—had no time or energy to spare. We cannot list the Demands in full; they presented China with a 48-hour ultimatum virtually imposing Japanese sovereignty on the country. Japan was to control Shantung, to extend her influence in Manchuria, to have special rights in Fukien, and to have mining and railway concessions elsewhere; China was to purchase most of her munitions from Japan, give Japan partial control of the Chinese police, and appoint Japanese political advisers. Through a variety of circumstances the Demands were watered down before they were accepted—partly as a result of vigorous protest from the United States, which insisted that the "Open Door" (equality of all nations in China) be maintained—but they clearly marked a new and ambitious stage in Japan's foreign policy.

In 1927—another milestone—came the Tanaka Memorial, which purported to be a statement by General Tanaka, then prime minister of Japan, of the trenchant aims of his country. It said: "For settling difficulties in Eastern Asia, Japan must adopt a policy of Blood and Iron . . . In order to conquer the world, Japan must conquer Europe and Asia; in order to conquer Europe and Asia, Japan must first conquer China, and in order to conquer China, Japan must conquer Manchuria and Mongolia. Japan expects to fulfill the above program in ten years." Japanese steadily have denied authenticity to the Tanaka Memorial, but the document, genuine or not, certainly contained some accurate prophecy. Japan has followed it almost as faithfully as Hitler has followed *Mein Kampf*.[2]

---

[2] One line in the Memorial is, "In the future if we wish to control China the primary move is to crush the United States."

The next great milestone was the Mukden (Manchuria) incident of September 18, 1931, from which all subsequent history of the Far East derives.

The Manchurian Complex

I pause now to inspect Manchuria. It is impossible to proceed without a survey of Manchurian background. Known nowadays as Manchukuo, it is one of the most fascinating regions in the world, a country twice the size of Germany (503,000 square miles), with roughly 35,000,000 people. For many years its chief characters were two great railroads and a war lord.

By almost every criterion—geography, language, history, the impact of several migrations—Manchuria was indisputably a part of China. It was the China "above the Wall."[3] But it is one of those unfortunate regions where permanent international conflict is inevitable. Its position gave it formidable strategic importance, because it had a common frontier with Russia, and was exposed closely to Japanese penetration. It has even greater importance now, because it is the tremendous buffer between Japan, China, and the U.S.S.R. When Japan took it in 1931 the march to empire really began.

Turn back a little. I have mentioned the Sino-Japanese War of 1894-95. This was a staggering catastrophe for China. What happened was that not only Japan but other powers took advantage of the Chinese defeat to grab loot, as noted above. The best loot was in the Manchurian provinces. But it was not the only loot. The chief thieves were Russia and Japan in Manchuria. But the Germans seized Kiaochow, the British "leased" the port of Wei-hai-wei and the Kowloon peninsula opposite Hong Kong, and the French took the Bay of Kwangchow in the far south. (What the United States did was enunciate the Open Door principle, without too sticky fingers.)

The rivalry over loot between Russia and Japan at this time is a germinal fact the sprouting of which we still see to-day. The story is complex. *First,* China was forced to cede to Japan not only Formosa but that crucially important Manchurian area known as the Kwantung or Liaotung peninsula—a sort of dagger pointing to Korea and Japan. *Second,* the great powers became alarmed that Japan should get this

---

[3] From this point on there will be considerable mention of Chinese affairs, but treatment of China proper does not begin till Chapter X. For the Great Wall, see Chapter X, p. 162.

Kwantung peninsula and formed a "Dreibund" (France, Russia, Germany), demanding that she give it back. Japan was forced to do so—but not to China. It went to China in theory, but a member of the "Dreibund," Russia, actually took it. So Czarist Russia seized the chief fruit of Japanese victory, which made the Japanese, a long-minded people, somewhat resentful of white imperial methods.

Third, China was assessed a considerable indemnity, and could not pay. So a Franco-Russian loan was floated, the proceeds of which went to China—in order to pay Japan—in return for which Russian interests (behind whom were French investors) obtained highly important rights and concessions. A Russo-Chinese bank was established, and its main function was to finance railway construction in Manchuria. Meantime Russia and China signed a secret treaty of alliance against Japanese aggression. Russia and France, in other words, were on one hand giving Japan its cash indemnity, on behalf of China, while on the other, Russia and China were attempting to freeze Japan out of further Chinese loot, especially in Manchuria. Result (following Russian occupation of Manchuria and penetration toward Korea): Japan's successful attack on Russia in 1904.

We must pause now to tell the story of the railroads, which is also germinal. The struggle between railways in Manchuria and Siberia is progressing to this day. First, the *Chinese Eastern Railway.*

This was the Russian line in Manchuria. It was built following the events just described. Nominally the Chinese had a share in its direction, but in fact it was almost totally a Russian institution. It ran from Manchouli, on the western frontier of Manchuria, to Vladivostok, the Russian port on the Pacific, and thus traversed Manchuria in roughly a north-west to south-east direction. Strategically it was of great importance, and for two reasons: (1), it ran parallel to the Trans-Siberian, which was exclusively on Russian territory, but by cutting through Manchuria shortened the distance to Vladivostok by several days; (2), it gave Russia a life-line into Manchuria, with all manner of derivative rights, for instance that of maintaining a military garrison—and Manchuria, be it remembered, was part of China. Presently the Chinese Eastern was extended with a spurline, running roughly north to south, from Harbin on the main line down through the Kwantung peninsula to Dalny (now called Dairen) and Port Arthur, which was then Russian territory.

Second, the *South Manchuria Railway.* Japan licked Russia in

1905, and by terms of the Treaty of Portsmouth promptly took back the Kwantung area, of which she had been deprived ten years before, and which thereafter became the spearhead of Japanese penetration into Manchuria. Also—and most importantly—Japan demanded and got most of the southern spur of the Chinese Eastern, which she renamed the South Manchuria Railway and promptly reorganized and extended. Thus began one of the greatest railway organizations in the world. The South Manchuria—commonly called the S. M. R. —was for twenty-five years and still is the artery of arteries through which Japan pumped money—and blood—into Manchuria. Japan got the right to keep troops in Kwantung—the origin of the Kwantung army I have already described—and in the railway zone. Southern Manchuria, by reason of the railway, became a Japanese sphere of influence. The Russians were forced to retreat into the north.

(It is convenient at this point, even if it means jumping ahead of the story, to deal briefly with the subsequent history of the Chinese Eastern. Friction was rife for years between the Japanese with their railway in the south, and the Russians with theirs in the north. After the Great War the Soviet Government, much less imperialist than that of the Czar, surrendered its extraterritorial privileges in China, and in 1924 partially turned back the Chinese Eastern to the Chinese, whose railway it should have been in the first place. But rivalries continued to bring trouble. First, the Chinese wanted more control, and provoked an incident in 1929 that brought actual if abortive warfare; Mr. Stimson had to invoke the Kellogg Pact. Second, tension between Russians and Japanese kept on mounting, and the Chinese Eastern remained the scene of interminable "incidents"—murders of rail guards, wreckages of trains, and so forth. In 1934 Russia sold the railway outright to Japan, after Japan had ousted China from the area. The Russians asked for 625,000,000 yen, and took 160 million, plus certain allowances. Promptly the Japanese changed it from the Russian broad gauge to normal, and incorporated it in the South Manchuria system. So the Chinese Eastern, after a history as noisy as that of any railway in the world, disappeared.)

To return. While after 1905 the Japanese and Russians resharp-ened their tongues and sabers, the government of Manchuria was vested theoretically in Chinese hands. Manchuria was legally part of China. What were the Chinese doing to protect and preserve this vital province? Very little—because from 1913 to 1928 Manchuria was under the control of a semi-independent war lord, the redoubtable Chang Tso-lin. We must have a paragraph about this gentleman. Enormous numbers of Chinese were pouring into Manchuria, which was empty, from the northern provinces of China proper, which were suffocatingly crowded. How was Chang Tso-lin ruling them? Mostly by playing China and Japan against each other.

Chang Tso-lin was born in 1873. Probably he was the most picturesque of all the great Chinese war lords. He was the son of a shepherd; he was a servant for a time and then a soldier; he became a guerrilla chieftain and was hired by the Japanese to harass the Russians. He maintained his connection with the Japanese until his death; but it was they who killed him. In 1922 he boasted to a group of American newspaper men that in the past few years the Japanese had given him eight million yen, and that before he was finished he would milk them of eighty. He said that he never rendered service for the money until the last moment, and then only when he could not avoid it. When he died he was worth at least fifty million Chinese dollars. At one time a great American bank set up a branch in Manchuria merely to take care of his investments. His fortune went largely to his son, the "Young Marshal" Chang Hsueh-liang, of whom we will hear much in this book.

Chang Tso-lin was unlettered; but a great gentleman. He was a bandit and a killer; and he had a tidy acquisitive mind. He was a small man, paunchy toward the end, and pale with opium; he had exceptionally small and delicate hands, and was proud of his neat, finely formed features. Once he dined at the American Embassy in Peking; his host was somewhat shocked that he brought a bodyguard of twenty-five men, who also had to be fed. One servant stood all evening before his chair, holding ready a succession of lighted cigarettes. The legend is that he drank tigers' blood as an aphrodisiac; the story is probably untrue, and derived from the fact that tigers' whiskers were popular among Manchurians of the period, since, tied together like a fly whisk, they were supposed to be a love charm. So were the powdered horns of a certain kind of deer. Chang Tso-lin was fond of this powder.

The Marshal rose by his own efforts, and by the sound practice of paying his troops well. The money of course he sucked out of the countryside. By 1913 he had become military governor of one of the Manchurian provinces and by 1918 he was in control of all Manchuria. He sided, but coyly, with the Kuomintang revolutionists who made the Chinese republic; his allegiance was a phenomenon subject to fluctuation. In 1924 he decided that Manchuria was too small for his ambitions, and he expanded into China below the Great Wall; he took Peking, made it his capital, and wanted to become Emperor of China under a new dynasty. He started making his own imperial porcelain (a sure indication of monarchical ambition); he prayed in those sections of the Forbidden City closed to all except the former Emperor; when he left his palace, the streets were shut off, and showered with golden sand. But rising in the south was Chiang Kai-shek, the new nationalist leader. Chang and Chiang had worked together —at a distance—but they didn't approve of one another. Chiang Kai-shek was setting out to unify China as a republic, and his armies approached Peking. Marshal Chang's allies melted away, and presently he himself had to flee. He had never surrendered his hold on Manchuria, and with this giddy Peking period apparently terminated, he decided to return to Mukden, his home and original capital. He never got there.

The bomb that killed him was carefully prepared and placed. The explosion took place just outside Mukden (June 4, 1928) as his special train, traveling on the Peking-Mukden line, crossed under the viaduct of the South Manchuria line to Dairen. The bomb, well within the Japanese railway zone, was apparently detonated by wires leading past Japanese sentries on the viaduct. Japanese workmen had been seen there in unusual circumstances during the day—protected by the concrete pillboxes guarding the line—and Chinese who attempted to approach are said to have been shot. Chang Tso-lin was not in his own carriage when the bomb ripped the train apart. He was in the next car, and the explosion was timed perfectly to get him. The presumption is that the assassins had confederates actually on the train. . . . Few people know the precise details. Few will ever know.

The Japanese—especially the young military—wanted to get rid of Chang Tso-lin for several reasons. First, he was too powerful; he was an essential obstacle in their plans to take Manchuria. Second, they feared that, even though he had left Peking, he might come to an arrangement with Chiang Kai-shek rather than with them for the future development of Manchuria. Another cause of Japanese dissatisfaction was that "patriotically" they resented his spending a vast

amount of Manchurian revenue in Peking instead of Manchuria itself. He was draining the country white. So they drained *him*—of the
blood in his small body.

The Young Marshal Chang Hsueh-liang, his heir, succeeded in
concealing for seven days the fact of his death, though everyone knew
that the attack had taken place. Thus the young man had time to
consolidate his position. Then he became a very serious disappointment to the Japanese, who had had certain hopes of him. He negotiated an agreement with Chiang Kai-shek when Peking fell, and
raised the Kuomintang flag in Mukden, thus denoting subservience
to the new nationalist régime. Manchuria became closer to China than
it had been for a generation. The Young Marshal accepted a high post
with the Kuomintang government, and it seemed that all China—
above as well as below the Great Wall—was becoming in truth united
at last.

This the Japanese could not countenance. New plans were laid.
For three years they maneuvered for position. After a period of
mounting tension there came another bomb explosion. It took place
on a section of South Manchuria track not far from the one that
killed Chang Tso-lin. The date was September 18, 1931. This explosion killed more than the one that killed Chang Tso-lin. It killed
Manchuria. Its echoes were heard around the world. They have not
ceased sounding yet.

The Mother of Incidents

The most extraordinary thing about the Mukden incident was that
quite possibly there was no incident at all.

Sometime between 10 and 10:30 P.M. on September 18, 1931,
according to Japanese accounts, Chinese agitators or soldiers blew up
a section of the South Manchuria track just north of Mukden, at a
place near the Peitaying (Chinese) barracks. (Remember: Manchuria was still technically part of China, except the Kwantung Territory and the narrow railway zone.) A fight took place between Chinese
troops and Japanese railway guards—according to the Japanese. The
explosion was an exceedingly minor one. The only evidence adduced
that the track *was* blown up was a collection of damaged plates and
splintered ties, plus one slightly bent one-hundred-pound rail. No
one was allowed to visit the scene; evidence may have been assembled
"later." A most amazing detail is that the regular express from

Changchun to Mukden arrived at 10:30 P.M. on time, suffering no harm. At first the Japanese explained this by saying that the train passed the damaged section of track before the explosion; later they unbelievably asserted that—although the track was ripped up for a yard or so—the heavy express had hurdled the broken rail without the slightest injury. No one on the train, so far as is known, heard any bump.

A great deal has been written about this affair. To date no evidence whatever has been produced to show that Chinese had anything to do with it. Nor is there any *direct* proof of Japanese complicity. We simply do not possess the details. The case is startlingly like the Reichstag fire in Germany, which prepared the way for Hitler to seize power; no one can *prove* that the Nazis started the fire (they blamed the communists for it), but their connection with it was suspicious to say the least, and they derived enormous profit from it. Similarly the Mukden incident was the signal by which Japan seized Manchuria. Of course a fire did actually burn in the Reichstag —perhaps two fires. But we are not absolutely sure of what happened at Peitaying. Lord Lytton himself, who led the League of Nations commission, is careful to point out that his report never refers to the explosion itself as a fact, but merely to the incident as a whole and the events which indisputably followed it. Possibly the Japanese military "framed" the whole thing. They might have exploded a harmless bit of dynamite next to the track, then placed there some bits of damaged wood and rail. As to the armed encounter with the Chinese, little evidence about it exists.[4]

Of what happened almost instantly after the incident there is overwhelmingly full proof. The Japanese seized on it even more thoroughly than the Germans seized on the Reichstag fire. Indeed proof is complete that the Japanese put their forces in motion—or knew that they were going to put them in motion that night—*before* the incident. Troops moved into Manchuria from Korea before midnight. The whole of the Japanese military establishment on the mainland marched with smooth precision. By dawn of September 19, a few hours after the explosion, their troops had captured the Chinese barracks and arsenal at Mukden, and were in action in the whole South

[4] A judicious account of this puzzling episode is given by Ben Dorfman, who was on the spot, in *Harpers Magazine* for September, 1934. I am following several of his conclusions.

Manchuria zone, from Dairen up to Changchun. The Chinese made
no resistance. Within four days Japanese conquest of southern Manchuria was complete.

There were several reasons why the Kwantung army chieftains
engineered the Mukden incident at this time. First, they were aware
that a critical period was imminent in China, with the Young Marshal
and the Chinese nationalists working closely together. Second, they
feared that they were losing influence vis-à-vis the civilians in the
Tokyo cabinet. It may, incidentally, be said with complete assurance
that Baron Shidehara, the Foreign Minister of Japan at the time, knew
nothing whatever of the preparations for the incident; probably he
first heard of it when he saw the morning papers. The Japanese military wanted to force the hand of the conciliatory element, and take
Manchuria while the taking was good. Third, the international situation was propitious, as I shall note later on; there was small chance
that America or England would interfere. Fourth, the military were
taking advantage of what is known as the Nakamura affair. Captain
Nakamura was a Japanese agent caught and executed by Chinese
soldiers near the Mongolian frontier. Indignation and rage had swept
Japan.

The international repercussions of the Mukden incident are hardly
part of our story. We must mention, however, that the League of
Nations sent an exploratory commission to Manchuria, headed by
Lord Lytton, and that Mr. Stimson, the American Secretary of State,
announced in January, 1932, his policy of non-recognition, by which
the United States refused to recognize "any situation, treaty, or arrangement brought about by means contrary to the Kellogg-Briand
Pact." The Japanese were held to have infringed this pact, to say
nothing of the Nine Power Treaty associated with the Washington
Naval Conference of 1922, which pledged the signatories—including
Japan—to respect the territorial integrity of China. In October 1932
the Lytton commission found Japan guilty. To forestall the Lytton
finding, the Japanese, working fast, set up Manchuria as an "independent state" under the name "Manchukuo"; soon afterwards Japan
left the League, the first great power to do so.

Meantime the Japanese extended their conquest in North Manchuria. And savage warfare broke out in China proper. Here the
Chinese did resist. There was bitter fighting in and around Shanghai
early in 1932. It came partly because the Japanese navy, not to be

outdone by the army, wanted an adventure too, partly as a result of the general strain in Sino-Japanese relations. The Chinese had established a damaging boycott on Japanese goods, and resentment at this by Japan led to local incidents, of which the Japanese took advantage to make unprovoked war. Fierce and heroic resistance by the Chinese 19th Route Army, a Cantonese force—Chiang Kai-shek stood aside—was unavailing, and Japan extended her sphere of influence in the Shanghai area. This was the second Sino-Japanese war. A truce was patched up, which lasted—more or less—till 1937.

Philosophy of Undeclared Warfare

Thus occurred the first in the modern cycle of undeclared wars. Later we had the Italians in Ethiopia and Albania, the Italians and Germans in Spain. Why did not the Japanese declare war frankly? There are several reasons.

First, the conflict in its earlier stages was *sub judice* by the League of Nations, and Japan was doggedly hoping at that period not to be condemned by the League.

Second, the word "war" still possessed an ugly connotation, even in Japan. The Japanese had their own public opinion to consider. The militarists were willing to wage war in the field, but not on paper. Overt warfare was not considered quite respectable in 1932.

Third, the Japanese had public opinion in China to consider also, and it would have been invidious to declare war while they concurrently claimed to have only the friendliest feeling toward the Chinese, whom they wished to "liberate." Additionally an open declaration of war would have added impetus to the boycott in China and perhaps other countries.

Fourth, Japan did not want to violate the Kellogg-Briand Peace Pact. This well-known document is, like one species of whale, devoid of teeth; nevertheless it is a potent instrument because no one knows just what the United States might do if it were openly repudiated. No war in Europe or Asia has been formally declared since the Kellogg Pact was signed in 1928. No one quite dares to ignore it juridically. The fact continues to be remarkable that many people will swallow painlessly a war which is not called a war, while openly declared war gives a moral headache. So long as war is undeclared, and the Kellogg Pact stays theoretically inviolate, the piece of parchment at least is safe.

Fifth, the Japanese did not want to risk denunciation by the United
States for violation of the Nine Power Treaty of 1922, which they
certainly did violate, but which they could claim they were not legally
violating so long as war was not declared. Subtle people—the
Japanese!

To-day the Japanese have a very much stronger motive for not
declaring war. It is the United States Neutrality Act of 1935. It is
quite true that the President of the United States may invoke this
act whenever he decides that a state of war exists, but its invocation
would be mandatory, not optional, upon formal declaration of war,
and such invocation would be exceedingly inconvenient for Japan.
For one thing, Japan could no longer purchase arms and munitions
in the United States; for another, Japan could purchase raw materials only on a cash-and-carry basis. And the President might at his
discretion place such items as petroleum and scrap on the embargo
list, which would be damaging to Japan in the extreme.

Politics by Jiu-Jitsu

From 1932 to 1937 the Japanese performed a complex series of
maneuvers in North China. A new period in expansion and penetration began. The Japanese were like their own wrestlers, grappling
with the much larger opponent by stratagems, by muscular coördina-
tion, by sharp awareness of the object desired. Among successive steps
were the following:

1. Japan extended the borders of the Manchukuoan state by con-
quering Jehol, the mountainous district which is the eastern section
of Inner Mongolia, and which lay between the old Manchuria and
North China proper. Jehol[5] like Manchuria fell without a struggle,
and its war lord, Tang Yu-lin, known as the "Opium King," fled
ignominiously. The story is well told in Edgar Snow's *Far Eastern
Front*, a book not so widely known as it should be. The obliteration
of Jehol was important; not only was the province rich—especially
in opium, which can be a highly lucrative commodity—but strategically its 65,000 square miles opened the way to Inner Mongolia.
Jehol fell to the Japanese in February, 1933. Snow quotes a Reuter
dispatch about its last disorganized and helpless hours: "Concubines

---

[5] Jehol is pronounced "Ruh-ho." But don't laugh. Think how we pronounce
Cholmondeley or Cirencester in contrast to the spelling, or how the French
pronounce St. Quentin or Rheims.

passed in and out of the palaces and an occasional telephone call disturbed the sleepy orderly. General Tang looked 'all-in.' He was still talking about fighting to the last man, but . . . asked about his army, he said he did not know where it was." Tang was one of the worst of the old war lords. He taxed everything from frying pans to water buckets.

2. In May 1933 came the Tangku Truce, which ended the Manchurian hostilities and by which the Chinese were forced to give up territory above the Great Wall. Additionally it further opened the way to Mongolia, which the Japanese coveted, by creating a demilitarized strip just *below* the Wall, in China proper. By the Tangku Truce the Japanese were able to claim new military rights within China itself.

3. What is called the "Amau statement" was issued in Tokyo in April, 1934. Mr. Amau (at present Japanese minister to Switzerland) was one of those famous "spokesmen" in the Tokyo foreign office who obliquely "explained" Japan's actions to the world. His statement of April 1934 told other powers to keep hands off China, especially in the matter of financial assistance (which was beginning on a considerable scale), demanded repayment by the Chinese of old Japanese loans (which had been inflicted on China on preposterous terms), and was in effect the declaration of a Japanese "Monroe Doctrine" for the Chinese hinterland.

4. General Doihara began his peregrinations to separate the Five Northern Provinces from China by intrigue and if possible without hostilities. Japan felt that the moment was at hand. First, Manchuria. Second, Jehol. Third, North China itself. Doihara very nearly succeeded. He *almost* got by facility in negotiation (of course he was negotiating mostly with prostrate and corrupt Chinese underlings) and without firing a shot what the Japanese army has, after almost two years of expensive and bloody warfare, failed to get.

5. Several steps accompanied the development of the Doihara "detachment" policy. The Japanese garrison in Tientsin[6] was increased, and General Tada, its commander, announced that the Five

---

[6] A result of the Boxer Protocol. In 1900 an uprising of patriotic Chinese, the famous "Boxer Rebellion," came to a climax in Peking against foreigners. China was punished by an indemnity, and by the establishment of the Legation Quarter in Peking where foreigners had the right to maintain their own troops; they also were empowered to garrison the railway line. A Japanese garrison was stationed at the port of Tientsin.

Northern Provinces would be set up in an autonomous government independent of the Chinese national government. Chiang Kai-shek could not protest; he was too busy chasing communists in the south. Came the Ho-Umedzu agreement of June, 1935. The Japanese forced the Chinese minister of war, General Ho Ying-chin, to accept demands which have never been published in detail, but which certainly diminished gravely Chinese suzerainty in the north. China was compelled to abolish the "Peking Political Council," one of the agencies of the national government in Peking, and to suppress Kuomintang activity in the north.

6. The first concrete result of detachment was the Hopei-Chahar Political Council created late in 1935. Hopei is the province which contains Peking and Tientsin; Chahar is part of Inner Mongolia. The new Council was "appointed" by the national government, and was in theory "responsible" to it, but on the understanding that it would be virtually autonomous under Japanese control. The Hopei-Chahar Political Council adumbrated a puppet state, but did not actually establish it. Its head, General Sung Cheh-yuan, had to take orders from the Japanese, though he continued to look to Chiang Kai-shek for "supreme" authority.

7. The Japanese carved out in part of Hopei an actual autonomous area, which did not maintain any pretense of allegiance to Chiang Kai-shek, called the East Hopei Autonomous Council. Here an overt puppet ruled, the feeble General Yin Ju-king, who had a Japanese wife and who spoke Japanese. East Hopei came to be of great importance, because it adjoined the sea, and the Japanese could thus smuggle goods into China customs-free. They filled North China with textiles, sugar, and other commodities, without paying a cent of duty; the Chinese government is said to have lost $50,000,000 per year revenue as a result. Here was a new technique in imperialism: conquest through smuggling.

8. In January 1936 Foreign Minister Hirota enunciated three points for Sino-Japanese "coöperation," which were to govern all future intercourse between the two countries. First, cessation of anti-Japanese activity in China, including the boycott; second, recognition by China of Manchukuo and inauguration of economic collaboration; third, joint action, presumably by military means, by Japan and China to wipe out the Chinese communists—who had become the chief anti-Japanese elements in China. The Nanking government could

not, obviously, accept these demands and remain an independent nation. Chiang Kai-shek, playing for time, made no definite answer.

9. The Japanese began actual military invasion of Suiyuan (one of the Five Northern Provinces, and a part of Inner Mongolia) though the attacking force was called "Manchukuoan." This was late in 1936. It was part of the Ishihara policy, in contrast to the Doihara scheme of conquest by negotiation. General Ishihara thought that Japanese occupation of Inner Mongolia was an essential part of Japan's "defense" against the Soviet Union. The invasion was a failure. Presently it was obscured by a much more important event—the kidnaping of Generalissimo Chiang Kai-shek at Sian by the Young Marshal and the Chinese communists, who resented his apparent yielding to Japanese demands. This event we deal with in detail later.

The Japanese had become somewhat too confident as a result of these five years of impenetration and maneuver. And the Chinese dragon, which had been a worm, showed signs of becoming a dragon again. Students in the north, members of the National Salvation Group of Mme. Sun Yat-sen, created serious agitation. There was uneasy stalemate for a few months, and in July 1937 the Japanese military precipitated the Marco Polo incident near Peking. Presumably this was to be merely the excuse for taking over the Peking area. But hostilities quickly spread to the south. So the third Sino-Japanese war began. So war—a real one—came. It is still going on.

Anti-Comintern and/or Anti-Russian Pact

Japan and Germany signed the treaty which came to be known as the Anti-Comintern Pact in November 1936. Its chief architects were the German ambassador in Tokyo and the Japanese military attaché in Berlin, and it is commonly said that the Tokyo foreign office, which had little to do with it, greeted it somewhat wanly. Meantime Germany and Italy established the Rome-Berlin Axis, and in November 1937, Italy joined the Anti-Comintern Pact between Japan and Germany as an "original" signatory. Thus the Rome-Berlin-Tokyo "triangle" came into being. The world saw the inception of a "Fascist Internationale."

Japan and Germany at least have strong community of interest. Both countries believe in race, and Japan has begun to flirt with anti-Semitism; both are expansionist states, which were once put in the "Have-Not" category; both fear and dislike the U.S.S.R. on nationalist grounds. Japan borrowed its constitution from a German model, and built its schools and trained its army with German methods. In Japan, conversely, I felt that I was beginning to understand something of Nazi religious impulses and ideas. Worship of the state, with Hitler as its prophet, is strikingly like Shinto and Emperor-worship in Japan.[7] In 1938 a "culture accord" was signed between Japan and Germany, and one of its first results—though one would not normally put it in the culture classification—was complete publication of *Mein Kampf* in Japanese. As regards economics Japanese-German collaboration has amounted to little, since Japan above all wants credit, a commodity which neither Germany—nor Italy, the other ally—can export. An Italian economic mission visited Japan in 1938, but did not accomplish much. An Italo-Japanese "culture treaty" followed in 1939.

The Anti-Comintern Pact is not an anti-Comintern pact at all, as even official Japanese will (after argument) concede. It is an anti-Russian pact. The Comintern (Communist International) has been about as dead as General Grant since 1935 when Stalin adopted the Popular Front policy, that is, coöperation with bourgeois parties abroad instead of revolutionary activity. Revolutionary communism may revive in time, but contemporaneously the German and Japanese fear, not communist propaganda in their countries, which they assert to be integrated states completely free of subversive elements, but the formidable geographic and military power of the Soviet Union. They have designs on Russia, as both have freely admitted; therefore they combined against her. The situation has changed little since the days of the Czars. *Russia,* whatever its internal politics, is the enemy, and the Germans and Japanese use the "anti-Comintern" phrase mostly as a blind.

The Anti-Comintern Pact is not popular in Tokyo, but is accepted dutifully. As it stands it means very little except as expression of a point of view. The Japanese were puzzled and hurt, when, during

[7] An interesting subsidiary point is that Japan, like Germany, has begun to cultivate assiduously Moslem sentiment throughout the world. Mohammedan missions have visited Japan, and the Japanese, like the Germans, warmly support the Arab cause in Palestine. This is partly reflection of a general anti-British attitude, partly an aspect of policy in China, where there are many Mohammedans—particularly in the Kansu region adjacent to Soviet Russia—whom the Japanese would like to win over.

the Sudeten crisis, it seemed to mean less even than that, since it was widely printed that in the event of general war Germany would give Japan no more than "moral" aid. Germany, it was said, would not support Japan if the Japanese attacked the Soviet Union. In January 1939, however, rumors were heard that the Anti-Comintern Pact might be expanded into a military alliance.

A Sense of Time

The Japanese have a wonderfully developed instinct for accurate timing. For instance they arranged the Mukden incident in September 1931 when Chiang Kai-shek was facing a new civil war, when England was about to go off gold, when America was distraught with economic crisis.

For instance they made the Marco Polo incident in July 1937, when the present war began, with full consideration of the fact that Stalin had just damagingly purged the Russian army, that China was becoming strongly united as a result of the Sian kidnaping, that Britain was too worried by Hitler to pay attention to much else, and that in Japan itself the army had met electoral rebuff.

Important events in Europe usually find quick repercussion in Japan. The Japanese make adroit trouble when Europe's back is turned. Immediately after the Munich settlement in October 1938 they took Canton; immediately after the fall of Barcelona two months later they took Hainan; immediately after the seizure by Germany of what was left of Czechoslovakia, in March, 1939, they stretched out a long arm and took the Spratly Island group near Singapore—the furthest extension of power they have yet dared to make.

Chapter VIII
Guinea Pigs of Manchukuo

~~~~~~

Japan is Manchukuo's head family and Manchukuo is Japan's branch family.
—WAR MINISTER GENERAL ITAGAKI

WE TURN now to Manchukuo to-day. Correctly we should say "Manchutikuo," which means **"Manchu Imperial** Land," whereas "Manchukuo" means merely "Manchu Land." In 1934 Japan decided that to make the country "independent" was not enough; it must be nothing less than an Empire, and Mr. Henry Pu-yi was crowned as Emperor. To say that Manchukuo is in reality independent is to talk preposterous nonsense. The country is nothing more than a Japanese colonial preserve, run by Japan for Japan; the myth of its "independence" is a glaring contemporary fiction.

What is a Manchu? The word means "pure." A Manchu history exists, but as a contemporary political reality the Manchus are extinct. Originally they were Tungu or Tartar tribesmen, who settled in the rich Manchurian plain; a thousand years ago at least they began to intermarry with the Chinese, who moved into Manchuria in great numbers and absorbed them. In 1616 A.D. a powerful leader, Nurhachu, rose against the Ming dynasty that ruled China; he overthrew Ming power first in Mukden, then in Peking. So (1644) began the Manchu dynasty in China, which lasted till 1911. Manchuria remained part of China. With the exception of a few isolated "pockets" mentioned in the Lytton Report, no pure Manchus survive. The language is a historical curiosity: only 250 books written in it are known, and these are translations from the Chinese. Manchukuo or Manchutikuo is, and has been for generations, ninety-five percent Chinese.

I have mentioned the great size of the country. Mostly it is a vast plain. It looks like Nebraska. It has never been fully surveyed, and no one—not even the Japanese who occupy it now—knows what riches they have to exploit. But it certainly contains very large deposits of coal and iron, tremendous timber regions, a considerable amount of gold, good agricultural land, and a foreign trade worth

$400,000,000. It is the home of the soya bean, that ubiquitous product which is food to the Chinese and Japanese (as well as oil, fertilizer, fuel, what not) and steering wheels to Henry Ford. Also it produces opium in great quantity, the trade in which has mounted staggeringly.

Kwantung Laboratory

The most interesting thing about Manchukuo is that the Kwantung army, which we have described in Chapter III above, is making of it a kind of proving ground, a testing station, for social and economic theory. Manchukuo to-day is rapidly becoming a collectivist paradise, though the army has met severe resistance from the South Manchuria Railway, the other agency which seeks to dominate the country. If the Kwantung officers decide that their Manchukuoan experiment is a success, then we may expect further extension of totalitarian economy in Japan—and China. Manchukuo is proof of the army pamphlet pudding. It is the great guinea pig of Asia.

The Kwantung army abolished extraterritoriality in Manchukuo, thus seeking to freeze foreign business out. It set up a rigid currency control, and inaugurated plans for collectivizing agriculture and controlling industry. Some farms are taken over by the state, and some are left untouched, so that the army authorities can see which system works best. The army has studied long-range planning in great detail—especially in regard to hydro-electric development and conservation—and has outlined a Five-Year Plan of industrial development which is startlingly similar to the Five-Year Plan in Russia.

Basic authority for control of industry came with Imperial Ordinance No. 67, promulgated in May 1937. The terms are sweeping. No new industrial venture may be launched without consent of the government, and the state is given authority to control those now existing. The state has power to scrutinize balance sheets and operating plans, to fix prices, and to inaugurate and suspend production. In other words, the state—that is, the Kwantung army—rules. Private capital, if it has no right to fix prices, to start new business, is helpless.

Ten industries are exclusively operated by the state:

Electric generation and supply
Electric transmission
Automobile manufacturing
Petroleum refining

Coal mining
Explosives manufacture
Aviation
Life insurance up to policies of 2,000 yen
Schoolbook publication
Opium refining and sale

The state does not operate, but controls, the following industries:

Aircraft manufacture
Woolen textiles
Matches
Cement
Oil crushing
Sugar
Beer
Hemp
Automobile transport

Finally, the state participates in the control of:

Forestry
Alcohol manufacturing
Light metals
News service
Liquid fuel
Cotton textiles
Fertilizers

In all these enterprises the state will "rationalize output." All reserves of raw materials are to be considered "defense resources" of the state. Finally, a stock company was set up as a sort of holding company for various industrial enterprises under these plans. The Planning Board of the Kwantung army estimates that a total investment of 2,450,000,000 yen ($661,500,000) will be necessary by 1942.

Struggle with the South Manchuria followed. The railway was asked to contribute not less than 900,000,000 yen of this great sum. The situation is peculiar. The South Manchuria is more than a railway. It is a huge industrial complex itself, with interests in timber and hotels, soya beans and steel and chemicals; it controls seventy-two industrial undertakings. The directors of the South Manchuria, who liked to regard the old Manchuria as their own province, became timid of the totalitarian aspects of the new policy, jealous of the

Kwantung army putting it through, and fearful of their good eight percent dividends. But—the critical point—the South Manchuria is, and always has been, owned fifty percent by the Japanese government. So the Kwantung army had simply to exert pressure on Tokyo to get its way. Yosuke Matsuoka, who in some respects is very close to the army, became head of the South Manchuria. The Kwantung officers were able in effect to dominate the South Manchuria in two directions: first by activity on the spot, second by pressure on the Japanese government, which it in part controlled, and which in part controlled the railway.

The army's point of view was simple. Let the South Manchuria retrench, and devote itself simply to the railway business, which was its proper business anyway. Let it continue to assist Japanese imperialism in the sphere of communications, especially in building strategic railways; let it drop its industrial and commercial accretions. So an organization known as the Japanese-Manchuria Trading Company was organized to replace the old sales and supplies division of the S. M. R., which is now handling the output of the collieries at Fushun and the other mining properties of the railway. The railway company still produces the goods, but the army, that is the Manchukuoan state, markets them. Likewise such S. M. R. subsidiaries as the Manchuria Chemical Industries Company, the Showa Steel Company, and the Manchu Electric Industry Company have been reorganized, with the army in control. Still the army is not satisfied. Recently the official Manchukuoan news agency announced that the S. M. R. was an "anachronism, intent on maintaining its kingdom and not understanding the post-Incident outlook," and demanding its "reformation."

To summarize: the Kwantung army feels that if the new Manchukuoan state is to be built on rational economic lines, the power of private capital as represented by the huge horizontal monopoly of the S. M. R. must be broken. Nevertheless the S. M. R. is useful at the moment, and therefore should be dealt with gradually.

Emperor Hank

His Imperial Majesty the Emperor of Manchukuo is almost certainly the only man alive who has been a monarch three different times in his lifetime.

Henry Pu-yi was born in Peking in 1906, the grandnephew of the old Empress Dowager.[1] He was crowned Emperor of China, Son of Heaven, Emperor of the World, Lord of a Million Years, at the age of two. His father (who is still alive but who lives in obscure retirement now) became Regent for him, but the dynasty was blasted out of China in 1912. Henry Pu-yi, then aged six, abdicated; no harm came to him, and the good republicans gave him a stipend of $4,000,-000 (Chinese) per year and permitted him to continue residence in the Forbidden City. In 1917 came a monarchical coup d'état and he became Emperor again, under the name Hsuan Tung, for a few days. Then he continued to live quietly in Peking, and in 1922 married a Manchu girl, Elizabeth Yuang, who had been brought up by American missionaries. In 1924 he was kicked out of the Forbidden City, and his friend Colonel Doihara smuggled him to Tientsin. In 1932 he was imported into Manchukuo as Chief Executive, and in 1934 became Emperor.

Henry's tutor for many years was a cultivated Englishman and Sinologue Sir Reginald Johnston. It was Johnston who first bought him a tennis racket, gave him a bicycle. When young Henry began practicing bicycle riding on one wheel, the court attendants were horrified; they said it would damage his manhood. Johnston also gave Henry the name he is best known by; he was studying English history, and Johnston suggested that he adopt the name of the English king he liked most. The young Emperor chose Henry VIII. Since coronation in Manchukuo his style of address has changed again, and he is called the Emperor "Kang Teh"; this name was chosen by a consortium of philosophers, and means "Exalted Virtue."[2] A

[1] More should be known of this wonderful old woman, who was a kind of Chinese Catherine the Great. Her career was bizarrely colorful. Originally she was a concubine; and she ruled the Chinese Empire for forty-seven years! Largely her technique was to establish the succession through minors, and then to dominate them from behind the scenes. She came to power in 1861. On November 14, 1908, her nephew, the then-Emperor, whom she had kept prisoner on an island in the Summer Palace, was found strangled. She then picked his son Henry Pu-yi for the succession. The next day she herself died suddenly. In her early days, before she went into the harem, she was called Yehonala. Then she was known as Kuei-fei (Concubine) I. As Empress and Regent she was named Tzu Hsi; as Empress Dowager she liked to be addressed by her full title, which was Motherly Auspicious Orthodox Heaven-Blest Prosperous All-Nourishing Brightly-Manifest Calm Sedate Perfect Long-Lived Respectful Reverend Worshipful Illustrious Exalted Empress Dowager. (See the *Encyclopaedia Sinica*, p. 614.)

[2] The present writer was somewhat horrified to discover that his own name, which the Chinese pronounce "Guan-teh," was best rendered in Chinese by the

few Chinese still maintain reverence for Henry. In one Peking museum is still preserved a can of dog biscuit from his childhood days.

Henry is very tall, almost six feet, but he weighs only 102 pounds. He was given an armored Lincoln motorcar, but could not sit in it in full regalia, because the special armoring raised the seat. The car was remodeled then, and the springs compressed. Henry almost never uses the car, because in effect he is a prisoner in his residence, which is the old Salt Gabelle building. He has no palace, but his salary is said to be $500,000 per year. The Japanese let him see no one. He is locked up like a case of mumps. One of his servants is reported to have said, "He hates the Japanese just as much as I do, but he gets paid more for it."

Unfortunately Henry has no children, which is one reason why his Japanese employers are now cool to him. They wanted him above all to found a dynasty. He is fond of his wife, and for a long time resisted Japanese demands that he take a concubine. He finally did, selecting one from photographs provided by a marriage broker, but after a time she left him. He has resolutely refused to take another. The Japanese, annoyed, have as a result treated him—and his wife—with even less consideration than before.

Henry is a mild, amiable and unfortunate creature, whose good qualities of modesty and intelligence have been obscured. As a political force he does not exist. The irreverent call him "Hank," and it can be said with complete assurance that he is the least consequential monarch on earth.

The Political Landscape

A totalitarian economy would seem to demand a mass political party to express its aims, and the Kwantung army set out presently to create one. This is a curious and revealing point: normally it is the party (as in Germany, Russia, Italy), which creates the government; in Manchukuo the equation goes backward, with the government creating the mass party. It is, I heard it said, "totalitarianism in reverse." The new party is an organization known as the Concordia Society.

It was also found necessary—again a reversal of the normal procedure—to establish a philosophy, an ideology or series of political myths, under which the new party should operate. Hence, with true

characters "Kang Teh." This puts the writer in a class above his friend Peter Fleming, who in Chinese merely becomes "Learned Engraver on Stone."

Japanese efficiency, an official philosophy was formulated, so that the new party could have something to believe in. The philosophy, which aims to resurrect the old Confucian virtues of diligence, filial piety, and the like, is named from the Chinese philosopher Mencius, and is called "Wang Tao"—the Kingly Way.

The aim of the Concordia Society is to broaden the basis of support to the régime, yet its printed matter is in Japanese, not Chinese. And there are at least 30,000,000 Chinese in Manchukuo, as against only 400,000 Japanese, almost all of whom are soldiers or officials, and who do not need conversion anyway. Concordia members—there are said to be 300,000—wear chocolate colored uniforms ("the national defense color"), go to culture meetings, attend athletic festivals, preach race harmony, build up "national" spirit, and have free vacations in Japan. The Concordia creed asks members to work for Wang Tao, to "eliminate the poison of a military system" (this in an organization founded by the Kwantung army!) and to "resist the possession of people's minds by capitalist philosophy or communist principles." The Emperor and Prime Minister are ex-officio Governor and President respectively of the Concordia Society; yet it is maintained that it is a "private" organization. Japanese always leave a loophole.

General Ueda, the Commander-in-Chief of the Kwantung army, Japanese Ambassador to Manchukuo, and undisputed ruler of the country (under Henry Pu-yi), said of the Concordia Society recently: "It was born at the same time as the state. It is a fixed political, cultural, and practical state organ. It guards the state, and educates the people so that the purpose of the state will be realized."

A law reorganizing the government of Manchukuo on a semi-totalitarian basis was promulgated in May 1937. It centralizes the administration, with the prime minister as head of what is called the State Council, and as the only minister of state. Under him is the General Affairs Board, which makes most important decisions in association with the Kwantung army. The prime minister of Manchukuo is a Chinese; but the head of the General Affairs Board, a Japanese civilian named Naoki Hoshino, tells him what to do.

Japanese have all the good jobs. They have, in fact, almost *all* the jobs. In the Department of Public Peace, for instance, eighty-two percent of the personnel is Japanese; in the General Affairs Board, seventy-two percent; in the Foreign and Home offices, sixty-three percent; in the courts, eighty-seven percent; in the Bureau of Capital

Construction, eighty-eight percent; in the Metropolitan Police Board, sixty-five percent; in industrial undertakings, eighty percent; in the Department of Public Welfare, sixty-one percent; in the provincial governments, at least sixty percent.

In July, 1937, Lieutenant-General Chikushi, the Japanese vice-president of the Manchukuoan Privy Council, resigned his post and left the country, in protest that Chinese were so rigorously excluded from jobs and opportunities for leadership. He was seventy-four, and the oldest Japanese official in the country. He said, "The policy of the Manchukuoan government is determined at present not by deliberations of the cabinet but by the whim of one or two powerful individuals." Surprisingly enough, this rebellious statement was freely printed in Japan, but suppressed in Manchukuo.

The first prime minister of Manchukuo was Cheng Hsiao-hsu, who died in 1938, aged seventy-eight. He was an old-style Chinese scholar and civil servant, a royalist who rejected the Chinese republic. For a time he worked well with the Japanese, then came to detest them, and when it appeared that his master, Henry Pu-yi, was to become nothing more than a puppet, he resigned. He was an exceptionally accomplished calligrapher. When the Japanese created their puppet state in North China early in 1938, they tried hard to get Cheng Hsiao-hsu to head it; he refused. But the Japanese respected him, and when he died they gave him an imposing funeral.

The present prime minister, General Chang Ching-hui, is much less a man. He is said to be largely illiterate (as the Chinese put it politely, he knows only "a few" characters) and like his late leader Chang Tso-lin, began life as a bandit. He held various posts in Chinese provincial governments, and joined the Japanese in 1931. He rose to be minister of war, and then got the premiership. In fairness to the Japanese it should be said that it is extremely difficult to find Chinese of any caliber who will take any jobs with them at all; they have to use what material they can get.[3] Chang Ching-hui was born in 1871.

[3] Some Japanese personnel in Manchukuo seem oddly chosen. Captain Amakasu, for instance, is Secretary-General of the Concordia Society. Early in the 1920's, a ferocious nationalist, he strangled the Tokyo labor leader Sakae Osugi, his wife, and seven-year-old son. He was convicted of the triple murder, and sentenced to ten years in jail. But many Japanese considered him a true patriot, and in 1931 he went to Manchukuo as one of the empire builders.

Imperialism Costs Money

I have heard Japanese proudly (and somewhat obtusely) say that Hsinking, the new capital of Manchukuo, would become to Tokyo what Alexandria was to Rome. A rather ominous comparison.

Imperialism is expensive. Other powers than Japan, gambling on great profit, have discovered this unfortunate truth. Estimates of the total sum spent by Japan in Manchuria are difficult to make, but one good calculation is that the mother country spent two billion yen there before 1931, and that expenses since the incident have averaged at least 500,000,000 yen ($135,000,000) per year. Not all of this is lost, since Manchukuo pays some return, for instance in profits of the S. M. R., emigrant remittances, and export trade. T. A. Bisson, an expert in Far Eastern affairs, calculated that in an average year, 1936, Japan spent 716,416,000 yen in Manchukuo, and received from Manchukuo 468,400,000 yen—a net loss of 248,016,000 yen. But these figures do not include the cost of upkeep of the Kwantung army, which are at least 200,000,000 yen per year additional.

For this sum Japan gets a good deal at present and in the future hopes to get a great deal more. A new repository for heavy industry. A wonderfully ample storehouse of raw materials. A market for Japanese exports. A potent lever on China. A good strategic frontier against Russia. Above all, an imperial domain.

It hoped too to get land for surplus population. But, as I have indicated, Manchukuo has been disappointing as a colonial enterprise. Emigrants so far have been of two classes only, the extremely poor, who could not resist the small subsidy offered for emigration, and the fanatic patriots; altogether only about ten thousand emigrants have arrived to date. This unimpressive figure has caused alarm, and recently official impetus was given to the emigration movement—which however is not called "emigration" but "mass movement of race"—by establishment of the Manchuria Colonization Society, capitalized at 50,000,000 yen. The object is to settle 1,000,000 Japanese families—say 5,000,000 people—by 1958, a program which will cost inordinately. "Manchukuo must have a sizable and well distributed Japanese minority to lead every phase of activity," it is proclaimed. The first batch of 500 immigrants under the new system were given three weeks' training in a national labor school, and then placed in a

10,000 hectare tract. The temperature when they arrived—Manchukuo is not a tropical country—was 38.3 degrees below zero.

One reason why Manchukuo has been so expensive is the enormous new railroad development. The Japanese took over the old Chinese lines which had fed the South Manchuria, and built out new spurs from the old Chinese Eastern. Three of these spurs prodded toward the Soviet frontier, which they reached in two places (the third points to Outer Mongolia) and were obviously planned for military purposes. Altogether the Japanese have built 2,800 miles of new railway in seven years. In Korea two ports have been developed, Seishin and Rashin—Rashin is entirely new—underneath the Soviet border and Vladivostok. By use of these new ports and the new railways serving them the Japanese hope to be able to pour troops into *North* Manchuria—adjoining the Soviet Union—several days more quickly than would be possible via Dairen and the South Manchuria route.

Another expensive item is banditry, but this has diminished from the terrific peak it reached in 1932-33. The Japanese keep accurate statistics on bandit activity, which is plotted like a fever chart. Day by day, carefully recorded, the graph goes up or down. I cannot resist some condensed quotations from the official *Japan-Manchukuo Yearbook*, 1938 edition:

TABLE 5. BANDIT ACTIVITIES IN MANCHUKUO. 1935.

	Jan.	May	Sept.	Total (1935)
No. of bandit raids	2,325	3,835	4,628	39,151
No. of bandits involved	93,880	193,737	205,405	1,783,880
No. suppressive expeditions	1,502	2,284	2,820	24,150
Bandit Losses:				
Killed	763	1,600	1,155	13,338
Injured	847	1,113	1,214	11,815
Captured	274	204	164	2,703
Arms	406	466	634	6,265
Ammunitions (rounds)	2,457	9,258	5,134	91,780
Horses	696	453	681	7,248
Captives (horses)	262	357	731	381
Suppression Troops Losses:				
Killed	61	136	143	1,361
Injured	107	150	275	2,276
Held captive	31	66	82	753
Arms	34	228	170	2,404
Ammunitions (rounds)	36,737	23,295	5,503	218,644
Horses	33	23	12	571

TABLE 5.—*(Continued)*

Civilian Losses:	Jan.	May	Sept.	Total *(1935)*
Killed	150	318	281	2,512
Injured	216	309	306	2,809
Held captive	835	2,282	3,560	27,531
Arms	123	827	157	2,184
Ammunitions (rounds)	1,447	434	1,375	20,723
Horses	2,882	2,470	5,005	36,877
No. of houses	961	2,028	1,868	19,326
Cash (Manchukuoan Yuan)	128,331	50,949	94,078	809,998

Another exhaustive table classifies the bandits by provinces; another (Table 7), concerns size of bandit raids.

TABLE 7. SIZE OF BANDIT GROUPS AND RAIDS CLASSIFIED. 1935.

	No. of Raids	Size of Groups		
		1–30	*51–100*	*301–500*
January	2,325	1,743	131	12
February	1,617	1,102	142	7
March	2,632	1,958	188	19

And so on.

Bandits were once classified officially in four categories ("Patriotic," "Religious," "Old Style," and "Bandits of Despair," i.e., desperately poor peasants), but now only three groups are recognized: first, communists, who are tied up with the national movement in China; second, "nationalists," who are pre-1931 insurrectionaries; third, bandits proper, i.e., desperadoes and brigands who do not dignify their activity by patriotic symbolism.

For a time suppression necessitated a form of punitive guerrilla warfare; as recently as 1937 Japan was supposed to have had to put 80,000 men in the field. But gradually a new technique developed, based partly on new roads, and the bandits were forced back into the mountains. The authorities took to surrounding disaffected villages with barbed wire, and literally padlocking them. The bandits sooner or later had to enter villages for food and ammunition; if they could not get in—and if peasants suspected of complicity could not get out—the problem was on the way to solution. There are several thousand Manchukuoan villages completely circled with wire and carefully guarded; they are a unique phenomenon, and have greatly reduced the guerrilla total.

The Imperial Japanese army, i.e., the Kwantung army, is never used in suppressing banditry. Instead there are the railway guards, the special force known as the Peace Protection army, and the Manchukuoan army itself, which is composed of Chinese officered by Japanese. Privates in the Manchukuoan army are allowed only five rounds of ammunition daily, though their service has been loyal—so far.

Chinese peasants and townsmen in Manchukuo have several complaints, though political fermentation hardly exists. First, they have been subject to forced labor. Second, crops bring the same price, but taxes are higher. Third, they are asked to join the Concordia Society (dues, 2.5 yen per year), and to contribute to the "independence" movement in Inner Mongolia. Fourth, they must grow tobacco and other export products, as well as the usual "pay" crops. Even so— professional banditry aside—the peasants have been numbed into submission.

The basic issue is whether the Chinese inhabitants do not prefer the stability and economic benefits of the Japanese régime, such as they are, to the risks of joining China's renascent nationalism. The war in 1937-39 seemed to give an answer. There was no Chinese revolt in Manchukuo, the revolt that China had anticipated. Manchukuo was quiet as a—tomb.

Elusive Foreigners

To date the independence of Manchukuo has been recognized only by Japan, Italy, and the minuscule Central American republic El Salvador. Even in Japan I heard that recognition by El Salvador came by mistake. It appears that, a year or two ago, on New Year's Day, the Manchukuoan government sent the usual holiday messages to all the countries of the world. A clerk in the El Salvador Foreign Office did not realize that, everywhere in the world except in Japan, these messages were by the rules of diplomatic etiquette rigorously ignored. The El Salvador official acknowledged the message. Hastily Japan seized on the contretemps, accepted the return of holiday greetings as recognition, and before anyone knew what was happening announced that El Salvador, splendidly isolated, had recognized the Manchukuo government.

Italian recognition of Manchukuo had its lighter note also. The Italian Consul General in Mukden, becoming minister to Manchukuo, duly traveled to Hsinking to present his letters of credence. He thought that the occasion demanded ceremony, and he asked for a cavalry escort. There was, unfortunately, no cavalry in Hsinking, the new capital. No escort, no credentials, said the new minister. So some police were collected, none of them horsemen by profession; they rented the uniforms of a local brass band hired for funerals, and borrowed aged horses from the ricksha coolies. The procession had ornate but temporary magnificence. It began to rain, the mounted police began to slip, the horses fled, and the colors in the uniforms ran. The Italian minister, a stubborn man, presented his credentials just the same.

Germany has been cautious in regard to Manchukuo. It has promised to recognize the country, but at the moment of writing has not done so.

Chapter IX
The Russian Position

A war between Japan and Russia would be as popular as could be imagined. The whole world would be cheering for both sides to lose.

—WALTER DURANTY quoted by DEMAREE BESS

I WROTE about the Soviet Union in *Inside Europe* three years ago. I would like to revise now some of my opinions (so would a lot of people), but this book is not the place for extended treatment of the U.S.S.R., even though Siberia covers such an enormous part of Asia. Most of this area belongs politically to the R.S.F.S.R. (Russia proper), whose issues and leaders are considered in *Inside Europe*. Here I should like to add a few words only about predominantly Siberian problems, three in number: industrial development, national minorities, and railroads.

Central Asia and Siberia have been the scene of a phenomenal economic development. The Kremlin leaders saw early the importance of the Siberian reservoir, which had been grossly neglected under the Czars, and the Five-Year Plans paid strong attention to the east. Soviet statistics show incredible potentialities in the region; for instance the eastern regions of the U.S.S.R. are supposed to contain eighty-five percent of the coal of the entire Soviet Union, eighty-seven percent of its copper, eighty-five percent of its water power, sixty percent of its wheat land, twenty-eight to forty percent of its iron ore. Moreover Siberia is not only rich; it is strategically impregnable, at least between Lake Baikal and the Urals. So development began. We must choose from a great variety of detail available. The gold fields in the Baikal region and Yakut began to be worked intensively, and it is said that presently they will produce not less than ten million ounces of gold per year. The far north was opened up, and the largest timber resources in the world are being tapped. Industrial production has increased 277 percent in Central Asia, 285 percent in Siberia, since the first Five-Year Plan. Finally, a great advance has been made in the Kuznetsk basin, where a coal-iron nexus has become the second Soviet producer of steel, rivaling the Magnitogorsk area in the Urals. A new steel town, Stalinsk, has been built, and the population of Novosibirsk, the central point of the region, has almost tripled in five years. The Kuznetsk basin is believed to contain four hundred *billion* tons of coal. A third "coal-steel base" will, it is said, be created later in the Baikal region. The Soviets, in a word, have turned to Asia intensively.

As to minorities Russia has pursued a careful policy. The fringes of Siberia, like the Caucasus, are a puzzling network of mixed tribes and nationalities. Political control by Moscow is absolute, though technically the chief minority groups have their own governments; the new constitution of 1936 divided the country into eleven republics (eight of which are in Asia) which stress autonomy in local administration and complete linguistic, racial, and cultural freedom. The R.S.F.S.R. is in turn divided into autonomous regions (fourteen of which are in Asia) which repeat the process. This is good sense. There is no attempt in Russia—politics aside—to assimilate non-Russians, no attempt like that of Germany to make a racially coördinated nation. The minorities appreciate this. Their local identities survive. Armenians, Georgians, Turkomans, Kazaks, Kirghis, Daghestanese, Bashkirs, Buryats, Kalmuks, Uzbeks, Tartars, Yakuts— all the bewildering medley of non-Russian peoples—are permitted to remain (politics again aside) non-Russian.

Third, the matter of railroads. I have mentioned that the Japanese built strategic lines in Manchukuo which reach the Amur River, i.e., the Russian frontier. These lines were a distinct threat to Russian security, since the Trans-Siberian railway—an absolutely vital link in Russian communications—is immediately adjacent to the Amur, and in the event of war might easily be cut. This would split Russia in half, and isolate the Pacific zone. It was a risk the Kremlin could not accept. Therefore at immense labor a new railway is being built —in April 1939 it was not quite completed—north of the Trans-Siberian and parallel to it, connecting a town called Taishet, just west of Irkutsk and Lake Baikal, with a new city which has had several names but which is most commonly called Konsomolsk, on the Pacific above Vladivostok. A spur connects it with the Trans-Siberian at Khabarovsk, the headquarters of the Soviet Far Eastern army. This new railway—if it works—will presumably enable supplies and troops to continue to pass across Russia if the Japanese pierce the

Trans-Siberian. Meantime, the Trans-Siberian has been double tracked, and in some places triple tracked.

Soviets and Japanese

Almost every Japanese I met thought that a war with the Soviet Union was someday inevitable. Vladivostok and Khabarovsk, where the Russians have air bases, are only seven hundred miles from Tokyo and the great industrial centers of Japan; which means, even in these days of modern mathematics, that Tokyo and the industrial centers of Japan are only seven hundred miles from Vladivostok and Khabarovsk; in other words they are extremely vulnerable to attack from the air. The Japanese will not bluntly say that they expect attack by Soviet Russia. But they are fully aware that the world is explosively agitated, that the Far East is a peculiarly sensitive area, and above all that their own ideas are expansionist. They will not rest content till they have pushed the Soviet frontier back as far as Baikal; they will not rest content till their precious capital, Tokyo, is safe from even remote possibility of air attack.

Not everyone remembers to-day that the Japanese, seizing the opportunity of the Russian civil wars, occupied the Maritime Provinces of Siberia in 1919, including Vladivostok, and did not depart till 1922. Following the Russo-Japanese war of 1904-5 Japan had annexed the southern half of the Russian island of Sakhalin, which has valuable oil deposits; the Japanese took the northern half too after the Great War, and did not vacate it till 1925.

That Japan should think of attacking Russia at the present moment, when it is so deeply imbedded in China, seems inconceivable. But I have mentioned the national tendency to *hara-kiri*. And it has been pointed out that the Japanese army, which certainly thinks that a Soviet war will someday be necessary, may choose to make it now rather than later, because Russia is getting stronger, Japan weaker, as the China conflict goes on. If stalemate continues in China, the Japanese military may fear that civilian rivals in Tokyo will strengthen their position, out of dissatisfaction with conduct of the China war; in this case, the military may think it necessary to regain prestige and power by striking elsewhere. On the other hand, war between Japan and the Soviet Union is more likely to develop out of a ramifying European crisis than a local incident, most Japanese believe.

The Russians are, if nothing else, realists. They know that Japan intends to make war—someday. Why, then, do not the Russians take advantage of Japan's contemporary troubles in China to strike now, and paralyze Japan with a swift blow while it is unable adequately to defend itself? The answer is twofold. First, the Russians, whose whole policy is defensive, have no more inclination to fight a "cold," preventive war than the British and French. They, like every one else, want these days to keep the guns at home. Second, if Russia should attack Japan, Russia might in turn be attacked by Japan's partner, Germany. Russia has two frontiers, with an enemy on each. Should the Russians become embroiled with the Japanese, they might find Mr. Hitler on their backs.

Peace serves Russian national interest, whereas activism is necessary to Japan. This is the whole story. Russian policy is defensive not necessarily because Russians are sweet people, but because to be defensive is good sense. Vis-à-vis Japan, they had only one possible tactic, which was to make themselves as strong as possible in the East, and to delay. So air strength was multiplied, the Amur frontier fortified, Vladivostok filled with submarines, and a great army concentrated at Khabarovsk. The Russians know that, if the Japanese fight, they will aim to strike at Baikal. So this sector is strengthened, and there is nothing else to do but wait.

The Russians (we will come to the matter of Outer Mongolia later) are proud of their pacific record in the Far East. Indeed their restraint in the face of incessant Japanese provocation has been considerable. From 1924 to 1927 the Soviets assisted the Chinese revolution; then they cleared out and did not resume normal relations with China until 1932. At about the same time they proposed a non-aggression pact with Japan; it was rejected. The Soviets, following trouble on the Chinese Eastern Railway, invaded Manchukuo (Manchuria then) to clean up; but they promptly left again, though the pretext to remain was much greater than Japan's pretext after the Mukden incident. Finally, at considerable loss, they sold the Chinese Eastern.

Russia has helped China in the present war, but not to any great extent. When I was in Hankow there were a few Soviet planes there. The temptation thus to encourage the Chinese was, presumably, irresistible. When the Japanese complained, Mr. Litvinov, tongue in cheek, told them off in their own language by saying that, after all, Japan refused to admit that a war was going on, and that therefore

Russian planes could not be taking part in hostilities. Russian supplies to China could be of inestimable value, but they are exceedingly hard to get in. The route across Mongolia is closed, and the trucks must take the long caravan route through Chinese Turkestan—an onerous undertaking. They start from a position on the "Turk-Sib" Railway—another comparatively new and highly important railway development—and go through Urumchi to Lanchow. This route takes at least eighteen days, and the trucks until recently had to carry their own gas and oil, which did not leave much room for pay load. The greatest aid Russia renders China is indirect. It is that, out of fear of complications with Russia, Japan must keep a huge army permanently mobilized on the Soviet frontier. At least 350,000 Japanese who might be fighting in China are thus sterilized into restless inactivity.

Troubled Waters

A perennial nuisance in international relations is the fisheries quarrel between Japan and Russia. The gist of it is this. Japanese fishermen have for generations collected a large part of their catch in Russian waters, off Sakhalin and Kamchatka. A convention establishing the rights of these fishers, and allocating certain special waters to the Japanese, was ratified in 1928 but expired in 1936. Japan had then just signed the Anti-Comintern Pact with Germany, which annoyed the Russians; for this as well as other reasons—some having to do with rate of exchange, some in regard to auctioning of fishing "lots"—the U.S.S.R. refused to extend the agreement for another long period, as the Japanese wished, but kept them on tenterhooks by extending it merely from year to year. Japan said that Russia was attempting to freeze their fishermen out of the area; Russia said that Japan was infringing on Russian sovereignty in territorial waters. In April 1939, a new agreement was patched up.

Fisheries are of vital importance to Japan, which has by far the largest catch of any nation in the world. Fish are a valuable article of export (the annual yield is worth 300,000,000 yen) and, above all, they fill a crucial rôle in making the country self-sufficient in regard to food.

An allied dispute concerns oil in Sakhalin. Japan not only takes oil from its own half of the island, but by terms of a treaty signed in 1925 has concessions in the northern half, which belongs to Russia. The

Japanese want these concessions elaborated and extended; the Russians want to conserve the supply.

"The Demon of Discord, with Her Sooty Wings"

The frontier between Manchukuo and the Soviet Union, almost 3,200 miles long, and for most of its length following two rivers, the Amur and the Ussuri, beyond doubt produces more dangerous "incidents" than any region in the world. About 2,000 of them have been officially recorded in ten years, ranging from catcalls across the border to pitched battles. One may ask how a frontier which is a river can detonate so easily. But the Amur is a difficult river, shallow, full of islands, and frozen for part of the year; moreover (an odd habit of Chinese rivers) it changes its course repeatedly. The incidents have been mainly provoked by Japanese. When a serious one occurs, the Russians can almost always produce a Japanese prisoner or two, taken on their territory, whereas Russian captives taken prisoner on Japanese territory have been very rare.

The two most famous of recent incidents occurred in June, 1937, on the Amur, and in July, 1938, at Changkufeng Hill near the eastern extremity of Manchukuo. Some experts say that both were aggravated by the Japanese, if not actually incited for reasons of policy, as deliberate tests of Soviet strength. Each told a different story.

In the 1937 incident Soviet gunboats were accused of landing troops on two islands near the Russian town Blagoveshchensk (which faces a new Japanese railhead with the cheerful name Heiho), which the Japanese said were Manchukuoan territory. The Japanese opened fire, and one Soviet boat was sunk. A crisis sharply ensued, but negotiations settled it. The Russians backed down precipitously and left the Japanese in possession of the islands. From this Japan deduced that Russia, harried by internal discontent and weak from purging, was in no condition to fight. Thus the importance of the incident: it led indirectly to the Chinese war, since the Japanese wanted assurance that Russia was not strong enough to intervene.

The incident at Changkufeng thirteen months later had an altogether different outcome. The Japanese say that the Russians occupied a commanding lump of territory which they assert is just inside the Manchukuo border. The hill had considerable strategic importance, and Russia claimed that it was Soviet territory by terms of an old Sino-Russian treaty. Serious fighting followed, and lasted for ten days with several hundred casualties. Many thought that the second Russo-Japanese war had begun. The Russians resisted stiffly; the Red Army seemed to have recovered from the purge. The Japanese receded, and negotiations ended the squabble. Russia remained in possession of the hill.

Another General Bluecher

The Far Eastern Army of the Soviet Union was for years an autonomous and self-contained command under the redoubtable Marshal Vassily K. Bluecher, one of the ablest military men of modern times. But in October, 1938—just after the Munich crisis—the Soviet War Minister Voroshilov traveled to Khabarovsk, and presently it was announced that the Far Eastern Army was no longer autonomous, and that Bluecher had been dismissed. Later he was reported shot. These reports, though generally believed, have not been confirmed, and Chinese rumors say that Bluecher is somewhere in Mongolia, possibly doing penance in remote confinement, possibly organizing Mongolian military forces. At any rate he has disappeared.

Bluecher was born in the Yaroslavl district near the Volga in 1889. His German-sounding name came remotely from Russo-German landlords nearby, but he is pure Russian; many Russians in this area have German names. He was a factory worker and mechanic, and in 1905—still a boy—joined the revolution. During the Great War he fought as a conscript. He was wounded and cited for bravery, and in 1917 helped organize the early military soviets in Leningrad. He rose rapidly, and led various detachments in the civil wars. He fought on the Siberian front, and in fact saved the Far East for Russia, because his armies defeated White leaders like Kolchak and Semenov, and beat the Japanese back to Vladivostok.

For a time he returned to Moscow, assisting Trotsky in the reorganization of the Red Army after the civil war. But his chief interest was the Far East. He conducted a mission into Mongolia. Later he found himself—quite by chance—a fellow passenger on the Trans-Siberian with a young Chinese officer named—Chiang Kaishek. The two became friends. Chiang invited Bluecher to Canton (where Chiang was reorganizing an officers school); Bluecher accepted, got leave from the Red Army, and began his great Chinese days. The Chinese called him "Ga-lin." So developed the "mystery" of his identity. Foreigners in China called him General "Galen" or

"Gallant," and for years he was better known thus than as Bluecher. To a considerable extent he was responsible for Chiang Kai-shek's early victories. When Chiang split with the communists, Bluecher fled; he returned to Moscow, and was sent to Siberia again. In 1929 he became Commander-in-Chief of the Far Eastern Army, the building up of which is largely his work. He created Kharbarovsk.

The Far Mongolias

"Europe seems to be quieting down, but now we have to worry about Asia once more. There are disquieting rumors that the Japanese have gone over into Outer Mongolia to wage peace in Russia's face."

—HOWARD BRUBAKER

I have an old-fashioned dislike of writing about places I have not seen, and travel in the Mongolias was impossible on account of the war. But in plain fact Outer Mongolia, at least, has been seen by very few people indeed in the last decade; it is such *terra incognita* that Tibet is practically Coney Island by comparison. There are two Mongolias, Outer and Inner, and the distinction between them is important. Outer Mongolia is a Russian sphere, whereas most of Inner Mongolia is Japanese. But first a word about Mongolia in general.

The Mongols are a world by themselves. They have not, like their neighbors the Manchus, been assimilated by the Chinese; they have preserved their racial and linguistic identity for centuries—even though they are nomads, and have intermarried broadly to produce "Mongoloid" peoples all over Asia. They have bitten very widely into history, though the bite is not deep. They were in the main wanderers and destroyers, not creaters. Some historians say that the Huns, who helped destroy the Roman Empire, were Mongols; we know that under Genghis Khan and Tamurlane the Mongols made fantastic conquests throughout Asia and Europe, with traces that persist as far west as Hungary; we know that they penetrated India, and played a great rôle in Indian history. Many Mongols became Mohammedans, and added the fire of religion to their expansionist zest. There are Mongol inheritances in Japanese, in Chinese, in Siamese, and in the Pacific peoples of the East Indies.

Their citadel remains Outer Mongolia. This is a tract almost unbelievably vast. It covers about a million square miles—almost one-third the size of Canada. A great deal of this is desert, especially the Gobi region; it is thinly occupied, and the total population is probably not much greater than 800,000. On the maps Outer Mongolia is almost invariably shown as part of China. This is nonsense. Outer Mongolia is no longer in reality part of China. To say that it belongs to China is to say that Roosevelt belongs to Hitler. Outer Mongolia since 1924 has been the "Mongolian People's Republic," and it is almost exclusively a Soviet sphere of influence. When they came into power the Soviets gave up the imperialist treaties with China. But in Outer Mongolia something very close to *Soviet* imperialism may be said to exist.

Russian penetration of Mongolia, like that of Manchuria, began with the Czars, and as early as 1915 Outer Mongolia had a peculiar and special status, being legally under Chinese sovereignty and Russian protection at the same time. During the Russian civil wars in 1921 the "Mad Baron" Ungern Sternberg, a White Russian adventurer, fled from Russia, took Urga (now called Ulan Bator), the Outer Mongolian capital, and set up one of the most extraordinarily sadistic rules in history. The Mongolians rose against him, organizing a revolutionary government, and the Russian Red Army came in to help. The Mad Baron was extinguished, and thereafter Soviet influence increased. Power had been in the hands of a ruling clique of Lamas (priests), under a gentleman known as the Living Buddha. He died in 1924 and a republic was set up. Events closely paralleling those of Russia then took place: redistribution of land, economic development, and creation of a semi-Soviet government. In 1934 came a mutual assistance pact with the U.S.S.R., though that this treaty existed—it is virtually a military alliance—was not revealed till two years later.

In 1936 Stalin categorically told Roy Howard in a famous interview that Soviet Russia would fight to prevent invasion of Outer Mongolia by Japan. At that time the Japanese—who know, in Owen Lattimore's words, that "no conflict in Manchuria can be anything but a prelude to struggle in Mongolia"—had been making incidents along the Manchukuo-Mongolia frontier. Since Stalin's statement Japan has tended to let Outer Mongolia alone.

The government of Outer Mongolia is vested in a People's Assembly called the Great Huruldan, and the prime minister is a man named Gen-dun. He is not merely a puppet, and his record has been excellent. There are no railways in the nomad-inhabited country, and most trade—wool and skins—goes by the caravan route to Soviet Russia.

Near Outer Mongolia are two Soviet substates. One is Tannu Tuva, which all philatelists know for the colorful quality of its postage stamps. It is supposed to be in the exact center of Asia, and it claims to be an independent republic. The other is the autonomous region called Birobidjan, above the Amur River, which the U.S.S.R. has set apart for colonization by Russian Jews.

.   .   .   .

Inner Mongolia lies closer to China, and therefore is more susceptible than Outer to Chinese—and Japanese—influence. Its precise area is hard to define, though normally it is considered to consist of the three Chinese provinces above the Wall, Chahar, Suiyuan, and Ninghsia (the first two are among the Five Northern Provinces) plus Jehol which is now administratively a part of Manchukuo. Before and during the war the Japanese penetrated Chahar and Suiyuan, which are rich in iron, coal, and wool, and which have been conquered in part. Ninghsia still remains Chinese.

The Kwantung army is undisputed lord of the Japanese area of Inner Mongolia, and it rules by puppetry. The region has been fragmented into several puppet states, including one in South Chahar, one in North Shansi (below the Wall), where the rich Tatung collieries are found, and one called the "Mongolian Autonomous Government." All have their own flags, their own administrations—under the Kwantung army. The idea is to combine them later into a Mongolian Federation; so we will have one of these days another new "country," a "Mongokuo." The strategy of the Japanese is to make the Mongol areas a second buffer against the U.S.S.R. Inner Mongolia is called the "main route of continental advance."

Leader of the Inner Mongolians is a remarkable man, a lineal descendant of Genghis Khan, named Teh Wang or Prince Teh. He is 37, and recently became "Chairman of the Federated Autonomous Government of Inner Mongolia." In November 1938 he went to Tokyo, and was received by the Emperor. But he is a sincere enough Mongolian patriot; he accepted Japanese support because he had no alternative. A fervent nationalist, he sought to work with Nanking, and create an autonomous Mongolia within China, but the Chinese government rebuffed him. Teh proceeded anyway to organize an

Inner Mongolian Political Council. The war came; the Japanese entered; and Teh, who considered himself badly let down by the Chinese, submitted to Japanese demands. He is a fattish young man, with little experience of the western world. He has never cut his queue.

. . . .

So now we finish the northern sector. We are not done with the Japanese yet. But it is time to turn to the magnificent world of China proper.

~~~~~~

> *To know what you know and know what you don't know
> is the characteristic of one who knows.*
>
> —CONFUCIUS

THE Chinese, a tremendously durable people, possess the largest
country and the longest civilization known to mankind. They have
uninterruptedly existed as a political and cultural entity for well over
4000 years, a record no country in the world can match. The Chinese
were old when ancient Greece was young; they produced Confucius
centuries before Alexander the Great or Julius Caesar; they were
having a magnificently mature development when Europe was a
medieval shambles. Chinese history goes back at least to 2800 B.C.
The birth of Solomon, the death of Socrates, the birth of Jesus, the
death of Charlemagne, the birth of Newton, the death of Bismarck,
all took place while China was the same nation. We do not know the
origins of the Chinese. They have always been there. They seem older
than the rocks.

So much for the dimension of time. As to the dimension of space.
Superimpose China on a map of North America; put Chungking at
Chicago. Then Peking will be near Quebec, and the eastern extremity
of Manchuria rests on Labrador. The southern frontier of China will
follow a rough line across Tennessee through Texas; the western
edge of Sinkiang touches Puget Sound almost precisely. In the northwest, the frontier between Outer Mongolia and the U.S.S.R. reaches
the extreme north of Saskatchewan. The total area of China, counting
Tibet, Sinkiang, and the Mongolias, is over 4,000,000 square miles, as
against 3,800,000 for the whole of Europe.

The Chinese call China *Chung Kuo*, which means "Middle Country." The word middle derives from geography, but has also come to
express "middle" in the sense of moderation. No one knows how many
Chinese there are. We have to decide what we assume "China" to be,
and to rely on estimates that vary widely. There has never been an
accurate census. The *China Year Book* (1938), as good an authority

as any, says that the population of China is 426,603,258. The World *Almanac* says 457,835,475. In any case the number is between one-fifth and one-quarter of the entire human race.

These proliferating numbers of Chinese, enclosed in their mastodonic circular area, are closely integrated, though five distinct "races" are recognized—Han (Chinese), Mongol, Manchu, Tibetan, Moslem. Since the Mongols and Tibetans are outside China proper, and since Moslems represent a religious rather than a racial criterion, the inner core of China is remarkably homogenous. The Chinese stem from Chinese aborigines, and thus may be said never to have been conquered; for centuries they have had the same social system, religious instincts, and written language. Even so, there are very considerable and striking differences between northern and southern Chinese, between a Turki nomad and a Shanghai coolie. Loosely one might say that China proper is more homogenous than Europe as a whole, less homogenous than the United States.

To generalize about China is obviously difficult in the extreme. We will confront the same problem when we come to India (though China is more uniform than India, largely because of the single written language), in that exceptions may be found to almost any statement one may make. However, in all diffidence, let us begin.

Some Qualities of the Chinese

"In the west, the insane are so many that they are put in an asylum; in China the insane are so unusual that we worship them."

—Lin Yutang

"The reason I don't trust Chinese surgeons is that I am afraid that when a Chinese surgeon cuts up my liver in search of a gall stone, he may forget about the stone and put my liver in a frying pan."

—Lin Yutang

The first thing to mention, it seems to me, is the great Chinese characteristic of rationality.[1] The Chinese are a sublimely reasonable people. They are suspicious of sectarianism; they are seldom violently partisan; they adore the Golden Mean, that is, compromise. This attitude may be carried to excess; sometimes it approaches the editorial policy of the American newspaper which was never able to say anything but "On the other hand." Lin Yu-tang writes in his beautifully eloquent and discriminating book, *My Country and My People,* that to

---

[1] Readers who happen to begin this book at this point are asked also to note "Japanese and Chinese" in Chapter II above, page 28.

the Chinese truth "can never be proved; it can only be suggested." It is of exceptional interest that in Chinese mythology—which is itself very rationally considered—man is supposed to have been created *before* heaven and earth. Man, in a word, is master; man is what counted. And what counts in man is reason, the life of the mind.

The Chinese are, I thought on cursory acquaintance, not mystics like the Japanese. They are packed with practicality and common sense; they have a wonderful feeling for the concrete and for their own concrete interests. The tennis anecdote is famous. Two Chinese pass an English club on a hot day, and see foreign players perspiring in exhaustion. One Chinese says to the other: "Obviously these foreigners are not poor. Why do they not hire coolies to play for them?"

Being rational, the Chinese are long-minded; their passivity, their patience, are notorious. Being rational, they are law-abiding; until the brink of modern times, there was no Chinese police. Being rational, they liked to be let alone; hence the early antipathy to "foreign devils" as whites were called. (But apparently Chinese first disliked foreigners because of their body odor. Westerners smell; Chinese don't. And westerners had—by Chinese standards—very big noses, which in China are the sign of Satan.) Being rational, the Chinese are sensibly opportunistic. Being rational, finally, they had little interest in political bickering; the best government was the one that no one heard about.

Above all Chinese rationality led to pacifism, a virtue carried so far that it became a vice. When a man fights, the Chinese adage says, it means simply that the fool has lost his argument. This tendency to pacifism became a serious political problem in modern times; to achieve unity and militance against Japan meant a tremendous evolution. The Chinese had to fight not merely a foreign war against a ruthless invader, but civil strife against their own good nature and civilized instincts. They are holding their own in both. Not for centuries has China been so strong, so united, so compact in defiance of an aggressor.

In Shanghai, early in 1938, I saw Chinese regions incredibly devastated by Japanese. In Canton, a little later, I saw Japanese property neatly padlocked and patrolled by Chinese police—to keep it from being harmed.

Even to-day, in spite of the surge and stress of war, the Chinese try to avoid chauvinism. My wife and I visited a village school near

Peking, and the children greeted us with songs. We asked for a patriotic song. The children looked blank. And we discovered that in this district no Chinese national hymn was known; there was no Star-Spangled Banner, no Marseillaise. Later we asked a group of professors at Yenching University to name some military heroes. We wanted to know who was the Chinese Grant, the Chinese Wellington. Our friends had to go back a thousand years to find one—and seemed embarrassed at the search.

Pearl Buck tells a pleasant story. Students at a missionary school, taught to play football, uniformed and exhorted valiantly to win, set out for their first big match at a neighboring school. They returned a few hours later—uniforms unspotted, hands unscratched. There had been no game. "We decided not to play as soon as we arrived," the captain said. "The other side was bigger than we were."

The Chinese guerrillas bewildered and maddened the Japanese because—among other reasons—they paid no attention whatever to the "rules" of warfare. Japanese kill their prisoners, and the sensible Chinese knew that uniformed men, if caught, would meet death. So the Chinese simply wore their everyday clothes. They fought without uniforms! (Result: Japanese, in some sectors, killed *all* Chinese they captured.)

The Chinese instinct to rationality is particularly remarkable in that China is a backward country by western standards, where many mythological concepts are entrenched. Even now most Chinese are fearful of evil spirits. Most huge ideographs on Shanghai buildings are not, as I first thought, advertisements, but designs to ward off devils, djinns, ghosts. The Chinese solve spiritual problems with their usual practicality: an evil spirit traditionally may not turn a corner, which is why screens are placed inside Chinese doors, and why bridges are sharply angled. The Chinese believe in *fengshui*, the spirits of wind and water, who bring good luck and who ought to be propitiated. In 1876 China got its first railroad. It had to be torn up, because it offended *fengshui*; the rails, ties, everything, were destroyed.

Another great Chinese characteristic is vitality, endurance. The Chinese withstand bad government, floods, disease, famine, corrupt administration, poverty of unspeakable nature, invasion from outside, civil wars, outrageous taxation, physical discomfort, physical labor almost unparalleled elsewhere in the world—and thrive cheerfully and multiply. Yet they are not, I think, masochists, as many Japanese are;

they endure their terrific and intolerable burdens not because they yearn subconsciously to be burdened, but because they enjoy and love life enough to attempt to overcome the burdens, to live in spite of them.

In Arthur Smith's *Chinese Characteristics,* a book not altogether friendly to the Chinese, I found the following:

A Tientsin man . . . had been in the habit of making a living by collecting spent shells around the ground where Chinese troops were engaged in artillery practice. On one occasion he secured a shell, when . . . it exploded and blew off his left leg. He was admitted to the hospital, and an amputation was performed below the knee. Instead of being cured of this dangerous mode of getting a precarious living, the man returned to it again as soon as possible, and about six months later . . . another explosion took place, which blew off his left hand about two inches above the wrist, leaving a ragged wound. Deep lacerations took place over the bridge of the nose and on the upper lip; punctured wounds, the result of exploding pieces of shell, were made on the right cheek, on the right upper eyelid, on the posterior edge of the frontal bone, and on the right wrist. There was also a deep cut over the right tibia, exposing the bone. On receiving these severe injuries the man lay in a semi-unconscious and helpless condition for four hours, exposed to the heat of the sun. A mandarin happening to see him, ordered some coolies to carry him to the hospital, himself accompanying them for two miles. The bearers apparently became tired of their burden, and as soon as the mandarin was gone, threw the poor wretch into a ditch to die. Though much exhausted by the haemorrhage, he managed to crawl out and hop for five hundred yards to a grain-shop, where he found a large basket of meal, which he overturned with his sound arm and coiled himself inside. To get rid of him the owners of the shop carried him in the basket to the hospital gates, where he was left outside to die. Although in a condition of extreme collapse, and with a feeble pulse, due to the loss of so much blood, the patient had no mental impairment and was able to converse intelligibly. . . . With the exception of diarrhoea on the fifth and sixth days, and slight attacks of malaria, the patient had throughout no bad symptoms, and left the hospital with a wooden leg four weeks after his admission.

Another interesting Chinese characteristic is classlessness. There are rich and poor in China, certainly, and there are illiterate coolies as well as brilliantly cultivated scholars. But there is no Chinese aristocracy, there is no *class* distinction among Chinese by blood. Consider the contrast to Japan, with its Samurai hangover, or India, multitudinously stratified by caste. In the old China there were four social categories—intellectuals at the top, then peasants, then artisans and merchants, and finally (at the bottom where they belong) soldiers —but this traditional cleavage no longer exists. In the old China, too, officials and administrators were chosen, uniquely in the world, not by criteria of birth or wealth, but purely on literary and intellectual merit. Every post was filled by competitive written test. Men could take the examinations at any age; dozens did so in their sixties or seventies or even later, after a life of preparation. This system lasted from the third century A.D. to 1911, and produced in the "Mandarin" class the first civil service in the world.

China got rid of its Manchus only in 1911, whereas Japan—a country anyway more susceptible to western influence—dropped the Shoguns in 1868, and thus had half a century headstart toward modernism. Three picturesque Chinese characteristics have died out in the last generation. One is the queue or pigtail; the 1912 republicans abolished it much as Kamal Ataturk abolished the fez. Originally the pigtail derived from filial piety and ancestor worship, as Confucius himself makes clear; one's hair belonged, strictly speaking, to one's parents, and so must not be cut off. When the Manchus came to China in 1644, however, they reintroduced the pigtail, as a sign of submission by Chinese. Second, bound feet, the origin of which was sexual; women bound their feet because Chinese men thought that tiny, plump, deformed feet were beautiful, and gave a peculiar titillation to a woman's carriage. With feet crushed, women quivered when they walked. Third, the kowtow or ceremonial bow.

Perhaps I am speaking of the Chinese too eulogistically; they have, like all people, defects as well as virtues. Many Chinese are cruel, at least by our standards; their passivity reaches insane and monstrous lengths; they have little sense of time, and an exaggerated tendency to optimism in moments of crisis. They say *mei-yu fa-tze* ("It can't be done") unendingly, and are debauched by procrastination; the phrase is a national characteristic like the Spanish *mañana*. Another familiar criticism is that Chinese are venal or avaricious; a basic vice is supposed to be "squeeze," the local expression for graft, corruption.

A foreigner arriving in Shanghai hears of "squeeze" almost as much as he hears of "face." Chiang Kai-shek can't do thus-and-so, because various underlings are "squeezing." China cannot get an efficient air force, because of "squeeze" in aviation contracts. From the aerial to the almost-earthly: a friend told me that his tailor arrived in his sixteenth floor hotel room terribly out of breath, because he walked up rather than pay 10¢ squeeze to the elevator boy. The story is—and it is shocking if true—that wounded Chinese soldiers are left behind if they cannot pay "squeeze" to rescuers, that in hospitals they are treated laxly if they are penniless.

Squeeze, it goes without saying, derives from the savage poverty of China, which is incontestably the most terrible in the world. Industrial wages may average—possibly—50¢ (Chinese)[2] per day; the average income of a peasant may average—possibly $10 (Chinese) per month. But write "income" in quotes. Because the peasant is in debt all his life. About 2,000,000 people die of starvation in China every year. In 1935, a normal year, *twenty-nine thousand* bodies were picked off the streets of Shanghai alone—one of the great metropolises of the world—of men, women, children dead of hunger. Many were female infants left by their parents to starve.

The Chinese are apt to be scamps about engagements, financial and otherwise. I tell this small story with no ill will at all. A Chinese friend summoned me to dinner, where gravely and ceremoniously he introduced me to my Chinese translator and publisher, and presented me with copies of the Chinese edition of *Inside Europe*. I didn't even know that it had been translated! No one said a word about contract or royalties. Indeed Chinese publishers are famous pirates. If any book of particular interest to the East comes out, a Chinese edition promptly appears, reproduced so beautifully by a kind of lithographic-photographic process that it is almost indistinguishable from the original.

The Chinese are superlative craftsmen with their hands, for instance in ivory, silk, pottery. But if I were asked what I thought their chief defect to be, I would say after brief acquaintance that it was a signal lack of mechanical sense. The Chinese are practical, yes; but not practical with machines. Which puts them at a disadvantage in the modern age. A single and tragic illustration is to the point. When warfare spread to the Shanghai area in August, 1937, a natural target for the Chinese was the Japanese battleship *Idzumo* which lay at anchor in the Whangpoo, just off the Bund. An analogous location would be the Hudson River docks at 42nd Street. The Chinese tried by every

[2] It is exceptionally difficult to express Chinese purchasing power or values in terms of western currency. Old parity for the Chinese dollar was 29½¢ silver. It has shrunk steadily. In April, 1939, $1 (Chinese) = 16¢ (U. S.).

possible means to blast that battleship out of the water. One result was an air raid that missed the *Idzumo* by at least half a mile and instead blew up, let us say, the Hotel St. Regis, Saks-Fifth Avenue, and part of Radio City. Several hundred Chinese were killed. Yet the Chinese aircraft had to journey only a few miles, and at that time there were few Japanese planes in the air. The *Idzumo* remains at anchor precisely where it was nineteen months ago.

Near Hankow early in 1938 the Chinese lost twenty-six planes in one raid, when the Japanese bombed their airport and hit a Chinese bomber, loaded with bombs itself, that was unprotected. The whole field blew up. The Japanese came back the next night—no Chinese dreamed that the attack would be repeated so soon—and destroyed the six Chinese planes that chanced to survive the first attack.

But to return to Chinese virtues. One could list them almost indefinitely. The Chinese are frugal, with a wonderful hatred of waste. They are polite, good-humored, tolerant, temperate, with a great sense of fundamentals. Like the Viennese, whom they rather closely resemble, they are discriminating and sophisticated, and they know how to relax with dignity. They like the good things of life, and they are packed with charm. Who but the Chinese, seeking a name for the wild aborigines near the Tibetan border, would think to call them the "*Shy People?*" Who but the Chinese would name a city "Nothing to Do," simply because it was a lonely spot?

When I arrived in Shanghai I shocked my Chinese friends by asking what Chinese civilization consisted of, concretely. I knew that old China had contributed silk to the world, paper, the compass, the art of printing. I knew a little—a very little—about Chinese painting, poetry, ceramics. But where, I wanted to know, was Chinese civilization *now*. Why had there never been a Chinese Nobel Prize winner? Who were some eminent contemporary Chinese musicians, philosophers, artists, scientists? The answer came: Chinese civilization consists of the way two Chinese greet one another on a street corner.

Almost all middle-aged Chinese look far younger than their years. I have seen men of fifty who might be twenty-five. This can mean, of course, only one thing: that they have led good lives.

Facing Face

The concept of face exists almost everywhere in the East (the Japanese have it too), but it is most strongly marked in China. Face is not easy to define, because it means more than one thing. It is at once the equivalent of dignity, prestige, and reputation. It means more than honor, partly because it is external; it is what people think of you, more than what you think of yourself. It means more than pride, since you can be without pride, and still have considerable face. One might say that it is the difference between the inner and outer self.

The best way to attempt a definition is to list some examples of face that I came across.

One of the Generalissimo's foreign pilots told me that he could not eat his own precious baked beans on long trips. His Chinese colleagues would lose face unless he ate their food.

I went in to see General Wu Te-chen, at that time governor of Kwangtung province. Others were waiting outside. When I emerged, my Chinese friends said admiringly, "You stayed a full hour. You got great face."

Generalissimo Chiang Kai-shek starved himself for some days when kidnaped at Sian, because to have eaten his captor's food would have entailed great loss of face.

I went to a luncheon party. A friend whom I had promised to bring could not come. My hostess wailed, "But think what face I lose!"

One of the German officers training Chiang Kai-shek's bodyguard rebuked a private for stealing a peach. The detachment had been marching through an orchard. The private killed himself that night. He had been disciplined publicly, in the presence of Chinese, by a white man; the loss of face was so great that he had to commit suicide, though suicide is very rare among Chinese. Items like this make military discipline a severe problem. Troops, for instance, may refuse to stay in reserve, where they belong, because they think they lose face. An incompetent officer, instead of being shot, is transferred to a new post, in order to save his face.

I heard several times that such-and-such a politician "didn't have much face left," though goodness knows how many times it may have been saved. Here the word is equivalent to reputation. It gives a girl great face if a prominent politician takes her to a cabaret.

I weigh 210 pounds. My wife weighs 110 pounds. I groaned for the ricksha coolies who carried me, in contrast to her, until I learned that the coolies preferred me as cargo *because* I was heavier. To carry my bulk gave them added face.

A foreign diplomat told me that he could usually get action from the Chinese foreign office, when all other methods failed, by pleading that he could not afford to lose face with his government at home.

The Most Charming Language

Every Chinese word is a single syllable. There are, moreover, only a very few syllables—sounds—that a Chinese can pronounce, perhaps six or seven hundred in all. The result is that in Chinese there are great numbers of words which, though they may be represented by different ideographs (symbols or pictures), are pronounced the same way. For instance the single sound *shi* (*Encyclopaedia Britannica*, Vol. V, p. 567), may mean:

history	an army
a lion	to rely on
to employ	solid
a corpse	to bestow
a market	poetry
a house	ten
a clan	power
to proclaim	officer
beginning	stone
to swear	generation
to pass away	

and has literally 41 other meanings. We have similar confusions, be it remembered, in English: *vain, vein, vane* or *new, gnu, knew* are pronounced the same way, but they mean entirely different things. But Chinese goes far beyond any other language in monosyllabic duplication. As a result, first, the Chinese learn to recognize meaning by context (so do we); second, they have a system of *tones* (four in the north, nine in Cantonese), whereby meanings may be differentiated by the tone of voice.

Chinese words *are* differentiated in writing; every "shi" above is a different written character (though they may be built from the same radicals or roots). Moreover, *every* Chinese word is unique. Each word is a picture, a different picture. There is no alphabet, though many words are compounded of several pictures, as we shall see. There are about 40,000 different words in Chinese, each with its own character or picture, and it goes without saying that it is a tremendous feat to memorize them all. Probably not a dozen men in China know every one. (Nor, for that matter, do more than a dozen men in the

United States know the meaning of every word in the English language.) A Chinese child going to school learns about 2,000 characters by the time he is ten. An average newspaper uses about 7,000 characters every day. The composing room of a big newspaper will have about 30,000 characters.

A most important point is that, though the pronunciation of Chinese differs widely throughout China, this written language of pictorial symbols is identical everywhere. Written communication is possible from Manchuria to Yunnan, without impediment. China is not, like India, splintered into different languages, and the uniform written language has played a colossal rôle in keeping China together. Take the numeral 5. Everywhere in Europe or the Americas we recognize 5 to mean 5, though it may be called "five," "cinq," "fünf," "cinque," and so on. (See Lyall, *China*, p. 22.) Similarly in China anyone who can read knows what important characters stand for.[3]

The "official" dialect of Chinese is what foreigners call "Mandarin," what the Chinese call *Kuo-yu*, national tongue, spoken chiefly in the north. Of other dialects there are many, chiefly Cantonese, the great southern "language." Various people whom I consulted differed drastically in their estimate as to how well Chinese in widely separated parts of the country understand one another. Differentiation is sharpest along the coast; in the interior the differences are, on the whole, not greater than those in various parts of the United States. In recent years considerable progress has been made toward introducing a simple variant of the classical Mandarin, called *pai-hua* (literally "white," hence "very simple," language) ; it was introduced through the efforts of Dr. Hu Shih, the father of the Chinese Renaissance. *Pai-hua* is colloquial, but oddly enough it is not so concise as Mandarin, since simplification demands more—rather than fewer—characters. Thus newspapers do not like to use it. The difference between Mandarin and *pai-hua* is roughly that between the language of Shakespeare and, say, Aldous Huxley. Official Kuomintang documents are still written in highly complex old-fashioned Mandarin. The modernist Red Army, on the contrary, uses simple *pai-hua*.

Chinese presents difficulties. It is so terse that Latin is windy by

[3] Japanese, I have noted, is written in the same characters as Chinese. But it is a quite different *language*. Analogy: "pain" and *pain* (bread) look alike in French and English, but they are pronounced differently, and they mean different things.

comparison. Because there is no alphabet it is extremely difficult to index books efficiently, or to use a dictionary, and until recently it was unpunctuated. But, since the language consists merely of a series of pictures, it has no need of grammar; there are no cases or declensions, and only two tenses. Ideas are pictorialized, that is, words are created, in a most fascinating manner; for instance, "gossip" is an ideograph symbolically portraying three women. "Plunder" is a man chasing a man. Others:

wife	woman with broom
hermit	man and mountains
law suit	two dogs
to think	brain plus heart (N.B.!)
good	woman and child
sincerity	man plus words
prisoner	man in a box
rain	drops of water
all	three men
worship	man kneeling
home	pig under a roof
west	bird flying to its nest
east	sun through trees
man	pair of legs

As Western ideas, Western inventions, came to China, the language struggled to adjust itself and absorb them. New concepts were represented by putting together symbols for old ones. For instance:

Capitalism	Money-as-Basis-Policy
Communism	Together-Production-Policy
Imperialism	King-Country-Policy (!)
Republic	People-as-Host-Country
Dictatorship	Single-Decision-Pattern
Parliament	Discuss-Govern-Country-Assembly
Democracy	Together-Peace
Government	Political-House
Election	Lift-Hand-for-Choice
Telephone	Lightning-Language
Railway Station	Fire-Wagon-Stop
Magnetism	Power-Pulling
Cigarette	Roll-of-Smoke
Fountain Pen	Automatic-Ink-Pencil
Camera	Take-an-Image-Machine

One cannot but note with delighted applause the extreme succinctness and concrete semantic intelligence embodied in this transfer of concepts to language. If we in the West said "Single-Decision-Pattern" instead of "Dictatorship," or "Together-Peace" instead of "Democracy," and kept on doing so for a generation or so, we might know better what we think. To the Chinese a word is a tool. And the tool is often beautiful. What could more admirably express the idea of "Republic" than "People-as-Host-Country"?

Chinese proper names seem appallingly difficult to foreigners, and for several reasons. For one thing, as I shall explain in the next chapter in reference to Chiang Kai-shek, most Chinese are known by several different names. For another, these names may be spelled and pronounced quite differently. It took me some time, for instance, to understand that Oong Wen-hao and Weng (or Wong) Wen-hao, were one and the same person, the excellent Chinese minister of economics. Dr. Sun Yat-sen, the father of the Chinese republic, may be called Sun-wen or Sun Chung-shan, depending on taste and circumstances. In Hankow I met a man named Tsur. But in the south his name is pronounced, not Tsur, but Chow, which elsewhere is pronounced "Jo." I have mentioned Mukden often in these chapters. Mukden is its Russian name; in Chinese it may be Shenking, Fengtien (the old Manchu word), or Liaoning; the Japanese have quite another name, Hoten. The city of Sian had its name lifted to Siking (western capital), in 1932, and to Changan (long peace), a little later. Hsuchowfu, Suchowfu, Suhsien, and Tungshan are all the same place.

Two slight supporting reeds. First, in Chinese the last name comes first.[4] The Chinese would say Dickens Charles or Bell Alexandergraham. The Generalissimo, if you wished to address him as a civilian, would not be Mr. "Kai-shek," but Mr. Chiang. Second, I have tried so far as possible to emphasize the last name, and omit the rest. Purists may protest, but let us think of the old war lord Wu Pei-fu simply as Marshal Wu, of Wang Ching-wei simply as Mr. Wang.

Religion, Filial Piety, Family System

"How lucky I am! Whenever I make a mistake, people are sure to discover it!"   —CONFUCIUS

Being rationalists, the Chinese are thoroughly sensible and realistic

[4] But some Chinese Anglicize their names; if they do so, they put the last name last, English fashion. For instance Sung Tse-ven is T. V. Soong.

about religion. There is no Chinese God, but very many Chinese belong
not merely to one religion but to three. They detest separatist dogmatism, and see no reason whatever why they should not jointly subscribe to the doctrines of Confucius, Buddha, and Lao-tse. Which is
roughly—very roughly—as if an American concurrently claimed to be
a Roman Catholic, a Seventh Day Adventist, and a Lutheran. The
Chinese say that each of their three religions has its special value, its
special spiritual impact, depending on circumstances, and that it is
parochial foolishness to believe in one creed fervently enough to exclude others. To every Chinese, religion is his own affair.

It is exceptionally striking and typical of the Chinese that their
grand old man and most important religious figure, Confucius, is not
considered divine, and that in fact he is most revered for what might
be called the extra-religious aspects of his teaching. That is, Confucius
stood for ethics rather than mysticism, for character in personal conduct rather than theology. He is unique among the great creators of
religions in that his followers invented no miracles, shibboleths, myths,
demonology, or witchcraft. The Chinese look for ethics in religion, not
hocus-pocus. Their attitude to God is mundane.

Confucius was certainly one of the most remarkable men who ever
lived. His name was Kung Fu-tze (Confucius is a Latinization), and
he lived from 551 to 478 B.C., a native of what is now the province
of Shantung. Apparently he knew Lao-tse slightly, the founder of the
"rival" Chinese religion, and the two worked in harmony for a brief
time—far cry from the usual competitiveness of religious systems.
Confucius was a civil servant and teacher by profession, hard-working
and with a great sense of detail. For years he was a competent political
administrator, but he found time to edit Chinese classics and to formu-
late his own code, which promptly became classical. He is extraordinarily like Plato in some respects.

It is all but impossible to concentrate in a few words what Confucius
stood for. What interested him most was right living. He believed
firmly in a fixed aristocracy of intellect and manners, and in orderly
and honorable government. He tried to classify conduct in five relationships—people to ruler, wife to husband, son to father, brother
to brother, friend to friend. He was supremely rational; he detested
the supernatural. He believed that a kind of central Authority existed
in the universe, which he called simply Heaven; he did not personify
it, and he is skeptical about immortality. Lin Yutang quotes his tre-

mendously succinct words when he was asked about the hereafter: "Don't know life; how know death?"

One series of concepts that Confucius, who like almost all aristocrats was a traditionalist, did believe in was filial piety, respect for ancestors, and the family system. This is heavily marked in his doctrine, and persists among most Chinese to this day. "If Confucianism can be called a religion," says Sansom, "it is the religion of filial piety." The *family* is the unit in contemporary as well as ancient China, not the individual. And the family system (plus the written language) has been the glue of China for 2,500 years. It promoted conservatism, a rigid code of manners, and complex patterns of social behavior. It also impeded such modern developments as patriotism and nationalism, since the loyalty of the average Chinese was primarily to his family group, not to his province or nation.[5] Inevitably filial piety and family system became associated with ancestor worship. The father is respected and obeyed when alive; therefore he should be revered when dead; indeed, it is not thought that the father—or anyone—actually dies. This is one reason why Chinese funerals are noisy, colorful, and full of fun. My first glimpse of ancestor worship was an almost monstrously cheerful Chinese funeral.

Of Lao-tse and Taoism we can speak little. Taoism was an ancient cult, the earliest of the Chinese religions, which became overlaid with Lao-tse's teachings in the sixth century B.C., and later was much debased with ritual and mythology. Lao-tse was a less interesting man than Confucius, and less is known about him; his doctrine, emphasizing a rightful mode of life called "the Way," is not so concrete as that of Confucius, not so primarily concerned with ethics. Taoism is supposed to be more "democratic" than Confucianism, more passive, since a Taoist need not obey so many rules of conduct. He is a much freer and simpler man; thus the instinct of Chinese to adhere to both faiths.

Buddhism I discuss briefly in Chapter XXIV below; it appealed greatly to Chinese because of its original reasonableness and because it emphasized fatalism. Mohammedanism too is discussed in Chapter XXIV, and again in Chapter XXXII. Some 25,000,000 Chinese are Moslems, mostly in the northwest and in Sinkiang. Finally the influx of Christianity in China is considerable. The country was a tremen-

---

[5] Bertrand Russell says acutely (*The Problem of China*, p. 41) in regard to filial piety: "It is probable that this doctrine has made the Chinese more prolific, in which case it has had great biologic importance." Economic and political importance too.

dous field for missionaries, both Catholic and Protestant, many of whom did and still do splendid work, especially in medicine and education. The Y.M.C.A. has great influence, partly because of its appeal to ethics and behavior.

Chinese History: Two Minute Glimpse

I have said that Chinese history begins about 2800 B.C., which is roughly the time of Sargon I in the Tigris-Euphrates valley at the other end of Asia. Of course actual written records come later than that. Apparently communities of Mongoloid people in the Yangtze and Yellow River valleys coalesced into vague groupings in the twenty-eighth century B.C., and presently expanded—by peaceful spreading out rather than military conquest—into what became a loose empire. There came a "Golden Age"—approximately at the time of Abraham and Isaac—when the Emperor became the "Son of Heaven" (though he was never worshiped as a god like the Emperor of Japan), when the rudiments of ancestor worship, the family system, handicrafts, and writing began. In 1750 B.C. appeared the first important dynasty, the Shang, which brought China to preliminary unity, and in which cultural development was considerable. The Chou dynasty (1122-221 B.C.) followed. It was the great feudal dynasty. Confucius and Lao-tse lived in this Chou period, which also produced the classical age of Chinese literature, and wonderful art in bronze. One subperiod in the Chou dynasty is known as the "Age of Confusion," when some hundreds of feudal states grasped for authority. But during all these generations, even during lapses into political anarchy, the essential features of Chinese civilization were maintained, and the written language, a great centrifugal force, spread out.

From 221 to 206 B.C. reigned one of the greatest men in world history. He ruled only fifteen years, but he was a giant. His name was Shih Huang-ti, and his dynasty was known as Chin, from which our word China derives. Emperor Shih Huang-ti was a kind of Charlemagne who wanted a politically united China. Vital, ambitious, patriotic, with a blasting ego, he called himself the "First Emperor," since he could not bear that others had preceded him. Like Henry Ford, he thought that history was bunk. To wipe out any traces of the China that antedated his majestic entrance, he ordered the burning of all books. In character he does not remotely resemble Dr. Goebbels, but he preceded him as the inventor of literary funeral pyres. He wanted to destroy Chinese classicism, which he thought stultifying; he spared only works dealing with medicine, agriculture, and astrology. (Luckily many books were hidden by priests and scholars and escaped; otherwise we would have no Confucius, no other Chinese literary records to-day.) The other accomplishment for which this Emperor was famous was more enduring. He built the Great Wall. The colossal nature of this feat rocks the imagination. The Mongols perpetually sought to invade the country; Shih decided to wall them out, literally. How, precisely, the Wall was built, we do not know; we do know that, to-day, it still stretches 2,500 miles from Mongolia to the sea, a colossal and unbelievably durable monument to the Chinese imagination. The Egyptian pyramids are mole hills beside this Great Wall; of all man's work on earth, it alone could be seen from Mars. . . . Exhausted by the conflagration of books he made with his left hand, by the Wall he built with his right hand, the Emperor Shih died after a brief reign. He is founder of "modern" China. Most Chinese to-day consider themselves to be his direct "descendants."

Thereafter came two tremendous dynasties, the Han (206 B.C.-220 A.D.), and Tang[6] (618 A.D.-909 A.D.). Under the Hans the classics were restored, Buddhism was introduced, sculpture began, and paper was invented. Chinese to-day call themselves the "Han" people; in this period began the examination system for the civil service which lasted till 1911. The Tangs, even more advanced, proceeded to develop and extend the stability of the Hans, and China reached its greatest area in about 650 A.D. This was a period of complete collapse in Europe, but in China the Tangs invented printing, developed the use of silk, created poetry and porcelain of unsurpassed loveliness, and began to paint. The Tang dynasty is usually considered the most productive and splendid in Chinese history. It was succeeded by a less exuberant dynasty, the Sung (960-1280 A.D.), which was politically decadent but which produced great art, especially painting.

In the thirteenth century, at the same time that Europe was invading another corner of Asia with the Crusades, the Mongols crashed through the Great Wall, broke up the Sung dynasty, and occupied large parts of China. Genghis Khan (1162-1227) made three Chinese

[6] Properly Tang is T'ang, just as Chin is properly Ch'in. The apostrophe in Chinese names indicates pronunciation. T, K, Ch, and P are soft; T', K', Ch', and P' are hard. T'ang is pronounced "Tong," but "Tang" is "Dong." Similarly K, P and Ch without the apostrophe are pronounced like G, B and J. Kuling is "Gooling," Peng is "Beng," and Chang is "Jong."

expeditions, and captured Peking in 1214; his tremendous successor Kublai Khan (1235-94), established the Mongol dynasty (which lasted only fifteen years) and penetrated as far south as Fukien. But Chinese civilization persisted, as witness the accounts of Marco Polo. Presently the Chinese, like a gigantic and imperishable sponge, began to absorb their Mongol conquerors. From 1368 to 1644 a true Chinese dynasty, the Ming—notable among other things for a wonderful florescence in porcelain—regained power and decayed after an ascendant period. Then, as we have seen, another northern group, the Manchus who were partly Chinese, took Peking and established rule. Gradually they in turn disintegrated, but the Manchu dynasty lasted till 1911. Which brings us to Dr. Sun Yat-sen, the Chinese revolution of 1911-12, the struggling republic, and the threshold of contemporary times.

Will the Japanese, new invaders from the north, repeat this history of conquest and then become assimilated? Future history contains no more fascinating question.

Imperialism and the Fat Chinese Melon

We sound now a drastic note, that of imperialism by the white western powers. We have mentioned imperialism before, we shall mention it again in the course of this long book. A standard definition of imperialism is that it is exploitation of an undeveloped colonial or foreign market, usually to the tune of military conquest. It is "extension of a nation's power beyond its boundaries," a policy of aggrandizement. The Marxist definition adds that imperialism is an essential corollary of capitalism, in that capitalism demands continually expanding markets. Imperialism is written deeply over Asia. Most of Asia is a European colony. There are, in fact, only six truly independent countries in all Asia—Japan, China, Siam, Afghanistan, Iran, and Saudi Arabia, and of these, Afghanistan and Saudi Arabia are, one might say, "independent" by courtesy only.

China was a fat and luscious melon. It is still incomparably the greatest unexploited market on earth. The western powers got interested in it early; traders and missionaries sought to settle on the coast, especially the Portuguese. But diplomatic intercourse with the Manchu empire was extremely difficult, because of Chinese ceremonial, Chinese isolationism. During the reign of Kang Hsi (1662-1723), for instance, Dutch and Russian ambassadors withdrew from Peking without seeing the Emperor, because they refused to kowtow to him. In those days to make a proper kowtow one had not only to kneel, but bump the head smartly on the ground. Other missions, however, representing several of the western states, and particularly Great Britain, wanted trade more than they cared about ceremonial humiliation. The process of initial penetration was laborious, but it succeeded. By 1800 the British were firmly fixed in Canton, the only port where they were allowed.

Came 1839 and the so-called Opium War, one of the most unpleasant wars in all history. British trade was based on opium; the East India Company dumped opium into China from India and got silver in exchange. Profits were enormous. But the Manchu government suddenly decided to stamp out the opium traffic; a Cantonese official, obeying orders, seized and burned a large store of British opium awaiting shipment to the interior. An analogy—not too close perhaps —might be drawn between this event and the Boston Tea Party a generation or so before. The British retaliated by making war. They fought China to inflict opium on it, and to "preserve the rights of trade." They invaded China not only near Canton but in the north, and the war lasted three years. The Manchu government, beaten, was forced to sign treaties which for the first time opened China as a whole to western trade. Five ports were set aside where foreigners had special privileges—Canton, Amoy, Foochow, Ningpo, and Shanghai. China was forbidden to set any tariff above five percent, which meant that foreign nations could sell goods at an enormous advantage. Finally, the British annexed the important island of Hong Kong.

Thus, in 1842, began western exploitation of China on a wholesale and "legal" basis. I have mentioned in Chapter VII above the progressive seizure of Chinese territory by Britain, France, Germany, and Russia. But territory was not the only desideratum. The foreign nations took and held special advantages in the *seaports* and on the great rivers, since these dominated intercourse with the immense interior. Overwhelmingly, their objective was trade. They used weapons cheaper and more efficient than direct conquest, like concessions in the "treaty ports," customs control, and, above all, the principle of extraterritoriality.

A *treaty port* was—and is—one wherein foreigners can do business under their own law. Originally there were five; now there are thirty-eight in China proper. Some of these ports are not on the ocean at all, but are far inland, like Hankow; some include "settlements" or "concessions" (like Tientsin and Shanghai) which are in effect outside any Chinese jurisdiction, though the fiction of ultimate Chinese "sovereignty" is maintained. White troops are the police; white officials are the government. They are hardly more part of China than Marseilles or Manchester.

Customs Control. This began in 1842 also, and was confirmed in 1854 by the formation in Shanghai of the Chinese Customs Service. The theory was simple: the Chinese appointed foreign officials who were exclusively in charge of customs administration. Ultimate authority was Chinese in theory, and revenue went into the Chinese exchequer, but foreigners controlled it. The head of the Chinese Maritime Customs has, since 1861, been an Englishman. Time came when China needed money and sought loans, and it was natural that customs revenue should be pledged as security. In 1928, China recovered —in theory at least—tariff autonomy, when Chiang Kai-shek told the bankers that he could not build up a national régime unless he had more money. But to this day at least thirty percent of Chinese customs revenue, which was in turn about sixty percent of total Chinese revenue until the present war, is earmarked for payment of foreign debt.

Third, *extraterritoriality.* (Efforts have been made to shorten this awkward word; first it was amputated to "exterritoriality," and some Chinese newspapers even say "extrality.") Extraterritoriality means that the foreigner in China—not merely in the concessions or treaty ports, but anywhere—is not subject to Chinese law, but only to the law of his own country. An American who, say, commits murder or any other crime in Fukien or Changsha is not tried by a Chinese court, but by a magistrate of his own nationality, usually the local consul. The system has its origin in remote Roman times, with the principle of "personal law"; every man was a Roman citizen, no matter where he lived, and the law followed him. Extraterritoriality has existed at one time or other almost everywhere in the world; for a time the French had extraterritorial rights in New Orleans. Now, however, it has virtually disappeared, except in China.

In the beginning, extraterritoriality was justified. There was no law worth the name in China, no judicial system. And in the present war extraterritoriality has turned out to be of great convenience to the Chinese; thousands of them took refuge in the foreign settlements, did patriotic work there, and were safe. But basically the system was an affront to China, and produced grave abuses. In 1925, in Shanghai and Canton, British police shot Chinese workmen; in 1927, British and American battleships bombarded Nanking. In Peking, the system has produced the revolting spectacle of Chinese not being allowed inside the best part of their own city. (The sanctity of the Legation Quarter in Peking derives, however, from the Boxer Protocol, not from the other "unequal" treaties.) Foreigners are exempt from Chinese law, but Chinese are not exempt from foreign police. In the early 1930's dozens of Chinese Left-wingers were caught by white police in the International Settlement in Shanghai and turned over to Chinese authorities. One had the Alice-in-Wonderland situation that Japanese generals—*on Chinese soil*—were comfortably directing a war against China.

It is taken almost for granted that extraterritoriality will disappear sooner or later. If China wins the war and is strong enough she will not be likely to permit alien troops on her soil, even if they are troops so friendly by and large as the British and Americans. (The United States maintains an extraterritorial garrison in Peking and a detachment of marines in the Shanghai International Settlement.) The story is that, when Chiang Kai-shek's troops took Shanghai, the big business interests were so certain that he would abolish extraterritoriality that they offered his agents a very considerable bribe—$10,000,000 gold is sometimes given as the sum—not to do so. In 1931, however, Chiang Kai-shek announced the "abolition of the unequal treaties." The announcement—owing to the struggle with Japan—has not yet been put into effect.

The case of the foreigner in China may be briefly put. It is that he brings wealth to China, and needs protection while doing so; it is that he is developing China commercially and industrially, not throttling it, and rightfully asks security in return for his services; it is that a prosperous, stable, efficient China is a better ornament to civilization than a corrupt, prostrate, and decadent Manchu empire. In the wake of the foreign merchant come mission schools, universities, modern medicine, sanitation, roads, railroads, bridges, electrification, movies, higher standards of living. What the foreigner is bringing to China is the civilization of the west; all he asks is modest profit, plus security. It goes without saying that many foreigners in China have unselfishly and even heroically worked for the good of the country. One need only mention railroad administration, medical research such as that of the Rockefeller Foundation, and especially famine and flood control.

Some die-hard westerners are apt to be pretty rough with the Chinese, and to flourish the strong white hand. Consider this passage from Rodney Gilbert (*What's Wrong with China,* 1932): "In recent years Great Britain . . . has followed America's lead and has substituted soft-soap and compliments for ultimatums, so that the Chinese are simply hysterical with self-complacency and contempt for the foreigner, and indulge in vociferous hate-feasts in every part of the country which inevitably bear fruit in an increasing number of outrages against foreigners, defalcations on loans, impertinent diplomatic notes, and assertions of 'rights' [*sic!*] every year."

It is not easy to calculate the foreign stake in China. Competent estimates, however, agree that the total British investment in China is approximately $1,250,000,000 (much greater than the total British investment in India, incidentally) and the total Japanese investment about the same if Manchukuo is included. Manchukuo excluded, Japanese investment in China is about $600,000,000. American and French investments are roughly $250,000,000 each. British capital is invested in a multiplicity of enterprises, chiefly banks, railways, shipping, tobacco. Japanese investments are mostly in shipping, mining, cotton. Japan and Britain between them handle fifty-seven percent of China's coastwide marine traffic. The American trade with China is comparatively slight, perhaps $100,000,000 per year.

The Not-So-Open Door

The Open Door is an American policy, enunciated by Secretary of State John Hay in 1889. Briefly, it means equal opportunity for citizens of all nations to trade in China or similar undeveloped territories; in 1921, at the Washington Conference, it was reaffirmed in the Nine Power Treaty guaranteeing the integrity of China, and became linked with the principle of Chinese independence. The motive behind Hay's original pronouncement is clear: the United States did not intend to be drawn into any territorial squabble over the China market, but fully intended to maintain its right to trade there. Nathaniel Peffer in a brilliant historical study (*Asia,* July, 1936) has indicated that Hay's doctrine was in fact first suggested by the British. The Open Door was very convenient to British aims, since, at that time, if threat of partition was removed, "no other country could successfully compete with Britain in trade or finance. On equal terms, Britain always won."

The Japanese have, of course, pushed the Open Door (for others) fast shut; as it was nicely said recently, they have "closed it so tight that there is not a Chink in it." Late in 1938 Japan announced the "New Order in Asia" doctrine, and by so doing jettisoned—as everyone knew they would—both the Nine Power Treaty and the Open Door. Mr. Hull protested. The Japanese paid no attention, and set out with redoubled activity to monopolize the China market, to push foreign enterprise out, to slam and lock the Door wherever possible. Ten days after capturing Canton they announced that foreign trade and business would be excluded there.

Shanghai

This complex political ulcer on the face of China demands a brief section by itself. Shanghai, the sixth largest city in the world, with almost 4,000,000 population in 1939, is the chief mart of Chinese trade, a splendid refuge for tax-dodgers, and the seat of the worst slums, the most grisly factories, some of the handsomest country clubs, and the finest night life on earth. In Shanghai, I have already stated, 29,000 dead bodies are picked off the streets in an average year. And in Shanghai is a restaurant where dinner may cost $600.

The foreign area of Shanghai is uniquely governed. It is divided into two parts, the International Settlement (population 1,023,300) and the French Concession, which together occupy 12.66 square miles. Outside and beyond it, in a swarming semi-circle, is the great Chinese city (320 square miles), now occupied by the Japanese. The International Settlement is administered by a Municipal Council, which is responsible in turn to the Consuls General of the Great Powers. Until 1928, no Chinese were allowed on the Council; now it contains five Chinese out of fourteen, but they have little power. Two Councilors are Japanese—which brings complications. The Council is in effect run by the British; the Japanese want more voice. As to the French Concession (population 478,552) it is de facto if not de jure part of France. It has no connection with the International Settlement, and the French Consul General runs it—and runs it well. Most well-to-do foreigners in Shanghai (as well as many Chinese) live in "Frenchtown," as it is usually called.

British, American, Italian, and Japanese troops and police each have a sector of the International Settlement to protect. Beginning in 1932, the Japanese transformed their sector, Yangtzepoo, into what is in effect Japanese territory. They used it in the 1932 fighting as their seat of operations against the Chinese; they claimed both belligerent and extraterritorial privileges, and have entrenched their position ever since. While holding Yangtzepoo exactly as if it were Tokyo, they continue to demand a share in the government of the rest of the International Settlement. Once prompt action by an American Marine officer, Colonel C. V. Price, prevented Japanese invasion of the non-Japanese Settlement area. During 1938 and 1939, when Japanese puppets were murdered in extraordinary number by Chinese who took refuge there, Japan was again tempted to seize the Settlement. Revenge was not the only motive. Sixty percent of total Chinese industry is in Shanghai, 41.5 percent of China's total customs revenue accrues at Shanghai. But the Japanese did not quite dare to take the whole Settlement over, because of the storm of protest it would arouse in Britain and the United States.

Shanghai is, I have indicated above, a paradise for the wealthy. *There are no taxes.* With the exception of an exceedingly small land tax foreigners pay no taxes at all, either to their own government, to the Settlement, or to China. This produces, inevitably, an emotion of shame, which produces worry; as Vincent Sheean once said, Shanghai is the city par excellence of two things, money and the fear of losing it. Some rich Shanghai families came originally from Bagdad and Bombay (with British nationality) and settled in China generations ago—the Hardoons, Ezras, Shamoons, Elis, Kadoories; some wealthy individuals settled there quite recently, like Sir Victor Sassoon. Several great Shanghai fortunes were based on opium; then came investment in land, in textiles, in native industry. Shanghai gas, waterworks, and local transportation are British; electricity, power, and the telephone system are American; much land is owned by foreign religious orders, like the French Jesuits, the Spanish Augustans. Shanghai real estate could be bought for a song fifty years ago. Land in the business district nowadays may be worth $1,500,000 per acre.

In Shanghai one finds most flamboyantly and conspicuously the westerner who hates the Chinese. He has done the Chinese an injury, that is, sucked wealth out of him; for this he cannot forgive China. In a Shanghai park was the famous sign, NO DOGS OR CHINESE ALLOWED. Some years ago an American newspaper man entertained no less a Chinese than H. H. Kung (now the prime minister!) in his office. The landlord would not allow Dr. Kung to enter the elevator reserved for whites; the American newspaper man protested; as a result the paper moved. Quite recently a British diplomat, a polo player, got into serious·social difficulties because he invited a Chinese (the mayor of Shanghai!), to witness a polo match on the club grounds. With my own ears I have heard a high consular officer say to his secretary, in the presence of a well-dressed young Chinese, "Throw that damned Chink out." Many rich foreigners in Shanghai hope that the Japanese will win the war, not the Chinese.

. . . .

Shanghai is also famous as the home par excellence of the Old China Hand. An Old China Hand is a white who has lived in China for thirty-five years without bothering to learn one word of Chinese.

A Word on Economics

Until 1938 not less than one-half of all Chinese industrial workers lived in the Shanghai area. The average wage of the semi-skilled was perhaps $15 (Chinese), per month, that is about $2.40 (!) at the present rate of exchange. A twelve hour day is the rule, and 15 to 16½ hours are not uncommon for piece work. Children may begin work at the age of five or six, and are delighted to get this early start, so terrible is competition for existence. The great mills are mostly Japanese owned, and in them contract labor is in force. An agent called the "sub-contractor" goes up-country, buys a group of girls from their parents—perhaps for a fee of $30 (U. S. $4.80) per girl for three years of work—and then sells them to the factory. He is more than the middleman, however; the girls remain technically in his charge. They pay *him* their wages, until his $30 is paid back—which may be never. This system cannot be rivaled for pure viciousness. The girls are in effect slaves.[7] British and Chinese mills are better run, with contract labor not allowed; but the fact that they are "better" does not mean that they are very good. A rudimentary trade union movement exists, and is growing stronger; there were frequent strikes in 1937 and 1938. The unions were crushed in 1927, when they were

[7] In one great Shanghai factory, where a modified form of contract labor exists, girl workers are given their wages in secrecy and at unstated intervals, so that middlemen and racketeers who prey on them may not know what money they have.

strongly Leftist; government (called "yellow") unions took their place; underground Red unions sprang up, and since the United Front have now tended to coalesce with the government unions. Red plus yellow equals orange, than which there are worse colors.

But the basis of economic life in China is agriculture. The life of China is the life of the land. At least eighty-five percent of Chinese are peasants; most of these are small tenant cultivators, though conditions vary province by province. Wheat and millet are the staple crops in the north; rice in the south. There are very few big estates anywhere, and as a rule the tenant—or proprietor—holds just as much land as his family can cultivate, which is something over an acre. Statistics are scarce, but I had it from competent authorities that the average income of a small farmer is probably under $100 (Chinese) per year, that is $16 U. S. If a landlord is a bad landlord, it means first that he is an absentee, second that he takes more than fifty percent of the crop as rent. The small landlords—tenants also—pay preposterous taxes, especially in remote provinces like Szechwan where war lords have collected taxes many years in advance. The agricultural debt is enormous—so enormous as to be incalculable. Two things I noticed, as any observer will notice them. First, the Chinese peasant is so close to the soil, so steeped in the soil, that the very color of his face is that of the soil. Second, grave mounds. By Chinese convention the dead are buried in hummocks on the surface, not deep underground. These hummocks stud the fields irregularly, and it is said that four percent of Chinese agricultural land is uncultivated, out of respect for the mound-like graves.

China, despite years of imperialist pressure, is still basically an undeveloped country. According to Snow, there are only 35,000 miles of roads (and most of them indifferent) as against some two million in the United States; there are only 6,000 miles of railways, as against 275,000 in the United States. The national budget is amazingly small for a country of 450,000,000 people—in 1936-37 expenditure was $990,700,000 (Chinese), in 1937-38 it was estimated at $1,000,600,000 (Chinese), which at present exchange is only $160,156,000 (U. S.). The chief exports are animal products, wax, tea, raw silk, raw cotton, hides, and tin, and the trade balance is adverse. (Japan, miraculously enough, still has an active trade balance.) China left the silver standard in 1934, to adopt a managed currency on lines suggested by the British expert, Sir Frederick Leith Ross.

A Chart of China

Finally, before proceeding to discuss Chiang Kai-shek and the other great Chinese political personalities, we must attempt to draw a brief chart of Chinese geography.[8]

First consider the Yellow River, called "China's Sorrow," which is the most anarchic of the world's rivers, and the most dangerous; it fills with silt regularly and overflows its dykes, causing almost unimaginable devastation. Ten times in history its course has changed radically; as recently as 1887 it took a sudden immense jump, and carved a churning path to the sea two hundred miles from its previous egress.

Above the Yellow River are the Five Northern Provinces, to which I have already alluded. They are Hopei, Chahar, Suiyuan, Shansi, and Shantung. Of these CHAHAR and SUIYUAN are not merely above the Yellow River, but above the Great Wall (as is Ninghsia also) and comprise Inner Mongolia, as we have seen. Chahar has about two million people, and its capital, Kalgan, is a famous junction of caravan routes to the north. Suiyuan, a wool-producing province of approximately the same size, is the center of Japanese activity in Mongolia.

HOPEI (or Hopeh), formerly known as Chihli, is rich in coal (the Kailan mines are the largest in the east), cotton, salt. It is the province, with more than 28,000,000 people crowded into the area of Arizona, where people eat millet, dodge camels, and see tourists. In Hopei are Tientsin, the second port of China, and Peking,[9] which many good folk will die for as the most beautiful city in the world.

One of the great provinces is SHANTUNG, population 38,000,000, with capital at Tsinan. Confucius came from Shantung; so did many modern war lords. It is the province of tall and strapping coolies, the greatest monastery in China, pongee silk, handsome women, and eggs,

---

[8] Carl Crow's *Handbook for China* is the best contemporary guide. I have used it considerably.

[9] Peking was the capital of China for 900 years till 1928, when Chiang Kai-shek's government demoted it in favor of Nanking. The name was then changed from Peking (Northern Capital) to Peiping (Northern Peace). Now the Japanese who occupy it have restored the old name, Peking. A journalistic anecdote is to the point. The London *Times* refused ever to acknowledge that Peking had become Peiping. For nine sturdy years it held out, saying Peking. Then the Japanese, in 1937, announced the resumption of the former name. The *Times* didn't know quite how to handle the story, since it had never admitted to its readers that the name had changed.

of which it produces 111,000,000 per year. Shantung men are good soldiers, strong workmen. The Japanese have occupied most of it, and have had less trouble than anywhere else in China, partly because there are no foreign concessions in Shantung.

SHANSI (which means West of the Mountains), is a more thinly populated province. It is the home of wool, opium, and bankers, and has been the scene of stubborn guerrilla fighting in the present war. For years its boss was Yen Hsi-shan, one of the most famous of modern war lords. Shansi has 11,000,000 people. Not considered one of the Five Northern Provinces, but adjacent to Shansi and Suiyuan, is SHENSI. The vowel changes confusingly. Shensi is a very important province indeed, though it contains only 7,717,000 people. It means "West of the Pass," and is the heart of old China; for four dynasties its chief city, Sian (where the Generalissimo was kidnaped), was the national capital. The old Japanese capital, Kyoto, was built to duplicate Sian. Shensi is a heart of new China too, since it is the headquarters of the Eighth Route (communist) Army, of which more later. Much of the land is "loess," dust or silt blown there by centuries of wind.

Further to the northwest are two remote and sparsely settled provinces, NINGHSIA and KANSU. Ninghsia, the western tip of Inner Mongolia, is still held by China. Kansu is the poorest of all the provinces, roughly the size of New Mexico, with the population of New York City; the people are largely Moslem, and live in caves carved out of loess. Both Ninghsia and Kansu are run by generals named Ma. Kansu and its capital, Lanchow, are of great strategic interest, because they control the caravan route, the old "silk road," from China to Sinkiang and Russia.

We turn now to the great provinces of Central China and the Yangtze valley. The Yangtze, the fourth largest river in the world, drains through China for 3100 miles before it reaches the sea near Shanghai. It is one of the most important of all Chinese phenomena, because it ties China together, and at the same time was the great avenue to penetration by the western powers. A whole book might be written about the Yangtze, as Emil Ludwig wrote an excellent one about the Nile. It probably has greater historical and geographic interest than any river in the world, except the Nile and Rhine. The word "Yangtze" means "willow."

HONAN does not actually border on the Yangtze (it is below the

Yellow River, as its name "South of the River" suggests, and adjacent to Shensi and Shansi), but it is one of the "central" provinces. About the size of Georgia, it has almost 35,000,000 people; it is a wheat growing province, with Kaifeng and Loyang as important cities. The Honanese are tough-fibered, conservative, proud of their tradition, inclined to rudeness. Honan is very fertile, and is often endangered by flood. Most Chinese peanuts come from Honan, and it is the fifth cotton province.

Below Honan is HUPEH, and below Hupeh is HUNAN. The north to south progression Hopeh-Honan-Hupeh-Hunan is a formidable business to get straight. Hupeh is a dull, rich, and busy province. It is first in cotton, and its capital is the great triumvirate of cities Hankow-Wuchang-Hanyang, collectively known as "Wuhan." Hupeh is often flooded. The name means North of the Lake. When we reach the next province, Hunan ("South of the Lake"), we are in the south. Here people eat red pepper, produce antimony, have soft voices, manufacture fireworks, and enjoy revolution. Hunan is called "the Balkans" of China. The population is almost 30,000,000, the capital, Changsha.

Eastward, converging on the Yangtze delta, are the vital provinces ANHWEI, KIANGSU, and CHEKIANG, with a total population of 85,-000,000. Anhwei, according to Chinese legend, is where two pairs of extremes meet; buffalo and camel, rice and wheat. Near Wuhu, in Anhwei province, the U.S.S. *Panay* was sunk. Kiangsu, incredibly fertile, containing Shanghai, Nanking, and Soochow, is the most densely populated area in the world, with 875 persons per square mile. Here is the industrial nexus of China, as we have seen. Chekiang (it means Curving River and is pronounced "Juh-jiong") is the smallest Chinese province, with the most enterprising people. Sailors the world over come from its Ningpo. In Chekiang are the prettiest Chinese women, the most fragrant wine, the smartest lawyers, the best developed roads, and the most advanced sericulture. In this region are the delightful cities Hangchow (in Chekiang) and Soochow (in Kiangsu). The Chinese say concisely "Above—Heaven; below—Hang and Soo."

Now to the south. FUKIEN is the hilly coastal province opposite Formosa, with Amoy as chief port; the Fukienese speak a highly difficult dialect, and are restless, good sailors, and fishermen. It is a great province for tea, oranges, and sugar. Behind it is KIANGSI (to be distinguished from Kiangsu above), which produces lemons, tungsten, camphor, tobacco, and communists. It is the area where the

Chinese Reds made their beginning, and where Chiang Kai-shek had his favorite residence, in the mountains at Kuling. The capital is the important city Nanchang, taken early in 1939 by the Japanese.

Furthest south are what are familiarly called the "two Kwangs," the great provinces of KWANGTUNG (capital, Canton), and KWANGSI, with combined population of 45,000,000. These are the provinces drained by the third of the dominant Chinese rivers, the Si-kiang. For some years these provinces were virtually independent of the rest of China, under the South West Political Council; the people are obstinate, impassioned, splendid craftsmen, enterprising; they are called the Irish of China. The great majority of Chinese who emigrate abroad, particularly those who go to America, are Cantonese; their remittances during the war helped save Chinese finance. Canton is the birthplace of Sun Yat-sen, and the nest of most Chinese revolutionary ferment; the proverb is that "everything new" comes from the Cantonese. They are marvelous cooks, too. The Kwangsi folk are poorer than those from Kwangtung, less developed, but with an even fiercer patriotism. Kwangsi has wood-oil, indigo, silver; it is a mountainous province, with the climate and scenery tropical. Tigers are still common in Kwangsi.

We turn now to the tremendous province of SZECHWAN in the West, where (May, 1939), having been pushed out of Kiangsu and Hupeh, Chiang Kai-shek now has his headquarters. The new capital of China is Chungking, which means (the pleasant Chinese!) "Happy Again." Szechwan has 431,309 square miles (bigger than France), and 52,000,000 people; the name means Four Rivers. For years it was the most backward province of China proper, with a large aboriginal population; it was looted by war lords like the Lius, and the peasants had to pay taxes literally sixty years in advance; there is not a foot of railroad in Szechwan, but from 1911 to 1939 the province saw no fewer than 475—believe it or not—civil wars. For a time the local boss threatened to shoot down any airplanes that traversed his area, though the national government was trying hard to extend civil aviation. Nowadays Szechwan is reaching modern times, and accepting its great responsibilities. The province has the greatest potential wealth of any in China, and the proverb says, "You never see a poor man in Szechwan." It is—or should be—China's bank and granary; it is extraordinarily rich in minerals, and can produce four crops a year.

Remote Szechwan, together with Yunnan nearby, are the strongholds of contemporary China.

Below Szechwan are KWEICHOW (literally "Sea of Mountains"), with what are believed to be the richest mercury deposits in the world, and YUNNAN, one of the critically important provinces. Yunnan, containing 146,000 square miles, 12,000,000 people, means "south of the Clouds"; it was in effect a French sphere of influence for some years, because an important French-owned railway penetrates it from Indo-China. Yunnan adjoins Burma also, and the new Burma-Yunnan road is a life-line of Chinese munitions. Yunnan is an immense, fertile, and healthy plateau; the chief products are tin and opium. For years the Yunnanese played little part in the Chinese revolution; now the torch of resistance to Japan has reached them, and because of its strategic position in regard to supplies it has become, next to Szechwan, the most important area in China. Like Szechwan, it contains aboriginal tribes in considerable number, such as the savage Lolos. Even these are learning loyalty to the national government.

Further west than Szechwan and Yunnan, in the mountain-and-desert land separating China proper from Sinkiang, are two remote and isolated provinces, where till recently the central government had small authority. One is KOKONOR, sometimes called Chinghai. Very little indeed is known about Kokonor, except that it is sparsely inhabited by Mongoloid nomads. The other is SIKONG, an immense rolling plateau of grasslands, which obtained its first regular provincial government in January, 1939. Kokonor is bigger than pre-war Austro-Hungary, and Sikong bigger than Finland.

China Beyond China

A very considerable part of China is not China. If you remove Outer Mongolia, part of Inner Mongolia, Tibet, and Sinkiang from China, enormous stretches of territory where Chinese rule is hardly even theoretical, you cut China almost in half, you reduce it from a total area of some four million square miles to something around two million. Tibet I shall consider in relation to India, since it is largely in the British sphere. The great area called SINKIANG (Chinese Turkestan) is technically part of China, but its northern sector is dominated by Soviet Russia, and in the south where it adjoins India, British influence is strong.

Sinkiang (the word means "New Dominion"), is one of the least known regions of the earth's surface. The area is colossal—some 700,000 square miles, or roughly the same as Mexico or Greenland— the population about 4,000,000. The capital is Urumchi, near the Soviet border, and trade naturally drains toward the Russian Turk-Sib railroad. The people are "Turki" by race and largely Moslem in religion; mostly desert nomads who raise sheep and wool. Soviet technical advisers are working on a "three-year plan" of economic development, with the sanction of the Chinese governor, General Sheng Shi-tsai; a trade treaty with the Soviet government dates from 1931. Various complicated wars between Turki, Tungan, and Chinese chieftains led to military intervention by the U.S.S.R. in 1934. Russia has been interested in Sinkiang from Czarist days.

Opium

"In Russia religion is the opium of the people; in China opium is the religion of the people."
—EDGAR SNOW

A vast lot of nonsense has been written about opium, and several libraries might be written about it. In excess opium is of course dangerous, as is any indulgence, and many Chinese take it in excess. But the widespread notion that a man's body, soul, and character are instantly destroyed by two or three whiffs of opium is somewhat exaggerated. In moderation, in fact, many doctors think opium to be no more harmful than whisky—perhaps less harmful than, say, American mixed drinks. The Chinese coolie or chairbearer smokes his opium exactly as a British navvy hoists a tall beer after a hard day; the Chinese intellectual sucks his pipe at nightfall exactly as a New Yorker takes one—or two—cocktails to brace himself for the opera.

Chinese work terribly hard. Many Chinese are hungry perpetually. Opium deadens hunger, and is surcease, relief, almost a kind of food, after exhausting physical or mental labor. One of the most eloquent foreigners in China told me, "Opium to the Chinese is an extra hour of daylight."

One thing is certainly true: opium is prodigiously important in the politics, the sociology, the economics of Chinese life. The bulk of people will not do without it, any more than most Americans would do without alcohol during prohibition. The hunger is deep, innate, fixed. Moreover opium is an exceedingly lucrative crop, and is steeply taxed. Some years ago opium revenue in Honan alone was

$10,000,000 per year, in Kwangtung $12,000,000, in Hunan $20,-
000,000. The Japanese certainly more than paid for the occupation
of Jehol by the revenue they took from that fat, opium growing
province. Today the government of Chiang Kai-shek is believed to
derive not less than $110,000,000 (Chinese) per year from opium
taxes, that is to say ten per cent of the national budget, though opium
figures are secret, and are never included in official statistics. The
important thing about opium revenue is that, by immemorial Chinese
tradition, it is earmarked for the military. Chiang created his national
army partly out of opium, just as warlordism was paid for by opium.
When Chiang set out to unify China, he struck first of all at the
provincial opium monopolies. When he captured a local chieftain's
opium revenue, his campaign was won.

Because Chinese will not give up opium, and because taxes on it
are so lucrative, the various experiments in China—which is by far the
largest opium producing country in the world—to "control" the traffic
need not be taken very seriously. However, a start has been made.
The government realizes that opium in excess is debilitating; it
realizes that peasants (even those who do not smoke) die of famine
because they grow opium instead of wheat. At present it is extremely
difficult to say whether opium is, or is not, legal in China. What the
government is attempting to do, under the "Six-Year Plan" introduced in 1937 to reduce the traffic, is the following:

First, growth of opium is legalized under severe restrictions. The
army, which considers opium its own province, has inspectors and
commissioners in every area.

Second, the government (theoretically) has the monopoly on opium
sales, which it taxes.

Third, the government takes severe measures against smuggling
and racketeering. A two-inch ball of illicit opium—it looks like tar—
may mean a year's living to a peasant who avoids taxes on it. Almost
everywhere in China, but especially in the French Concession in
Shanghai, gangsters "muscle in" on the opium trade, try to fatten on
opium sales themselves. Rival gangsters then "muscle in" on these
gangsters, so that no one will be cheated except the government. The
situation is startlingly like the heroic days of underworld Chicago,
when Capones "hi-jacked" O'Donnells and vice versa to control beer
and booze.

Fourth, a campaign to cure addicts got under way. It was never true that the Chinese government intended to execute all smokers; what it did do was set up hospitals for addicts, and attempt to treat them. On taking the cure addicts were forcibly branded, to show that they were "cured"; if an addict was found smoking again, he could be executed. And many smokers were thus executed. The campaign, however, lost momentum during the war.

Of much greater importance than Chinese attempts to control the traffic are Japanese efforts to extend it. The Japanese have flooded every area they occupy with opium; competent neutral observers are witnesses to the shocking increase in opium smoking in such cities as Peking, Tientsin, and especially Nanking. The Japanese do not merely enthusiastically encourage the sale of opium, but of such narcotic derivatives as heroin, which Chinese do not normally take, and which is a vicious poison. Heroin cost $800 per ounce before the Japanese occupation, so that no one but a millionaire, if there were such witless millionaires, could use it; the Japanese now distribute it at an easy price, so that according to Dr. Searle Bates, the vice president of the University of Nanking, about *fifty thousand* people in Nanking— one-eighth of the population—have become heroin addicts, including women and children. Japanese motive is double: heroin debauches the population, and at the same time, no matter how cheaply it is sold, produces handsome revenue.

An Octet of Critics

I asked eight representative Chinese recently what China needed most. The eight answers:

1. Men of character.
2. Greater industrialization; agrarian reform to produce more wealth.
3. Honesty. Abolition of squeeze and Face.
4. More technicians, more engineers.
5. End of the old shiftlessness, defeatism, passivity.
6. Artillery.
7. More men like Chiang Kai-shek and T. V. Soong.
8. Abolition of the Japanese.

Chapter XI
Generalissimo Chiang Kai-shek

〜〜〜〜〜〜〜〜〜〜〜〜〜〜〜〜〜〜〜〜〜〜〜〜〜〜

*If we perspire more in times of peace, we will bleed less in
times of war.*

—GENERALISSIMO CHIANG KAI-SHEK

CHIANG KAI-SHEK, the inconspicuous son of a village merchant
who became leader of China's four hundred and fifty million people, is commander-in-chief of army, navy, and air force, President of
the Supreme War Council and the National Military Council, President of the National Aviation Commission, and Director-General of the
Kuomintang, China's single political party. He is also a psychological
puzzle of considerable magnitude.

He is the strongest man China has produced for generations, and a
terrific disciplinarian; but the enemies he has forgiven—and given
jobs to—are many. His dominating mission is to unite China, consolidate it, and indeed he has united it (with certain help from Japan!)
more than any man in centuries of history—but he spent ten dreary
years fighting civil wars against his own people. Like that of Masaryk,
whom he doesn't otherwise resemble, his life is shot full of paradox.
He is a popular leader of the stature of Stalin or Mussolini—but he is a
bad politician, the last possible alternative to rabble-rouser or backslapper. He is a strong Chinese nationalist—but he got much of his
education in Japan. He is an extremely typical Chinese—who nevertheless believes in Christianity and the Y.M.C.A.

Mr. Gandhi, the Indian nationalist leader, is a politician who makes
good use of mysticism. The Emperor of Japan is an imperial puppet,
whose mystical characteristics are utilized by politicians. Chiang Kai-
shek's mysticism is of a peculiar kind. He has no supernatural qualities. One might almost call him supernormal. He does not serve a
religion, as do Gandhi and the Emperor of Japan; he makes religion
serve him. Chiang Kai-shek is almost a missionary. He is certainly a
reformer.

In the preceding chapter I have sought to sketch something of the immense backdrop of China. Let us attempt to pin on this backdrop the stubborn figure of the Generalissimo.

Boundary Stone and Central Righteousness

He is slight, straight, wiry, with delicate features. He carries himself with a curious elastic grace, but stiffly. He is quite tall—five feet nine—but is rather short-legged, and likes to be photographed sitting down, or wearing the broad black cloak that is his favorite costume. He weighs 141 pounds. He dresses in a simple khaki uniform almost always, and likes big-brimmed hats. His eyes are remarkable: a very dark gray, deep, both piercing and luminous, and never at rest. His face, his speech, seem somewhat arid, until the eyes light them up. He was severely injured by a fall during the Sian kidnaping, but now his health is excellent.

He rises early—at dawn usually—and works hard till nightfall. He thinks that the time between dawn and breakfast is the best hour of the day. After lunch he takes a brief nap, usually falling asleep to the tune of a wheezy gramophone. His favorite record is Schubert's *Ave Maria*; his friends in the next room know that he is asleep when the record stops. After tea he has half an hour for prayer or meditation. He goes to bed early. He likes to lie down, and does as much of his work as he can on a sofa.

He is abstemious and methodical. He does not drink or smoke, he avoids even coffee and tea, and for many years has kept a full diary. (The Emperor of Japan shares several of these qualities, incidentally; he too gets up at dawn, keeps a diary, and doesn't drink or smoke.) Chiang's diary, it might fairly be said, once saved his life; the mutineers at Sian read it, together with some of the Generalissimo's letters to his wife, and were impressed enough to change radically their attitude to him.[1] The Generalissimo eats both Chinese and European food, the latter in particular when he is dieting.

The things he likes best are poetry, mountains, and his wife. His idea of a really good time, if he ever has time to have a good time, is to walk in hilly country on a sunny day, or to have a picnic lunch outdoors. His friends can make him do almost anything by promising him a day outdoors. When he walks he recites poetry. His favorite abode is Kuling, in the mountains near Kiukiang, where he has a small cottage; he hasn't been able to visit it since the war. His family

---

[1] The precious episode of Sian is considered in Chapter XIV below.

life is happy, and Madame Chiang is his indispensable and beloved associate, but he is definitely a lonely man, a person who admires solitude. His closest foreign friend is W. H. Donald, the Australian newspaper man who has been his unofficial "adviser" for some years. Another good friend is an American missionary, Dr. George Shepherd. Once Shepherd dared to tell him that his troops treated the peasants in Kiangsi worse than the Reds, and rebuked him. Later he and Shepherd became close friends.

The Generalissimo is sensitive and sometimes stand-offish. He seldom sees people socially, and he never gives himself away. When touring the provinces he gives the proper official dinner to the local dignitaries, and then makes no further attempt to see them. He is not what you would call chummy. When thousands of deliriously happy Chinese sought to celebrate the victory of Taierchuang in March, 1938, by gathering outside his house in Wuchang and cheering, he wanted to send them home without a word; his advisers had to appeal to him not to clear the streets. He does not like people in the abstract—or even the particular.

But when the Generalissimo and Madame Chiang see a foreign visitor, they are conspicuously urbane. Madame Chiang receives her guests; after a brief introduction the Generalissimo comes in, and tea is served. Usually Chiang stays just half an hour; then Madame Chiang may carry the conversation further. She interprets for him, since his only foreign language is Japanese; I had the feeling, however, that he knew more English than he admitted. The interpretation is so fluently expert that it is hard to determine who is speaking; Madame (everywhere in China she is known simply as "Madame") knows his mind so well that there are no pauses, no interruptions. The Generalissimo is not a time waster. When I saw him he first paid a pleasant compliment to my wife, then asked if I would explain the "European situation" in "one or two" sentences. I did my best. He talks deliberately and interrupts his remarks with a queer guttural snap. He receives journalists for official interviews only very rarely; I was the first foreigner he had seen for a long interview since the war. When the conversation was over, he gave me a Chinese translation of the written questions and answers, and signed it with an imposing flourish.

On occasion the Generalissimo is closely guarded—for instance, he

has a bullet-proof limousine with windows almost an inch thick—
but on that same day I had occasion to see that the stories were not
true that he never moved without a strong armed guard, never showed
himself among the people. My wife and I, leaving his villa, went to
call on Dr. Kung, the prime minister, in the Bank of China Building.
The scene was the Hankow Bund; a rough analogy would be the
Thames embankment. There, walking along, apparently quite alone,
was the Generalissimo, who himself had just visited Dr. Kung. He was
so inconspicuous in the crowd that he saw us before we saw him, and
stopped and greeted us. Then, as he walked deliberately toward the
jetty, we noticed that members of his bodyguard did accompany him,
but about twenty feet away. Very few people in the crowd noticed
that the Generalissimo was there.

The official head of the corps of picked troops who guard Chiang
is Captain Walther F. N. Stennes, a German officer with a remarkable history. He was a prominent member of the Storm Troops before Hitler came to power, and once led a revolt against Dr. Goebbels. Later he quarreled with Hitler, spent some time in prison, and
eventually came to China. He is a splendid officer. The Generalissimo's
personal pilot for his surviving private plane—a Douglas DC3—is an
American, Royal Leonard. Formerly Leonard was pilot to the Young
Marshal Chang Hsueh-liang, who kidnaped the Generalissimo at Sian.
The Generalissimo loves to fly.

The Generalissimo's name is a source of much confusion. His family name was Chiang, and as a boy he was called "Jui-tai"; Chinese
children are usually given a temporary name, so that when they grow
up they can change it if they wish—a pleasant convention! Reaching
adolescence, Chiang decided that the name he wanted was "Kai-shek,"
which means "boundary stone," an interesting choice psychologically
in that it forecasts the idea of a fixed frontier. But the Chinese
ideographs for "Kai-shek" may be Latinized in two different ways:
the Mandarins would say "Chieh-shih," the Cantonese "Kai-shek."
In some books the Generalissimo is called "Chiang Chieh-shih"; many
people in China still pronounce his name thus. The approximately
correct pronunciation of Chiang Kai-shek is, incidentally, "Jiahng
Gai-shek."

When he became prominent, he adopted, as most Chinese do, quite
another name, his "official" name. This is Chiang Chung-cheng,

which means, according to one translation, "central righteousness";
note that he retained his original family name, which not all Chinese
do. His adoption of the word "central" is an obvious clue to his character. In official proclamations, in signing government papers, even
in reference books, his name is given as "Chiang Chung-cheng."

In conversation, he is officially addressed as *Weiyuchang* (Mr.
President), or *Chungszeling* (Generalissimo). In the party, according
to Madame Chiang, he is called "Mr. Chiang"; some old soldiers
call him "Mr. Principal." A considerable source of power has been
the group of officers whom he trained at the Whampoa Academy, a
closely knit clique which was the nucleus of his army. Sometimes he
is called "Lao (old) Chiang," an affectionate diminutive. Madame as
a rule calls him "Kai"; Donald, who cannot take time to pronounce
all of Generalissimo, says "Jissimo."

Chiang has several times been chairman of the Executive Yuan,
that is, prime minister of the Chinese government, though he is not
prime minister at present; for a time he was "president" of China,
that is, official head of the Chinese state, but he does not hold this
post now. His main job, like the main bent of his mind, has always been military; since 1926 he has been commander-in-chief of
the armed forces, and head of various military bureaus and commissions, except during brief intervals. In March, 1938, he became general director (*Tsungtsai*) of the Kuomintang party, a post previously
held only by the founder of the party, Dr. Sun Yat-sen. This step had
importance beyond its prestige value, since for the first time Chiang
became *party* as well as military and governmental leader. The
Kuomintang, in other words, merged with the state.

Chiang has no hobbies, no relaxations, except reading. He plays no
games, but he likes to read, especially the Chinese classics. His favorite passage from Confucius—note the tendency to "uplift"—is the
following:

In order to propagate virtue to the world, one must first rule one's
country,
In order to rule the country, one must first rule one's family,
In order to rule the family, one must first regulate one's body by moral
training,
In order to regulate the body, one must first regulate one's mind,
In order to regulate the mind, one must first be sincere in one's inten-
tions,

In order to be sincere in intentions, one must first increase one's
knowledge.

(Quoted in Hollington K. Tong's official biography, p. 606)

Among character traits of the Generalissimo one must mention
first, and above all, his stubbornness, his tenacity. This delicately
featured Chinese soldier is a bulldog. He has no tact. Anyone who has
read his diary describing the Sian kidnaping knows what I mean. He
dug himself in, emotionally, physically, morally, and never budged—
and kept begging his captors to kill him!

There is cruelty in his character, and the ruthlessness of his war
against the communists is well known. Thousands of people were
executed, many of them for no crime except that they disagreed with
him.

He has a kind of inflexible inner egoism, an egoism so enormous
that it becomes almost *im*personal. For instance, he gravely noted in
his Sian diary that Shao, the civil governor, advised him to be more
"lenient" in his next conversation with the Young Marshal, his
captor! Chiang talked to the Young Marshal with complete un-
mitigated confidence, and never glossed over his contempt for those
who had captured him.

He is shrewd, suspicious, calculating, and not above the use of
guile. On the other hand, both his physical and moral courage are
indisputable. He has proved more than once that he has no fear of
death.

Another quality which is a source of power is his peculiar concept
of responsibility to the nation. Continually he emphasizes the factor
of discipline, and the necessity for those above to be responsible for
the behavior of their inferiors. It is characteristic that, at Sian, he
"assumed responsibility" for the mutineers who kidnaped him.

He makes wonderful use of enemies. He has a knack of making

them work for him. He resents hotly any aspersion on the characters of his associates, even if they attempt to betray him; he forgives— and doesn't forget. This is caused not merely by loyalty or by calculation that the enemy, in the unstable condition of China, may turn out to be useful, but by a curious *moral* attitude; Chiang feels that he knows himself to be right, and is willing to wait until the others see their errors, admit that he is right, and come to him repentant. He likes to have everyone, even those whom he dislikes, dependent on him. He is so sure of himself that, in time, he is convinced that he can convert anybody, or that the power of events will effect conversion. Thus the extraordinary succession of war lords and such who, after revolts, have been pardoned, paid soundly, and sent abroad to "recuperate their health."[3]

He has a distinct tendency to jealousy. No single officer was an outstanding hero during the 1937 defense of Shanghai; and for a reason. Chiang remembered that in the fighting in 1932 the world's homage and admiration went to the commander of the 19th route army, General Tsai Ting-kai. Chiang didn't like this—especially since he himself had not fought. When war came again he saw to it that no single officer was too conspicuous.

Another characteristic is his almost illimitable, dogged patience. He develops slowly. Early in 1934 he delivered three lectures to the Officers School at Kuling which to-day make amazing reading—such amazing reading, in fact, that unfriendly critics have hinted that they might be bogus. The lectures, secret and confidential at the time they were delivered, have now been published. At the time they were delivered Chiang was submissively bowing to Japanese attacks and demands. He lost Manchuria; he lost Jehol; he saw the Japanese in-

[3] For instance, in 1935 the Kwangtung war lord Chen Chai-tang led a revolt against him. Chen started a "punitive expedition" against Chiang, which, however, fizzled out, because the war lord's private air force flew over to the central government. Chen took refuge in the foreign settlement in Canton, and a British gunboat spirited him to Hong Kong. What did Chiang do? He began negotiations, not to punish this obvious insurrectionist, but to see that he had a pleasant trip abroad. Chiang knew that he was rich. And, when the war with Japan began, he got some millions of dollars out of him for the national exchequer. This episode, however, was not without its unfortunate results. As part of the deal whereby Chen was not punished, Chiang agreed to appoint as military governor in Canton a general known as Yu Han-mou. This somewhat inefficient gentleman, to whom otherwise Chiang would never have given the post, was partly responsible for the subsequent fall of Canton to the Japanese.

trench themselves in North China; he saw Inner Mongolia threatened; yet for years he stood aloof, made no resistance, said nothing against the Japanese, and, indeed, punished Chinese who did. Several of his best officers, appalled at what they called his weakness, his pro-Japanese policy, flared up in civil wars. Still Chiang did nothing. Then the war of 1937 came. Chiang fought. But the lectures prove that even in 1934 he was passionately telling his best officers in confidence that eventually they must fight Japan; he cited Japan as the flagrant and inevitable enemy; he implored them to prepare themselves for the fight that was bound to come; he tuned his whole mind to one pitch—the implacable necessity of winning it. How may this apparent paradox be explained? Only by assuming that Chiang knew that, in the early thirties, successful Chinese resistance was impossible; that at all costs the Chinese must do everything possible to appease and mollify the Japanese until they were ready, and had some chance of fighting a successful war; that at all costs, at the risk of any indignity, the Chinese must buy off Japanese attack until the last, the final, the uttermost minute, at which time they might have a chance to win.

The lectures show great grasp of history, shrewd understanding of both Japan and China, and an intense Chinese patriotism. Chiang has done very little writing for publication; these lectures are a state paper of considerable significance.

Chiang's sense of humor may be described as occasional. He does not laugh much. Once in Sian, at a moment of terrible tension, W. H. Donald whipped a pack of cards from his pocket, and said to the Generalissimo, "Let's play casino!" (Occasionally Donald and Madame play casino or rummy for golf balls.) The Generalissimo was so stunned that he burst into incredulous laughter. Once he and Donald were motoring in Chekiang. Donald exploded, "Good heavens, some damned fool has taken down the English road signs!" He was surprised then to hear Chiang chuckling with mirth. It had been he who had ordered the English signs to be removed. The Generalissimo likes to collect Scotch jokes, which he tells "on" Donald.

The humor is bitter sometimes. Once Donald said, "What you've got to do is shoot all the crooks and traitors in China."

The Generalissimo sighed, "Unfortunately there is not ammunition enough."

Attitude to Money

The Generalissimo's salary is $1,000 (Chinese) per month. His private fortune is not believed to be great, though he made money freely in his early Shanghai days; the fortune of the Soong family into which he married is quite another matter; the Soongs are among the richest folk in China. The General and Madame do not need much money, and do not have to spend much. They do not live like coolies, but their tastes are frugal.

Chiang has a house in his native village Chikow, and a cottage in the mountains near Fenghua. His residence in the French Concession in Shanghai is unostentatious. The lodge at Kuling, which he likes best, he rents from missionaries. The government built an official residence for the head of state at Nanking, a kind of White House, but the Generalissimo and Madame lived instead in a small bungalow borrowed from the military academy nearby.

The Chinese are not prone to flamboyant demonstration of wealth. The best houses have, as a rule, tawdry exteriors; which is a form of protective coloration. A high official in Nanking bought a cream-colored limousine just before the war; hurriedly he painted it over—black—when kidnapers became interested. . . . On the other hand, the Chinese, sensible people, realize that successful generals must have private fortunes, because otherwise they could not pay their troops. Money has always been a vital adjunct to political power—which, for that matter, it is in most other countries.

Chiang makes shrewd use of money. Early in the war he invented a system of wound bounties unique in military annals; he paid bonuses for wounds. Every private soldier wounded in action in China gets $10 (Chinese) per wound, which is solider satisfaction to the realistic Chinese than a stripe on the sleeve. Officers get $30 to $50, and generals $100. The success of this system was immediate.

Attitude Toward Religion

"There is Methodism in his madness."
—Frances Gunther

On October 23, 1930, Chiang Kai-shek was baptized into the Christian church. The Rev. Z. T. Kuang, a Methodist minister in Shanghai, performed the ceremony, which took place in the Soong family home. All the Soongs are strong Christians, and it was largely the influence of his wife that led to his conversion. Indeed, when the Generalissimo was courting Madame, his suit was rejected at first, because he was not a Christian. Old Mme. Soong demanded that he adopt Christianity; the General, stubborn as always, said that she would think less of him if he assumed a new religion merely to make marriage possible. She was impressed by this; then he promised that if the marriage took place, he would study Christianity seriously for a long period and become a convert if he came to believe in it.

His turning Christian is not quite so sensational as it sounds. It has been said that an analogy would be for President Roosevelt suddenly to become a Buddhist, or Hitler a Jew; this is not quite correct, because the Chinese care little for religious stratifications, as we have seen.

The Generalissimo is asserted to be a devout and even ardent believer in Christianity. He and Madame pray daily, the first thing every morning; they say grace before all meals, and observe Sunday fairly strictly. In his speeches Chiang talks incessantly about Christ; he chose "Why We Believe in Jesus" as the text for an important radio address in 1938. When he was kidnaped at Sian, he delivered himself into the arms of the Lord, and prayed for strength from Jesus; when Madame arrived to rescue him, his first impulse was to quote Scripture: "Jehovah will now do a new thing, and that is, He will make a woman protect a man."[4]

Nevertheless, the Generalissimo still reveres his ancestors, like all good Chinese. This raises a nice theological point, because strictly speaking it would not appear that an orthodox Christian, who must believe in hellfire and salvation, can also believe that his ancestors survive as physical entities, to be worshiped and adored. Chinese ancestor worship has no place for hell, purgatory, or a sense of sin, which is one reason why the Chinese are the pleasant people that they are.

Schoolmaster Dictator

Every Monday morning in Hankow, or wherever Chiang's government happens to be, occurs a remarkable ceremony. It gives sharp insight into his character.

About six hundred men hop off the Yangtze ferry, walk briskly to

[4] Quoted in Madame's Sian diary which is published in America as *General Chiang Kai-shek.*

a hall near his headquarters, file into the big building, and wait. They do not have to wait long. The Generalissimo is punctual. He arrives, mounts the platform. The military band plays a march, and the audience comes to attention.

The music stops, then everyone in the hall uncovers and bows three times to a portrait of Dr. Sun Yat-sen, the founder of the Chinese republic. One—two—three. The bows are made with precision and *éclat*. Officers put caps on again. The Generalissimo then reads the testament of Dr. Sun Yat-sen, uttering it a sentence at a time, which the audience repeats. It is exactly like a prayer meeting and the reading of the gospels.

The Generalissimo asks silent meditation for three minutes and then delivers a lecture which lasts at least an hour, and may last two hours or longer. He discusses the military situation, exhorts his officers and civilian ministers to further efforts, scolds slackers, points out abuses, and issues moral injunctions. One recent lecture developed the theme that not only must soldiers be trained to make good officers; good officers, on their side, must learn to be good soldiers. During the entire performance, the audience—which includes everyone of consequence in the government, even cabinet ministers—must remain standing. When it is over, the Generalissimo does not say thank you, or au revoir, but simply a single abrupt word: "Completed!"

Life Story of the Generalissimo

"No nation can ruin us, unless we first ruin ourselves."
—CHIANG KAI-SHEK

Chiang was born in the village of Chikow, in the seaside district of Fenghua, Chekiang province, in 1887. The inhabitants are mainly fisherfolk, traders, and the like, who for generations have been exposed to foreign influence; it is not impossible that, far back, his ancestors may have had admixtures of Portuguese or Arab blood. He was certainly not of a rich family, but he was never desperately poor. His mother, like the mothers of Hitler, Stalin, and Kamal Ataturk, appears to have been a remarkable woman; of his father, who died when he was a child, little is recorded. His father married three times, and had five children; Chiang was the eldest son by the third wife. The family slaved to send him to school, where his record was not brilliant. In 1907 he cut off his queue—symbol that he intended to be "modern."

He went to Japan when he was about nineteen to become an officer. He was not allowed, however, to enter a Japanese military school without recommendation from the Manchu (Chinese) government; so he returned to China, and studied at the Paoting Military Academy near Peking. Then he went to Japan again, and entered the Military Staff College. He actually served several years in the Japanese army: which is as if, say, some great French revolutionist had been an officer in the German army, after a thorough German training. But also in Japan he encountered an influence destined to alter the course of his life. He met some one much more important than any Japanese officer. He met Dr. Sun Yat-sen.

This was in 1909, when he was twenty-two. Dr. Sun Yat-sen was in exile. Promptly young Chiang became infected with Chinese nationalism. He stayed in Japan two more years, but he joined the Tungmeng-hui, a secret society of patriotic Chinese which was the forerunner of the Kuomintang. When, in 1911, the Manchu régime was overthrown in Peking and the Chinese republic was born, Chiang set sail for China to join the revolution, though this meant technical desertion from the Japanese army.[5] It is recorded that punctiliously he sent back his sword and uniform—by mail!

For five years, roughly from 1911 to 1916, Chiang fought in the variety of minor civil wars and insurrections that implemented the revolution. Once his regiment saved Dr. Sun's life; he became known as an officer of integrity and vision. He was one of Sun's best subordinates, but in 1917 he quit the army suddenly to go into business. This may have been foresight. He was roughly in the position of a young American who decides to enter politics; he knew that for a successful political career he had to have money—a lot of money—first. He set out to earn it. First he worked as a clerk in a brokerage house. His personality must have been strongly marked, because he was successively "adopted" by two rich and influential men, who became his patrons. One was Chen Chi-mei, who brought him into an underground secret society, devoted to Chinese nationalism among other things, and who was later assassinated; the other was Chang Chin-kiang, a wealthy merchant who helped him win his fortune.

[5] But he returned to Japan at least twice in the next few years. It should be remembered that in those days most Chinese students, intellectuals, and revolutionaries went often to Japan. The Japanese had won the war with Russia and the Chinese considered Japan the savior of Asia from western domination.

By 1921, Chiang was busy with military affairs and politics again; i.e., he was a revolutionist. On one occasion he spent fifty-six days aboard a warship, in steady conference with Sun Yat-sen; in 1923, Sun sent him to Moscow, where he spent six months as a liaison officer; this was the first period of Russian association with the Chinese national revolution. In Moscow he saw Trotsky among others. His official biography takes note of a bit of advice given him by Trotsky: "Patience and activity are the two essential factors for a revolutionary party, and the one complements the other." The next year Chiang, returning to China, became first principal of the newly organized Whampoa Military Academy in Canton. Among his advisers was the Russian Marshal Bluecher. By 1925 Chiang was chairman of the standing committee of the Kuomintang, and when Dr. Sun Yat-sen died, he assumed office as commander-in-chief of the nationalist army.

He has always been simple in manner and approach. Lewis Gannett, for instance, records his meeting with him in 1926:

When I went to see Chiang Kai-shek in Canton I presented my card at the door of an inconspicuous two story modern dwelling-house; the boy studied it and silently pointed upstairs. At the top of the stairs I met a pleasant-looking young man in an officer's uniform without distinguishing marks of rank.

"Where Chiang Kai-shek?" I asked in simplified English.

"Yes, Chiang Kai-shek," the young man replied.

"Where, where, Chiang Kai-shek?" I repeated, puzzled.

The young man pointed to a bedroom; I entered and sat down. A moment later Chen Tsu-yen, a former Lehigh University student, came in and explained that the pleasant young officer was the Commander in Chief himself. The bare bedroom was his; it was also his workroom. . . . The general ate nothing, and instead of tea he sipped hot water.

(*Young China,* published by *The Nation,* New York, p. 28)

At this time he told Gannett that he would conquer and unify all China, which then seemed an utterly impossible dream; he said too that he would cancel the unequal treaties (with foreign powers) and "set China free." He stated, "It will not be difficult; in one, two, at most three years, it will be done." But a good many things happened to deflect Chiang from this course, including one of the biggest turnabouts in modern history. Chiang may have unified China—but not in the way he then anticipated. And he certainly didn't kick the foreign powers out.

Dr. Sun did not directly hand the succession to Chiang Kai-shek, who was merely one of a triumvirate. Dr. Sun's idea was that he should be military leader of the revolution, while the left-wing patriot Wang Ching-wei was political leader. Dr. Sun liked Chiang because he stood midway between Wang, on the Left, and the third member of the triumvirate, Hu Han-min, on the Right. But presently Hu died, and gradually, with many ups and downs, Chiang maneuvered Wang (who fled China in 1938) to second place.

In 1926 began Chiang's most amazing exploit, and one of the most amazing ever performed by anyone anywhere. He set out on the gigantic, the illimitable, task of unifying China by military conquest. At this time, it should be recalled, the Kuomintang held power only in the extreme south; the Nationalists were considered in Shanghai to be little more than a gang of undisciplined reds; Chiang Kai-shek was thought of as an obscure "Bolshevik," as Dr. Sun had been dismissed as an impractical visionary. It is quite true that many forces helped Chiang in the campaigns that then electrified the world. The country was sagging with corruption and decay. Rival warlords were eliminating each other endlessly. Not much stiff resistance was encountered. There was no granite Chiang had to hew through. Even so, his achievement was remarkable. He fought with arms; he fought with money. His armies (he himself was sometimes in the background) captured Wuchang in October, 1926; Hangchow in February, 1927; Shanghai and Nanking in March, 1927; Peking in July, 1928. This campaign is one of the seminal facts of modern history. Chiang made China, which was a continent, into a country— at least for the time being.

Then, a most extraordinary event, having consolidated China into what might have been a permanent modern entity, he disrupted it. Having won his fight, he lost it. Having gained victory, he all but threw it away. Ten weary years of civil war began. Why?

.   .   .   .

At this point we must pause briefly and perform a task that will have to be done often in this book; viz., inspect background.

Dr. Sun, who was one of the greatest men of the modern age, but who died[6] before his work was finished, was a prophet. He was not a man of action. His vision, however, was tremendous; his creation of the Kuomintang (literally, Kuomintang means "National People's Party") as a modern instrument of revolution in decadent and medieval China, has historical rank with, one might say, the invention of Islam by Mohammed. (Indeed, Chiang could be said to be a sort of Caliph Omar to Sun Yat-sen's Mohammed.) Let us compress Dr. Sun's life into a paragraph.

He was born a poor boy near Macao, in South China, in 1867. He became a convert to Christianity, and in 1894 was the first doctor of medicine to be graduated from the new medical school in Hong Kong. As a revolutionist he spent twenty years in and out of China, creating the Kuomintang. Once he was kidnaped by Manchu agents on the streets of London, and for a time there was a price of £100,000 on his head. Like Masaryk, he was not in his own country when finally the revolution occurred; he returned from England in 1912 to become provisional president of the first Chinese republic, as Masaryk returned to Prague from Washington.

The Chinese, who are not a mystical people, come as near to revering Dr. Sun as to revering anybody, except perhaps Confucius. (They do not revere Chiang; they respect and fear him rather; perhaps they may get to the point of reverence when he dies.) Dr. Sun's tomb is a national memorial; everywhere in China parks and streets are called by his familiar name, Chung Shan. When he was dropped from *Who's Who in China,* after his death, so many protests came to the editor, Mr. J. B. Powell, that his name had to be reinserted; he is the only dead man in the Chinese *Who's Who.* His widow, Mme. Sun, a sister of Mme. Chiang Kai-shek's (Dr. Sun and Chiang were posthumous brothers-in-law), is still a strong moral force in Chinese affairs.

In 1921, Dr. Sun announced his Three Principles, which in theory at least are still the determining motives of Chinese political action. They are (1) Nationalism, (2) Democracy, (3) People's Livelihood. By this the eminent doctor meant that China must, by abrogating the foreign concessions and extraterritoriality, achieve proper national unity and integration; that the country must be prepared for self-government through the establishment of democratic principles, with free elections to a national legislature; and that livelihood must be

[6] Of cancer, in Peking, March, 1925.

assured the starving millions by social reform, economic advance, and the redistribution of wealth. The gigantic nature of Dr. Sun's task may be gathered from the fact that, until he invented it, no *word* for democracy existed in the Chinese language. Dr. Sun said that the revolution should be accomplished in three stages, first of military consolidation, then of political tutelage, finally of constitutional development. The constitutional period was to have begun with elections for the first Chinese legislature in November, 1937—but war with Japan came instead. Sun knew fully what a modern China needed. He said (as Lenin in Russia talked about electrification) that China could never be strong until, first, it had 100,000 miles of railways, then 1,000,000 miles of roads.

In 1921, Dr. Sun needed help—badly. The western powers would have nothing to do with his struggling revolution—which, indeed, they opposed bitterly. The British, the French, were not too friendlily disposed to a national movement which might end their own privileges. They didn't want China strong; they didn't want China united. Dr. Sun turned to the U.S.S.R. He sent Chiang to Moscow, and made an entente with the first Soviet emissary to nationalist China, Adolf Joffe. Sun and Joffe hammered out a vitally important agreement, which should be quoted in full:

Dr. Sun holds that the communistic order or even the Soviet system cannot actually be introduced into China, because there do not exist here the conditions for successful establishment of either communism or sovietism. This view is entirely shared by Mr. Joffe, who is further of the opinion that China's paramount and most pressing problem is to achieve unity and attain full national independence, and regarding this great task he has assured Dr. Sun that China has the warmest sympathy of the Russian people.

Russian political advisers then came to Canton, like Michael Borodin; Russian influence in the Kuomintang spread, though the Kuomintang never was, it is important to state, a communist organization. When, in 1927, Chiang captured Hankow, a government influenced by Borodin and the communists was established, though it was never a "communist" government. But a Chinese variety of communism, which was largely a program of agrarian reform, surged through the left wing of the Kuomintang, inflaming and irradiating the landless peasants. It was perhaps inevitable that the Kuomintang should split. The right wing, thinking mostly of Dr. Sun's first principle, nationalism, found itself more and more at variance with the left wing, which emphasized the third principle, social equality. The breach widened; the split became irremediable; and civil war broke out. The leftist government in Hankow was overthrown (1927). Chiang overthrew it, and he established the "National" government in Nanking.

Chiang went to the Right. Why? His friends were dumbfounded; his family split. He seemed to be destroying wantonly a large part of the program of the revolution; he seemed to be betraying his pledges, his friends, and the memory of Dr. Sun. Chiang, the revolutionist, became a counter-revolutionary. His former associates and brothers-in-arms, who joined the Left, were ruthlessly hunted out and extirpated. A white terror of unexampled ferocity struck China.

The deepest reason for this must certainly have been an innate conservatism in his character. He may have been a revolutionist; he never was a "radical." The chief note in his life is the idea of the national unity of China; like so many modern chieftains, Hitler and Pilsudski for instance, he has been a prisoner all his days of one idea. So he came to feel that the revolution was bound to be destroyed unless he could make it respectable, i.e., get the support of the powerful business and foreign interests in Shanghai and the Yangtze valley. He went to Shanghai, bowed to the bankers and international concessionaires (whom he had threatened to throw out) and became their man. They gave him money; and he promised to trounce the Reds.

Later his anti-Red campaigns served several important corollary purposes. For one thing, so long as he was fighting communism himself, he removed a pretext for Japanese interference with China, since the Japanese themselves wanted to "save" China from communism. Again, his long pursuit of the Reds gave him an excuse to put his national army in many Chinese provinces which otherwise he could not easily have invaded. Again, it gave actual combat training to his troops. Finally, the Red heresy gave him something concrete to attack persistently: an item useful to a nationalist dictator. The Reds were Chiang Kai-shek's Jews.

The left-wingers and communists, after various adventures and escapes, withdrew to Kiangsi province, where the first Chinese Soviets were set up. Chiang's ten-year series of "pacification campaigns" were unsuccessful. He tried literally to bleed China "white"; he didn't quite do it. The communists never succumbed, and never surrendered; presently we shall describe their Long March, their government in Shensi province, and the extraordinary personalities, like Mao Tse-tung and Chu Teh, who led them. Finally came the kidnaping in Sian and as a result a *volte-face* as astonishing on Chiang Kai-shek's part as the first one. The communists had Chiang at their mercy, he who had had so many of their men murdered; and they let him go. The reconciliation was as remarkable as the original split: Chiang made a United Front with these "enemies," which is as if Stalin resurrected and gave jobs to all the Trotskyists, after having been kidnaped and then released by Mr. Trotsky. After terrible dilemmas, terrible delays, a new chapter in Chinese history began.

.   .   .   .

Chiang spent most of his time from 1927 to 1937 Red hunting. But other things did happen. He was continually resigning his job, getting reappointed, and taking on new spheres in administration. He organized a semi-secret group known as the Blue Shirts, which became his Gestapo. There were various complicated civil wars quite aside from the major motif of the Red civil war, for instance the Fukien rebellion of the 19th Route Army in 1933, and the northern war against the old warlords, Feng Yu-hsiang and Yen Hsi-shan, in 1930. (This was a real civil war, even though warlords of the traditional variety were involved; people actually got killed.) In 1936, he faced a serious revolt of the powerful Kwangsi generals, Li Tsung-jen and Pai Chung-hsi, who resented his apparent acquiescence to the aggression of Japan; a Southwestern Political Council was set up virtually independent of Nanking.[7]

Though these military preoccupations were recurrent and severe, Chiang did manage to cultivate other fields. His accomplishments in ten years were considerable. He traveled by air over almost all of China,[8] and at one time no fewer than twenty-two provinces were

[7] The Kwangsi generals were annoyed with Chiang for a number of reasons. One was opium. Kwangsi province collected a transport tax on opium delivered from Yunnan to the Generalissimo's control bureau. To discipline the rebellious Kwangsi generals, Chiang diverted this transport tax, thus seriously reducing their revenue. Later these generals became his best allies in the struggle with Japan.

[8] One of his biggest tours started almost by accident. In 1934, the Generalissimo was in Loyang. Donald mentioned that he could visit Sian, the ancient capital of China, by traveling another three hours. Chiang had never been

loyal (that is, paying taxes) to him, a record no other recent Chinese ruler has approached. He hired competent foreign advisers; Professor Kemmerer of Princeton and Sir Frederick Leith Ross put his currency in order; he outlined a splendid capital at Nanking. He built roads, and coöperated in famine relief. He made a beginning toward control of the opium traffic, and at Madame's inspiration inaugurated the curious experiment in manners and sanitation known as the "New Life Movement." He created a national army, something unknown before, "and made soldiering respectable." Above all, he gave the country a modern political sense, and the bulwark of a national spirit.

He was too successful. So at least the Japanese thought. He went too far. So they attacked.

Family Affairs

When he was fifteen Chiang married the daughter of a neighbor, a Miss Mao of Fenghua. The marriage, arranged by his family, was terminated by divorce in 1921. This Madame Chiang lived in Suchow until the war, and then moved back to the home of her parents; she is believed to be an old-style Chinese, with bound feet. The Generalissimo never sees her these days, though he continues to support her dutifully. She bore him one son, Ching-kuo, now about thirty.

After his divorce the Generalissimo met Mei-ling Soong in Canton and fell madly, desperately in love with her. For some years he pursued her with stubborn determination, but she rejected his advances, on the grounds that she was "not interested"; her family strongly disapproved of the match. But he was persistent. He interrupted the war; he interrupted the revolution; he rushed back and forth between Canton, Hankow and Shanghai; he was a man possessed.

In 1927, Madame Kung, elder sister to Mei-ling, summoned a small group of newspaper men. They were surprised to find the Generalissimo there. She introduced him, and said, "The General is going to marry my little sister." Commotion and surprise. The marriage took place on December 1, 1927. First came a private religious ceremony in the Soong home, performed by a secretary of the Chinese Y.M.C.A., and then an imposing public celebration in the

---

there, and was overwhelmed by the warmth of welcome he received. Donald then suggested going on to Langchow, the capital of Kansu, which was risky and remote *terra incognita.* Chiang agreed. They proceeded in this wise, visiting almost all of the west of China.

Majestic Hotel, to which more than a thousand guests were invited, and on which, it is reported, the General spent $50,000. Flags were draped over a portrait of Dr. Sun Yat-sen, and the political implications of the union were emphasized. Immediately after the ceremony Chiang said, "After our wedding, the work of the Revolution will make greater progress, because henceforth I can bear the tremendous responsibility of the revolution with peace at heart."

The Generalissimo is said to be as much in love with Madame to-day as in the days he courted her. She is part of his blood; his indispensable friend, companion, and adviser. They have no children. His last message to her from Sian, when he thought he would die the next day, was, however, couched rather impersonally:

As I have made up my mind to sacrifice my life, if necessary, for my country, please do not worry about me. I will never allow myself to do anything to make my wife ashamed of me or become unworthy of being a follower of Dr. Sun Yat-sen. Since I was born for the Revolution I will gladly die for the same cause. I will return my body unspotted to my parents. As to home affairs, I have nothing to say further than that I wish you would, to gladden my spirit, regard my two sons as your own.

> (Quoted in Madame's account of the Sian kidnaping, *General Chiang Kai-shek*, p. 156)

The son by the first wife, Ching-kuo, was estranged from his father for a decade. A pronounced communist, he went to Russia when the civil war began, and remained there as an industrial engineer. On at least one occasion the Russian press quoted him in vitriolic denunciation of his father. But in 1937, after the United Front, young Ching-kuo returned to China, bringing with him a Russian wife and their son. Reconciliation followed, and Ching-kuo got the important job of Pacification Commissioner in Kiangsi province, where he is a liaison officer to the communist army.

Chiang's other son, known as Wei-ku, was adopted. His father, a Kuomintang politician, asked the Generalissimo to take care of him as if he were his own child. Wei-ku is said to be partly Japanese on his mother's side. He is about twenty, and is at present in Germany, where he was a student at the University of Berlin and a cadet in an officer's training school.

For Madame Chiang herself—and the remarkable family to which she belongs—we must await the next chapter.

Unity and Power

I have sketched several of the sources of Chiang Kai-shek's power. The most important is that he has become, for good or ill, the symbol of Chinese unity. The communists did not let him go because they loved him; they released him because they knew that he was indispensable to their cause, that no other man could hold the country together, give it some chance for a successful fight against Japan. Chiang is the symbol, the personification, the cement, of Chinese unity and resistance against Japan. The Japanese know this very well; they have announced that they will kill him if they capture him; they would do almost anything, even to the point of surrendering much territory, to get rid of him.

Chiang is no supreme bowlder across the path of history; he is no Lincoln, no Alexander. But probably he is the strongest Chinese individual since the third century B.C. when the Great Wall was built. And it is another Great Wall he is doing what he can to build—a wall to keep the Japanese out, to permit China an authentic national development, to allow China to belong to the Chinese. His friends say that he is happier now than they have ever known him, more poised, more confident. It is not hard to guess the reason. He is fighting a foreign invader, and not his own people.

Chapter XII
A Song of Soongs

*Putting new wine into old bottles is not an easy task. . . .
I have often spent one hundred per cent of effort to get one
per cent of result.*

— MADAME CHIANG KAI-SHEK

LET us sing a song of Soongs. This extraordinary family rules
China. It represents what is beyond doubt one of the most striking agglutinations of personal power in the world, since it includes
not only the three Soong sisters, but Generalissimo Chiang Kai-shek,
Dr. H. H. Kung (the prime minister of China), T. V. Soong (China's
best financial mind), and the spirit of Sun Yat-sen. The three Soong
girls make the Chinese republic what might almost be called a
matriarchy or a sorority. They accomplished the complex and unprecedented miracle of marrying a continent.

Nothing like this has been known in history before, and probably
nothing like it will ever happen again, though participation by women
in politics is an old Chinese tradition. Women have been politically
active in China since the Shang dynasty in 1550 B.C.; the last Manchu
ruler, the Empress Dowager, was a woman. But no one has ever
rivaled the present position of the Soongs. The origins of the family
are obscure; it is doubtful if the girls know the names of their grand-
parents. Official records are contradictory even on the immediate
background. *Who's Who in China* says that Madame Kung is the
daughter of "the late Mr. and Mrs. K. T. Soong, well known in
Chinese business circles," but the biography of Madame Sun gives
the father's initials as "C. J." It says of Madame Chiang that her
father was "a native of Kwangtung and her mother a native of
Kiangsu," but other information has it that the family originated in
Hainan, an island near French Indo-China.

The father, who called himself Charles Jones ("Charlie") Soong,
emigrated to the United States in 1879 when still a boy.[1] The family

[1] One story is that he was born a foundling and took the name Soong from
the captain of the clipper which brought him to the United States.

was not rich, reports to the contrary notwithstanding. Father Soong
had friends in America, and worked his way through school and then
Vanderbilt University. He was converted to Christianity, and became
a strong Methodist. He returned to China as an English teacher and
missionary, helped organize the first Y.M.C.A. in Shanghai, and
then made a living as a Bible manufacturer and salesman. Some fifty
years ago he married a lady named Ni, also a highly religious Methodist. Both Charlie Soong and his wife are dead. But they lived long
enough to see their amazing family flourish.

They had six children. The eldest daughter, Ai-ling, born it is
believed in 1888, is the present Madame H. H. Kung. Second, in
1890, came Ching-ling, who married Sun Yat-sen. Third came Mei-
ling (often anglicized into Mayling), born in 1898, the wife of
Chiang Kai-shek. Ai-ling means "Loving Mood," Ching-ling means
"Happy Mood," and Mei-ling "Beautiful Mood." There were three
sons, Tse-ven (T. V.) the eldest, Tse-liang (T. L.), and Tse-an
(T. A.). All were brought up in a religious atmosphere, all went to
missionary schools in China before completing their education in the
United States, and all—most importantly—were associated from
childhood with the Chinese revolution.

Politics in China is inveterately personal. A great deal depends on
the shifting flow of personal relationships—which is one reason why
the Soong sisters are so important. We begin with Madame Kung.

Madame H. H. Kung and Family

She is the most formidable of the Soongs; she is, in fact, one of the
most formidable women anywhere. A hard-willed creature, possessed
of demonic energy and great will-to-power, violently able, cunning,
and ambitious, she is as powerful a personality as any in China. It
would be an exaggeration to say that she dominates her husband, the
prime minister, completely; but her influence on him is obviously
profound. Her passionate interest is money. She is a first-rate
financier in her own right, and takes a fierce joy in business manipu-
lations and enterprises. To her shrewdness, her financial ability, the
growth of much of the great Soong fortune is attributed.

Madame Kung, like Madame Sun Yat-sen, was educated at the
Wesleyan College in Macon, Georgia. She returned to China, joined
the revolution, and became Dr. Sun's secretary. The story is that it
was she, not Madame Sun, to whom the great doctor first paid court;

but she married H. H. Kung instead. She met him on a trip to Japan, where he was secretary of the Tokyo Y.M.C.A. She was also a close friend of Chiang Kai-shek's. The Kungs have four children.

All Chinese revere their ancestors, and Dr. H. H. Kung, a stoutish, friendly, solid-looking person, has a special advantage in having an important one to revere—Confucius himself. He is a descendant of Confucius in an unbroken line that has persisted for seventy-five generations. So the Soongs, it may be said, married not only a continent; they married into the family of what might loosely be called the Chinese God. Dr. Kung, however, is a Christian. He went to Yale. For twenty years he has been an important figure in the Chinese revolution, and is now both prime minister of the national government and finance minister.

When I saw Dr. Kung I thought he had what seemed to be a rather wistful sense of the past. He would like to see China united, tranquil, gracious, under the tremendous heritage of its old civilization, and unperplexed by modern pressures. He talks in what seem almost anachronistic terms of restoration of the old gentry virtues, with China ruled by paternalism. He has little of the fierce modernism of his brother-in-law T. V. In 1937, he represented China at the Coronation of King George VI, and when the war started traveled all over Europe seeking credits.

None of the sisters—except when Madame Chiang Kai-shek was head of the air force—participates in public affairs officially. They work in the background. And the implacable Madame Kung's clique of rich and ambitious friends is sometimes resented by purists in Chinese affairs. There is talk of malign influence, of "squeeze." Efforts to abolish corruption in office have at times been unaccountably blocked. The Kungs are of great importance to the Generalissimo, and they know it. So does he. This is because they control the national finances, and in addition are independently very rich. When Chiang needs money—for political purposes, of course—it is to the Kungs that he must go. T. V. is rich too, and has often been minister of finance, but Chiang and T. V. don't always agree.

David Kung, the eldest son of the Kungs, became at the age of twenty-two the joint managing director of the Central Trust Company, which is the purchasing agent for government supplies. That such a highly important job should, in wartime, be given to such an extremely young man, naturally provoked much criticism. He had only just been graduated from St. John's University in Shanghai. Young David has the reputation of being a rather spoiled youngster. Once, the story goes, David was stopped by a traffic policeman; playfully the young man pulled out a small revolver and started shooting. No one was hurt, however.

Madame Kung is very close to Madame Chiang Kai-shek—which is not true of the next sister, Madame Sun Yat-sen.

A Woman of Important Virtue

Here is a great lady. Soong Ching-ling, the widow of Dr. Sun Yat-sen, at once a delicate and heroic figure, lives in virtual retirement now. If Madame Kung is the tigress of the Soong family, Madame Sun is a gazelle; if Madame Chiang is the glittering diamond in the Soong dynastic crown, then Madame Sun is other things: a hidden flower; a beautifully luminous bit of porcelain; a source of spiritual continuity and power; a shadow with flame behind it. She is beyond doubt the most important person in the family, because basically its power derived from her; had she not married the father of the revolution, the others could not have got so far.

Madame Sun is a small and graceful woman, with an infinitely lovely voice. She is also very beautiful. When I went to see her, especially since she has been outside the *grande ligne* of Chinese politics for a decade, I expected to find a sort of Queen Victoria, a resigned and perhaps forbidding figure, widow's weeds and all. But Madame Sun, even to-day, looks like a girl of twenty-eight. Her grace and vivacity, frail as she is, as well as the carved perfection of her features, gave an impression not of a historic revolutionary character, but of a young woman at the threshold of a career. Almost all Chinese look younger than their years; Madame Sun is no exception.

She, like Madame Kung, finished high school in Shanghai, and went to Wesleyan in Georgia. On her return to China she became Sun Yat-sen's secretary, and then married him. She was his affectionate companion until his death. When the Kuomintang split, Madame Sun stayed with the Left, believing that she thus performed the only possible service to her husband's memory; she joined the Hankow group, separated from her family, and went to Moscow when the Hankow government collapsed. She did not return to China for years, though she could have had any position for the asking. At great cost of physical hardship, she gave up everything for what she said her husband stood for. She gave up family, wealth, and privilege. Few women ever gave up more.

Nowadays in China Madame Sun hovers on the fringe of politics. Under an assumed name she lives in a secluded apartment building in Hong Kong, high on the cliff over that beautiful city, and sees few people. When the other sisters come to Hong Kong, they visit her, but they are not really close. She has not seen Chiang Kai-shek for years, because she believes that he betrayed the revolution. Her influence on her brother T. V. is, however, considerable. She is the inspiration of a contemporary left-wing movement in the Kuomintang, known as the National Salvation group, and she belongs to another organization, the China Defense League, devoted to fighting to a finish with Japan. Her friends have repeatedly offered to buy her a motorcar, to make it easier for her to live. She has refused to accept anything, and gives every penny she has to relief work.

After years of withdrawal Madame Sun became conspicuous early in 1937, when seven members of her National Salvation group were arrested in Shanghai, by agents of the national government, for their *anti*-Japanese activities. (This was, of course, before the war, when Chiang was ostensibly pursuing a course subservient to Japan.) The group, including one woman, was whisked away to Suchow for a secret trial. Madame Sun followed her friends there, and staged a sort of sit-down strike before the court, whereafter the prisoners were released.

By 1938, the United Front between Chiang and the communists had become concrete; which made it easier for Madame Sun to express herself again. She became a member of the Central Executive Committee of the Kuomintang. Vincent Sheean's *Personal History* contains a portrait of Madame Sun of great beauty and distinction.

Madame Chiang Kai-shek

"Was this the face that launched a thousand airships?"
—FRANCES GUNTHER

And now the diamond of the crown. Madame Chiang, the youngest, is the most brilliant of the three sisters, and the most conspicuous. She is exceptionally good-looking, though not so beautiful as Madame Sun; she is not, oddly enough, very photogenic, and is much better looking in life than in pictures. Also she is very *chic*. Madame Chiang, who went to Wellesley, and is perhaps a bit more Americanized than her sisters, gives the impression of an American woman of social rank and executive ability; one might almost say that she is like the president of a really first-rate American woman's club: alert, amusing, smoothly polished, full of graceful small talk, and enormously efficient. Like Madame Sun, she has beautiful hands, arms and ankles, and a lovely voice.

Madame Chiang, it should be said forthrightly, is not the "dictator" of China. She is not the single most important and powerful personage in China. She is not the uncrowned "empress" of 450,000,000 people. She does not "run" the Generalissimo. On the other hand, she is probably the *second* most important and powerful personage in China. She comes immediately after the Generalissimo in influence. She is China's No. 2 individual. This is partly because Chiang trusts her so deeply, and because her advice is good. He put her in charge of the air force because in the person of his wife, incontestably, he had trust. But she does not dominate him, or make his major decisions. He makes his own decisions. She is an adviser, a counselor, an indispensable agent for contact with foreigners and foreign opinion, a collaborator. I asked her once to what she attributed the powers of the Generalissimo. (Her reply was, interestingly enough, "His feeling of duty to the Chinese people.") My wife laughed, pointed to her, and said "You!" It is all but impossible to describe the grimace that Madame Chiang then made, compounded at once of pleasure at the compliment, denial of it, horror that the idea should be expressed, and amusement.

She has a highly western mind. This is one of her strengths, especially in association with Chiang, who is exceedingly Chinese in temperament. W. H. Donald once paid her the best compliment at his command: "She thinks just like a man!" (Yet, withal, she is very feminine; for instance she took her *amah*, maid, with her to Sian, despite the strenuous ardors of that trip.) She has a great sense of fundamentals, a sense of structure; she likes to look at engineering works and the like; when she was in Hong Kong recently she admired the great walls holding up the cliff, and said she wished Chiang could see and admire them too.

Yet, for all her admirable capacity for administration, it seems that she lacks *political* sense. Her friends say that she grasped the significance of Sian more quickly than did her husband, but she talks about the communists, not merely with distaste which would be understandable enough, but with a curious glib lack of comprehension. She did not appear at all to understand the significance of the Young Marshal's Eight Points, the program presented to Chiang by the mutineers. An odd point is that she could never bring herself to read Edgar Snow's *Red Star Over China,* one of the most valuably informative books on China ever written, because she thought it presented only one side.[2] Some people say that—since she was educated in America from childhood—she does not know China "well."

Her positive qualities are many. She has wit and a lively sense of phrase. "Not only God but everybody else is on the side of the big battalions," she wrote once. One of her epigrams is worth recording, that too many foreigners think that "in China the men wear the skirts, and the women the trousers." She is very quick. The Young Marshal complained to her that Chiang, his captive, was scolding him. Madame instantly replied that "the Generalissimo only scolds people of whom he has hopes." When I saw Chiang, he asked about Hitler, and I said that I thought Hitler wanted a "digestive interval." Madame asked flashingly who would proffer "international soda mints" to assist the process of digestion.

Her devotion to China as well as to Chiang, and her energy, her lively courage, are beyond dispute. She goes everywhere; she does everything; she is like Mrs. Roosevelt. When an air raid comes, Madame Chiang drives up to the scene, sometimes in slacks or any costume, to superintend care of the wounded. Only once have her friends seen her a trifle nervous—when she was returning to Hankow by plane, with the radio out of order, and the pilot pushing up to 17,000 feet to get bearings from the sun, although ice kept breaking from the propeller and smashing against the windows of the plane.

Her egoism is, as is proper enough, considerable. She says, for instance, that the Sian kidnaping would not have happened if she had been present, and indeed she is probably right. (She was ill at the time; it was the only considerable flight Chiang ever took without her.)

The military folk in Hankow assert that she is quicker to understand

---

[2] A recent book Madame Chiang enjoyed was Stuart Chase's "The Tyranny of Words." Magazines she subscribes to are the *Atlantic Monthly,* the *Ladies' Home Journal, Asia, Reader's Digest, Good Housekeeping, Harper's Magazine,* and the *Forum.* Occasionally she sees the *Contemporary Review* (London), *New Statesman* (London), the *Saturday Evening Post* and the *New York Nation.*

technical problems than the Generalissimo. If, for instance, an adviser tells Chiang that a division of troops cannot reach a certain point in a given time, he is apt stubbornly to refuse to accept the fact, if it is inconvenient to his aims. But Madame understands at once—usually.

Her achievements have been considerable, especially in fostering rehabilitation work in rural areas, in encouraging development of simplified language instruction, and in the creation of the New Life Movement. This movement, which borrows largely from the Y.M.C.A., was an attempt during the days of civil war to steal Red thunder by a positive program of self-help and betterment. Villagers are organized, children are instructed, with emphasis on "orderliness, cleanliness, diligence, and propriety." Mass meetings are held all over China, with slogans repeating simple ethical and hygienic principles, like "Don't crowd; keep in line"; "Don't spit—cleanliness prevents disease," and "Avoid wine, women, and gambling." Madame thinks the New Life Movement is the biggest thing the Kuomintang has done.

Her "last" message to Chiang at Sian, sent by T. V., expresses a good deal of her character: "Should T. V. fail to return within three days I will come to Shensi to live and die with you." (Chiang, reading this, records, "My eyes got wet.") But Madame did not wait the stipulated three days; she arrived the next afternoon to make her husband's cause, his life, her own.

The Generalissimo asserts that he has one bone to pick with Donald—that Donald has taught Madame to swear. But the oath has seldom exceeded a mild "Damfool!"

T. V.

Of all the Soongs T. V. is probably the most complex in character. Stocky, glossy, with hair stiffly *en brosse*; diffident and direct by turn; not afraid to be rude, and intolerant of bores; industrious and honest as the day; stubborn, sometimes vain; enormously competent, and the best financier China has ever produced; an intellectual and a liberal who has lately swung far to the Left—T. V. presents a variety of qualities. He went to Harvard, then to Columbia, where he was a brilliant Ph.D. in economics. He has never written anything, because he fears his opinions may change, and is horrified to recall what he might have written a decade ago.

T. V. was finance minister for nine years until 1933. He was an unequivocal foe of graft and corruption in administration; he fought with a mop, cleaning up. His record was superb; he put Chinese finances on a western basis, introduced the budget system, abolished domestic tariff barriers like the *likin*, got taxes even out of such warlords as Han Fu-chu, established a central bank, and unified the currency. He left the finance ministry largely because Chiang resented the purse strings being in his hands; he continually sought to reduce military expenditure, which Chiang opposed. These brothers-in-law have not always been good friends. T. V. violently disagreed with Chiang's early policy of conciliation to the Japanese.

Of all Chinese politicians, indeed, T. V. is the one with the most consistent and honorable record of opposition to Japan. He put his own Salt Gabelle troops into the fighting in Shanghai in 1932, when Chiang stayed aloof; they were annihilated. The story is that, when the Chinese determined to resist Japan in Shanghai in 1937, the generals held their first secret conference in T. V.'s house. The Japanese hate him, especially since he became a chief pillar of the United Front.

Not everybody likes T. V. But there are few in China who do not respect him.

.   .   .   .

T. L. Soong, the next brother, went to Vanderbilt, like his father. He is a very prosperous young man who, until the war, paid little attention to politics; during the war he took charge of transportation of war materials and supplies from Kwangtung to the front, as director of the Southwest Import and Export Bureau, a highly important post. He has also served on the Whampoa Conservancy Board and as a director of the Central Bank of China. Of T. A. Soong, the youngest brother, little is known. He was a student of exceptional brilliance at Harvard, and for a time was director of the Salt Monopoly.

T. V., at present in charge of the Chinese air force—note how this remarkable family keeps the key jobs in its hands—likes to assert that he is comparatively poor, though the family fortune *in toto* is the biggest in China by far. He has told friends that he would rather be penniless under the communists than a millionaire under Japan. T. L. has a considerable fortune also. But most of the family money is believed to reside in the Kung branch. The Kung wealth alone is esti-

mated by competent observers to be in the neighborhood of 80,000,000
Chinese dollars.

Don

"A faithful friend is the medicine of life."
—ECCLESIASTICUS, VI, 16.

W. H. Donald is not, it goes without saying, a member of the
Soong family. But no picture of the fountainhead of China would be
complete without him. He is a most extraordinary human being.

Donald has saved the lives of various Chinese ambassadors; he
helped overthrow the Manchus, and with his own hands dragged the
guns into position that blew them out of Nanking; thirty years ago
he helped Madame Chiang and her sisters adjust their pigtails; he
wrote several of Sun Yat-sen's early proclamations; he first revealed
Japan's "Twenty-one Demands" on China, and almost single-handed
brought China into the World War in 1917; he cured the Young
Marshal of the dope habit, and held the balance between the Young
Marshal and the Generalissimo at Sian; he sings lullabies to children
of missionaries; he helped unseat the usurper Yuan Shih-kai in
Peking in the counter-revolution of 1916; he has been matchmaker
to Chinese politicians, confidant to generals, handyman to warlords,
and the bottomless receptacle of more news, information, chitchat,
and, above all, state secrets, than any foreigner who ever lived in
China.

The incredible Donald, let it be said further, speaks no single word
of Chinese. He has never bothered to learn the Chinese for as much
as "Please" or "Be damned to you." He never touches Chinese food
—after more than thirty years in China! He asks no questions and
requests no favors. He talks like the wind and never betrays a confidence. He is an incomparable raconteur—who practically never goes
to dinner parties. He is a recluse—who has a thousand friends.

As fantastic as anything about Donald is the manner of his arrival
in China. He was born in Australia in 1875; he decided early to
become a newspaper man. One morning thirty-four years ago, arriving in his office on the *Sydney Daily Telegraph*, he found a letter
from an editor in Hong Kong, offering him a job and notifying him
that $600 had been transferred to a Sydney bank for traveling ex-
penses to Hong Kong. Donald was bewildered. He had never heard
of the Hong Kong editor. He asked his own editor for advice. His

own editor said, "Maybe it's a hoax. Go to the bank. If the money is there, then it's real. And go to Hong Kong if you wish." Donald found the money and shipped for Hong Kong. He went to his new boss, who said, "Good day, Mr. Donald, I shall be obliged if you start work at once. Your desk is in that corner." Still bewildered, Donald asked, "Would you mind telling me first why you hired me?" The editor replied, "Easy. Seven years ago I asked a friend, who travels incessantly around the world, to notify me immediately if he ever found a newspaper man who doesn't drink. Seven years passed. A few weeks ago I received a cable from him. '*At last have found your man. His name is Donald, and he works on the Sydney Telegraph.*' So I wrote to you. Thank you for coming. Your desk is right there."

And indeed Donald, who is loquaciously convivial, has never touched a drop of alcohol in his life.

Donald is ruddy, with big glasses; upright and a trifle stout; white-haired, bright-cheeked; he is kind, gusty, forthright, and full of vitality and laughter. He has a retentive and anecdotal mind; his sense of humor is famous on several continents, and he has never forgotten anything. He is blunt in character, very cheery, and he insists on finishing any story he begins.

Donald worked for a while on the Hong Kong paper, then turned to bigger fields. He was *New York Herald* correspondent for a time, and then became so fascinated by the Chinese that he dropped his foreign connections, except for occasional special work. He joined the revolution at about the same time the Soongs did. From the beginning he had a very special capacity to gain the confidence of people. Some years ago he established the Chinese Government Bureau of Economic Information; this paid his living expenses, and it still exists. More than a modest living he has never asked for. He eats with the Chiangs every day—they have to cook foreign food for him—but he does not live in their house, and has no official title as Chiang's adviser; indeed, he refuses to admit that he is his adviser.

In 1928 Donald was "adopted" by the Young Marshal, Chang Hsueh-liang,[3] the son of the Manchurian warlord, Chang Tso-lin. Donald made the Young Marshal over. He negotiated his rapprochement with Chiang Kai-shek in 1929-30, took him to Europe, and for some years was the Young Marshal's "man." Then, in 1934, he entered the service of Chiang Kai-shek. It happened in this manner. The

[3] Of this bizarre young man we shall hear later in Chapter XIV.

Young Marshal was quarreling with the Generalissimo. He called him every name under the sun. Donald watched attentively as Madame listened and translated. He had known Madame all his life, but for some years had not been in close touch with her. He was impressed and amazed at her reaction to the Young Marshal's furious tornado of objurgation; he could hardly believe her courage when she did not tone it down. They began to work together—Chiang, Madame, Chang, and Donald. Immediately Donald began to harp on his favorite theme, the necessity of making China strong, the necessity to wipe out inefficiency, corruption, defeatism. The Generalissimo listened and agreed. Donald gave up his plan of leaving China. A few days later Madame, overwhelmed with routine work, with letters piled high on her desk and an immense amount of secretarial detail to handle, turned to Donald and said, "Won't you join us, won't you help *me*?" Donald said Yes, and has been their friend and ally ever since.

Donald's great strength is that he has no ax to grind. He asks nothing. He is free to quit any day—and sometimes threatens to. He tells the Generalissimo exactly what is in his mind, without fuss or hesitation; he is the only man in China who can say No to Chiang —and he says it repeatedly. He is a kind of "No man"—though not like Ulysses to Polyphemus—and Chiang respects him for his fearlessness.

Donald pays scant attention to Chinese ritual or sensitiveness. He raises hell with anybody. He is the greatest enemy of Face in China. He scoffs at the purists who try to pronounce Chinese words in Chinese fashion. No "Jiahng Gai-shek" for him. He pronounces it still in an exaggeratedly foreign manner, "Cheeee-ang Kai-shek," and so on.

He was never ill in his life till sixty, when he had a serious pneumonia after a tonsillectomy. Thereafter he was in bed for six months with a mysterious stomach malady. He is a complete fatalist. Once his airplane had a forced landing in a snowy field near Sian. Donald had heard one motor splutter and then fail. The pilot, after the landing, found him stretched out in the sofa the plane carries. Donald had never budged. After inspecting the situation the pilot said that he had perhaps one chance in three of getting off again on that one motor. Donald said, "Go ahead."

He noticed that the day the Generalissimo was released at Sian happened to be Christmas. (There were a few other things to think about.) Madame Chiang describes touchingly how "Don" managed to find a tree and ornaments and a few gifts, and how he used his own golf socks for Christmas stockings. He is blindly devoted to Madame Chiang.

He forthrightly denounced the Nanking generals after the kidnaping, asserting that Chiang was in much greater danger from these somewhat precipitous folk—Chiang's own men who wanted to get his job—than from the Young Marshal and the Reds. The generals were furious, and demanded that he be expelled from China. Chiang refused to let him go. For seven months Donald and the minister of war, General Ho Ying-chin, never exchanged a word.

Donald bought a small yacht in 1933, intending to leave China. But just before he planned to go, he met Madame Chiang. He has scarcely ever seen the yacht. It is lying empty in Shanghai harbor. Donald built a huge desk in it, on which he planned to write his memoirs. If he ever does, they will be remembered. In 1939, Donald——

But one could proceed for a whole book writing about Donald alone.

Chapter XIII

The Chinese Reds, Who Wear Blue

~~~~~~~~~~~~~~~~~~~~~~~~~~~~~~~~

Land to those who till it.—DR. SUN YAT-SEN

THE so-called "Red" area is a new Chinese world. Here is China alight and alive. The Chinese Red Army, since 1938 incorporated into the national forces as the "Eighth Route Army," fights in the north, and its redoubtable guerrillas are an essential item in the national struggle. But to think of the Chinese Reds merely as guerrilla Robin Hoods is to miss the point. Overwhelmingly their immediate preoccupation and task is to lick Japan. Behind that is a vision of a new China, powerful, forward-looking, incorruptible, and free. Already, in spite of the incessant daily pressure of warfare, and the necessarily limited materials they work with, the Reds have done things in education and social reform to make you blink.

By all-China standards the achievement is local, of course; the Red region is severely circumscribed. The Eighth Route Army is impregnable in Shensi, has occupied much of Shansi, and is pushing hard in Hopei and Honan. That is all, though it is a good deal. But listen to the chairman of the Chinese Soviet government, Mao Tsetung, quoted with admiration by the London *Times*, which does not ordinarily admire communists. Above all, Mao has vision. The *Times* correspondent asked him what he thought the new China should be. Mao replied:

Every man has food to eat and clothes to wear. Every man understands the rights and duties of citizenship and has a fair chance of education and amusement. The marriage customs are to be reformed, roads built, industry developed, a six-hour day established. There is no foreign aggression. No man oppresses another. There is equality and freedom and universal love. Together all build the peace of the world.

I have sketched briefly the origin of the Chinese Soviets. Chiang Kai-shek, as noted above, chased the left wing Kuomintang out of Hankow in 1927; the Leftists who escaped the White Terror organized a vestigial Red government in Kiangsi. Its power spread till it commanded a large area, no matter how hard Chiang fought to beat it down. Chiang began his long series of "pacification operations" and "extermination" campaigns, which were extraordinarily costly in men and wealth; he put 900,000 men in the field at last, and fought five wars. To kill a single Red, Edgar Snow[1] calculates, the Generalissimo had to spend $80,000. The Kiangsi Soviet held out for seven years, till 1934, when things finally got too hot. The Reds, beleaguered, had to move. With nice Chinese practicality they decided to move their entire "nation." Thus the celebrated "Long March," one of the most extraordinary feats in modern annals.

It began in October, 1934, in Kiangsi which is southwest of Shanghai; it ended a year later in Yenan in Shensi, far to the west of Peking. The Reds began with 100,000 men; they finished with 50,000. They marched 6,000 miles, across twelve different provinces; a remote parallel would be the march of a European army from Constantinople to Stockholm by way of Sicily and Spain. From the moment when, making the most scrupulous preparations, they broke Chiang's blockade and escaped at night from their Kiangsi capital, till their final arrival in Yenan, diminished in number and exhausted, but intact, 368 days later, they had to fight every mile of the way. The official record of the Long March shows fifteen major battles, three hundred skirmishes. There were one hundred days of "rest," 268 of actual movement, which means an average speed for the entire march of fifteen miles per day. Military experts are staggered by these figures. The Reds had to traverse incredibly fractious and difficult country, some of it inhabited by aborigines and virtually unknown; they climbed eighteen mountain ranges, occupied sixty-two cities, and crossed half a dozen rivers. They carried radio, a printing press, and their archives. Once Chiang Kai-shek thought he had finally trapped and surrounded them. The Generalissimo does not give way to emotion often, but near the Tatu River he burst out, "Now we have them!" The Reds managed to cross the Tatu and escape, however, with Chiang's breath on their heels. He thought the Long March would be the Red funeral march. It almost turned out to be a funeral march for *him*.

So, surviving its ordeal, the Red Army arrived in the isolated northwest. At Yenan in Shensi it joined other communists who had

[1] Anyone who writes of the Chinese communists must be indebted to Edgar Snow, his wife Nym Wales, and Miss Agnes Smedley. Snow's *Red Star Over China* is one of the best books of historical journalism ever written.

come from Honan, and established a new Soviet. It proliferated powerfully, set up an "independent" state, declared war on Japan, and became one of the most interesting communities in the world. It is still there. The Generalissimo never seriously attacked the Reds again. In 1936 came the Sian kidnaping. The Reds intervened in this fantastic imbroglio, used their influence to let Chiang go scotfree, and made a United Front with him. From this event all subsequent history of China derives. It united China—in a manner of speaking—after ten years of civil war—and made full-dress attack by Japan inevitable, since Japan had perforce to prevent Chinese unification at any cost.

The Red Napoleons

The leaders of the Chinese Soviets are Mao Tse-tung and Chu Teh. They are associated so closely that for a long time people thought they were the same man; one heard of the famous "Red general" Mao-Chu, or Chu-Mao. Mao Tse-tung (pronounced roughly "Mow Tzuh-doong"), the chairman of the Central Executive Committee of the communist party, is political chief. General Chu Teh ("Joo Duh") is military leader. An odd point is that "Chu Teh" literally means—Red Virtue!

The two are intimately close friends, but differ widely in character and attributes. They complement each other nicely. Mao is a philosopher, an intellectual; Chu Teh is an executive, a soldier. Mao, I heard it said, is the Red brain, Chu Teh the Red heart. A calm man, of peasant stock, Mao is a builder, a dreamer, a creator; he has never been outside China. Chu Teh, much warmer in temperament, less aloof, has traveled widely; he has great human quality, and people talk of him as they might talk of Lincoln. Mao could hold his own anywhere among Chinese intellectuals; Chu Teh talks little. Both have a considerable sense of humor, though Mao's is more sardonic; both have highly modern minds. Mao, perhaps, is the greater man; but he would not be where he is had not Chu Teh developed and led his unique army. I have heard Mao described as equal intellectually to Lenin.

Mao Tse-tung was born in 1893 in a village in Hunan. His father was a peasant, and he began to work at the age of six on the small family farm. His mother was a considerate woman, his father exceptionally severe; Mao records that he was never allowed eggs or meat, though the other farm boys had these luxuries occasionally. He had remarkable strength of character and ambition, and a fierce urgency for education; he struggled to go to school, and at seventeen tramped alone to the near-by city of Changsha where there was an academy. Came a tremendous event: he saw for the first time a map of the world. He pored over it gluttonously. He writes, "I went to the library in the morning when it opened. At noon I paused only long enough to buy and consume two rice cakes, which were my daily lunch. I stayed in the library every day reading until it closed." He studied Adam Smith, Darwin, Spencer, Mill. One book that influenced him was called *Great Heroes of the World*, which contained biographies of Napoleon, Peter the Great, Rousseau. He read about the American Revolution and came across a pregnant sentence: "After eight years of difficult war, Washington won victory and built up his nation."[2]

Mao began to write, turned to journalism, and found himself on the threshold of politics. With his Chinese practicality, he put an advertisement in the Changsha newspaper, asking that "hardened and determined" young men interested in patriotism and politics get in touch with him. Changsha became too small for him. He had seven dollars. He bought shoes and an umbrella, and set out to see the world. His instincts were predominantly nationalist at first; he wanted to free China from foreign domination. Imperialism, he proceeded to see, was inextricably associated with capitalism, and he became a socialist. His revolutionary career began in 1927, when he was appointed president of the first Chinese Peasants Union; his rise was rapid, and by 1930 he was chairman of the Workers and Peasants Revolutionary Committee. Then came the Long March; the great years began. Chiang Kai-shek offered a reward of $250,000 (Chinese) for him, dead or alive; his first wife and sister were caught and executed. His present wife—a typical enough touch—learned many details of his life for the first time when, in her company, he dictated his autobiography to Edgar Snow. She was severely wounded during the Long March, when she walked 6,000 miles.

Chu Teh's history is remarkably different in detail, though the same sting of nationalism-*cum*-socialism flavors it. He is about fifty, and was born in Szechwan. I have heard experienced western military men call him, not merely "the best officer in China," but a military figure "as generous as Lee, as stubborn as Grant, as competent as

[2] Snow, *Red Star Over China*, p. 121.

Wellington." Chu Teh is a friendly, quiet man, gentle and full of heart. One hears of the "smiling Chinese"; he is one of the smilingest, if that is a word, in China. I have never seen a photograph of him without a broad, gleaming, confident, gum-exposing grin. Yet for ten years the price on his head was, like that on Mao, $250,000. He and Mao topped the market.

Chu Teh was not a poor boy. Quite the contrary. He came of a rich land-owning family, he was well-educated (for a time at Göttingen in Germany), he passed his youth—as he himself admits—in "luxury and dissipation." He had concubines; he smoked opium (and later drastically cured himself of the habit); he was a fashionable young officer. The 1927 revolution came; it hit him like a mallet on the head. He went to Moscow, studied Marxism, and dropped his career as an official in Yunnan. He joined the communists, showed extraordinary military competence, and in 1931 was unanimously elected commander-in-chief of the Red Army by the first Chinese Soviet Congress. Next to revolution and the Red Army, his great passion is basketball.

Other Eighth Route Army leaders have had remarkable careers. It is a pity to have to compress them in a paragraph or two. About each a chapter might easily be written. There is, for instance, the shrewd and competent Chou En-lai ("Jo En-lie"), who is No. 1 to Mao on the political side, and who now represents the communists at the Generalissimo's headquarters. A good man for the job: since it was he, one of the chief actors in the Sian kidnaping, who saved Chiang's life. When, in Hankow later, I asked him why, he said it was because Chiang was the one person indispensable to United China. I asked him also what guarantee the communists had that they might not be betrayed by the Kuomintang when the war was over; he said that education among the masses, realization during the war that the communists fought well against Japan, and were real patriots, would keep them safe. Chou En-lai was the son of a Mandarin (official), and was educated—in part at foreign mission schools—to be a scholar. He went to France, and helped organize Chinese communists abroad. In the early revolution he was secretary of the Whampoa Military School at Canton, where Chiang Kai-shek and General Bluecher trained officers. Later Chiang put $100,000 on his head. Chou En-lai is about forty-one.

The ranking military man after Chu Teh is General Peng Teh-huai, the field commander. He is a young man, only thirty-seven, and a professional officer. But his origins were humble; he told Snow how, at the age of nine, he was tossed into the street alone, because he had dared to kick over his grandmother's tray of opium, and was there-upon (!) sentenced to death by a family council. "My life was spared," General Peng relates, "but I had to leave home. I was nine at the time, it was cold October, and I owned nothing but my coat and trousers." A man of great endurance, General Peng walked almost the whole of the Long March, though as second-in-command he was entitled to a horse. In 1928 his wife disappeared in the revolutionary turmoil; isolated in Kiangsi or Shensi, he has not seen her since.

A terrific fellow is General Ho Lung, the most Robin Hood-like of all. He was one of the earliest Red organizers, and he stuck it out in Honan even after the Long March started. He was rich, and gave up a fortune of $5,000,000 to join the Reds. . . . Another notable character is General Hsu Hai-tung, born a coolie. For years $100,000 was on his head, and *sixty-six* members of his family in Hupeh were executed by the Kuomintang, which sought to exterminate the entire Hsu clan, even babies. General Hsu has been wounded eight times. . . . Another Hsu is Hsu Teh-lih, the Red minister of education, who cut off his finger as a token to Mao in the early days, and wrote his allegiance in his own blood. . . . General Tsen Ken is only thirty-two; he is a Whampoa graduate, once commanded Chiang Kai-shek's bodyguard, once saved his life. He was trapped and arrested in Shanghai when he joined the Reds, but the Generalissimo, in gratitude, let him go.

How Red Are the Reds?

Not very, by our standards. The party calls itself communist, true; it subscribes to Marxist doctrine, and organizes itself on the Soviet model. But if you ask a Red Army chieftain if he has plans or even desires for the nationalization of Chinese production, which is what communism would in theory entail, he looks at you almost bewildered. Any such prospect is for the remote future. Mao is a realist. In his own words: "For a people being deprived of its national freedom, the revolutionary task is not immediate socialism, but the struggle for independence. We cannot even discuss communism if we are robbed of a country in which to practice it."[3] Trotskyists, kindly note.

What the Chinese Reds do stand for is agrarian reform. The move-

[3] Snow, ibid., p. 415.

ment is not communism, in that it does not even advocate nationalization of the land; what it advocates is a tremendous land reform with land assigned—not to the state—but to the peasants themselves. Even so, in most Red areas, land has not been actually expropriated by the peasants; landlordism is attacked, but the landlords have not been liquidated. There has been little confiscation. Rents, however, have been reduced twenty-five percent, a moratorium on debts declared, and interest cut to one percent. Chinese communism is "rural equalitarianism," with the object of freeing the land from the terrible burden of corrupt and absentee landlords and from the stifling, unimaginable agrarian debt.

There are no Russian advisers or officials with the Chinese Red Army, nor do Russian supplies reach it in any quantity. Back in 1923 and 1924, when Bluecher worked at Canton, Borodin at Hankow, there was profound Russian influence in China, as we know. To-day it is slight in China proper, though considerable in Outer Mongolia and Turkestan. The Chinese Soviets run their own show. They are autonomous. On the other hand, the Chinese communist party is an "official" communist party, and as such—at a remote distance—is associated with the Third Internationale, and the Red constitution calls the U.S.S.R. its "loyal ally."

The chief non-military manifestations of the Chinese reds in their northwestern stronghold have been social and cultural. There is a Red Academy under the veteran soldier-teacher Lin Piao, a former Whampoa cadet; a publishing house employs 800 men and issues a stream of textbooks; literacy in the Red Army is uniquely high. Education—education above all—more and better education—is the motto. Not satisfied with using simplified Mandarin, the communists are flirting with Romanization of the language. Opium is barred, cooperatives are encouraged, child marriages forbidden, radio worshiped, athletics stimulated, and old-style Confucianism scorned.

Red Army Technique

The main concept of the Eighth Route Army is that it belongs indissolubly to the people. This gives it a morale, a solidarity, a patriotism, unmatched by any other Chinese army, though Chiang Kai-shek's newly trained divisions run it close. It is unbelievably advanced compared to the old provincial armies. The Reds fight because they are defending their country and their ideals, not because they are paid to do so. Indeed, privates get only $1.00 (Chinese) per month; Chu Teh himself, at the top, gets exactly $6.00 (Chinese), or 96 cents. There is no "squeeze," and no war lord can sell anybody out.

The officers, called simply "leaders," have no distinguishing rank. Fighters are in three categories, all volunteers. First come troops of the line, most of them hardened by prodigious service in the civil wars; next the "Volunteers" or "Partisans," who are the reserve; finally the people themselves—technically nonbelligerent—in occupied areas, who coöperate with the troops and are an essential item in Red strategy.

Officers are very accessible, and eat the same food as the troops; they may have individual sleeping quarters if their work demands it. Any private may see Chu Teh to present a grievance or for any other reason. Discipline is strict, but is "by persuasion." There are three categories of punishment: (1) confinement to quarters, (2) public rebuke and self-criticism, (3) expulsion from the army. The army takes prisoners (as against the Japanese custom of shooting them), and tries to convert them. Soldiers are taught a few words of Japanese, and when they go into action they shout at the Japanese troops, "Join us! Kill your officers." The Red Army is unique in that it has no prostitutes, no camp followers.

The great strength of the Red Army is in guerrilla warfare, at which it is marvelously adept. It retreats when the Japanese advance, and advances when the Japanese retreat; it harries Japanese communications, and raises the country behind them; it cuts railways, burns villages, traps isolated columns, bites exposed flanks—and then melts into the country again. It is delighted, actually, when the Japanese take a considerable town, because it can get its own adherents out, then isolate the town and starve the Japanese. "Foreigners," a Red chieftain says, "pay far too much attention to towns."

When warfare spread after 1937, new Red or semi-Red armies were organized in other districts on the Eighth Route model, for instance, the Fourth Route Army in Anhwei and Kiangsi under the redoubtable communist General Han Ying, who had fought in this area for years. Guerrillas, mostly communist, pinched off parts of Chekiang in 1938, and fought fiercely at the gates of Shanghai and Nanking, a thousand miles behind the Japanese front lines. For a time this "front" was not more than a mile or two from the French Concession in Shanghai. In the Tientsin-Peking area guerrillas persistently attacked and disorganized communications; to run a train 150 miles to Paotingfu became a perilous adventure.[4] In Hopei, early in 1939, a well-developed communist government was functioning *inside* the Japanese occupied area; a new Red state, like the one in Shensi, with 4,000 square miles and 7,000,000 people, became a big island in "Japanese" territory.

United Front Problems

The Eighth Route Army and the other communist-guerrilla armies are no longer independent forces in theory. They have been "absorbed" (again in theory) by the Chinese national forces, with Chiang Kai-shek as their supreme commander. This was part of the United Front arrangement after the Sian kidnaping. The communists refused to dissolve their party, but they agreed that the Red Army should lose its identity, which nowadays wears the blue uniform of the Kuomintang.

Thus the communist party still exists, de facto. But the Kuomintang has never abrogated its outlawry of the communist party, and technically communism in China is still a crime punishable by death. The Kuomintang, de jure, is the only political party in China, but continually the communists are allowed to increase their membership. This anomalous situation produced considerable dissatisfaction and a perpetual struggle for power within the United Front. Chiang met Chu Teh for the first time in 1937; Chu Teh flew down from Shensi to see him again late in 1938. In 1939 the United Front is still operating fairly smoothly, but anti-Red pressure by Kuomintang conservatives remains a serious problem.

Two additional items should be noted. One is that the Japanese, who say that they waged war to "save" China from communism, have served to strengthen it. Chinese communists now hold a much greater area of China than they ever held before, and are better organized, more deeply intrenched. Second, Chiang Kai-shek, if he wins the war, will almost certainly face extension of communist influence which the war promoted. Communist aim in regard to land reform has spread widely and is imitated widely, and the Generalissimo must pay his debt by reckoning with it.

[4] The canny Chinese do not merely destroy the rails, but remove and *bury* them, so that the Japanese cannot repair and reuse the metal.

Chapter XIV
Young Marshal at Sian

~~~~~~~~~~~~~~~~~~~~~~~~~~~~~~~~~~~~~

The commander of the forces of a large state may be carried off, but the will of even a common man cannot be taken from him.

—CONFUCIUS

THE Young Marshal, Chang Hsueh-liang (pronounced roughly "Jong Shweh-liahng"), is a marvelous psychological puzzle. I have mentioned several baffling characters in this book, like Prince Konoye, and soon we will have others, for instance Mr. Gandhi. Of them all, I should put the Young Marshal first from the point of view of purely personal interest. He has little political importance at the moment, but so long as he is alive he is fascinatingly unpredictable. Young Marshal Chang Hsueh-liang is, I think, the most difficult, the most refractory, the most engaging human being I have to write about.

Consider his looks. Like so many Chinese, he has great physical charm and intense animal magnetism. There is electricity in this man's supple finger. Yet he is ugly. The wide, loose, sensual lips; the nose un-Chinese and beaked; the disdainful but appealing big eyes; the humor, the reserve, the sophistication in his voice; his poised, careful, wary gait—all this marks an exceptional personality. He has been unbelievably weak, and then unbelievably powerful. The gamut he runs is shadowy and long.

The Young Marshal inherited the domain of his father, the great Chang Tso-lin, in 1928. None of his generals thought that this narcotized youngster could hold Manchuria. The two most ambitious and corrupt were Yang Yu-tin and Chang Yun-hui. Both fawned on the new ruler, both were willing to unseat him. And the Young Marshal suspected them of complicity in the murder of his father. He invited them to dinner, entertained them regally, and with the coffee had them taken out and calmly shot. He then gave $100,000 each to their widows, a generous man.

The story is that, until the last moment, young Chang did not decide whether to kill his two generals or not. That afternoon he spent some hours tossing a silver dollar up and down; heads I shoot them, tails I don't. He couldn't make up his mind. He called in his wife, a pretty girl, and asked her to witness the last throw. It came tails. Chang was dissatisfied. He said he would try again. Finally heads came up. He ordered the execution, happy. Then he tossed the lucky dollar in a big chest, as a souvenir, and locked the chest. Two years later the Japanese, as we know, took Manchuria. They sent the Young Marshal all his belongings, except that chest.

The Young Fellow

Those who know him well call him the Young "Fellow," and his courtesy name is Han Ching. He was born in Mukden in 1898. He is impish and impulsive. His name means, according to one translation, "Learning to be Virtuous"; in his early campaign he once pursued a bandit with the identical name, whereupon he decided that, though he would retain this translation for his own name, the identical name for the bandit should be translated as "Dirty Wolf."

He is a stanch fellow. He has all the courage in the world, and his common sense—in some respects—is almost startling. Royal Leonard, who was his private pilot before entering the Generalissimo's service, found him a highly impetuous aviator. He invented a new method for determining the direction of the wind; he would order the plane to fly so low that frightened sheep would kick up dust, which the wind carried. Then he invented a signal system new to aviation, whereby his troops threw themselves on the ground as he approached, and with their bodies spelled out words and messages.

The Young Marshal has always been extremely sociable, and he likes his friends. They are, however, sometimes alarmed when he plays bridge and draws a revolver to indicate the seriousness of his bidding. He loves bridge, golf, tennis, and companionship. Once, while he was reviewing troops, an American newspaperman who was his guest fell off his horse and floundered in the mud. Instantly the Young Marshal dived into the mud too, ruining his white uniform, because he did not want his guests to be embarrassed. Their Face was his.

Chang Tso-lin, whom we have already described, trained him for rule from an early age. When he was a youngster Chang Tso-lin took him to pay obeisance to the Prince Regent. The Young Marshal, a democrat then as now, refused to kowtow, and merely shook hands. Chang Tso-lin was impressed at the irreverent courage of his son, but beat him soundly. "I have no brains," the Young Marshal moaned.

For years he was very rich. An American friend, James C. Elder, took care of his investments. When the Japanese kicked his government out of Manchuria in 1931 (he himself was absent during the Mukden incident, ill in Peking), they sent some of his property after him, but not all by any means. To-day the Japanese use his Mukden house for breeding police dogs.

In about 1928 the Young Marshal came strongly under the influence of another westerner, W. H. Donald, who "adopted" him and for five years took care of him like a son. At that time Chang was taking opium. He sought a cure, and fell into the hands of an unscrupulous doctor who, pretending to wean him away from opium, surreptitiously gave him heroin instead, an infinitely more dangerous drug. This was a Japanese idea; they thought they could make use of the Young Marshal, and wanted him to be pliable. Donald, rugged, cheerful, vehement, swept the drugs away. He put the Young Marshal in hospital,[1] saw to it that he had a real cure, made him a new man.

The Japanese are not fond of Chang Hsueh-liang, though once they gave him the Order of the Rising Sun. In a Japanese newspaper recently I came across a "biography" of the Young Marshal, of which the following is a quaint quotation. Chang is portrayed quarreling with a lady, whom he accuses of betraying him. But first he "draws her closer, gives her a kiss." Then his accusation:

Chang Hsueh-liang sprang up to his feet and kicked her off the sofa. "Get up, you wretch," he ordered. He stood still and cold, a revolver in his hand.

"I was a fool to believe you," she said. "You never loved me."

"Wretch!" he roared. His revolver went off at the same moment. Madame Li dropped down. The white shirt was marked with spots of blood. Hsueh-liang, grey from excitement, drew close to her side. He pressed the point of the revolver upon her heart.

In the same moment her hand made an arc, and her dagger flew at his breast. With a sharp cry, he retreated a step. He was not hurt. "So that's what you'd do to me!" he said in an angry voice.

[1] Dr. Miller of the Seventh Day Adventist Hospital in Shanghai did the job by means of rectal anesthesia, blistering the patient's stomach, and producing an autogenous serum.

"I hate you!" she said. "I hate you because I loved you . . . I love you now. I'll always love you. Oh, I am happy. I am sleepy. Take me in your arms. Take me, please . . ."

With his foot Chang rolled her over on her back. He fired the revolver at her heart [*Sic!*]. A score of excited guards appeared.

"Take this body to the hill back of the northern mausoleum," the general ordered.

"Men!" he added, calling back the soldiers. "See that this lady is left unburied—else a wolf or mad dog may miss a square meal."

All this is perfect nonsense, of course. Nothing remotely like it ever happened.

Five different times the Young Marshal has saved Generalissimo Chiang Kai-shek from critical embarrassment; on at least one of these occasions he saved his régime, and once his life. Yet there is little love lost between them. Enemies of Chiang Kai-shek say, in fact, that he disliked the Young Marshal so intensely that he was willing to lose Manchuria rather than help him save it. The five occasions when the Young Marshal enormously helped *him*: (1) the Young Marshal, immediately his father died, raised the Kuomintang flag in Mukden, which gave Chiang's central government nominal authority over Manchuria for the first time in generations. Against the advice of all his generals, and in face of threats by the Japanese to kill him, he acknowledged Chiang Kai-shek as commander-in-chief. (2) In 1930 the Young Marshal intervened to save Chiang in the "Northern War," when a coalition of northern war lords was close to beating him. (3) In 1931 Chiang Kai-shek resigned from the National Government in a huff. The Young Marshal went out with him, which made the position of the new government untenable. (4) In 1933 he took the responsibility for the loss of Jehol, though he had nothing to do with it, in order that Chiang and the National Government should not lose face. He publicly accepted punishment, and went to Europe in disgrace, though it was he, not Chiang, who was passionately anti-Japanese. (5) In 1936 he helped save the Generalissimo at Sian—after kidnaping him.

W. H. Donald first brought Chiang and the Young Marshal together. They met in a railway coach at Paotingfu, and the young man gave over his armies to the Generalissimo. Donald accompanied Chang on his European trip, and the young man had a superlatively good time. Came word that his northeastern army was rising against the Generalissimo. Donald rushed back to China. The Young Marshal was terrified of being left alone in Europe, though he was consoled, the evening Donald left, by at last understanding all the jokes in a music hall. He followed Donald home, and the three—Donald, Generalissimo, Young Marshal—began to work together. I have already described Chang's first fury with Chiang, and how Donald then started to work for Chiang. At first the Young Marshal, desolate at losing Donald, was to share him with the Generalissimo alternate months.

We approach the Sian episode. The Young Marshal's former Manchurian troops, known as the Tungpei Army, were now stationed in the northwest. Chiang warily watched the Red Army arrive safely in Shensi after the Long March; he sent the Young Marshal's forces to Sian to engage them when the moment was propitious. He was performing a double maneuver: giving Chang a tough and ticklish job and getting ready to attack the Reds once more. But what happened was that, instead of fighting the communists, the Young Marshal's men began to fraternize with them. Lonely in Sian, without Donald (who could always keep him out of trouble), young Chang flirted with the Reds. He decided that he liked and admired these enemies whom he was supposed to suppress. His motive was genuine patriotism. Like T. V. Soong, he was disgusted with the Generalissimo's incessant civil wars. He wanted to unite the country, not split it asunder. He wanted to make it strong—against Japan.

Chiang Kai-shek smelled soon that something was amiss on the northwest frontier. He decided to fly to Sian and investigate. What occurred then everyone knows. The Young Marshal snatched him.

Kidnaping at Sian

This was one of the most unusual dramas in history. Analogies are misleading and sometimes intellectually fraudulent. But consider the sensation that would be aroused if Neville Chamberlain, say, were kidnaped in a remote part of Ireland and held prisoner for thirteen days by Winston Churchill assisted by Jimmy Maxton and the communist party, and was rescued at last by Mrs. Chamberlain, Bill Bullitt, and Montague Norman, while the bigwigs of Westminster sent bombing planes to blow up everybody.

The Generalissimo arrived in Sian to dress down the Young Marshal on December 7, 1936. They quarreled furiously. Young Chang said that, far from being in a position to fight the Reds, his troops were on the point of joining them. Chinese simply refused to fight Chinese any longer. The civil war game was up. The Young Marshal pleaded to be given a chance to fight Japan. He said in effect to Chiang: "You have lost a sixth of China without firing a shot. All you do is chase and murder peasants." The Generalissimo, black and red with rage, ordered him to keep his mouth shut and obey orders. Why did not the Young Marshal resign his command? This is what Donald had suggested. But the Young Marshal said he could not resign while the body of his father lay outside Chinese soil. He would not resign because he must regain Manchuria.

I must foreshorten drastically the actual events that began December 12. Far away in Nanking, Donald had taken an hour off to go to the movies. He returned to find a host of telephone messages. He rushed to Madame Kung's house, where he found Madame Chiang Kai-shek. They burst out with the shocking news: "The Young Fellow has kidnaped Kai!" Donald asked simply if they were sure that it was the Young Marshal who had done the job. If so, he said, and it was not a regular military mutiny, the Generalissimo was safe. Donald then posthaste flew to Sian.

What had happened at Sian was this. The Generalissimo was living outside the city proper. Students were rioting; the army was quivering with anger and excitement. This was the night of December 11. The Young Marshal ordered the city gates locked, and, to save the Generalissimo embarrassment, personally headed off a crowd going to his villa to demonstrate. He prevented what might have been an ugly incident. Then he and General Yang Hu-cheng (note well this name), the Pacification Commissioner of Shensi province, called on the Generalissimo for a final talk and protest against the impending mobilization order. Again violent but shadowy words. The Generalissimo noted something behind the conversation; he was surprised at the Young Marshal's "uneasy manner" and "apparent distraction of mind." Young Chang returned to Sian with General Yang, apparently beaten. One can imagine the turmoil in his brain. It was all over. The Generalissimo refused to understand the issue. He continued to rebuke them for not fighting the communists, when fighting was utterly impossible. Something drastic had to be done, and at once. The Young Marshal almost expired at the decision he had to take. "Let's arrest the stubborn son-of-a-blank," he finally blurted out.

On the 12th Chiang Kai-shek, dressing at 5:30 A.M., heard gunfire. One of his bodyguards rushed in. Mutiny! Chiang grabbed his clothes, forgot his false teeth, slipped out a back door, climbed a wall, fell into a moat, and scrambled toward escape in the mountains. His small party was surrounded; his nephew, a notorious Blue Shirt leader, was killed. Chiang was captured actually by Captain Sun, a member of the Young Marshal's bodyguard. The scene has Chinese overtones and undertones; Captain Sun, almost paralyzed at the enormity of what he was doing, *knelt* before Chiang weeping, as he arrested him; Chiang shouted, "Hold your tongue, you rebels! If you want to kill me, kill me right now!"[2]

Chiang's fall injured his back. He was carried to confinement. Then came that extraordinary series of dialogues between the Young Marshal and the Generalissimo, captor and captive, as a result of which, before long, their rôles were reversed. The Generalissimo refused to eat, refused to talk, refused to listen. He lay like a rock. At one point the Young Marshal said to him, "If Your Excellency accepts my suggestions I shall obey your orders." Chiang replied:

Which are you, my subordinate or my enemy? If my subordinate, you should obey my orders. If you are my enemy you should kill me without delay. You should choose either of these two steps, but say nothing more, for I will not listen to you.

At another point the Young Marshal said:

I think you are the only great man of this age, but why won't you yield a little, comply with our requests and lead us on in this revolution so that we may achieve something instead of your merely sacrificing your life?

To which Chiang was adamant:

If I stand firm and would rather sacrifice my life than compromise my principles, I shall be able to maintain my integrity till death, and my spirit will live forever.

The conversation remained on a very superior level, until, curtly, Chiang refused to listen any longer. Meantime the Young Marshal was reading Chiang's diary: one can imagine his thoughts when he found that a few nights before Chiang had written that he had "no

[2] This and most other quotations in this chapter are from *General Chiang Kai-shek*, by General and Madame Chiang Kai-shek.

character." He then told Chiang that he quite agreed with this. Chiang was violently irritated when, at last, the Young Marshal— cringing now—dared to present a formal list of demands. There were eight points:

1. Reorganize the National Government.
2. End all civil war, and initiate resistance against Japan.
3. Release the "National Salvation" leaders recently arrested in Shanghai.
4. Pardon all political prisoners.
5. Guarantee liberty of assembly.
6. Give the people a free hand to express themselves patriotically.
7. Carry out the will of Dr. Sun Yat-sen.
8. Call a conference immediately for "national salvation."

These points had been put to the Young Marshal by the communists, who were close in the background, though they were actually written by a group of army commanders.

Meantime Donald arrived. Bad weather delayed his flight. He greeted the Young Marshal cheerily, and went in to see the Generalissimo, whom he found lying on his side in a freezing cold room, silent, immobile. Chiang looked up, and saw Donald with surprise; he had had no idea that anyone would come to rescue him; slowly tears rolled down those iron cheeks. Donald persuaded him to move to more comfortable quarters. Already Donald had a plan, though he carefully did not disclose it. He knew the Young Marshal better than any man in the world; he thought he could wean him away from his associates, persuade him to ignore his colleagues and release Chiang, and then fly them *both* to safety.

But it was not too simple. First, Donald had to keep the Generalissimo from killing himself. The Chiangs have a black terrier, Blackie. The Generalissimo had lost face, and wanted to be a martyr. Donald kept whistling, "Better one live Blackie than a hundred dead lions." Second, the Young Marshal collapsed, and kept pleading with Chiang to forgive him. No one paid attention.

In Nanking the strain was terrible. No one had accurate information. The Kuomintang generals had to be restrained by Madame Chiang from attempting to crush the mutiny by force, which would almost certainly have led to Chiang's death. They did go so far as to bomb Loyang close to Sian. They thought the Generalissimo was probably dead anyway. They felt that they should make this gesture to his memory; some felt too that if they got there first they might get his job. Chiang, when he heard that Nanking intended to march, was happy, even if it meant his death. The supreme effort of Donald and Madame Chiang was not to free Chiang from the Young Marshal, which was easy, but to prevent the government itself from blustering in and killing everybody.

Donald's own words for Madame's struggle with the Nanking generals—which is minimized in her book—are that "she fought on two feet like a man."

He had telephoned her from Loyang. Her account reads:

"Fly back to Nanking from Sian," I urged him.

"No, I'll stay here," he replied. And my last words were: "Then you'll be killed if I cannot stop the fighting."

"There may be another way," Donald said, "but I cannot say more."

On the 20th Chiang's brother-in-law T. V. Soong started for Sian as intermediary. Donald turned to Chiang. One star shone in the cold sky. He said: "You are a Christian. I don't know why God should save you, but He is; T. V. will be here to-morrow." Then "Jimmy" Elder, the Young Marshal's friend and financial adviser, arrived. It became quite a party. On the 22nd, at 4 P.M., arrived Madame Chiang herself.

The Generalissimo wrote in his compact, stubborn diary:

I was so surprised to see her that I felt as if I were in a dream. I had told T. V. more than once the day before that my wife must not come to Sian, and when she braved all danger to come to the lion's den I was very much moved and wanted to cry . . . My wife tried her best to be cheerful . . . I was very much worried about her safety. For ten days I have already put away all thoughts about my own safety, but from now on I shall have to worry about her. She is so courageous, wise, kind, and affectionate. . . .

When Madame Chiang arrived in Sian her poise and presence of mind were enormous. The Young Marshal met her at the airport:

I greeted him as I have always done, and when we left the plane I asked him quite casually not to let any of his men search my baggage, as I disliked having my things messed up.

"Oh, Madame, I would never dare do that," he apologetically replied.

Then she shook hands with General Yang (as if nothing whatever had happened), and told the Young Marshal she would have tea with them *before* going in to see the Generalissimo, in order "to show that I took him to be a gentleman and was quite prepared to put myself in their hands." But she had already given Donald a loaded revolver, ordering him to shoot her "without hesitation" if his plan failed.

Settlement was patched up at last, though the Generalissimo signed no documents, and made no promises. The Young Marshal pitiably demanded that he be duly disciplined. Then a new crisis came. General Yang wanted to know where *he* came in. Everyone else was being nicely taken care of, and Yang, a tough customer, did not intend to be the victim, did not want *his* throat cut. He, as the phrase is, "hijacked" the kidnaping. He and his men refused to release the Generalissimo, though the plane was ready to carry him back to Nanking, with motors warming up.

This was the most severe crisis of all. It was at this point that the communists entered the scene openly. Their intermediary at Sian was Chou En-lai, whom I described in the preceding chapter. When the deadlock was complete Donald came to Madame and said, "There is a way out, but it is difficult. Will you and the Generalissimo consent to receive a communist?" Appalling request! General and Madame Chiang had not talked to a communist for ten years; they had spent a decade chasing communists all over China, their mortal enemies. But Madame has good sense. She withstood the shock. She recovered her poise, and agreed to receive Chou En-lai. They whittled out a new agreement, and on Christmas Day the Generalissimo was released. The final suspense was terrific. Everything was in the hands of Yang and Chou En-lai. Though she accepted communist aid, Madame still must feel uneasy at what happened, because this last struggle and compromise is very lightly glossed over in her book. She never mentions Chou En-lai.

The Generalissimo told the Young Marshal—after giving him a final lecture—that he need not return to Nanking. The Young Marshal insisted on accompanying him, and crawled into the cockpit next to the pilot when the plane took off.

Then came an elaborate process of general face-saving. Everybody's Face got scrubbed. The Generalissimo, convinced that he was humiliated, that he had lost his usefulness, repeatedly resigned; each time the resignation was refused. The Young Marshal begged to be tried, and was; he was removed from his command, "pardoned," and then placed under "disciplinary observation." For a time he was kept in custody near Fenghua, Chiang's birthplace, and then moved to Kiangsi, where, early in 1939, he still was. He insisted on talking violently at the "trial"; had he not made such provocative observations, he might have been released.

As to the communists, they gained enormously from these events. The Sian episode convinced the Generalissimo that civil war was impossible any longer; it opened his eyes to the fact that Chinese communists might also be Chinese patriots. He is a realist; he could not but be impressed by these "enemies" who had him at last—after ten years!—and then let him go. Although Chiang never accepted them officially, the Young Marshal's eight points became the basis of agreement and future policy. The communists played their hand, of course, with considerable shrewdness. The temptation to get rid of Chiang, he who had fought them so ruthlessly, must have been tremendous. They withstood it. What they got—instead of Chiang's head—was cessation of civil war, and a unity of China against Japan.

As to General Yang, he got $300,000 and a trip around the world.

Chapter XV

Course of the War

~~~~~~

*Even a Buddha will get angry if slapped in the face often
enough.*

—CHINESE PROVERB

*Cet animal est très méchant; quand on l'attaque il se
défend.*

IN JULY, 1937, the third and greatest Sino-Japanese war began. The
Japanese struck when they did for several reasons. First, China
was becoming stronger economically. The currency was stabilized, and
a new central bank operating; Dr. Kung was in Europe collecting
loans, and Chinese industry was rising to compete with Japanese. Second, Chinese military strength and unity were increasing, following
Sian and the United Front. The Japanese knew that it was now or
never. Finally, the international situation was propitious, with Russia
weak.

The Generalissimo and Madame Chiang knew that conflict was inevitable. Once the civil wars were over, once China became united,
Japan was bound to strike. But they thought that they had one more
year for preparation; they anticipated assault in 1938, not 1937. They
thought that Japan—despite the Soviet purges—was still afraid of
Russian intervention, and that the Japanese financial position would
serve to defer war another year. They were wrong. But they were not
caught napping. They fought back—at last.

The most striking thing about the war as a whole is that, although
Japan fought for one overwhelming purpose, to keep China from
becoming strong, the war has united what is left of China into a
more cohesive and effective fighting organism than anything known
for generations. The Japanese have carved out much territory; what
remains of China is more Chinese than it has ever been before.
Japan, by waging war, served to produce just what it sought to
prevent.

Worms do turn sometimes. So do dragons—even Chinese dragons.

Incidents and Chronology

The course of the war may be sketched in a paragraph or two.[1] The precipitating incident took place at Lukouchiao, near the Marco Polo bridge ten miles from Peking, on the night of July 7. Japanese troops of the Tientsin garrison were holding night maneuvers, and one man—a private—disappeared. The Japanese decided to teach the bumptious Chinese a lesson. They attacked the Chinese to recover this missing man. Fighting started. Then the lost private reappeared. He had been in a brothel apparently. No matter. The incident was a "good" pretext; within twenty-four hours thirty-five thousand Japanese troops poured through Tientsin toward Peking. Everything was ready. Whether this Marco Polo incident of 1937 was, like the Mukden incident of 1931, made by local Japanese officers without knowledge of the Tokyo government, is unknown. In any case, the Tokyo government had no choice but to support what the army did.

Chiang Kai-shek kept his head. He still did not want to fight if warfare could be avoided. But he could not hold his own people back. This was quite a different matter from Manchuria and Jehol; here China proper—almost its heart—was involved. At Kuling, on July 16, he made a speech quite unlike any other he had addressed to the Japanese or to his own people. He demanded the evacuation of Japanese troops from the Peking area. He told the nation that it must fight or perish, if the Japanese did not withdraw. He did not propose to yield another inch. The Japanese replied by marching on Peking itself, which fell, without firing a shot, on July 29, 1937. Tientsin was taken the next day.

Then, just as in 1932, fighting recrudesced spontaneously in Shanghai. The Chinese were maddened by events in the north. And fearing extension of the conflict, the Japanese had filled the river with warships. Large numbers of Chinese troops drew into the suburban area beyond Shanghai, though this was supposed to be demilitarized. A Japanese officer, in uniform, was discovered prowling near the Hungjao airdrome. This was a dangerous thing to do. He was challenged by a Chinese sentry, he shot the sentry, and then was shot himself. This was on August 9. Within two days a stream of Japanese troop ships was converging on Shanghai. Fighting—real fighting—began.

[1] There is a complete and concise account of the early part of the war in T. A. Bisson's *Japan in China*.

In 1932 Chiang Kai-shek had stood aside while the Nineteenth Route Army fought. This time he did not do so. He poured the best of his new army into the Shanghai area, and had there not been some bad staff work, his troops might have pushed the hard-pressed Japanese into the sea. The battle lasted till November 9. It was the biggest battle the world had seen since Verdun; Chinese casualties alone are calculated at not less than 450,000 in three months. Chinese resistance was stubborn, the Japanese attack was violent; the Chinese receded, gave up the Shanghai triangle in November, and lost Nanking, the national capital, on December 13. There is fierce dispute among military folk as to whether Chiang, at such gigantic cost, should have attempted to hold Nanking. His German military mission thought not. He decided to try to save Nanking, no matter how many men he would lose, because of its emotional and historical importance.

For a long time experts said that the Japanese, by taking Nanking, "lost the war." They had the bear—or dragon—by the tail; they could not go back, once they were so far inland; Chiang enticed them deeper and still deeper into the interior, which cost them tremendously in men and yen. They had to proceed to an attempt to *conquer* China. Most good observers do not think that, originally, the Japanese planned to attack Central China at all. They wanted to nip off the Five Northern Provinces once and forever; they didn't want a major war if a minor one could as easily serve their purpose. So Chiang initiated a process of what might be called attrition in reverse; he fought, he receded a little, he stood, he receded again, always with the object of making any Japanese advance extremely expensive. There was one important Chinese forward movement and victory, at Taierchuang in Shantung, in March, 1938.

The primary Japanese objective during the first half of 1938 was junction of their northern armies, in the Hopei-Shantung area near the Yellow River, with their central army in the Yangtze Valley, based on Nanking. This was achieved by a long battle at Hsuchow, in May. The Japanese then gained control of the Lunghai railway, the great west-east Chinese railway (built and formerly administered by Belgians, incidentally); they began to push southwestward in a great expanding arc. Hankow, where the Generalissimo moved after the loss of Nanking, fell in October, 1938. Chinese troops retreated west, and took up new positions in Szechwan. The guerrillas, meantime, fought hard in the north, and held most of Shansi. They developed the technique of getting the people to rise *behind* the Japanese front line.

But in October, 1938, the Chinese lost Canton. This was a crippling blow, more serious than the loss of Nanking and Hankow together. The great bulk of Chinese munitions had come from Honk Kong via Canton to Hankow, although the Japanese incessantly bombed the railroad. With Canton gone, this route was cut. The Japanese took Canton while Europe was recovering from the Munich crisis. The Chinese had not bothered to defend it seriously, never dreaming that Japan would invade China so far in the south and so close to Hong Kong and Kowloon, British territory. But the Japanese decided after Munich that the British no longer had the will—or power—to protect what had hitherto been considered their vital interests in the Far East. Mr. Chamberlain sold out Czechoslovakia at Munich; he very gravely damaged China too.

No important battles took place—up to the end of April, 1939— after the loss of Hankow and the Canton catastrophe.

Totalitarian Paradox

I have just mentioned Generalissimo Chiang Kai-shek's German military advisers. Not everything is totalitarian in this totalitarian world after all. Germany is Japan's ally in the anti-Comintern pact, and Japan is engaged in a death struggle with China; one would normally take it for granted that Germany would assist Japan in every way. But in Hankow I found the amazing spectacle of a variety of Germans helping *China*, the enemy of their ally. What is more, I found Russians—aviators mostly—in Hankow also working on the Chinese side, fighting in coöperation with Germans against Japan. I blinked. The German military mission, the Russian aviation mission, were headquartered within a few blocks of one another—in the old Japanese concession! To preserve diplomatic proprieties, neither Germans nor Russians would admit that the others existed, and they never met officially.

German help to China came in several ways. It was so conspicuous when I was in Hankow that young Dr. Trautmann, the son of the German Ambassador to China, arrived from Berlin with a German Red Cross unit. The Chinese announced that $500,000 worth of medical supplies were coming to China, donated by German factories and other organizations. Again, indispensable communications between Chinese cities were—and still are—provided mostly by German civil aviation. The Lufthansa Company operates Junker planes all over the west and southwest of China. I flew from Hong Kong to Hankow and back in a German plane, with a German pilot and Chinese radio operator. Again, until the fall of Canton, about sixty percent of all Chinese munitions came from—believe it or not—the German Reich.

Above all, there was the German military mission. This followed tradition. In 1928 or thereabouts the Generalissimo began to import officers from Germany to train his troops, and Colonel Max Bauer, General Von Seeckt (former chief of staff of the Reichswehr), and General Baron von Falkenhausen, were successively in command. There were between sixty and seventy German officers in all, most of them retired from the Reichswehr, some trained by Ludendorff, and superbly competent. Officially they were instructors, and in the first months of the war they whipped into shape thirty-one Chinese divisions, 500,000 men. Also they were consultants; the Generalissimo saw how good their advice was when Nanking fell, and thereafter he followed them closely in strategy and tactics. German officers helped plan the Chinese victory at Taierchuang.

This exasperated the Japanese. It enraged them that their ally should help their enemy. Tokyo put pressure on Berlin, and after months of negotiation the German military mission was withdrawn. At about the same time (June, 1938), German munitions shipments to China were sharply cut. The Lufthansa, however, still maintains its aviation service, and a handful of German officers of the military mission refused to return home. They had signed contracts and sworn loyalty to China, and, good officers, they would not break their word. Some were anti-Nazi; they surrendered German citizenship, and stayed with Chiang Kai-shek.

There was plenty of reason for German interest in China, for the long reluctance of Berlin to meet Japanese wishes. Germany does not, it might be said, passionately want Japan to conquer all of China. The Germans might not mind if the Japanese nipped off the Five Northern Provinces, but Japanese occupation of China as a whole does not suit German ambitions. First, it might cut down German trade with China, which was soaring until the war broke out. Second and conversely, in the event of a general European war, or a world war, Germany would not like to see Japan weakened by a long and indecisive Chinese campaign.

Outrages and the Panay Episode

"The Tokyo Foreign Office asks that the powers in China refrain from any action calculated to give misgivings to the Japanese forces. Anything that smacks of brute force is distasteful to the sensitive little fellows."
—HOWARD BRUBAKER

I have mentioned that I have seen Japanese soldiers, in uniform, beat old women in the streets; I have mentioned the slaughter in Nanking, when civilians were executed—some burned alive, some tied in bundles and used for bayonet practice—by the thousand. Such things happen in warfare. Wars are unpleasant. There has never been a war without an atrocity. War itself is the atrocity. But the Japanese make war even more horrible than it usually is. Almost everywhere they have gone, they have burned, looted, raped, and murdered.

In Shanghai is one of the most extraordinarily gruesome sights in the world. I have never seen anything to approach it. Parts of Chapei and Hongkew, where fighting was hottest, are in ruins paralleling those of the Western Front in France. The Japanese looted this area, which comprises several square miles, not merely of furniture, valuables, and household possessions, but of every nail, every window wire, every screw, bolt, nut, or key, every infinitesimal piece of metal they could lay hands on. Houses were ripped to pieces, then the whole region set on fire. No one lives in this charred ruin now. No one could. The Japanese have, however, maintained street lighting; the lighted avenues protrude through an area totally black, totally devoid of human life, like phosphorescent fingers poking into a grisly void.

What is known as the Garden Bridge separates this Japanese-occupied area with one rim of the International Settlement proper. Barbed wire and sandbags protect it. Japanese sentries representing army, navy, and police stand at one end; British sentries are at the other. I have seen these tall Englishmen go white with rage as the Japanese, a few feet away, kicked coolies or slapped old men with bamboo poles; they could make no protest. The Japanese have life-and-death power over anyone in their area. Chinese, passing the Japanese sentries, have to bow ceremoniously, and doff their hats. Yet the Japanese—at the same time they may playfully prod a man across the bridge with their bayonets—say that they are in China to make friends of the Chinese people!

Lest it be thought that I exaggerate, I append the following Reuter dispatch from Shanghai, of date March 30, 1938:

Feeling is running high in British military circles here today as a result of an incident which occurred this morning on a bridge over the Soochow Creek. . . . Japanese soldiers set upon and beat an old Chinese man who happened to be on the bridge, and then threw him over into the water.

The whole action was in full view of sentries of the Durhams, who were on duty at one end of the bridge. The British soldiers, unable to leave their posts, were compelled helplessly to watch the old man drown, while the Japanese soldiers laughed and cheered.

In Nanking a totally scrupulous American observer, arriving in April, saw decapitated bodies of Chinese servants still lying unburied in British compounds. Nanking was captured in mid-December.

The most famous Japanese outrage was the sinking of U. S. gunboat *Panay*, in the Yangtze a few miles above Nanking, on December 12, 1937—a year to a day after the Sian kidnaping. Aboard were American diplomatic and other officers rescued from beleaguered Nanking; the *Panay* was escorting three Standard Oil tankers, which provide a slight imperialist touch. The river had been extremely agitated for several days. On the 11th Japanese land forces fired on a British gunboat, the *Ladybird*, and two British officers went ashore to protest; other British ships, the *Scarab* and *Bee*, were attacked, but not sunk. The Japanese officer in command nearby was Colonel Hashimoto, who had organized a sub-Fascist party in Japan after he was (temporarily) discharged from the army for alleged participation in the 1936 mutiny. He said that he got orders from Shanghai to "clear the Yangtze of shipping." Later it was "explained" that the message reached him imperfectly, and that the word "enemy" before "shipping" had been omitted.

At 1:38 P.M. on December 12 the bombardment of the *Panay* began. Those aboard had seen Japanese planes circling above; they never dreamed, however, that they would be bombed. Though American flags were clearly visible, the attack continued until 3:54, when the *Panay*, blasted full of holes, finally sank. The Americans tried to beat off the attack with machine-gun fire: in other words, actual military engagement between the armed forces of Japan and the United

States took place. American survivors were machine-gunned as they took off in small boats to reach the shore; attacks continued even after they were on land, hiding in the freezing marshes. Extreme heroism was shown by the American commander, Captain J. J. Hughes, who suffered a broken thigh in the first bombardment, and by Lieut. A. F. Anders, who succeeded to the command. Anders, shot in the throat, could not talk. He then wrote his orders in chalk on the slanting, blistered deck—until he was shot in the wrist and could not write.[2]

The Japanese in Tokyo were terrified by possible *Panay* repercussions. They took up collections for the survivors, and paid on the nail the bill for $2,214,007.36 submitted by the United States government. American officials in Tokyo thought immediately after the incident that suspension of diplomatic relations was inevitable. The Japanese had been notified by Admiral Yarnell exactly where the *Panay* was—two hours before the attack began. It seemed wanton and deliberate. Motive for it was probably Face, plus jumpy nerves; the Japanese wanted to show the Chinese that they could afford to be contemptuous even of white military power.

Another famous outrage was the shooting of the British Ambassador, Sir Hughe Knatchbull-Hugessen, on August 26. It is held, however, that he did not warn the Japanese military of his presence on the road that day, as he might have done. The Japanese were gunning for Chiang Kai-shek, who did pass down the same road a few hours later.

Three Precepts Which May Be Illusions

First, a nation of 70,000,000 people cannot conquer a nation of 450,000,000. True, maybe. But the proposition becomes somewhat dubious if the 70,000,000 are well armed and mechanically equipped, and the 450,000,000 are not. You cannot fight a machine gun by whistling at it.

Second, the Chinese always absorb their "conquerors." This has been the lesson of history, though the Chinese have lost territory by the process. But circumstances to-day are not quite parallel to those of former centuries. The Japanese are mechanized. They have radio.

[2] An Italian journalist was among those killed. He was a good Fascist even in death. He is quoted by an Italian comrade as having said that he died happy, in the conviction that Russians (!), not Japanese, had killed him. This of course is total nonsense.

They have aircraft and swift means of communication. Moreover, it is small comfort for the Chinese to think that in a century or two they may have "absorbed" the Japanese. To tell a woman whose child has been stabbed in the stomach to-day that, in a few hundred years, the Japanese will have become Chinese, is invidious to say the least.

Third, the Chinese can retreat indefinitely, draw the Japanese in after them. This is true to a certain point. But, the further west the Chinese forces retreat, the greater mechanical difficulty they face in communications. There are no railroads in the west, and railways are almost vital. The Chinese want to stand before too much is lost. They have had a Borodin; one might add that nowadays they need a Borodino.

The Chinese Position: Supplies

Advantages to China in the 1939 deadlock are several. First, time is on the side of the Chinese, and time is a very important factor. The longer the war goes on, the better it is for China, because the standard of living in Japan is depressed every month the war continues, while the Chinese can—and do—live on the country and fight naked. Second, the Chinese army, rebuilt after the Shanghai-Nanking debacle in 1937, has improved immeasurably, though it could be still better. Third, defense is less expensive than attack. The Japanese must *win* in order to win; the Chinese can, more or less, stand pat. Fourth, guerrilla warfare, as we know, has played havoc with Japanese communications and morale.

Perhaps the greatest advantage to China is the inordinately difficult military and administrative job facing the Japanese. The front runs 2,350 miles, and the Japanese are trying to hold eleven great provinces, covering at least 800,000 square miles, and with a population of at least 200,000,000 people. China, I heard it said, is like a blanket: the Japanese hold the seams, i.e., the canals, the railways, the rivers, the great cities. But to hold the seams is not enough. Japan has almost 800,-000 troops below the Wall, and hesitates to increase this vast army, the upkeep of which costs money. There are another 350,000 above the Wall—the Kwantung army of occupation in Manchukuo and Mongolia —which costs money too.

Disadvantages to China are several also. First, though the army has improved greatly, it is by no means a first class fighting force. Chiang has about 1,500,000 men under arms, but only about one-third of them are capable of front-line work. The Chinese army is composed largely of provincial levies, which differ considerably in quality. Some Kwangsi troops have been superb; some others have not been superb. Recruits do not spring from a well-integrated system of national conscription, and they are thrown into the front with insufficient training. It is, moreover, exceptionally difficult to weld different provincial units into a compact, cohesive, national force. After a battle divisions cannot be reformed of remnants of other divisions; troops from different areas may not speak the same dialect, may not even eat the same food. The greatest military problem in China is to melt and cast these varying strains into a single solid ingot. Another point is that the Chinese gravely lack aircraft and artillery.

Second, financial considerations. China has lost all its important seaports, most of its railways; it has lost its richest tax-collecting provinces, and 90 per cent of the Maritime Customs. By arrangement with the British, the Japanese now collect Chinese customs in the ports they control; technically they do not seize the revenue, but merely "block" it in earmarked accounts at the Yokohama Specie and other banks. But China loses this revenue, and Japan has the use of it. Almost sixty percent of Chinese revenue came normally from the Maritime Customs. Finally, the Chinese export trade has severely suffered, and there is virtually no silver left. One talks glibly of the economic drain in Japan. The economic drain in China is probably worse.

Third, the whole matter of supplies. When I was in Hankow a man indisputably in a position to know said that the outcome of the war depended on supplies. For this reason among others the loss of Canton was so serious, as we have seen. The Canton-Hankow line had been the great trough for shipment of supplies. Now the Chinese have three routes left:

1. The old caravan route in the north, Sian-Lanchow-Urumchi, into the Soviet Union. I have already hinted at its difficulties. The route is long; much of it is across desert and difficult terrain; when supplies do reach Lanchow or Sian, they must be transshipped—again overland—to the central front, since the Japanese have cut the northern railroad. The Chinese have now got gasoline dumps along this road, and have worked heroically to improve it.

2. The French narrow-gauge railway from Haiphong and Hanoi to Kunming (Yunnanfu), the capital of Yunnan. For many months

the French held down shipments on this line, though they grieved bitterly at the lucrative freight hauls they were missing, because the Japanese threatened to seize the great Chinese island of Hainan, which lies athwart northern Indo-China, if France continued to assist China by keeping the line open. Early in 1939 the Japanese seized Hainan anyway. The French, angry, then opened the line freely to traffic. The Japanese tried to exert pressure to close it again, but it remains the single most important source of Chinese shipments. It is a technical problem of some difficulty to transship arms, once they are in Yunnan, on to Chungking and the front, since there is no railway. Thousands of coolies, however, keep the road in good repair.

3. The new road from Burma (British territory), on the other side of Yunnan, to Yunnanfu and Chungking. The American Ambassador to China, Nelson T. Johnson, and his military attaché, Major James M. McHugh traversed this route in January 1939, covering the 2,100 miles in a light car in thirteen days. Heavy munitions traffic was expected to begin promptly. The chief difficulty is tropical rain, which may wash out the bridges.

Finally, one must mention Chinese morale which is, in a word, magnificent. China is fighting for self-preservation, for national integrity and survival. Against almost inconceivable difficulties, the Chinese have put up a fight against the better equipped Japanese to make the imagination dance. The Japanese thought that the war would be over in three months. They know now that it may last three more years; they are talking of getting rid of the guerrillas in the north "in 1941." Bombs have brought Japan's menace into remote Chinese villages that had scarcely ever heard of Japan. The Japanese have deliberately destroyed not less than fifty-four universities or seats of learning, burning the libraries, smashing the equipment,[3] and refugee students have carried their story of renascent nationalism to the remotest parts of the interior. Boys in far-off Szechwan have volunteered for the national army by the thousands, and have marched barefoot to join the united command; in villages buried for generations, young men are training with broomsticks, cheering the name of Chiang Kai-shek, preparing to defend their country.

[3] See the London *Times*, Jan. 3, 1939, for a horrifying account of these atrocities against the mind of man. In many instances Japanese aviators made raids on distant cities purely to destroy universities and especially libraries, which often contained irreplaceable material. In every city, the Japanese burn the books first.

The Japanese Position

"He who rides the tiger may find it difficult to dismount . . . A dragon stranded in shallow water furnishes amusement for the shrimps."
—CHINESE PROVERBS

The immediate Japanese aim in 1939 was double. First, hold the front and consolidate it. Second, exploit the occupied areas, so that China will in effect be made to pay for its own destruction. Behind these immediate aims are, of course, others: the Japanese want to prevent the unification of China, to attack British influence and prestige, and to get something *out* of the war, to derive concrete benefits to parade before its people.

Point One. The Japanese hold the great north-south railway from Peking to Canton at each end, and at Hankow in the middle. What they want is to gain complete control of this railway, so that their armies will have maneuverability, which the Chinese have not. They then hope to entrench immediately in front of this railway, and make it their impregnable Chinese frontier, above the Yangtze at least. Then, behind these entrenchments, they plan to turn backward, fight the war over again—in reverse—from the railway to the sea, and thus liquidate passive resistance, individual terrorism, and the guerrillas. This campaign, it is hoped, will give them complete military security. It will take a long time, since the railway itself is by no means entirely taken. What is left of China if this plan succeeds will be almost railroadless hinterland. The Japanese do not envisage Chinese offensive power sufficient to throw them out. The Chinese, be it remembered, have very little aircraft, and almost no artillery—the weapons which an attacking army needs above all.

Point Two. Politically the Japanese are attempting to administer the conquered areas by puppet governments, which we shall inspect soon, while economically they exploit them by several agencies. The new "China Federal Reserve Bank" has been set up, with capital furnished fifty percent by the Yokohama Specie Bank, though the Japanese barefacedly deny that they control it. It issues banknotes, paper *yuan* convertible into Japanese yen, with which it seeks to drive out Chinese dollars, which by fiat have been reduced forty percent in value. But the Chinese peasants will not sell their goods for *yuan*. What might be called a currency war is in progress—especially since

Britain and the United States have each helped to prop up the legitimate Chinese dollar with $25,000,000 loans.

The Japanese—without much success—have tried to suck Chinese dollars, which are backed by silver, out of the peasantry. These they sell for foreign exchange, which drives the Chinese currency down. So China has imposed a strict currency control, with British backing. This has infuriated the Japanese against the British, even though the British coöperate with Japan in the new customs régime. Britain, says Japan, is the chief factor maintaining Chinese strength, first because of its support of Chinese currency, second because of Hong Kong— British territory—which is the Chinese capital so far as finance, supplies, trade, are concerned, as well as a perfect home for Chinese officials who go in and out with impunity.

Two huge mechanisms of industrial exploitation have been set up by Japan in conquered territory, the North China Development Company (capital 350,000,000 yen, half of which was contributed by the Japanese government), and the Central China Development Company (capital 110,000,000 yen). Both are under the supervision of the new "China Board" in Tokyo, which is controlled by the army and which has frozen out the Foreign Office from control of Chinese affairs. These companies will attempt to develop electric power in China, build up transport, collect crops, manufacture salt, explore mineral deposits, and otherwise assimilate the country. The idea is to transform China into a solid Japanese monopoly, with the Open Door shut, and foreign business as far as possible excluded. Thus the Yangtze has remained closed and Canton has been cut off. The best Chinese weapon of resistance to this plan of economic conquest has been the "scorched earth" policy. Rather than turn over their industries to Japan, the retreating Chinese burn the factories if they cannot move them. The textile mills at Tsingtao were burned, with a loss of $100,000,000 (Chinese). Rather than let the Japanese feed on their crops, the Chinese burn the fields.

The greatest Japanese advantage is that they have command of the air, plus good artillery. The greatest danger to the Japanese is overconfidence following the capture of Canton. Before Canton they had little ambition to chase Chiang Kai-shek beyond Hankow. So long as they entrench along the northern railway and the Yangtze, they are in no military danger except from guerrillas. If they over-extend themselves by attempting to penetrate Yunnan and Szechwan, they may meet disaster.

The Japanese, fighting China, have seemed fairly impressive. But I heard one of the best military men in the east say, "Any first-class European army, even the Italian army, could drive the Japanese into the sea in six months."

The material damage caused by the war is all but incalculable. About seventy percent of Chinese industry has been destroyed or taken over by the Japanese; industrial damage in the Shanghai area alone is stated to be $600,000,000. Above and beyond this staggering dislocation is human suffering almost without parallel in recent history. I do not mean military casualties, which are considerable enough. I mean refugees. We have heard of several kinds of European refugees. In China, in the Shanghai-Nanking area alone, there are sixteen *million* refugees; sixteen *million* men, women, and children have had to flee for their lives, permanently displaced, forced out of their miserable homes, destitute, shattered, starving.

A final word on western attitudes. Both Britain and the U.S.S.R. play roughly the same game, to help the Chinese—a little—against the Japanese, in order that Japan shall not become too strong. Some observers, however, feel that Britain may eventually make an agreement with Japan, whereby Japan remains in control at least of North China, in return for cessation of the war which is seriously damaging British trade. If the war lasts long enough, all foreign powers might derive profit from it: defeat of the Japanese would break the power of the military in Japan, and perhaps make China a progressive, stable, pacific state.

The Trek to the West

"The journey of a thousand miles begins with one step."
—LAO-TSE.

By the "Trek to the West" China is attempting to retrieve itself. The Long March of the Red Army was a very considerable achievement; a hundred thousand men crossed China to create new life. The Trek to the West is more diffuse, and much bigger. Against unbelievable obstacles, pushed from the splintered ruins of their homes, their mangled dead behind, penniless, with their lives ruined by the Japanese, several million refugees have set out from the sea coast and the Yangtze provinces, have walked a thousand miles westward, are starting to build a new China in the undeveloped west. This migration is comparable to nothing except the march to the west in American frontier days, and has produced strikingly analogous episodes of heroism and endurance, determination and recuperative ingenuity and sacrifice.

Details would demand a whole chapter. The remnants of the old universities are consolidating into new institutions of learning. Old railways have been torn up, and the actual rails carried by terrible physical labor by patriotic coolies to safety in the west, where they will be used for new railways. Several hundred industrial enterprises have been bodily moved, machinery and all, and are laboriously being set up and made to work in cities hundreds of miles from their original location. New highways are planned and built. Resources—especially gold in Szechwan, tin in Yunnan—are being explored. Rewi Alley, a young New Zealander, formerly an inspector of factories in the Shanghai International Settlement, has organized the "Chinese Industrial Cooperatives" which are beginning to function, partly following initiative by Madame Chiang Kai-shek.

Moving the factories was a heroic undertaking. Difficulties were not always technical. One big cotton mill in Hankow refused to move, or to make any provision for its several thousand workers after the Japanese occupation. Arrangements had to be made in haste, as the Japanese were closing in on the city. The government asked the factory to dismantle its machinery. The factory refused. It happened that labor conditions were particularly bad in this factory. One morning at 5 A.M., Madame Chiang appeared just as the night shift was going home, the day shift going on duty. She appealed to the workers, and her intervention was so spectacular that the factory was forced to move.

Peace and Deadlock

When the Japanese captured Nanking in 1937 they thought that Chiang Kai-shek, having lost his capital, would sue for peace. He did not do so, and cautiously the German Ambassador, Dr. Trautmann, acting as an intermediary for the Japanese, presented their "peace terms." Madame Chiang, who received him, did no more than glance at the document. She said quietly, "It is pleasant to see you again, Mr. Ambassador. Might I ask—how are your charming children?" There was no more talk of peace.

The Japanese, as noted in Chapter I above, were furious; they "withdrew recognition" from Chiang Kai-shek, and from that day to this have refused to concede that he exists, except to say that they will behead him like a common criminal if they catch him. There have been no negotiations between Japanese and Chinese since. In December 1938 the Japanese announced their peace terms, including (1), Chinese recognition of Manchukuo and adherence to the Anti-Comintern pact; (2), Inner Mongolia to become a special "anti-communist" area; (3), Japanese troops to be stationed in various parts of China; (4), opening up of China—especially Inner Mongolia and the Five Northern Provinces—to Japanese development; (5), abolition of the Kuomintang. To this the Chinese made no answer; such "terms" were impossible to answer. In January 1939, however, Madame Chiang announced China's minimum conditions—peace with honor, which must include the territorial integrity of China, administrative sovereignty, and "equal treatment."

The present position is a complete stalemate, which may persist a long time. The Japanese are not strong enough to push the Chinese into Tibet; the Chinese are not strong enough to push the Japanese into the sea. The Japanese—if they maintain their present strength—may follow their invention of the concept of Undeclared War by making an Undeclared Peace. They cannot easily resuscitate the Generalissimo in order to negotiate with him—even if he would negotiate on such terms as those above; they may choose instead to let the fighting fray out, hold what they have, and attempt to proceed with economic exploitation without calling off the war. But they must face the united and regenerated force of the Chinese nation. They are fighting a people that have never before been permanently beaten.

Chapter XVI

Chinese Generals and Politicians

〰〰〰〰〰〰〰〰〰〰〰〰〰〰〰〰〰〰〰〰〰〰〰〰

Better a diamond with a flaw than a pebble without.
—CONFUCIUS

THE Kuomintang (pronounced "Gwomindong"), the single political party which rules Chinese China, is now headed by Chiang Kai-shek in person. I have sketched briefly its origins under Dr. Sun Yat-sen, who founded it before 1911 among Chinese political refugees in Japan, and who established the Three People's Principles (nationalism, democracy, people's livelihood). "Kuo" means country, "min" means people, "tang" means party. The Kuomintang—in theory at least—is the supreme authority in China, since it appoints the government. It is the Chinese equivalent of totalitarian parties elsewhere.

It differs from other mass parties, however, very widely; indeed it is unique among them. First, it stands for democracy as one of its three major tenets; it considers itself the repository of the ideals of the Chinese revolution, which it hopes to develop gradually: not by a process of crude dictatorship but by organic evolution. It is not, like the communist party in Russia, a close-packed nucleus of the devout; it is not, like the Nazi party in Germany, a mass ballyhoo movement. Although it dominates the Chinese government, cabinet ministers do not have to belong to it. Anyone who wishes may become a member if he has a satisfactory sponsor and record; no one is compelled to join. There are no dues, and few duties except to memorize the will of Dr. Sun Yat-sen, which reads as follows:

For forty years I have devoted myself to the cause of National Revolution, the aim of which is to secure for China a position of independence and equality among nations. The accumulated experience of these forty years has fully convinced me that to attain this goal it is necessary to awaken the mass of our own people and associate ourselves with those peoples of the world who treat us on a footing of equality in the common struggle.

The Revolution is not yet achieved. Let all my comrades follow my writings, "Plans for National Reconstruction," "Fundamentals of National Reconstruction," "Three Principles of the People," and the Manifesto issued by the First National Congress of the Party, and work unceasingly for their consummation. Above all, the convocation of a People's Convention and the abolition of unequal treaties, which I have recently advocated, should be accomplished with the least possible delay. This is my will and behest.

I heard widely varying estimates of Kuomintang membership; most insiders think it has perhaps 100,000 men—hardly more—of whom some 20,000 are the active cadre. Membership is semi-secret. There is very little feeling, however, between members and non-members, nothing remotely like that separating sheep from goats, party members from non-party members, in Germany or the Soviet Union. I have several times dined with both Kuomintang and non-Kuomintang men; all laughed together, and even joked about party membership.

The Kuomintang is organized rather like the communist party in the U.S.S.R., though its spirit is different in that it is not an exclusive party. The highest organ is the Party Congress, which meets every two years. This delegates authority to two standing committees, the Central Executive Committee, which carries out the decisions of the Congress, and the Central Supervisory Committee, which has advisory powers. From these a smaller group derives, the Central Political Council, which handles routine and current business. Responsible to these organizations in a closely interlocked pattern is the actual Government of China, which is composed of five broad councils, or "Yuans."

The war inevitably led to creation of auxiliary organizations. It was urgently necessary to centralize control. Thus the Kuomintang appointed a Supreme War Council, and the Government established a Supreme Council of National Defense, of which Generalissimo Chiang is chairman. An offshoot of the Supreme Council of National Defense is the all-important Military Affairs Commission, which the Generalissimo also heads, and which supervises the activity of military branches of the government.

The Yuan system was invented by Dr. Sun Yat-sen. It took over from Chinese tradition, borrowed ideas from the Soviet Union and the West, and was in general a broad, fluid series of channels through which Chinese administration could learn to develop. One should remember that China never had a political party in the Western sense of the term until 1911; China became a republic overnight, after having been a decadent empire for centuries. Dr. Sun had to feel his way with caution. His whole idea was to *prepare* the people for self-government. China is the only great country in the world which has never had an election. It has never had a real parliament.

Of the five yuans which comprise the government the first, the Executive Yuan, is the cabinet. We call Dr. H. H. Kung the prime minister or premier of China; in Chinese diction he is simply chairman of the Executive Yuan of the National Government. It meets every Tuesday morning. Second, Legislative Yuan. This is the vestigial legislative body from which a true national parliament was to arise. It is empowered to initiate legislation, but has little actual power. Third, Judicial Yuan. This was to create a judicial system consonant with the times. Fourth, Examination Yuan. An obvious offshoot of the old examination system, it was to build up the civil service anew. Fifth, Control or Supervisory Yuan, a general overlapping body to correlate activity, superintend execution of decisions, and make common plans.

Politics in China is inveterately personal, and personalities rather than issues dominate the Kuomintang and the Five Yuans. The Kuomintang is full of furiously competing cliques and counter-cliques, which sometimes merge, then separate again. Since the United Front, cliquism has diminished, perhaps, but at least half a dozen special groups may be distinguished.

1. The National Salvation group. This is dominated by Madame Sun Yat-sen, and is strongly left wing. Groups of National Salvationists, especially students, began the revival against Japan in the north in 1935, as noted above. This was in a sense the origin of the United Front.

2. The Cantonese group, also markedly left wing, led by Sun Fo, the son of Sun Yat-sen by his first wife. T. V. Soong and other strongly anti-Japanese politicians are members of this group. For a long time it violently opposed Chiang, since it wanted cessation of the civil wars, unity against Japan.

3. The "C. C." or "Chen Brothers" group, which for some years was the Tammany Hall of the Kuomintang. It is strongly on the right; it led the fight against the communists, and was closely associated with the big merchants, *compradores,* Chinese bankers and so on in Shanghai and the treaty ports. It has diminished in influence lately, partly because the Japanese have occupied its strongholds,

Kiangsu and Chekiang. Undercover work against the United Front, inside the Kuomintang, comes mostly from this "C. C." group.

4. The "Political Study" or "Political Science" clique. This is very fluid, very personal; it is important, but it is difficult to tell what it stands for. Its leader is General Chang Chun, a former foreign minister; for a long time it tended toward conciliation with Japan, and is still very anti-Red. A great many Chinese politicians, as we shall see, are Japanese-educated; most of them belong to this "Political Science" group.

5. The "Whampoa" group, which is composed mostly of officers trained by Chiang Kai-shek (and General Bluecher in the early days) at the Whampoa military academy near Canton. Several are classmates of officers now with the Red or Eighth Route Army. Basically they have been a neutral officers cadre, slightly on the anti-Red side. The leader is the well known general Chen Cheng.

6. The Western Hills group, which had headquarters in Peking, and which is now almost extinct. It was led by Hu Han-min, and was violently right wing and reactionary. It associated with a pro-Japanese group outside the Kuomintang, the Anfus, from which most Japanese puppets in China come.

These groups, dissimilar as they may seem, have a common denominator, in that all have the same single ambition: to gain power by being closest to Chiang Kai-shek.

At this point one should mention the Blue Shirts, which are in effect Chiang Kai-shek's *own* clique, muscle men, private army, GPU, and Gestapo. Something to note: they do not wear blue shirts. The term blue shirt is, in fact, a loose translation of Lan Yi Shih, which correctly means "blue clothes"; the name was chosen because blue is the national color, and most Chinese wear blue blouses. The organization began in 1932, when Chiang's influence over the Kuomintang seemed momentarily waning; the party was riven by dissension, and he thought he could hold it together—and keep his own power—only by the most hard-boiled means.

The Blue Shirts have lost some of their importance, because their main function was to root out and destroy Reds. Since the United Front the Reds are not seriously molested, and the Blue Shirts—especially with a war going on—have turned to other work. A detachment of Blue Shirts went with Chiang—as it accompanies him everywhere—to Sian, under the supreme Blue Shirt leader Tai Li, one of the most important men in China.[1] There the Young Marshal dared to seize and shoot several of them, which caused the organization to lose face severely, and is incidentally one of the reasons why the Young Marshal is still in "voluntary" confinement. The Blue Shirts won't let him go.

The Blue Shirts began frankly as a terrorist semi-Fascist organization. Some members were renegade communists; others, in disguise, were *real* communists—Reds inside the Blue—who became counter spies, and risked not only their lives but terrible torture to get inside the Blue Shirt organization. An early Blue Shirt exploit was the murder of Yeng Chien, the secretary of the Academia Sinica and a friend of Madame Sun Yat-sen's. For a long time what remained of white terror in China was in Blue Shirt hands.

The Blue Shirt organization is one of the few really hush-hush things in China. Not only are its present status and duties obscure, but it is even denied that it continues to exist. All Chinese smile politely when you mention Blue Shirts, and change the subject—after looking covertly behind the door. *Asia* Magazine published an article about the Blue Shirts once, whereupon *Asia* was suppressed in China for some months; and a high Chinese official in New York demanded that *Asia* retract. He said that the Blue Shirts were a myth.

Finally, a word on secret societies, which at one time flourished in China, though they never had anything like the importance of secret societies, the Black Dragon for instance, in Japan. The most important is the Ching-Pang, Blue Society or Green Society depending on taste, since *Ching* means literally "middle color" and can be translated as either blue or green. Another is the Hung-Pang, Red Society. The Green Society, of which Chiang Kai-shek was a member for some years, flourished in the French Concession in Shanghai, though the organization is on a national basis. It was anti-communist, anti-labor, anti-Japanese; it had patriotic aims, an interest in opium, and not too scrupulous methods. For years its leader was Chen Chi-mei, the political boss of Shanghai and father of the Chen brothers who formed their own clique in the Kuomintang, as we have just noted. It was this elder Chen who was an early patron of Chiang Kai-shek and who started him on the practical road to being Generalissimo.

[1] Unofficially he is head of the secret police. He was educated, perhaps fittingly, in Germany.

Two on the Top

We have talked of Chiang Kai-shek and the Young Marshal, of Madame Chiang and Madame Sun Yat-sen, of Dr. H. H. Kung and T. V. Soong, of the Red leaders Mao Tse-tung and Chu Teh. These might be called the eight most important individuals in China,[2] though two more names should belong to any dominant list, the Kwangsi generals Pai and Li. These eight—or ten—outstanding names are by no means the only names in China that count. There are a great many other Chinese of important personal and political distinction.

From the hierarchical point of view we should begin at the top, that is, with the venerable Lin Sen who is President of the National Government. His importance is nominal; he is Kalinin to Molotov and Stalin, or King Victor Emanuel to Mussolini. President Lin, a native of Fukien, was born in 1864; he lived in California for many years, and returned to China in 1911 to join Sun Yat-sen's revolution. He has been a good Kuomintang wheelhorse ever since, and was elected to his present post in reward for a career remarkably free from intrigue or ambition. He is a frugal man, who once wore one pair of foreign shoes for five years. The peasants call him Lin "Hu-tsu" (whiskers), because he has a dangling white beard. Once, tramping up the mountain walk to Chiang's house in Kuling, he sat on a stone bench to rest, and scribbled on it, "Those who have concubines, do not sit." His salary is $800 (Chinese), or $128 U. S. per month.

A quite different type of man is Sun Fo, known as the "Crown Prince." He was born in Kwangtung in 1891, the only child of Sun Yat-sen by his first wife. This old lady is still alive, a recluse in Macao (Portuguese territory near Hong Kong); the great Doctor divorced her to marry the marvelous Soong sister now known as Madame Sun Yat-sen. In reality, two Madame Sun Yat-sens exist. The elder one, Sun Fo's mother, is a Baptist (the Soongs are Methodist); the old lady lives quietly, has no interest in politics, and is a simple, pleasant character.

Sun Fo went to school for a time in Hawaii, then at the University of California and Columbia University. He returned to China in 1917 to assist his father, whose secretary he became; later he was mayor

[2] Note that five of these eight belong to a single family group, Generalissimo and Madame Chiang, Madame Sun Yat-sen, Dr. Kung, and T. V. Soong.

of Canton, minister of railways, and president of the Legislative Yuan, which post he holds in 1939. He will, it is assumed, be the next deputy leader—under Chiang Kai-shek—of the Kuomintang. Sun Fo's allegiance to Chiang has been by no means uncheckered, however. For a brief interval he managed to squeeze him out as prime minister, and in 1930 was sympathetic to the "Northern Coalition" which made war on him. Sun Fo has always been radical. He wanted to fight the Japanese, not the Reds. He is to-day very close to the United Front. In 1938 he made two trips to Moscow, seeking to arrange closer Sino-Soviet coöperation.

The Japanese dislike Sun Fo intensely, though once—when his temporary opposition to Chiang Kai-shek made it necessary for him to get out of China quickly—they flew him out. This was in 1930. Times change. In October 1938 one of the airliners jointly operated by China and an American company was shot down by Japanese, and the fourteen passengers killed. This was one of the very few civil airplanes that the Japanese have ever attacked; the reason, it is believed, is that they thought Sun Fo was a passenger.

Sun Fo is an intelligent man, pleasant in appearance, rich, cultivated, ambitious. He may go far. But, like Lin Sen, he is not a general; he has no army, and for this reason it is difficult for him to retain really high office except by the favor of others.

The Kwangsi Twins

These are among the finest and ablest men in China, or for that matter anywhere. The two Kwangsi generals, Li Tsung-jen (pronounced "Lee Tsung-ren") and Pai Chung-hsi ("Buy Joong-shee") have had such inseparable careers that they are usually spoken of together as a joint entity like Hindenburg-Ludendorff; like the Red generals Mao Tse-tung and Chu Teh, they are sometimes thought of as actually the same person, under the name "Li-pai." They are signally complementary. Li is a plain man, unpolished; Pai is more sophisticated. Li has been called the iron fist inside Pai's silk glove. Li is older, and remains senior in rank; Pai does more work in the field, and is in active command.

The importance of these two generals is simple, and may be simply expressed. First, they are the best officers Chiang has. Second, their army is incontestably the best in China for general operations, better even than the Red Army, which specializes in guerrilla warfare. Li and Pai are poor men, intensely honest, hard-working, and patriotic. In 1935, angry because Chiang Kai-shek was wavering before Japan, they seceded in their stronghold Kwangsi[3] and set up a virtually independent régime. Immediately after the Marco Polo incident they offered themselves and their armies to the United Command. Pai— who had been Chiang's indispensable assistant in the early years— flew to Nanking; he had not shaken hands with the Generalissimo for eight years. Promptly Chiang made him chief of staff of the national army, which he still is.

Li Tsung-jen looks like a hard-bitten and husky Mongoloid long-shoreman. He was born in 1890, a native of Kwangsi. In his early days he was—unusual among Chinese—a gymnasium instructor. By 1925 he had joined the revolution, and became one of Chiang's best soldiers. Three things distinguished him, as they distinguished Pai, from the old-style Chinese military: he was not in the business of feathering his own nest, he was not "squeezing" for himself; he had real military training under actual combat conditions; he had a firmly integrated political ideal—the unification of China against Japan. Good observers call Li "the most sincere man in China."

General Pai Chung-hsi was born in 1893. Like Li, he went to the Paoting Military Academy, and promptly joined the revolution. He is a Moslem: which gives him special and particular importance. During the present war he took a long trip through Kansu and the Northwest, sounding out Moslem opinion and counteracting Japanese propaganda, seeking to keep the Mohammedans safe for China in the critical region where they control the supply route to the U.S.S.R. He is the only man in China, it is said, who has dared to countermand Chiang's military orders in the field if he thinks them incorrect. He is called the best professional strategist in the Chinese army.

I have mentioned in Chapter XI that incredible campaign in 1927-28 when Chiang Kai-shek, marching north, performed one of the most extraordinary of modern military feats by capturing Shanghai, Nanking, Hankow, Peking, and thus unifying China provisionally. Let us not detract from the splendid fixity of vision and organizing skill which directed that accomplishment. Let us also say, however, that very nearly all the actual fighting was done by Pai and Li. They led their hard-bitten and beautifully disciplined southern troops into the Chekiang area; Li took Shanghai (with Pai an inch behind

[3] The only province in China with universal conscription, incidentally.

him), and Pai beat off the northern war lords later; together they took the Wuhan cities; Pai got actually beyond Peking, the first Chinese in more than a generation to push through the Great Wall, and reach the borders of Manchuria.

Pai Chung-hsi has at times attacked the Reds, though he winked at their passage through a part of his Kwangsi domain during the Long March, on severe conditions. The story is told that he once saved the life of Chou En-lai, the communist intermediary at Sian, whom he admired. Chou was caught in one of Pai's early purges. Pai knew who he was, though Chou had taken another name. Pai arranged to sit in justice on him himself, let him go, and never revealed his identity, which if known publicy would have made execution unavoidable.

General Pai thinks that the war will last three more years. He said recently that China has supplies ample for that time. If Chiang Kai-shek should by some misfortune be eliminated, opinion is general that Pai is overwhelmingly the strongest candidate as his military successor. If the Japanese could buy off Pai and Li—they have tried hard with no success—China might meet disaster.

Chen Cheng and Chang Chun

These two Chinese generals, both of cardinal importance, are confusingly similar in name. Arriving in China, I had two dominant ambitions: first, interview Generalissimo Chiang Kai-shek, the Soong family, and the Red Army leaders; second, learn to tell Chen Cheng and Chang Chun apart. The pronunciation of their names is almost identical.

General Chen Cheng. We will call him simply Chen. He is, I have mentioned, the leader of the Whampoa Officers group in the Kuomintang. He is also former military commander of the Hankow area, minister of political training in the National Military Council, and ex-minister of war. He combines very strong party affiliations with military strength, though he has no army of his own. He was born in 1900 and looks unbelievably youthful. The Generalissimo likes him extremely, and acted as personal go-between or matchmaker for his marriage; he was captured with Chiang at Sian. It is generally believed that he has been chosen by the Generalissimo as his political successor. Most people in China would say that he was No. 2 to Chiang in a political sense, as Pai is No. 2 militarily.

General Chang Chun. We will call him simply Chang. He is a

former mayor of Greater Shanghai, a former foreign minister, secretary general to the Military Council, and at present vice president of the Executive Yuan, that is assistant prime minister. He is very close to Chiang Kai-shek. They met in Japan in 1910, returned to China together to join the revolution, and have been good friends ever since. His wife is a Christian. His tenure as foreign minister (1935-37) was extremely difficult; he was continually pressed by Japan to make concessions, while his own people called him pro-Japanese. He is anti-Red.

Four More Chens

The Chen brothers, leaders of the "C. C." clique in the Kuomintang and sons of the old Shanghai millionaire and Green Society leader who gave Chiang Kai-shek his start, are a waning influence nowadays, though for a long time they were the party bosses; in the Nanking days the Chen boys really ruled the Kuomintang. Chen Kuo-fu, the elder, was born in 1892, and for a time was in the exchange business in Shanghai; he helped finance Chiang Kai-shek, became governor of Kiangsu, and is now minister of education. Chen Li-fu is seven years younger, and is rather effeminate in appearance. In *Who's Who in China* it is said that "he is the founder of a new system of philosophy based on Sun Yat-sen's teachings and set forth in a two-volume work" that has sold 100,000 copies. He was the main organizer of Madame Chiang's New Life Movement, the attempt to create an antidote to warlordism in the shape of Y.M.C.A. uplift. Both Chen brothers, as befits party bosses, are public-shy.

.   .   .   .

Another Chen, Eugene Chen or Chen Yu-jen, is the furthest possible remove from the Chens above. He was born in the British West Indies of mixed blood, in 1878, and became world famous as foreign minister in Hankow in 1927, the Left government dominated by Borodin and later overthrown by Chiang Kai-shek. Born and educated abroad, he does not know the Chinese language well. A violent radical, something of a bombast, a careerist politician, he is not popular these days, though he was reinstated into the Kuomintang in July 1938, along with Chou En-lai, Mao Tse-tung, and others who had been in the wilderness for long years. Eugene Chen has been foreign minister in three different Chinese governments, but never in the

National Government since the Kuomintang turned Right: first in Hankow, then in Canton during a short-lived Cantonese independent régime in 1931, then in 1934 in Fukien when the radical 19th Route Army set up a government there. Chen has one considerable achievement to his credit: he negotiated what is known as the Chen-O'Malley Agreement whereby the British voluntarily gave up their concession in Hankow—something it is not always easy to persuade the British to do. Chen has several interesting children, including a boy, Jack, who is the best political cartoonist in China, and a girl, Sylvia, who is a talented dancer. He flits in and out of China. Whenever he returns, people say that something must be in the wind, since he has a great reputation as a trouble-shooter.

·   ·   ·   ·   ·   ·   ·

Another Chen, and one widely variegated from the rest, is Chen Tu-hsiu, born in Anhwei in 1879, who was one of the organizers of the communist party in China and its secretary general for some years. Later he took a Trotskyist position, and was known as the chief Trotskyist in China. He is a literary man and great scholar, and was educated in France. In 1932 he was arrested, and after a sensational trial sentenced to fifteen years imprisonment. He is said, however, to be well-treated in jail, especially since the United Front, because of his early services to the literary revival in China and to the revolution.

There are 131 different Chens, Chengs, Chuns, and Chungs in the Chinese *Who's Who*. Many deserve a word. But we must press on.

Ambassador Dr. Hu Shih

"Our armies are now undergoing the hardships and trials of China's Valley Forge."   —DR. HU SHIH

I began this chapter by stating that many more important Chinese remain to be discussed; I might have added that almost beyond doubt the single most distinguished living Chinese, from any point of view not narrowly political, is some one so far scarcely mentioned in this book, Dr. Hu Shih (pronounced "Hoo Shur"), the Chinese Ambassador to the United States. It is an impertinence to attempt to compress his life in a paragraph or two. I must, however, give the bare facts.

Charming like almost all Chinese, convivial, graceful, a realist, Dr. Hu Shih is father of what is called the Chinese Renaissance, the literary and social movement which came after the fall of the Manchus, and which complemented and assisted Dr. Sun's political revolution. As with most great movements, its driving line was simple. Dr. Hu had started learning Chinese when he was three, and knew thousands of characters at ten; he remained appalled at the enormous, the inconceivable difficulties and multiplicities of the language. So he invented Pai-hua, the simplified tongue I have already alluded to. He sought to give his people a simple language they could learn easily and understand easily, one they could *use*. Pai-hua spread, as Dr. Hu and his disciples wrote poems and philosophies in it, instead of in the intolerably obscure and complex Mandarin. This attempt by Hu Shih to simplify Chinese may rank historically with the reformation of English by Chaucer, or with the replacement of Latin by French in Europe after the Middle Ages.

Hu Shih is one of those extraordinary men starred by fortune from the beginning, and endowed with intellectual strength of an almost abnormal nature. A man like the Christian general, Feng Yu-hsiang, is a physical giant; so, literally, Hu Shih is a mental giant—though he is not a monstrosity like Feng.

He was born in Shanghai in 1891. His father was an elderly scholar and geographer; his mother, the father's third wife, was much younger, under twenty when he was born. The father died when he was three; to his mother he says he owes "everything." At twelve the youthful prodigy had memorized most of the Chinese classics—a feat comparable, say, to memorizing Shakespeare, Dante, Milton, Lucretius, Racine—and sought new intellectual worlds. His family was poor; he had to support himself and his mother teaching, and he became a journalist. He got a scholarship for study abroad, and went, of all places, to the agricultural school at Cornell University; he thought that China might be regenerated by scientific agriculture, and decided to become a farmer! He began, however, to read western political and philosophical works—incidentally discovering on reading Darwin that his own name meant "survival of fittest"—and left Cornell for Columbia, where he studied philosophy and literature. Here he came strongly under the influence of John Dewey. In 1914 he wrote a prize winning paper on Robert Browning; in 1917 his Ph.D. thesis at Columbia was "The Development of Logical Method in Ancient China," which promptly became a classic. Hu found himself famous—almost. He returned to China, wrote vastly (confounding the critics by producing excellent verse in the vernacular language), and began to be interested in politics. Variously he was professor of philosophy in Peking National University, author of an immense work on Chinese philosophical history, editor of a weekly political newspaper called the *Endeavor*, an indefatigable lecturer and political theorist, and (1927-30), president of the China National Institute at Woosung. He traveled abroad, wrote twelve volumes of collected essays, began a translation of Shakespeare into Chinese, published other literary works, edited another magazine known as the *Independent Critic*, and in 1931 became Dean of the School of Literature in Peking University. Though he was not a member of the Kuomintang (which indeed he had often severely criticized), and though he had never held a political post, he was named Chinese Ambassador to the United States in 1937. When the Japanese heard of his appointment, they decided to send "three" Japanese ambassadors to Washington, in order to match his prodigious energy and talent.

Do not think from this sketch that Dr. Hu is an ivory tower type of student, a recluse. On the contrary. He is crammed with enjoyment of life. He loves to talk, smoke, have dinner parties, meet friends, and is devoted to his family.

Hu has been called the Voltaire of China. From the age of eleven or twelve he set himself against Buddha and mysticism. For a long time, however, he flirted with the concept of non-violence; apparently the necessity to resist Japan blasted it out of him. He is now the best type of discriminating Chinese nationalist.

. . . .

China has been particularly rich in her ambassadors. There is Dr. Alfred Sze, who competently represented China at the League of Nations, and the learned Dr. C. T. Wang, who was Hu Shih's predecessor at Washington. In London China has Quo Tai-chi, one of the most engaging of all Chinese; quick-witted, brilliant with humor, an astute and incisive politician. He was once editor of the *Pennsylvanian* at the University of Pennsylvania, once secretary and publicity director to Sun Yat-sen. He has been a delegate to the Paris peace conference, president of a university, and a vice-minister of Foreign Affairs.

In Paris is the positively mythical Dr. Wellington Koo, who—quite aside from his accomplishments in China—has been called the most brilliant student in the history of Columbia University. He arrived scarcely knowing English; in three years he had both B.A. and M.A. with various honors, and found time meantime to run the debating team and edit the *Columbian* and *Spectator*, two of the university publications. His LL.D. (Causa honoris) is from Yale. Koo became Chinese minister to the United States at the unearthly age of twenty-seven. He brought China into the League—which later let China down. His career has been greatly assisted by his competent and beautiful wife.

The Mysterious Mr. Wang Ching-wei

There is distorted genius in this man. His name is not well known abroad. Until a few months ago he would have been on any Chinese list of the dozen most important living Chinese.

When I met Wang Ching-wei I gasped. He is fifty-three; he looks twenty-eight, an extraordinarily handsome man, slight and supple. Here is one of the fathers of the Chinese revolution. He might almost be a schoolboy.

It is very difficult to write about Wang, because his career has been marked by such variegated inconsistencies. He is a poet; yet all his life has been pursued by violence. He started on the extreme left wing; he ended as an implacable Red-hunter. He is one of the most disloyal men in history, in that his life vis-à-vis Chiang Kai-shek is a checkerboard of allegiance and repudiation; yet he would say that it was Chiang Kai-shek who alternately supported and repudiated him. Wang is something of an individualist and egoist—to put it mildly.

Wang Ching-wei was born in Canton, though his family came from Chekiang. He finished his education in Japan, where he met Dr. Sun and joined his group of exiles. He was first a voluble journalist and party organizer, and then a terrorist. He returned to China, and assisted by his fiancée attempted on March 28, 1910 to blow up the Prince Regent (father of Henry Pu-yi) by bombing a bridge. Normally he would have been beheaded, after torture; the Empress Dowager, however, became interested in this young firebrand—and his extraordinary good looks—and he was sentenced merely to life imprisonment. The collapse of the monarchy in 1911 freed him.

Wang promptly went to Canton, rejoined Sun Yat-sen, and was his chief assistant until Sun's death. It is quite clear that the great Doctor intended Wang to be his political successor, whereas Chiang Kai-shek was scheduled for military leadership; Wang himself wrote Sun's last will and testament. At this time Wang was emphatically on the Left; he was chairman of the Leftist government at Hankow in 1927, though obscured by Eugene Chen and Borodin.

Came the split. Wang went to exile in France to think it over. Gradually he turned Right, and finally joined Chiang. They had their ups and downs. In 1930 he joined the Northern Coalition to fight Chiang openly. More exile. He returned, reëntered the fold, and with Chiang's connivance became prime minister. The Generalissimo, surpassingly long-minded and wily, needed Wang to unify the party. He himself receded temporarily into the background. In 1935 Wang was shot by an assailant who disguised himself as a newspaper photographer, with a revolver ingeniously concealed in his camera. He was terribly wounded, but recovered. The motive for the shooting is obscure, and is still, four years later, being investigated. Wang had had a Right period, and seemed to be settling back to a middle leftist course. Both Rights and Lefts had reason to hate him. Patriots said that he was inordinately pro-Japanese. But possibly he was pro-Japanese on Chiang's order; possibly the Generalissimo was shrewdly using him to buy off Japanese attack. The Blue Shirts hated Wang too.

Wang went abroad and stayed away until the Sian kidnaping. He rushed back to China, still a great influence in the party, and now leader of a special group known as the "Reorganizationists." In 1937 he was made deputy leader of the Kuomintang under Chiang. Yet insiders felt that he was sympathetic to the Japanese. Chiang, however, still had use for him. But in December 1938 came another—and major—shift. He jumped right out of China. He bolted suddenly after the capture of Canton. He fled to Hong Kong and then Indo-China.

Wang's poems have been issued in English translation.[4] They have great color and feeling for nature. Samples:

> The quiet lake gleams as if covered with snow,
> And lovelier than snow appear the plum flowers;
> Endlessly the track winds among the hills,

[4] *Poems of Wang Ching-wei*, Translated into English by Seyuan Shu. London, Allen and Unwin, 1938.

Scarcely have I finished my song before a subtle fragrance
comes this way in the breeze.

And one called "Arising at Dawn":

How ravishing is the morning air above this quiet vale,
Fresh as early autumn and soft as spring;
The fading moon looks at the vanishing stars,
On these bowers of jade no dust can ever settle.

When in China Wang likes to live in his big house in Shanghai.
He is rich, but not ostentatious. He has six children; he likes bean
milk; he is kind to his servants; everyone in the house must retire
at 10 P.M. promptly, and rise at 6; he is an atheist, but has built a
small Buddhist temple in the garden for his mother-in-law; the house
contains an elaborate system of alarms, sirens, searchlights, and elec-
trically charged barbed wire entanglements.

The Generalissimo was in Sian inspecting the front with Madame
and Donald on Christmas Eve, 1938—two years to a day after their
release—when they heard of Wang's last defection. Previously their
suspicions were aroused. Wang had seen the Generalissimo in Chungking on the eighteenth, and said he was going to Chengtu to make a
speech. Then came a telegram from the governor of Yunnan stating
that Wang had arrived there by plane, and was talking about peace.
"Do you know anything about this?" the Yunnan governor telegraphed
the Generalissimo, who replied that peace on the recent terms enunciated by Japan was utterly impossible, and that Wang had no authority to discuss peace terms. Then the Generalissimo heard that Wang
was outside China. He told Donald to pick up the phone, and notify
the American and British embassies in Chungking that Wang was
disavowed.

Next—a wonderful Chiang Kai-shek touch—he telegraphed Wang
suggesting that he return freely to China as soon as he had recovered
from the sudden "illness" that had taken him away.

Others were not so forgiving. In the press Wang was called a
traitor, "a piece of rotten meat," and an "undesirable horse." On New
Year's Day the Kuomintang, meeting in special session, expelled him
and deprived him of all his posts.

Chiang Kai-shek, with his prodigious instinct never to be finally
quit of an enemy, on the chance that some day, some day, he might
become useful again, was content to let Wang keep what miserable

face he had left. Not so some young Chinese direct-actionists. They followed Wang to French Indo-China, and on March 20, 1939, shot him. Again—enduring man, with indomitable vitality—he survived his wounds.

Later, in May, it was reported that the ubiquitous Japanese General Doihara had arrived in the south to prevail upon Wang to head a coalescence of Japanese puppet governments in China. The story sounds too facile, but may be true.

Final unpleasant touch. The great city Changsha, capital of Hunan, was destroyed by fire late in 1938, following a panicky rumor that Japanese troops were just outside the city. (As a matter of fact, they were ninety miles away, and still have not captured it.) Wang, it is said, took advantage of this conflagration—stupidly made by precipitous scorched-earthers—to urge a Kuomintang split. He accused the communists of responsibility for the fire, though Chou En-lai, who was there, almost perished in it. Now the communists say that Wang's men may have had something to do with this disastrous fire—60,000 houses were burned and hundreds of them died—themselves.

Another Wang

There are several million Wangs in China; there are several hundred Wangs in the Chinese *Who's Who.*[5] Let us mention one more, who is utterly unlike Wang Ching-wei, although his name is very similar—Wang Chung-hui, the minister for Foreign Affairs in the National Government. A scrupulously devoted public servant, his record goes back a long way. His career has been mostly in law. He went to Yale, translated the German Civil Code into English, co-edited the journal of the American Bar Association, progressed to England, was called to the Bar of the Inner Temple. He was several times Chinese minister of justice, and for some years served on the Permanent Court of International Justice at The Hague.

Dr. Wang is an intensely shy man, a trifle bowed, with a passion for detail and great love for his work. As wartime foreign minister he has not, unfortunately, had a great deal of attractive work to do.

A Brace of Ho's

General Ho Ying-chin is minister of war. His importance is largely titular. I have heard him described as a jellyfish. He was born in

[5] Exactly as in the American *Who's Who* there are 281 Smiths.

Kweichow, in the far southwest, in 1889; his courtesy name has charm—Chin-chin. He is another of the group of early friends of Dr. Sun educated in Japan; his record of military activity is long, and he is conspicuous in having never once swerved in loyalty to Chiang Kai-shek. For some years a member of the "Political Science" clique of the Kuomintang, he wanted conciliation with Japan; it was he who, as minister of war, signed the Ho-Umedzu Agreement opening up part of north China to Japanese penetration. But, obeying Chiang Kai-shek who at that time was following an apparently pro-Japanese policy, he had no choice. He was the leader of the Nanking group which most strenuously wanted to rescue Chiang from the Sian kidnapers by force of arms.

Another Ho is General Ho Chien, ex-governor of Hunan, and minister of the interior. He was born in Hunan in 1887, and has literary pretensions; he is the author of a book called "The Five Human Relationships and the Eight Virtues." For some years General Ho Chien was Commander-in-Chief of the First Route Army of Communist Suppression Forces; as such he was the most merciless of all the anti-Red generals; the communists say that in his native province alone he caused to be executed not less than 20,000 people. He has one of the cruelest faces I have ever seen.

The Capone of Shanghai

This is an engaging ruffian. I have heard him called "the most interesting man" in China. He is variously known as Dou Yung, Dou Yu-seng, Tu Yueh-sheng, and Tu Tuh-hseng; he was for years the opium boss of Shanghai, and built up a colossal fortune from the narcotic traffic. He is in his late forties, and was a potato vendor by origin. He has, of course, lived down his salad days; his occupation is officially given as "banker and public welfare worker," which is indeed correct, since he is president of a very important local bank, the Tung Wai Bank, and is a director of the Bank of China; moreover, he went into philanthropic work quite seriously, and was the efficient —and strongly anti-Japanese—head of the Shanghai Civic Association for some years.

Tu (or Dou) "muscled into" the opium traffic in the early days, and became a powerful leader of the Green Society. He inevitably turned to politics. All patriotic revolutionary organizations are, in effect, secret societies which at the proper time become public societies.

This is true of the communist party in Russia, the Fascist party in Italy; and it was almost true of Tu's Ching-Pang. Tu rendered considerable service to Chiang Kai-shek, then also a Green Society man, and he is one of the few men whom the Generalissimo listens to attentively. With the Chen brothers who at that time bossed the Kuomintang, Tu is supposed to have been the intermediary between Chiang and the local bankers when Chiang turned Left to Right. Some five thousand Red workers were killed in Shanghai as a result in the next few weeks.

Tu's headquarters are in the French Concession in Shanghai, on the Rue Doumer; his house, hidden behind a high stone wall, adjoins a charming garden containing a small shrine. He is perfectly "respectable" to-day and patriotic. Not only is he a banker and philanthropist; he controls newspapers (he is managing director of the *China Press* and *China Times*, for instance), electricity plants, produce marts, and mills.

Doubtless the story is apocryphal, but in his early days it was said that Tu was strongly displeased at a very high official indeed of the National Government, who was so tactless as to interfere with the narcotic trade. The high official found a large, handsome coffin delivered to his door one morning. He reformed.

Late in 1938 Tu moved to Hong Kong. The French authorities thought that he was so conspicuous helping Chinese refugees that his continued presence in Shanghai might provoke an "incident." Tu has the reputation of fairly eating Japanese for breakfast.

Assorted Generals

Until Canton was taken by Japan the governor of Kwangtung was one of Chiang Kai-shek's ablest subordinates, General Wu Te-chen, a big strapping man with a friendly smile, attentive and alert, and one of the most attractive personalities in China. Responsibility for the loss of Canton was not his. He learned English, which he speaks with a fantastic accent, in Honolulu; one of his sons is a student at the Massachusetts Institute of Technology. General Wu was born in 1888, and joined the revolution in 1911. For some years he was Chiang Kai-shek's chief of police, and then the competent mayor of Shanghai. With infinite patience and tenacity, he withstood the early assault of Japanese surliness, truculence and provocation in the Shanghai area. General Wu is supposed to have been the intermediary who persuaded the Young Marshal to join forces with the National Government after the death of Chang Tso-lin.

Attached to Wu's staff—Wu is now fighting in the field—is one of the most picturesque of foreigners who have devoted their lives to China, General Morris Cohen, a massive Englishman who was for many years Sun Yat-sen's chief aide-de-camp and bodyguard. He now performs the same service for General Wu.

General Sung Cheh-yuan, a Shantung man of the old war lord type, who was originally one of Christian General Feng's army commanders, was chairman of the Hopei-Chahar Political Council. As such, he was adjudged responsible for the loss of Peking and Tientsin in 1937, and removed from his command. He was never, however, as is sometimes said, a Japanese puppet; he had the thankless job of trying to keep the Japanese in check, while officially serving Chiang Kai-shek. His main policy was to try to outmaneuver the Japanese by willful delay; his weakness was that he never knew if Chiang would back him up. He was conveniently—or inconveniently depending on the point of view—not in Peking when the war started, but visiting the graves of his ancestors in Shantung.

An attractive character is General Tsai Ting-kai, the commander of the Nineteenth Route Army which defended Shanghai in 1932.[6] He fought like a tiger. A strong left winger, he then collected remnants of his demolished force, retreated to Fukien, and in 1934 set up a short-lived independent régime there, with Eugene Chen as foreign minister. By using air power, the Generalissimo crushed it. Tsai Ting-kai was in hospital with a broken leg when the 1937 war came. Promptly, like his Kwangsi friends Pai and Li, he offered his services to Chiang when it appeared finally that the Generalissimo was going to resist Japan.

Another fighting general is Chang Fah-kwei, known as "Old Ironsides" for his defense of Pootung in 1937. He was for a long time military boss of Chekiang, and one of the Generalissimo's best men. He has considerable political strength, which derived partly from his

[6] This famous army, a Cantonese force, happened to be in the Shanghai neighborhood in 1932 for a curious and very Chinese reason. Chiang Kai-shek had just arrested one of the early Kuomintang founders, Hu Han-min. Civil war loomed. Chiang released Hu at last, with the understanding that the Cantonese army should be near by to watch him. So the Nineteenth Route Army drifted north. When the war began, an excellent force, it fought. One reason why Chiang did not support it was jealousy both of Hu and the Cantonese.

close association with overseas Chinese; he lived for some time in the United States. He is to-day army commander in Kwangtung, in charge of counter-operations to regain Canton, after a period directing the guerrilla struggle in the Shanghai area. He is a member of the Central Supervisory Committee of the Kuomintang.

Cabinet Officers and Politicians

An exceptionally able official, Dr. Oong (also Wong and Weng) Wen-hao, is minister of national economy. He represents a new and healthy trend, that of disinterested civilian experts giving up private life to join the government, thus helping to form a new administrative cadre. A geologist by profession and a graduate of the University of Louvain, Dr. Oong was once a university president; he left academic life to become a mining engineer. He is one of the best men in China. Largely through his efforts the immense transplantation of Chinese industry to the west got underway. Dr. Oong and his staff bodily moved not less than 138 factories by the end of 1938, including sixty-four machine shops, eighteen electrical plants, twenty-two chemical plants, five glass factories, seven cotton mills, twelve printing plants, four dockyards, four other plants. This was a literally stupendous undertaking. The total weight of the machinery moved and transplanted on coolie back for hundreds of miles was 24,919 tons.

In a similar category is the minister of communications, Chang Kia-ngau. A banker by profession and for years the managing director of the Bank of China (he was sometimes called the "best banker in China"), he had been outside politics until 1936, and even now is not a member of the Kuomintang, though he holds one of the most important government posts. He was the first high official I met in Hankow; I was impressed by the acute sense he gave of technical experthood putting itself at the disposal of the government. Oong, just mentioned above, and Chang Kia-ngau resemble in a way the great industrial chieftains like Bernard Baruch who were mobilized for government service in the United States in 1917. His importance is considerable, as is the movement he represents.

Attached to the Executive Yuan, though not actual cabinet ministers, are a group of officials with special departments. Head of the Anti-Opium Commission is Kan Nai-kuang, a journalist, writer, and professor of political science. Mongolian and Tibetan affairs are managed by General Wu Chung-hsin, who was formerly governor of

Kweichow. Chairman of the Famine Relief Commission is Hsu Shih-ying, once ambassador to Japan; a small man, weighing under a hundred pounds, his province includes the immense task of refugee relief. He is a former supreme court justice and prime minister. Overseas affairs are handled by Chen Shu-jen, educated in Japan and formerly an adherent of Wang Ching-wei.

The chairman of the second Yuan, the Legislative Yuan, is, as we know, Sun Fo. Chairman of the Judicial Yuan is Chu Cheng, a graduate of a Japanese law college, who has a long record of Kuomintang service; he is a veteran, one of the old Sun Yat-sen followers. The Examination Yuan is headed by Tai Chi-tao, a scholar born in 1890, who wrote poems when he was nine years old. He was a revolutionist at sixteen, and is a Buddhist and a vegetarian. Yu Yu-jen is chairman of the Control Yuan; he was born in Shensi, educated in a French school, and a journalist who joined the revolution in 1911. He has the longest beard in China, and is one of the elders of the movement.

The present secretary general of the Kuomintang, who can make of his post an extremely important job, is a younger and more active figure, Chu Chia-hua, formerly minister of communications. Born in Chekiang in 1892, Chu is a Ph.D. from the University of Berlin, and was for some years professor of physics at Peking University, then president of Chung Shan University at Canton, then minister of education. A graceful, sensitive, accomplished man, he represents a new type of Kuomintang party boss.

Parties Outside the Kuomintang

Until the war these were not permitted to exist. Then came the United Front with the communists, and concurrently Chiang Kai-shek performed one of his typical all-sides-of-the-fence maneuvers by suddenly recognizing the legality of a minuscule National Socialist group, led by Carson Chang. This Chang was born in Kiangsu in 1886, and describes himself as jurist, author, and lecturer; he studied in Japan and Germany, and has written a book *Social Democracy in the New Germany*. His semi-Fascist party is supposed to have 10,000 members. When he was "recognized" by the Generalissimo in April 1938, he announced his fidelity to the Three People's Principles, and pledged himself to resist Japan. He has fiercely attacked the United

Front, however, and early in 1939 demanded that the Red government in Shensi give up its semi-autonomy.

The Chinese Youth Party, led by Tso Hsun-sun, a 46-year-old native of Hunan, who was educated in France, is also theoretically independent of the Kuomintang. It was founded by nationalist refugees in Paris, and has little concrete importance. It is very left wing, and seems to be vaguely Trotskyist; it does not officially belong to the United Front. In April 1938, Chiang Kai-shek permitted it to come up from underground and establish itself as a legal organization. One thing cannot be denied about the Generalissimo: sooner or later, he takes everybody in.

Chapter XVII

War Lords and Puppets

~~~~~~

*China is the greatest mystifying and stupefying fact in the
modern world, and that not only because of her age or her
geographical greatness . . .*

—LIN YUTANG

THE Chinese, reasonable people, are easier to understand than the
Japanese, who are mystics, or the Indians, who are crushed in a
perplexing way between mysticism and the British Empire. A puzzling
old-time Chinese phenomenon was that of warlordism. If the Chinese
are pacifists, why did they have so many civil wars? If they are
reasonable, why did they let war lords flourish?

One could write at considerable length about the great war lords. I
shall not do so, despite great temptation. First, it is time to be getting
on; this book is half done, and still we have covered only Japan and
China. Second, warlordism is a declining phenomenon. The expanding strength of Chinese nationalism has swallowed and almost di-
gested it. No war lord to-day plays remotely the rôle that Chang
Tso-lin once did, or even Wu Pei-fu in his blazing days.

In simple fact the war lords were not war lords at all. They were
political bosses who gained control of large provinces and milked
them. They were really Land Lords. They did not fight often; when
they did, the wars were—with one notable exception, the Northern
War against Chiang Kai-shek in 1930—tame affairs. Very little actual
fighting took place, and then only between professional retainers,
whose object was that of bullfighters—to come close to danger without getting hurt. The people seldom had anything to do with it. As a
rule wars were concluded by financial arrangement, not by combat in
the field. The agent of one war lord would buy off the troops of the
other in a monetary flanking operation.

The war lord epoch was roughly 1916 to 1927, when Chiang's unification of China got under way. The phenomenon derived from the
breakup of the Manchu Empire and the temporary incapacity of the
young republic. The old dynasty collapsed, the old viceroys fell, and

ambitious soldiers and officials recruited armies out of bandits (= unemployed soldiers) and grabbed what territory they could. Breakdown of authority produced get-rich-quick-ism on a fantastic scale.

I confine myself to six war lords, three dead and three alive. Let us begin with those alive, Wu Pei-fu, Feng Yu-hsiang, and Yen Hsishan.

The Philosopher Marshal

He is a very considerable gentleman indeed. Marshal Wu Pei-fu, born in Shantung in 1878, in retirement since Chiang Kai-shek slapped him out of politics ten years ago, was educated to be an officer, served in the Manchu army, and gave his services to the struggling republic. He did not, however, see eye to eye with Dr. Sun Yat-sen and the Cantonese, and from 1920 to 1924—after campaigns and vicissitudes too complicated to mention—asserted himself as national leader in Peking. At that time many people thought that Marshal Wu, not southerners like Chiang Kai-shek who at that time were scarcely heard of, would dominate China during the next generation. In 1924 he was ousted from Peking by General Feng, the turbulent Christian General who had been his subordinate; he spent two years in retirement in a monastery, and returned fitfully to influence in 1927. When the Hopei-Chahar Political Council was organized, he took a nominal post as special adviser, and received a salary which came from Chiang Kai-shek's Nanking government; but he never declared formal allegiance to the Generalissimo. He is almost certainly the best known Chinese outside the Chiang Kai-shek fold. Therefore the Japanese made tremendous efforts to procure him as their chief puppet in China. They besieged him with every compliment and artifice. Late in 1938 reports said that he had succumbed to the Japanese proposal, but by May 1939 he had not confirmed this by taking office. For a long time he stated that, rather than work for the Japanese, he would climb into his coffin. He has something of a sense of humor; when first approached by General Doihara, and the Japanese, he said he would be delighted to head their "Chinese" government if (1) all Japanese troops left China, and (2) Chiang Kai-shek gave permission. The Japanese were wild.

Wu Pei-fu has courage; he is one of the very few war lords who, in their various complicated dodging in and out of power, always stayed in China proper; he never took refuge, as would have been easy, in Japan or a foreign settlement. He is supposed to be very superstitious; during his retirement in Tientsin he worked on a commentary on the Chinese classics in a room scribbled with cabalistic charms. He has cared little for money; unlike most war lords, he never looted the countryside, starved the peasants. Again unlike most war lords (Feng is another exception) he has only one wife. He is a modest man, with only one conspicuous ostentation: a private spittoon bearer who follows him wherever he goes.

One of Wu Pei-fu's poems, written after defeat in battle:

The cold wind from the West stirs my old battle cloak,
To look upon the bloodstain on the cloak brings sorrow to my heart,
My only possessions now are my loyal heart and brave soul.
These will be with me forever, despite the ice and snow of the present
        situation.[1]

Marshal Wu is unusual among war lords—among most Chinese for that matter—for his appearance. He has reddish hair, and pale brown eyes. Bertrand Russell tells a story that indicates his special quality. He won a battle, but it took place in the rain, which was considered unorthodox. Promptly the Marshal informed his adversary that he would give up his gains, revert to his former line, and fight the battle over again in sunshine.

The old Marshal, without exaggeration, is said to be one of the most learned Chinese of his time; he has had a fine scholastic record since the age of eleven.

The Christian General

General Feng Yu-hsiang (pronounced "Fung You-shahng"), is sterner stuff. This sprawling hulk of a man—he is six feet four, shaped like a pyramid, with a melon-sized head—is as typical a Chinese peasant-soldier as is Wu Pei-fu (with whom he has had an exceedingly complicated relationship) a scholar-soldier. Feng is out of the soil. He is of the earth earthy.

He wears peasant clothes, and looks like a coolie projected to monstrous size. He never wears officer's uniform, and likes a wide straw hat (size ten) which he ties under his neck with a string. He eats only the simplest food, and cares nothing for either intellectual or physical luxuries. He has never eaten delicacies like sharks' fins in

[1] Quoted in J. Hampden Jackson's *Post War World*, p. 299.

his life. Once Chiang Kai-shek sent his limousine to bring him to dinner. Feng scorned the limousine, and drove up to Chiang's headquarters sitting next to the chauffeur of the rough truck used by his bodyguards. When he first came to Nanking as minister of war, he refused to live in the headquarters provided him, but took a mud hut near by. Once an American newspaper man came to interview him. Feng sat in the courtyard with his soldiers, squatting on the ground in his underwear, chewing watermelon seeds.

Feng is a Christian, and leads an exemplary personal life. His young Christian wife, who was secretary of the Peking Y.M.C.A., is his constant companion. Once she prevailed upon him to address the chapel in the Peking Union Medical College; the authorities were somewhat shocked that, arriving, he brought four bodyguards who mounted machine guns on the stage, and stood watch beside them.

Feng exhorts his troops with Christian sermons before every battle; they march into action singing "Onward, Christian Soldiers." It is not, however, true—as is almost everywhere said—that he baptized his troops wholesale with a firehose. The story originated when an American newspaper man remarked to Dwight L. Edwards of the Y.M.C.A. that Feng could more easily baptize a large contingent of troops whom he had just "converted," if he used a firehose. Feng became a Christian, it is thought, because as a boy in Paotingfu he saw some Christian missionaries massacred by Boxers, and was struck by their great courage as they were executed.

General Feng was born in Anhwei in 1880. In his autobiography, which has never been translated into a western language, he describes his early struggles. His father was a mason, and the family was unbelievably poor; Feng had six brothers and sisters, of whom five died of starvation. Apparently his terrible childhood experiences marked him deeply; he left his birthplace as a boy, and never returned—in contrast to the habits of almost all Chinese—to see the family graves until 1937. Both his father and mother were opium addicts, he writes; he loathes opium himself. In 1891 he entered the village school and stayed fifteen months, which is all the schooling he ever had. His real name was Keh-poa. He got Yu-hsiang (which means "jade" and "good luck") by accident.

He tells frankly in his autobiography of his first hatred of white foreigners, then of the Japanese. As a boy of twelve he picked up a

rifle and fired shots into a western church, on the general principle
that the fewer foreigners in the neighborhood the better. No one was
hurt, however; and six or seven years later, Feng joined the same
church he had fired upon. He fought in the first Sino-Japanese war in
1895, though he was only fifteen, and has detested the Japanese ever
since. When he became a full fledged soldier he was nicknamed what
may be translated as "Apple Pie"; his comrades thought he was so
lusciously big that the enemy would eat him alive.

A simple man, he has only two ornaments in his home—a pair of
Japanese shell-cases. He cares nothing whatever for money or display.
The Generalissimo and Madame Chiang came to dine with him re-
cently in Hankow; they got rice and black beans, and nothing else.
Recently misfortune of a personal nature crushed him; his only son—
by a first wife—was killed fighting the Japanese.

Feng's career of conspiracy and counter-conspiracy, of alternating
allegiances and shifting power, is far too complex to include in this
brief sketch. An excerpt from his official biography has charm:

1923. Director General for Defense of Northwest.
1924. Married Miss Li Teh-chuan [Christian girl].
1924. Betrayed Wu Pei-fu. [He quite candidly uses the word "be-
     trayed."]
1924. Expelled Boy Emperor Henry Pu-yi from palace.[2]

In 1920-24 he was one of Wu's trusted subordinates. He wanted
power himself, and he tossed Wu out. Later, however, he and Wu
rejoined. Along came Chang Tso-lin in 1926, descending from Manchuria; he fought and expelled both Feng and Wu. Feng fled to
Russia and stayed a year in Moscow. On another occasion, temporarily out of power, he retired in the best war lord tradition to the
Taishan monastery in Shantung, where Confucius is buried. In 1927
or thereabouts Feng became aware of the growing power of Chiang
Kai-shek. They played cat and mouse with each other for several
years. Obviously this massive peasant puzzled and impressed the
supple Chiang. He could not be bribed; he was difficult to fight. For a
time the two made an uneasy alliance; then Feng formed the "Northern Coalition" against Chiang, with two other war lords, Yen of
Shansi and Han of Shantung, plus the elusive Kuomintang politician

[2] A lively year for Feng Yu-hsiang. In 1924 also he managed to capture and
kidnap the then president of China, Tsao Kun.

Wang Ching-wei, as allies. The coalition fought Chiang almost to a standstill. Then Feng was sold out by Han, and the war collapsed.[3]

Now Feng and Chiang are closely collaborating, because Chiang is anti-Japanese, which Feng always was. When Chiang was released at Sian, old Feng was so overcome with relief and happiness that he drank three glasses of wine, the first he had tasted in many years. Feng is, however, a general without an army these grim days. He is vice-chairman of the Military Affairs Commission, a reasonably important post, but one which entails no duties in the field.

Model Governor

General Yen Hsi-shan ("Yun Shee-shahn"), the "model governor" of Shansi province, is a suspicious man. When he is shaved, one of his soldiers holds a gun at the barber's temple, in case the barber has been bribed to cut his throat.

Also the model governor is a good man in his fashion. He taxed his peasants mercilessly, but sought to give them something in return. Except for one brief interlude he has been governor of Shansi since 1911 (he seized power immediately the Manchus fell), a record no other war lord can match, and for long years Shansi was considered the best administered province in China. General Yen abolished opium, at least in theory, and built railroads and schools. While doing so he made a nest egg of $75,000,000 (Chinese). He lost it all, however, as a result of the Northern War. On being defeated he escaped to Dairen, Japanese territory, with his nest egg; the Japanese flew him back to Shansi presently, but the nest egg remained in Dairen.

General Yen's strength has been that, with the exception of the disastrous Northern War interlude, he has never sought to extend his influence beyond Shansi. He is a localist. He is not an adventurer like Feng. No one disturbed him in Shansi, which anyway was inaccessible and not particularly rich; he disturbed no one outside. As a result his province was seldom ravaged by civil war, and had a fair chance to develop prosperously. He was clever enough, incidentally, to build his railway narrow-gauge: which made it impossible for outside rolling stock, carrying soldiers, to get in.

Yen was born in 1883, and educated partly in Japan. Two things to his credit: he came under the influence of Sun Yat-sen, and sup-

[3] Feng attempted another revolt against Chiang as recently as 1933, in Inner Mongolia.

ported Chiang Kai-shek as early as 1927; in the turbulent years
1935-37 he, as much as any man, served to defeat the machinations
of General Doihara in attempting to sever the Five Northern Provinces from China. One of these is Shansi; but the Japanese could
never make Shansi's boss, General Yen, budge one inch in their
direction.

Something to his discredit: unlike Feng Yu-hsiang, who is strongly
pro-United Front, General Yen has old-style antipathies, and thinks
that the Eighth Route Army now fighting in his province (to help
save it for China) is worse than poison—though not worse than the
Japanese.

Three Dead Ones

The late General Han Fu-chu, war lord and governor of the great
province of Shantung, came to an evil and untimely end. He was a
great fence-sitter. It was his doom.

Han, born in Hopei in 1890, was a poor boy; he began life as a
coolie, and was a teamster for a time; his mother said, "Some day
you will be a war lord, and eat three meals a day." He did. A person
of great natural ability, simple, well-meaning, close to the soil, he
became attached to Feng, and fought with him for many years; in
1930, however, he betrayed him. Chiang Kai-shek recognized this
service, and in reward—but with some cautious misgivings—made
Han governor of Shantung. General Han had other titles. He was
"Commander-in-Chief of the General Reserve of the Communist
Suppression Force, member of the Peiping Readjustment Commission, member of the Peiping Branch of the National Military Affairs
Commission." He worked hard; he tried to do something for the
crushed, miserable peasantry; he was no great "squeezer," and when
he was shot had only $4,500,000 (Chinese), in the bank, a minor
sum—veritable tiddlywinks—for the man who ruled Shantung.

The war came; the Japanese offered Han $80,000,000 (Chinese) to
give up Shantung. Han refused. But he was cautious; he pursued a
double game, wanting to be on the right side when the war was over.
He withdrew from Shantung without offering serious resistance; he
let the great towns Tsinan and Tsining fall without a shot.

I have described in Chapter III above how, on one occasion, Han
fooled General Doihara. On another occasion—the last event in which
he participated—General Han got fooled himself. He was summoned

to a conference with the Generalissimo. Still sure of himself, sure that he could "explain" the loss of Shantung, he came, bringing with him a large bodyguard which could certainly protect him in the event of trouble. But immediately Han arrived at Chengchow for the rendezvous, there came a curious event: a sudden air raid alarm. Chiang rushed Han hurriedly to a special dugout. Han was thus separated from his men. Placidly he was then arrested. The air raid alarm had been invented for the purpose of capturing him. He was tried for cowardice and treachery, found guilty, and shot. This made a great impression on China. It was early in the war, and no one knew how hard-boiled Chiang was going to be with subordinates who did not toe the line.

. . . .

The fabulous creature General Chang Tsung-chang demands mention as a bizarre historical curiosity. He was Han's predecessor as war lord of Shantung. He was an utterly different type of person. Han was a rustic, an exemplary man if a traitor; Chang was vicious, if patriotic. Chang Tsung-chang was called the "Three Don't Knows." He didn't know how many soldiers he had, how much money he had, how many concubines he had. It was, however, conceded that Chang had concubines of twenty-six different *nationalities*; each had a wash-bowl marked with her flag. When not called simply "The Monster," he was called "Old Fifty-Six," for reasons, alas, which as they say cannot be mentioned in a family newspaper. A youthful American consul was summoned to Chang's palace once. He was somewhat shocked to find the general still in bed. Nor was the general alone.

Chang was six foot six. He was illiterate. He began life as a wharf coolie in Vladivostok. He could speak Russian. When he became eminent, he discovered the good Chinese need of ancestors; he prodded through Shantung, and duly found a grave thereafter attributed to his "mother." Early in the 1930's he visited Japan, and there murdered a Japanese aristocrat whose wife he fancied. The matter was hushed up, because the Japanese saw that they might have use for this man. In 1933 he was assassinated on the Tsinan railway station by a relative of a journalist whom he had executed. Chang Tsung-chang did not like newspapermen.

General Liu Hsiang ("Lyoo Shahng") was, till 1937, the war lord of great Szechwan. He was corrupt, an extortionist, cruel, illiterate, powerful, and backward. He had never been outside Szechwan till 1933; he had never seen a street car or a skyscraper. From 1920 he fought an interminable series of civil wars with members of his family; in one of these, a three-cornered fracas, all three contestants had the same name, and all were cousins. They united in one thing only: to suppress the peasants. Szechwan was till recently the most despicably looted province in China.

General Liu, lukewarm, but finding it necessary to declare fealty to Chiang Kai-shek when war came, visited Hankow in 1937. He died of a sudden illness a few days after Han of Shantung was shot. Perhaps it was just as well.

The Japanese Puppet Governments

"We are puppets . . . Do we move ourselves, or are we moved by an unseen hand at a game that pushes us off from the board?"
—ALFRED, LORD TENNYSON

I have talked much of puppets in this book. Let us finish a tiresome subject with a final brief blast of puppetry.

The Japanese, developing a new technique in imperialism, thought that their interests would be best served by employing Chinese to administer the occupied areas; they could thus assert—if the scheme worked—that Chinese were still ruling Chinese; they could call Chiang Kai-shek an outlaw, recognize their "Chinese" government, hope that other powers would recognize it; in a word, create a new "legal" China, under complete Japanese control, that would ostensibly be "Chinese," but which the Japanese would run.

Thus in the north, in and about Peking, we have what is called "The Provisional Government of the Chinese Republic," and in central China, centering on Nanking, "The Reformed Government" of China. Each is an adjunct to the Japanese military in command of the area, and the Japanese have been very careful not to consolidate them into a single puppet state. The Japanese want to keep them apart, to keep them powerless, and to stimulate jealousy between them. If, in time, the Japanese get some really prominent Chinese, like Wu Pei-fu or Wang Ching-wei, to become puppet-in-chief, then coalescence between the rival régimes is possible. In South China, following the capture of Canton, a third puppet state has been set up, but it is still embryonic. In Shanghai and the chief cities sub-puppets are in being.[4]

The Japanese have had extraordinary difficulty in getting good men to work for them. Finally they picked Wan Keh-min to head the Peking "Provisional" government. He was the seventeenth different man they had approached, and a nonentity by all-China standards. When a Chinese does accept puppethood from the Japanese, he is in grave danger of assassination. Not only do Chinese patriots set out to murder every prominent Chinese who consents to work for the Japanese; in some cases they have searched out and despoiled the graves of their ancestors, which to a good Chinese is worse than death.

The list of murders mounts daily. By May 1939 there had been about eighty political assassinations, most of them in the Shanghai area, which made Shanghai—particularly the International Settlement—the explosive focus of Japanese-Chinese conflict. Among Chinese (who worked for Japan) murdered by nationalist Chinese:

Li Lieh-wen. Puppet commissioner of police, Pootung.

Chen Yun. Puppet chairman of the Nantao District Administration.

Dr. Hsi Shih-tai. Police secretary of Greater Shanghai puppet government.

Mao Yu. Secretary general to puppet Nanking government.

Koo Ping-tsung. Financial councilor of Nanking puppet government.

Wang Chu-lin. President of the Tientsin Chamber of Commerce.

Chan Lo. Foreign Minister of the Nanking puppet government.

General Chow Feng-chi. Scheduled to be minister of war, Nanking puppet government.

Jen Pao-an. Land commissioner in the Shanghai "Ta Tao" government.

Loh Pah-hong. Catholic businessman and philanthropist, who was accused of friendliness to the Japanese.

Murder on such a wholesale basis produced retaliation. Japanese

[4] That in Shanghai is called the "Ta Tao" or "Great Way" government. The name derives from Confucius. The Japanese want to obliterate the China of the last thirty years, built anew on old Chinese doctrine. But the personnel of the Shanghai government and other city governments near by is largely Formosan. Chinese who accept jobs are imported from Formosa, where they have been under Japanese influence for a generation. Most Formosans are, in fact, not authentically Chinese.

gangs were organized and armed, especially the Huang Hwei or "Yellow Society." Among loyal Chinese killed in rebuttal was the eminent Dr. Herman C. E. Liu, president of the University of Shanghai, who was supposed to be using his great influence to prevent old Chinese friends from becoming puppets. In February 1939, a group of American journalists friendly to the Chinese in Shanghai were threatened with death, including Randall Gould, J. B. Powell, and Edgar Snow.

Wan Keh-min, president of the Executive Yuan of the "Provisional" government in Peking, was born in 1879 and educated partly in Japan; he became a banker, and for a time—circa 1924—he was finance minister. He then retired, and took no part in political life until the Japanese, desperately searching for someone to head the Peking régime, found him in Hong Kong. The negotiations were carried on by the Japanese General Umedzu. Wan's daughter has publicly denounced him for treason. But this is an overstatement. Not an unattractive personality, Wan is in a peculiarly delicate position. He took office on the understanding that the Japanese were only to "advise" him; his object was to attempt to hold something for China, to play with the Japanese hoping thus to prevent outright annexation of Chinese territory. Most Japanese in the north dislike him heartily. Wan is blind in one eye, and wears dark glasses.

The Japanese, with Wan as "front," tried to adumbrate a totalitarian régime in the Peking area closely paralleling that of Manchukuo. Occupying the same position—a mass party created after the state was set up—as the Concordia Society in Manchukuo, is the Hsin Min Hui, or New People's Association, in the Peking area. Associated with Wan in his feeling that he can—still—be something of a check to Japanese penetration in the north, is the ablest member of his cabinet, the education minister Dr. Tang Erh-ho, whom the Japanese wanted more than they wanted Wan, but who refused to be prime minister. Dr. Tang, an eminent medical man and scholar, is one of the very few Chinese who has married a Japanese.

Japan had difficulties enough in setting up the Peking government; establishing the "Reformed Government" in Nanking was even harder. Although Prime Minister Wan in the north is not at all an outstanding Chinese, he outranks by far anyone whom the Japanese could get to work with them in Nanking. The prime minister in Nanking is Liang Hung-chih, a poet and civil servant, who had no other dis-

cernible qualifications for the post except that he had (like Wan)
been a member of the "Anfu" clique, the body of pro-Japanese Chinese
who ruled Peking twenty years ago.[5]

General Ma Chan-shan of the Nonni River

This general has great and picturesque quality. He has been called
the pluckiest man in China. His name means horse, but, after all, in
England and America there are thousands of people named Lion, Fox,
or Wolf. General Ma, a northern Moslem, born in extreme poverty
of a shepherd's family, was one of the old-time guerrilla chieftains on
the Russian border. When, after the Mukden incident in 1931, the
Japanese began to advance northward to occupy all of Manchuria,
General Ma was in command of the region and decided to withstand
them. He was the first Chinese since 1895 to have courage enough to
fight a pitched battle against Japan.

He did a good job of it. He retreated, blew up a bridge over the
Nonni river, and beat the Japanese back when they tried to cross. He
appealed (vainly) for help from Chiang Kai-shek, and addressed a
remarkable telegram pleading for intervention by the League of Nations, since the Japanese had such big guns! Ma kept fighting as he
retreated, although the Japanese got reinforcements; he fought on
the Chinese eastern line, then at Tsitsihar, then finally was pushed
across the Russian border.

The Japanese decided that this man was worth having. Doihara got
in touch with him. He offered Ma a fantastic sum to join the new
Manchukuoan puppet régime, which Ma promptly accepted. Then Ma
suggested that he make a tour of the north to tranquilize his people
and adjust them to Japanese rule. The Japanese agreed. Ma promptly
decamped with all the money, used it in an attempt to re-create his
own army—*against* Japan—and established himself at Heiho, on the
River Amur, until the Japanese, boiling with rage, sent another force
to throw him out. Meantime General Ma proceeded good-humoredly
to reveal to the world what Japanese secrets he had picked up.

In the battle that followed the Japanese thought that finally they
had squared accounts with Ma. He just managed to escape, but the

---

[5] The Anfus met, in fact, at Liang's house in Peking, which was on a street
called Anfu; thus the name. It was also chosen because *An* means "peace," and
Fu is "joy."

Japanese advance guard captured his horse and equipment. This was sent to Japan, and presented to the Emperor himself, with the glad news that Ma was dead at last. Unfortunately he reappeared a few days later, escaped across the Russian border once more, and made an incredibly circuitous journey through the Soviet frontier regions and Mongolia to rejoin Chinese forces in the south.

In the 1937 war the indomitable Ma was at work again. He led guerrilla resistance to Japan in Suiyuan province.

Ma is neither a war lord nor a puppet, but a simple Chinese soldier, with guts and charm.

Chinese Miscellany

Chinese, the most civilized people on earth, keep ink in a box, and send invitations on blotting paper. Chinese smoke in church, and wear white, not black, for mourning. No long division is possible with Chinese numerals.

Chinese do not perspire; they have no ear wax and very little bodily hair. At Chinese dinners the guest of honor faces the door, presumably so that he can see his way out. Chinese houses usually face south, and are not numbered in sequence. They never kiss in public, and dislike cheese.

Chinese seldom wash the umbilicus, because this is the place where evil spirits gain entrance to the body; they celebrate birthdays of their dead relatives by playing mah-jongg; at funerals they burn paper representations of ships, houses, and elaborate conveyances and furniture which the departed may need in heaven; funerals await—sometimes for months—a propitious day.

Chinese have no word for either Yes or No; Chinese adore noises, porcelain, and philosophizing; children of Chinese concubines kowtow not to their mothers, whom they call their aunts, but to their fathers' first wives.

Chinese drug stores are identified by triangles of metal hanging outside, and noodle shops by coils of tissue paper. Chinese sign their names with a chop (rubber stamp), and pay bills on the fifteenth day of the harvest moon. Chinese are a year old the day they are born, and use bewildering "small" and "large" money. There are only twelve hours in a Chinese day, and New Year's Day is somewhere between January 21 and February 19.

Note in Diagnosis

One of the most accomplished and experienced of American diplomats abroad told me recently that one must not look for "solutions" in Sino-Japanese relations, that there is no "solution." Three dilemmas, he recounted, were "insoluble." I am sorry he is so gloomy.

First, Japan must have land, must expand: expansion can come only by conquest, which makes war inevitable for a long time.

Second, China cannot beat Japan back, but is nevertheless unconquerable: which means that the war will be "permanent."

Third, Japanese imperialism may come into conflict with Western imperialism, which will extend the war elsewhere.

Chapter XVIII
Manuel Quezon

~~~~~~

My loyalty to my party ends where my loyalty to my country begins.

—MANUEL QUEZON

ELASTIC, electric, Manuel Quezon is a sort of Beau Brummel among dictators. Here is an extraordinarily engaging little man. The prankishness of Quezon, the rakish tilt to the brim of his hat, his love for the lights of pleasure as well as the light of power, his dash and roguery, the spirited elegance of his establishment all the way from the yacht cruising on Manila Bay to the refulgent pearls—so luminous they seem—cruising on his shirtfront, combine brightly to indicate a character straight off Broadway or Piccadilly Circus, a lighthearted playboy among eastern statesmen.

But such an interpretation would express only a fraction of the complex, composite truth. Mr. Quezon, the first president of the Commonwealth of the Philippines, is a great deal more than a playboy. He is full of nerve—and nerves. He is one of the world's best ballroom dancers; also one of the world's supplest and hardest-boiled practical politicians. He loves cards and alcohol; also he loves his country and his career. He likes to laugh—even at himself—but he is a genuine revolutionary, as much the father of his country as Kamal Ataturk. The history of the Philippine Islands in the twentieth century and the biography of Manuel Quezon are indissolubly one.

When Quezon was a boy of eighteen or so he returned to his native village in the north, feeling himself a grand cock of the walk with his newly gained academy degree. Both his father and mother were school teachers. His father took him to see the chief authority of the village, a local priest who had come there while Quezon was away at school. The tradition in those days was that anyone visiting a priest must kiss his hand. The priest was a very fat man who sat with one leg sagging over the arm of a chair. He extended his pudgy hand for the boy to kiss, not otherwise moving. So young Manuel grasped and shook the hand instead of kissing it. Sensation. The priest begged

Quezon's father to punish him for his irreverence. Young Quezon bided his time. He discovered that the priest was having a liaison with a girl in the village. Quezon became acquainted with her himself, and then paraded the main street—with the priest's handkerchief stuck jauntily in *his* pocket!

At about the same time he came in conflict with the other source of authority in the village. He quarreled with an officer of the civil guard over another girl. He managed to insert himself in the girl's place at a rendezvous with the officer, knocked him down, and fled. It was a bitterly serious offense then to assault a Spanish officer. Quezon was caught, arrested, and sentenced to imprisonment. But the authorities chose to mask the real reason for the quarrel, not caring to mention the female element; they justified Quezon's arrest merely by asserting that he was a revolutionary—which was untrue. He had scarcely heard of the Filipino independence movement at this time. He began to get interested in it. The affair gave him the idea that the revolutionaries—no matter what their politics—must be nice people.

These two anecdotes, lost in years and trivial as they may seem to be, were important. Quezon would have become a revolutionist anyway, since it is his nature to expand and rebel, but this early conflict with authority sharpened him for the struggle to come, told him with irresistible pressure on which side he belonged.

Anecdotes about Quezon are abundant. Yet they do not build up into a legend. There is nothing hazy or mythological about him. He is an exceptionally concrete and compact man. He has a genius for directness, and also for the unexpected.

His nephew, training to be a cadet in an army preparatory school, was one of a group recently convicted of a hazing offense. Quezon is an enemy of nepotism—indeed it is a rule in the civil service that no two relatives may work in the same office—and he expelled the entire group of cadets, nephew included. His wife pleaded with him; Quezon was adamant, asserting that the punishment must be a lesson to the army as a whole. A month later, he gave the cadets a chance to get their commissions after all, by serving for eighteen months as privates. Once the nephew was on guard duty at Malacañan palace, the residence of the president. Quezon heard that his wife was secretly feeding the lad in the palace kitchen. He ordered her to stop this, or else feed the entire two hundred privates in the guard.

He is exceptionally impulsive and generous. Once when Malacañan was being restored he noticed a workman who didn't seem to be the ordinary type of Filipino laborer. Quezon talked to him, found that he was a student out of a job, and gave him clerical work inside the palace. The next day the whole working crew struck and asked for the same kind of easier work.

Nothing daunts him. Crossing the Atlantic once he taught the ship's orchestra to play the Filipino national anthem by tapping out the tune with one finger on the piano—though he hadn't touched a keyboard for years—and though Paderewski was a fellow passenger and startled onlooker!

He is something of a scamp. Once, courting his wife, he arrived wearing a spray of orange blossoms. She asked him why. He said airily, "Oh, I've just been married!" The poor lady burst into tears, so that Quezon knew that she really loved him.

His approach is inveterately personal. When a political prisoner is arrested, which isn't very often, Quezon usually talks to him himself. Once a prisoner had been arrested for making amateur bombs. He was the driver of a *carabao* (buffalo) cart earning fifteen cents a day. Quezon said, "This is ridiculous. No wonder you are a bomb-thrower. No one can live on fifteen cents a day." And he ordered his release.

His temper flashes quickly over little things. He may violently rebuke a secretary, and twenty minutes later completely forget what the trouble was about. He likes to quote a saying of his father's: "Better one day red than three days blue."

He is full of histrionics. His agile, intensely mobile features make him an excellent mimic and actor. When he is bored or petulant, anyone who knows him well knows it instantly, because his thick eyebrows shoot up, and his long and expressive nostrils twitch.

He is almost startlingly informal; he makes his very informality dramatic. Saying good-by to his great friend Roy Howard when Howard was in Manila last, he called alone at Howard's hotel, and simply walked in unattended and unannounced. He takes guests out yachting; he drives them home to their dwellings himself. But woe to anyone who abuses this informality by wanton insult to the dignity of his position. Swift and stinging rebuke came once to an American who, dancing at a party where Quezon was a guest, slapped him on the shoulder with a gay "Hi, Manuel!"

He is very Latin and expansive with great affection for his own roots, his own past. In his home in Pasay, a suburb of Manila, he has a large airplane photograph of the village where he was born, marked: "Here I First Saw the Light of Day." In his official residence he has built up a veritable museum of Quezoniana. Last year he was pleased beyond measure to recover at last a knife he lost when he was captured in 1899 by American troops. But he has never been able to trace and find the sword he sold for twelve *pesos* when the war was over.

Loyalty, gratitude are good political weapons, and Quezon knows it well. Dozens of friends who helped him in the early days have been rewarded with jobs or pensions. He held a man named Antonio in such affection—Antonio fed and housed him when he was poor—that he adopted his name as part of his own. He has great sympathies for the old and poor. When he was a young lawyer he charged the poor no fees, and soaked the rich.

His wife told him recently, with considerable perturbation, that she had discovered their cook, whom he greatly admired, to be a communist. Quezon went straight to the kitchen. He returned and told his wife, "The cook is not a communist. If he were a duke, he would be for the dukes. But he's a cook, and so he's for the cooks."

He likes to do things quickly. He got General Douglas MacArthur to come to Manila as his military adviser and superintendent of the military establishment of the islands in five minutes of talk. He said to MacArthur, "I want your answer to just one question: Are the islands defensible?" MacArthur said, "Yes," and Quezon offered him the job.

He seldom stands on ceremony and he always knows when it is wise to recede. Recently he stated that Tagalog, his native dialect, should become the official language of the islands. Then it was discovered that Tagalog did not contain enough of the technical vocabulary necessary to modern government. So he dropped the idea without a murmur.

After his election to the presidency he called together the rich Manilans who had supported him and paid for his campaign. "Gentlemen," he said in effect, "let there be no misunderstanding between us. Of course I know, now that I am in office, that you do *not* anticipate any political favors. You have contributed to my campaign, but surely you do not expect to derive profit from having done so. If you should have such an assumption, you would be dishonoring yourselves, by suggesting that you had attempted to bribe the President, and also myself, by suggesting that the President could be bribed." The rich Manilans were too staggered to say a word.

Once, years ago in Washington, he was chatting with friends in the office of Secretary of War Henry Stimson. Stimson turned to him suddenly: "Quezon, do you really want independence for the Filipinos?" Quezon smiled and told the anecdote of the young Spaniard who always asserted that it was his ambition to become bishop of the church. The Spaniard ended up happily enough as a janitor for the church property. Quezon winked.

A superb politician, he knows all the approaches. Once a group of legislators wasn't doing the work he expected of it. He announced, "I won't fire you, but if your job isn't finished by next Monday, I'll write a letter to the newspapers under my own name denouncing you as incompetent." The job was done by Monday.

Once Lloyd George said of De Valera: "He is like trying to pick up mercury with a fork." Quezon has something of this defiantly fluid quality.

.   .   .   .

Don Manuel Luis Quezon Antonio y Molina was born in Belar, a small town on the island of Luzon, on August 19, 1878. His father was a Filipino schoolmaster, certainly not rich, but not desperately poor, a member of the *illustrado* class; his mother, Molina by name, who also taught school, was partly Spanish. Young Quezon was a bright lad, but lazy. As a schoolboy his nickname was *gulerato*— bluffer. The family pinched itself to send him to Manila, eighty miles away, where he studied first at San Juan de Letran, a junior college, and then at the law school of the University of Santo Tomas. His studies were interrupted by the revolution against Spain in 1898.

The Philippine Islands, discovered by Magellan in 1521, were forlorn and almost forgotten remnants of the Spanish Empire. That Empire, corrupt and decadent, was governed by remote control from Madrid, but most actual power was in the hands of the local Catholic Church plus a few Spanish grandees and landowners. The Filipinos— about 9,000,000 of them then and perhaps 14,000,000 now—are in the main Malay by race, Christianized by Spain and with strong admixtures of Spanish blood. They are an easygoing people, but they rose against Spanish oppression under the patriot Aguinaldo, and were fighting a bloody and successful revolution when the Spanish-American War broke out. America attacked Spain in Philippine waters, promising to help the revolutionaries. Then America, victorious, took the islands over; Aguinaldo continued his revolt against the United States, but he was captured in 1901, and the fighting fizzled out.

Young Manuel Quezon plunged melodramatically into this situation. He joined Aguinaldo, in a year rose from private to major, and fought the Americans. Advancing under a flag of truce he was told Aguinaldo had been taken and that the revolt was over. Quezon refused to believe this. The Americans took him to Manila and showed him Aguinaldo in captivity with his own eyes. Quezon spent six months in jail; his cell was a dungeon in the city walls near the southeastern gate, and not more than a hundred yards from the Letran school he had attended. When fifteen years later he returned to Manila from Washington with the Jones Law (which prepared the way for Philippine independence) in his pocket, the gate was renamed Quezon Gate in his honor.

Quezon was furious at the United States when the rebellion collapsed. The insurrectionists who fought with the Americans in the original struggle considered themselves betrayed. Out of jail, Quezon was so angry that he refused to learn English. But he met an American officer, General Bandholtz—the first American he had ever known well—and discovered promptly that Americans were not Spaniards. Bandholtz said that Quezon must learn English and that *he* would pay Quezon, instead of vice versa, to take lessons from him! Then Bandholtz was transferred from the islands; Quezon dropped English, and did not take it up again until he became Philippine Commissioner in Washington in 1909, when he learned it with astounding speed.

Quezon's first years after the revolution were difficult. He resumed the study of law, while scratching out a living at odd jobs. His father died, and he returned to Belar to settle the family estate; then he began practice in Tabayas province. He was at once successful. Politics beckoned. He gave up his job, at which he was earning $500 per month, to accept a position as local *fiscal*, or prosecuting attorney, at $75. He got a national reputation almost at once by daring to prosecute a prominent American lawyer for fraud; this was as early as 1904, when it was almost unheard of for a youthful Filipino to attack a foreigner. By 1906 he had become governor of Tabayas; by 1908, when he was thirty, he was floor leader of the Filipino Assembly, and obviously the coming man.

The next twenty-five years were all variations on a single theme: the stubborn and wary campaign of Manuel Quezon to achieve independence for his country. Battles with ill-health; spectacular junkets;[1] a local struggle for power with Senor Osmeña, alternately his rival and running mate in Filipino affairs—these were subordinate to the unchanging main current of his life. Two things helped Quezon cardinally. One was the very considerable anti-imperialist sentiment in the United States which steadily favored liberation of the islands on political grounds. The other was the sugar lobby in Washington, which I will touch on later. Very early Quezon saw that the key to everything was Washington. So he contrived to become Resident Commissioner there, a post which he held from 1909 to 1917. He was an effective lobbyist. He helped arrange the appointment of the Pro-Filipino Francis Burton Harrison as governor general in 1913. and he was spiritual if not temporal author of the Jones Bill in 1916. He knew also that complete independence—too soon—might wreck the islands economically; he had continually to plot a sinuous middle course. By 1917 he saw that Manila was a better strategic post than Washington; he became President of the Philippine Senate and as such the first man of the islands. He had years of passionate struggle with General Wood, a governor who reversed the Harrison policy; he ingratiated himself with other governors, cajoling, bluffing, threatening. He dodged back and forth to Washington. Finally in 1934 came the Tydings-McDuffie Bill, which tentatively at least won the fight. The Philippines became a commonwealth of autonomous status, with complete independence promised in 1946.

Quezon went to the country and won its first presidential election. His chief opponent, whom he overwhelmed, was old General Aguinaldo, who wanted independence without compromise and at once. Quezon moved into Malacañan palace, and the American governor, now known as the high commissioner, rented a house in town.

. . . .

Quezon is sixty-one. He doesn't look it. He lives hard still, and

[1] In 1908, when chairman of the committee of appropriations, he sent himself to St. Petersburg as delegate to a navigation congress. Cost: 34,000 *pesos* or $17,000.

works a long and restless day. Usually he is up at dawn, and he likes to entertain at breakfast. As chief executive of the islands he has to face multitudinous administrative decisions; on anything important his is the final word. He reads the papers carefully, and a clipping bureau in America sends him by weekly airmail a big packet of news. He receives visitors in a comfortable airy room on the second floor of Malacañan, decorated in gamboge and orange. He has what seems to be a velvet swivel chair, and photographers snap pictures of El Presidente and his guest as they converse. Next day the photographers try to sell the pictures to the visitor.

The President two or three times a week makes surprise inspections anywhere in Manila. Without warning, without ceremony, he drops in at a local police station, a tobacco factory, a prison or any government department; if all is not in order, the feathers fly. He likes to listen to grievances. Sometimes he eats luncheon with workmen out in the yard.

He loves good clothes; the splendor and multiplicity of his shirts are famous. For his own dress he has invented a semi-uniform of high russet riding breeches, a soft white shirt, and a high buttoned military tunic with a high collar. But often he receives visitors informally, wearing a polo shirt open at the neck. At home he wears native Tagalog dress, which he claims to be exceptionally comfortable.

If he ever lost his job he could make an easy living at cards. He is indisputably one of the best poker players in the world. Lately he has taken up bridge, too, and likes it even better than poker. Most of his relaxation nowadays comes on his yacht, the *Casiana,* on which he cruises and dines when the day's work is done. He got it, a bargain at a reputed price of 100,000 *pesos* ($50,000), from an American oil magnate. He reads a good deal in a utilitarian way, especially when he wakes up, restless, very early in the morning, but he is an impatient reader who finds it hard to finish books he has begun. He plays golf a little, and sometimes practices mashie shots in Malacañan garden. He likes to ride, and is a tolerable horseman.

There is a bar in the palace, and he asserts that he has never refused a drink, but in fact he drinks rather little. At one reception at Malacañan that I attended, no alcohol was served at all. The President likes to joke about liquor as he likes to joke about the ladies. Old photographs show him with wonderful twirling mustachios over a jaw-breaking collar; he says he cut them off because they tickled the girls too much. Once he said,[2] apropos of alcohol.

When I left Manila the doctors told me that I could drink nothing intoxicating. When I reached Java I saw a doctor and he said a glass of beer would not hurt. So I drank beer from Java to Paris. In Paris another doctor said, "You should not drink beer; wine is the thing." So I changed gratefully to wine. Then a French specialist told me, "You should drink only champagne; it is the only drink for you." So I drank champagne for a time. Then I reached the United States, and the physicians said, "Don't drink wines or beer at all, but only whisky." So now, if I want a drink, all I have to do is decide which physician I shall obey.

He is fond of good food, but of his trim figure too. Before he underwent a serious operation at Johns Hopkins in 1934, he asked for *adobo*, a highly seasoned Filipino specialty consisting of beef steamed in vinegar, then fried with garlic. The doctors wouldn't let him have it. He enjoyed his operation, which was for gallstones, immensely; he dramatized every detail, and the newspapers in Manila carried front page photographs of all the instruments the surgeons used. He said afterward, "All I have is a thin red line that looks like a pin scratch, and I can say that it is even elegant."

But what he likes most of all is a junket. His political pilgrimages have carried him all over the world, and nothing is lacking to make the journeyings impressive. El Presidente travels with a flash and a flourish. Special trains, mass meetings, speeches are in order, and the entourage is huge. Usually Quezon takes with him a doctor, two or three secretaries, a military aide, and a half dozen hangers-on. He has learned more than one lesson from the politics of the United States: he is a junketeer par excellence, and his expense accounts are wonderful to behold.

In Manila Quezon goes from place to place in a big Chrysler Airflow with special glass which impedes the view inside. Contrary to report it is not armored or bullet proof. But there is a small revolver in the side compartment which contains writing materials, cigarettes, and the like. It bears license plate No. 1.

He wanted to attend the coronation of George VI of England during his European trip in 1937, but the British foreign office didn't

[2] Quoted in the biography, *Manuel Quezon,* by I. P. Cabellero and M. de G. Concepción, p. 376.

know quite what precedence to give him, and informally persuaded the Americans to ask him not to go. On this trip he had planned to go to Ireland and Denmark, also the U.S.S.R., to study agrarian problems; time cut his itinerary short. In Germany he saw Schacht, but not Hitler. On the way he visited Cuba and Mexico; for the Mexican President Cardenas he has terrific admiration.

About Mussolini Quezon once said, "He talks loudly but everyone can rely upon him to do the right thing." About Hitler: "That's not my idea of a leader." The President calls himself "almost a communist" except that he believes in the right of private property. But he also believes that the government has the privilege of curbing the right of private property "if and when public good demands it."

His wife, whom he adores, and who has considerable influence over him, is his first cousin. Her name was Aurora Aragon; he eloped with her to Hong Kong in 1918 after an interrupted boyhood romance. She is a pretty and cultivated woman, and a good Roman Catholic. When they were in Mexico she told her husband that perhaps she might skip going to church for once, if church-going should embarrass his conversations with Cardenas; the President replied that she could blankety-blank well go to church any time and any place she chose. The Quezons have three children, Maria Aurora, who is eighteen, Zenaida, seventeen, and Manuel, Jr., twelve.

Donna Aurora doesn't pay much attention to politics—her hobbies are orchids, her collection of dolls, and her two thousand books —but she did contribute something to the woman suffrage movement in the islands. Quezon was lukewarm on the issue, and, hoping to forestall it, arranged a compromise providing that suffrage should come if 300,000 women voted for it within a year. No one thought that 300,000 women could be found who would vote. But Mme. Quezon plunged into the campaign, and the votes were found. Quezon was uneasy, because most women voters are in the hands of the priests, whom he thinks have enough power already. But he did not want to oppose his wife's wishes.

Quezon and Paul V. McNutt, the present high commissioner, are not intimate friends, but relations between the governments are quite correct. Quezon hoped that another man would be appointed and that in any case he should be consulted on the appointment; McNutt's name was rushed through before Quezon got to Washington, and for several days he sulked, refusing to call on McNutt until Roy Howard

smoothed the matter over. Quezon says that nowadays he likes to
see McNutt in order to get away from the local politicians. He records
that his friendship with him was cemented by a poker game, in which
both were winners—Quezon, however, by a bigger margin.

The McNutt toast story set tongues wagging on several continents.
What really happened was this. When McNutt arrived on the islands
the Japanese Consul General gave him an official dinner, at which
the first toast was to the Emperor of Japan, the second to the President of the United States, the third to President Quezon, the fourth
(after rather a long pause) to High Commissioner McNutt. The
next day McNutt wrote a private and confidential memorandum to
the consular corps asking that this procedure be henceforth corrected,
since officially he, as representative of the President of the United
States, outranked Quezon. He didn't want a scandal; he was as
embarrassed as was Quezon when the story got out, which it did when
the Japanese tipped off the newspapers.

Some time later, asserting his prerogative to be consulted in all
international matters, McNutt asked that correspondence between the
various consuls and Malacañan be routed, as was correct, through him.
The Japanese sought to get around this by using the telephone instead
of writing.

Quezon has a fabulous number of friends all over the world. In
Manila those closest to him are probably his secretary Jorge Vargas,
who is his man-about-politics, and his aide-de-camp Major Manuel
Nieto. Nieto is the Brückner of the régime, the confidential bodyguard.
He knows all the secrets; when Quezon went on the operating table
at Johns Hopkins, he dictated to Nieto the letters that were to be
opened only in the event of his death. Nieto, a fine athlete and boxer,
was in the tobacco business before taking his present post. Also close
to Quezon are the four Elizalde brothers, of an old and distinguished
Spanish family who took out Filipino citizenship recently. They are
very rich; the four compose their own quite good polo team. Another
person close to the President is Adong, the seventy-year-old Chinese
body servant who goes with him everywhere, who has been with him
forty years, and who sleeps on a bench outside the master's bedroom.

Like most good American politicians Quezon gets on nicely with
newspaper men. Once he promised Dick Wilson, Manila correspondent of the United Press, some letters of introduction to friends in
China; he was suddenly stricken with appendicitis and actually while

being wheeled to the operating theater he saw Wilson in the hall, and remembered to call a secretary to tell him not to forget the letters. His press conferences are quite informal. Ninety percent of what is said is off-the-record. Once the correspondents asked him about a matter in connection with his personal religious history. Quezon couldn't remember a date exactly. He reached for the phone, telephoned his wife, and got it from her.

No one knows with certainty who will succeed Quezon when his six years are concluded in 1941. Resolutely the President has stated that he will take no second term, which indeed is forbidden by the new constitution. One obvious candidate is Vice-President Osmeña, who, incidentally, is partly Chinese in origin as Quezon is partly Spanish. Another is Manuel Roxas, a lawyer for the sugar interests and former speaker of the assembly, who like Osmeña has a checkered career of affiliation and opposition to Quezon. Another is the present minister of the interior, Elpidio Quirino, dictatorial in tendency, whom the President finds useful, but who is said to be rough and too anxious for the job. Insiders say that another possibility is Judge Teofilo Sison, who was a good secretary of the interior and chairman of the inauguration committee when Quezon became President.

Quezon's religious history is curious. He was, of course, born a Roman Catholic, but he was not confirmed until he was fourteen, although the usual age is three or four. Then he joined the revolution and became a Freemason, when Masonry, forbidden by the Spanish régime, was a symbol of the independence movement. He rose to be a thirty-second degree Mason, but was reconverted to Catholicism in 1928 after two decades of apostasy. His wife strongly wanted him to reënter the church for the sake of the children. He was ill with tuberculosis; he took communion when he thought he might be on his deathbed, but only—a typical enough Quezon touch—after saying he would refuse to believe in miracles. He is a Catholic, like everything else, on his own terms.

Stories to the contrary notwithstanding, Quezon is not particularly rich. His salary is only 30,000 pesos ($15,000) per year, and he needs every cent of it. He was always an easy spender; after several years of successful law practice in 1905, he made a great ceremony of giving a friend all the money he had saved—four dollars! He has some real estate, but he is no millionaire.

One could list many of the sources of Quezon's power. For instance, he is indisputably the best orator in the islands in any of three languages, English, Spanish, or Tagalog. His considerable charm, his patriotism, his executive capacity, his curious combination of American characteristics, like aggressive practicality, plus a Latin heritage of suppleness and adroit facility in negotiation, all contributed to his career. But his knack of getting along well with both rich and poor, with the miserably fed peasants of the countryside as well as the Spanish millionaires in Manila, is probably his single most valuable characteristic, according to the best informants in Manila. The masses adore him, because he gives them something. The rich like him too. By using both he has built up an irresistible machine.

·   ·   ·   ·   ·   ·   ·

The question of independence is alluringly complex, even if we do not touch upon the question whether or not the Filipinos are capable of self-government. Early in 1939 the situation provided one of the most attractive paradoxes we shall find in all this long tour of the East. It is that Manuel Quezon, having devoted the whole of his life to Philippine independence, isn't so sure that he wants it; it is that the people of the Philippine Islands, after forty years of agitation which have brought them to the threshold of nationhood, are increasingly alarmed that they are going to get—what they asked for.

A word on background. The Tydings-McDuffie Act provides an interim period until 1946 in which the United States retains certain rights in the islands, and is responsible for their defense. America is to give up its military bases in 1946, though the question of naval bases is left open. Until 1946, American law controls matters of tariff, immigration, debt, currency, and foreign trade. In 1946 all this is cut off. The country becomes the Philippine Republic, and swims—or sinks—alone. The theory behind the Act was to provide a ten-year transition during which the islands could learn—to swim.[3]

Now there are several points of view among Filipinos in regard to independence. Some outright folk like Aguinaldo want unconditional independence at once. They call Quezon a trimmer. Some would like

[3] In December, 1938, the Philippine-American Joint Advisory Committee, after a year and a half of investigation, advocated that the Philippines should remain on preferential trade relations with the United States for a further period until 1961. President Roosevelt has submitted the proposal to Congress. In February, 1939, Mr. Quezon asked for a Philippine plebiscite in regard to the date of full independence.

a "Permanent Commonwealth," i.e., the status quo extended in perpetuity in the form of something resembling Dominion Status. There are some who stand by the Tydings-McDuffie Act. And there are the Retentionists, who do not want independence at all, though they are not often bold enough to say so outright. Among Retentionists are the reactionary clergy, who fear social revolution when the islands are left to themselves, and the sugar interests, who know that they will no longer sell sugar profitably to the United States—and sugar is by far the most important item in the economic life of the islands —when it becomes a foreign commodity and must pass an American tariff wall. At present Filipino sugar enters the United States duty free.

The Tydings-McDuffie Act provides that beginning in 1940 the Filipinos will be charged a five percent export tax on sugar, rising five percent per year until a full tax of twenty-five percent is reached by 1946, so that the economy of the islands may adjust itself to the loss of the free American market. No one at this moment can calculate the effect of this arrangement. Thus any long range attitude to national affairs is difficult if not impossible. No one knows what future revenue will be. No one can dare to estimate future programs of public work, national finance, and the like, planning of which ought to begin to-day.

In essence the struggle for Filipino freedom is a struggle between two competing spheres of sugar interests. This is basic fact.

American sugar, and Cuban sugar which is controlled by New York finance, want the islands to be independent, so that Filipino sugar will have to pay duty in America and enter the American market at a severe and possibly fatal handicap.

Filipino sugar fears full independence. It prefers the status quo, so that it may continue to flourish by free entry into the American market, which will be lost when the islands become a foreign state and have to climb a tariff barrier.

Thus an odd situation: American interests tend to support the liberation of the Philippines, whereas Filipino interests tend to prefer the present situation, i.e., their own servitude. Patriotism? But the Filipinos say that real patriotism is to avoid independence if its result is suicide. Seventy-two percent of Philippine trade is with the United States; sixty percent of this is sugar.

American imperialism has never been as tenacious or grasping as

European imperialism; the United States is not a one hundred percent imperialist power. The Filipinos know this, and are grateful.
If you ask a Filipino why almost no one harbors deep or passionate
resentment against the United States—as an Arab, say, may harbor
resentment against an Englishman—he will say that, first, America
was a veritable fairy godmother compared to Spain, and second that
America has always been willing to clear out.

Immediately after Quezon's inauguration a curious thing occurred.
The President took Roy Howard for a cruise on the *Casiana*. When
Howard returned he wrote an obviously inspired story—this was in
1935!—to the effect that the "dream of Philippine Independence was
fading." If Quezon, having just won his fight, was indicating by
this that he hadn't wished to win it, he might justly have been accused of monstrous hypocrisy. But probably the story was a *ballon
d'essai* to sound out political opinion in the United States; Quezon
didn't want America to cut the Philippines adrift too soon.

In 1937, Quezon took the uttermost opposite line. He came to
Washington and asked for complete independence at once. He said:

The Philippines have been assisted economically and schooled politically by the United States for almost forty years. No people in history, coming under a foreign flag, have ever been treated so gener-
ously. . . . We are as competent to govern ourselves now as we can
possibly be eight years hence. . . . Under actual test the terms of the
Independence Act are proving surprisingly capable of creating irrita-
tion. One high commissioner, even if of the highest character, if
lacking in sympathy could create a most unfortunate clash. . . . One
[American] Congress apparently cannot bind the action of a suc-
ceeding Congress. Consequently, as long as we are bound by the
present Independence Act, which we have no power to alter, the
Philippines will continue to be at the mercy of every self-seeking
group of lobbyists capable of log-rolling a tariff or commercial quota
to our disadvantage.

Also Quezon must have feared that President Roosevelt might be
succeeded by a Republican Administration in 1940, which might
repeal the Tydings-McDuffie Bill.

This was in early 1937. By 1939 the situation had changed again.
Reason: the Japanese campaign in China.

The flamboyant MacArthur, former chief of staff of the United
States Army and now a Philippine Field Marshal, believes firmly that

the Filipinos, even if absolutely cut off from America, could defend
themselves. General MacArthur has a battery of technical reasons to
support his claim. The Filipino general staff agrees with him. For
one thing they say that air power would not be effective against the
islands, and that an infantry invasion is hardly possible. The Filipino
army is training 40,000 recruits a year, and is turning into a good
fighting force. But the islands have little of the industrial equipment
upon which modern war depends. They have no navy, and to assert
that they could *alone* withstand a major war seems childish. A war
would be a disaster.

Very many in the islands have genuine fear of Japan. They think
that if America goes, Japan will come in.

There is a close-knit and powerful Japanese colony in Davao,
perhaps 15,000 in all, growing hemp—and possibly trouble.

In July, 1938, Quezon made a sudden brief holiday visit to Tokyo.
He had been there several times before, and the Japanese do their
utmost to be nice to him. Quezon denied hotly a story to the effect
that he sounded out official opinion in regard to Japanese intentions
toward the Philippines. Japan, he said, was willing after 1946 to
adhere to an agreement neutralizing the islands, according to former
pronouncements of policy. Yet it would be an insult to Mr. Quezon's
very active intelligence to suggest that he does not know that Japan
is hungry for just the sort of loot the riches of the Philippines, including very large gold deposits, provide.

One can be sure that Quezon has heard of Czechoslovakia. He
will not be caught and squeezed out like Dr. Beneš.

One can be sure at least of one thing: if the islands are alone,
Quezon will make the best terms with Japan that he can get.

.   .   .   .

Politically the Philippines are an advanced democracy, at least in
theory; economically they are still in the feudal age.

Spain left its ugly heritage. Industry is largely in the hands of a
few Spanish aristocrats; the land is held largely by great landowners
or by the Church. Less than one-fifth of one percent of the landowners own twenty-one percent of the total arable land. They give
staggeringly lavish parties in Manila; their tenants pay the taxes;
the peasants starve. In one district in central Luzon ninety percent
of the land is owned by two percent of the people. The landless prole-

tariat numbers ten percent of the total population. Agrarian wages may be as low as fifteen cents a day. The Church has vast properties, some gained by gifts or purchases through the tithe, some donated by the penitent.

Quezon has begun cautiously a program of breaking up the big estates. He would like, as he says, to "complete the revolution," and abolish feudalism; he must move very slowly. He promises much. But he is roughly in the position that President Roosevelt would face if, attacking Wall Street, he knew that all his cabinet and perhaps seventy percent of his majority were Wall Street men. Quezon knows that to make a real revolution he must destroy feudalism, i.e., the power of the Church. This he can do only by destroying himself too.

Opposition to Quezon is feeble. In 1935, a group known as the Sakdalists staged an uprising, and its leader, Benigno Ramos, fled to Japan. Nowadays a Popular Front embracing everyone from communists to the "national socialists" of Aguinaldo has been organized to combat the President, but it has not got very far. One dissident leader of consequence is the liberal head of the Philippine Independent Church, Bishop Aglipay. The popularity of Quezon is great—and carefully nurtured—and no real opposition leader is in sight. In the last election Quezon won every seat. There is not a single opposition deputy.

Indeed, members of the Popular Front do not dislike or oppose Quezon, whom they regard as the father of the country, as a man or a leader; they simply want him to modify his policy. Their complaints are that he has created a bureaucratic dictatorship; that he controls not only the executive, but the judiciary, the army, the legislature, the entire complex of government; that he is afraid of the Church and the big landowners; that his economic program is too slow. They do not want to replace Quezon; they want to swing him to the Left.

Quezon was profoundly impressed by Roosevelt and Cardenas in 1937; he returned to announce a kind of New Deal for the islands under the name of the "Social Justice" program. This, he announced, gave expression to a "distributist" philosophy, a middle path between capitalism and socialism; he said that it was the duty of the government to use every means it had to force the distribution of wealth so that the rich would be less rich and the poor less poor. "I do not believe," he said, "that any one man can earn a million *pesos* by his brain alone. If that is communism, then I am a communist." He inaugurated a minimum wage for government employees (one *peso* per day), and set about a new tax program.

Thus Quezon at sixty-one. Perhaps a tongue is in that roguish cheek. The next few years will tell.

Chapter XIX
Singapore Base

〜〜〜〜〜〜〜〜〜〜〜〜〜〜〜〜〜〜〜〜〜〜〜〜〜〜

FIELD MARSHAL LORD ROBERTS once said that the history of the world would be decided at Singapore someday. There is reason to think that the British are getting ready for the day. For they have built Singapore Base, a new, bigger and better Gibraltar, one of the most formidable concatenations of naval, military and strategic power ever put together anywhere.

The major advantages of Singapore as the site for this giant base are three. First, geography. It is not, like Malta, vulnerable to attack from a near-by neighbor; Singapore controls the trade route to Japan, but Japan is 3,000 miles away. Second, it has a completely peaceful hinterland in which politics scarcely exists; Malaya has no nationalist movement. Think by contrast of British bases in Egypt, Iraq, or India, which have seen acute political trouble. Third, it is beautifully equipped for aircraft. Think by contrast of Gibraltar, gravely handicapped because there are no convenient landing fields, with Germany reported to be arming the opposite shore near Algeciras with heavy guns.

The agglutination of power at Singapore performs a number of functions. It provides oil storage for the British fleet, as well as dockyards for naval repair. It backs up what is left of Hong Kong and is a factor in the protection of Australia. It guards Colombo and Calcutta. It drives a great armored stake into a great imperial pivot, the junction of the trade routes from India and the West to China and beyond.

But above all else, Singapore Base is a warning to Japan. Hardly an aggressive gesture. But somewhat of a threat, something of a warning. Singapore Base tells the Japanese, in a language they understand, that the British still mean business in this part of the world.

This is precisely why what appeared to be an innocent enough announcement caused so great a flurry in January, 1938. The announcement was that three American cruisers, the *Trenton*, the *Milwaukee*, and the *Memphis*, would participate in the formal opening of the naval base on February 14 last. It caused an outburst of speculation in Tokyo, among other places. Authorities in Singapore professed to be ignorant of the source of the arrangement. The Admiralty in London kept very quiet. So did the Navy Department in Washington.

It now appears that the visit had been projected for some time. The cruisers had been scheduled to make a visit to Singapore after their call at Sydney, Australia, where they participated in the one hundred fiftieth anniversary celebration of the settlement of Australia. It happened that the date very nearly coincided with the Singapore ceremony, and, since it might have looked strange if the American cruisers came to Singapore and just missed the inauguration, arrangements were made so that they would come in time to participate.

Heartburnings and tremors bothered Singapore editors. They didn't want to be unfriendly to the United States. But they did not want to have to ask other countries to attend, chiefly Japan, and they feared that if the United States came, other nations—again notably Japan—might ask to be invited. At least one editor went out on a long limb by saying that the Admiralty had not been informed of the American visit and that if the American ships did come, there would be no question of their "participation" in the ceremony. On February 3, the Singapore Free Press chimed in with the remark that some lesser official of the Admiralty had apparently failed "to realize the repercussions" of an invitation to just one power, and that "an error has been committed that will tax the ingenuity of the British Government to rectify."

Journalism isn't exactly free in Singapore. When it appeared that more editorials on the same line might come out, which would put British hosts in a position of being ungracious to American guests, the authorities saw that they were modified. The explanation of this editorial nervousness is easy enough: Singapore folk, despite the strength of their base, don't want to offend Japan.

The American cruisers duly arrived; they were greeted with the utmost courtesy; they stayed a full week, and the visit was a great success. When they left on February 21, two British warships, the *Norfolk* and the *Emerald*, left with them. It was announced that, whereas the American ships would go to Manila, the British vessels would proceed to Colombo, "more or less directly." So immediately the rumor spread of joint maneuvers. It is a point to note that the American ships took a week to get to Manila, though the ordinary cruising time is about three days.

One thing is clear as the eye of a pike. The visit, whatever its origin, had much greater significance than an ordinary courtesy call of units of one navy to another. The opening of the Singapore Base, a cardinal event in British rearmament and the evolution of British Pacific policy, cannot be viewed in a vacuum. It must be viewed in the light of events in Europe, of the war in China, of Japanese pressure to the south and east. Maybe the American visit wasn't exactly a joint demonstration. But it came very close to it, and it gave Japan a good deal to think about.

The sequel seems conclusive. In March, 1938, Geoffrey Shakespeare, parliamentary secretary to the Admiralty, announced in the House of Commons that Britain was prepared to "lease the facilities of the new Singapore naval base to the United States in case of necessity." In other words, in case of war. "Lease" the Singapore facilities? In case of war, the British would turn handsprings to get us there for nothing.

But Singapore docking would be a very great convenience to the United States in the event of war in the Far East, since we have no base west of Hawaii capable of repairing large ships. Manila is too small. And anyway we may be leaving Manila in 1946.

The Fortress Isle

Singapore is an island. It measures twenty-seven miles by fourteen, and is connected with the mainland of Asia by a causeway over the Strait of Johore. Probably Manhattan is the only small island in the world to outrank it as an extraordinary combination of geographical position, commercial development and strategic importance. At the tip of Malaya, where the boats must turn upward for the voyage to China and Japan, it commands the sea route to the East.

The British are courteous to visitors in Singapore. But they have caught a bit of what is called "yellow fever" locally—that is, spy mania. The Japanese see spooks and spies almost everywhere; now the British see them too.[1] Pretty severe precautions are taken to keep people out of the defended areas, and some of the defense details are still secret. All the workmen in the dockyard are fingerprinted, which

[1] The British say that Japanese espionage in the region began during the Great War, when Britain and Japan were allies. Japanese officers went all over the place freely until 1918.

is a reasonable precaution, considering the amount of espionage said to be going on.

But Japanese technique in espionage arouses coarse laughter in the British. For instance, Japanese "fishing boats" take supposedly "secret" soundings in waters which are completely and accurately charted by the Admiralty—and anyone may buy these charts. Recently the Japanese took over a fashionable restaurant, the Tamagawa, where food is served at exceedingly cheap prices—maybe because the Tamagawa commands a sweeping view of the Johore beach. At Pongon near the air base, there is a cluster of Japanese beer gardens and fish ponds. During the maneuvers in 1938 a Japanese freighter, the *Borneo Maru*, anchored off Blakang Mati, one of the fortified islands about 600 yards from the Singapore docks. The anchorage was quite legal and maybe it was an accident. But at the last moment the British had to change the routine of the maneuvers.

Our host drove us along the water front the day after the inaugural ceremonies at the base. There was quite a lot to see. The naval base is at Seletar, on the north shore of the island and about twelve miles from Singapore City. Immediately to the east, below a small inlet, is the air base. There are three designs in Singapore. One was written by the British army, the second by the navy, the third by the air force. "Singapore Base" is the term used to embrace all three.

One of the officers with us looked a bit red-eyed. He had been up most of the night before, checking photographs of the inaugural ceremonies. Every photographer had a soldier in attendance; each one knew just where he could and could not go. Of one hundred-odd prints exposed, about six were forbidden circulation.

"There was a river here," our host said. "We moved it over yonder."

The last time I saw a river that had been bodily moved was at Dearborn, Michigan, when my guide was an official employed by Mr. Henry Ford. And the gigantic engineering problem of the naval base at Singapore, which was created out of mangrove swamp, reminded me of some things back home.

On one side, the glittering blue ribbon of the Strait of Johore, intersected by the white causeway. Except on special provisioning missions, no ships of any kind—not even British merchantmen—

are allowed in these waters. On the other, the tawny hills, the tropical jungle, of Singapore island, a backdrop to the prodigious excavations which made the base.

The dull pewter-colored oil tanks on the right hold 1,000,000 tons of fuel. Each is built in a sort of saucer, to prevent the spread of fire, if there should be an explosion. Ahead are three wireless masts nearing completion. The higher up the Chinese laborers work on these Eiffel Tower-like structures, the higher is their pay. Underground are the munition dumps. Enough stuff underground, safely hidden, to blow the whole base to kingdom come.

The naval base as a whole covers twenty-one square miles. Its chief ornaments are the two immense docks, one floating, one a graving dock, which lie at right angles within half a mile of each other. The docks are the citadels of Singapore; without them the base would have little utility or function. What are the docks for? To make possible the quick repair of big warships in case of a fleet action. Suppose there were a naval engagement in the Pacific; if Singapore didn't exist, damaged ships would have to go all the way to Malta for refurbishment. The war might be over by the time they got back.

Of the two docks, the floating dock was put into position first. Almost 900 feet long, almost 200 feet wide, it is the third largest floating dock in the world. It can lift any battleship afloat; 60,000 men can stand in its giant bottom. The dock was built in England, then towed in sections from Wallsend-on-Tyne to Singapore, 10,000 miles. The tow has been termed one of the most remarkable of modern marine feats.

The new dock, the graving dock, was the one inaugurated in February. It is 1,000 feet long; to make it took six years, about £1,000,000 and 500,000 cubic yards of concrete. Any ship in the world will fit in it readily; it held 68,000,000 gallons of water in a recent test. The floating dock could, in case of necessity, be moved somewhere else; the graving dock is stationary. Adjacent to both docks are the paraphernalia of ship repair—machine shops, power plants, storehouses, and the largest crane east of Suez. This, of course, is to lift the big guns from the ships in case of need. Everything is in duplicate except the crane, so that air raiders—if they got through—would have to do their job twice.

Contrary to general opinion, the Singapore Base does not include a large naval establishment. Headquarters of the British naval forces in the Far East, called the China command, are at Hong Kong, not Singapore. In Singapore itself only one warship is permanently stationed, the old monitor *Terror*; it has fifteen-inch guns and saw service off the Belgian coast during the Great War. Singapore has one defect from a naval point of view. The surrounding waters contain submerged reefs which make pilotage of submarines difficult. Of course this works both ways.

The air base in Singapore is likewise a complex and highly efficient group of units. There are three different military landing fields on Singapore, as well as one of the finest civil airports in the world. It was built on reclaimed land on the water's edge, so that both land and sea planes use it—the Douglas DC 3's of the Royal Dutch Air Lines as well as the new Empire flying boats of Imperial Airways. The airport is unique in that it is only about seven minutes' drive from the business section of the city.

The chief military field, closely adjacent to the naval base, similarly provides facilities for both land and sea craft. There are about twenty miles of what Sir Shenton Thomas, the hard-working governor, has called "perfect water" for flying boats. About forty aircraft are permanently stationed at the base. This isn't many, but the number may be quickly augmented by squadrons flying from India, as the maneuvers last year proved.

Technically, Singapore is a fortress. About 7,000 regular troops are stationed in the area, but they are not what counts. What does count is the one thing about which Singapore is really mysterious—the secret fortifications, the great land batteries, which dominate the coast. There are batteries at Changi, on the extreme eastward tip of Singapore island, and on several of the small islands in the Straits and off the roads. These islands house permanent garrisons of artillery and engineers. Some of the batteries contain eighteen-inch guns which are the heaviest and most powerful in the world.

Opium into Howitzers

Is Singapore impregnable? This is the question the military and naval experts like to ask. It is, of course, unanswerable. No one knows. Each year maneuvers are held—very elaborate and dramatic maneuvers, too—and it is always officially understood that they are "successful." But no one can tell what actual war may bring.

There are two schools of thought among the British. One, represented mostly by men on the spot, says that Singapore is as nearly perfect a fortress as geography and the mind of man can contrive. They say that it is stronger than Gibraltar, and believe that no enemy could possibly attack it with success.

The other school of thought, stationed mostly in London, admits that the defenses are very good, but would like to see them augmented and improved, especially air defense. This school is the big-stick school which, no matter what armament it has, wants more. For instance, the British magazine *Aeroplane* wrote recently that the defense forces of Singapore are "a laughing stock" to any intelligent Asiatic—certainly an extreme view.

The British air estimates for 1938 included considerable expenditure in the Singapore area. The strength of the Royal Air Force Far East Command, which has headquarters in Singapore, is to be doubled by the end of the year. New airdromes have been completed not only on Singapore island but in Sarawak and Borneo, and others are planned for Malaya above the Strait.

There are designs "in" Singapore; there are also designs "on" Singapore. No one in the area thinks of anyone except Japan, if you mention possible aggression. The best military information available is that the island is open to attack only from the mainland to the north. A sea approach is almost impossible, and though an air attack might do damage, it could hardly result in the investment or occupation of the island. To take Singapore, an enemy would have to land infantry detachments somewhere in Malaya, or possibly Siam, and march south.

Singapore's chief advantage is its location. It is only 1,578 miles from Manila and 1,674 miles from Hong Kong, friendly territory, but it is 3,345 miles from Yokohama, Japan. It is true that the Japanese are building an important air base in Formosa, considerably nearer. But the air isn't everything. To make a full-dress attack on Singapore, the Japanese fleet would have to steam at least 3,000 miles, which is pretty far.

Singapore is convenient for offensive action also. A British fleet action against Japan would be as difficult as a Japanese fleet action against Singapore. But the essence of naval war is attack on trade. A Pacific war would be largely a business of intercepting merchant vessels, plus blockade. The British would try to destroy Japanese ship-

ping—as the Germans tried to destroy British shipping in the Great
War—and thus isolate and starve Japan. For this purpose, Singapore
is ideal.

If—or when—the United States leaves the Philippines, the situation will greatly change. Should the Japanese occupy Manila Bay
both Hong Kong and Singapore would be gravely threatened. Some
British experts go so far as to say that Singapore is "useless" if Japan
has the Philippines. And already Japan has the Spratly islands.

Work on the base began after the War. In 1919, Admiral Lord
Jellicoe toured the British dominions and recommended that a
British Pacific fleet be created and based on Singapore. He wanted
battleships instead of mere cruisers in Far Eastern waters; he wanted
a two-hemisphere naval policy for Britain. Soon after, a conference
of British admirals met in Penang; it seconded Jellicoe's suggestion.
The British were worried about the new postwar situation and the
growing power of Japan, but their nearest base equipped to handle
big British warships in case of trouble was Malta, 8,000 miles away.

In 1921, the Imperial Conference met in London, pondered the
Jellicoe statement, listened to the cabinet and the Committee of
Imperial Defence, and took the plunge. It decided to build Singapore.
In 1922—mark the sequence—the Washington Naval Limitation
Treaty was signed which established naval ratios among the great
powers and ended the Anglo-Japanese Alliance.

Considerable outcry came from England. First, critics said that
the new base was an unreasonable extravagance; second, that it
would needlessly irritate and provoke Japan. And Japanese indignation was high and hot. Also, purists in politics claimed that the new
base was a moral infringement of the Washington Naval Treaty,
which forbade fortifications or naval bases east of 110 degrees
east longitude. Singapore lay outside this zone, but only just outside
it—by six degrees. One M.P. put it this way: "It is contrary to the
spirit of the Washington treaty to move a few hundred miles from
Hong Kong and then embark on an expenditure of £10,000,000."

Plenty of people talked about British "duplicity" at Washington.
The allegation was formally denied by officials who took part in
the conference. For instance, Mr. Bruce, prime minister of Australia:
"Australia understood when the treaty was signed that Singapore
was to be built. Australia would have never agreed to the treaty if
Singapore had been included in the area where the building of bases

and docks was prohibited." The British say that all the powers at
Washington were cognizant of British plans to embark on the Singapore undertaking.

Work on the base began late, because the Labor Government reversed the decision of the previous conservative government and
canceled the project. Pacifist Ramsay MacDonald called it "wild and
wanton folly." The Conservatives came in in November, 1924; policy
was changed again and work resumed; Mr. MacDonald lived to be
prime minister of a national government which pushed the base almost to completion. The work took about fifteen years in all.

To date the base has cost a pretty sum, about £16,000,000 (the
official estimate) for equipment, and perhaps £50,000,000 if the cost
of maintenance, garrison and so on is included from the beginning.
Oddly enough the mother country, England, has had to furnish only
a minute fraction of the cost of the base itself. Contributions have come
from Hong Kong, New Zealand, the Straits Settlements, the Federated Malay States and neighboring potentates like the Sultan of
Johore. The upkeep of the base is calculated at £500,000 per year,
but this is almost covered by the annual assessment of 4,000,000
Straits dollars or £464,000, paid by the Straits Settlements, the
crown colony of which Singapore is the capital.

In other words, capital expenses excepted, the Singapore Base costs
the home government almost nothing. Where does the government
of the Straits Settlements get the money from? Two sources of
revenue are unusual. One, direct, is opium. The other, indirect, is
the American importer of tin and rubber.

Opium is a government monopoly in the Straits Settlements and
it is highly profitable. The British buy raw opium from Iran or
India and prepare it into what is called *chandu*. The raw opium costs
perhaps one Straits dollar per "tahil" (one and one-third ounces);
chandu sells for twelve Straits dollars per tahil. The profit is obviously enormous, but the price is put so high in a deliberate effort
to diminish sales. The *chandu* is sold on a strictly controlled basis,
like liquor in Scandinavia; only registered addicts may buy, and no
one can get on the addict list except upon medical authorization.
The shops are rigidly inspected. The addicts are about ninety-nine
percent Chinese; Singapore, be it remembered, is largely a Chinese-
populated town.

The revenue from opium for many years made up not less than

one-third of the total revenue of the Straits Settlements; in 1936 it provided 23.23 percent of the total revenue, in 1937, 24.48 percent. There are about 35,000 registered opium addicts, that is to say, roughly five percent of the Chinese population. In other words, 35,000 registered Chinese opium eaters pay one-quarter of the colony's share in the cost of the Singapore Base, which is perhaps ninety percent of the total cost.

The American importer contributes indirectly to Singapore's upkeep because the Federated Malay States, on which Singapore is economically dependent, have affixed high export duties on the two chief articles of export, tin and rubber, for which the United States is a very substantial customer. In 1937, of the total revenue of the F. M. S. (50,900,000 Straits dollars), the export tax on tin contributed 16,215,000 Straits dollars or 31.6 percent, the export tax on rubber 5,634,065 (eleven percent). American importers paying a steep tax contribute to the solvency of the F. M. S., which in turn make the contributions of the Straits Settlements to Singapore possible.

Notes on Empire

If you look at a map of the British Empire, neatly colored pink by tradition—an odd color to choose, when you come to think about it— the temptation is great to consider it as a unit, as something uniform. As a matter of fact the British Empire, with its 485,000,000 people, its 13,290,000 square miles, is very far from being uniform. Its vast "mixture of growths and accumulations" is by no means governed by a single law.

The Empire includes dominions like Canada and Australia, which are self-governing, sister states of Britain virtually independent since the Statute of Westminster, except for the common bondage of the Crown. It includes the colossal subcontinent of India, itself subdivided into British India and princely states, which we shall deal with soon. It includes some crown colonies which are administrative dictatorships, and some which have constitutions and legislatures. It includes "free states" like Eire, mandated territories like Palestine, protectorates like the hinterland of Aden, condominiums like the Anglo-Egyptian Sudan, territory held jointly with France like the New Hebrides, and political curiosities such as Bhutan or Sarawak

which fit into no normal categories. There are even regions ruled
by chartered companies like the old East India Company.

Parts of the Empire were rented and then purchased, like Zanzibar.
Some were gifts, Bombay for instance. Some were gained by conquest, and some by luck in exploration, like Australia. Some came
to Britain as the result of warfare thousands of miles away, like
Canada; some were grabbed locally, like Hong Kong from the
Chinese. British Honduras was won by woodcutters from the West
Indies, and Malta by a revolution of the Maltese. Togoland was
captured from the Germans, the Gold Coast from the Dutch, Cyprus from the Turks, Jamaica from Spain, and parts of India from
the Portuguese. Some divisions of the Empire were gained by original settlement, like Barbados and Fiji; some, like Nigeria, were
ceded by native kings. Some were almost lost by war, like South
Africa, some regained after mutiny, like Oudh and Agra, some were
loot, like Tanganyika.

Aside from the dominions and India, which have their special
offices, the executive force over the Empire is the colonial office,
which until recent years—now it is in the excellent hands of young
Malcolm MacDonald—was the most backward of the great British
government departments. Governors of colonies sent out by the colonial office are of several categories. I heard one incisive critic say
that there are four classes of colonies. First, the "unicellular," like
Gibraltar, where the colony is merely a fort; there is no native population, no political problem, and the governor may happily be a
retired admiral or some similar figure. Second, what my friend called
the more advanced or "mollusk" type, like Uganda or the Bahamas,
where the governor has considerable preoccupation with local problems like public health and administration, but where politics is not
acute. Third comes the lower "mammalian" category of colonies like
Cyprus or Ceylon, where the governor is—or should be—some
one competent to deal with highly difficult political problems, where
he must face politically advanced native populations. In jobs like
these the old-style soldier-administrator governor, who may be admirable in the remote interior of Africa, is utterly hopeless. Finally
come the "human" colonies; for instance, Palestine (technically
Palestine is a mandate, of course), where a good governor must be
a good politician above all else.

The British rule their colonies by a subtle combination of power and prestige. The power is always there, but often it is in the form of battleships a thousand miles away; meantime the young officer may boss 10,000 people with a swagger stick and dinner jacket.

A common denominator is, of course, imperialism. The root reason why the colonies exist is exploitation. The British are there to get something out of being there. But exploitation is paid for by a variety of services; the British bribe the natives whom they exploit to enjoy the process of exploitation by a double reward: first, attention to such matters as public health, public order, education; second, by gradual training of the people toward self-government. No British colony is a slave state, though political mastery may be complete. In most British colonies the eventual result of British imperialism is held to be freedom from the strictures of that imperialism. Obviously the process thus envisaged is an extremely gradual one. Development of self-governing institutions is never allowed to interfere with the immediate demands of empire. Ask Mr. Gandhi or Mr. de Valera. They will confirm this view.

One psychological factor helping the British in their imperial rule is their innate, impregnable unassimilability. Once an Englishman, always an Englishman. I have met British officials, British merchants, who have lived in Malaya or Baluchistan for forty years; for all the effect on their character, their habits, they might have spent all that time in Nottingham or Bournemouth. The British Empire is the furthest possible remove from a melting pot. The British do not Mix.[2]

The most pleasant locality in almost any Asiatic city is—and has been for twenty or forty years—the site of the British club; the best embassy, consulate, or local bank is the British one; in every capital in the East from Cairo to Peking (except Teheran) there is a daily British newspaper, usually edited by Scotsmen. The British never become, as Americans become, expatriates.

A trip from the Atlantic to the Pacific through waterways largely British controlled is an extraordinary experience of British omnipresence. The entire route is staked out by British fortresses or bases: Gibraltar, Malta, Suez, Aden, Colombo, Penang, Singapore, Hong Kong. It could not have been done more neatly with a slide rule.

The threat of Italian naval power in the Mediterranean, the dan-

[2] One interesting minor point is that no English prostitute or even female night club performer is allowed anywhere in British territory in the East.

gerous entrenchment given Germany near Gibraltar as a result of
the Spanish civil war, the riotous instability in Palestine, above all
the Munich "peace" in September, 1938, and its consequences, gravely
weakened British prestige, British power too, all over the world, as we
well know. As a friend of mine said: "The lion tried to show his
teeth, and it was all bridgework." In fact some teeth were still there.
Mr. Chamberlain preferred to smile instead of biting—but he may
have to bite before too long.

Malay Medley

What is known as British Malaya consists of three different types
of territory. The Straits Settlements including Singapore and Penang
are a crown colony; the Federated Malay States are native principalities ruled by Britain; the Unfederated Malay States are hardly
more independent than those federated, but technically their sultans
enjoy autonomy. The region as a whole is dominated by one
momentous consideration, namely, that acre for acre it is the richest
British possession or sphere of interest on the face of the globe. It
produces forty-five percent of the world's rubber, thirty-five percent
of its tin; the annual foreign trade is over half a billion dollars,
which is greater than that of many western countries.

Malaya is from several points of view a wonderful imperial preserve.
Labor is infinitely cheap, the people are indolent and affable, nationalism hardly exists. The Malays are Moslems by religion, but they
have never used religion as a spearhead for political expression, as
Moslems almost everywhere else in the world have done.

As a typical crown colony the Straits Settlement is governed—
by a governor. He is chairman of what is known as the legislative
council which meets perhaps for an hour every month or so; there are
thirteen official members, i.e., those who hold government posts, eleven
unofficial members appointed by the governor, and two members
"elected" by the chambers of commerce in Singapore and Penang.
Of the group all are British except one Malay (a former government
civil servant), one Eurasian, one Indian, and three Chinese. The
governor initiates legislation. The structure of government has not
been changed since 1867 when the colony was separated from India.
There has never been a political campaign or an election.

The Federated Malay States, the most important of which are
Sekangor and Perak (this latter region of 7,800 square miles produces

not less than twenty-seven percent of the total world output of tin), are ruled by a Federal Council of which the Governor General of the S. S., in his capacity as High Commissioner of the Federated Malay States, is chairman, though each native ruler in state council is theoretically vested with "supreme" authority. The sultans are a mixed bag. Some do not even speak English. One has forty-three children. A political issue in the F. M. S. is what is known as "decentralization," which means extension of the power of the sultans. Until recently they were regulated with iron authority by the Chief Secretary in Kuala Lumpur, the capital, who reported direct to the colonial office in London. Now this post has been abolished and the sultans have more elbow room, so that they may be persuaded that they are as well off as the unfederated sultans. This process is roughly analogous to that which has led to provincial "autonomy" in India.

But the British remain very distinctly in a position to make any sultan do what they wish. The old sultan of Selangor, known as His Highness Aladdin Suleinan Shah, had both his first and second sons rejected for the succession by the colonial office, which found the third son more satisfactory as a ruler.

The unfederated sultans have a good deal more power. The most important and picturesque of them, the Sultan of Johore, is a robust character, a great huntsman and bon-vivant, who has been forty years on the throne. He is an absolute sovereign in his own domains, though the British have full control of his foreign policy. His state is just across the causeway from Singapore, and thus has great strategic importance; he contributed £500,000 to the expenses of Singapore Base.

The Sultan of Johore was for some years married to a Scotswoman, a Mrs. Wilson, whose previous husband had been the Sultan's physician. His three sons are said to be of different mothers, but all three, an odd point, married sisters. The Sultan is very rich. Of the total revenue of Johore, 16,660,594 Straits dollars in 1934, some 5,400,000 are written in the budget as "personal emoluments." He has a prodigious sense of humor. One of his good stories describes a visit to a Czechoslovak spa, where he couldn't get a bath until he had seen a doctor, to visit whom cost £20.

In the Malay states we pick up the Japanese trail again. Espionage I have mentioned. Trade also should be mentioned. Japanese exports to Malaya have more than doubled in eight years. Cheap Japanese textiles flood the peninsula. There are several big Japanese-owned iron mines, especially in Trengganu state; Chinese workers in these mines have repeatedly gone on strike. About a million tons of iron ore per year go from Malaya to Japan.

Mui Tsai

This Chinese phrase occasionally crops up in the news dispatches. It means a Chinese girl in her teens or even younger purchased from her family and employed as a domestic servant, without wages, by another family. The employing family feeds and clothes her, and presumably on growing up she gets married. But the system was open to rank abuses, and many children became prostitutes. A government commission investigated the *Mui Tsai* question in Malaya and Hong Kong, and the system is to be eventually abolished. Meantime every *Mui Tsai* is supposed to be registered, and a law has been proposed forbidding domestic labor by children under twelve.

Borneo and Sarawak

Near the Malayan peninsula are the British portions of the vast island of Borneo—as large as Germany before the Czechoslovak conquest—which are in three distinct divisions.

One is Sarawak. This state, ruled by a white rajah, is unique, and has an extraordinary history. In the middle of the nineteenth century the local ruler, facing a rebellion, asked a retired English officer of the Indian army, James Brooke, for help. Brooke was what might be called a counter-buccaneer. He was a mercenary professionally engaged in suppressing pirates; he had his own boats, his own crew. As reward for his services the local Bornean potentate *gave* him Sarawak, a territory as big as England, and Brooke became its first rajah or ruler. The British government recognized the independence of Sarawak in 1888, and this fiction that it is a sovereign state is maintained to this day, though the British have, of course, the right to control its foreign relations, and the ruler of Sarawak looks to the governor general in Singapore for advice.

In 1868 the first Brooke died; he was succeeded as rajah by his nephew, Sir Charles Johnson Brooke. The family lived between England and Sarawak, cultivated its preserve, kept everyone else out, and married able women. The Dowager Ranee of Sarawak, widow of Sir Charles, died in 1936; she was born in Paris as Margaret de Windt, and was a brilliant patron of music and the arts. She lost four children through illness (three tragically died of cholera on the same trip to England); her fifth child, Sir Charles Vyner Brooke, is the present rajah. He succeeded to the title in 1917. His wife, the Honorable Sylvia Brett, a daughter of Lord Esher, was a great friend of Shaw, Barrie, and literary figures of the day. When she and the rajah became engaged Shaw sent her a jingle:

> *Ride a cock horse*
> *To Sarawak Cross*
> *To see a young Ranee consumed with remorse.*
> *She'll have bells on her fingers,*
> *And rings through her nose*
> *And won't be permitted to wear any clo'es.*

The present rajah, Sir Charles Vyner Brooke, has three daughters but no sons. His heir is his brother, Captain Bertram Brooke, known as the Tuan Muda; in effect they divide rule, since each takes over from the other while one is on holiday in England. The three daughters all made remarkable marriages, one, Valerie ("Princess Baba"), to a professional wrestler, Bob Gregory; one ("Princess Pearl") to a jazz band leader, Harry Roy; the third ("Princess Gold") to Lord Inchcape, heir to the P. & O. shipping fortune. When Princess Pearl was married a popular song saluted the occasion:

> *Sarawaki's skies of blue,*
> *And a meeting beneath the golden bamboo . . .*

Rather testily Rajah Brooke announced recently that none of his daughters are "princesses." He said:

The title is a pure fabrication by the Press, a slogan which has been used and misused until not only our country, but every country in the world, is heartily sick of the sound of Sarawak. . . . I wish to state definitely here and now that none of my daughters are Princesses. Before they married their names were: Miss Leonora Margaret Brooke, Miss Elizabeth Brooke, and Miss Nancy Valerie Brooke. At least, that is what they were christened. . . . I would be extremely grateful if the gentlemen of the press would realize once for all that there are no such people as Princess Gold, Princess Pearl, and Princess Baba, but that I have three daughters whose names are: The Countess of Inchcape, Mrs. Harry Roy, and Mrs. Bob Gregory.

Aside from the Brooke family no one knows much about Sarawak. No foreigner may buy land in the territory, and outside enterprise is severely discouraged. Annual revenue is $2,135,000, and there is no public debt.

The other divisions of the British part of Borneo are Brunei and North Borneo. Brunei has a sultan but he is subsidized by Britain, and the real ruler is the British Resident. Its revenue was $100,000 per year a decade ago, and now ten times that, because oil was recently discovered there. Its single town is hard to reach, because junks filled with stone were sunk across the river bed as a barricade during the days of piracy, and have never been removed. North Borneo is in still another category. It is ruled by a chartered company, which has a "Court of Directors" in London and its own civil service. The board appoints a governor, who is de facto and de jure ruler of the state, but with the consent, of course, of the colonial office. There is a big Japanese colony in North Borneo.

Here arises a detail which concerns the United States. The Moslem tribesmen in the Philippines, known as Moros (it is not usually realized that a large number of Mohammedan semi-savages still live under the American flag), have as titular leader the Sultan of Sulu, who also claims to be Sultan of North Borneo. The British North Borneo Company paid him a subsidy or land rent, so that his territorial ambitions did not become too pressing. This is the first but not the last time in these pages that we will come across British subsidies to undeveloped kings or countries in obscure parts of the world.

At the end of 1938 a quarrel was raging between two rival candidates for the sultanate of Sulu.

Chapter XX
Dutch Treat

~~~~~~

THE Netherlands Indies are a great world of their own in this swing around Asia we are making. Some 65,000,000 people live in the Indies, Malay-Polynesian by race and predominantly Moslem or heathen in religion, ruled from afar by the 8,000,000 stout burghers of the Netherlands, ten thousand miles away by crow or the K. L. M. air line.

The Indies have a European as well as an Asiatic function. The life blood of the Netherlands comes from here. Pumping into Holland from Insulinde, as the Indies are called, is a stream of invigorating wealth. The Indies tail is what wags the Dutch dog. As a consequence Dutch policy in the East is to conserve this precious appendage, to see that the Japanese are held off and that the Malays do not rise.

There are some two thousand islands in this extraordinary archipelago. If you put the western tip of Sumatra at San Francisco, then the eastern extremity of the Indies, in New Guinea, would almost reach the Atlantic coast, the Dutch extremity of Borneo would be in North Dakota, and the southern extremity, below Timur, would lie somewhere near New Orleans.

The dominating fact about the islands is that, like Crœsus and John D. Rockefeller, Jr., they are rich. They are the Big Loot of Asia. They are packed tight with natives, under the steaming sun, who both produce and buy wealth. Java is the most densely populated country in the world, exceeding even Japan. In the old days, the days of the Dutch East India Company, trade was a simple business of profitable barter: glass beads, which cost little, for spices and cinnamon, which brought profit. Nowadays it is a tremendous international process. The Netherlands Indies pour out an illimitable stream of pepper, sugar, rice, tea, coffee, oil, iron, gold. If necessary they could totally supply the world's rubber. They produce to-day ninety-five percent of its quinine, fifty percent of its tobacco, twenty percent of its tin, ten percent of its petroleum.

The government of the Netherlands Indies is a complete but in effect a benevolent autocracy. If you compare the Dutch system of rule with that of, say, the British in India, several points of contrast and analogy arise.

One cardinal item to note is that the Dutch encouraged intermarriage with natives in the old days, and still do not outlaw it. What would make the *pukka* Sahib in British India go gray with horror is accepted in the Netherlands Indies without moral or ethnic shame. This was because the first Dutch settlers came out alone, and often stayed their lives in the Indies without returning. They married natives because there was no one else to marry—to say nothing of the manifest charms of those ladies from Bali and similar islands which nowadays grace the shipping advertisements. In British India, a Eurasian (half-caste) is considered an Indian. As a rule he is outlawed socially. In the Netherlands Indies, a Eurasian, no matter how slight the amount of white blood in his veins, is considered a European, and may reach almost any position.

Another point is that the Indies have at times been more independent of the colonial office in The Hague than British India has ever been independent of London. The Indies have what is practically their own foreign policy; they appoint trade commissioners abroad who may in time have the status of ambassadors. The islands are a big show in themselves. On the other hand, the home parliament has the right to veto laws passed by the Volksraad of the Indies. Relations between Batavia, the capital of Insulinde, and The Hague are apt to shift depending on the political situation at home and the person of the governor general. The present governor general is known as a "Holland man." His predecessor in contrast virtually wrote his own policy.

Another point is land. In British India land is held by the British Crown. In the Netherlands Indies the title of the land (in Moslem districts anyway) is theoretically in the hands of Allah; it is vested in the people, and only administered by the government. No foreigner, not even a Dutchman, may own, buy or sell land. He can only lease it. Land is never alienated from a native, and no peasants are dispossessed for debt. The land is supposed to belong to the people as a whole. This does not, however, prevent exploitation of land; for instance, almost half of Sumatra is held under lease by the Handels-Vereeniging of Amsterdam, the biggest enterprise in the islands, which produces sisal, hemp, palm oil, and so on. Its chairman was once Dr. Colijn, the Dutch prime minister.

There are native princes in the Indies just as in Malaya and India. The Dutch permit them a mild kind of autonomy. In Java two native potentates are the Soesoehoenan ("Emperor") of Soerakarta, sometimes known for short as Solo, and the Sultan of Jogjakarta, this last a considerable character. Recently he divorced his twelve wives. The gentleman from Solo is highly picturesque. He has fifty or sixty decorations, which he inveterately wears, and his own little army; one of his numerous and resplendent titles is "Nail of the Universe." He rests one day a year in ceremonial fashion, so that the universe, which revolves upon him as on a pivot, may rest likewise.

Very large rubber and tobacco properties in Sumatra are in the hands of native sultans, and are held on lease by American and British companies—for instance, U. S. Rubber, Goodyear Rubber, Hawaii-Sumatran Rubber, and Standard Oil of New Jersey. Some of these leases are expiring soon, and the sultans may hold out for bigger rents. This puts the Dutch administrators in a quandary. They don't want to interfere with the right of powerful sultans like those in Deli and Langkat to make good bargains, but on the other hand they do not want to set precedents to future Dutch disadvantage.

The Sultans of Sumatra are important for another reason; namely, that if a Japanese invasion of the Netherlands Indies should ever occur, the Dutch would regard Sumatra as their final bastion and refuge. Java they might lose; Sumatra they think they can hold. Java is of course the most important island in the Indies, with 40,000,000 people or two-thirds of the total island population. But Sumatra is nearer Singapore and British help—if the British should choose to help.

The governor general of the Netherlands Indies, like the viceroy in India, is appointed by the Crown for five years. The viceroy may nowadays return on home leave once during his term of office; the Dutch governor general is not allowed this privilege. He must spend his five years in the islands without a break. The governor general is usually chosen from among distinguished civil servants, politicians, or even business men. The job is the supreme plum in the political life of the Netherlands.

A British King usually visits India for his Durbar; in contrast, Queen Wilhelmina has never seen her island empire. The distance was thought to be too great, and the risks of travel too onerous. Her heir, Juliana, may visit the Indies some day. The idea is constantly mooted.

The governor general has very wide powers—wider probably than those of a British viceroy. Like the viceroy, he is assisted by a council of state—in India it goes by a different name—which is both a cabinet and a rudimentary upper house. One interesting detail is that members of the council of state are usually civil servants who also serve five years, but their terms do not necessarily correspond with the governor general's term. This theoretically leads to steadiness and continuity in administration.

In British India the overwhelming problem, the problem which every viceroy must face every minute of every day, is that of relations to the Indians. This hardly exists in Netherlands Indies. The Indians in British India, led by Mr. Gandhi and Pandit Nehru, are a terrific political force; the Indian National Congress, pledged to freedom from British rule, is governing in eight out of eleven provinces. But in Netherlands Indies political consciousness is primitive, the autonomy movement is closely held in check, and the governor general rules supreme.

Yet despite the rigidity of the Netherlands system of administration, it has characteristics which tend to bring closer relations between Dutch and native than between British and Indian. The Dutch civil service, called the Binnenlandsch Bestuur, is probably nearer to the people than the Indian Civil Service in British India. This is because of the system of *native* administrators called Regents, who work under Dutch residents or governors, but who have considerable local influence and authority. The Regents serve to decentralize the administration.

In British India, however, there is an electorate of some 35,000,000 people, and provincial autonomy under native governments has begun to function. In the Netherlands Indies there is hardly an electorate at all, and provincial autonomy is a distant dream. A Volksraad, or People's Assembly, does exist, but twenty-two of its sixty members are appointed, and the others are elected on an extremely limited franchise, perhaps one percent of the population. Nor has the Volksraad anywhere near as much power as, say, the Congress legislatures in Bombay or Madras.

The present governor general of the Netherlands Indies is an official out of the diplomatic service, very young for his post—he was appointed at forty-four—with the jaw-breaking name of Jhr. Dr. A. W. L. Tjarda van Starkenborgh Stachouwer. Young as he is, he looks younger. His eyes are among the most piercingly blue I have ever seen. He is a tremendous worker, and something of a stickler for punctilio. His wife is an American, the daughter of a diplomat.

In 1933, a very severe series of "crisis measures" was introduced in the Netherlands Indies. The object was to counteract the ravages of the world depression; in four years, the total trade of the islands had fallen sixty-nine percent. The new decree gave the governor general the right to limit and license both imports and exports, to control local trade and industry, and to fix prices. The budget was slashed almost in half, from a 1929 figure of 763,364,000 guilders to 485,706,000 in 1933. Taxes went up, salaries went down. The operation was almost herculean, and the patient just managed to recover.

Accompanying the crisis decrees came some severe exercises in political dictatorship. The governor was given power to outlaw any political party, to regulate public meetings, to forbid political activity by government servants, and to control the posts, telephones, telegrams, and local transportation.

The pinch of the crisis decrees plus resentment at what seemed excessive political regimentation produced much grumbling. One result was what came to be called the Dominion Status bill. The Volksraad may not introduce legislation, but, by majority vote, it may petition the queen asking for legislation. So a deputy rose in October, 1936, and petitioned her "to take steps to see that the government of Netherlands Indies was administered in accordance with terms of Article I of the Constitution." This meant Dominion Status, since Article I of the Constitution provides for equality of the Dutch colonies and the home country under the Crown. The petition was passed on June 15, 1937. The Eurasians, who are usually more Dutch than the Dutch, voted with the native nationalists to make its passage possible.

The nationalists are in two groups. The moderates are afraid of Japan, which tends to dampen their ardor, since they prefer Dutch rule to Japanese. So they do not want to cut the ties with Holland, which might make Japanese penetration possible. The extremists, on the other hand, who call themselves "non-coöperative," want independence. The nationalist leader, Mohammed H. Thamrin, the son of a civil servant who was for a time acting mayor of Batavia, is an able man in his early forties; he dominates the thirty natives in the Volksraad.

The grievances of the nationalists are several. They say, first, and most important, that Holland sucks all the wealth out of the country, that the Indies are run for exploitation and profit by the home government. The Indies give Holland life blood, and get little in return. Until the depression, the home country got almost $150,000,000 per year from Insulinde.

Second, they accuse the Dutch administration of deliberately starving the educational system. This tends to keep the people in subjection, and to prevent the normal growth of political aspirations. Dutch policy, it has been said, is "to keep the bellies of the people full, their minds empty." Indeed, the record of the Dutch in education is miserable. Illiteracy is ninety-five percent, and the public school system is a myth.

Some parts of the islands are inhabited still by aborigines,[1] who occasionally cause trouble. For a time a focus of discontent was the Atjeh region in northern Sumatra, where Moslem tribesmen resisted subjugation. What brought them to settlement was mostly the steady advance of roads, automobiles, and movies, which gave them better (and less risky) amusement than headhunting. Also on Sumatra are the Minang Kabau Malays, who consider themselves the fathers of the Malay race; they are the purest in language and blood of anyone on the islands. They revolted briefly, in 1926, largely because they had no share in government. In West Java there is a wild tribe, the Bantamese, who likewise had to be crushed in 1926.

In Batavia, in 1926, occurred a serious rising partly communist in origin, partly straight nationalist. The putschists gained control of the telephone system, but were put down. The leaders were shipped to Boven Digoel in New Guinea, an isolated camp in cannibal territory, where they were let pretty much alone—since the character of the

[1] Most of the remaining cannibals and headhunters are in New Guinea. Aviation in Insulinde developed through splendid air services which now penetrate territory hitherto almost unknown. Recently a plane flew over a backward stretch in New Guinea. The tribesmen below decided that it could not be a bird, because it made too much noise. They consulted the medicine man who informed them that it was the devil himself. The apparition, devil or not, had come from the south, and the villagers—just to play safe—marched southward and slit forty-odd throats in the next community.

country almost precluded the possibility of escape—and told to make their own utopia there.

Partly as a result of criticism, partly to strengthen itself, the government of the Netherlands Indies in 1938 embarked on a far-reaching reorganization. The Indies are always considered to consist of two units: Java and the adjacent island of Madura comprise one, and everything else—the "Outer Possessions"—are the other. Hitherto the Outer Possessions—Borneo, Sumatra, New Guinea and so on —have been parceled up among a number of local governors or residents; there were ten in Sumatra alone, for example. Now the whole Outer Possessions—covering a territory almost as widespread as the United States—are to be consolidated into three big governorships: one for Sumatra, one for Borneo, one for the remaining islands which will be lumped together as the *Groote Oost* (Great East). This will have two effects: it encourages autonomous development, and at the same time strengthens the center if, some day, there should be trouble with Japan.

Overwhelmingly the great worry of the Netherlands Indies is Japan. The war in China threw into vivid spotlight the possibility of eventual Japanese penetration to the south. In Malaya and Singapore, by and large, I found an atmosphere of confidence. The Singapore Base is in a way a monument, a tribute to Japan's potentialities, but it serves to reassure Britain. The Dutch are frightened—though they don't like to admit it—because they cannot defend themselves. Holland is not a poor country, but it could not afford a military expenditure sufficient to make the Indies impregnable. One might think that the Dutch would assume that the Japanese will be busy in China for a long time, their hands too full for other adventures, but on the contrary the success of Japan in China is what worries the islands most. One adventure sometimes suggests another. An additional point, the Dutch say, is that the Japanese army in China earned such kudos that the Japanese navy might be tempted to imitate its success in adjacent fields.

Japanese agents are everywhere busy on the islands. The Dutch tell scare stories of Japanese reserve officers disguised as laundrymen, of Japanese fishing boats which are eyes for the navy. Recently a Japanese trawler, prowling in coastal waters, was fired on and sunk by Dutch guards. One story, which I could not confirm, described a Japanese timber concession near Balikpapan, in Borneo, where tracts of forest were supposed to have been cleared as secret landing fields for aircraft. Another story tells of a landing field— Dutch—near Samarang, Java, supposedly secret in location. Japanese spies found it. But the Dutch continue to call it their only "secret" field in the hope that the Japanese won't find others which really are tucked away.

The Dutch appear to be rather suspicious of their own natives in military matters. The native troops, for instance, are not allowed to train with machine guns, and natives are not permitted to visit Dutch warships. So when a Japanese cruiser called at Cheribon, Java, it was intelligent of the Japanese to invite the native population aboard. The Dutch accuse the Japanese of encouraging and secretly subsidizing the more outspokenly anti-Dutch of the native political groups.

Dutch military preparation is active. The experts know that the islands could not be defended—not all of them, at any rate—from comprehensive or major attack, but they are busily intent on making an attack expensive to the attacker. This costs money. The defense budget went up from about 90,000,000 guilders in 1936-37 to not less than 135,000,000 in 1937-38. Part of the cost is being defrayed by a two percent export tax. The rule is that the home government supports the navy, the Indies government the army. As there is no separate air force, wings being attached to both army and navy, aviation cost is split.

The Dutch navy in Indies waters would be no match for Japan; it has no battleships and only four cruisers. There are eight to ten destroyers and perhaps a dozen submarines; nine more submarines are being built. A naval base exists at Sourabaya, at the other end of Java from Batavia. The army is proportionately stronger, and it is believed that the Indies could put about 50,000 fighting men in the field, perhaps more. There have been large purchases of foreign— mostly American—bombing planes. American engineers and instructors are on duty at Bandoeng, the mountain town three hours from Batavia which is army headquarters.

The major line of Dutch defense is to rely on diplomacy, which means support from England. And British support should be forthcoming if anyone remains in London with any regard for empire policy, because an enemy in the East Indies would cut the line from Australia to India and would endanger Singapore. If diplomacy fails, the Dutch hope to fend off attack by mines, by submarines, and by

air power. I heard hush-hush talk of a secret air base on Ambon, an
islet between Borneo and New Guinea. Recently Batavia was treated
to an experimental blackout. It was judged successful, though one
American bomber crashed. But probably the Japanese know by this
time where Batavia is.

Japanese commercial penetration is also a preoccupation in the
Indies. For many years Japanese business was unimportant; roughly
from 1914 to 1929 it did not exceed ten percent of the total import
trade. But after the crash of 1929 the Japanese began to undersell
the countries of the West and to multiply their exports to the Indies.
In 1928, for example, Holland contributed 20.05 percent of the
islands' imports and Japan only 9.54 percent. But, in 1934, the Dutch
share of imports dropped to 12.98 percent, and Japan's share rose to
31.88 percent. Alarmed, the Dutch proceeded to impose quota restrictions on Japanese products, and decreed that a certain proportion
of Japanese exports to the Indies—thirty-eight percent—must be
carried in Dutch ships. Even so, Japanese textiles, shoes, chemicals,
rubber goods, bicycles, cotton, continued to pump into the islands.
The home country found it impossible to compete with Japanese
low wages plus the depreciation of the yen. A Japanese-Dutch trade
conference took place in Batavia, but broke up after six months of
wrangling when the Japanese demanded not only trade rights in the
Outer Possessions but the right to "develop" them, development presumably meaning agricultural and mineral concessions.

Note on nationalism. It is a striking phenomenon, as Frances
Gunther has pointed out, that native peoples tend to take on the
complexion of the folk that rule them. Human and political nature
does change—at least in the East. For instance, the Filipinos, after
forty years of Americanization, are more American than the Americans. A barman in the Hotel Manila, a deputy in the Filipino legislature, could have lived all their lives on Broadway so far as general
attitude is concerned. Similarly in British India most of the great
nationalist leaders behave strikingly like Englishmen. They go to
school in England; they learn about that extraordinary concept, "fair
play," and they look at "gentlemen"; back in India, they become
English gentlemen themselves, even when bitterly attacking British
rule. The same thing is true in the Netherlands Indies. Most of the
nationalist leaders I met were almost indistinguishable from Dutch-
men.

The Dutch watch American Philippine policy with mistrust and apprehension. They think that the United States government, if it lets the Philippines go, will have committed a mad act of treachery to the white race.

The Japanese probably would prefer the Dutch East Indies to the Philippines as a possession, because the native population is not so advanced and the islands are richer. The Dutch fear that if the United States give liberty to the Filipinos, the Japanese will skip over them and grab Insulinde.

. . . .

And now we return to the Asia mainland for a quick glimpse of Siam and Indo-China, and then assault on India.

Chapter XXI
The Incredible Kingdom of Siam

~~~~~~

S IAM, about the size of France, is a country of rice, rubber, four-teen million good-natured peasants, and a boy king. On the map it looks rather like an octopus with one tentacle dangling into Malaya toward Singapore. It is the country where no one needs to work more than three or four months a year (because the climate is so propitious and rice so abundant), where the pronunciation of names is fantastically at variance with spelling (for instance "Guam-chitiphol" is pronounced "Kunchit"), where Japanese influence is increasingly active, where there are 17,408 monasteries and 225,000 priests, and where white elephants are sacred.

Its capital, the town of Bangkok, is a charming place where the tramcars are yellow and the priests' robes orange, where one-fifth of the total area is covered by temples, where rice husks are used as fuel, where the most expensive daily newspaper in the world—in English—is published, where silver plated tiger skulls are sold as ash trays, where rickshas are drawn by bicycles, and where you put your feet in bags up to the thighs to keep the mosquitoes off.

Siam is the only independent country in Asia between Japan and Persia, the only eastern territory that did not become booty of the great powers during the imperialist expansion of the nineteenth century. The Siamese call their country "Muang-Thai," which means land of the free. They have been an independent state since about 1350, and originally their kingdom extended to the Yangtze. The Siamese are a distinct racial and linguistic group, but with very marked affiliations with China, and some Malay admixtures. They performed the miracle of surviving as an independent kingdom partly because their territory, half of which is even to-day unex-plored jungle, was hard to penetrate and conquer, partly because it was convenient to both Britain and France to have a buffer state between Burma, Malaya, and Indo-China.

But Siam may not remain an independent state forever—if the acknowledged Japanese dream of domination over "East Asia" becomes a reality.

Siam was—and is—not only an independent country; until 1932

it was one of the last absolute monarchies remaining in the world. Since 1782 it has been ruled by members of the staggeringly prolific Chakri dynasty. Until 1932 it was a backwater, a stagnant and not unhappy land where the monarch, although with absolute powers, chose as a rule to govern mildly. There was no constitution, no judicial system, no legislature, until 1932. Siam was a remnant, picturesque in the extreme, of Oriental medievalism. Then the first flush of modern ideas reached Siam. The flush spread, and became a fermentation. The people demanded reforms, they demanded the extension of governmental institutions. So in June, 1932, a curious bloodless revolution took place. The Siamese are mild people. The only casualty was one general wounded in the leg.

King Prajadhipok, a small smiling man, with great subtlety of mind and an astute sense of humor, promptly accepted the ultimatum of the revolutionaries. There was no need even to declare martial law. The revolutionaries apologized for the bluntness of their first manifesto, which had attacked the king, and prepared a provisional constitution, which was followed by another one. The movement was directed mostly against the topheavy clique of royal princes and noblemen who monopolized the political power and economic privileges of the land. The king was permitted to remain.

The revolution was made by a group of officers and students. They had strong leftist tendencies. They wanted to democratize Siam. Soon a split came, and in June, 1933, occurred another coup d'état. The first prime minister of the revolution, Phya Manoprakorn, fled to Penang, and was succeeded by an army officer with a more forthright policy, Colonel Phahol. Then in October, 1933, came an attempt at counter-revolution. Several disgruntled noblemen and landowners, led by a Prince Bovaradej (who is now an exile in French Indo-China), sought to overthrow the new régime. The revolt—granting the extreme difference between Spanish and Siamese character—was strikingly similar to that of General Franco in Spain. The propertied classes and aristocrats had been ejected from domination of the government; they refused to stay ejected; they rose against the revolution. They were put down (unlike General Franco) largely because the counter-revolutionary leader—gentle like almost all Siamese—refused to take the responsibility for further bloodshed when fighting began.

The government passed death sentences on several of the captured counter-revolutionaries. King Prajadhipok meantime had begun a long trip around the world searching for relief from eye trouble. It became clear that he did not want to return to Siam, though the government insisted that it had only the friendliest feelings toward him, and would treat him with respect if he remained faithful to the new constitution. Crisis came when royal assent was necessary for the execution of the rebels. The King refused this assent—this was in 1935—and therefore abdicated. He was in London at the time; the abdication was by mail. (Incidentally the rebels were executed, Japanese fashion, through a curtain.)

The quality of Siamese political life before the revolution may be judged from the fact that a great many words, not existing in Siamese, had to be invented to express the ideals of the movement. A brilliant young Siamese, Prince Varnvidya-Vavarane, who chose to side with the new government despite his royal blood, and who was trained in philology at Balliol, had the task of creating words hitherto unknown to the Siamese language. For instance:

Constitution	Revolution
Political Science	Proletariat
Reform	Political Party
Civil List	Policy (in the sense of statecraft)

Actually these concepts had never found expression before in Siamese. (On the other hand, words did exist before 1932 for such terms as "Democracy," "Privy Purse," "Cabinet," "Education," "Taxes," "Legislature.")

A revolution may be judged by two things, first its transfer of political power, second its transfer of economic power. As regards the first item the Siamese revolution is complete. A legislature functions, an independent judiciary has been set up, and the paraphernalia of western democracy are closely imitated; power is in the hands of the People's Party, an outgrowth of the original revolutionary clique. Economically the revolution is not complete. Beginnings have been made to equalize taxation, to distribute wealth, and a social reform program of some consequence has been inaugurated; but Siam still has a long way to go before it becomes an integrated people's state.

The actual technique of the revolution was unusual. It was a technological coup d'état of an advanced type. Its chief authors had read Trotsky and Malaparte. They acquired power not by force of arms but by seizing the sources of power—the telephones, the power plants, the railway, and so on. Also the Siamese revolution differs from many others in that there was no punitive assault on the class represented by the previous régime. The great bulk of the princes and aristocrats continue to live in peace; they were not eliminated, even after their attempt at counter-revolution. Their privileges, how-ever, were severely curtailed. Before 1932 the royal princes usurped a tremendous proportion of the national revenue. Now the civil list, which includes the expenses of the regency, is only 445,200 *ticals* (1 *tical* = 45¢) out of a total budget of 104,891,114, or .004 per cent.

King Prajadhipok continued after his abdication to live in England. His successor was his nephew, the boy Ananda.

Royalty in Siam

Because Siam is still a kingdom, because the princes of royal blood may someday choose to reassert themselves, it is necessary to inter-polate a word about what by all odds is as improbable and ornate a group of characters as the Asian world can show.

The great Siamese king Phra Chula Chom Klao, known as Chula-longkorn, the most impressive figure in Siamese history, ruled from 1868 to 1910. It was during this long reign that Siam heard the first enticing whispers of the modern world outside. Chulalongkorn was an enlightened despot. Railways came; so did posts and telegraphs; so did treaties with foreign nations. But the most interesting thing about him was his family. Reputedly he had eighty-four wives and 362 children. In the current Directory of Siam nine and a half pages are necessary merely to list the male descendants of Chulalongkorn who survive to-day. They are grouped in twenty-five main families, presumably offspring of the twenty-five chief royal wives.

In a polygamous country like Siam, if more kings came with the vitality of Chulalongkorn, practically the entire population would eventually become admixed with royal blood. So the Siamese invented a system unique in royalty whereby the progeny of kings gradually resume the status of commoners. Thus the son of a Siamese monarch is known as a Royal Highness; the grandson is merely a "Mom Chao" or Serene Highness; the great-grandson is a "Momrajawong" or Lord; the great-great-grandson is plain mister.[1] Even this gradual but drastic de-royalizing of royalty did not seem sufficient precaution

[1] There are, however, several categories of minor nobility in Siamese; a man may successively be a "Luang," a "Phra," a "Phya," and a "Chaophya."

in view of the inordinate number of surviving princes, so that recently a law was passed inflicting monogamy on the Siamese monarch. Moreover, it has become a custom that the monarch—if he can find anyone—should marry some one not of royal blood.

The marital affairs of King Chulalongkorn, quite apart from the number of his wives, were incredibly complicated. Incidentally his senior wife, known now as the Dowager Consort, is still alive; she prays daily in the great temple of the Emerald Buddha, and is the richest person in Siam. King Chulalongkorn's first wife had two sons. The King then married in turn three sisters. The third sister had six sons. She had great influence over him, and persuaded him to skip the *second* son by his first wife when arranging the succession, in favor of *her* first son and then her other sons. Another complication is that the three wives who followed the first wife were not only sisters, but moreover were half sisters of the King himself. All had the same father (the previous king) though the mothers were different.

So King Chulalongkorn's heir was his eldest son by his first queen; he reigned from 1910 to 1925 as King Rama VI. He was an exceptionally engaging creature, a spendthrift and wonderful gambler, with a very fat stomach; his people nicknamed him "Tum-Tum." He translated Shakespeare into Siamese, wrote plays, and acted in them. .

According to King Chulalongkorn's rule of succession, Rama should have been followed by his eldest half brother whose name was Mahidol. But Mahidol was far from being interested in kingship. He refused the succession. He went instead to Harvard and Johns Hopkins, became an excellent doctor, and married—in Albany, New York—a Siamese girl who was a hospital nurse. The succession then passed to Mahidol's next brother Prajidhopok. When Prajidhopok abdicated, the next heir was adjudged to be Ananda, the son of Mahidol.

Ananda, born abroad in 1926, is being educated in Switzerland. In November, 1938, he made his first state visit to Siam. He reaches his majority at sixteen, that is in 1940, when he will be bathed, anointed, and crowned in a picturesque ceremony. First he must pass some time as a novitiate in a Buddhist monastery. Among his titles are Supreme Arbiter of the Ebb and Flow of the Tide, Half Brother to the Sun, and Keeper of the Twenty-four Golden Umbrellas.

Three regents were appointed in 1935 for the period of Ananda's minority. They are Prince Aditya (pronounced "Odit"), a cousin of King Prajidhopok's, who represents royalty—he looks like an extraordinarily gifted child, though he is in his forties; Chao Phya Yomaraj, of humble birth, who was a monk for many years, who represents the government; and General Bijayendra (pronounced "Pitchian") who represents the army.

Of the great mass of survivors of King Chulalongkorn who are still Royal or Serene Highnesses, very few occupy conspicuous positions to-day. By terms of the new constitution none are allowed to become government ministers, though they may be advisers or department heads. The most noteworthy of them lives in Java. He is Prince Nagor Svarga (pronounced "Nakan Sawan"), who was King Prajidhopok's uncle and minister of defense, and who was the power behind the throne until 1932. He has pledged himself never to return to Siam.

One pleasant little anecdote is told of Prajidhopok. His sight was saved by an operation performed in America by the late Dr. John M. Wheeler. "I can see," muttered the King, as the cataract was removed under local anæsthetic. Wheeler wondered about the etiquette of presenting a bill to royalty, and in the end simply gave him a receipted bill with no amount mentioned. The King then reputedly sent him a check for $86,000!

Siamese Triplets

Siam to-day is ruled by a junta of thirty or forty men, the nucleus of the People's Party, who were the active conspirators in the 1932 coup d'état. These thirty or forty officers are bound by an oath of blood brotherhood. They are still young; most of the cabinet ministers are under forty-five. In effect they rule Siam, but Siam is not a dictatorship. The ambition of the junta is to create a Siamese democracy, though in the present transition period only one political party is allowed, and half the members of the legislature are appointed. Even so, opposition may be spirited; for instance, it took the government three months to hammer the 1938 budget through the chamber.

Three men dominate the junta. They are the prime minister, the foreign minister, and the minister of defense.

Of these the foreign minister, Luang Pradist Manudharm, is probably the most interesting. He is a shy, chunky man with a shrewd peasant's face; he is partly Chinese in origin, and has the familiar Chinese characteristic of looking younger than he is; though he is thirty-six one might think him to be twenty-five. Pradist was a poor boy who struggled for education; he won a scholarship maintained by the old government, and went to Paris to study law. Returning to Siam he became a teacher and then entered politics.

Pradist (some spellings of his name omit the "s" and it is pronounced merely "Pradit") was the civilian organizer of the coup d'état. A convinced radical, he began at once to agitate for agrarian coöperatives, a land reform, and educational advances; his colleagues thought that he was going too fast and he left the first government soon after it was formed. He went into exile for a time, and visited Japan, Britain, and the United States. He was accused of being a communist, and ultimately was cleared of this heinous charge by a parliamentary committee. In 1934, he returned to Siam to be the left-wing leader of the junta and foreign minister of the government.

The prime minister, Colonel Phya Phahol Pholphayuha Sena (pronounced simply "Pa-Hoon"), is an older man, with considerable force of character; his function seems to be that of arbiter between his brilliant and radical foreign minister, and the minister of defense who is on the conservative side. He chuckles a great deal; he has a wide, white smile; he suffers from asthma; his wife has great influence over him. Phahol was educated first in Denmark, then Germany. An army man, he went to the same cadet school as did General Goering, who was a class ahead of him. His nickname is "The Buffalo."

When I saw him he stressed the liberalism of Siam. He scoffed at the idea that the government should more stringently protect itself against the possibility of counter-revolution. He took a glass of water on the table, and tipped it first one way, then the other, without spilling. That, he indicated, was the path of moderation Siam was following. The budget for education, he said, had jumped from about 3,000,000 *ticals* before 1932 to 14,000,000 now. He said that defense cost one-quarter of the national revenue, and denied vigorously that his country could ever become a vassal of Japan.

The army minister, Colonel Luang Pibul Songgram (pronounced "Peebun"), is called the "strong man" of the régime. His enemies are apt to say, first, that he has totalitarian ambitions *à la* Mussolini, second, that he is not likely to accomplish them because he is not strong enough. What power he has comes from the fact that he controls the army, especially the new mechanized units, like the tanks. The colonel is a quiet and retiring individual, educated in France. There were two attempts on his life in the autumn of 1938. Some people call him pro-Japanese, and he is obviously a man to be watched.[2]

These are the Siamese triplets who rule the country. Other politicians of consequence are the minister of public instruction, Captain Luang Sindhu, who is also chief of the naval general staff; the minister of the interior (also a naval officer) Lt. Commander Luang Dhamrong; and the chief of police Colonel Luang Atultej Charas. One of the original leaders of the coup d'état, Colonel Song Suradej, didn't like the foreign minister's radicalism, left Bangkok in disgust, and is commander of military training in the north. He is held to be an important character.

. . . .

Siam is not a rich country. Only thirty people in the kingdom pay tax on incomes greater than $10,000 per year. There is no middle class, and no feudalism any more; the great bulk of the population is the peasantry. Siam lives on rice, the principal article both of consumption and export; teak and tin are its other important resources, most of which are controlled by British capital. The British also hold the small foreign debt.

Yet Siam has great untapped possibilities of wealth; it is one of the few countries left in the world with a vast public domain; perhaps fifty per cent of the country is still not surveyed. Covering about 200,000 square miles, it contains only 14,000,000 people; it is practically a vacuum compared to the suffocatingly crowded provinces of China and India near by. A future problem is bound to be that of foreign capital. The Siamese want keenly to develop their country, but they cannot do it alone, and they remain suspicious of outside help.

Though Siam is not rich the finances are admirably in order. The trade balance is always favorable, and the budget has never been out of balance. The public debt is small; the currency cover is no less than 124 per cent. Recently a foreign expert said that he had never known a sounder financial state. There is, however, a very considerable agricultural debt, since the peasants borrow against their crops,

[2] Colonel Pibul Songgram became prime minister in December, 1938, shortly after a reported attempt to unseat King Ananda.

as in China, and the money-lenders try to suck them dry. The best customer is Malaya; most imports come from Japan.

The only political issue recently has been a scandal. Until 1932 all of Siam was technically the property of the king, as an absolute monarch; now different categories of royal property have been marked out, and some have been bought by the nation from the crown. It was alleged that several very high officials of the government gained by these transfers of property. People like the minister of war were compelled to defend themselves in public addresses. The Regency Council resigned, but was reappointed after a few days of crisis.

Foreign Affairs and the Legend of Kra

The foreign policy of Mr. Pradist in particular and of Siam in general is strict neutrality, with no external engagements or entanglements. The Siamese are an independent nation, and want to remain so. The greatest care is taken to steer a neutral path. For instance, Siam employs several foreign experts; an American is chosen by tradition as adviser in the foreign office, an Englishman in the ministry of finance, a Frenchman in the judiciary, and so on. Recently Siamese nationalism has found expression in many small particulars; for instance, government reports, hitherto always written in English, are now done in Siamese.

Obviously the war in China and the steady growth of Japanese influence in southeastern Asia constitute a serious problem for Siam. The country has a certain strategic importance in that it lies between Burma and Singapore; the Siamese know this—and so does Japan. Siam does not dare to offend Japan (yet the considerable Chinese population of Siam maintains an unofficial boycott of Japanese goods), and must base all its calculations on the assumption that Japan may someday become an enemy. So Siamese policy is double-edged, a kind of wary friendliness; fear of Japanese aggression combined with cautious attempt to buy it off. The Japanese have gone far with economic penetration. For instance, Japanese shipping does a thriving Siamese business; Bangkok harbor is being dredged and rebuilt by Japanese companies; new units of the Siamese fleet have been purchased from Japan. Yet to state that Japan absolutely dominates Siamese policy would be an exaggeration.

Siam and China are good friends, although—a curious point—there have been no diplomatic relations between the two countries for several hundred years. This is because the Chinese insist on claiming Chinese nationality for children born of pure Chinese parents no matter where they live. There is a very large and powerful Chinese community in Siam, probably numbering 2,500,000 in all, and the Siamese cannot accept the thesis that those of them born in Siam are Chinese by nationality, not Siamese.

The Isthmus of Kra, as one may readily see from any map, is the narrow bridge of land near the junction of Siam and Burma. For several years this otherwise unremarkable strip of rock, swamp, and jungle has been responsible for a fancy crop of rumors to the effect that the Japanese are building a canal there. There is no foundation to these rumors—at least not yet. The Kra Canal is purely a myth at present—though conceivably it might be a reality at some future date. London newspapers have printed picturesque stories about Japanese laborers already at work, assiduously digging between sea and sea. They are without foundation.

The reason for the Kra legend is, of course, that a canal at the Isthmus would permit Japanese or other shipping to progress from European or Indian ports to China or Japan without passing Singapore. It would short-circuit Singapore Base. Technical experts disagree as to its feasibility. The canal would have to be only thirty-three miles long, but difficulties of construction are believed to be formidable. A not unimportant point is that the western orifice of the canal, should it be built, would be directly adjacent to British territory—Victoria Point in Burma, which could easily be fortified.

The Kra project, if it can be called a project, dates back a good many years. King Rama VI, a madly generous person—he could refuse nothing to his friends and he gave untold wealth away—once voluntarily offered the Isthmus to a French concessionaire. But Rama's foreign advisers stepped in and persuaded him to withdraw the gift.

In Siam we strike a new foreign trail. It is that of Germany. In Siam, as in Afghanistan, the Germans have subsidized radio broadcasting stations. News comes from Berlin, and is broadcast in Bangkok in English and other languages; the Siamese news report, furnished by the Deutches Nachrichten Buro, is heard all over India and the East. We shall pick up this kind of radio news and propaganda again—in Italian throughout the Middle East—before this book is done.

Note on Climate

Most of the westerners who live in Bangkok like the Siamese. Customarily the Siamese and Burmese are called the "nicest" people of the East. But the westerner will be apt to say that the Siamese, for all their admirable qualities of gentility and intelligence, are inept, slothful, lacking in push, and incredibly timid of accepting responsibility. One foreign engineer told me that among the natives of all Malaysia, including Siam, there were only half a dozen "adults."

Whether this childishness is real or not I don't know. A reason sometimes put forward for it is—heat.

In Japan, in China, it may be hot; Manila knows scorching days, and Singapore and Batavia are warm and humid; but the real heat of the East begins in Bangkok. Here temperature becomes an enemy; here sunshine is a vice. Siam is hot, with the terrible debilitating heat of the deep tropics, as India is hot. And often the white man says that heat is what ruins the natives. The inexorable sun wrings vitality from their very blood; its sucks wit and gumption from their brains, it reduces them to impotence and slavery. I have heard Europeans say that true autonomy, true independence, is impossible to a tropical country. So the white man, who can outwit heat, is tempted to adduce climate as a pretext for imperialism.

French Indo-China

Indo-China, the chief bastion of France in the East, "the French balcony in Asia," resembles Siam very closely. The people are mostly Annamese, who once had a mighty kingdom; travelers who have been impressed by the magnificence and heroic scale of Angkor Wat know what a civilization once existed in this obscure corner of the world. Indo-China is roughly the size of Siam, but with twenty million people instead of fourteen. Like Siam, it lives on rice. The French, as we have seen, took it from China late in the 19th century.

French colonial methods stand roughly midway between those of British and Dutch. The French, who are good administrators, believe in decentralization and local autonomy—but some of their colonies are considered to be actually part of France. French officials do not encourage as much admixture with natives as do the Dutch, but they are less self-conscious than the British about their presumptive superiority to the local populations. The French keep iron watch on local political activity, and have ruthlessly suppressed strikes in Indo-China; but they have covered the country with good roads, good hotels, and so on. By comparison Siam is still a wilderness. The standard of living is much higher than in Siam.

The French, as we will see when we reach Syria, are great partitionists. Their method of administration is to divide and subdivide. Indo-China, for instance, contains five quite distinct and separate régimes, though as a whole it is under the control of a governor-general who is responsible to the Minister of Colonies in Paris. First is Cochin China. This is precisely in the category of a French *department*; like Algeria it elects representatives to the Chamber of Deputies in Paris; it is legally an integral section of France itself. The capital, which is also capital for Indo-China as a whole, is Saigon.

Then comes Annam. This is a protectorate. A youthful "Emperor," known as Bao-Dai, is theoretically vested with authority; the real ruler is of course the French Resident-Superior. Cambodia is likewise a protectorate, ruled in theory by a native king with the nice name Sisowathmonibong. Another division, Tonking, with its capital at Hanoi, is an independent unit under the theoretical rule of the Emperor of Annam. Finally there is Laos, which has a sort of sub-king, or kinglet, of its own. Annam is the most highly developed of these separate states. The warmest political discontent comes from Cambodia.

France in Indo-China is perpetually alarmed at complications that the Japanese invasion of China may bring. There is, uniquely in southeastern Asia, little problem in regard to Japanese economic penetration, since the hard-boiled French shut out Japanese goods with a very high protective tariff; but the political issue may become acute. Recent reports state that France is building a naval base at Cam Ranh, on the Indo-Chinese coast above Saigon. And, as we know, early in 1939 the Japanese seized the Chinese island of Hainan, which commands the Indo-China coast.

Chapter XXII
Mr. Gandhi

I am not a visionary. I claim to be a practical idealist.
—M. K. GANDHI

MR. GANDHI, who is an incredible combination of Jesus Christ, Tammany Hall, and your father, is the greatest Indian since Buddha. Like Buddha, he will be worshiped as a god when he dies. Indeed, he is already literally worshiped by thousands of his people. I have seen peasants kiss the sand his feet have trod.

No more difficult or enigmatic character can easily be conceived. He is a slippery fellow. I mean no disrespect. But consider some of the contradictions, some of the puzzling points of contrast in his career and character. This man who is at once a saint and a politician, a prophet and a superb opportunist, defies ordinary categories.

For instance, his great contribution to India was the theory and practice of non-violence or civil disobedience. But at the very time that non-violence was the deepest thing he believed in, he was supporting Britain in the World War. The concept of non-violence is a perfect example of Gandhi's familiar usage of moral weapons to achieve practical results, of his combination of spiritual and temporal powers. India, an unarmed state, could make a revolution only by non-violent means. Non-violence was a spiritual concept, but it made revolution practicable.

There is again the matter of his celebrated fasts. He fasted purely for moral reasons, but they served a considerable practical convenience, because if he began a fast in jail, the British had to let him out. A sort of etherealized Houdini, he was in a position to escape from prison any time he chose because the British would not accept the onus of his death from starvation while in confinement. Yet—the point is important—Gandhi himself never consciously thought of fasting as a method of escape. His last fast came early in 1939.

His inconsistencies seem remarkable, until you note that his objective seldom varies, but that he is willing to compromise on contributory details. He is interested in substance, not form. For instance, he devoted the major portion of his career to a titanic struggle with Britain, yet now he is coöperating more or less freely with Britain under the new constitution. His point in this case is that his objective, Indian independence, may be the more easily achieved by coöperation than by struggle, now that civil disobedience is over. Yet the paradox is enormous: Mr. Gandhi, who fought the British Empire to a standstill, in 1939 is almost the best friend the British have in India.

Another great paradox is his attitude to caste and the Untouchables.[1] Mr. Gandhi devotes the largest share of his energy nowadays to uplifting the Untouchables, but he resisted with his life an attempt to remove Untouchability from Hinduism, which would have been the effect of the British plan (which he succeeded in modifying) to give Untouchables a separate electorate. He adores the Untouchables, and would do anything for them—except remove them from Hinduism, which makes them what they are.

There are other paradoxes and contradictions. To Gandhi modern science is anathema, but he uses a thermometer and wears eyeglasses. He pleads for Hindu-Moslem unity, but he wouldn't gladly see a member of his family become a Moslem. He is the soul, backbone, eyes, and fingers of the Indian National Congress, but he is not a member of it. His approach to everything is religious, but aside from Hinduism it is difficult to tell what his religion is.

Nevertheless, Mr. Gandhi adds up to a great deal. The record of his life is heroic in the best sense of that word: he is a man who fought—and almost won—an elemental struggle against the nature of his environment. This tough and rubbery little man, dressed in a loin cloth and sitting by his spinning wheel, who weighs 112 pounds, took on the greatest empire the world has ever known—an empire with every recourse in man power, accumulated wealth, tradition, skill and strategy in administration—and almost vanquished it. He fought fate—and what used to be stronger than fate—the British Empire.

Nowadays people are apt to assume that Mr. Gandhi, with his score of great years behind him, is played out; they even think that he no longer counts in India. Nothing could be farther from the truth. He is still incomparably the most important living Indian. One cannot be in India two hours without finding out incontrovertibly that he still rules the Congress. (The Congress, of which we shall write much, is

[1] The reader is asked impatiently to await Chapter XXIV for discussion of religion in general and caste in particular.

the nationalist political organization, the strongest in India, devoted to Indian independence.)

Some young nationalists are impatient at his mysticism, and even his most devoted admirers occasionally blink at his unpredictable vagaries. They think, for instance, that his willingness to compromise with Britain—now—passes proper limits. But his hold on the great mass of the Indian people is unshaken. He is a unique kind of dictator, one who rules by love. He is adored as well as worshiped. His photograph is enshrined in a million cottages; children, sick, are touched with his likeness to make them well. Peasants may come twenty miles simply to see his train pass, even if it does not stop and he is not visible. To the submerged masses, the "dumb half-starved millions" as he frequently calls them, he is a man of miracles. All over India I noticed how the faces of people lit up when his name was mentioned. And he is the only man in India who by a single word, by lifting his little finger, could instigate a new national revolt, who could start civil disobedience again among more than 350,000,000 people—roughly one-fifth of the human race.

What explains the hold Mr. Gandhi has on India? What has he done for India? The outline of his career is known to everyone, but we must sketch it briefly. Let us try to take this extraordinary man apart, and see what it is that controls his unique behavior.

St. Francis in South Africa

Mohandas Karamchand Gandhi was born in Porbander, one of the small native states in the Kathiawar peninsula, on October 2, 1869. Thus he is seventy, which is old for an Indian, whereas it may be comfortable maturity to a Japanese. He came of a solid official family, members of the third or Vaisya caste; both his father and grandfather were *Dewans*, that is, prime ministers, of local Kathiawar states. The name "Gandhi" means "grocer" in his native language. His father, whom he describes as being brave and incorruptible, married four times, and Gandhi was the youngest child of the fourth wife. His mother, a passionately devout woman, given to strict observance of Hindu fasts and customs, profoundly influenced him.

The best source of material for Gandhi's early years is his autobiography, called *The Story of My Experiments with Truth.*[2] It is a

[2] Gandhi wrote the book in his native tongue, Gujerati, and his faithful secretary Mahadev Desai translated it into English. It has been published in India but

work of very peculiar and original texture. I know no autobiography quite like it. Artlessly it sets down details of almost shocking intimacy; peacefully it explores the origins of Gandhi's character, like a brook rising to a river. It gives an impression of almost biblical restraint, and yet is full of naïve candor. It varies between passages of great nobility and literary force and of preoccupation with idiosyncrasies almost meaningless to a western reader. Its last words are—after 1,090 pages—"I must reduce myself to zero."

His picture of his mother is worth recording:

> The outstanding impression my mother has left on my memory is that of saintliness. She was deeply religious. She would not think of taking her meals without her daily prayers. As far as my memory goes back, I do not remember her having ever missed the *Chaturmas* [a semi-fast period that lasts four months during the rains]. She would take the hardest vows and keep them without flinching. . . . To keep two or three consecutive fasts was nothing to her. Living on one meal a day during *Chaturmas* was a habit with her. Not content with that she fasted every alternate day during one *Chaturmas*. During another *Chaturmas* she vowed not to have food without seeing the sun. We children on those days would stand, staring at the sky, waiting to announce the appearance of the sun to our mother. . . . She would run out to see with her own eyes, but by that time the fugitive sun would be gone, thus depriving her of her meal. "That does not matter," she would say cheerfully, "God did not want me to eat today."

(*The Story of My Experiments with Truth,* Vol. I, pp. 19-20)

A friend told young Gandhi that Indians are a weak people because they do not eat meat. "The English are able to rule over us, because they are meat-eaters." Secretly Gandhi decided to taste the forbidden substance, but a furtive meal of goat's meat made him sick. That night he had a horrible nightmare, in which a live goat kept bleating inside his stomach. . . . At about the same time a friend took him to a brothel. Gandhi says, "I was almost struck dumb and blind in this den of vice. I went into the jaws of sin, but God in His infinite mercy protected me." He fled, "saved." On another occasion he smoked a forbidden cigarette, and almost committed suicide in remorse. He says that he never told a lie in childhood.

---

not in England or the United States. Gandhi records his hesitation to write it, because "writing an autobiography is a practice peculiar to the West."

He married at thirteen. Before this he had been betrothed three times, but the little girls all died. His ten-year-old wife was chosen from a neighbor's family, and he was married in a joint ceremony with his elder brother and a cousin. Marriage is a complicated festival to Hindus, and it was cheaper and more expedient to have the three weddings together. Gandhi writes, "Little did I dream then, that one day I should severely criticise my father for having married me as a child. Everything on that day seemed to me right and proper and pleasing. There was also my own eagerness to get married." He "draws the curtain" over the first encounter of the two nervous, frightened children, and then says that he lost no time in "assuming the authority of a husband."

His wife, Kasturbai, was illiterate. "I was very anxious to teach her, but lustful love left no time . . ." As a result Kasturbai to-day— a half-century later—can only barely read and write. "I am sure, that had my love for her been absolutely untainted with lust, she would have been a learned lady today; for I could then have conquered her dislike for studies."

When he was fifteen, Kasturbai had their first child, who died. His father died at about the same period; the event, in addition to its normal consequences, had tremendous moral significance for Gandhi, because at the moment of his father's death he and Kasturbai were in bed together. His "shame" at this is "a blot I have never been able to efface or forget."

The sexual motif is strong throughout Gandhi's book. He continually writes of his carnal impulses and desires; as late as 1933 he says that he has not finally conquered them. Four times God saved him from going to brothels. His first great struggle for emancipation from earthly needs, earthly wants, was in regard to sex; all his fantastic experiments with diet, and his final choice of goat's milk as ideal food, were caused by his desire to diminish sexual ardor. In 1900, when he was thirty-one, he gave up sexual intercourse; in 1906, he confirmed his abstention with a perpetual vow of continence. This he considered his first step forward to self-mastery; it was the essential preliminary to the doctrine of *ahimsa*, non-violence.

Having finished high school and the University of Ahmedabad, young Gandhi decided to go to London and study law. This was a very unconventional thing to do in those days. Orthodox Hindus are supposed to be defiled by crossing water and especially by ocean travel, and he had to seek permission for the voyage from his uncle. Reluctantly the uncle gave consent—incidentally, Gandhi had to travel five days by bullock cart and camel to see him—but the subcaste of his community excommunicated him. Note the strength of character of this young man. The worst social consequences could not deter him from the trip. He calmly relates how he sold his wife's trinkets to help pay his way—he left her behind—and describes his solemn vow to his mother to eat no meat, drink no wine, and have no women. At this period his ultimate ambition was to become a *Dewan*, like his father.

His adventures in London—he arrived there in September, 1888— make strange reading now. He set about learning the ways of this remarkable island people who kept his own people in subjection. An Indian friend told him, "Do not touch other people's things"—(this after he had innocently stroked a silk hat the wrong way)—"Do not ask questions on first acquaintance; do not talk loudly; never address people as 'sir' as we do in India." Young Gandhi bought a dress suit for £10, learned French and Latin, took dancing lessons, and went through miseries trying to find palatable vegetarian food. (He would not eat eggs, or even sauces made of eggs, and had to question waiters to find out how the food was cooked.) He made many friends in the Indian colony in London, became a member of the executive committee of the Vegetarian Society, and was so frightened and shy that he could not talk—he was unable even to read from manuscript—at his first public speech.

Three years later he returned to India, and set up legal practice in Bombay. In his first case, when he rose to cross-examine a witness, he was too timid to speak, and had to sit down again without asking a question. A little later came a disconcerting experience: he was bodily thrown out of an Englishman's office when he came to ask a favor on behalf of his brother. Directly he sought to bring suit against the Englishman—note his pepperiness—but was prevailed upon not to do so. He swallowed the insult, but profited from it as well. He records, "Never again shall I place myself in such a false position; never again shall I try to exploit friendship in this way."

In 1893, feeling himself a failure in India, he went to South Africa, where the large Indian colony offered him the chance of a good practice. Almost before he knew it he was a leader of the community, and he remained in South Africa, hardly realizing how the time slipped

by, for more than twenty years. These were his great years of preparation. South Africa was a rehearsal for what was coming.

When he arrived in South Africa, and indeed for a long time thereafter, he was a loyal citizen of the British Empire. He early became
interested in Indian Home Rule through the influence of Gokhale and
other leaders, but he was distinctly a gradualist. Indeed, he helped
organize medical work during the Boer War and the Zulu rebellion,
supporting the British forces; he received citations for bravery in the
front line, and in 1914 went straight to London to offer his services
for establishing an Indian ambulance corps. This, too, despite the
indignities he and his compatriots suffered owing to race and color
prejudice in South Africa. In the early days he was kicked, beaten,
spat upon as a coolie. He could find no rooms in hotels, no restaurants
to eat in.

Gradually in South Africa the two main streams in his life came
forth. Later in India they converged. First was his conversion to the
doctorate of non-violence. He read Ruskin, Tolstoi, Thoreau, and set
himself to follow their example. He was a highly successful barrister,
earning £5,000 a year, but he dropped commercial practice to found
an agricultural colony devoted to poverty, non-violence, and the simple
virtues. Second was his growing interest in Indian nationalism. He
did not fight the British directly, but he roused a tremendous tumult
in defense of Indian rights. He founded a newspaper, *Indian Opinion*,
and wrote his first book, *Hind Swaraj* (Indian Independence),
showing that he had not forgotten the great peninsula to which he
must return. He became the undisputed leader of the nationalist
Indians in South Africa, following a series of semi-political campaigns
and efforts to remove discriminations against Indians. He tested out
his theory of passive resistance as early as 1906, and three times went
to jail.

Meantime he was broadening, developing, both spiritually and
practically. The autobiography contains fascinating nuggets from these
forgotten days.

For instance, he decided that he was not well enough grounded in
the Hindu scriptures. But he was busy, with little time to spare. So
he copied out the Gita verses, hung them on a wall, and memorized
them during the fifteen minutes each morning he devoted to cleaning
his teeth.

He discovered a good deal about the law. From the beginning he refused to take any case the justice of which he doubted. He learned that if he were sure of facts, the law was apt to take care of itself. "Facts mean truth, and once we adhere to truth, the law comes to our aid naturally." Also he saw that the winning party seldom recovered all his costs, and that compromise was an excellent technique. "The true function of a lawyer is to unite parties riven asunder. A large part of my time during the twenty years of my practice was occupied in bringing about private compromises."

One of his early spiritual struggles was over life insurance. "Man," he told himself, "you have sold almost all the ornaments of your wife. If something were to happen to you, the burden of supporting her and the children would fall on your poor brother." So he took out 10,000 rupees ($3,700) of life insurance. Then he canceled it. What reason, he asked himself, had he to assume that death would claim him earlier than the others? The real protector was, he decided, not his brother, but God Almighty. And he concluded, "In getting my life insured I had robbed my wife and children of their self-reliance. Why should they not be expected to take care of themselves? What happened to the families of the numberless poor of the world? Why should I not count myself among them?"

Note the curious emphasis here. He is willing that even his family should suffer provided that his conscience is square with the Almighty. We shall meet this trait again. Mr. Gandhi is a supreme egotist, willing to shoulder this difficult responsibility, because of his conception of mankind, under God, as a whole.

He had many political tussles and tumbles. He learned to handle men, and to handle crowds. He was absolutely inflexible on any matter of principle, and wonderfully supple on minor details.

He was continually exasperated by diet. He tried countless experiments. Finally he gave up salt, tea, and meals after sunset. He began, too, to observe Monday as a day of silence. Goat's milk seemed an ideal food for the observation of *brahmacharya* (self-restraint), but it was only after a terrific struggle that he consented to take it, since, after all, it was not strictly a vegetarian substance. Meantime, he struggled to maintain his vow of continence.

Such was the man, aged forty-five, who returned to India in 1914. Then the great years, the tremendous years, began.

Entrance to India

"Out of South Africa there came a wizard across the seas."
—Mrs. Sarojini Naidu

We cannot deal with Mr. Gandhi and the British from 1914 to 1939 in any but the briefest fashion. To discuss the subject in satisfactory detail would demand an entire book. The chapters that follow will, I hope, add some color and spice of detail to the general story of the political development of India, but here we must confine ourselves to the barest outline.

Mr. Gandhi, smelling his native soil again, spent a year in travel and social work, getting close to Indian affairs, and in 1915 founded his *Satyagraha* hermitage near Ahmedabad. This word, *Satyagraha,* needs careful definition. Gandhi invented it. Literally it means no more than "right effort," but "force of truth" or "soul force" is the usual translation, and later it was used loosely to indicate "non-coöperation," "passive resistance," and "civil disobedience." To the hermitage he brought the poor, including a group of Untouchables; he founded a colony, much like his colony in South Africa, devoted to poverty and the law of love. His word swept India. Also he was tackling practical jobs in investigating and helping to redress the grievances of peasants in several districts. By 1917, at least, he was already known as the Mahatma (literally "Great Soul"), a title not directly given him by anyone, but spontaneously bestowed by a willing people.

At the end of the war the political situation was boiling over. India loyally supported Britain during the war; in fact, she sent 1,215,000 men overseas, of whom more than 100,000 were casualties. In return the Indians, Mr. Gandhi among them, assumed that Britain would lighten the burden of its rule. And indeed the British did introduce the Montagu-Chelmsford reforms which gave India a limited—a very limited—measure of self-government. Mr. Montagu, the secretary of state for India, announced in 1917 that

the policy of his Majesty's Government . . . is that of increasing association of Indians in every branch of the administration, and the gradual development of self-governing institutions with a view to the progressive realization of responsible government in India as an integral part of the British Empire.

But the "dyarchy" system, by which Indian ministers in the provinces had rights over certain minor subjects, did not promise to work well. The Indian movement for home rule continued to grow. To check the rising tide of political discontent, the British introduced the Rowlatt bill, giving the police special powers; it was furiously resented. The country seethed, and Gandhi became the head of the nationalist movement. Even the Moslems joined him. He declared a *hartal*, general strike, in protest at the Rowlatt bill; then in April, 1919, came the grotesque tragedy at Amritsar, when a British general gave the order to fire on a crowd of mostly unarmed Indians—men, women, children—who had no method of escape, and killed and wounded hundreds of them. India rose—but not with a roar. It rose with *Satyagraha*.

Commonly it is said that Amritsar[3] turned Gandhi finally against the British. But already the machinery of civil disobedience—in 1919-20 it was called "non-coöperation"—was in motion. Amritsar hurried up the policy, made it inevitable, and to the great mass of Indians gave civil disobedience a tragic reality, a tragic necessity, that it might otherwise have taken longer to achieve. *Satyagraha* swept the country. Mr. Gandhi made it a political weapon as well as a spiritual force. It was as if his teaching struck deep through the skin of India, and touched a sensitive nerve long concealed. The people were on the brink of revolution; the Mahatma showed them the way. The call of non-violence, of self-mastery through abnegation, was something that the majority of Hindus—who are inclined to masochism—instinctively understood. It appealed directly to their religious nature; it made lions out of Hindus.

The British were bewildered. What could they do with people who let themselves be beaten to a pulp without lifting their hands? What to do when literally thousands of young Indians besieged the jails, demanding to be arrested? Mr. Gandhi's precepts to his *Satyagrahi*, as the passive-resisters were called, are almost more than the western mind can comprehend. The Mahatma insisted that *Satyagrahi* must harbor no anger, must not swear or curse, must never retaliate to attacks, must voluntarily submit to arrest, must never insult an opponent, and must *assist* British officials assaulted by forgetful Indians.

[3] The British, too, were profoundly influenced by Amritsar. It might be argued that what reforms have come to India since 1919 have been penance for the Amritsar shame.

Mr. Gandhi broke off relations with the British. He wrote to the Viceroy:

It is not without a pang that I return the Kaisar-i-Hind Gold Medal granted to me by your predecessor for my humanitarian work in South Africa, the Zulu War medal for my services as an officer in charge of the Indian Volunteer Ambulance Corps in 1906, and the Boer War Medal for my services as assistant superintendent of the Indian Volunteer Stretcher-bearer Corps during the Boer War of 1899-1900.

I can retain neither respect nor affection for a Government which has been moving from wrong to wrong in order to defend its immorality. . . . The Government must be moved to repentance.

I have therefore ventured to suggest non-coöperation, which enables those who wish to disassociate themselves from the Government and which, if unattended by violence, must compel the Government to retrace its steps and undo the wrongs.

The Mahatma was wrong; the government did not retrace its steps. Instead, the lines of battle were marked out. The Indian Congress declared for *Swaraj* (Home Rule—literally, "oneself-country") "by all legitimate and peaceful means" and worked out a practical program under Mr. Gandhi's guidance. He became dictator of the Congress. Nationalist Indians agreed to boycott British goods, to take their children from government schools, to withdraw from the law courts, to give up public jobs, to pay no taxes, to surrender titles and honors, and, above all, to use *Khadder*, i.e., homespun cotton. This, like the invention of *Satyagraha*, was another example of Gandhi's astute political sense. Nothing so dramatized the movement—down to the remotest village in the peninsula—as the revival of home spinning and weaving. It at once starved British imports, revived village economy, and gave the Congress a badge, a uniform.

In 1921 came the episode of Chauri-Chaura. An infuriated mob of Indians hacked and burned to death a group of police. Gandhi was horrified. He was about to push civil disobedience further, but he suddenly and startlingly called off the entire campaign. It is difficult to know who were the most astonished by this volte-face, the British or the Indians. Gandhi said simply that Chauri-Chaura proved that India was not ready for *Satyagraha*. The people could not yet be fully trusted with this new weapon. He talked of his bitter humiliation, his "Himalayan blunder"; he denounced mob violence and said that he, the person responsible, must undergo cleansing; he set himself the penance of his first great fast.

In 1922, he was arrested. He knew this would come. Listen to his logic:

What can be the motive of the Government in arresting me? The Government are not my enemy; I have not a grain of enmity toward them. But they believe that I am the soul of all this agitation, that if I am removed, the ruled and ruler will be left in peace. Not only the Government but some of our leaders also share this belief. How then can the Government put the people to the test? How can the Government ascertain whether the people do understand my advice or are simply dazzled by my utterances?

The only way left for them is to arrest me . . . I desire that the people shall maintain perfect self-control and consider the day of my arrest as a day of rejoicing.

(Speeches and Writings of Mahatma Gandhi, p. 690)

The trial was a tableau to stagger the imagination. Mr. Gandhi told the prosecutor that his crimes were greater than those in the indictment; gravely, placidly, he pleaded with the judge to give him the maximum sentence. The judge rose to the occasion, and matched the Mahatma's courtesy with his own. The testimony reads like the proceedings of some court of honor under a code of chivalry. The judge sentenced Mr. Gandhi to six years' imprisonment, and the Indian leader courteously thanked him.

He adored jail. It gave him rest and seclusion. His own words are that he was "happy as a bird" in confinement. After a sudden operation for appendicitis, he was released in 1924.

The next year he undertook a twenty-one-day fast following an outbreak of trouble in Kohat between Hindus and Moslems. By his example, he hoped to bring friendship between the two. He wrote, "I was writhing in deep pain. News of Kohat set the smouldering mass aflame. I passed two nights of restlessness. I knew the remedy . . . My fast is a matter between God and myself. My penance is the prayer of a bleeding heart for forgiveness, for sins unwittingly committed. It is a warning to Hindus and Moslems who have professed to love me." Breathless, a whole continent waited the three weeks in anguish. When finally the Mahatma, on the twenty-first day, took a sip of orange juice, he was too weak to talk.

Came then five years of tension, feeling for position, and delay.

The British sent the Simon Commission to India to prepare the way for a new constitution, and the Congress steadily expanded in strength and spirit; in 1930, Congress came out flatly for Complete Independence (*purna Swaraj,* which is more than just *Swaraj*), at about the same time Lord Irwin, the viceroy,[4] announced that the British government considered that the natural issue of India's constitutional progress was—Dominion Status. Battle lines were drawn again, and tempers rose. Gandhi wrote Irwin, even though he always addressed him as "Dear Friend," that he considered British rule to be "a curse." He opened a renewed course of implacable opposition. He presented demands to the "satanic" government, which were rejected; thereupon, in 1930, civil disobedience began again—more vigorously than before.

It opened with Gandhi's "salt march" to Dandi on the sea. Salt was—and is—a government monopoly; the tax on it bore especially hard on the poorer people, and Gandhi chose it as a symbol that everyone could grasp. The march—except perhaps that of the Red Army in China—is the most remarkable in modern history. With a group of volunteers, the Mahatma slowly traversed the country, and a fire of rebellion followed in his wake. When he began it, he said, "On bended knee I asked the Government for bread, and I got a stone instead." With his friends bowed beside him, he finally reached the sea, and scooped illegal salt from the water, saying, "I would rather die a dog's death and have my bones licked by dogs than that I should return broken."

But he was broken. Rather, since he is Mr. Gandhi who makes his own rules, he was broken and patched up again. Civil disobedience became a great national revolution, but it did not win victory. By 1934, it had fizzled out; thousands of people were in jail, the British ruled by pure repression, and the country was prostrate. What happened then was a double course of events. First, the British hammered out the new constitution at the Round Table Conferences and in meetings of the Joint Select committee, a constitution which did very considerably advance India toward self-government; second, the Congress, under Mr. Gandhi's lead, came around, by 1937, to reluctant participation in its working. So the net result of civil disobedience was a compromise. The British gave way to

[4] Now Lord Halifax, the British foreign secretary.

some extent; the Indians grudgingly consented to work with them. This is the present situation.

Mr. Gandhi's own career from 1931 to 1939 contains perplexities. He patched up a preliminary truce with Lord Irwin in 1931, after a period in prison; he went to the London Round Table as the *sole* representative of the Congress, which seemed to many to indicate excessive self-assurance. When he returned to India he was jailed again, and he began his great "fast to death" for the Untouchables. Later he fasted again for twenty-one days to purify himself, and was released from jail; and then—much as in the 1921 campaign— he abruptly called off civil disobedience on what seemed to his colleagues a comparatively minor personal issue. Came jail again, and a fast again. In 1934, he "retired" from Congress and politics in order to devote himself to village welfare—but nevertheless continued to run Congress from behind the scenes.

Daily Life of the Modern Saint

Nowadays the Mahatma lives most of the year in a remote village called Segaon, near Wardha, in the very center of the most backward part of India. He chose it, with his customary combination of foresight and crankiness, just because it was peculiarly inaccessible, surrounded by mud and dust, and populated largely by *Harijans* (children of God), which is the name he has given the Untouchables. He wanted to demonstrate that even the most unbelievably backward village in India—and he searched hard to find it—could benefit by Gandhism.

He rises every day at 4:30 for his morning prayers, then takes a brisk walk, rain or shine. He did this even in London, when he exhausted the two detectives assigned to guard him. When I write "brisk," I mean "brisk." He walks as Paavo Nurmi runs. I have enjoyed watching Europeans in good condition try to keep up with him. He sails along, carrying a long staff, like some extraordinary bird.

The prayers are very important, even more important than the ritual of stiff daily exercise. In London he would interrupt any meeting without a trace of self-consciousness to sit down on the floor and pray—even in a committee room of the House of Commons. He prays twice a day, morning and at sunset. The sunset prayers are in the nature of a public ceremony, because his household joins him, together with the villagers. First his attendants lay a rectangle of straw mats on the ground. Quietly the people gather, squatting on the periphery of the open rectangle, and lamps are lit. The evening I saw the prayers on Juhu beach (Mr. Gandhi was having a holiday near Bombay) a Japanese priest joined the ceremony, and Miss Madeline Slade, the daughter of an English admiral who is the faithful manager of his household, sang from the Hindu scriptures. The moon rose at one end of the beach just as the sun was setting; the night was calm, still, and very beautiful. Mr. and Mrs. Gandhi walked quietly up, and the Mahatma took his place at the short end of the rectangle, facing the sea. He sat there cross-legged, head bowed, for precisely thirty minutes. There was no other ceremony. No one spoke; no one moved; but the Hindu chants continued plangently. Suddenly he rose; the enchantment broke, and the prayers were over.

He eats no meat, of course, and in fact only seldom takes any cooked food; but it is not quite correct to say that he eats very little. A mug of goat's milk, dates, nuts, a tablespoon of honey, garlic, a bowl of chopped fresh vegetables, and plenty of fruit—oranges, pineapples, mangoes, peaches—this is the general menu.

He works very hard, seeing people incessantly, receiving visitors, consulting subordinates. Wherever he is is the capital of Indian India. Any particularly interesting conversations appear later in his newspaper, the *Harijan*. So no words are wasted. He keeps up a considerable correspondence with people all over the world. His chief relaxation is his bath; he bathes in very hot water for forty minutes before retiring, and usually reads in the tub.

Monday is his day of silence. He will not interrupt it no matter what urgent business is clamoring outside the door.

Mostly his work at present, except when the Working Committee of Congress is meeting, centers on the village. To revive the village, and thus prevent the countrymen from being sucked into the terrible slums of the towns, is his plan. He has a five-point program for village welfare and economy. Encourage home spinning. Make village education vocational. Improve sanitation. Bring the Untouchables into the community. Above all, stimulate village industry. He is doing his best, for instance, to create work from by-products of dead cattle, fertilizers and the like. Of course no Hindu would kill a cow, which is sacred in India, but the Mahatma is trying to persuade the villagers to utilize those that die naturally—not an easy thing to persuade them to do.

Gandhi has very little need of money, and the financing of his household doesn't seem to be a problem, because what he needs he gets from charity. Rich friends flock across his path. He has small interest in economics in the abstract, and has driven young Congress socialists to despair by his refusal to think in economic terms. Once he told a socialist friend that he believed in both private property *and* nationalization. "I purchase a mill, for example," he explained. "Then I give the people good wages; that is socialism!"

His epistolary style is quite his own. Consider this telegram of condolence to his friend Pandit Jawaharlal Nehru, the second man of India, when Nehru's mother died:

Mother lived nobly, has died nobly. She was model wife, mother. No sorrow. Let our women copy her example. Love. Bapu.

"Bapu" is what his friends and intimates call him; it is the Gujerati word for father. In his early days he was called "Bhai"—brother. Few people in India call him "Mahatma"; he has always been embarrassed by the phrase. Ordinarily—in fact, universally—he is called "Gandhiji," "ji" being an untranslatable suffix which informally means "Mr." but which connotes affection also. Sometimes he is called "Bapuji" or even "Mahatmaji." When I arrived in India and talked to Congress people, I was puzzled by frequent use of the phrase, "High Command." This means Mr. Gandhi, too.

His health is quite good, except that he suffers intermittently from high blood pressure. He looks made of rubber. He is not nearly as frail, as brittle, as his photographs indicate; the torso is well-formed, and the muscles hard and smooth. His personal physician, Dr. Roy, one of the first doctors of India, told me that he was "superbly normal." But then Dr. Roy admitted that Gandhiji could do things that normal men could not do.

His experience of fasting has, for instance, given him peculiar powers over his body. Once—indication that he is not given to self-delusion—he noted that fasting could be "as great a weapon of indulgence as restraint." Once he was down to ninety-seven pounds and eating only 400 calories a day. Dr. Roy said he must get up to 104 pounds, and that he could do this only by doubling his intake of food. Gandhi listened patiently, refused to change his diet, and asserted that he could take on the necessary seven pounds in one week without changing his diet by one calory. Which he did.

He will say, "I will go to sleep for twenty-five minutes." Then he can fall asleep instantly, and sleep for twenty-five minutes and no more. On the trains his attendants know that he will be asleep within thirty seconds of getting into the compartment. Once he was asleep in an automobile, returning from Pandit Motilal Nehru's funeral. The car overturned. Mr. Gandhi was thrown out, but when his worried friends went to him on the roadside he was asleep again.

He owes much to Roy and other doctors, but he detests modern medicine. He calls medicine "the concentrated essence of black magic"; he once argued quite seriously that modern medical science created more tuberculosis and venereal disease than it cured. He once studied nursing, and he has made a hobby of home cures. There are pages in his autobiography about the "earth cure" for constipation, which he invented; it consists of wrapping some good clean dirt around the tummy.

Mr. Gandhi is much less oppressive a personality than most people think. He loves laughter. He bubbles and chuckles in talk. Once he told a friend that he might have killed himself long ago but for his sense of humor.

His tributes to Kasturbai, his wife, are touching. She is a small, round, cheerful woman, with a face like a Dresden china shepherdess, close to him but never obtrusive; he quite calmly notes the wide difference between them intellectually, and says that he has no doubt that she does not approve of many things he does. "She is blessed with one great quality . . . willingly or unwillingly, consciously or unconsciously, she has considered herself blessed in following in my footsteps, and has never stood in the way of my endeavor to lead a life of restraint." In another passage, he writes, "I can no more describe my feeling for Hinduism than for my own wife. She moves me as no other woman in the world can. Not that she has no faults. I daresay that she has many more than I see myself. But the feeling of indissoluble bond is there."

The Gandhis have four sons and several grandchildren. In his autobiography he criticizes himself for not having given his children a better education. One son, indeed, has been a disappointment, but two others have made excellent careers as journalists. The fourth son married the daughter of Mr. Rajagopalacharia, the prime minister of

Madras. This caused a great commotion, because the Gandhis are not Brahmans, and the Rajagopalacharias distinctly are. Another Gandhi contradiction—the good Hindu thus breaking the laws of caste!

The Gandhi Gambit

"Means and ends are convertible terms in my philosophy of life."
—Mr. Gandhi

The record of Gandhiji's positive qualities is a long one. The brief narrative I have given of his career indicates some. There are many others, which perhaps help to explain his enormous power and hold on Indians.

For one thing, his unbelievable simplicity. This sometimes reaches the borderline of comedy. Once he went through a minor spiritual crisis before allowing his wife, a third-class passenger, to use a second-class bathroom. Once on shipboard he persuaded a friend to toss into the sea an expensive pair of binoculars. In prison in South Africa he offered to clean the latrines himself, although the warder asked him to choose some one else for the job. Once a Christian was his guest; Mr. Gandhi himself tended to emptying the chamber pot. In South Africa he learned laundrying, starched his collars, and taught himself to cut his own hair. One possibly apocryphal story describes the Englishman who shouted "Coolie" at him at a railway station. Obediently Mr. Gandhi picked up the Englishman's bags and took them to the train.

Again there is his very considerable charm. He hasn't had sexual intercourse for almost forty years, but he adores the company of women, and he likes to flirt. His charm is such that, according to the legend, the Secretary of State for India, Sir Samuel Hoare, ordered a new Viceroy, Lord Willingdon, not to see Gandhi, in order to prevent his succumbing to his formidable charm.

His intelligence is quick and shrewd. One could write a thousand words about Miss Mayo's *Mother India* and not describe it better than did Gandhi with his famous remark, "It is a book that no European and every Indian should read." His political sense is acute on other than merely Indian questions. He called the Munich agreement "peace without honor," and doubted that it would bring peace.

He is uncommonly intuitive, and not only catches the moods of people very quickly, but is capable of quick changes of mood himself. He senses it instantly if his friends are tired; he talks nonsense, laughs, gossips, makes jokes. But he can resume serious discussion instantly.

His consideration for others is very detailed. Nehru records how he found time during a serious crisis to send word to him that his little daughter had taken on weight. (Nehru was in jail at the time.) When, after the Round Table Conference, he wanted to give presents to the two detectives who had risen at 4:30 to jog with him through Kensington Gardens, he didn't know what to select, since Congress was boycotting British goods; so he sent for two Swiss watches. Once, leaving Bombay on a long trip, he saw a friend's wife among the concourse of people seeing him off; he remembered to tell her not to buy a new house she was interested in—this was his method of hinting that civil disobedience might begin again, and that none of them would need new houses. Another woman friend told me that Gandhiji had certainly saved her life, merely by seeing her occasionally, talking to her, during a severe nervous breakdown.

He has this tact, charm, consideration, but he can be brutal for a principle. Consider for instance the story of the illness of his ten-year-old child Manilal.

The doctor found Manilal with a high fever, caused by pneumonia after typhoid. He said that eggs and chicken broth might save him, but Mr. Gandhi refused to allow him either. "Manilal was only ten years old. To consult his wishes was out of the question. I had to decide." The doctors implored Gandhi to give the boy nourishing food, since his life was in grave danger, but the father continued to refuse. He told the doctor that he would treat Manilal in his own way, if the doctor would consent to come in from time to time and examine him. He gave Manilal hip baths and orange juice, and Manilal bravely said, "I will not have eggs or chicken broth." But the boy grew worse. His fever reached 104°. Gandhi proceeds:

I began to get anxious. What would people say of me? What right had parents to inflict their fads on their children? . . . I was haunted by thoughts like these. Then a contrary current would start. God would surely be pleased to see that I was giving the same treatment to my son as I would give myself . . . The doctor could not guarantee recovery. At best he could experiment. The thread of life was in the hands of God . . .

It was night. My mind was torn between these conflicting thoughts. I was in Manilal's bed lying by his side. I decided to give him a wet sheet pack. To the head I applied a wet towel. . . . The whole body was burning like hot iron, and quite parched. There was absolutely no perspiration . . .

I was sorely tired. I left Manilal in charge of his mother, and went out for a walk. . . . Very few pedestrians were out. Plunged in deep thought I scarcely looked at them. "My honor is in Thy keeping, oh Lord, in this hour of trial," I repeated to myself . . . After a short time I returned, my heart beating in my breast.

No sooner had I returned, than Manilal said, "You have returned, Bapu?"

"Yes, darling."

"Do please pull me out. I am burning."

"Are you perspiring, my boy?"

"I am simply soaked. Do please take me out."

I felt his forehead. It was covered with beads of perspiration. The temperature was going down. I thanked God. . . . I undid the pack, dried his body, and father and son fell asleep in the same bed.

(*Story of My Experiments with Truth,* Vol. I, pp. 571-577)

The point of this story is, of course, that his honor, his faith, were more important to the Mahatma than the life of his son. Years later an almost identical episode occurred, when Kasturbai was taken ill. The doctors said she would certainly die unless she got nourishing food. Gandhi consulted with her; they decided that she would not take it. And she got well, after a harrowing experience.

Another source of power is his tremendous knowledge of India. There are 700,000 villages in India, and Gandhiji has visited an extraordinary number of them. His travels have been epochal. In the third-class trains and especially on foot, he has covered the entire peninsula. In November, 1938, he was hard at work on the Northwest Frontier.

The things Gandhi likes most are children, fresh air, laughter, friends, the truth. What he dislikes most is a lie.

This is another source of power. People cannot lie to him. I heard this all over India: as if the Mahatma had some special supernatural quality which overcame temptation to falsehood in other people. His own sincerity, his own love of truth, is so great that he brings out truth in others. Jahawarlal Nehru, who admits that his language is sometimes incomprehensible, talks of his wonderful "knack of reaching the hearts of the people," by this means.

His colossal spiritual integrity on the one hand; his earthly command of politics on the other—this is the Gandhi gambit.

He invented *khadder* and village spinning, which plunged his revolution into the heart of the countryside; he *walked* to Dandi and the sea, and behind him spread the wildfire of revolt. He likes to choose a small concrete objective that the starved, illiterate millions can easily grasp. Recently the Bombay government wondered how to reach the peasants quickly with concrete proof of the Congress program. Gandhi suggested abolition of a grazing fee that hampered movements of their cattle, and in a few days word of the new program had spread widely. When he decided to hold the annual sessions of Congress, where a hundred thousand people congregate, in tiny villages instead of the great towns, people said that it would be impossible. They pointed to the lack of sanitary arrangements; they were terrified of cholera. But Mr. Gandhi simply let cholera go hang, and nobody got sick—at least not of cholera.

When he left Congress in 1934, he did so in order to make himself more honest, more neutral. He wanted to be in a position to adjudicate, not merely between different factions within Congress, but between Congress and the British. This is as if Abraham Lincoln, say, had quit the presidency in the middle of the Civil War, in order to see that the North behaved with proper honor to the South.

Science of Mahatmatics

When people in India talk about Mr. Gandhi's defects, they are apt to mention half a dozen things.

First, he is dictatorial. "If you choose to follow my lead, you must accept my conditions," he said once. As I have mentioned, he went to the Round Table Conference alone—and as a result was drowned in detail and outmaneuvered—and he has stated that he *alone* must decide whether or not civil disobedience is ever to be renewed.

Second, his medievalism. Even his closest friends object to his extravagant use of religious symbolism. There was a great earthquake in Behar in 1934; Mr. Gandhi promptly announced that this was punishment sent to India for the sin of Untouchability; Nehru has a wonderful passage describing how this staggered him.

Third, his meekness, his masochism, have played into the hands of the British in negotiation.

Fourth, he may love flowers and open spaces, but he seems signally to lack general æsthetic sense.

Fifth, his sense of proportion is off-balance. He will stop work all day to deal with any sudden small problem, for instance a forlorn mother in a village, or a crying child. His friends were horrified at several of his fasts, in which he risked his life for what modern minds thought were minor issues. He twice canceled nationwide civil disobedience, as we have seen, because of isolated cases of impurity or violence. (But, with wonderful political instinct, he knew that each campaign was lost, that it was wise to recede at just that time.) One story is that he held up negotiations for the Gandhi-Irwin truce because an officer in Gujerat impounded a peasant's cow. The Mahatma stopped everything until that cow was released.

Sixth, and above all, his inveterate love of compromise. He is a staunch antagonist, but he infinitely prefers settlement to struggle. Gandhiji wants compromise with the socialists, with the princes, with the industrial magnates, with the government in Delhi. Surely no man has ever so quickly and easily let bygones be bygones. He has no hatreds, no resentments; once a settlement is made, he coöperates with enemies as vigorously as he fought them.

Associated with this quality of compromise is his dislike of hard and fast definitions. Once during the Round Table Conference he offered the Moslems a blank check in settlement of communal[5] difficulties, provided they would subscribe to the Congress program of complete independence. Thereupon Mr. Jinnah, the Moslem leader, confronted the Mahatma with seven different definitions of independence which he had at one time or other made. No one in India knows precisely, beyond shadow of a doubt, where the Mahatma draws the line between "Dominion Status" and "independence." He seldom defines his terms. Once he was asked by a political writer of the *Times of India* to give an important statement on provincial autonomy. He dictated it rapidly, and the writer was delighted with his scoop. He took the statement back to the office—there were only four sentences—whereupon it was discovered that each of the four sentences could be interpreted in different ways.

There are important nuances even to his concept of civil disobedience. He abhors violence, but he admits that some things are worse than violence—cowardice, for example. He dislikes "passive resistance" as a synonym for *Satyagraha*, because he feels that *Satyagraha* is not passive; it is non-violent resistance, which is quite a different thing from non-resistance *per se*.

[5] This tricky word doesn't refer to "communism" but to "communities."

He adores formulae. When the Working Committee of the Congress meets these days, Mr. Gandhi stays away, waits until the members are in disagreement, and then finds a formula for straightening them out. This science is known throughout India as "Mahatmatics."

Grace Notes

In London his friends took him to see Charlie Chaplin. He noted the considerable crowds around Chaplin's hotel. The two had an amiable talk. Leaving, Gandhi asked his companions, "Who was that delightful man?" He had never heard of Chaplin before.

Once a snake dropped on his ankle, and involuntarily he twitched and shook it off. He has regretted this ever since, because it showed that his devotion to non-violence was not really perfect.

One of his friends was accused of complicity in a minor scandal. Gandhi heard about it, summoned the friend, and said, "Tell me the whole truth by tomorrow morning." Then he added that if the friend denied the charges, he would investigate them anyway. The friend confessed, whereupon the Mahatma forgave him.

A Congress prisoner behaved badly in Bijapur jail. The British warder threatened to inform Mr. Gandhi, who would start a new fast if the congressman didn't reform. The congressman reformed.

Indian students in London went to a great deal of trouble to collect 200 goats with which to greet Gandhiji's arrival. The India Office, informed by the police, frowned; the Mahatma was heartsick that the goats weren't allowed to welcome him.

The Working Committee of Congress decided to break off the 1931 negotiations between Lord Irwin and Mr. Gandhi, since the British claims were too great. The Mahatma went to Irwin to tell him so. He returned at 2:30 A.M. and informed his waiting colleagues that he had agreed to Irwin's demands! Consternation. Mr. Gandhi explained that he had succumbed because at the crucial point Irwin rose and said in effect, "Mr. Gandhi, why should you disbelieve in my sincerity, why cannot you accept my word, as I freely accept yours?" Deciding that he had no moral right to assume that his opponent was less honorable than he, Gandhiji gave way. His colleagues remained stunned.

Once he was tempted to ask his followers to eat fruit only after it had fallen from the tree. To pick it while it was still on the branch might touch the borderline of violence.

The Religious Factor

"I worship God as truth only. . . . Truth is like a vast tree, which yields
more and more fruit, the more you nurture it."   —Mr. Gandhi

The attitude of the Mahatma to religion is obviously important,
but it is not easy to define. No one knows just what faith he believes
in. His insistence on rendering good for evil, his feeling that one can
win justice only by giving justice to the enemy, his injunction to hate
the sin but not the sinner, are the essence of practical Christianity.
He believes in original sin, and is probably more like Christ than any
man in the political sphere who has ever lived. But he does not call
himself a Christian. When, watching him pray, I asked his intimate
friends whom he prayed to, they did not know.

The following passage is illuminating:[6]

I do perceive that whilst everything around me is ever-changing
and ever-dying, there is, underlying all that change, a living Power
that is changeless, that holds all together, that creates, dissolves,
and recreates. That informing Power and Spirit is God . . . I see it
as purely benevolent, for I can see that, in the midst of death, life
persists; in the midst of untruth, truth persists; in the midst of dark-
ness, light persists. Hence I gather that God is life, truth, and light.
He is love, He is the Supreme Good. . . .

He is a devout Hindu, but he believes that the scriptures of *all* the
great religions are equally the word of God—Bible, Talmud, Zenda-
vesta, Koran, and the Buddhist canon.

He writes:

I cannot account for the existence of evil by any rational method.
To want to do so is to be co-equal with God. I am, therefore, humble
enough to recognize evil as such, and I call God long-suffering and
patient precisely because He permits evil in the world. I know that
He has no evil in Himself and yet if there is evil He is the author of
it and yet untouched by it.

In an article written in 1920 he says:

Why should we be upset when children or young men or old men
die? Not a moment passes when someone is not born or is not dead
in this world. We should feel the stupidity of rejoicing in a birth
and lamenting a death. Those who believe in the soul—and what

[6] Made in, of all places, a record for the Columbia Gramophone Company.

Hindu, Mussulman or Parsi does not?—know that the soul never
dies. The souls of the living as well as the dead are all one.

Then there is the famous passage about suffering:[7]

Suffering is the mark of the human tribe. It is an eternal law. The
mother suffers so that her child may live. Life comes out of death.
The condition of wheat growing is that the seed grain should perish.
No country has ever risen without being purified through the fire
of suffering. . . . It is impossible to do away with the law of suffering which is the one indispensable condition of our being. Progress
is to be measured by the amount of suffering undergone . . . the
purer the suffering, the greater is the progress.

"Swaraj" is the ordinary word used by Indians to denote "independence." Lately the Mahatma has used "Ramraj" instead. "Ram"
means "God."

Next Avatar?

In February 1939 Gandhi undertook a new fast, following trouble
in the tiny native state of Rajkot (where he had been educated and
where his father was prime minister), in which every aspect of his
character showed true-to-form. The ruler of Rajkot's 282 square
miles had been repressive to the population. Congress negotiated
with him and prevailed upon him to introduce reforms. Then apparently British advisers insisted that the Rajkot princeling change his
mind.

In Mr. Gandhi's own words: "There is evidence of a cold-blooded
breach of a solemn covenant entered into between the Rajkot ruler
and his people. And the breach has been committed at the instance
and bidding of the British Resident, who is directly linked with the
Viceroy."

First Gandhi sent Kasturbai, his wife, to Rajkot, and she was
arrested. Then he came himself, determined to make this a test case.
He was not so much intervening between the ruler and his people,
but between the ruler and the British *raj*. India knows that the next
great struggle will be on Federation, amalgamation of British India
and the princes, and Gandhi's object was to focus attention on the
plight of the people in the princely states. He determined to "fast

[7] Quoted in Romain Rolland's eloquent little book on Gandhi, p. 47.

unto death" once more, and—just as in the early years—the world breathlessly watched.

He fasted 98 hours and 25 minutes, when the British gave way. It was announced that there would be a "compromise."

Despite this episode, it was clear early in 1939 that Gandhi was still definitely a force for moderation in Indian politics, a check against extremism. He resisted left wing influence in the Tripura plenary session of Congress, and carried the bulk of Congress with him.

Gandhi has told friends that in moments of vanity he believes he has been destined to deliver India from British bondage, but the British will view it as a catastrophe when he dies. The immediate future of India is from one point of view a medical or actuarial question; namely, Gandhiji's survival. For while he lives very little can happen; his death will on the other hand liberate forces almost certainly tending to increase the strength of Indian nationalism.

But what a tremendous, dazzling career he has had! His greatest accomplishment is that he has given the Indian people new spirit, new unity. His God, Whoever He is, should treat him fondly, when he is gone.

Chapter XXIII
Beginnings in India

〜〜〜〜〜〜〜〜〜〜〜〜〜〜〜〜〜〜〜〜〜〜〜〜〜〜〜〜

If there is a paradise on the face of the earth, it is this, oh!
it is this, oh! it is this!
—INSCRIPTION, HALL OF PRIVATE AUDIENCE IN DELHI FORT

IT REALLY is a sub-continent. The opening words of the Simon report phrase it well. "The central mass of Asia throws out to the west, beyond the Urals, the sub-continent which we call Europe, and to the south, behind the higher barrier of the Himalayas, the sub-continent which we call India."

Superimpose a map of India on a map of Europe. Put Karachi at London. The western edge of India will protrude into the Atlantic, and the eastern edge will be about two hundred miles east of Moscow. Peshawar will be in mid-Norway, Bombay will just touch the border of Switzerland and what was once called Austria, and Cape Comorin, the southern tip of the peninsula, will be in the Mediterranean between Sicily and Tunis.

It is not only a sub-continent of vastness, but of the vastest extremes. Here are the highest mountains in the world, the broadest plains, the most torrid heat, and the most torrential rains. Here is every imaginable contrast in fauna, flora, geography, architecture, domestic manners, religious customs. Here are 350,000,000 people, or roughly one-fifth of the human race; they include statesmen and professors of the highest intellectual attainments, as well as mendicants and fakirs degraded almost outside human form; they include Maharajas of the most fabulous wealth, as well as starving peasants and aborigines in 700,000 villages, some of whose habits could fill a new *Golden Bough*. Here is a fixed and fierce climate which extracts its toll from European and Indian alike.

The vastness of India, its conglomeration of confusions, make investigation seem difficult. How give a bird's-eye view of a society four thousand years old? How simplify—without succumbing to the danger of oversimplification—the illimitable diversity of its peoples, problems, creeds? How elucidate even the simplest facts about a country where—to take a few instances—the comma is in the wrong place in numerals,[1] where men worship animals like rats and herons, where names are polysyllabically unpronounceable, where a bewildering technical jargon masks ordinary meaning? "Communalism," for instance, a word used often, has nothing to do with "communism"; it derives from "community" and means Hindu or Moslem separatist tendencies.

Bewildering it all is—but not quite so bewildering as the first glance forebodes. Which is fortunate enough.

There is a vast welter of peoples, yes; but one must grasp the fact—and hold tight to it—that a Punjabi and a man from Mysore, even if they differ as much as an Englishman from a Spaniard, are both Indians, as the Englishman and Spaniard are both Europeans.

Indian names are difficult, yes, but not so difficult as Chinese names. Some sound comical to western ears, especially Parsi names like Sodawaterwala or Cocanutwala (*wala* means "man of"); but after all, these do not differ in kind from names like "Shoemaker" or "Marchandeau," which do not cause laughter in England or France. As a rule the last name of a Hindu is a kind of community or clan name rather than a family name. The father's name (except in Bengal) is commonly put in the middle. Take Bulhabhai Jivanji Desai, for instance, the leader of the Congress in the central legislature. Bulhabhai is his given name, Jivanji is his father's name, Desai is his clan name. Perhaps as a result a great many Indian politicians are most often called simply by their first names, at least by friends and in informal talk.

There are probably several thousand religions and sub-religions, yes; but for immediate practical purposes we have to deal with only two, Hinduism and Mohammedanism.

There are 222 different languages and dialects, according to the 1931 census, but only about eight or ten have serious political importance.

When I arrived in Bombay I happened to inspect a rupee note carefully, and saw that the words "One Rupee" were written on the back in eight different Indian languages, each in its own alphabet

---

[1] For instance the number 10,000,000 is written 1,00,00,000. This is because big figures are calculated in units of *lakhs* (one hundred thousand) or *crores* (ten million). Thus one says, not five hundred thousand people or acres or what not, but five *lakhs* of whatever it is, written 5,00,000. Or one says seven and a half *crores*, 7,50,00,000.

and script. Thereupon I asked everyone I met, Indian or British, to identify the eight; it was several weeks before I could find anyone who knew them all.[2] As a result, perhaps unwarrantably, I grasped the inference that language fissures were not a very close pre-occupation of most people. The language used by most Indians—about 139,000,000 according to the last census—is Hindustani.

Now Hindustani (I do admit that this is confusing) exists in two vocabularies and two scripts, Hindi and Urdu. Experts will seize by the throat anyone who tries to talk about it simply, but the easiest explanation is that the original language of the Aryans in India, Sanskrit, became strongly intermixed with Persian during the course of Moslem infiltration. So the resultant mixture, Hindustani, exists in duplicate. The dialect with more Persian words, written in a script similar to Persian, is Urdu; the dialect with more Sanskrit influence, written in characters like Sanskrit, is Hindi. About eighty percent of the words are the same in speech. Another definition calls "Hindustani" the colloquial name of the *spoken* language, whether it is Hindi or Urdu. The obvious connection of Moslems with Urdu, and of Hindus with Hindi, has made a minor political issue of this question. Extreme nationalists in each camp shout for their separate scripts.

Closely allied to Hindustani, written in approximately the same alphabet, are Gujerati, Punjabi, Marathi, Bengali. Of a quite different category are the great Dravidian languages of the south, like Tamil. The difference between Hindustani and its derivatives is roughly that between the various Latin languages of Europe. But between Hindustani and the southern tongues the difference is at least as great as that between English and Arabic. A man from Peshawar and a Tamil from Madras cannot understand each other. This does not, however, necessarily impede political contact between them.

A word as to illiteracy. It is terrific, but not so terrific as in China. Accurate figures must await the next census; at present about eighty-five percent of the men and ninety percent of the women of India are believed to be illiterate.

Finally there are half a dozen important *political* stresses, or oppositions of force. Indians versus British. Moslems versus Hindus. British India versus the princely states. Congress versus Moslem

---

[2] Urdu, Hindi, Bengali, Burmese, Tamil, Telegu, Kanarese, Gujerati.

League. Congress versus princes. And so on. Most of these overlap into ramifying and interlaced sub-stresses. The only one, however, upon which all the rest depend is the first—Indians versus British.

The modern explorer, e.g., journalist, has one tremendous advantage in India, which is that it is one of the most hospitable countries in the world, a veritable paradise for ease of contacts on both Indian and British sides. I have never been in a country where it was pleasanter to work.

Historical Interlude

Now let us undertake a dangerous and perhaps foolhardy but necessary task—an attempt to telescope the history of India in a paragraph or two.

About 1500 B.C. or earlier, a series of invasions of India began by light-skinned nomads who came through the Afghan passes and settled in the Ganges plains. They were great warriors and soon they spread out all over northern and central India, as far as the barrier of the southern mountains. They were people of the grasslands, nomads originally, but the rich land of India, the ease of cultivation, turned them into settlers and agriculturalists. These nomad invaders were the Aryans; in Sanskrit the word "Arya" means gentleman or one high born. The Aryans had their own literature; their early books are called Vedas, or scriptures. "Veda" literally means "knowledge."

The Aryan invasion displaced the original inhabitants of India, who were dark-skinned people, the Dravidians. No one knows much about these Dravidians; probably they were similar to the peoples who inhabited Egypt, Mesopotamia and other parts of Africa and Asia ten or twelve thousand years ago. The interloping Aryans were contemptuous of the Dravidians; one theory of the origin of caste (the Sanskrit word for caste is *varna*, which means color) is that it was invented by the Aryans to prevent intermarriage with the dark Dravidian people. The Aryans very early developed an exceedingly complicated form of worship, which became Hinduism. To this day Aryan influence is predominant in north India, while Dravidian traces are more conspicuous in the south.

India became a melting pot. In spite of the caste system Aryan and Dravidian culture coalesced to some extent. Hinduism spread all over the peninsula. There were other influences: Darius of Persia reached the Indus, and after Alexander the Great's expedition in 326 B.C. came a considerable influx of Hellenic culture. Winds from China drifted across Tibet. By 264 B.C. the great emperor Asoka, one of the most enlightened monarchs who ever lived, united all but a small portion of India under his sagacious and benevolent control. A great creative upheaval followed to produce the golden age of Indian art. Asoka disliked the religious excesses of Hinduism, and made a new creed, Buddhism, the state religion; after his death, however, Buddhism began gradually to recede, and the Hindu Brahmans reëstablished their privileges and power.

After Asoka, Indian history for centuries is a record of various conquests. The Huns, the Turks, the Persians, the Mongols, the Moslems invaded the peninsula. But strong native dynasties, like the Rajputs, also grew up and held power tenaciously, and Hinduism, entrenched by caste, maintained its grip on the masses. Along about the fourteenth century A.D. the Mongols (called Moguls in Indian parlance) began to penetrate India; Genghis Khan captured Lahore in the Punjab and Tamurlane took Delhi. This Mogul period reached its climax in the tremendous reigns of Babur, who became emperor of Hindustan, and his grandson Akbar (1556-1605) and great-grandson Aurungzeb (1658-1707). The Moguls, who almost united India again, were Moslems, and not only built things of enduring and entrancing beauty like the Taj Mahal and Delhi Fort, but furnished the seed of the communal disputes between Hindu and Moslem that go on to this day.

After the Moguls the next invaders (omitting the Persian Nadir Shah who captured Delhi in a brilliant raid in 1738) were the British. The struggle for imperial and commercial power of the western nations occurred in India just as it did in the Americas, and at about the same time. The first aim of the British was trade, and their instrument was that remarkable organization, the East India Company; by 1761, they had largely ousted their French and Dutch rivals from the peninsula, and were turning it into a great commercial dependency. In 1798, the British were strong enough to appoint a Governor General who ruled most of the country, though still in the name of the East India Company. Various wars reduced native peoples like the Mahrattas and Sikhs. In 1858 came the Indian Mutiny—a rising of what would to-day be called militant Indian nationalism—and following it India came formally under control of the British Parliament and Crown. The Mogul Empire ceased to be, and Queen Victoria was crowned Empress of India and the Dominions Beyond the Seas.

In the preceding chapter we dealt briefly with the growth of the Indian independence movement concurrently with the career of Mr. Gandhi. After the end of civil disobedience the next great step in Indian history was the new Government of India Act, 1935, the longest act in the history of the British Parliament, passed after seven years of bitter argument in Whitehall. This Act embodies the new Indian constitution. It is the basis of rule in India to-day. It is the framework of Indian government and law. We must inspect it before proceeding further.

Government of India Act, 1935

The Act is in essence a compromise. It was opposed just as grimly by Winston Churchill and pro-Empire diehards in England as by Jawaharlal Nehru and the Congress nationalists in India. It does not in any sense modify the central fact of British sovereignty in India, but it goes a considerable way beyond the reforms of 1919 in giving India a measure of self-government.

British policy since the War has been, in a sentence, to give India something, but not too much, with Dominion Status as the distant end in view. Anything else, men like Stanley Baldwin knew, would stiffen Indian nationalism so intensely that revolution might recur.

Indian nationalist policy, as represented by the Congress, has been, in a sentence, to get what it could, with complete independence instead of Dominion Status as the end in view. Mr. Gandhi and his followers think that the 1935 Act is a vehicle toward this end.

The Act gives enormous powers to the Viceroy or Governor-General. A new federal legislature is established, to which in theory the executive is responsible, but the Viceroy has unrestricted veto power over any act of the legislature. Moreover, three key subjects —defense, foreign affairs, and ecclesiastical affairs—are "reserved" to the hands of the Viceroy, besides which he has special powers to deal with:

(1) the prevention of any grave menace to the peace or tranquillity of India or any part thereof,

(2) the safeguarding of the financial stability and credit of the government,

(3) the protection of the rights of Indian states and the interests of the minorities,

(4) the prevention of commercial discrimination,

and certain other matters. For instance, in case of emergency he may (like the Emperor in Japan) suspend the entire constitution.

By terms of the Act, India is made a federal country. This means coalescence between British India and the native or princely states. For reasons which I shall explore later, federation has so far been delayed, although a new federal court is sitting, and a federal banking system has been set up. Congress bitterly opposes full federation for many reasons, among which is the fact that the composition of the new central legislature has been so devised as to give the British members, plus the representatives of the princely states who in most matters will certainly vote with them, an unshakable preponderance.

The Act gives the Governors in the provinces of British India— who like the Viceroy are Englishmen appointed by the Crown— powers roughly similar to those of the Viceroy at the center. Nevertheless a system of *Provincial Autonomy* is far advanced. The new Act abolishes the reserved subjects which the old provincial assemblies were not allowed to touch; it gives the provinces almost full powers over items like local finance, police, prisons, education, land revenue, health, public works, agriculture and forests, and above all law and order. Moreover, the new cabinets in the provinces are elected by the Indian people and have fairly complete administrative authority.

The Act contains 451 clauses and roughly 120,000 words. It would need a book the length of this one to explore its highly controversial texture thoroughly. Out of the forest of recommendations and decisions I can mention only a few. Burma, for instance, was separated from India. Two new provinces in British India were created, Sind and Orissa, and the Northwest Frontier Province, hitherto excluded, was brought into the field of progress and reform. On the other hand, certain regions like Baluchistan continue to be "excluded areas" outside provincial autonomy. The electorate was considerably increased—from 7,315,000 in 1919, about three percent of the population of British India, to approximately 35,000,000, or fourteen percent.

The political position in 1939 was that the non-federal provisions of the constitution are in force. In Delhi, the old legislature, as set up in 1919, still sits. But in the provinces, autonomy as established by the new Act is working. Elections in February, 1937, gave Congress majorities in seven out of the eleven provinces, and later an eighth province, Assam, went to Congress. Congress had spent years in attacking the Act, and at first it refused to take office, though it did not boycott the elections. After some months of haggling and delay, Mr. Gandhi evolved a compromise. So in eight provinces Congress governments, elected by the Indian people, are ruling.

Chart of British India

The eleven provinces[3] of British India differ widely from each other, and provincial spirit till lately has been very strong. A marriage between individuals of different provinces is almost as rare as one between members of different castes. A man in one province is apt to know little about the others. Even the British succumb to provincial stratifications, because as a rule an official having learned the ways and language of one province, serves his entire career there; this is one reason for the narrow outlook of many members of the Indian Civil Service.

Generalizations are risky, but let us attempt here what we attempted in China—a rough description of each province. In India the names at least are easier.

The first British settlements in India were in Bombay, Calcutta (Bengal) and Madras, and these three great provinces, called "Presidencies," are the top of the tree. Governors to these Presidencies are not taken from the civil service, but are political appointees direct from London. Bombay or Madras may be given to young M.P.'s or exceptionally able sons of peers, like Lord Brabourne, who inherit peerages and thus have small parliamentary opportunity in England.

BOMBAY, covering 77,000 square miles and with a population of 17,000,000—in other words it is a good deal bigger than pre-Munich Czechoslovakia—is the smallest and most heterogeneous of the Presidencies. It is the home of the Parsis of India; of the great cotton mills at Ahmedabad; of exchange speculators, Gujerati merchants, and Mahratta farmers; and of the cosmopolitan society of Bombay City.

[3] Nothing in this section refers to the native or princely states, which I shall discuss later.

The city is an island (like Singapore) linked to the mainland by a causeway. Originally it was settled by the Portuguese, who gave it in 1661 to Charles II of England; a few years later Charles bestowed it on the East India Company for ten pounds a year! No important island except Manhattan has ever been gotten so cheaply.

Bombay the city is unique in India from a social point of view. Calcutta is still snobbish, but in Bombay you may find Indians and Englishmen eating together, working together, partaking of what is almost a joint social life (except at the Bombay Yacht Club, which no Indian may enter); in Bombay I have dined with a Parsi industrialist, two Moslem writers, a socialist Hindu, a Congress lawyer, two women out of purdah, and a Maharaja, at the same table.

The Congress is strong in the Bombay district. Gandhi's birthplace is not far away, and Bombay was the scene of the first great civil disobedience struggles. It is a predominantly Hindu province.

MADRAS, in area as big as Italy, with a population greater than that of Great Britain (over 47,000,000), is the great Presidency of the south. It is mainly agricultural, growing rice, cotton, tobacco, sugar cane, coffee. Almost completely cut off from the rest of British India by native states, it has developed special characteristics of its own. Linguistically it is cut up into four distinct areas, where the people speak Tamil (a pure Dravidian language which has resisted Sanskrit influence more than any tongue in India), Telegu, Kanarese, and Malayalam.

Madras is the home of two things, first, of most of the intellectuals of India, second, of Hinduism in its most intensive form. The intellectuals become lawyers, bankers (a common proverb is that no one in India understands finance except Scotsmen and Madrasis), and journalists. Ninety percent of the newspapermen in India are Madrasi Brahmans, even on English papers like the *Statesman* and *Times of India*. As for Hinduism in Madras, it is virtually a disease. Madras is the place to go to inspect rigidity of caste, orthodoxy in observance, and misery among Untouchables.

Whether the phenomenon is a result of intellectualism and religious extremism or not, I don't know, but Madras is also the poorest of the great Presidencies. Recently an English scientist, to test this out, picked several groups of albino rats, all the same age, sex, and weight, segregated each group, and gave each group the diet of different Indian communities. Eighty days later the rats were weighed. The rat eating the normal Sikh diet weighed 235 grams; Pathan diet, 230 grams; Mahratta diet, 220 grams; Gurkha diet, 200 grams; Kanarese diet, 185 grams; Bengali diet, 180 grams; Madrasi diet, 155 grams.

Madras is strongly Congress. Its political boss is that wonderful old Brahman fox, Mr. Rajagopalacharia.

If we turn north to the UNITED PROVINCES—always abbreviated in India to U. P., which made me think for a time that the United Press or the Union Pacific had a great deal to do in India—we find quite a different story. Madras and Bengal are peasant provinces, with farmers holding their own tiny tracts of land; the U. P. is the home par excellence of great landowners, the *zemindars*, who sublet the soil to tenants. According to the Simon report, some 260 zemindars own two-thirds of the sub-province of Oudh, but pay only one-sixth of the land revenue. Agrarian unrest and agitation has been more pronounced in the U. P. than any Indian province except adjacent Bihar. It was here that Jawaharlal Nehru began his agrarian campaigns.

The U. P. has a population of almost 50,000,000 people, or about forty percent of that of the United States. Eighty-five percent of the people are Hindu. The province is often called the most "typical" in India; in it are Agra and Benares, with Delhi and Lucknow near by. The people are the most cultivated in India, the most sophisticated (Bombay perhaps excepted), with the greatest tradition for activity in politics.

Below the U. P. are the CENTRAL PROVINCES, called C. P. for short; if the U. P. is the most advanced province in India, the C. P. is probably the most backward. The C. P. is surrounded by native states, and is eighty-five percent Hindu; ninety percent of the people speak Hindi or Mahratti. In the C. P. are the great untrod jungles of India, the giant waterfalls, most of the aborigines, tribes of incredible backwardness, pythons and tigers, animists. Also in the C. P. is Mr. Gandhi.

BIHAR, though it is a smallish province—population 25,000,000—is exceptionally important. It is a valley between the U. P. and Bengal, largely agricultural, eighty-two percent Hindu, and the seat of the worst agrarian exploitation in India, the fiercest agrarian unrest. Its leader is the Congressman Babu Rajendra Prasad. Near by is ORISSA, which till the 1935 Act was part of Bihar. Orissa is the smallest of the states, with a language—Oriya—all its own. Its peasants, exceptionally religious, are among the most ignorant in India. In some parts of the state the title of the land is supposed to be God's, and men must plow instead of women, because men can impregnate the fields.

These, with the North West Frontier Province, are the seven which Congress prime ministers and cabinets began to govern.

The Presidency of BENGAL, with Calcutta as capital, has more than 50,000,000 people; it is as populous as the whole United States from the Mississippi to the Pacific; probably it is the richest Indian province, as it is the most densely populated. Traditionally the Bengalis are the poets of India, emotional and sensitive; their physique is generally poor, their resistance weak. Bengal is the home of Indian terrorism, of the jute industry, of most of the *babus* (clerks) of India, and of Rabindranath Tagore. Bengalis are not recruited into the Indian army.

Bengal is homogeneous physically and in language, but not religiously; there are 27,500,000 Moslems (54.87 percent of the population), and 21,570,000 Hindus (43.04 percent). By and large the Hindus are the merchants and landlords; the Moslems are the proletariat, though much labor is imported into Bengal from Madras and Bihar. Land is held in Bengal by the incredible terms of what is known as the "Permanent Settlement Act," which in 1793 determined what land revenue should be assessed property; the rates have not changed since.

Hindus in Bengal complain severely of discrimination. For instance, although they are a minority they pay eighty-five percent of the taxes. They say that the Moslems not only have a guarantee of a permanent majority in the local chamber, but that what is called "weightage" gives them additional seats. Bengal will have only thirty-seven seats out of 250 in the new Central legislature, though its population is almost one-fifth of British India. This the Bengalis say is punishment for terrorism. Bengal is governed by a non-Congress coalition in which Moslems predominate.

ASSAM is a small province, now under a Congress ministry, to the east of Bengal; in population it is the size of Belgium, but most of the people, hill tribesmen, are backward and undeveloped. The chief industry is tea. Far to the other end of India is a small non-Congress province, SIND, which is predominantly Moslem. Sind, in

the words of the Simon report, is nearer to Iraq or Arabia than the
rest of India. Karachi, the chief Indian airport, is in Sind. When
it was first conquered by a British General, he telegraphed simply
"Peccavi" (I have Sind).

Finally, one of the great provinces—the PUNJAB. Its capital is
Lahore, and with 105,000 square miles and 24,000,000 people it
is half as big as France. Here religious stratification is triple, because
there are not only thirteen million Moslems and six million Hindus,
but some four million Sikhs. Thus the Punjab has always been the
heart of fierce religious tension, as Bengal is the heart of revolutionary terrorism. The Punjab is mostly a great plain, watered by five
rivers; it is the India of Kipling, of open spaces, of the summer
capital Simla; the India of the tallest men and fiercest forces of nature, of agricultural coöperatives and colossal irrigation projects—
and of Amritsar.

The Punjabis, especially the Sikhs, are staunch fighters; the region
was the last in India to be taken by the British. The Punjabis say
that the great invasions of India stopped at Lahore; perhaps some
riffraff went on into deeper India, but the real men stayed. And
Punjab supplies fifty-four percent of the troops of the Indian army;
it is the country's military reservoir. The bearded Sikhs are the police
everywhere in the East, all the way to Shanghai and Singapore. Like
Bengal, the Punjab is governed by a coalition ministry dominated
by Moslems.

Indian Village

We almost missed the train. Our bearer shoehorned us aboard
somehow. The trains in India are like none I have ever seen anywhere. They pant, scuffle, scream over the gigantic peninsula, seldom
late, always jammed, shaking their passengers like dice, torrential
monuments to British engineering and capacity to endure discomfort.

The first class cars are divided into coupés for two people or com-
partments for five or six. The beds, a thin smear of black leather
over wood and iron, pull out of the walls; you bring your own bed-
ding, of course. You get no ticket for your berth. Instead your name
is placarded outside the car. When changing at a junction, you tear
along the incoming train as it rolls in, searching for your name as the
cars flash by. There are no conductors. At least, in six or seven

thousand miles of travel in India, I never saw one. During two months of those trains, I never had a ticket stamped or punched.

The windows of the cars have two screens each, coarse to keep out cinders and gravel, fine to keep out dust; there is also a glass, and all three fit into parallel grooves, which interminably fall out of place with discordant bangs. Within twenty minutes of the start of any journey, the compartment is thick with sand or dirt, despite the screens; thus the shower bath which comes with each first class berth. There are very few corridor trains in India; once you are in your compartment, you stay imprisoned till the train stops. The train halts at widely spaced intervals to let you get out and walk up to the dining car, if there is a dining car.

We were traveling from Bombay to Mysore. The terrific spectacle of native India spilled out as we prodded south.

The railway station is the heart of each village, and the heart of each railway station is the water pump. Rather, there are two hearts, because Hindus and Moslems must have their different pumps, their different water. The train grinds to a stop; the heavy clanking doors fly open and the people gush out; they rush to the pumps, and, if it is early morning, clean their teeth first; no toothbrush, but the forefinger working like a piston inside the mouth. (A toothbrush, made of animal bristles, would be considered unclean. Hindus are very careful about what they put to the mouth. Many Orthodox Hindus will not lick postage stamps.)

The villagers surround the train. Sick children, beggars, half-starved dogs, mothers combing their daughters' hair, children rounding up stray cattle, old men with foreheads covered with caste marks, denoting esoteric significance. Women with diamonds in their noses (which means merely that they can afford them). Untouchables, hovering near their isolated pump. Many Brahmans wear their hair long, braided into an untidy topknot. If they are also bearded they look astoundingly like the circus creatures advertised as both men and women.

The village of Vajamangala is about ten miles from Mysore. Here we spent a morning.

The houses are built of mud, glazed by the sun to a whitish color, but with tile roofs. That the roofs are tile means that Vajamangala is a prosperous village, that is, the average income of a peasant may be as much as $50 per year. The roofs slope upward from the exterior walls, then stop. There is an open rectangle of sky over the center of each house, which is an inclosed courtyard. It doesn't rain much in Mysore. The exterior walls of the house are windowless. This is the rule all over India. No windows. Solid walls keep thieves and evil spirits out.

Inside the windowless exterior wall, bounding the courtyard and opening on to it, is a series of partitions on one side where the human beings live. One room is the kitchen, which we could not enter, since, being foreigners, we would have defiled the food. Another houses the family gods. On the other side, twelve or fourteen feet across the court, live the cattle, who are quite obviously part of the family. The horns of the cattle are painted. The bullocks get blue horns, the cows red. Piled to the side is a heap of incredibly primitive wooden farm implements.

Children welcomed us; soon they were a long tail to the kite of our procession. They offered us limes and wreaths of flowers. When bored by our company, they returned to their business, which was to make mudpies of cow dung and stick them on the walls to dry. Flowers and cow dung—these are the antitheses of southern India. The dung is used mostly for fuel, though in one corner of the village we saw the common fertilizer dump. Dung is important. The steps of every house are washed with a solution of it every day; it is ammoniac and antiseptic, and believe it or not—clean. Dung is the great cleanser, the great purifier. Sheep dung has a lesser place than cow dung in the community. Sheep are kept only for their dung, but it is considered second class dung. Chickens are not kept at all, because Brahmans consider poultry to be unclean.

The house we first visited was scrawled outside with signs, an open hand and an interlocked sort of figure eight; these are freshly chalked up every day, after the bath of dung, to propitiate the household gods. The tenant, a blacksmith by profession, was a Siva worshiper. Carpenter and blacksmith are usually among the most important citizens of the village, and the carpenter in Vajamangala was also the mayor, elected to this position by his fellows to serve three years. The tax-collector, known as the *patel*, who is also important, holds his job by heredity; father passes it on to son, as do executioners in France. The village, population 1,400, has four policemen, none of them armed.

In the village shops, which are open sheds facing the main lane,

you find coconuts for sale (they are used in one form of worship);
cigarettes—though I never saw anyone in an Indian village smoke;
six or seven kinds of grain, like *ragi* and *jola*, the staple foodstuffs of
Mysore; condiments for curry and bright red chilis; and some cheap
manufactured goods and kerosene. The show cases are square gasoline cans set on end like filing cases and open to the street. Very little money circulates. It isn't necessary. Once a year the laundryman
and so on are paid in goods—usually grain.

Beyond the shops, some hundreds of yards from the village proper,
is the section reserved for Untouchables. Even this quarter was—
in this model village Vajamangala—clean. Here we heard the clatter
of chickens, which Untouchables will eat. The houses were smaller,
the children timid.

Further beyond are the fields. There are few homesteads in India
with fields surrounding the house. The people live in villages, and
may have to trudge several miles to reach their land. Often a family
has to work in widely separated fields.

Before I visited this village I felt like a man with boxing gloves,
fumbling at marbles; afterwards I began, I thought, to get just a
little of the hang of things.

. . . .

India is eighty-nine percent rural. Well over 300,000,000 people live
in the 700,000 villages of India. Probably one-third of the entire population lives in villages of less than 500 inhabitants each. The land
is overwhelmingly the great Indian problem. On the life of the land,
India depends.

There are two different types of land tenure. In the north, land
is as a rule held on the *zemindari* system; that is, by big landlords, the
zemindars, who farm it out to tenants. In the south the *ryotwari*
system is in force; that is, peasants hold the land themselves, mostly
in very small tracts. In each case what is known as "land revenue" is
paid to the government; as a rule this is both rent and tax. The
zemindar collects rent from the peasant and pays "land revenue" to
the state; the ryot pays rent direct to the state in which tax is included.
Normally land revenue accounts for about *one-half* of the peasant's
earnings; fifty percent of his produce goes in rent or taxes. This
system is not a harsh British invention; it was indigenous by early
Hindu custom, and both Moguls and British took it over.

The peasant labors under enormous disadvantages. Electricity is a myth; running water is a dream; mechanization is nearly everywhere impossible. There is no primogeniture in India as a rule, and when the peasant dies his land is subdivided among all his sons, with the result that most holdings are infinitesimally small. In one district in the Punjab,[4] following fragmentation through generations, 584 owners cultivate no less than 16,000 fields; in another 12,800 acres are split into actually 63,000 holdings. Three-quarters of the holdings in India as a whole are under ten acres. In many parts of India the average holding is less than half an acre.

Poverty is unspeakable; for instance, agricultural wages are about eight cents a day. The agricultural debt is enormous; a modest calculation puts it at $3,295,000,000. Because of the system of land tenure there is no satisfactory basis for loans with security, and the peasants are at the mercy of rapacious money-lenders. Interest rates run anywhere from twenty-five to one hundred or even two hundred percent—sometimes higher. Most peasants are in debt from the day they are born till the day they die. Their position is intolerable, and a virtual moratorium reigns in several provinces; the courts refuse to convict for debt, and generally speaking no one is dispossessed.

Poverty produces several of its necessary concomitants. One is disease. A startling survey of rural areas by a director of the Indian Medical Service, Sir John Megaw, states that forty-one percent of the population of India is poorly nourished, twenty percent badly nourished, i.e., they are perpetually hungry. There are fifty to one hundred million cases of malaria a year, and two million of tuberculosis.

Another is lack of physical vitality. In Bengal alone about 750,000 children under fifteen die every year, a quarter of them from preventable diseases. "The peasantry of Bengal are in large proportion taking to a dietary on which even rats could not live," says an official report. The maternal mortality rate for India as a whole is 24.5 per 1,000, as against 4.06 for England and Wales. The death rate as a whole is 26.8 per 1,000 as against 11.7 per 1,000 in England. The average expectation of life is, incredible detail, only twenty-five years, as against England's fifty-five.

And another is political discontent. In several provinces, notably

[4] See M. L. Darling's admirable books on the Punjab peasantry.

the U. P. and Bihar, the peasants, *kisans,* are well organized and they have refused to pay taxes in mass campaigns. Agrarian turmoil has more than once reached the point of virtual revolution. The socialists in the Congress have paid particular attention to the agrarian movement.

"I came from a good village," a young Moslem told me one day in Delhi. "We were not so very poor. There were only a handful of us so poor they could not afford loin-cloths, and almost all of us had meat—once a month."

Patriotic Indians are chauvinistic even about their poverty. I remember a friend in Lahore who turned red in indignation when I dared to say that Chinese poverty was as acute as Indian.

Despite poverty, the birth rate is enormous; despite disease, the increase of births over deaths is very great. It is believed that the census of 1941 will show the population of India to be over 400,-000,000, which means an increase of about forty millions—almost the population of France—in ten years. Fecundity, Indians know you well.

Industry—Two Kinds

The basis of Indian life is agriculture, but India is a very important country industrially; it is in fact the eighth industrial state in the world according to production of manufactured goods. Cotton textiles lead the rest, but India produces very important amounts indeed of iron and steel, jute, manufactured woolens and silks, sugar, cement, leather, wax. The largest iron and steel works in the British Empire, bigger than anything at Sheffield, is at Jamshedpur, operated by the great Parsi company, the Tata Iron and Steel Company. Tata is the nearest thing in India to organizations like Mitsui in Japan or U. S. Steel in the United States.

For more than a generation Lancashire fastened and fed on India, virtually controlling its industrial economy. Lancashire bought raw cotton from India or elsewhere, processed it, and sold it to the tremendous Indian market in the form of cheap textiles. During this early period free trade was forced on India. Since the War Lancashire's hold on India has slipped somewhat. First, the British were alarmed at India's lack of self-sufficiency, and reversed their first policy by imposing heavy tariffs in India on imported manufactured goods. So Indian mills sprang up and because the labor market was inexhaustible and wages incredibly cheap, Indian cotton was soon underselling Lancashire cotton. Second, the Japanese began to exploit India with textiles even cheaper than Indian textiles themselves.

To India belongs the doubtful honor of having the worst slums in the world. The *bustees* (hovels) of the jute workers near Calcutta are worse than anything in Poland, worse than Naples or Glasgow or even Shanghai. Workmen getting three or four rupees (say $1.20) a week live in cells with no light, no water, no sanitation; the entrance to the hovels is a tunnel streaming with sewage; nine to ten people may live in rooms eight feet by six. Disease, squalor, degradation of the human being to the level of animals are rampant as men live in stinking filth.

The environs of Calcutta are the worst, but one should not think that Cawnpore or Bombay are much better. In Cawnpore (in the U. P.) the textile workers may not see their families for months on end, because there is no room for a family in a cave below street level the rent of which may be two rupees per week, or half the worker's wage. In Bombay medical examiners found that *one-third* of the population, i.e., 370,000 people, lived in single-room tenements holding four to five persons each. There were 15,000 rooms in which twenty people or more lived—if "live" is at all an appropriate verb.

Profits are high in many of these mills, but wages are the lowest in the world, next to Chinese. For a long period after the war a fifty percent dividend was common in the jute mills, owned mostly by English capital; recently it was revealed that textile mills in Sholapur, Indian-owned, had for a period paid one hundred percent in dividends. But a coal miner, employed in dangerous work, gets ten cents per day; a textile worker is lucky to have five rupees ($1.85) per week; industrial wages generally average no more than $5 to $6 per month. In theory the nine-hour day is in force—but only in theory. Labor of children is supposed to be prohibited under the age of twelve, but some industries continue to employ children for ten or twelve hours a day from the ages of five or six. The children get from ten cents to seventy-five cents per *month*—and this pitiful sum may go to help pay their father's debts.

An especially hideous feature of the industrial system is the rôle played by the jobber. This exceeds in primitive viciousness even the indenture system in China—or a racket in New York. As a rule in India there is no direct contact between employer and employee; all labor relations are in the hands of a jobber who hires, fires, and has practically rights of life and death over the workmen.

Suppose you want a job. You go to the jobber, who demands his fee for giving you one. This in Cawnpore is usually twenty rupees ($7.40). You have not got twenty rupees. But this tribute, this extortion, is necessary before you can work. So you borrow the twenty rupees—from the jobber, who is also the money-lender. You then get credit for food at the company's store—from the jobber who is also the storekeeper. The normal rate of interest on your debt is two annas (five cents) per rupee (thirty-seven cents) per month, which works out to 150 percent a year. Of course the jobber does not want you ever to repay the debt. He gets rich on the interest. A case is on record in which a man with a debt of 110 rupees had paid 570 rupees in interest on it—when at last the police presumably stepped in. But of course the police may also be corrupt—in the pay of our friend, the self-same jobber.

The jobber, if he needs some quick cash, may simply discharge the whole establishment of a factory. (Be it remembered, there are twenty-five million industrial workers in India—twice as many as in the United States!—but twenty million of them are in factories employing fewer than twenty men each.) Then he extorts his original contribution from the new staff he hires.

It should be noted that abuses of this dreadful kind take place in Indian-owned factories as well as those British-owned. Indian experts in the field are inclined to think that on the whole the British factories are more humanely run than the Indian. Some Indian industries, like Tata, have model plants. But certainly the British *raj*, which is to both British and Indian factories as an elephant to mice, even though it does not control them directly, bears its share of responsibility for the system which permits such outrages.

Recently a Workman's Compensation Act was inaugurated, but in many parts of India it seems to be a dead letter. Trade unions are permitted, but they have been split by internal fissures and are poor. The dues are usually one day's wage per year. There are about 200,000 trade-unionists in India—no more. Strikes are legal and frequent. In 1937, no fewer than 8,982,000 work days were lost in strikes throughout India.

Indian Miscellany

India is the country where locks turn the wrong way, where hotels have no doors or bells, where soda water bottles are sealed by a glass ball, and where the price of elephants has fallen fifty percent.

It is the country where railway trains run on three gauges, where a politician may have the name Rao in his name in three places, where American cigarettes are cheaper than they are in the United States, and where a double whisky soda is called a *burra*-peg.

It is the country where rupees are known as chips, where 315,-000,000 people are illiterate, where a man's profession may be Sucker of Bad Blood or Grasshopper Salesman, and where the British sahib obeys the ritual of shooting his first panther before he tackles tigers.

It is the country where most patients in mental hospitals are Eurasians, where every coconut palm tree is numbered, where the streets of the great cities seem strangely empty, and where the remarkable religion known as Hinduism flourishes—something which we must now inspect.

Chapter XXIV
A Word About Religion

Religions are different roads converging to the same goal.
—MR. GANDHI

THE continent of Asia, as everyone knows, is the birthplace of all the great world religions: Judaism, Christianity, Buddhism, Confucianism, Zoroastrianism, Hinduism, Mohammedanism. Two of these, Buddhism and Hinduism,[1] began in India. A common but very erroneous assumption is that these two are similar, and that Buddhism flourishes in India still. But they are as different as sunshine from twilight, and Buddhism disappeared centuries ago from the Indian peninsula. An exile from its home, it proceeded then to conquer China.

Buddhism was founded by one man, one of the greatest who ever lived; Hinduism was a proliferation from many sources. Buddhism, before it became corrupt, had no sacrifices, miracles, or temples; Hinduism lives in a welter of all three. Buddhism acknowledges no god as a supreme being; Hinduism has a whole caravan of gods, and worships monkeys, cattle, the phallus, and a great deal else. Buddhism is a mode of conduct, an experiment in rationalism—therefore it appealed so greatly to the Chinese; Hinduism is mythology.

A word or two about Gautama Buddha. He was an Aryan prince, born in Nepal some time between 600 and 500 B.C., a wealthy and cultivated young man, vastly intelligent, who lived until about thirty in a conventionally luxurious manner. Then suddenly he gave up his family and home, his title and wealth, and went into the wilderness to inspect his soul. He became aware of poverty and disease; he set about seeing what service he might perform for miserable mankind, if his own soul could be made pure. First he underwent a period of extreme asceticism, then gave it up; he decided that some golden mean—if he could reach it—was better than either indulgence or asceticism. Under the Bo tree (plantings of which still exist in

---

[1] Sometimes called "Brahmanism."

Ceylon) he found enlightenment, and in the deer park at Benares his followers listened to him rather as the Athenians listened to Socrates.

Buddha's basic teaching is the concept of Nirvana, which means roughly the peace of mind and soul that comes to man after he has overcome three cravings, those for riches, sensual enjoyment and immortality. In its original form Buddhism differs from other world religions in denying life after death. Later, however, it became corrupted with Hinduism, and Buddhists to-day believe in *Karma* (reincarnation) as Hindus do. Buddha taught that the way to Nirvana was the eightfold "Aryan Path"; these precepts, guides to good living, are correctness in speech, aspirations, effort, opinions, and so on. When he died peacefully at eighty, he was known as the greatest teacher of his time. The word Buddha means simply "Enlightened."

.   .   .   .

Hinduism is an infinitely difficult concept to identify or describe. It is more than merely a creed, because it embraces social categories (caste). It began apparently in the days of the first Aryan invaders as a kind of nature worship; it developed into what is certainly the most complicated theology known to mankind. It holds that one supreme being, Brahma, exists in several forms or manifestations, and is the universal spirit which pervades everything. It believes also in *Karma*, the transmigration of souls, and the doctrine that your next life is dependent on your behavior in the present.

"There is (in Hinduism) a bewildering maze of sects which overlap each other in the most extraordinary manner," says the 1911 Census Report. "Hinduism shelters within its portals monatheists, polytheists and pantheists; worshipers of the great gods, Siva and Vishnu, or of their female counterparts, as well as worshipers of the divine mothers of the spirits of trees, rocks, and streams, and of the tutelary village deities; persons who propitiate the deity in all manner of bloody sacrifice, and persons who not only will not kill any living creature but who must not even use the word 'cut'; those whose ritual consists mainly of prayers and hymns, and those who indulge in unspeakable orgies in the name of religion."

A host of gods exist. They are as numerous and as complicatedly interrelated as the denizens of Mt. Olympus in Greek mythology. Brahma, the Creator, lives in three concurrent forms: as himself, as Vishnu the Preserver, and as Siva the Destroyer. The wife of Brahma, known as Sarasvati, is the goddess of music and the arts. As Vishnu, Brahma has a different wife—Lakshmi—and has been reborn nine times; in one avatar he was a fish, and in another a wild boar; in another he was Rama, the hero of the Ramayana, one of the great Hindu epics, and in another Krishna, who is a sort of Hindu Hercules, the hero of the Mahabharata. Orthodox Hindus also consider Buddha to have been an earthly incarnation of this very important god Vishnu.

Siva the Destroyer is almost as popular as Vishnu—although he has some unpleasant characteristics—because he is associated with fertility and reproduction. His wife, a highly difficult lady named Kali, demands sacrifices of goats. Of their sons, Ganesh, who has an elephant's head, is the god of learning, and Kartikkeya is the god of war. There are dozens upon dozens of other gods—one, Hanuman, exists in the form of a monkey, for which reason most Hindus think monkeys sacred.

Hindus, by and large—I know of course that there are almost as many exceptions as rules—do not eat meat, use no intoxicating liquors, kill no animals, and adhere to the laws of caste. They revere the cow, and burn their bodies after death. They like to die on the shore of the Ganges at Benares—that blot on the face of India— because then their souls proceed at once to heaven, without the un- certainties and inconvenience of other avatars.

The doctrine of Karma has considerable political consequence. Ob- viously it embodies an extreme form of fatalism, which impedes ambition. Obviously too, if a man thinks that his present life is merely an interlude between other lives which may be vastly more important, the spur to such a mundane consideration as nationalism is lacking. Then too it gives us a clue to such phenomena as Mr. Gandhi's doctrine of non-violence, since it destroys man's inclination to resist. Gandhi is inflexibly a Hindu.

And now let us come to grips with the problem of the cow.

The Cult of Cows

Cow worship is an essential fact of Hinduism. Let me quote the Mahatma. "Cow-protection is to me one of the most wonderful phemonena in human evolution. It takes the human being beyond his species. The cow to me means the entire sub-human world. Man through the cow is enjoined to realize his identity with all that lives. . . . She is the mother to millions of Indian mankind. The cow is a poem of pity. Protection of the cow means protection of the whole dumb creation of God."

This extraordinary veneration of the cow goes back to the remotest Indian times. The cow gave the early Aryans everything that kept them alive—food, fuel, shelter, and work in the fields. Used as a draft animal it made agriculture possible. It still does.

It performs other functions too. When a Brahman must purify himself, remove corruptness from his body and soul, he swallows a pellet made of the five excretory products of the cow: milk, butter, curds, urine, dung.

The economic consequences of cow worship are enormous. For one thing, no one may kill a cow, and yet many cattle are wretchedly cared for; thousands of half-starved beasts roam the country, pitiable creatures mostly skin and bone; they devour crops, and they cannot be turned into useful byproducts, leather, bone dust, fertilizer. It is all but impossible to raise the standard of breeds, since castration of bulls is severely frowned upon. As a rule dung is not used for fertilizer, but is instead burned for fuel, so that the land is incredibly impoverished. One might assume that India, where cows are sacred, should at least have a plentitude of good milk, but the contrary is true; the condition of the cattle is so miserable, the period of lactation so abused and the quality of milk so poor, that less milk is consumed in India than any comparable country. There are, it is estimated, something over 200,000,000 cattle in India, which is almost a third of the world's total cattle population; of these 200,000,000 at least sixty per cent are considered a liability economically rather than an asset. But they cannot be killed off, they cannot be utilized. Man is victim of the holy cow. The cow lives on the man, instead of vice versa.

Among orthodox Hindus even *dead* cows—cows that have died a natural death—may not be used for fertilizer or in any other fashion. Shades of the packing industry of Chicago! Of course no caste Hindu will touch leather, alive or dead; leather work is the most menial in India, on the same level as scavenging or lavatory sweeping; only Untouchables work in tanneries.

To kill a cow in Hindu India is a highly serious offense. In some native states, death was the penalty for deliberate cow-killing until recently; even now *seven years* in jail—literally—is the punishment in the native state Kashmir, even if the cow is killed accidentally.

O'Malley[2] records the practice of one sect; if a man should happen by accident to kill a cow, he must beg for his food for a long period thereafter, and may not speak but must *moo*. Beef is unprocurable in some of the princely states, even by Englishmen. I have met British officials, crazed for red meat, who cook ducks disguised as filet mignon.

The cow is by no means the only animal whose veneration produces serious economic drain. The peacock is holy in Rajputana and other parts of Hindu India, and peacocks every year destroy thousands upon thousands of tons of grain. The pigeon may not be killed, and useless pigeons are thick as flies. The monkey, sacred also, eats anything, and eats a considerable amount. The rat is holy to some sects; not only does it carry disease, it consumes grain. The pig is not holy, but Hindus may not kill any beast, and pigs eat their way through India, instead of Indians eating their way through pig.

Caste of Characters

Caste is as old as India. It is the inner citadel of Hinduism. It is the institution which makes India unique, the device breaking up Indians into fixed categories that has no approximation elsewhere in the world. "Every Hindu," says a recent census report, "is born into a caste and his caste determines his religious, social, economic, and domestic life from the cradle to the grave." No man may ever leave his caste, except to be expelled. It is impossible to progress from caste to caste.

Caste came with the early Aryan invaders. I have already noted that the Aryans invented it, according to one theory, as an instrument, a function, of their own supremacy. But the classifications grew up slowly; even in the time of Buddha, at least a thousand years after the first invasions, they were not final. Then they became final. The caste structure became fixed, and has not altered since. Frequently a newcomer to India asks when the last Brahman, as it were, "got in." The answer is that, with rare exceptions, his ancestors "got in" twenty centuries ago.

There are four castes, named in the ancient law of Manu: first the *Brahmans* or priests and scholars, second the *Kshatriyas* or warriors, third the *Vaisyas* or merchants, artisans and traders, fourth

[2] *Indian Caste Customs* by L. S. S. O'Malley is a brilliant guide to these matters. I have drawn on it considerably.

the *Sudras,* servants or serfs. Members of the third caste are still, by and large, the shopkeepers of all India, though the others have come to admit other occupations. Of these castes the Brahmans are considered to be "twice-born," that is they have both physical and spiritual lives; as symbols of this headstart toward Karma, they wear a sacred thread. The other castes do not have this advantage. Below the fourth caste—outside of caste—are the Untouchables. Possibly the Untouchables were originally the Dravidians whom the Aryans wanted to subdue.

The great, the overwhelming characteristic of the caste system is that marriage between castes is forbidden. This rule is of course what enables caste to survive unshaken. Nowadays the rule has been somewhat relaxed, but marriages between a Brahman, say, and a Sudra, are extremely rare. Marriage between a Brahman and an Untouchable would be unthinkable; if one should even joke about such an outrage, highly westernized Hindus, as I know from my experience, are horrified. The analogy in America would be marriage between a member of the House of Morgan or the faculty of Harvard University and a negro share-cropper who lived by cleaning toilets.

The legend is that the Brahmans rose from the mouth of Brahma, the creator; the Kshatriyas from his shoulders; the Vaisyas from his thighs, the Sudras from his feet. When a Brahman, even to-day, meets a Kshatriya, he is supposed to say, "May prosperity attend you," to a Sudra, "May you live long." To an Untouchable, of course, he will not speak. (Not that one Brahman out of fifty really obeys this ritual, except perhaps in avoiding Untouchables.)

Another important point is that there are multiform sub-divisions —sub-castes—in each caste. The cleavages are bewildering, and follow several stratifications; all told some two thousand different sub-castes exist in Hindu India. Locality, for instance, determines whether a man is a Rajput or Kashmiri Brahman. Occupation creates vast numbers of sub-castes; the Marwaris, for instance, devote themselves to financial speculation. Religious differences divide the Brahmans; followers of Vishnu, for instance (who wear a trident on their foreheads), differ widely from the Krishna worshipers (who carry a stamp of yellow over the brows) and devotees of Siva who smear their foreheads horizontally with ash. Another cleavage is social custom. The Nairs in south India, for instance, have a matriarchal society; inheritance is through the mother.

Expulsion from caste is, in theory, a terrific excommunication. It abolishes the Hindu's right to talk, live, and eat with his friends, and his family and children likewise suffer. Expulsion from a sub-caste is, however, a minor matter; Mr. Gandhi, for instance, was expelled from his group in Gujerat in early manhood and is still excommunicated, but it certainly has made little difference in his life.[3]

Nowadays the Brahmans are by no means exclusively scholars, professors, priests. The abominable complexities of caste know no end. For instance, Brahmans are by and large the cooks of India. This is because, whether or not they can cook, their superior touch does not defile food and water, and thus non-Brahman families employ them. The Brahmans in their more intellectual professions are extraordinarily dominant in India considering their number. There are only about nine or ten million Brahmans in all, but they control the politics of the country. Most leading congressmen, like Nehru and Rajagopalacharia, are Brahmans. In other words, a Brahman can, without sacrificing Brahmanhood, be a nationalist, a revolutionary, or a socialist. The leader of the communist party in Bombay is a Brahman. Naturally Brahmans of a modern intellectual type do not swallow the pernicious nonsense and hocus pocus associated with their creed. Mr. Nehru wears no ashmarks on his forehead.

Caste, most observers believe, is beginning to break down. I asked dozens of people, some of whom were somewhat appalled at the question, to which caste they belonged; if they were not Brahmans, most of them answered simply "Non-Brahman"; they made no distinction among the other castes. The growth of train travel has damaged caste fixity and caste observance—because a Brahman cannot easily avoid an Untouchable if he is locked in the same compartment with him—as has the progress of modern education and influx of western influence. Most modern Indians deplore and dislike caste heartily.

Caste is, of course, profoundly, devastatingly, undemocratic. Moslems especially (who have no caste) say that the basis of the Hindu system is discrimination, and that as long as Hinduism retains caste a modern political development bestowing equal rights to all sections of a community will be impossible to India. Obviously, too, caste

---

[3] In January, 1938, when a meeting of the Brahman conference in Benares decided to sanction intermarriage among Brahmans of different categories, the news got big headlines in the Indian press.

impedes Indian nationalism. Like the Chinese belief in ancestor worship, it divides man's loyalties, it inhibits freedom of choice, it promotes rigid sectional attributes. The evil genius of India is the Hindu caste system.

The Untouchables

Untouchability may be defined easily; it is Jimcrowism on a fantastic scale. Imagine a Jew in Germany ten times worse off than he is; that will approach the position in India of the Untouchables, who are even more literally pariahs. Gandhi calls them Harijans, literally Children of God; the British call them "the depressed classes" or "the scheduled castes." All told there are fifty-one million Untouchables in India, out of a total Hindu population of 238,000,000.

Let us say something on the Brahman side. A Brahman, defending the social cleavage which distinguishes Untouchability, says rightly that a Park Lane aristocrat in London would not normally dine with his janitor, with a street cleaner, or with a lavatory sweeper. On the other hand, in England, janitors, street sweepers, lavatory cleaners, are not outcasts, and the British lord does not feel polluted if he sees them on the street. To which the Brahman might reply that the Englishman would change his mind, if England were India where in the great mass of the villages sanitation is unknown, and where Untouchables seldom get a chance to wash properly.

Untouchability hinges in essence on the Hindu doctrine of pollution. A Hindu is defiled, and must go through a complicated ritual of ablutions, if any person whom he considers "unclean" touches him or his food or water; this derives from fear that such uncleanliness impedes his possibility of successful reincarnation. Foreigners as well as Untouchables may pollute orthodox Hindus.

Untouchables, as if to copy caste, stratify themselves in various classifications of Untouchability. Laundrymen are usually Untouchables; leather workers and shoemakers; oddly enough barbers; workmen on canals; undertakers; peons or servants of a low class; the police often; scavengers and sweepers. Untouchables, being outside caste, carry no caste marks.

The plight of most Untouchables is appalling; not only are they the poorest of India's poor, but they suffer consequent social indignities. The child of an Untouchable in some parts of India may not enter a schoolroom; Untouchables may not use water from the ordinary village well or otherwise in any way mingle with the community; they may not ordinarily enter temples. In south India an Untouchable may pollute a caste Hindu even from a distance; the unfortunate creature, as he walks along the road, must retreat into the fields when a Brahman passes. In Tamiland a variety of Untouchable defiles actually on sight, no matter from what distance, so that he can go out only at night.

Mr. Gandhi, that complicated man, believes firmly in the caste system, but Untouchability he thinks is a degradation, a disgrace. "I would far rather that Hinduism died than that Untouchability lived," he said once; he calls it a "rotten excrescence" on Hinduism. He denies that Untouchables are less clean than other Hindus; early in his attempts to uplift them he is delighted to find that their houses —"the entrances well swept, the floors beautifully [sic] smeared with cowdung, the few pots and pans clean and shining"—and latrines are cleaner and better kept than those of the rich of the town.

In 1933, the Mahatma began his greatest fast—the fast that was to have been unto death—for the Untouchables. This followed a decision by the British, supported by the orthodox Hindus, to make the Untouchables an entirely separate community, to cut them off from Hinduism in the new electorate. One might think that such divorce would have advanced their position. Not Mr. Gandhi. "I have to resist your decision with my life," he wrote Sir Samuel Hoare, on the ground that the Hindu community must not be split up, and that the lot of the Untouchables must be ameliorated *within* Hinduism. His point of view, in a word, is to make the Untouchables touchable, i.e., to create a new fifth caste.

Terrified that the Mahatma might die, with the whole world breathlessly watching the progress of the fast, the British and the orthodox Hindus patched up a compromise; Mr. Gandhi accepted it. He broke the fast in solemn company with a few friends, Dr. Rabindranath Tagore, and a leper.

Family System

Let us continue to burrow among these Indian complexities— hoping that they will turn out to be less complex than they seem— with the family. A word of warning. What is true for the north may not be true of the south, what is true of Hindus may not be true of Moslems. A description of affairs in Bengal may be totally erroneous if applied to Travancore. This qualification must be maintained throughout these chapters. Let us say it once again: India is a sub-continent.

As in China, the unit of Indian life is the family, not the individual. But Indians, unlike Chinese, have two families. Their own—and their caste. In regard to family life proper, Hindus as a whole are distinguished from most other peoples by three phenomena.

The first is child marriage. We have had a glimpse of this in connection with Mr. Gandhi, and anyone who has read Katherine Mayo's heartbreaking *Mother India* knows its colossal cost in blood, suffering, and degradation. Little girls are betrothed sometimes before they can talk; they are married at puberty or before, and not all husbands wait even till puberty to begin sexual relations. Men of fifty may marry girls of ten. Shattered by excessive child-bearing, deprived of the possibility of education, often treated worse than cattle, the girl children of India have a good cause for grievance against the laws, the customs, inflicted on them by the mythology of their country.

The origin of child marriage is probably associated with sacrifices attending the propitiation of crops. The instinct to fertilization, of women or of land, is very strong. Hindus make a considerable fetish of virginity; to marry a girl before the age of puberty, when she is almost certain to be a virgin, is a sort of insurance of the husband's rights. There is a proverb in Punjabi: "No Hindu father sleeps well if he has a daughter in puberty," i.e., he fears that the virginity and hence marriageability of his daughter is in danger. Also most Hindu families are eager to marry off their girl children for economic reasons.

Second, remarriage of widows is forbidden by orthodox Hindu custom, and is still very rare. This condemns to a virtual serfdom thousands upon thousands of young women, who are made to do the most menial work by the rest of the family, who are cast out by their friends as unclean, who must wear black for the rest of their lives. The fate of the widow is appalling; but not so appalling as it once was. Until the British came, orthodox Hindu widows were obliged to incinerate themselves on the funeral pyres of their husbands—the ceremony known as *suttee*. The origin of *suttee*, and, derivatively, of the perpetual widowhood of women, is the feeling among old-fashioned Hindus that the woman has no authentic life of her own, and must in effect cease to exist when her husband is removed.

The first thing everyone notices on arrival in India is the red spot worn by most women in the center of the forehead. This is not a caste mark; it means simply that the bearer is not a widow.

Third, *purdah*. This exists in other countries, for instance Egypt and Iraq, but not quite so formidably as in India. Purdah, literally "curtain," means that the woman must conceal her face from all but members of her own family circle, or must even live perpetually inside her home. Purdah came to India with the Moslem invaders; the Hindus were quick to copy it, largely it is said to preserve their women from rape. It has caused untold suffering among the poor and backward; medical reports are testimony to the growth of such diseases as tuberculosis among women who, after marriage, literally *never* again breathe fresh air. But purdah is dying out among the educated.[4] All over India one may meet officials who proudly ask you home to dinner, introduce you to their unveiled wives, and announce that they came out of purdah last year, or the year before.

Marriage is a tremendous sacrament in India. Preparation begins for it before the child is born; cases are reported in which *unborn* children have been "betrothed." It has been reported that in one backward caste, girls who, because of some deformity, may not get a husband, are "married" as puberty approaches to a sword, an arrow, or a tree; in another, if an unmarried girl who has reached puberty should chance to die, a man of the village goes through a ceremony of marriage with the dead body.

The worst thing that can happen to an orthodox Hindu male is not to have a son. The very word "son," in Punjabi, means "deliverance from hell." Thus the extreme accent on marriage. The son is so important because only he, officiating at his father's funeral pyre, can save the soul from contamination. The doctrine of Hindu reincarnation depends on descendants on earth, in order to make avatars in heaven possible. The line between death and life must not stop.

Another aspect of the family system is that when an Indian gets a good job, hundreds of retainers and obscure and distant members of his family may fasten on him for a living. The poverty of India—caused in part by British exploitation—is overwhelming. The legend is that the first Indian to become a peer, Lord Sinha, had to retire

---

[4] But some social climbers in the middle class take it up, because to have purdah means an extra room in the house, which is a sign of wealth.

from public service—he was a governor—because the pressure of his clansmen to support them became too much to bear.

Moslem India

We cannot in this chapter discuss in detail the career and philosophy of Mohammed or the theology of Islam. We can touch upon Mohammedanism only as it exists in India and affects the Indian problem. More Moslems live in India than in any other country in the world; they form a vast pool in the vaster pool of Hinduism. There are about 77,000,000 Moslems in India, as against approximately 238,000,000 Hindus; the ratio of Moslems to Hindus is thus roughly one to three. They make what is beyond doubt the most difficult minority problem in the world.

Everything in this chapter to this point refers only to Hindus. The Moslems are a distinctly dissimilar people. Moslems believe in one god, Allah, and in the unity of God; they believe in one prophet, Mohammed, in contrast to the pluralism of the Hindus. They do not worship idols; they do not believe in caste; they tend to individualism rather than excessive devotion to a family system, even though a Moslem may have four wives. Hinduism is a passive faith; Mohammedanism is distinguished from other great creeds by its proselytizing activism. The Mohammedan, by and large, has a more concrete attitude than the Hindu both to the reality of earthly existence and the joys of the hereafter. Their creeds differ drastically in minor details. Hindus play music at festivals; Moslems don't. And the Moslems have an important feast called Baqr Id in which the cow—the selfsame wretched beast that the Hindus worship—is killed by sacrifice. The Mohammedans were invaders of India, but they never assimilated Hindus as the Hindus, previous invaders, assimilated the earlier Dravidian culture. Nor have the Hindus had much success in assimilating Moslems.

It is difficult, however, for a newcomer to tell a Hindu from a Moslem on sight if costume is not considered. Both may smoke tobacco; neither may drink alcohol. As to costume, Moslems tend to wear loose-fitting garments and turbans; plenty of Hindus, however, wear turbans too. One clue is that Moslems, most of whom have beard and mustache, clip the hair away from the lips so that it cannot touch food.

Hindu theology is staggeringly medieval, but one should not assume that the unitarian Moslems are much more modern. The Moslems are just as parochial, just as tenacious of their faith, as the Hindus; they are fiercely jealous of their prestige as inheritors of Mogul glamour, and at the same time they suffer acute pangs of inferiority because they are numerically a minority. Most communal trouble in India derives from Moslems, not from Hindus.

The Moslems are by a considerable degree the poorer community. Their share of the wealth of India by no means follows the one to three ratio. They have much less. One curious point is that the Koran forbids Moslems to charge interest; therefore the orthodox are automatically excluded from being bankers or big creditors. It is difficult for a Moslem to be a *banya* (shopkeeper), the most profitable trade in India, since most *banyas* make more on loans and interest than on sale of goods.

Sources of dissension between Hindu and Moslem are multiform. Superstition, politics, cash and credit, turn the two communities against each other. Almost everywhere in India they live side by side, and it is almost impossible to avoid tension during such festivals as Baqr Id, for example. It is difficult, however, for a foreigner quite to appreciate the fanatic intensity of Hindu-Moslem bitterness. I heard it said that "several million" in each community would rather die of thirst than take water from the other. Small wonder that scarcely a week passes without some communal riot, some disturbance of the peace.

The Moslems, being the minority, consider themselves the injured party. Their list of grievances is long. But when one analyzes them in detail, they become hard to grasp. The Moslems complain generally of political discrimination; they say that their religious and cultural homogeneity is "endangered." But there is very little that the British or the Hindus can do to ameliorate this general grievance, since the Moslems *are* that most unfortunate of all things, a permanent and unassimilable minority.

The Moslems assert that the Hindus get the best jobs in India. But as a rule the Moslem fails to get the job, not because he is a Moslem, but because he is apt to be inferior to the Hindu in brains.[5] The Moslems complain that their form of the native language, Urdu, is being supplanted by Hindi. But surely, if they are so confident of

[5] For instance in Bengal ninety-two per cent of those with university education are Hindus, though Moslems are a majority of the population.

the culture, their language should be able to defend itself. The
Moslems say that they are politically generous to non-Moslems in the
provinces that they control, and that the Hindus are not. But in
Bengal for instance they not only have fifty-four per cent of the
people; they are assured by a special law of a permanent majority
in the chamber.

The Hindu attitude varies widely. Some die-hard communalists
among the Hindus are deplorably, shamefully backward; most of the
more modern leaders want coöperation. "Hindu-Moslem unity is not
less important than the spinning wheel; it is the breath of our life,"
says Mr. Gandhi. Pandit Nehru thinks that the Hindus, as the majority race, must take the lead in generosity, but he resents it that communal Moslems like Mr. Jinnah have split the nationalist movement
by their tactics. Most Hindu congressmen, I think, have a subconscious grudge against Moslems because they say that the Moslems
did not keep up their end in civil disobedience; the Hindus went to
jail, but many Moslems sat outside and watched.

The attitude of the British toward communal tension is complex.
As humanitarians and men of the West they deplore it and perhaps
do what they can to ameliorate it. But as imperialists they find it a
useful convenience in that it furnishes a very strong pretext for
remaining in India. The British *raj* claims that only the British can
keep order in the peninsula, because they have no religious ax to
grind; they must maintain peace between the rival factions, and adjudicate between them. Thus the Hindu-Moslem quarrel has great
derivative importance aside from its intrinsic quality. The British in
effect use Mohammed and Sri Krishna as pillars of the Empire. They
use communalism as a justification for conquest.

In 1932 came the remarkable document known as the Communal
Award. Hindus and Moslems failed at the Round Table Conference
to reach agreement, and in order to make the constitution even
tentatively workable, a scheme had to be devised whereby seats in
the provincial legislatures were blocked off for the various communities. Moslem voters, for instance, vote only for Moslem candidates, and it is determined in advance how many Moslem members
there shall be. In Madras twenty-eight out of 215 seats are thus reserved for the Moslem community, in the Punjab eighty-four out
of 175, and so on. Later this scheme will be extended to the federal
legislature, in which Moslems are assured eighty-two seats out of

250—a proportion rather greater than strict numerical justice would provide. The British government will withdraw the Communal Award at any time that Hindus and Moslems can get together and devise a satisfactory plan for a normal or joint electorate.

On the whole Moslems are less nationalist than Hindus. They may freely join the Congress, and many do, but the avowed aim of the Moslem League is merely Dominion Status, whereas Congress wants complete independence. This, too, nationalist Hindus resent. On the other hand, Moslems are even more bitter than Hindus in opposing federation, because a federal India will tend to increase Hindu strength.

The Moslem community is a good deal more homogeneous than the Hindu community, since Moslems do not have caste. There is, however, a main cleavage on religious grounds in the Moslem world, that between Sunnis and Shias. The Sunnis are, one might put it roughly, orthodox historically; the Shias, numbering twenty-eight percent of the Moslem population, are the dissenters, though in religious practice they are on the fundamentalist side. The Shias do not concede that Abu Baqr, Omar, and Othman were true caliphs in succession to Mohammed; they are followers of Ali, Mohammed's cousin and son-in-law, the fourth caliph. Ali will come back to earth, they believe, and lead the faithful to new glory and conquest. Shias are in general more limited in outlook than Sunnis.

Among Moslem sub-sects the most interesting are perhaps the Bhoras and the Khojas. Both originated within the last hundred years, comprising groups who were *converted* to Islam from Hinduism, and both retain some Hindu characteristics. The Khojas are subdivided further; one group, the Ismailis, believes that the present Aga Khan is the thirteenth *Imam* after Ali, and thus is vice-regent of God. The other, the Ishnasharias, do not believe in the divinity of this gentleman.

One other branch of Moslems should perhaps be mentioned: the Ahrars who are the left-wingers in the Punjab and who have joined the Congress. They are a curious combination: fanatic communalists in religious attitude, and at the same time political radicals. They have adopted the religious approach, their critics say, the better to reach the uninformed masses. The only civil disobedience conspicuous in India today is practiced by Ahrars at the Shahidgunj Mosque in Lahore, which has been a historic scene of religious tension.

The chief political organ among the Moslems is the All-India Moslem League. This dates from 1906, when conservative Moslems in Bengal determined to found an organization to advance their political aims. In 1916, the so-called Lucknow pact united Congress and Moslem League in a home-rule program; Hindus and Moslems continued to work together politically under Mr. Gandhi, but began to split after 1921. The League passed several years between death and life, mostly as an instrument of Moslems close to the British, and then revived during the Round Table Conference, after which it adopted Dominion Status as its aim and intensified its communal program. The Moslem League fought the 1937 elections against Congress,[6] and Moslems won majorities in Bengal and the Punjab. These Moslem governments are not, however, nearly as closely tied to the Moslem League as the Hindu governments are tied to Congress.

Jains

The Jain sect, numbering about 1,200,000 people mostly in the south of India, is an offshoot from Hinduism; originally like Buddhism it represented a revolt against doctrinaire Hindu theology; the Jains reject the Veda scriptures and do not accept caste. They do, however, believe in Karma, and Jains carry to an extreme point Hindu vegetarianism and veneration of animals. Orthodox Jains may not eat before sunrise or after sunset, for fear of swallowing an insect in the dark; they wear white gauze strips over their mouths during the day as a similar precaution. Most Jains carry a small brush, with which to dust places when they sit down, so that they may not inadvertently squash an ant or other insect. If a Jain should chance to kill an animal, even a tiny bug of some sort, he would turn into that bug for several hundred generations.

Jains are a prosperous community despite these strange strictures; they are traders, jewel merchants, and the like.

The Stalwart Sikhs

The Sikhs, who come exclusively from the Punjab area, are neither Hindus nor Moslems; they comprise an autonomous religious community numbering 4,500,000, who are also a sort of military caste.

---

[6] One may ask how much competition can take place under the Communal Award which reserves seats to each community. But the Congress ran *Moslem* congressmen for the Moslem seats.

Sikhs are closer to Hindus than to Moslems—they hate the Moslems fiercely—but they are monotheistic, believing in a single God who has been represented on earth by ten Sikh *gurus* or prophets. The Sikhs deny that they have caste, but in practice they discriminate against menial workers and the like. They may, like Roman Catholics, be converted; indeed, no Sikh is born a Sikh, but only becomes one when he is initiated into the creed during adolescence.

The thing that makes any Sikh instantly identifiable, the stigmata that automatically distinguishes him from all other Indians, is long hair. No Sikh cuts his hair from birth to death, and the stuff, a weird mixture of beard and backhair, is braided together and tucked inside a turban. Sikh boys at the age of ten or twelve are a curious sight, because their hair is long although they have not yet begun to grow beards. The long hair is one of the five "K's." Orthodox Sikhs must wear their hair long (*kes*), carry an iron bracelet on the right wrist (*karra*), wear short underpants (*kachh*), use a comb in the hair (*kanghi*), and carry a short knife (*kirpan*). Sikhs may not smoke, but most of them drink like fish.

Almost all Sikhs use the name "Singh" in their names. This is the Rajput word for lion. Rajputs are called Singh too, but you can tell a Rajput named Singh from a Sikh named Singh because the Rajputs cut their hair. Most Sikhs call themselves "Sardar"—chief.

The Sikhs have a national history quite their own, and very martial it is. They were not subdued by the British until 1849. Now they are the best troops and police in India. One group of Sikhs, however, the Akalis, are anti-British. They belong to the Congress and take a strong left-wing line.

Parsis

This community is utterly distinct from either Hindus or Moslems; the Parsis differ from each at least as much as Lutherans differ from Jews, or Swedes from Fiji Islanders. The Parsis are worshipers of Zoroaster and their sacred books are the Persian Zend Avesta; they have one deity, Ahurmazd, the giver of life and all that is good, together with his counterpart, Ahirman, who is the devil; they maintain and worship sacred fires which Zoroaster brought from heaven. Parsis are neither buried nor burned on death, but are given to the vultures, in order not to pollute the elements.

This grewsome "vulturization" aside, the Parsis are probably the most progressive community in India. They bear importance far beyond their numbers—there are only about 120,000 of them in India, mostly concentrated near Bombay—because they are the best business men, the richest industrialists in the land. Parsis run the new Indian air service; they operate the best hotels; they control Tata, India's greatest industrial concern. And they add greatly to the sophistication, the cosmopolitan quality of Bombay.

Chapter XXV
Jawaharlal Nehru

~~~~~~

*Socialism is for me not merely an economic doctrine which
I favor; it is a vital creed which I hold with all my head and
heart.*

—JAWAHARLAL NEHRU

*Believe me if Jawaharlal is not in jail today, it is not be-
cause he is afraid of it. He is quite capable of mounting the
gallows with a smile on his lips.*

—MR. GANDHI

THE remarkable human being whose name is Pandit Jawaharlal
Nehru is, next to Mr. Gandhi, the most important Indian in
India. This handsome, cultivated, and exceptionally fastidious and
sensitive Kashmiri Brahman, who is slated to be the Mahatma's
successor in the nationalist movement, is not so baffling a creature
as Mr. Gandhi, but he has complexities enough. The struggle in
Nehru is triple. He is an Indian who became a westerner; an aristocrat who became a socialist; an individualist who became a great
mass leader. More than this, he is a man with a modern mind, a
man of reason, a devout—if this is the proper adjective—rationalist.
And in India!—the continent of caste and holy cattle, of religious
fanaticism in an extreme degree—India, which is a sort of cesspool
of rival faiths, but in which faith, any faith, is a paramount desideratum. Nehru the agnostic, Nehru the modern man, faces the colossal medievalism of India. He fights the British, but he fights the
entrenched ritualism of his own people too. His position—in reverse
—is roughly that of an American politician, say, who dared to come
out *against* radios and two-car garages. His struggle is that of a
twentieth-century mind trying to make a revolution of material that
goes back beyond the middle ages. Think of the backdrop of the
preceding chapters. This is the curtain on which Nehru has to write
a modern, a contemporary story.

. . . .

Nehru was born in Allahabad on November 14, 1889, the son of Motilal Nehru, one of the greatest lawyers and richest men in India. It is difficult to call him "Nehru," because in India he is universally known just as "Jawaharlal." Possibly this use of his first name became common in the early days to distinguish him from his father. Sometimes he is referred to as "Panditji" but as a rule the diminutive "ji" is not used with Nehru. Jawaharlal is enough. One thinks of him only as Jawaharlal. "Pandit," incidentally, which means "wise man," is a Kashmiri title he took on from his father.

The Nehru family, originating in the hills of Kashmir, settled first in Delhi, then Allahabad. One ancestor, Raj Kaul, was a Persian scholar in the good graces of the Mogul emperor of the time. The family name was Kaul for several hundred years; Nehru, which means "canal," was added later. Nehru's grandfather and great-grandfather both held posts under the last Moguls, and one of his uncles (like Gandhi's father) was a *Dewan* or prime minister of a small native state.

When one says that Jawaharlal is a Kashmiri Brahman and the son of Motilal Nehru, it is as if one were to say that a man was a Boston Cabot or Lowell whose father was like Mr. Justice Holmes. He comes not only of the bluest blood in India, with a tremendous pride of race and heritage, but of a family with a deep tradition of public service and utility to the community.

Young Nehru had an English tutor from his earliest years; in 1905, at sixteen, he went to England, where he studied at Harrow and Cambridge and read for the bar—curious background for an Indian revolutionary! During this period his influences were largely literary. He was shy and lonely; he read Pater and Wilde and was devoted to what he calls a "vague kind of cyrenaicism," though he came early in contact with social and scientific ideas.

Nehru, like Gandhi, has written an autobiography[1]—but it is a very different kind of book. The Mahatma's placid story compares to Nehru's as a cornflower to an orchid, a rhyming couplet to a sonnet by MacLeish or Auden, a waterpistol to a machine gun. Nehru's autobiography is subtle, complex, discriminating, infinitely cultivated, steeped in doubt, suffused with intellectual passion. Lord Irwin once

---

[1] *Jawaharlal Nehru: An Autobiography*. London: John Lane. It has never been published in America.

said that no one could understand India without reading it;[2] it is a
kind of Indian "Education of Henry Adams," written in superlative
prose—hardly a dozen men alive write English as well as Nehru—
and it is not only an autobiography of the most searching kind, but
the story of a whole society, the story of the life and development of
a nation.

In 1912, when he was twenty-three, Jawaharlal returned to India.
Life smote him promptly. It was in any case impossible for him not
to be close to politics—for instance the coalition between the Congress
and the Moslem League in 1916 was made in his father's house—
and he joined the nationalist movement. He met Mr. Gandhi ("All
of us admired him for his heroic fight in South Africa, but he seemed
very distant and different and unpolitical to many of us young men")
and soon made his first speech. He was dumb with shyness and
doubtful of his capacity even to speak his own tongue, Hindustani.
But after his talk the renowned leader, Dr. Tej Bahadur Sapru,
rushed up on the platform and embraced him.

Then came the Rawlatt bills and Amritsar. Nehru writes:

Toward the end of that year (1919) I travelled from Amritsar to
Delhi by the night train. The compartment I entered was almost full
and all the berths, except one upper one, were occupied by sleeping
passengers. I took the vacant upper berth. In the morning I discovered that all my fellow passengers were military officers. They
conversed with each other in loud voices which I could not help
overhearing. One of them was holding forth in an aggressive and
triumphant tone and soon I discovered that he was Dyer, the hero
of Jallianwala Bagh[3] and he was describing his Amritsar experiences.
He pointed out how he had the whole town at his mercy and he had
felt like reducing the rebellious city to a heap of ashes, but he took
pity on it and refrained. . . . I was greatly shocked to hear his
conversation and to observe his callous manner. He descended at
Delhi station in pajamas with bright pink stripes, and a dressing gown.

(*Autobiography*, pp. 43-44)

Soon after, a turning point in Nehru's life occurred. He took his
mother and wife, both of whom were ill, to Mussoorie in the north.
It happened that an Afghan delegation, negotiating peace with Brit-

---

[2] See an excellent survey, *India Reveals Herself*, by Basil Mathews.
[3] Dyer was the British general in command. Jallianwala Bagh was the place
where Indians had to crawl on their bellies to pass into the city.

ain after the 1919 Afghan war, was housed in the same hotel. Nehru
never talked to any of the Afghan plenipotentiaries, but after a month
he was asked by the local police not to have any dealings with them.
This struck him as being unreasonable; he had no intention of talking
to the Afghans, but—a young man of fiber—he refused on principle
to obey the order. Thereupon he was formally "externed" from the
Mussoorie district. This was his first conflict with British authority.
In the next two weeks he had nothing much to do, and as a result
became aware of the *kisans*, peasants, and their grievances. The accident at Mussoorie helped turn him to the land.

Already he had had vague socialist leanings. Now these began to
be entrenched. With some colleagues he visited the peasants on the
little farms. He saw their sufferings first hand, and heard their
grievances. He learned to survive the Indian sun, and to speak to
large gatherings. He discovered his capacity to arouse people. He
even—unwittingly—sent several peasants to jail, because when they
had been guilty of looting homes of landlords he—filled with *Satyagraha* spirit—demanded that they give themselves up to the police.
"Many received long sentences and in later years, when I went to
prison, I came across some of them, boys and young men, spending
their youth in prison."

Here is his first picture of the peasants in their "miserable rags"
fighting the lords of the land:

They showered their affection on us and looked on us with loving
and hopeful eyes, as if we were the bearers of good tidings, the guides
who were to lead them to the promised land. Looking at them and
their misery and overflowing gratitude, I was filled with shame and
sorrow, shame at my own easy-going and comfortable life and our
petty politics of the city which ignored this vast multitude of semi-
naked sons and daughters of India, sorrow at the degradation and
overwhelming poverty of India. A new picture of India seemed to
rise before me, naked, starving, crushed, and utterly miserable.

(*Autobiography,* p. 52)

Nehru first went to jail during the 1921 non-coöperation campaign.[4] This was the time of the first tremendous enthusiasm for civil

[4] He handles irony nicely. He says, "My offense was distributing notices for a
hartal (strike). This was no offense under the law then, though I believe it is
one now, for we are rapidly advancing towards Dominion Status."

disobedience, and hundreds of Indians, guilty of no crime or mis-
demeanor, fought for the privilege of being arrested. Young men
and women mobbed the police lorries going through the streets, and
scrambled to get inside the jails.

Next he was arrested in a native state called Nabha, where a
British administrator ruled in place of a deposed Maharaja. With
two comrades Nehru went to investigate conditions there; they were
arrested, led down the street handcuffed, and thrown into a filthy
jail. Apparently the charge was that they did not have permission
to enter Nabha territory. Nehru was handcuffed to one of his companions for twenty-four hours; at night, as he slept on a muddy
floor, rats crawled over his face. It took two weeks before he was
released. The "trial," before a judge who knew neither English nor
Hindustani, was an unbelievable farce, and Nehru was sentenced to
two and a half *years'* imprisonment. Luckily the sentence was suspended—but Nehru and his comrades all came down with typhoid
fever, caught from the foul drinking water in the hovel where they
were confined.

"The state of Nabha was under a British administrator, a member
of the Indian Civil Service, and he had the full powers of an autocrat, subject only to the Government of India. And yet at every turn
we were referred to Nabha laws and procedure to justify the denial
of the most ordinary rights. We had to face a combination of feudalism and the modern bureaucratic machine with the disadvantages of
both and the advantages of neither," Nehru writes.

Altogether Jawaharlal has served seven terms in prison. Jail or
threat of jail took the best years of his life. He was sentenced to an
aggregate of ten and a half years; several sentences were suspended,
and he was discharged before time, so that he actually served five and
a half years in all. The last sentence came as late as 1934, after civil
disobedience had been called off; he was arrested following an alleged
seditious speech in Calcutta, and given two years.

Mr. Gandhi (who only served four brief terms) adored jail;
Jawaharlal did not. But he is seldom bitter. There are beautiful passages in his book, describing the stars he managed to see, peering
upward from the compound, and the animals—squirrels and monkeys
and parrots—he learned to play with. He knows the emotional
starvation of jail, the chafing of steady confinement, the terrible

dreariness of day after day, season after season, without change. He found harshness, and also consideration. With wistful eye he looked

"Upon that little tent of blue
Which prisoners call the sky,
And at every drifting cloud that went
With sails of silver by."

In one jail he lived in a large barrack, with holes in the roof and crannies in doors and windows. "I lived in solitary grandeur. But I was not quite alone, for at least two score sparrows had made their home in the broken-down roof. Sometimes a wandering cloud would visit me, its many arms creeping in through the numerous openings and filling the place with a damp mist." It is in this passage that he writes that suffering, even if it may be necessary for clear thought, will cloud the brain in excess. He does not like suffering as Gandhi does. He was not an introvert by nature, he says, but prison made him so. Jail has deeply marked and pitted this man. He cannot bear cruelty.

Continually he brooded not merely on the nature of repression but on the fundamental reasons for it—reasons even beyond the political struggle in India. To test his courage he withstood a *lathi*[5] charge, and was bruised and beaten; his own mother was likewise hit on the head with canes, and knocked down by the police; his wife followed him to jail. He heard of such incredible sentences as that of the youth who got nine years' rigorous imprisonment for carrying a revolver, and he knew schoolboys who were flogged in jail for political offenses. But his mind kept ranging above the particular.

Jail alone did not make him a socialist, but it gave him the time and opportunity for exhaustive political study and introspection. Generally he was well treated in jail; he was permitted books and writing materials. His ideas on socialism took concrete form, and merged gradually with his nationalism. He began to see the Indian problem as more than a struggle between rebel nationalists and British nationalists. He became convinced that British imperialism as a capitalist growth was the real enemy, and that it must be fought from the socialist as well as from the nationalist point of view. British imperialism rests on capitalist exploitation as well as on the political

---

[5] A *lathi* is a long bamboo staff, the familiar weapon of the Indian police.

demands of empire; therefore a logical opponent of British imperialism must be not merely a nationalist but a socialist too.

This is the root of Nehru's creed. In every possible way he tried to hammer it home to the Indian people.

Most Indians are distinctly not socialists—remember the backdrop I have tried to sketch!—but Nehru rapidly became, next to Gandhi, the most important Indian leader. It is a question, however, if most of his followers are devoted to him because he is a socialist, or in spite of it. At any rate for ten solid years he was either secretary or president of the Congress; he is the only man who has ever been president of Congress three times. He was powerfully instrumental in making Gandhi come out for *purna Swaraj* (complete independence) at the Lahore Congress; in 1931, at Karachi he persuaded the Working Committee to accept a few vaguely and guardedly socialist planks. In 1937, he opposed the taking of office by Congress, but then he went to the country and, in an unparalleled stumping campaign, almost single-handed brought victory to Congress in seven provinces.

He is adored throughout India—revered and adored almost as Gandhi is.

"This My True-Begotten Father!"

His father Motilal was a very important influence on Jawaharlal, which is not surprising considering how sensitive Jawaharlal was and considering the vitality of the old man. Many important men have had great mothers; to find a great father passing on his qualities to his son is more unusual. The equation in the Nehru family worked both ways; Jawaharlal influenced Motilal almost as much as vice versa. One is reminded of the psychoanalytic phenomenon of countertransference, wherein the patient attracts and influences the doctor, instead of the doctor attracting the patient.

The story of Jawaharlal and Motilal, their love, their conflict, their hunger to understand each other, their eventual community of ideas, is well told in the autobiography. Motilal was solidly rich, a lawyer with an extensive practice, an intimate friend of governors and viceroys. He had, in Jawaharlal's words, "strong feelings, strong passions, tremendous pride, and great strength of will." Jawaharlal paints a beautifully revealing portrait of him as man, patriot, father.

The youth, barely twenty, began to drift toward extremism, toward rebellion. Motilal strove to understand his son, to check this drift away from him which horrified him. At that time Motilal was a moderate; he had been a member of Congress for years, but Congress was a very pale body in those days. Motilal wrote an article which Jawaharlal disagreed with; he chided his father by saying the British would approve it highly. Motilal was wild with rage. Yet Motilal's career depended largely on British policy and peace.

Came Gandhi and non-coöperation. Jawaharlal joined up. Motilal was dumbfounded. "He was not in the habit of being swept away by new proposals." He wasn't at all sure that civil disobedience would work; he resented it that his precious and beloved son should risk jail. The conflict grew. "We tried to be as considerate to each other as possible . . . night after night I wandered about alone, tortured in mind and trying to grope my way out." Then Jawaharlal discovered that Motilal was sleeping on the floor—to see what life in jail would be like for his son!

Within the year Motilal came over completely to his son's side. He took his stand with Gandhi and civil disobedience. This meant giving up his great house in Allahabad, his wealth, his practice; it meant giving up most of the friends, the political acquaintances with Indians and British alike, of a generation; it meant complete remaking of his life at sixty. And promptly old Motilal became the lion of the movement. When Jawaharlal went to jail, his father went with him.

For nine years the two worked together, fought together. Motilal was treated with the utmost consideration in prison, but imprisonment hurt his health. By 1930 he was an invalid. "He pulled himself together and banged a table in front of him, saying that he had made up his mind to be an invalid no longer." But the machine was burned out. "There he sat like an old lion mortally wounded and with his physical strength almost gone, but still very leonine and kingly." Sometime later Gandhi came to see him. Motilal said, "I am going soon, Mahatmaji, and I shall not be here to see *Swaraj*. But I know that you have won it." Early in 1931 he died.

Jawaharlal writes:

I was watching by his bedside. He had had a troublesome and restless night; suddenly I noticed that his face grew calm and the sense of struggle vanished from it. I thought that he had fallen asleep, and I was glad of it. But my mother's perceptions were keener, and she uttered a cry. I turned to her and begged her not to disturb him as he had fallen asleep. But that sleep was his last long sleep, and from it there was no awakening.

Then:

There were some ceremonies at home, and then the last journey to the Ganges with a mighty concourse of people. As evening fell on the river bank that winter day, the great flames leapt up and consumed that body which had meant so much to us who were close to him as well as to millions in India. Gandhiji said a few moving words to the multitude, and then all of us crept silently home. The stars were out and shining brightly when we returned, lonely and desolate.

Later:

I found it difficult to realize that he had gone. Three months later I was in Ceylon with my wife and daughter, and we were spending a few quiet and restful days. . . . I liked the place, and it struck me suddenly that it would suit father. Why not send for him? He must be tired out, and rest would do him good. I was on the point of sending a telegram to him in Allahabad. .

(*Autobiography,* pp. 247-248)

Finally a curious thing happened. Returning home Nehru found a letter from his father awaiting him! It had been sent many months before, and had been forwarded and reforwarded without ever reaching the destination. And it was a letter of farewell.

Word of Legend

Legends aplenty grew up about the Nehrus. One is that Motilal, a highly fastidious person, sent his laundry weekly all the way to Paris. It is nonsensical, of course. Another to the effect that the Viceroy (who had a very high regard for him) sent him champagne in jail is equally without foundation.

Another story, which has been widely garbled and distorted, has it that Motilal's sudden turn away from the British began when Jawaharlal was blackballed by an English club. The facts are these. Many years before, when Motilal was beginning his practice, an English friend offered to nominate him, Motilal, for membership in the European club in Allahabad. Motilal thanked his friend courteously, but declined the offer, because he did not want to risk rejection and because election of an Indian might make English members uncomfortable.

Another story of a different category is that Jawaharlal is a communist and that he has frequently been to Moscow, there to listen to the party line. But in fact he is not a communist, but a kind of social democrat; he has been in Moscow only once, and then for a few days in company with his father. They went as tourists to see the tenth anniversary festivities in 1927.

The Man Jawaharlal

At forty-nine Nehru is strikingly handsome—especially when he wears the Gandhi cap, a sort of white forage cap—and he is one of those fortunate people who photograph even better than they look. Usually he wears the Congress uniform—white *khadder*—and manages to appear courtly and impressive even when shrouded with yards of cheesecloth apron. His friends say that he has aged a good deal in the past two or three years, mostly as the result of fatigue, incessant traveling, and the giving out of energy. He is tall for an Indian—about five feet ten—with excellent bearing. He exercises methodically, and loves winter sports and swimming.

He lives as a rule in a house called the Anand Bhavan at Allahabad. Motilal gave his tremendous house to the nation, renaming it Swaraj Bhavan; for the family he then built what was to have been a simple cottage, but Motilal was an exceptionally expansive personality, and the simple cottage—the Anand Bhavan where Nehru lives—turned into a house almost as big as the original one. The big house is now the headquarters of the Congress party; part of it is used as a hospital.

But Jawaharlal isn't in Allahabad very often. His travels are formidable. He lives on the railway trains, and by choice travels third class. Anyone who has been in India knows what an ordeal this is.

India—Indian India—has no capital. Gandhi is in Wardha, Nehru in Allahabad; Bombay and Calcutta are important centers to Congress, and so are Lucknow and Madras. The Working Committee of Congress—its executive body—meets once every six weeks or so. As a rule it rotates between different cities. The annual session is held nowadays in a remote village. So Congress committee members are incessantly, unendingly traveling. The trains roar across dusty India, bringing them together.

Nehru's wife, Kamala, who came from a Kashmir Brahman family like his own, died in 1936. She had been in ill health for many years, and he was released from his last term of imprisonment in order to visit her in Switzerland. Previously, when she was in India, the British volunteered to free him so that he might see her if he would pledge himself informally to give up politics for the period corresponding to the rest of his term. He refused. She begged him to refuse. Their only child, twenty-year-old Indira, is in school in England. Nehru has two sisters; one, Lakshmi, married Ranjit S. Pandit and is the thoroughly competent minister for local self-government and health in the United Provinces government—the first Congresswoman to reach ministerial rank. As a child she was called Sarup (the Beautiful One), and nicknamed Nan.

Nehru keeps closely in touch with the outside world. He subscribes to the *New Statesman*, the *Manchester Guardian Weekly*, *Time & Tide*, the New York *Nation, The New Republic*, the *Living Age*, and *Vendredi* and *L'Europe Nouvelle* from Paris. Additionally he would like to see regularly several leftist magazines which are forbidden circulation in India. Recently he went for a brief vacation in the Himalayas. The books he took with him were Aldous Huxley's *Ends and Means*, Bertrand Russell's *Which Way to Peace*, John Dewey's *The Quest for Certainty*, Edward Thompson's *Life of Lord Metcalfe, The Tongues of Man* (a book on comparative philology) by J. R. Firth, and Levy's *Philosophy for a Modern Man*.

His knowledge of English poetry is profound, and his love for it passionate. Incessantly he quotes classic verse.

He has a great number of acquaintances, but very few intimate friends. He speaks often of his loneliness. He loves children, light-heartedness, laughter, but he is no backslapper; he hates promiscuous effusiveness; he is moody and ingrown, and finds it hard to meet people half way. They must come to *him*. He made even his father come to him: to meet his growing mind and soul. In one passage he says that he took to the crowd and the crowd took to him, but that he was never able to lose himself completely to it; he was in it always, and *of* it never. This diffidence, this inner loneliness, is probably the mark of jail.

He is the furthest possible contrast to the mob leader like Hitler or Mussolini. American newspapers tag him with the adjective "fiery," which is singularly inappropriate, though he is capable of flashes of temperament. When he talks, he deliberately understates his case; he sounds like a lecturer at Oxford, even at a political meeting. Frequently he confesses his failings; he is sometimes bored by politics; he is the victim of competitive emotions; occasionally he is unsure of himself and divided in judgment. Dogmatism does not become him. He talks frankly of his inner conflict, of "subconscious depths struggling with outer circumstances, of an inner hunger unsatisfied."

In one despondent moment he wrote that he represented no one. "I have become a queer mixture of the East and West, out of place everywhere, at home nowhere." Much in India disheartens him, and he confesses "retreating into his shell."

He detests ritualism and mysticism, except perhaps in poetry. Religion he calls a killjoy. He is all for modernization, westernization. "The spectacle of what is called religion, or at any rate organized religion, in India and elsewhere, has filled me with horror, and I have frequently condemned it and wished to make a clean sweep of it." This—from an Indian leader! And there are many to say that his hatred of religion will keep him from supreme heights in India, because it is inconceivable that India should surrender herself finally to an agnostic.

He has no faddisms, like the Mahatma. He ate meat from childhood, but gave it up under Gandhi's influence in 1920. He reverted to meat again in Europe, though he felt that it "coarsened him"; now (like Hitler, whom he in no other way resembles) he is "more-or-less" a vegetarian. He smokes occasionally, and outside India may even take a little light wine. His father drank wine; in fact young Jawaharlal saw him with a glass once, and was thunderstruck; he thought old Motilal was drinking blood.

His general health is so good that even in jail he had no insomnia, he says. He has, however, recorded some curious dreams. A favorite dream is of flying over open country. Once he dreamed that he was being strangled.

He gets no salary for political work, and the family fortune has gone mostly to the cause. What little money he needs he gets from writing.

The things he likes most are mountains, running water, children, glaciers, good conversation, and all animals except bats and centipedes. Once he had a moment of intense enjoyment in prison; the temperature was 116° F. and his wife sent him a thermos flask filled with sherbet. The things he dislikes most are "exploitation, cruelty, and people who, in the name of God, truth, and the public good, are busy feathering their nests"; in a word, most politicians.

He wrote to me recently, "I suppose my father and Gandhiji have been the chief personal influences in my life. But outside influences do not carry me away. There is a tendency to resist being influenced. Still influences do work slowly and unconsciously. My wife influenced me considerably in many ways, though unobtrusively." He was influenced for a time by Bertrand Russell, and then found him ineffective. He disliked Spengler at first, but found a "certain fascination" in his book.

Nehru proceeds to say that Marx and Lenin had a powerful effect on him, partly from the content of their writings, even more by reason of the way they wrote. He was tired of mysticism and metaphysics; he liked the unadorned, scientific, analytical point of view. He says that he is certainly a socialist in that he believes in socialist theory and method. His general approach is Marxist. But he wrote me, "I am not a communist chiefly because I resist the communist tendency to treat communism as holy doctrine; I do not like being told what to think and do. I suppose I am too much of an individualist. . . . I feel also that too much violence is associated with communist methods. The ends cannot be separated from the means."

He likes moderation. He believes in the rational approach. He says of the Hindi-Urdu controversy: "Open the way to both scripts everywhere." As to communal troubles, which he thinks the British deliberately keep to the forefront, he says that the real struggle is not between Hindu and Moslem, but between both and modern ideas.

One of his defects, people say, is that he is too decent, too honorable, to be a good politician. He is a gentleman. Worse, he is an English gentleman! He has devoted his life to freeing India from Britain, but the British imprint is deep upon him. The old-school tie has turned to homespun cheesecloth, and he still follows a code of chivalry. Another defect is, of course, his ingrownness, his hatred of give-and-take and political hurlyburly.

The sources of his power are numerous. Consider, for instance, his courage and obvious strength of character. Then there is his technical competence at a job; he was, for instance, a successful mayor of Allahabad for a time. Consider too his industry, both intellectual and physical. In jail he not only wrote most of a closely printed 617-page autobiography, but a history of the world in the form of letters to his daughter, 1,569 pages long. During the last election campaign, he traveled 110,000 miles in twenty-two months, and reached villages everywhere in India. He used vehicles ranging from bullock carts to airplanes; he had to give up airplanes because peasants in remote parts of the peninsula, never having seen a plane before, would overrun the landing fields. Once he made 150 speeches in one week.

Then again there are his modesty and complete honesty with himself. By 1929, he was a hero, almost inundated by the applause and enthusiasm of the masses; by 1930, he had to face hero worship such as no man in India, Gandhi alone excepted, had ever known. He writes that "only a saint or inhuman monster could survive" the praise that came his way without being a little affected. He was distrustful of his popularity but he couldn't help being exhilarated and impressed by it. His family quickly chastened him with raillery; his wife and sisters, and even his small daughter, began to call him in the home the names he was given by the crowd. They would say, "Oh Jewel of India, what time is it?" or "Oh Embodiment of Sacrifice, please pass the bread."

His political integrity is unshakable. Nothing can deflect him from the path he has chosen, if he believes it to be right; he dislikes compromises and he has nothing of the occasional slipperiness of Mr. Gandhi. He makes definitions scrupulously, and abides by them. He is certainly one of the finest characters in public life I have ever met.

One small anecdote is to the point. In 1928 came a crucial vote in the Calcutta Congress session, over which his father was presiding. Gandhi and Motilal were strongly backing a proposal that Congress should adopt officially what was known as the "Nehru Report," a document prepared by Motilal to answer the Simon commission. Jawaharlal and his group—he was at the time head of a separate organization, the Independence League, as well as secretary of Congress—opposed this. The vote was close; Jawaharlal's side won. Then he discovered that there had been a technical error in the voting. As Secretary of the Congress he brought this to the attention of the meeting, even though he knew that it would mean overriding his victory and that in the next vote his group would lose.

He has great detachment. Recently—this is a curious oblique side-light on his character—he wrote a character sketch of himself, and carefully arranged so that it was published in a magazine anonymously. No one knew that he was the author until he let the secret out to a few friends months later.

It begins with a resounding *"Rashtrapati Jawaharlal Ki Jai!"* (Long Live Jawaharlal, Chief of State), and describes in somewhat indignant detail his manner as a conqueror of the multitude.

The Rashtrapati looked up as he passed swiftly through the waiting crowds, his hands went up and his pale hard face was lit up with a smile. . . . The smile passed away and the face became stern and sad. Almost it seemed that the smile and gesture accompanying it had little reality; they were just tricks of the trade to gain the good-will of the crowd whose darling he had become. Was it so? . . . Watch him again.

Is all this natural or the carefully thought out trickery of the public man? Perhaps it is both and long habit has become second nature now. The most effective pose is one in which there seems to be the least posing, and Jawaharlal has learned well to act without the paint and powder of the actor. . . . Whither is this going to lead him and the country? What is he aiming at with all his apparent want of aim?

For nearly two years now he has been President of Congress. Steadily and persistently he goes on increasing his personal prestige and influence. . . . From the far North to Cape Comorin he has gone like some triumphant Caesar, leaving a trail of glory and a legend behind him. Is all this just a passing fancy which amuses him . . . or is it his will to power that is driving him from crowd to crowd and making him whisper to himself:

"I drew these tides of men into my hands and wrote my will across the sky in stars."

What if the fancy turns? Men like Jawaharlal with all their great capacity for great and good work are unsafe in a democracy. He calls himself a democrat and a socialist, and no doubt he does so in all earnestness . . . but a little twist and he might turn into a dictator. He might still use the language of democracy and socialism, but we all know how fascism has fattened on this language and then cast it away as useless number.

Jawaharlal cannot become a fascist. . . . He is far too much an aristocrat for the crudity and vulgarity of Fascism. His very face and voice tell us that. His face and voice are definitely private. . . . And yet he has all the makings of a dictator in him—vast popularity, a strong will, energy, pride . . . and with all his love of the crowd an intolerance of others and a certain contempt for the weak and inefficient. His flashes of temper are well known. His overwhelming desire to get things done, to sweep away what he dislikes and build anew, will hardly brook for long the slow processes of democracy.

The article—Jawaharlal must have had a good time writing it—ends with a stirring appeal that he be defeated if he runs again for Congress president. In the document he was outlining possible dangers of the future quite unconnected with himself. He was anxious *not* to be president of Congress for another term.

Attitude to Gandhiji

Jawaharlal's relations to Gandhi are more complex than those of a disciple to a master. Poles apart as they are mentally and emotionally, they are devoted to each other—recent rumors that they quarreled are quite without foundation—and they complement each other nicely. Nehru needs Gandhi because Gandhi alone can carry the mass of the Indian people. Gandhi needs Nehru because he is his indispensable second-in-command.[6]

When Nehru first came in close contact with the Mahatma, he thought that in time Gandhi would turn gradually toward socialism. Years went by, and he saw his mistake. He worried terribly about it. It seemed to him an unreasonable paradox that Gandhiji, with all his "love and solicitude for the underdog," should "yet support a system which inevitably produces it and crushes it." He was impatient with Gandhi's ideas of trusteeship by the upper classes; he could not endure it that the Mahatma, who believed in non-violence, could support a system, capitalism, which was based on violence. Now he has given up Gandhi as incorrigible on this issue.

Nehru, strictly speaking, is not the leader of the Left in Congress. There are many others much more to the left than he is. He is not, oddly enough, even a member of the Congress Socialist party, a sort of autonomous block within Congress. This—another Indian paradox—is partly because the organized and official socialists fear that his identification with them might embarrass his leader-

[6] In February, 1939, Nehru resigned—presumably temporarily—his membership in the Congress Working Committee to side with Gandhi in a party split. See next chapter.

ship of Congress as a whole. Jawaharlal holds an approximate left center position, just as Mr. Gandhi is right center. There are many Congressmen to the right of Gandhi.

Sometimes young men in Congress think that, in the future, Jawaharlal may turn out to be Trotsky to Gandhi's Lenin. Jawaharlal himself quotes grimly a prophecy that he will some day be hanged by his own Congressmen.

Nehru likewise differs basically from Gandhi in that he cannot follow his leader all the way on non-violence. He admits the political value of non-violence, but he says frankly that non-violence *alone* cannot carry India to the final goal.

But what a beautifully warm and compelling picture he draws of Gandhi, what a waterfall of tribute his pages are! He talks of his tremendous debt to Gandhi, his "amazing and almost irresistible charm and subtle power over people," his capacity to make "heroes out of clay," his "inexhaustible reservoir of spiritual power." He defends him vigorously against the socialists who call him a reactionary. "Reactionary or revolutionary, he has changed the face of India, given pride and character to a cringing and demoralized people, built up strength and consciousness in the masses, and made the Indian problem a world problem."

Relations to the British

Nehru doesn't hate the British. He hates British imperialism and its exploitation of India, but he freely admits his intellectual debt to British culture. When he takes a holiday, he heads straight for England. He has tried to forget the long agony of jail, to dissociate the responsibility for it from Britain as a whole.

Nor do the British, a few retired Colonel Blimps aside, really hate Nehru. But they *fear* him deeply. It is enlightening to compare British opinions of Gandhi and Nehru; very few Englishmen are worried about the Mahatma any more, but for Nehru they have a healthy apprehension. They attack him as a socialist unendingly, as a blind for their alarm of him on purely nationalist grounds.

The British should realize that the fact that he is a socialist— and a gentleman—is a great asset on their side. Nehru, since he is a socialist, is impeded from any projection of the Indian struggle internationally, for the reason that the only countries which could help him are Fascist states, and he will have nothing to do with them.

The British are enormously curious about Nehru. They all know Gandhiji; rather few know Jawaharlal. The present Viceroy, for instance, until the end of 1938 at least, had never met him. Everywhere one goes in India, the first political question is, "Have you seen Jawaharlal? What's he like—what's he doing—what's he up to now?"

Chapter XXVI
The Congress Structure

~~~~~~

. . . And India shall soon be seen, proud and self-reliant, strong and free, the radiant splendor of Asia, as the light and benediction of the world.

—Mrs. Annie Besant in 1917

IT goes almost without saying that the Indian National Congress was founded—you've guessed it—by an Englishman. The British add to the story of their imperialism with methods, sometimes inadvertent, that are wonderful to behold.

In 1885 Allan Octavian Hume, who had been a British civil servant in India for thirty years, brought the Congress into being. He thought that Britain owed a debt to India, that the British should take a lead in encouraging the development of Indian institutions. As first envisaged, however, the Congress was planned to be humanitarian and social rather than political in aim; the story is that when Hume went to the Viceroy of the day, Lord Dufferin, to get his blessing for the project, Dufferin himself suggested that the movement should have a political basis, on the ground that governments need a "loyal opposition." On December 28, 1885, the first Congress met in Bombay, with 72 delegates. Within a few years it became noisy enough for Dufferin himself to dismiss it as "a contemptible minority," but for a long time it remained basically loyal; in fact it had English presidents in 1904 and again in 1910. Only during the Great War did it become provocatively nationalist, when Mr. Gandhi got control of it and turned it into a revolutionary weapon. In 1929 the Congress reached full stature, and came out officially for complete independence.

The Indian National Congress, let it be understood, is more than a political party; it is in a sense the organized expression of the aims and will of the Indian people. It includes Moslems as well as Hindus, though in smaller number; rich industrialists as well as homeless radicals; agitators in the native states as well as prime ministers in the eight Congress governments; socialists and reactionaries both. Anyone may join the Congress who pays the annual sub-- scription of four annas (about ten cents) per year—even this minuscule sum is too much for many Indian peasants—and who signs the pledge to work for the independence of India by all legitimate and peaceful means. At present the Congress has 3,102,113 members. It is both the reservoir and attacking stream of Indian man-power, a sort of giant People's Front against the British *raj*.

The Congress structure is complex. First come the private "four anna" members in the villages; of the four annas, incidentally, three go to the local Congress organization, one to the central secretariat at Allahabad. The primary members choose delegates to the provincial congress committees; a constituency is 250 primary members. The provincial committees choose the All-India Congress Committee, a sort of parliament. The president of the Congress—Nehru, as we have seen, was president three times—is appointed by this committee and is responsible to it. The presidency changes each year as a rule, and the new president selects fourteen or fifteen men who are his cabinet, though by tradition he chooses them on an All-Congress basis rather than as a reflection of his personal opinions. The President and his fourteen associates, the top of the Congress structure, are called the Working Committee. None—an interesting point —receive any salary. Some committee members remain on it year after year, no matter who is President.

The Congress is indisputably the best organized and most powerful organization in India. It is by far the largest party in every province of British India except the predominantly Moslem Punjab, North West Frontier, and Sind. In Madras, for instance, it holds 159 seats; the next biggest party has 21. In the U.P. it has 134 seats, and the next party 29; in Bombay it has 85, and the next party 19. The great manifestation of the Congress each year is the annual plenary session, which now takes place in some remote village. These plenary sessions, where at least a hundred thousand people congregate, are magnificent spectacles, not to be forgotten by one who has attended them.

The Congress has its uniform—white homespun and the Gandhi cap. It has its army in the shape of the Volunteers, who keep order at public meetings, though members are not armed. It has a foreign department, a propaganda bureau, and so on. It has its flag, composed of three stripes, saffron, white, and green, with a spinning wheel.

It has its national holiday—"Independence Day"—on January 26. This celebrates the 1929 decision to come out for complete independence instead of Dominion Status, but the actual date was chosen at random; January 26 happened to be a convenient Sunday far enough ahead for word to get around.

The Working Committee of Congress is a fascinating study in human and political nature. Devoted, disinterested, of varying beliefs and creeds, but all united by faith in Indian nationalism, the members are somewhat like the old Soviet Politburo. The membership is variegated; when I saw most of the members in Juhu, waiting in Mr. Gandhi's anteroom for a word with the master, I thought I had never met such different types of men bound by common aim. Here a wealthy and sophisticated lawyer, and at his side a peasant chieftain from Bihar; here a Moslem theologian, and next to him a soldier from the Northwest frontier.

The Left began to emerge as a distinct political group inside Congress when civil disobedience was called off in 1934. The revolt against Britain failed; the Congress had to become legal again. It turned "respectable," and many prominent politicians of the Right became members—because it was so powerful, even when illegal, that no one could have a political career outside it. At the same time, largely under Nehru's influence, an irrigation of socialist thought watered India. Hitherto the Congress had been dominated exclusively by nationalism. Thereafter a strong socialist streak developed. The Rightists resented this, and have opposed it. Thus an intra-Congress struggle tended to begin.

It reached an unpleasant climax in the Tripura plenary session in February, 1939. Mr. Gandhi suggested the Moslem theologian Moulana Abul, who is on the Right, as new president. His election was presumably assured, but something happened. The 1938 president, Subhas Chandra Bose, decided to run for reëlection, as a test of Leftist strength; also he was annoyed that Gandhi's chief Rightist lieutenant, Sardar Patel, had allegedly circularized Congress without his knowledge about Abul's candidature. So it became a fight between the Gandhi-Patel Right and the Bose Left. Bose won: at least he was elected president. The rank and file was with him. Then—obviously under Gandhi's influence—the rest of the Working Committee resigned. This was the most serious split in Congress history, but negotiations began at once to patch it up. Nehru, though ostensibly on the Left, sided with Gandhi, who was finally vindicated in a vote of the Agenda Committee of Congress by 210 to 131.

Working with the British

In 1937 came the tremendous event I alluded to briefly in the chapter on Mr. Gandhi above. It is the controlling factor in the situation to-day, the core of the whole story. The tremendous event was that, after the passage of the new Government of India Act, elections were held in the eleven provinces of British India, and Congress won in seven of them and took office. "Provincial Autonomy," as promised in the new Act, came into being. Thus the Congress, the same Congress which had so bitterly fought Britain, came into the British structure.

Nehru and his Leftist followers violently opposed taking office. They thought that autonomy, as defined in the Act, did not go far enough; they thought that acceptance of office, working under British governors, was a fatal compromise. But after almost four months of final negotiation Mr. Gandhi invented a formula which seemed to permit Congress to rule without loss of face. A kind of gentleman's agreement appeared to bind—perhaps not quite bind—the Viceroy and the governors not to use their veto powers except in circumstances of great public crisis. The right wingers in Congress were satisfied, and the Congress governments took office.

Now a curious point. The "high command" and the Working Committee under Nehru decided not to accept jobs personally in any province. Logically one might have assumed that the Working Committee leaders, if they stood for election and were returned, would be the new prime ministers. But they determined not to take jobs themselves. Instead, they deputed a second line of leaders to assume office. The Working Committee, again like the old Politburo in the Soviet Union, decided to keep out of actual administrative work, and to guide their governments from behind the scenes. So second-line Congressmen (I know that one or two of them may dislike this appellation, but I do not mean it personally) became the prime ministers and finance ministers and all the rest, and the Working Committee was transformed into a sort of composite *Eminence Grise*.

This has turned out to be something of an embarrassment, though not a serious one. Almost at once certain dissidences arose between the Working Committee and the Congress governments. The Working Committee held the whip hand, of course. It could break any provincial government, and in fact it turned out of office one of its own prime ministers, Dr. Khare in the Central Provinces, when it accused him of being disobedient. But it is awkward for the Working Committee to have to attack its own ministers openly. Thus negotiations have to be very delicate when there is divergence of opinion.

Two dangers, from the Left point of view, faced the new governments. First, as in the case of the Wafd nationalist organization in Egypt, they found that the sweets of power were—sweet. They were tempted by the comforts and advantages of their position to modify the pure fervor of their nationalism. Second, they found that running a government is a great deal more difficult than criticizing it; this too tended to seduce them into "moderation," which word Congress radicals are apt to interpret as subservience to Britain.

Provincial autonomy was a highly shrewd gesture by the British, though many Englishmen think—and fear—that it gave the Congress "too much." But in essence it was masterly, because it brought Congress for the first time within the fold of governmental responsibilities; it gave Congress most of the prickly things to handle, while the British continued to hold veto power, defense, foreign affairs, and federal finance.

Most Congress ministers are right wingers. This follows the complexion of the Working Committee, which numbers roughly ten right wingers to four left wingers. So the ministers began their legislative programs cautiously. In several provinces they declined to have social relations with the governors, though official relations were quite correct;[1] in Bombay the prime minister introduced a bill banning the British titles and honorifics which flood India every New Year's Day. But they did not attack the fundamentals of British power anywhere; their program of social reform—housing, educa-

---

[1] This is because Congress people will not "sign the book" in Government House, or contribute in any way to "Imperial ritual or prestige." It has led to episodes which would delight authorities in etiquette. In the old days a social-minded Indian might be willing to do almost anything for an invitation to a Government House reception; now, if he is a member of the government, he cannot accept it although the invitations are freely given. He may talk with the Governor in his office; he cannot accept a cup of tea in the drawing room next door. When a new Governor of a province arrives, the Congress ministry which *is* his government cannot even greet him at the railway station. Even Mr. Gandhi, in order to have a social word with a Governor, must go through elaborate stratagems.

tion, reduction of agricultural debt, and so on—got under way slowly. They cut their own salaries to 500 rupees ($185) a month—while their British secretaries might be getting five times that sum—and promised as a first effort at economy to slash salaries in the provincial civil service. Twice—in the U. P. and Bihar in February, 1938, and later in Orissa—Congress governments came into conflict with the governors, and resigned. In each case the issue was compromised, with Congress coming out on top.

In five provinces at least the Congress ministries began to introduce prohibition. It is difficult for an American who saw our prohibition debacle to sympathize with this. But prohibition is a foremost Congress point. It can be introduced only at great cost. Revenue from "toddy" and other alcoholic drink amounts, by and large, to almost *one-quarter* of total provincial revenue. Moreover, the cost of enforcement will be very considerable. Altogether prohibition will mean that Bombay, for instance, may lose almost one-third its revenue, which must be met by other means. The Congress ministers, when they take toddy from the peasant, must cut salaries of school teachers from, say, forty rupees a month to twenty-five.

Most Congress governments, especially Bombay, the United Provinces, Bihar, and Madras, have been unendingly perplexed by the problem of extremism. The situation is peculiar. Here is Congress in office at last, after many years of electoral propaganda and promises. But no matter how well disposed it is, it cannot begin to fulfill these promises at once. In the United Provinces, for instance, Congress held out the bright beacon of land reform. The restive peasantry in the U. P. is demanding action, like liquidation of the agricultural debt, which Congress cannot now perform. Any drastic solution of the land problem like collectivization would instantly lead to severe conflict with the British. In Bihar the *kisans* (peasants), awaiting the promised reforms, refused to pay rent to the landlords, who thereupon refused to pay taxes to the government. Refusal of tax payment to a British government was one thing. Congress sympathized with this and indeed advocated it for years. But boycott of Congress taxes is quite another thing.

Again, the Congress governments, particularly in Bombay, are worried about political agitation by extremists. Take the case of the Congress Minister for Law and Order, Mr. Munshi. For years Mr. Munshi has been part of a movement which taught the people to hate and despise the police; Mr. Munshi himself, like almost all Congress leaders, went to jail for civil disobedience. But now Mr. Munshi is in charge of the police, and sometimes he finds that he has to use them even against his own people. It is an unenviable situation to say the least.

Several Congress ministries have had actually to arrest Congressmen under an act of the Indian penal code which defines sedition and which all good Congressmen, for twenty years, learned to hate like arsenic. Yet in one case all that the offender did was make a speech against recruiting. He got six months. The case has been appealed. The Leftists say that it is intolerable for Congress to prosecute a man for sedition when Congress by its basic nature is itself seditionist, that is, advocates complete severance of the tie with Britain. Another highly unpopular act which gives a magistrate summary right to quell disturbances has had to be invoked by Congress ministers in connection with strikes at Sholapur and Cawnpore—which enraged the rank and file of Congressmen.

It would be easy to make out too harsh a case against the Congress governments. No one can blame them for holding on to office when retirement from office would mean that reactionaries would get the jobs. Administrative experience, which the governments are getting a-plenty, is something Congress has badly needed; these transition years may be a precious interlude for practice. Again, the new legislative programs have begun excellently, even if the governments have held office only a comparatively short time. The experience is just beginning, and it makes a challenging spectacle.

Congress President

The President of the Indian National Congress, reëlected for a second term in 1939, is the remarkable character Subhas Chandra Bose, a stubborn mystic turned politician, who represents an extreme left-wing view. Bose has suffered more than any man in India except perhaps Nehru, whose devoted disciple he is. He has had no fewer than ten terms in jail. His last release came as recently as March, 1937.

Bose was born in 1897 in Cuttack of a good middle-class family; his father was an eminent lawyer. He is one of the comparatively few first-rank Hindu politicians who is not a Brahman. When young Bose was about sixteen he ran away from home and wandered alone in the Himalayas, seeking spiritual refreshment. Like Buddha, he gave up family, wealth, material comforts, and secular affairs, and took youthful refuge in mysticism. But he did not find the guidance he sought. He left the Himalayas after perhaps a year, and continued his pilgrimage in holy cities like Benares. Then suddenly he was stricken with typhoid fever; a friend discovered his identity and returned him to his anguished family, who had had no idea where he was.

Bose had several stormy years of education. He went to the Presidency College in Calcutta, and joined a group which sensationally thrashed an unpopular English professor who, they said, insulted the Indians. He was dismissed from college, and after an interval resumed his studies in England. At the Scottish Church College he took a B.A. with first class honors in philosophy. Then he was graduated with honors at Cambridge, and passed the examinations for the Indian Civil Service; he stood fourth in the list. It was his intention (Nehru had a similar idea) to enter the I. C. S.; but at the end of the war Gandhi and civil disobedience captured him as it captured almost everyone else, and he joined the Swaraj party.

Since that time his whole career, like that of Nehru, has varied between public work as a Congressman and periods in jail. He was the most turbulent of the Indian leaders. He organized the Independence League with Nehru in 1928, and was president of the All-India Trades Union Congress from 1929-31. Several times his health broke down, and he took one brief cure in Europe. In 1930 he was elected Mayor of Calcutta while serving a jail term in Burma.

The British don't like Bose. They fear him, as they fear Nehru. His book, *The Indian Struggle*, is forbidden circulation in India, even though Nehru's more outspoken autobiography is allowed to be sold. Once when Bose was interned in Burma he saw a note in a Calcutta newspaper to the effect that he was "the soul" of the terrorist movement in Bengal; this was not true—Bose is not in any sense a terrorist—and he sued for libel. The newspaper appealed to the Government of India for evidence to back up the charge, but none was forthcoming, and Bose won the case, getting damages.

What Bose stands for is complete severance of the tie with Britain. He said as much frankly in his presidential address at the Haripura Congress in 1938. He is unalterably opposed to the provisions of the Government of India Act in regard to Federation—incorporation of the princely states with British India—and he has stated that if necessary he will oppose Federation, as at present envisaged, with civil disobedience.

Bose is a sturdy figure, despite bouts of ill health. He is stubborn, a good talker, something of a fanatic, and an implacable nationalist. He is unmarried. During the 1939 Tripura Congress, when Gandhi turned against him to the Congress split, he was too ill to take the president's chair in person. Then, in May 1939, he suddenly resigned.

. . . .

Other Congress Leftists of consequence are Govind Vallabh Pant, the prime minister of the United Provinces government; young Jayaprakash Narayan who is general secretary of the Congress Socialist Party; and M. R. Masani, the joint secretary. Masani, a brilliant young Parsi, was for years forbidden to leave India by the British authorities; now, however, since a Congress government has gained power in Bombay, he has his passport back.

Pant (pronounced "Punt") is one of the ablest Congress prime ministers. Massive in build, untidy in appearance, a man gentle and serene in casual talk, but deadly in debate, he was born in the Himalayas of a high Brahman family, and settled in the U. P. as a youth. He had an exceptionally good academic career, and then a period as a lawyer; he soon left the bar, however, to join Congress and devote himself to public work. Though not an extremist, he is very much on the Left. In his cabinet is Mrs. Pandit, Nehru's sister. He is called the best financial mind in Congress.

Thirty-seven-year-old Jayaprakash Narayan, the founder of the Congress Socialist party, is a restless soul who has had a varied and picturesque career. He was born in a tiny village in Bihar; it is recorded that he never saw a street car till he was 19. Then he went to—America. In eight years in the United States he studied at five different universities, starting in California, progressing to Iowa and Wisconsin, and steadily working his way east. He worked in a California orchard first, then as a packer in a jam factory, a mechanic, and a waiter. He became a Marxist, returned to India, joined Nehru, and was put in charge of the Labor Research Department of Congress. He went to prison, and emerged in 1933 to organize the first session of the Congress Socialist party, the left-wing bloc inside Congress.

The socialists include various types of Marxists. Most are fairly radical, though their main preoccupation is of course nationalist opposition to British rule. By and large they are anti-religious, and most of them do not believe in caste; indeed they are contemptuous of caste strictures, and consider the Untouchables from a class point of view, namely, that they are merely the submerged proletariat. The socialists want to organize India in terms of workers and peasants, not on the basis of religious community. The Right in Congress, on the other hand, generally conservative, tends to cling to caste.

The communist party is illegal in India, but many individual communists join Congress. This is a recent development; the old communist line toward India was to consider Congress a bourgeois "agent of imperialism," but in these Popular Front days communists are urged to become Congressmen. The socialists are inclined still to resent the former communist attitude. Communists are of several sorts, with Trotskyism becoming popular. The most interesting personality among communists or ex-communists—he has been disavowed by Moscow—is the well-known M. N. Roy, who has his own group, the "Royists." These are independent radicals within Congress, but whom conservative Congressmen disavow. Roy, a handsome creature, has been a figure in three revolutions: Russian, Chinese, Indian. The Comintern sent him to Hankow in 1927, and his advice, overriding that of Borodin, helped to precipitate the break in the Kuomintang. On his return to India he spent several years in jail.

The Three Zonal Chieftains

We turn now to the Working Committee, that extraordinary organization which is the heart of Congress. Officially there is no precedence within the Working Committee, but the three men nearest the top, each of whom is a kind of district boss—in fact the political organizer and virtual dictator of his region—are Sardar Vallabhbhai Patel (Bombay, Madras, Sind, C. P.), Moulana Abul Kalam Azad (Bengal, Punjab, North West Frontier, and U. P.), and Babu Rajendra Prasad (Bihar, Assam, Orissa).

These three names are unfamiliar. New to most western readers, they are difficult to pronounce, to remember. Yet these three men, quite aside from the fact that next to Gandhi and Nehru they are the most important political personages in India, are tremendous personalities. Their names may mean little. But their histories, their characters, mean much. Behind the difficult names are living human beings of the utmost interest and appeal.

Sardar Patel ("Sardar" is a kind of title) is the chief right winger in Congress. He is the party boss par-excellence. He is the Jim Farley, the ruthless party fixer and organizer. Once Gandhi has determined the line to take, it is Patel who rams it through, as happened at Tripura in 1939. He is creator of the political machine, and he virtually controls the eight Congress ministries.

Patel is sixty-one. He is a solidly built man with a great bald skull; he looks rather like a Roman emperor in the heroic tradition. He calls himself a "simple farmer"—which he most distinctly is not— though he was born on a farm; some one said of him once that his only culture is "agriculture." He has nothing of Nehru's grace and intellectual precision, and very little of Rajagopalacharia's subtle inflections of mind and mood; he has no vision beyond the immediate task in hand, and almost none of Gandhi's religious impulses—for instance it is said that he never had read the Hindu scriptures till last year; but he is a man of action, of practicality: the man who gets things done. As such, he is one of Gandhi's very closest collaborators.

Patel was born in the Kaira district of Gujerat. His father fought in the Sepoy Mutiny against Britain, and his elder brother was an eminent Congressman, but as a youth he showed little interest in politics. He was a pertinacious student; he decided to become a lawyer, and his subsequent career in criminal law was distinguished; he was a great defense attorney in murder cases. When Gandhi returned to India from South Africa Patel came under his spell. But it took some time to convert him. The story is told that, when Gandhi first entered the Ahmedabad club to convert the members to non-violence, Patel sat in a corner shrugging, playing cards, and cynically smiling. Then he saw Gandhiji's tremendous self-assurance, and, a strong man himself, came to admire him. When the Mahatma began the civil disobedience campaign Patel gave up his flourishing law practice, like Motilal Nehru, to join him.

Years ago Patel, whose nerves are filaments of ice, was arguing a case in court. A telegram was handed to him. It announced the death of his wife. He read it, folded it, put it in his pocket, and continued the case without interruption or change of mien.

Many expert observers of Indian affairs think that Patel may turn out to be Stalin to Gandhi's Lenin—perhaps with Jawaharlal as Trotsky. Certainly if an open split should occur in Congress Patel would be leader of the Right.

The next member of the "zonal triumvirate," Moulana (roughly "Very Reverend") Abul Kalam Azad, is as different from Patel as is conceivable. The two represent utterly different worlds; but the link of Congress bridges their variegation. Moulana Abul, who is 50, is a Moslem theologian and philosopher, one of the most learned men of the East, a bookworm-intellectual, a savant, the author of the best modern commentary on the Koran. He was born in Mecca in 1888, and went to Al Azhar University in Cairo, the most famous institution of learning in the Moslem world. Something of a prodigy, he was at fifteen a serious scholar in Persian, Arabic, and Moslem theology. He went to India (where his father had lived) and in 1912 founded an Urdu newspaper, *Al Hilal,* which had a sensational success. Abul was, though an orthodox Moslem, a modernist. His attitude toward Islam is reformist. He sought to bring the Moslems into the nationalist movement; he is one of the few Indians who began important agitation before Gandhiji's great entrance to the arena. As early as 1916 Abul was interned on a charge of revolutionary activity. He was released in 1920 and promptly joined the non-coöperation movement.[2] In 1923 he was elected President of Congress—the youngest in its history.

Abul's unique characteristic is his combination of classic theological training and modern outlook. He went to Al Ahzar; but he wants to Latinize the various Indian scripts. He is an excellent political speaker and journalist, despite his absorption in holy books. Nowadays he lives in Calcutta when he is not traveling on Congress jobs. As we have just seen, Gandhi wanted Abul as President in 1939.

If Patel is the ruthless fist of the Congress triumvirate, and Moulana Abul a part of the brain and spiritual enlightenment, then Babu Rajendra Prasad is the heart. This man has great personal quality.

Prasad was born in 1884. He had a first-rate career at Calcutta

[2] He was also a very prominent figure in what is known as the "Khilafat" issue; Gandhi worked closely with the Moslems in attacking the British because of the peace treaty with Turkey and the consequent reduction in power of the Turkish (Moslem) Caliph.

University—his scholastic accomplishments are still talked of—and then successively became teacher and professor of English, History, and Economics, until he decided to devote himself to the law. He is one of the great lawyers of modern India. He earned a great deal of money, but when, in 1920, he resigned his practice to follow Gandhi and non-coöperation, he had exactly 15 rupees in the bank. He had given his entire fortune to poor students. He is one of Gandhi's warmest friends, and next to him is probably the most beloved man in India; he is mild and engaging in manner, and without an enemy. Prasad is a simple person, with little regard for personal appearance; he looks like an unkempt peasant. Once when he was in jail a delegation of British officials passed by his cell. "Obviously a criminal type," said one Englishman, pointing to him. Prasad smiled—not bothering to add that he spoke seven languages. Had he not joined Gandhi, he would have certainly reached the highest position possible to an Indian in British India; he would have been a Supreme Court Judge or a Provincial Governor. Since 1912 he has been a member of the All-India Congress Committee, and since 1922—seventeen uninterrupted years—a member of the Working Committee. He was Congress President in 1934. He is undisputed leader of Bihar.

. . . .

Two other men should be mentioned in particular connection with Vallabhbhai Patel,[3] because they too are far on the Right. One is Jamnalal Bajaj, the former treasurer of Congress; he is a very rich and successful business man, who renounced his titles and went to jail when he came under Gandhi's influence. He lives in Wardha, in the Central Provinces, which is one reason why the Mahatma lives there; usually he accompanies Gandhi on his travels. The other is Ghanshyamdas Birla, a Calcutta industrialist and millionaire. Like Bajaj, he belongs to the Marwari community (Hindus traditionally of the occupation of money-lenders) ; like Bajaj, he resists socialist influence in Congress. Commonly it is assumed that Birla very conspicuously helps to finance Congress. The organization could not live on its four anna subscriptions alone, and contributions from Birla and his friends are important. Birla, however, unlike Bajaj, is not a member of the Working Committee.

[3] Pronounced to rhyme with "lullaby," incidentally.

Congress Center

Three more members of the Working Committee, each in a special category, are the poetess Mrs. Sarojini Naidu, the soldier Khan Abdul Gaffar Khan, and the lawyer Bhulabhai J. Desai.

How can one possible imprison Mrs. Naidu's tremendous and aggressively radiant personality in a paragraph or two? One of the great women of Asia, she is a poetess, a revolutionary, a passionate worker for Hindu-Moslem unity, an eloquent orator in several tongues, a politician, a soldier. For a time, when other members of the Working Committee were in jail in 1932, she was in charge of the civil disobedience movement. Mrs. Naidu is an exceptionally dominant individual. The story is that, on one occasion, the police were terrified by having to arrest her, and she visited police station after police station demanding to be jailed; the police, once they had her, dutifully took her advice on what to do next.

But her arduous career has not masculinized her. Mrs. Naidu is a woman. She loves laughter. She loves her children, her friends. She is the gayest politician in India, and the first Indian hostess of the land. She likes to bring people together, and her salon in the Taj Mahal Hotel in Bombay is famous.

Mrs. Naidu was born in 1879 in Hyderabad, Deccan, of a distinguished Brahman family. Her father was a Doctor of Science who went to Edinburgh University; her mother was a poetess of distinction, her husband a physician. She began writing poetry at the age of twelve, and next to Tagore she is the best known poet in India. She has traveled widely out of India, and is probably the most cosmopolitan of the Indian leaders. She was President of Congress in 1925. She worked for days on her inaugural speech—she hates to write her speeches out—and then decided that she could not be bound by a mere manuscript and at the last moment delivered, extemporaneously, a different one.

Once I asked Mrs. Naidu what made all the members of the Working Committee revolutionaries, what was the common denominator between them. She answered that it was because Indians were a subject people. She is a vibrant and emphatic nationalist. But she is other things too. She has worked forty years for the rights of women, against the abuses of *purdah* and child marriage, and for the intellectual and moral advance of India.

"The one sin," she wrote once, "is fear . . . We are cowards by compulsion . . . How shall I bring together the scattered, demoralized, and conflicting forces of the Indian people? If only I could destroy this patience of yours!"

Khan Abdul Gaffer Khan ("Khan" means chief, and most Pathans use the word at least once in their names) is the tall soldier from the north west frontier who is leader of the Red Shirts, the Congress private army in the frontier area. Their shirts are not red to indicate political conviction, but because brick dust provides the cheapest local dye. Khan Abdul differs from Moulana Abul, the only other Moslem on the Working Committee, considerably. He is a fighter, not a theologian; he is six feet six inches tall, and from head to heel a soldier. A devoted follower of the Mahatma, he is often called "the Frontier Gandhi." His political importance is that he, a Moslem, has great prestige in the frontier region, and made the victory of Congress possible there; the North West Frontier Province is the only Moslem province with a Congress government. The prime minister, Dr. Khan Sahib, a doctor of medicine with an English wife, is his brother. Their grandfather, incidentally, fought in the Indian mutiny —on the British side.

If deadlock should some day come between Nehru on the Left and Patel on the Right for supreme headship of Congress, Bhulabhai Desai might be a compromise choice as leader. He is in charge of Congress in the Central Legislature at Delhi, and thus is Leader of His Majesty's Opposition in India; he will probably be the first federal prime minister of India, if Federation comes. Desai is a distinguished lawyer. Everyone refers to him by his first rather than his last name. He is a late-comer to Congress, having been active in politics only since about 1932. He then joined Civil Disobedience and dutifully went to jail; the British considered him to be extremely respectable, however, and his confinement was not arduous. Desai is a Brahman, but his religious sentiments are inconspicuous. He was born in Gujerat in 1877, his manner is suave and graceful, and Gandhi likes him.

The Brahman Savonarola

The prime minister of Madras, though not at present a member of the Working Committee, is one of the half dozen most important men in India. He bears the complicated name of Chakravarti Raja-

gopalacharia (in Sanskrit Chakravarti means "World Conqueror"!),
which is quite a mouthful even for Indians; everywhere he is known
simply as "C. R." Rajagopalacharia, born of a distinguished Brahman family about sixty years ago, became a lawyer and then a politician; for twenty years he has been closer to Gandhi (whose son
married his daughter, as I have noted) than any other man in India
except possibly Patel and Nehru. He is unchallenged boss of Madras,
and a dominant figure—very much to the Right—in the party councils.

Rajagopalacharia looks like Savonarola. Indeed he might have been,
as Mrs. Naidu has said, a wonderful Renaissance prince or prelate.
An accomplished dialectician, he is sometimes called the "Tamil
Mahatma"; the story is that at those supreme moments when even
Gandhiji cannot devise a formula, C. R. is called in to invent one.
His intellect is so subtle, so refined, so delicate, that one is tempted
to ignore his capacities as an administrator, which are considerable.
He could, like Rajendra Prasad, have reached any height in British
India; like so many other Indians, he gave up everything to follow
Gandhi.

C. R. is a fanatic about three things: the first is prohibition. As
soon as he assumed office he introduced the first prohibition legislation in India; he turned his own home district dry—oddly enough it
has the name Salem, redolent of other puritanism across the sea.
Second, he believes in *khadder* and village spinning. Third, he wants
economy in administration, and has drastically cut provincial salaries.
Rajagopalacharia is deeply religious, a fanatic Brahman, and a confirmed ascetic. He is probably the only man alive—except John Tunis,
the American tennis expert—who until last year had never seen a
moving picture. Some friends prevailed upon C. R. to go to a
Mickey Mouse film. The great Brahman was bewildered.

* * * * * * *

Among other Congress prime ministers I have mentioned briefly
Mr. Pant of the U. P. and Dr. Khan Sahib on the Frontier. One more
who deserves a word is certainly Balghanghader G. Kher, the prime
minister of Bombay. He was a dark horse, little known before 1935;
he became prime minister partly because of rivalry between two
more conspicuous men for the post, and Mr. Gandhi took him as a
compromise candidate. He is an exceptionally modest man. The
British governor of Bombay offered once to give him a large placard,

"I Am Prime Minister of Bombay Presidency," to hang in front of his bed, so that he would see it on arising every morning and thus become more conscious of his importance. Kher, a Brahman, was a poor boy who—of all odd things—got his education by reading to a blind man. His record in office has been excellent, though Bombay, like all the other provinces, has been crippled by lack of revenue. Tremendous programs of social welfare and reform must await complete fiscal authority. Kher's most prominent cabinet minister is the eminent and quick spoken Gujerati scholar and lawyer, K. M. Munshi, who is in charge of law and order.

Chapter XXVII
The World of the Great Princes

~~~~~~

IN THESE Indian chapters so far we have been discussing British India. But there are two Indias. Unlike Gaul, India is divided into two parts. On the one hand there are the eleven provinces and various administrative districts of *British India*, ruled in the last analysis by the Viceroy and the India Office in London (which is responsible to the British parliament), but to which the machinery of democracy has come since the new Government of India Act in 1935. On the other hand there is the India of the native states, *Princely India,* which is totally a distinct and different matter.

British India is, in a word, the three-fifths of India which the British, beginning with the East India Company, carved out of the great sub-continent by force of arms. It is the direct result of imperialism of a very direct sort. Princely India in a word is the two-fifths of India which the British did not choose to conquer by this means. They control it as indisputably as they control British India, but in a different manner, through a series of complex treaties and the doctrine known as "paramountcy." The Princes recognize the suzerainty of the British Crown, but in everything except foreign affairs they consider themselves autonomous.

There are 562 princely or native states. Not being a part of British India, British law or laws made by Delhi do not affect them. They are not in the sphere of Provincial Autonomy. They have their own armies, governments, prime ministers, law courts, police; some have their own customs, railways, postage, coinage. No British troops are allowed in princely territory: but conveniently the British have "enclaves" at adjacent strategic points. The people in princely India are not, technically speaking, even British subjects, though they need British passports if they travel outside India. British imperialism again shows its amazing elasticity. . . . Princes claim to be representatives of the original populations of India. Some, like the Rajputs, had ancient and distinguished kingdoms; some were Mahratta invaders and marauders; some came with Islam.

A word as to statistics. British India comprises roughly 818,000 square miles, with a population of 256,534,000 by the 1931 Census, more than twice the population of the United States. This is 58.2 percent of the area of All-India (excluding certain tribal areas), and 75.8 percent of the All-India population. Princely India covers 690,000 square miles (roughly 41.7 per cent of the All-India total), and contains about 80,000,000 people, which is about 23.6 per cent of the total population. Thus, whereas about two-fifths of India belongs to the Princes, their peoples number less than one-quarter of the total population.

The main characteristic of the princely states is that they are autocracies. They are anachronistic pools of absolutism in the modern world, and they control the lives and fortunes of 80,000,000 people. Slowly, stertorously, the route of democracy—however incomplete and hedged in with restrictions—has advanced in British India. But whether a native state should relax its autocratic absolutism—or not— has been purely its own business.

In most of the native states there is no habeas corpus. In only about 40 is judicial authority separated from executive authority. Only about 40 out of 562 have High Courts; only about 30 have any so-called legislatures, and these are consultative in power, with nominated members in most cases. In some states newspapers are forbidden; in most the ruler has life and death powers over his subjects; in some the people may be bought and sold like serfs. In most states the ruler, who may be recklessly extravagant, commands the entire state income. There are, it should be noted, a few—a very few—"good" states, like Mysore and Travancore, where administration is in general as good as in British India, or better. But states like Mysore are exceptional.

The anomaly, the paradox, between the law of British India and the lack of law in the native states, became too glaring. It was impossible for fairminded people to envisage the spectacle of three-fifths of India progressing toward self-government, no matter with what lurching interruptions, while two-fifths remained purely feudal. It was bad morals. It was bad politics. It was unworkable and archaic.

Thus came the tremendous project of Federation. The Government of Asia is in two parts; the first set up Provincial Autonomy in British India, as we know, the second proposes federation of British India with the Princely States, in order to abolish the anomaly of two Indias, and to bring the princes and the provincial governments into a single federal structure. The British had several motives for this. We will discuss them later. The point to make now is that the project of Federation, or coalescence, is the biggest problem of contemporary India. It is in fact one of the biggest—and most onerous and exacting —problems in the world, that of trying to create a United India for the first time in centuries.

And what manner of men are these princes, these maharajas, who now face the threshold of modern times?

The Late Maharaja of Alwar

Last year a man died in Paris. His name was Alwar. More completely, his name was Colonel His Highness Sewai Maharaj Shri Jey Singhji, G.C.S.I., G.C.I.E., Maharaja of Alwar. He ruled a state in Rajputana, near Delhi, 3,158 square miles in extent (half the size of New Jersey), with a population of 750,000, and an annual income of 3,680,000 rupees ($1,261,000). He had an army of about 1,250 men, and a police force of 883. His salute was 15 guns.

This Maharaja of Alwar was one of the most extraordinary human beings of recent times. He was a little bit of a saint; and a good deal of a sadist. He was double-natured to an amazing degree, combining extreme purity of motive with the most savage cruelty. He was like a prince in 16th century Italy: crazy, cruel, brilliant, devious, and indescribably arrogant, a bizarre creature of pride and vice.

He could not bear that anyone should touch him. Once at dinner a lady, admiring a ruby on his finger, asked to inspect it. Promptly he took the ring off and gave it to her. She handed it back. He gave the ruby to the servant behind him, with the words, "Wash it."

But this was an unusual occurrence, because as a rule the Maharaja of Alwar wore gloves in company. One story is that, when he was about to be received at Buckingham Palace, the court chamberlains were paralyzed with embarrassment, because they knew that Alwar never took his gloves off, and also that the late King George V had said that he would not shake hands with "that man" with his gloves on. Until the last possible moment, as he advanced, Alwar kept his hands concealed—and all the servants in suspense. Then, with an arrogant gesture, he did condescend to expose his right hand.

Alwar had a savage sense of humor. On a trip he got word that his "guru," or spiritual adviser, had died at home. Alwar wanted to see him again, and ordered the body to be pickled in spirits until his return.

He was insanely proud. He once telegraphed a friend that he could not keep an appointment in Bombay because he had missed not his train, but his "special train." As if a man could miss a special train! The point was that his credit was exhausted, and the railway people would not give him any more special trains.

He spent a very considerable share of the state revenues on himself. For some years he blocked stubbornly an attempt by the British to push a road through his territory which would link Delhi and Jaipur by a direct route. He protested that the road would spoil his tigers! He would order ditches dug across the new road every night, to obstruct it.

He was a wonderful shot. This, however, did not assuage the feelings of native women, his subjects, when he took their living babies for bait at tiger shoots. He would say calmly that they should not worry, he was sure to get the tiger before the tiger got the baby.

Sometimes, to improve shooting, he would remove, tear up, eradicate, destroy whole villages, and let the people roam away to starve.

He constantly quarreled with the British in his capital. One British official plead with him not to be "vindictive." It was the word of rebuke the Englishman always chose. One day he came to see Alwar; he was in a horrified rage. Before he could say anything, Alwar walked to the writing table, scribbled on it, and said, "I know what you are going to say. I will write what you are going to say." And he handed the official a piece of paper scrawled with the word "vindictive."

What Alwar had done was to take a pony which had disappointed him in a polo match, pour gasoline over it, and set it afire, alive.

Finally the British deposed Alwar. In extreme cases, the government of India will "extern" an errant prince. But only half a dozen have been so externed in recent years, and usually it is for a political, not a personal, offense. The British eliminate a Maharaja only with extreme reluctance, and as a rule only if the ruler gets politically unruly. Alwar might have gone on murdering polo ponies for years. But he was considered politically "unreliable." Also part of his realm had risen in revolt. . . .

Alwar died in Paris in exile. His body was shipped home to India, embalmed by a special process so that the corpse might be properly exhibited. He wished this. He was carried through the streets of his capital, his dead face haughty, dressed in his most blazing uniform, his jewels resplendent—and with sunglasses to "protect" his eyes!

And some of the Alwar citizenry lined the streets, watched the grisly procession, bowed to the ground as they did when the ruler passed in life, groaned, and wept.

A Bouquet of Princes

Alwar was not typical. There are maharajas of many groups and breeds. Indeed it is almost impossible to generalize about them. There are maharajas of subtle and sophisticated intelligence, like the late Gaekwar of Baroda, and men of the highest morality, like the Maharaja of Mysore; there are others in the Central Indian Agency who are literally savages. There are maharajas with rubies on their toes worth $100,000; there are others whose annual income is only a few rupees.

Their names and titles are fantastic, like the Jam of Nawanagar or the Wali of Swat. To address the Maharaja of Patiala correctly, one has to insert somewhere in the name, which is elephantine in length anyway, the word "Sri" (lord) 108 times. To shorten the process (I am cutting out innumerable sub-names), the Maharaja of Patiala is called simply Lieutenant-General His Highness Farzand-i-Khas-i-Daulat-i-Inglishia Sri 108 Maharajadhiraj Mohinder Bahadur. The "108" goes in like an algebraic device.

Some maharajas in Rajputana belong to the "Solar" or "Lunar" branches of Rajputs; some derive from the Abbasid caliphs of Bagdad; one, Jaisalmer, claims descent literally from Krishna, the Hindu god. One maharaja, the ruler of Aundh, has written a book on physical culture; another, Rewa, aged only 34, asserts that he has already shot five hundred tigers. Several rulers, like Vadia, enforce prohibition in their states; others have consumed more than a normal budget of champagne. In one state the chief justice was also chief inspector of dancing girls.

One maharaja, young Cooch Behar, went to Harrow[1] and Trinity College, Cambridge; several have never been to school at all. One maharaja, Ihrangadhra, has married five times, and one, who shall be nameless, has at least one hundred children; others are as ascetic as Mysore or frugal as Hyderabad. One maharaja, Rajpipla, won the Derby in 1934 with Windsor Lad; one, Indore, lost his throne over the affair of Mumtaz Begum, a dancing girl; one, Gondal, is an M.D. from Edinburgh and has written a history of Aryan medical science.

[1] And sat at Jawaharlal Nehru's old desk!

Sometimes the language of maharajas is flowery. One, Balasinor, belongs to people "famous not for their kingly pomp, dignity, and splendor, but for their luxuriance of benevolence and exuberance of magnificence." Sometimes floweriness in speech is all they have. Some maharajas are as poor as others are inordinately and fantastically rich. Hyderabad is enormous, but Banka has an area of five square miles. Consider Amrapur, population 407, area two square miles; Bihora, population 266, area 1.75 square miles; and Bilbari, population 27, area 1.65 square miles. The annual revenue of Bilbari is solemnly given as 80 rupees ($29.60).

The princes have, and have had for more than fifteen years, a sort of trade union. It is called the Chamber of Princes; every maharaja with a salute of eleven guns or more is a member with one vote; 127 states with fewer guns share twelve other votes. In recent years the chancellorship has more or less alternated between the maharajas of Patiala and of Bikaner. The Chamber does not do too much. Most members are jealous of their comrades, and states like Mysore and Hyderabad participate little. It has no legislative powers.

The things the maharajas are proudest of are not their jewels, not their harems, not their medieval splendor (if they can afford splendor), but their guns. Take a gun away from a maharaja; it means more than losing an arm. Sometimes people suggest that giving certain princes more guns would be a convenient form of bribery. But it wouldn't work. The gun structure is more complex, more zealously guarded, than the hierarchy of Burke's peerage. Some states, like Jaipur and Jodhpur, are, the British admit, "undergunned," but to step them up would cause no end of trouble.

The maharajas with guns are so sensitive about them because they are a symbol of sovereignty; the British *raj* salutes them thus. The guns make a considerable racket. When the Chamber of Princes meets in Delhi, and each prince gets his salute on arrival at the railway station, the noise is cataclysmic. The princes, like children, adore this. The rule is that no salutes are fired on Sunday. Some princes wait in their royal trains all day Sunday, if they arrive that day, so that the proper salutes may be fired Monday morning.

149 of the 562 states have guns. The others are condemned to silence. There are only five 21-gun states; these are the lush states, the states with biceps and heavy shoulders. They are Hyderabad, Mysore, Baroda, Kashmir, Gwalior. There are six 19-gun states—

Kalat, Indore, Bhopal, Kholapur, Travancore, and Udaipur. And there are twelve with 17 guns—Rewa, Cochin, Patiala, Bahawalpur, Jaipur, Jodhpur, Bundi, Bikaner, Kotah, Bharatpur, Tonk, and Kutch.

The British control the princely states through an organism known as the Political Department. This is the branch of the Delhi governments, responsible directly to the Viceroy, which appoints the British Residents and Agents-General scattered throughout Princely India. Not every state has a British resident; for instance the Maharaja of Bikaner is permitted to rule without one. Several states, like Jaipur and Jodhpur, share one resident; the smaller states are grouped together into agencies, and one British agent-general may have thirty or forty different states to handle. The residents in the 21-gun states are usually distinguished members of the Indian Civil Service who are near retirement but have missed becoming governors of provinces in British India, the supreme job. They get Mysore or Hyderabad as compensation.

Often it is said that the British residents directly rule the states. The generalization is too broad. Circumstances vary. The ordinary maharaja takes care to be on good terms with the Resident, and as a rule sees eye to eye with him. Residents seldom have to dictate to maharajas. All the states admit the sovereignty of the British crown, but the Resident seldom interferes with internal administration. "The most important part of a Resident's job," I heard it said, "is what he doesn't do." In the event of grave crisis, of course the British *raj* can do anything it likes.

Almost every maharaja has, if not a complete cabinet, a prime minister, the *Dewan*. The maharaja may himself be the head of the cabinet council, in which case the Dewan becomes vice-president; in most cases the Dewan, whatever his official title, does the work. These Dewans are a curious phenomenon. They are chosen from any part of India and from any profession, though most of them are lawyers; they are not necessarily citizens of the states they administer; often they circulate, serving several states in succession, as a kind of special caste of itinerant prime ministers. Some are exceptionally able and distinguished men. As a rule a maharaja choosing a Dewan consults the Political Department as to the talent available, and—as a rule but not always—consent of the Political Department is necessary before an appointment takes effect.

Now, an illuminating point, some twenty Dewans are not Indians but British. These are usually retired members of the Indian Civil Service who are offered private jobs with maharajas and who accept; they are—I mean no offense—political mercenaries. They have no formal or official relation with British India; they owe sole allegiance to the native state that employs them. Jaipur, Jodhpur, Cooch Behar, Bundi, Tonk, Kapurthala, are among important states with British Dewans. The only 21-gun state ever to have a British Dewan was Kashmir. In addition many states, like Hyderabad and Rampur, employ British experts as finance ministers; many choose British retired colonels as military advisers, like Jaipur; several, like Mysore, appoint retired British judges as justices of their High Courts.

The Political Department, it goes without saying, knows everything it needs to know about every maharaja. There are secret files and dossiers.

The Miser of Hyderabad

Hyderabad is the premier Indian state. It is a solid block of territory in the center of India, with a population of 14,500,000, an area of 82,698 square miles (as big as Kansas, almost as big as England and Wales), and an annual revenue of 85,000,000 rupees. Its ruler, the Nizam, is the only Indian potentate entitled to be called His "Exalted" Highness. He was born in 1886, and is a slight, shy, strange, and cultivated man.

H. E. H. the Nizam of Hyderabad is popularly reputed to be the richest man in the world, though the Emperor of Japan would outrank him by some standards. No one can estimate the amount of his fortune accurately, but competent guesses put his annual income at $50,000,000, his fortune in gold bars at $250,000,000, his collection of jewelry at no less than $2,000,000,000. Not everyone knows that, despite his incredible wealth, the Nizam is afflicted with almost pathological tendencies to parsimony. His palace is shabby; his habits are frugal; he drives a 26 year-old Rolls-Royce. The story is that he selects his own mangoes, haggling over the price, that to save laundry bills he wears one ancient white suit, and rests in his bath while it is being patched or washed.

The Nizam often writes poems in Persian; recently he broke into print in English with a Christmas lyric:

Blest in his birth, the son of Miriam came,
Heaven's secret—and man's glory at its height!
Auspicious fate! the Magic of his name,
Fills votaries' hearts with love, their eyes with light.

Auspicious hour that to the Temple brought
The living Word, the Messenger ordained,
As though the breath of Morn life's garden sought
And Rose and Nightingale in love enchained!

Spring blew its breath into the crystal bowl,
To give a brighter color to the Wine;
And that December for the World's dead soul
Held in the Cup of Life a draught divine!

Osman! He came as Prophet and as Guide
To lead the Nations in the Righteous Way.
The Faith was firmly planted ere he died,
His destined task completed in his day.

—Reprinted from the *Madras Mail*.

The Nizam is a Moslem of distinguished lineage; under the ruling clique of Moslem landlords and aristocrats, however, the people are 90% Hindus. This makes the chief political issue in Hyderabad. The wives of the Nizam's two sons are cousins; one is a daughter, one a niece, of the last Sultan of Turkey. No Nizam, incidentally, has ever left India.

The Nizam is fortunate in that his Dewan or prime minister is quite possibly the most distinguished Indian politician outside Congress, 70 year-old Sir Akbar Hydari. Born in Bombay of a good but not rich Moslem family, Hydari had a brilliant scholastic career, then entered the Indian Audit and Accountancy Service, which in those days was the only imperial service in which Indians had much chance. He rose quickly, went to Hyderabad, and became finance minister to the former Nizam, though the British resented his appointment. He was considered too able, too independent; he did not get a knighthood till 1928. Now, however, the British admire him, and recognize the great rôle he may play with the advent of Federation; he is one of the very few Indians who is a Privy Counsellor. His son, a civil servant, is married to a Swedish lady. A great humanist, Hydari is proud of two achievements; he founded the Osmania University in Hyderabad, and he was largely responsible for the restoration of the incomparable Ajanta caves. Pavlowa once created and named a dance for him.

The Nizam has been supposed to be somewhat cool to the idea of Federation, because he knows that inevitably it will produce some democratization of his domain; an era will end, and neither Hyderabad nor any state will be quite the autocracy it was. But Akbar Hydari, of all the Dewans of India, is the one who favors Federation most.

The State of Mysore

Mysore, in the deep south, with almost as many people as Belgium or the City of New York, is called a model state. In education, public health, electrification of villages, irrigation, industrialization, it has accomplishments that British India might emulate. Two remarkable men are largely responsible for this, the Maharaja of Mysore and his prime minister, Sir Mirza Ismail.

The Maharaja is an absolutist, but his autocracy no more resembles that of princes like the late Maharajas of Alwar or Patiala than tea resembles ink. They have a generic relationship; that is all. Mysore is one of the saintliest men in India. He has no vices, no interest in the life of the flesh; he lives remotely in his palace, a recluse and an ascetic; he spends each week-end in prayer and meditation. Almost uniquely among maharajas, he lives on a civil list, with his personal moneys separate from State funds. He has a Moslem Dewan, a British private secretary, and a Christian aide-de-camp.

The Maharaja of Mysore takes Hinduism, his religion, with extreme seriousness, though he is not a Brahman. For many years he refused to leave India, because orthodox Hindus lose caste by crossing water; in 1936, however, he made his first trip to Europe. The Maharaja travels always in a special train to avoid pollution; the story is that he bathes, to remove pollution, even after receiving such a foreigner as the British Resident. On the other hand, once he got to London he went about almost as an ordinary tourist, insisting with alacrity on seeing everything. Recently he made a pilgrimage to Tibet.

Sir Mirza Ismail, his Dewan, is a shrewd, industrious, highly competent administrator who knows every stick and stone in Mysore, who looks under the carpets in public buildings to see if any dust is there, who is a kind of super-efficiency expert for the whole state. He is a Mohammedan, whose family came from Persia three generations ago; his father was an A. D. C. to the Maharaja's father, and he and the present Maharaja grew up together; they have been friends for forty years. Ismail has a passion for neatness, for precision. He has considerable political sense, and keeps in touch with everything;[2] he wants to industrialize Mysore by sound engineering methods. He and Gandhi are good friends, though he does not get on with Nehru.

Sir Mirza's family only recently came out of *purdah*. He has strong instincts for public service, and his son, too, recently became a Dewan—the youngest in India—in the small state of Banganapalle, near Madras. Ismail has influenced and trained several young maharajas elsewhere; the rulers of both Travancore and Gwalior, for instance, are his protégés. His salary is modest considering his job—5,000 rupees per month, or $1850.

Ismail is an emphatic proponent of Federation. He thinks princes who oppose it are foolishly obscurantist, since Federation will turn out to be a kind of insurance for their survival. But he wants a *quid pro quo* for Mysore's entry to the federal scheme. It is in two parts, (a) removal of the British garrison from the vicinity of Bangalore, (b) reduction in the "tribute" which Mysore pays the British *raj*.

The Congress has recently renewed political agitation in most of the princely states, especially the advanced ones like Mysore. This is, of course, so that Congress will have a good foothold when—or if—Federation comes, and in order to exert pressure on the maharajas. Most of the princely authorities have vigorously opposed such agitation. Congress has been declared illegal in Hyderabad and Travancore, and late in 1938 demonstrations were put down with serious bloodshed in several states.

Travancore

This—if you forget its opposition to Congress—is one of the most progressive states in India. Like Mysore, it is run by an exceptionally competent Dewan, Sir C. P. Ramaswami Aiyer. Aiyer was for a long time a Congressman, who once worked closely with Nehru; he left Congress, had a scholarly career at the bar, went to London with the

[2] He subscribes to the New York *Times*, the Books supplement of the New York *Herald-Tribune*, the New York *Nation* (to tell him about the Left), the Chicago *Tribune* ("to get the point of view of the Middle West" he told me), the *Reader's Digest*, and of course all the British political periodicals.

Round Table Conference, wrote a constitution for Kashmir, and for a time was an acting cabinet minister in Delhi. In 1936 he entered the service of the youthful Maharaja of Travancore. The state has the best literacy rate in India—41 per cent—and has had a legislative council since 1888.

One reason why both Mysore and Travancore have had such good administrations—though one must keep in mind that, like all the states, they are autocracies—is that each was ruled for long years by a very exceptional woman. Before the present Maharaja of Mysore began rule his mother was Regent for ten years, and a wise old woman she was; similarly Travancore had a decade of regency under the present Maharaja's able mother. Incidentally in Travancore and other regions in the extreme south, like the Malabar Coast, inheritance is not from father to son but from uncle to nephew; society is matriarchal, and succession—in the matter of ordinary property rights and inheritance as well as princely rule—is through a woman.

Travancore became famous in 1936 for opening its temples to the Untouchables. This was an unprecedented step, particularly notable because Travancore like the rest of southern India was a hotbed, a citadel, of extreme religious conservatism. The youthful maharaja, on Aiyer's advice, decided nevertheless to give the miserable Untouchables the right to pray. The sensation was considerable. At least one political reason led to the decision, namely that Untouchables were turning Christian by the thousand, and joining the large Christian population of Travancore (mostly agricultural workers descended from Syrian settlers) to make political agitation. A proposal was on the books to enlarge the Travancore legislature with a new suffrage law. The Untouchables and Christians started a boycott which took an anti-Maharaja tinge. This frightened the dominant Brahmans. The reform has also been useful in that Untouchables from all parts of India have poured into Travancore, in order to pray, which has increased tourist revenue.

The nearby state of Cochin early in 1938 initiated a considerable political reform, creation of a ministry actually responsible to a legislature. This shows how the democratic wind is blowing in the native states. A nephew of a former Maharaja of Cochin recently resigned from the ruling house, joined Congress, and became a Congress organizer.

Kashmir and the Former Mr. A.

In considerable contrast to Mysore and Hyderabad is the third of the great 21-gun states, Kashmir in the far north. Its complexion is the reverse of Hyderabad's, since it is a ninety-two percent Moslem state ruled by an infinitesimal Hindu oligarchy. It is bigger than Hyderabad, (85,885 square miles), but its population, 3,646,000, is much less. The maharaja, born in 1895, faced severe internal discontent which grew into an armed uprising in 1932. A commission of inquiry headed by the present head of the Political Department, Sir Bertrand Glancy, reported on a number of grievances and suggested reforms. For instance Kashmir has 1,990 villages, but only 842 primary schools; there were complaints of forced labor for the benefit of the state; widespread corruption was found in the police and other administrative officials. Kashmir is one of the backward states of India. The Hindu oligarchy demands the strictest observance of religious principles, though the population is overwhelmingly Moslem. And the Moslems don't like it that they have to go to jail for seven years if they kill a cow.

The Maharaja of Kashmir and Jammu is named Sir Hari Singh. In 1925 in London, as "Mr. A.," he was the central figure and victim in a celebrated £300,000 blackmail case. In court Sir John Simon called him "a poor, green, shivering, abject wretch."

The Three Mahratta States

Baroda is one of the great states. The venerable Gaekwar, its ruler for 63 years, ascended the throne as a boy of 13; this was in 1875, before Queen Victoria became Empress of India. For many years Baroda was probably the most modern and progressive native state, but lately others have been catching up, especially since the Gaekwar was too old to pay close attention to administration. Baroda is rich, it faces the sea, and its people are hard-working and lively Gujeratis and Mahrattas. It is the scene of much of Louis Bromfield's novel, *The Rains Came*. The Gaekwar died in January, 1939.

He was an extraordinarily compelling old man—and with an extraordinarily compelling old consort—who was the son of a poor shepherd; nevertheless, he was adjudged the rightful successor to the previous maharaja. He got into trouble at the 1912 Durbar by not bowing low enough to King George V. Beyond dispute one of the ablest men in India, he was also popular and respected elsewhere. He was the first native ruler, be it said to his honor, to introduce free and compulsory primary education in his realm. He had a jeweled sword worth $1,200,000.

The ruler of the nearby state Gwalior, also a 21-gun state, is a young man of 22, very much dominated by his mother. He is one of the richest men in India, and his army is supposed to be the best native force. He has a British finance minister. He is unmarried. The story is that in 1937 he set out with a retinue of 5,000 to pay court to a lady in Bengal, the sister of the Maharaja of Tripura; his mother disapproved of the match and went on hunger strike until it was called off. Gwalior is one of the states advanced enough to encourage civil aviation, which till recently has been backward in India; like Indore and Bhopal, it helps to subsidize the new Tata air service. Gwalior has 3,500,000 people.

Indore, a 19-gun state, is also ruled by descendants of the Mahratta conquerors. The Maharaja, born in 1908, went to Christ Church, Oxford, and was invested with ruling powers in 1930 following the abdication of his father. Indore is one of the progressive states; recently it followed Travancore to give temple entry to the Untouchables. The army head is British. Indore's father, the previous Maharaja, left India and married an American, Nancy Miller, following the Mumtaz Begum affair. Mumtaz was one of his dancing girls; she was abducted by a rich and madly infatuated Bombay merchant, Bawla by name; whereupon some of the Maharaja's retainers followed her to Bombay and murdered Bawla.[3]

Patiala, Bikaner, Others

One of the grimmest and most backward states, until recently at least, was Patiala. If the Nizam of Hyderabad is known as His Exalted Highness, the old Maharaja of Patiala was called His "Exhausted" Highness. He had a prodigious harem, and a considerable part of his activity was the acquisition of young ladies to freshen it. In 1930 an organization known as "Patiala Enquiry Committee," appointed by the Indian States Peoples Conference, wrote a long report charging the old Maharaja with most of the crimes and sins in the calendar, from lechery to murder. He was said to have spent

[3] Early in 1939 the young Maharaja also married an American, a lady who had been his daughter's nurse.

sixty percent of the state income on himself, and to have had 3,500 servants. The old man had a special title—"Favorite Son of the British Empire"—and was an A. D. C. to the King-Emperor.[4] He was suspicious of the Federation idea, and hired the eminent lawyer Bulhabai Desai to give his legal opinion of the scheme; Desai told him that it was probably the best he could expect. The old Maharaja died in 1938.

Patiala is the premier Sikh state. Of its 1,625,520 people the males never cut their beard or hair. For many years it was as completely repressive an autocracy as India could show. Recently a committee was appointed to set up a constitutional assembly, but it was announced that the sovereign would have the right of veto over any acts of the legislature. In Patiala's capital, according to Sir William Barton, are dog kennels of unrivaled splendor. For the 95 royal dogs three English trainers are provided; the dog hospital has three wards and an operating theater, which "put to shame" military hospitals in the rest of India. The kennels are "specklessly clean, with tiled walls and electric light." Tiled walls and electric light are not, however, among the ornaments of civilization which have yet reached the human beings of Patiala's realm.

．　　．　　．　　．　　．　　．　　．

Probably the most "typical" Maharaja, the perfect picture of proud and glittering regality, is Bikaner. This tremendous fellow, born in 1880, has been on his throne since 1887, and celebrated his golden jubilee last year. Always very close to England, during the Munich crisis of September 1938 he was the first Indian potentate to offer his services to the British crown. By November 8, 98 out of 562 princes had done likewise. Handsome, despotic, magnificent, the Maharaja of Bikaner is a complete autocrat, with no nonsense about cabinets or legislatures, but he has tempered autocracy with a good deal of practical benevolence; his state is well run. It is largely his creation, in that before his reign, with only 17 guns, it was not considered one of the two or three which really count. Bikaner was one of the fathers of the Federation idea, but now has cooled to it. *This* scheme is not quite the Federation he had counted on.

[4] British morals are very odd. No one objected to Patiala's fondness for hosts of Indian women. But if a Maharaja takes a *foreign* mistress, the British are extremely severe, and do not receive her officially.

Tragedy dimmed the later years of the Maharaja of Bikaner as it did those of the Emperor Franz Josef of Austria; his favorite son was found shot, together with his A. D. C., in circumstances which like the Mayerling tragedy in Austria have never been fully explained. The Maharaja has a very large harem, and his wives are in the strictest kind of *purdah*. A visitor may see the harem building outside, humming with activity and full of lights; no one can get in. Not even the British Vicerine, visiting Bikaner on a state visit, has met any of the wives. Bikaner's present heir, a plump young man, is one of the first shots in India.

.   .   .   .

The Rajput states are fascinating. They are in the west of India, and are strongly Hindu. Udaipur, with its enchanting capital built on glimmering lakes, considers itself the senior Rajput state, a title to which Bikaner jealously objects; but Udaipur has not the political importance of Bikaner. According to legend, there is a "curse" on the house of Udaipur, and no eldest son except the present one has ever inherited rule. Many centuries ago the Maharana of Udaipur had a beautiful daughter; the rulers of nearby Jaipur and Jodhpur paid court to her. They invaded the Udaipur realm when both suits were rejected, determined to win her; the Udaipur ruler then solved the dilemma and escaped from invasion by the simple expedient of murdering the young lady. She was forced to walk through fire. Then her true beloved laid the curse on the house. . . . The present Maharana (which is supposed to be a "higher" title than Maharaja) of Udaipur is an invalid.

Jaipur, another great Rajput state, is ruled by an attractive lad who is quite possibly the best polo player in the world. He inserts the word "Sawai" before his name; this means "one-and-a-quarter," since the Jaipur tradition is that the ruler is not merely a maharaja, but a maharaja and one fourth.[5] Underneath each royal flag in Jaipur city, built of beautiful pink stone, is a little flag, one-quarter the size of the big one, to denote this twenty-five per cent bulge on rivals. Jaipur is supposed to be descended from the sun, like the Emperor of Japan. In fact he was actually an adopted son of the previous Maha-

[5] Incidentally, both Jaipur and his neighbor Jodhpur detested Alwar, whom they refused to call with the title "Highness." So Alwar added the word "God" to his name!

raja, who was frightened by a soothsayer who told him that he would lose the throne if any legitimate son reached maturity.

The administration of Jaipur is excellent, under a first-class British Dewan, Colonel Sir H. Beauchamp St. John. The state is feudal in economic organization, and the big political issue is the attempt by the *Thakurs* or great landowners to retain their power. The Maharaja will no longer send police to help the *Thakurs* collect their rents, which makes them angry. Jaipur is a citadel of intense Hinduism; recently the Brahmans stirred up an unpleasant riot because some Untouchables dared to have a banquet, with their food cooked in butter. The penalty for killing a peacock in Jaipur, even accidentally, is six months in jail.

A familiar problem of intelligently run states like Jaipur is lack of men. The British make every effort to get order into things, to find good men who can be built up into an administrative *cadre*. One reason why Jaipur and Jodhpur are in good condition is that the rulers had long minorities. The British like this; it gives them opportunity to spend some years in training the potentates and their officials in responsibility.

.   .   .   .

An interesting state is Bhopal, ruled by a young Moslem, the Nawab Sir Mohammed Hamidullah Khan. Until 1926, Bhopal had been governed for eighty years by a line of able Moslem women; four of them—a unique occurrence in India—took the throne in succession. Then in 1926 the reigning lady abdicated in favor of her third son, the present ruler, whom she had trained as her secretary. Abdication was necessary because, had she died, the succession would have gone to a nephew by another son, whom she thought not to be capable. Young Bhopal is a conscientious and accessible ruler. Every day he walks alone down the palace avenue, slowly, and any person may approach and address him; at the same time his consort, the Begum, receives any Moslem woman who wishes to talk to her.

Federation Versus Congress

We now come to the attitude of the princes to the project that will determine their future, namely Federation.

That they will lose a good deal by Federation goes without saying. First, though they may maintain their legal status as separate entities, they are bound to be bereft of some sovereignty. The laws of the new Central Legislature will, for the first time, extend to Princely India.

Second, they may lose a number of special privileges. Federation will be a myth or a joke if states are permitted to retain such ornaments to "national" dignity as their own postage stamps and coins.

Third, some of them will suffer severe financial losses. Many states have their own customs regimes; about twenty per cent of the state revenues of Jaipur, to take one example, come from import tariffs. Yet internal tariffs must disappear if Federation is to be more than a fiction. As the Government of India Act is now drawn, the native states will not be subject to federal income tax, but other British Indian taxes, notably a corporation tax, will hit them.

Fourth, most of the states think they will lose what is more important to a despot than rubies, namely, prestige. They feel that "they will become pawns in a British game to set off the radicalism of British India."

On the other hand, the native states are bound to derive certain considerable advantages from Federation.

First, at least when the project was first broached, the princes thought that it might release them from the occasionally onerous demands of the Political Department. They would, they thought, be partners in a free union, not vassals of the government of India.

Second, while Federation would tend to reduce certain of their rights, it would also be a fixed and final guarantee that the states should survive as separate organisms. The princes would be surrendering minor privileges in return for permanent security against demands by Congress to abolish them.

Third, Federation as envisaged at present gives the princes stronger representation in the Central Legislature than their numerical proportion justifies.

In curious fact, Federation was first suggested by the princes themselves. Two Dewans, one of Bhopal, the other of Bikaner, were the fathers of the idea, together with the great Allahabad lawyer Sir Tej Bahadur Sapru. The project was presented suddenly by the maharajas at the first Round Table Conference in 1931, partly to British surprise; London didn't think the princes were ready for such an evolution. The British then seized the chance to push it.

The present position is that the federal provisions of the 1935 Act are not yet in force. "Instruments of accession" have been several times prepared and early in 1939 a final draft was submitted to the various princes; each instrument differs according to the special treaty rights and privileges of each state. It has been an extraordinarily complicated legal job to draw them up, 562 in all. Most observers think Federation will finally come in 1940 or 1941.

Federation goes into effect as soon as states comprising fifty-one percent of the total population of Princely India sign the instruments of accession. Thus if Hyderabad, Mysore, Kashmir, Baroda, and a few more of the big states signify their consent, the others must follow or be left out in an unpredictable cold. What is going on now is a process of blackmail and bickering. The princes want concessions and special favors as a price for signing up. But if Federation were merely a matter of the British and the princes, it could come into force to-morrow. There is a third great factor to consider—the Indian National Congress.

The Congress is a split on some issues. On one issue it is unanimous and solid—opposition to Federation. It opposes it—at least this scheme of Federation—for a variety of reasons:

First, coming into force of Federation would set the seal on the whole Government of India Act, many provisions of which Congress still bitterly opposes, for instance the Viceroy's right of veto and his reserved powers on matters like Defense and Foreign Affairs. Federation would serve to "freeze" the present situation.

Second, Congress claims that Federation is simply a device whereby the British procure a conservative anti-national majority in the Central Legislature for many years. The princely delegates, it is presumed, will vote with the British. The British are using the princes, the Congress feels, as their bulwark against the Indian people.

Third, the princes have too much representation in the projected new legislature. They represent only one-quarter of the population of All-India, but they are given 104 seats in the projected Council of State, as against 156 for the rest of India, and 125 in the projected Legislative Assembly, as against only 250 for the rest of India.

Fourth, according to the Act at present, the princely delegates to the new legislature will be nominated, not elected, i.e., they will be nothing but mouthpieces of the rulers. The Congress, which stands for Indians on an All-India basis, cannot possibly "desert" the people of the native states, who will have fewer privileges under Federation than the people of the provinces. Even the British agree that this is an anomaly. As Congress infiltration into the states began, the Delhi authorities hinted that the maharajas might wisely "prepare the way" for democratization. Early in 1939 Lord Linlithgow, the Viceroy, warned the states pointedly to put their domains in better order.

Fifth, elections to the new central legislature are indirect, which puts Congress at a disadvantage.

All this Congress believes. Whether or not Congress can be made to back down, to dilute its opposition, remains to be seen. Congress opposed provincial autonomy almost as fiercely as it opposed Federation—at the beginning. Later it was willing to accept a compromise. But as things stood early in 1939, Congress was pledged even to the extreme of civil disobedience to ward Federation off.

Chapter XXVIII
Aga Khan and Others

~~~~~~~~~~~~~~~~~~~~~~~~~~~~~~~~~~~~~~

*Germany is the only country in the world that has practical
socialism . . . I found myself there nearer to constructive
socialism of a practical kind than I have ever been in my life.*
THE AGA KHAN quoted in the *Congress Socialist*

THAT fabulous creature the Aga Khan, a bon-vivant on several
continents, a man who loves to chuckle, Derby winner and owner
of one of the greatest racing stables in the world, is of course an
Indian prince, but his position is peculiar in that he is not ruler of
a state—he has no territory—but of a sect. Thus he belongs in a
different category from the maharajas of the preceding chapter. The
Aga Khan was born in 1875. Properly his name is Aga Sultan Sir
Mohammed Shah; his followers call him simply the "Sahib," which
means Lord. He is one of the most picturesque and unusual potentates
on earth—partly because his domain is heaven. The adherents of his
sect consider him to be a God.

Perhaps not quite a God. But the Aga Khan is the leader of
those Khoja Moslems who are known as Ismailis; there are about ten
million of them in India and elsewhere in the world, notably the
Middle East and Zanzibar. They are an odd mixture, very religious
Mohammedans who have absorbed certain Hindu customs; for instance they believe in reincarnation, and they think that the Aga
Khan, the present leader of the community (the position is hereditary)
is the *living* incarnation of their deity. In addition the Aga Khan
is a lineal descendant of the Prophet Mohammed in the forty-eighth
generation. He is also said "to represent an incarnation of the *Hindu*
trinity." (India, Census Ethnography, 1901-31.) He thus assumes
one of the most comprehensive religious positions ever held by anybody.

Thirty years ago it seemed that the Aga Khan might reach almost
any position in Indian politics. The promise of his career was exceptional. The great Indian leader Gokhale addressed his last testament to him, and it seemed inevitable that he should become leader

of all Indian Moslems at least. He was shrewd, competent, good-humored, emancipated, intelligent. But he chose to take the English rather than the nationalist side, and his political career has been largely that of a British mouthpiece. He might have been a Moslem Gandhi; instead he has "represented" India at the Round Table Conferences and the League of Nations—as well as at Deauville, Biarritz, and most of the resorts of Europe.

Jawaharlal Nehru wrote of him with some trace of bitterness, referring to the Round Table Conference: "It was fitting that in this assembly of vested interests—imperialist, feudal, financial, industrial, religious, communal—the leadership of the British Indian delegation should usually fall to the Aga Khan, who in his own person happened to combine all these interests in some degree . . . He would have been an able representative of Imperialist England at that Round Table Conference. The irony of it was that he was supposed to represent India."

The wealth of the Aga Khan is, as everyone knows, almost inconceivable. He is probably one of the four or five richest men in the world. His revenue derives in the first instance, not from land, but from the offerings of his Ismaili followers. These, who are for the most part fanatically loyal, are supposed to pay him ten percent of their incomes every year, as a faith offering and fee for religious services which the community provides; of course by no means all of the ten million pay him so much, but the amount is nevertheless very considerable. In every city where Ismailis live, there is a "Jamat Khana" or community house, the equivalent of a mosque or temple. Here the Aga Khan's worshipers come to pray twice a day, usually leaving an offering. The entire property of all the Jamat Khanas everywhere belongs to the Aga Khan in person.

On his twenty-fifth Jubilee a few years ago, the Aga Khan was weighed ceremoniously, and presented by his community with gold equivalent to his weight. He is not exactly slim, and the amount came to 300,000 rupees. It was returned to charity. This picturesque ceremony derives from the Great Moguls, who were weighed in terms of gold once a year. Incidentally the legend is apocryphal that the Aga Khan's bathwater is piped off and sold for good sums to the faithful.

The Aga Khan is not particularly orthodox. He likes to drink, which is forbidden ordinarily to Mohammedans. Once some one asked him about this. "Ah," he replied, "you forget that wine turns to water as soon as it touches my mouth." On another occasion one of his followers protested at his luxurious manner of living abroad. "I only live so," he replied quick-wittedly, "in order to test your faith." It is indeed a puzzling phenomenon that a man so obviously worldly in tastes and temperament should be the object of devout religious worship.

He became a Highness during the War. His position as leader of the Ismailis would not in itself entail this rank, and his son does not necessarily inherit it. His services were valuable, because he staunchly took the side of the Allies, and thus served to check what might have been a tendency among his Moslem followers to sympathize with Turkey. Several years ago he is reported to have asked the Indian government for a grant of land, so that he might become a temporal as well as spiritual ruler. But there was no important territory available, and the project fell through.

The Aga Khan is a marvelous host, and he likes good conversation. He is occasionally temperamental, is full of vitality and humor, and has lively political sense. He loves food, and it is worth crossing several oceans to see him eat a mango, a fruit of which he is inordinately fond. When he travels to Europe crates of mangoes follow him by each fast boat. Also he adores ice cream; he is one of the greatest individual ice cream consumers in the world.

He was a dutiful son for many years, and his mother, who died in Bagdad in February 1938, had great influence on him. He flew from Karachi to her deathbed, but arrived half an hour too late. The Aga Khan has been married three times, first to one of his cousins, then to an Italian lady, who is mother of his heir, finally to a French lady, who has given him one young son. His heir, the Ali Khan, an attractive and ambitious young official in Hyderabad, married the former Mrs. Loel Guinness. Thus the Aga Khan's successor after the next generation may be only one-quarter Indian.

In October 1938 the Aga Khan wrote a letter to the London *Times* that aroused salty controversy. Surveying the Munich crisis, he asked for a better understanding of Germany, and suggested that *Mein Kampf*—something of a bar to good relations—might no longer represent Hitler's present views. Whether the Aga Khan would write a similar letter in April 1939 is—doubtful.

Mr. Jinnah and Other Moslems

Mohammed Ali Jinnah, the president of the All-India Moslem League, which is the Moslem analogy to Congress (though it is not nearly so powerful), is a prominent lawyer who was born in 1876. He is a Khoja Moslem, but his attitude toward religion is by no means fanatic. For many years he fought for Indian nationalism, but recently he has all but ruined his position by adopting a fierce separatism. His opposition to the Hindus is bitter and inflamed; he tours the country making attacks on Congress, which splits and weakens nationalist sentiment. Jinnah says that he was driven into communalism and the resurrection of the Moslem League by the intransigeance of the Hindus.

An eloquent orator, Jinnah led a joint Hindu-Moslem agitation in Bombay to attack a proposal for a public memorial to Lord Willingdon, then retiring as Governor of Bombay. It was decided to name a public hall in Jinnah's honor, and it was dedicated—the People's Jinnah hall—with appropriate ceremonies. But nowadays the Congress folk call it simply the "P. J." hall, because their differences with the Moslems are such that they hate to use Jinnah's name. Congress accuses Jinnah of being a flagrant opportunist. He deserted the nationalist movement, they say, at the time of the first non-coöperation movement, and invented the Moslem League as a crassly obvious method of re-entering politics. His appeal to religious feeling only strengthens the reactionaries, Congress feels.

Mr. Jinnah has one distinction so far as the brief acquaintance of this reporter is concerned. He is beyond doubt the thinnest man I ever saw. Next to him a certain character in the works of Mr. Dashiell Hammett is an obese monster.

Another eminent Moslem politician is the prime minister of the Punjab government, Sir Sikander Hyat Khan, a soldier, business man and banker, and one of the few notable Indians not a lawyer. Sir Sikander, a pleasant man, is a member of the Moslem League, but his opinion of Mr. Jinnah is not high. The Moslem governments (Punjab, Bengal, Sind), are by no means as close to the Moslem League as the Congress governments are to Congress; in fact in the Punjab election the Moslem League got only three seats. Sir Sikander's grandfather was a soldier loyal to Britain in the Great Mutiny; he was an orderly to the celebrated General John Nicholson, and carried him dying to his house; Nicholson then asked that he be taken care of. Sir Sikander served briefly in the army, and was the first Indian ever to command a company on active service; then he went into business, and finally politics. He is leader of the Unionist party in the Punjab, and takes a strong conservative line.

Another Punjab politician of consequence is a Moslem woman, the Begum Shah Nawaz. She and Mrs. Naidu were the only women at the Round Table Conferences. It is continually striking to see the increasing rôle able and intelligent women play in Indian public life.

The Moslem attitude toward Federation is very important. They fear Federation even more than do the Hindus, because almost all the princely states (Hyderabad and Bhopal are the only important exceptions) are ruled by Hindus; thus a federal structure would increase Hindu predominance in India. Mr. Jinnah has been fighting Federation for almost a decade. A recent proposal is to unite the Moslem areas in the north west in a new province, "Pakistan."

Leader of the Untouchables

In the Bombay telephone book you will find the following entry. Behind it is one of the most interesting men in India:

> 60486. Ambedkar, Bhimrao Ramji, Bar-at-law,
> Residence, "Rajgraha," Dadar.

Dr. Ambedkar, son of a soldier and Untouchable leader, was a poor boy in Bombay. As a child he learned quickly and painfully what the stigma of Untouchability meant. Somehow, showing rare initiative, he got to Baroda, where the old Gaekwar became interested in him and financed his education. Ambedkar went to Columbia University in New York (class of '17), where he took courses in anthropology, economics, and law; later he went to Bonn University in Germany and the London School of Economics; he is both a Ph.D. and a Sc.D. Returning to India he could get no decent job because he was an Untouchable. He joined the Baroda civil service, but the other clerks would not let him approach, and no landlord would rent him rooms. For a time he risked severe punishment by disguising himself as a Parsi; Untouchables who obtain work, especially in factories, by pretending that they are not Untouchables, have been beaten to death. Ambedkar returned to Bombay in humiliation and disgust and set himself up, alone, in practicing law. Almost at once he was successful. He wrote several books, including a work on finance, and then entered politics. A career such as this is very remarkable for an Untouchable, indeed unique.

Ambedkar stands for the abolition of caste. He thinks caste must be approached from the religious as well as the economic attitude, and that to say facilely that the Untouchables are merely the proletariat is not enough. The Untouchables are the proletariat—certainly—but the proletariat that cannot, at any price, get jobs except as agricultural serfs or laborers of the lowest category. He differs sharply from Gandhi, who wants to improve the lot of the Untouchables *within* caste. Also he is contemptuous of the Temple Entry experiment in Travancore. The orthodox Hindus, he says, embark on these partial and minor ameliorations not out of genuine concern for the Untouchables, but to purify themselves in penance for their own sins.

The British sent Ambedkar to London as representative of the Untouchables at the Round Table Conference. This was smart politics, because it served to split the Hindu front. Ambedkar assumed a strong anti-Congress line, which forced Gandhi to take up the Untouchables as a political issue. When the Mahatma made his great fast for the Untouchables, he certainly had politics partially in mind; if the Untouchables became a separate community, they might vote against instead of with the Hindus. When it appeared that Gandhi might die, the British desperately brought pressure on Ambedkar to agree to revision of the Communal Award scheme, so that Gandhi would have a loophole for calling off the fast; Ambedkar did so, but only after getting more seats for his community than was first planned.

Ambedkar is 46. Every taxi driver in Bombay knows his address, though he lives in an obscure suburb. He is a widower, a non-smoker, a teetotaler. His conversation is stubborn and vigorous. He is studious, and has a library of 8,000 books—but he is on record for wanting to burn the Hindu scriptures. He fiercely hates Congress, and has founded a new Independent Labor League. Recently he stated that he was no longer a believer in democracy in all circumstances, "and that India needs the strong hand of an enlightened autocrat."

Pandit Malaviya

And now to the extreme opposite pole. There must be a word about what is known as the Hindu Mahasabha, the political organization which stands for Hinduism in its most orthodox form, which believes fanatically in caste and all the strictures of medieval Hinduism. Yet the Mahasabha has a modern outlook too, since it is almost the only group in India wholeheartedly in favor of Federation—which it assumes will entrench Hinduism in government. The most prominent figure in the Mahasabha is the venerable Pandit Madan Mohan Malaviya, who has been president of Congress twice (1909 and 1918), who joined civil disobedience gallantly, but who founded a nationalist party of his own several years ago when he could not understand the way Congress was growing up. Malaviya—it is lamentable to have to give him only a very few words—is the creator of the Hindu University at Benares. He is a renowned scholar, a great money-raiser, and a hot communalist. He is, of course, a Brahman, and has never touched tobacco, alcohol, tea, coffee, or even eggs. In 1939 he undertook a remarkable rejuvenation cure at the hands of a Yogi reputed to be 172 years old. Malaviya, who is seventy-seven himself, went into a special room without light or ventilation, and took drugs and a special herb diet. After twenty days of it he said he felt twenty years younger, and could walk upright again.

The Old Liberals

The great Indian liberals are those who, in a way, have outlived their historical function, which was to help pave the way for Indian democracy. We must at least mention them. They are distinguished men. But events have thrown them into the background, since Congress, to which most of them once belonged, has advanced far beyond their former views.

The most famous of the liberals is Sir Tej Bahadur Sapru, whom we have several times briefly named; born in Allahabad in 1875, he is a very prominent lawyer, and one of the few Indians to be a Right Honorable, i.e., one of His Majesty's Privy Counsellors. Closely associated with Sapru in much of his career was M. R. Jayaker, now a judge on the Federal Supreme Court. The Rt. Hon. V. S. Srinivasa Sastri, an old friend of Gandhi's and a great figure in Madras, was for a time Indian High Commissioner to South Africa. The chairman of the National Liberal Federation, Sir Chimanlal Setalvad, is a Bombay lawyer.

Most liberals are inclined to favor Federation, and believe in Dominion Status as the goal. They work with the British closely.

Chapter XXIX
British Rule in India

∿∿∿∿∿∿∿∿∿∿∿∿∿∿∿

> *As India must be bled, the lancet should be directed to parts where the blood is congested . . .*
> —Lord Salisbury

> *I am unwilling to set up an Indian Empire of Great Britain in opposition to the general interests of mankind.*
> —Mr. Gladstone

> *The key to the Indian problem is sympathy.*
> —King George V

ALMOST the greatest shock I had in India was the discovery in Delhi that the Indian Civil Service, the steel brace of British administration in India, contains exactly 591 Englishmen. I had thought, as almost everyone else thinks, that there were many thousands.

The total personnel of the I. C. S. is 1,107. Of these not less than 416 are Indian. By 1940, moreover, by terms of a recent arrangement, the service will become a full fifty percent Indian. This is yet another example of the remarkable English facility of transforming subject races into actual agents of British imperialism. By offering first class jobs, first class pensions (the highest ranks of the Indian Civil Service retire after thirty-five years of service at £1,000 per year), the British skim the cream of the Indian educated class and make it work for them. Outstanding nationalists do not succumb; but I have noted that both Nehru and Bose were at least tempted to become civil servants. The British say that by this process they are educating Indians to the responsibilities of government; meanwhile in effect they buy off discontent with good jobs, good careers. This is probably the most successful imperialist device ever invented. India—under the British—is staffed by Indians. Gold is cheaper than guns . . . Aside from the chosen 416 Indians actually in the Civil Service, there are of course multitudinous thousands of Indians of every race and class and category employed as minor officials, schoolmasters, clerks, and the subordinate like.

The I. C. S. is by all odds the most notable civil service in the world. It has a massive tradition and tremendous prestige. The initials "I. C. S." after a man's name mean more than a Ph.D.— though it is not true, as was once suggested, that members of the I. C. S. form a special category of the human race. It means, if he is an Indian, that he is of good family, good education, and arduous training. It means, if he is English, that he has gone to public school and (usually) Oxford or Cambridge, that he has passed a rigorously severe competitive examination, that he has learned at least one Indian language, that he has started the ladder as a Deputy Commissioner or "Collector" and then worked up. He is magistrate, administrator, and executive; a boy of thirty may be in charge of 4,000,000 people. (With the advent of provincial autonomy, of course, the I. C. S. men in the provinces are in theory at least subject to orders from Indian governments.) The top in the I. C. S. is a governorship or membership in the Viceroy's Executive Council. After that—retirement at sixty or so with a smacking good pension, life in England or the Riviera, a comfortable old age, and usually a nostalgia for India that never fades.

The I. C. S. is called narrow. It is called parochial. Many of its members, stiff-necked, straight-laced, especially those nearing retirement, are incompetent to understand the modern stresses in India, and are horrified privately at Provincial Autonomy and its developments. Some live all their careers in one province; they have no All-India sense. I have met members of the I. C. S. who have been in India twenty-five years, and have never seen Madras or Lahore; I have met army officers—much more liberal minded as a rule—who say that the I. C. S. has tried to throttle every reform in India since 1919. On the other hand, the organization contains many splendid men, administrators of the highest competence who are unselfishly devoted to India, and who have given their lives to it.

The I. C. S. costs about 25,000,000 rupees ($9,250,000) per year, which is approximately 1.25 percent of the total budget. There is one I. C. S. officer for every 256,000 of the population, one to each 868 square miles.

The administrative framework of India is the I. C. S. Behind it of course is armed force. And let us note that whereas Englishmen in the I. C. S. are infinitesimally few, the number of British troops in India is very considerable—about 56,000. They are in two categories: officers and men of the Indian army, which is an autonomous command, and officers and men of the British army in India, i.e., purely British regiments serving for a time at Indian posts. In the Indian army the troops and non-commissioned officers are mostly Indian, the officers mostly British. Here again the skillful British employ Indians to do the actual dirty work—a technique now copied by other colonial powers; the French use Senegalese troops, the Italians use Askaris, and—notably—in Manchukuo the Japanese use Chinese. The British are absolutely convinced that their Indian troops are loyal. They even allow them to train with machine guns, which has horrified some foreign observers. As Norman Angell has said—to repeat it annoys nationalist Indians hotly—"India was conquered by Britain with man power supplied by Indians."

Whereas the I. C. S. is to become half English, half Indian, the British are very careful to see that no such equilibrium exists in the army command. Theoretically an Indian officer (there is a training school, the Indian Sandhurst, at Dehra Dun) could become a field marshal; in actuality none has ever risen beyond major. And only ten Indians per year are chosen to come to England to get what are known as "King's Commissions," that is officerhood in the British (not the Indian) army. There are comparatively few Indians in the Air Force, and none in the Tanks Corps.

Surrogate King

At the top of the British structure is, of course, the Viceroy, who is sole representative in India of the Imperial Crown. He is never chosen from the I. C. S., but is an eminent peer or politician sent from England for a five-year term. When he arrives he meets his cabinet or executive council, members of which likewise are appointed for five years, for the first time; their terms are not necessarily coterminous with his, and he is thus in the odd position of not choosing his own cabinet. Of the seven members of the executive council at present, four are I. C. S. men, and three are Indians. If Federation comes, this type of appointed executive council will cease to exist, and quite possibly the present one is the last in history, since—after Federation—the cabinet will have a prime minister, and will be chosen by western parliamentary procedure from whatever political party commands the new (and first) federal legislature. It will be a political instrument, not the instrument of a civil service.

Quite possibly the Viceroy of India is the most powerful single human being in the world. In Chapter XXIII we surveyed his enormous powers. If crisis comes, he has in his hands (together with the India Office in London of course), the fate of one-fifth of the human race. (But after Federation, incidentally, the title of Viceroy will disappear; he will be merely the Governor-General.)

The present Viceroy, whose term expires in 1941 (no Viceroy has ever been reappointed) is a Scotsman forty-eight years old, Victor Alexander John Hope, the Most Honorable the Marquess of Linlithgow, P.C., K.T., G.C.I.E., O.B.E. He was a banker by profession, but he is probably the best educated Viceroy in Indian history. For years he studied India, and he spent almost three years there as chairman of the Royal Commission on Indian Agriculture; it was he who pushed the Government of India Act through the House of Lords, as Sir Samuel Hoare superintended it in the Commons, after he had been chairman of the Joint Select Committee on Indian Constitutional Reform, which wrote the bill. He was made Viceroy by Baldwin, and like Baldwin is a middle-of-the-road man basically.

Lord Linlithgow is tall, hard-working, prudent, and confident, with a gift for quiet eloquence, great tact, and great capacity for difficult and detailed exploration and negotiation. He works twelve or fourteen hours a day at least, with one hour off. His decision is vital on a great number of detailed affairs; he tends to everything himself, and meticulously writes his own minutes on documents, something that not all Viceroys do. A rather shy man—but very charming and supple—he cares little for display; he is not the elaborately caparisoned Viceroy of tradition. When he arrived in Delhi he addressed the nation on the radio—something utterly unprecedented in India— and even put in the speech some passages addressed to Indian children. He arranged almost at once that Gandhi should meet him, though his predecessor had managed to avoid the Mahatma for five long years.

It is Lord Linlithgow's great dream to be the first Viceroy under Federation. When he came he pushed the Federation project almost too hard.

What Britain Gets Out of India

Pages could be written on this. Britain gets imperial power out of India. It gets imperial prestige. It gets ports of communication en route to Australia, and a comfortable habitat for a large army in the east. It gets experience for its soldiers and politicians, and opportunity for its young men. It gets trade: thirty-eight percent of all United Kingdom exports go to India, and thirty-two percent of all Indian exports go to the United Kingdom. Above all it gets booty, loot.

Call it money. Call it profit. Call it what you like. Some £250,-000,000 in gold went to England from India in the early 1930's. A great deal of this came from the maharajas and other wealthy men, who, when sterling was devalued, sold gold for paper pounds, and thus made forty percent profit on any amount they cared to risk; some of it was "distress gold," coming from the villages, because people could only pay their taxes by selling hoarded jewels and the like. Meantime, the exchange value of the rupee was arbitrarily manipulated in favor of the British; the rupee was fixed at 1s. 6d., instead of 1s. 4d., which helped the British importer of Indian goods, in that he had to pay twelve percent less for rupees.

The total amount of British investment in India is extraordinarily difficult to compute; a moderate estimate is £850,000,000, which is about one-quarter of all British overseas investments. Of this £365,-000,000 is held in sterling bonds, and is India's debt to Britain; the rest is made up of industrial investments, shipping, railways, insurance and the like. It has been calculated that the average return on British overseas investments is 4.9 percent. (*Times of India,* January 14, 1938.) So in a word what Britain gets out of India is this: roughly 4.9 percent per year on a total investment of perhaps £850,000,000.

What Britain Does for India

When one asks an Englishman in Delhi what the British have done for India he is apt to be painfully but honestly surprised that the question should even be asked. It takes him a moment to collect his thoughts. He is inclined to take the whole question of the *merit* of British rule for granted. It may be right morally; it may be wrong; but surely, he will say, it is indisputable that British rule has produced an infinitude of good works, of worthwhile benefits to the Indian community. And presently he will produce a comprehensive dossier of accomplishments and reforms.

The first point invariably made is that Britain has established peace, unity (almost), and order. It has ended disruption and civil strife; it has imposed on foreigner and Indian alike a strict regime, not only of British imperialism, but of British justice. It has brought tranquillity (almost) and law to India. It has established complete public security, and given one-fifth of the human race the benefits of an administrative machine—the civil service—which is unparalleled elsewhere in the world.

Then our Delhi friend will go into details. He will mention conspicuously the work of the British, which indeed is valuable beyond dispute, in irrigation. From about ten million acres in 1879, the area irrigated directly by state works rose to 31,000,000 acres in 1928—by far the largest irrigation scheme on earth. There are 79,000 miles of government canals. This work is important, because it abolishes threat of famine. (On the other hand, it should be noted that the canals have been expensive, and that the people pay soundly for them with high taxation.) Closely associated with irrigation and famine control is work in agriculture—creation of seed depots, experimental stations for improvement of crops, and the like—and in forestry; not less than one-fifth of British India is carefully regulated forest area, part of which is in reserve and protected. Again, among concrete physical accomplishments, there will be mention of the colossal railway system, in which alone £150,000,000 of British capital is invested. Indian railways carry over 500,000,000 people a year; it is the fourth largest railway system in the world. If China possessed a system of communications like that of India, the history of China in recent years would have been very different (though one might also say that if China had it, China would not have been China, but a British preserve). Finally the British have given the country an excellent postal administration and telegraph and radio service. You can send a telegram anywhere over the length and breadth of India for one anna (about 3¢) per word.[1]

Accomplishments in other spheres are, perhaps, not so notable. But the British point out that they have made a beginning in industrial legislation with a Workman's Compensation Act and an act—not fully operative—reducing hours of work to fifty-four per week, that

---

[1] But on Sundays oddly enough the price is double.

new laws forbid the employment of female labor in mines underground, that child labor is—in theory at least—restricted. As to matters of public health, the British say that in fifty-four years they have reduced the death rate from 26 to 24 per thousand (still shockingly high), and raised the birth rate from 24 to 35. As to education—an uncomfortable subject—official figures have it that fifty percent of boys of school age are now going to school (in British India, of course, not the princely states), and seventeen percent of girls. But illiteracy as a whole is still eighty-five percent for men, ninety-seven percent for women, a grisly total.

The Indian Grievances

Grievances by nationalist Indians, especially by Congress, may be outlined approximately as follows:

First and overwhelmingly, the Congress claims the inalienable right of a people to be free. British imperialism throttles the legitimate expression of national development, that is, full and authentic independence. The British say that Indians are not competent to govern themselves. Congress denies this strenuously.

Mr. Gandhi makes an interesting point. "You English committed one supreme crime against my people. For one hundred years you have done everything for us; you have given us no responsibility for our own government, nor enabled us to learn by making mistakes. If we are deficient in the character and experience necessary to enable us to take over the control of our own affairs, it is because you have never given us the opportunity to develop those qualities in practice. We demand responsibility at once." (In a talk with Lord Lothian, New York *Times*, April 2, 1937.)

In another place Gandhiji says that the British have (a) impoverished the dumb millions, (b) established political serfdom, (c) sapped Indian culture, (d) caused spiritual degradation.

Derivately there is the matter of repression. Here Indians sometimes exaggerate. There is no repression in India comparable to repression in Germany, Italy, or the more spectacular Balkan States. In the whole of India—now—there are only a few hundred political prisoners, and of these most are convicted terrorists. The Congress governments have done a great deal to force the liberation of prisoners, and in Bengal the last of the "detenus"—this pretty word is an Indian invention, and describes some one arrested without trial for a political offense and held in a kind of concentration camp—was released in 1938. At one time there were 2,700. What Indians object to most at present is surveillance and pinpricking. The Congress leaders are closely watched; even Delhi is a whispering gallery. I asked a friend in Madras for his address. He replied, "Just Madras is enough; the police will forward any mail." (His is a common name, and there are 647,230 people in Madras!) Some books are suppressed, and some Leftist literature may not enter India. Newspapers are theoretically free, but in fact they are mostly edited with caution, because every newspaper must post a bond, confiscation of which may stop publication.

By ordinance anyone in India may be arrested and detained without trial. No offense need be proved. This law is still on the statute books even in Congress provinces, because—as we have seen—Congress sometimes wants protection against its own extremists. But nowadays it is seldom invoked . . . The British, incidentally, find police work more difficult since Provincial Autonomy. Law enforcement is handled by Indians, and except in the event of grave national crisis the British may only "consult and advise." The authorities can no longer step so freely from one province to another. On the other hand it goes without saying that the British could—if they wanted to and had enough policemen—arrest to-morrow every Congressman in India.

I have heard a very high British official—so high that I shudder to think of his name—say that in the event of renewal of civil disobedience every Congress leader and subleader and sub-subleader would be in jail in twenty-four hours. Every man is spotted. (He added: "It is our only hope.")

Second—and hardly less overwhelmingly—the Indian Congress resents and condemns what it calls "exploitation." It is referring, of course, to the booty—£850,000,000 at 4.9 percent—described above. The British, the Indians say, have sucked wealth out of India, giving no fair return; they have impoverished India, bled it dry. They refer among many other things to British tariff policy; for generations England imposed free trade on India, when this gave stimulus to the cotton manufacturers of Lancashire; now it imposes protection on India, which starves local Indian industry. No matter which turn British commercial policy took, it was calculated to Indian disadvantage. Experts state that tariffs imposed on India by the British at present cost the Indian consumer about 250,000,000 to 300,000,000 rupees a year. The Indians refer also to the colossal sums paid British officials in India, which are paid for by the Indian budget, i.e., the Indian taxpayer. The Viceroy, for instance, gets 256,000 rupees ($94,720) per year aside from various allowances. A governor of an important province gets 120,000 rupees ($44,400) per year, and members of the executive council get 80,000 rupees ($29,600)—sums which Indians rightly consider staggering. Again, the Indians assert that the railways, such a proud accomplishment of the British, are inefficient, that they have been built for strategic rather than basically commercial purposes, that they discriminate against internal markets, and favor the seaports at which they may deliver cargoes to British ships. And the Indians say that British agricultural policy, even irrigation work, is either woefully deficient or far too expensive. The Punjab irrigation canals return a revenue of twenty percent on the investment.

Closely associated with the general subject of exploitation is the army question. Indians say first that Britain has taken good care to see that no real Indian army exists, so that the country, should it become free, would be defenseless. Second, they say that the British army in India serves no legitimate Indian need, but only imperial interests. Third, they bitterly complain at the cost of the army, which is indeed terrific. The expenditure on defense is 503,819,000 rupees per year ($186,413,030), which is almost *half* the entire budget of the central government. If provincial revenue is counted, the army consumes about twenty-six percent of the total budget. All but a minute fraction of this sum is paid for by the Indian taxpayer. At first it was suggested that the British at least support their own troops, then that India pay not more than twenty percent of its own budget on defense, finally that the British pay at the very least the difference between upkeep of the British army in India and what its upkeep would be at home (which is the system in Palestine); this was all rejected as being too expensive, and until three years ago the British treasury paid *nothing* toward the cost of British troops in India. Now it pays the preposterously small sum of 20,000,000 rupees ($740,000) per year.

These two general and basic grievances—political bondage and economic exploitation—are dominant. Beyond them there are almost any number of detailed complaints. For instance:

1. The British starve education. They spend uncounted millions

on defense, and a few wretched pennies on public schools. Their efforts in education, as well as results obtained—even if some recent statistics are mildly encouraging—are miserable. Their aim in education is to produce *babus* (clerks) and minor officials. They pay scant attention to the education of women, or to technical or vocational training.

2. The British point to their "record" in public health, and emphasize famine relief; but in India there are still one hundred *million* cases of malaria every year, of which not ten percent get proper treatment. As we have seen, not less than twenty percent of the entire population is "badly" nourished, which means in simple language that 50,000,000 people don't get enough to eat.

3. The British record in the field of social reform is negligible. The "Sarda Act" does, it is true, prohibit in theory the marriage of girls younger than 14 and boys under 18, but it is full of loopholes. A law passed in 1937 conferred on Hindu widows the right of inheriting property, but it is too early to see how effective it will be; a similar law proposed in regard to Moslem widows provoked such opposition (from the Moslems) that it had to be withdrawn. Since 1933 it has been an offense under the Indian Penal Code for a parent to pledge his child's labor for payment of a debt; the British had been in India more than one hundred years before this shocking outrage began to be checked; even now the law is continually evaded. In 1938 a woman deputy proposed a law to prohibit Hindu polygamy, and another authorizing divorce of Hindus in certain circumstances; these laws have not yet been passed, and probably will not pass. The British attitude toward social and religious reform is very simple. It is never to interfere with the social and religious customs of Indians if it can possibly be avoided.[2] (It should, of course, be added on the British side that social reforms are bitterly opposed by orthodox Indians too.)

4. Social discrimination is perhaps not quite the bitter point it once was. But it remains ridiculous that men like the Aga Khan or the Nizam of Hyderabad may not enter the Bombay Yacht Club. British color snobbery has left more than one unpleasant trace.

5. The British assert that they have given India an equitable taxation and revenue system. Indians deny this, pointing out the terms of

[2] Probably this derives from the Mutiny in 1857, one cause of which was fierce resentment by both Hindus and Moslems at having to lubricate their guns with grease made of holy cattle and unholy pigs.

the somewhat antiquated Permanent Settlement Act, which still determines the character of land revenue in Bengal, and which was promulgated in—1793!

6. The new Government of India Act gives India no control of foreign policy. An interesting incidental point is that there is no diplomatic corps at Delhi, and consuls of other powers are permitted only at the seaports.

7. The new Government of India Act, with its creation of a federal bank, nullifies fiscal autonomy. The rupee is linked to sterling, and the British will continue to be in charge of about eighty percent of the federal budget.

8. The reserved powers of the Viceroy and the various governors serve to make effective Indian independence impossible. One detail is that considerable portions of British India, like Ajmer-Merwara and Baluchistan, remain outside the scope of provincial reform, and continue to be ruled direct from Delhi. (In 1938 certain villages in Ajmer-Merwara were transferred to their neighbors the Rajput states, Udaipur and Jodhpur. Instantly Congress suggested that this was a territorial bribe to entice the maharajas into Federation.) There are about 13,000,000 people in the "excluded areas."

9. Finally, Congress folk say bitterly that Britain has given them peace—yes—but that it is "the peace of the looted graveyard."

British Attitudes

And, of course, the British blame the Indians exactly as the Indians blame the British for many phases of the deadlock. . . .

The debate could be endless. Take the single point of education, for instance. How, the British ask, can you have free and compulsory primary education when neither Hindus or Moslems will countenance boys and girls in the same school, even when they are tiny children? Take social reform. It is the Hindu religion which blocks and stultifies any effort at amelioration. Take labor conditions. Indian-owned mills are worse than British.

The British feel that the Indians are incompetent, shiftless, supersensitive, bribable, and torn by religious fissures. They say that Indian "capacity for self-government" is a fantastic overstatement.

If I heard it once, I heard it fifty times from Englishmen that Indians "have an inferiority complex" and that "Indians never tell you what they really think, because they are not *sincere*." Probably this indicates that the British are secretly beginning to doubt their own capacity to govern the country indefinitely; they can't, therefore, bear to concede that Indians can be "sincere" in the belief that they *can* govern it. The Indian sense of inferiority derives mostly from generations of being snubbed, atop a craving to be liked; when they are not "sincere," it means mostly that, hoping to be liked and accepted, they tell you what they think you will approve.

Indians perplex the British terribly. Recently in the U. P. the Congress movement ordered that Indians in official correspondence be addressed as "Mr." or "Esquire," rather than with Indian appellations like Babu, Lala, Maulvi, and the like. The British could not get over it that a revolutionary Indian government wanted to use *their* Anglo-Saxon terms. But Congress took up this small issue merely to indicate its striving for equality. Perhaps Indians may not enter British clubs. They will at least demand that the British call them "Esquire."

In one province recently a British civil servant employed harsh language to an Indian officer. The case was carried straight to the top; the British civil servant had to apologize.

In Delhi I met a member of the I. C. S. who told me with what I think was genuine sadness, "I have lived in India thirty-four years and I have never met an Indian I can absolutely trust. They always let you down." (But if I print this the objurgation of a million Indians will crash on my head.)

Another eminent Englishman, not an I. C. S. man, suggested to me that Britain had made four "great mistakes" in India. But he was quick to add that they were not "vicious" mistakes:

1. Importation of a western judicial system into an eastern country incapable of understanding it. Too many lawyers.

2. A totally faulty policy in education. Indians came to feel that the only object in life was to become a clerk.

3. The high standard of living emphasized by British, which led Indians to try to imitate it.

4. Snobbery. The color line. (But, he pointed out, the institution of *purdah* made social intercourse between British and Indians extremely difficult.)

All of which leads to a conundrum often posed. Is the docility, by and large, of Indians, and the lack of gumption (speaking generally) in their character, caused by something inherent in Indian nature—

the product of a savage climate, perhaps, and centuries of poverty and underdevelopment before the British came—or is it the result of British rule in the past hundred-odd years? In other words, as Basil Mathews has put it, is India a subject state because it is weak, or is it weak because it is a subject state? The best answer evades the issue. It is—both.

Coda

British policy in India in a word is to "yield the appearance of power while keeping the substance of power." Indian policy in a word is to defeat this aim. The resultant situation at the moment—early in 1939—is a compromise. The British know that suppression of a fixed and arbitrary type is no longer possible; they know that to quit India is impossible if the Empire is to survive; so somehow, by some miracle, they have to make the Indians their friends.

Crisis will probably come in the event of a European war, since a real smash-up on the Federation issue is unlikely. Will India be loyal as it was in 1914; will India send troops to France, let alone remain passive at home?[3] The easy thing to say is, of course, that if Congress played its cards correctly it could gain enormously by any such crisis. It could promise to remain loyal—*in return* for an advance in independence—if the British are risking war on any issue that Congress could even remotely approve, as over Czechoslovakia in 1938. This will probably be the Indian line.

[3] The Sino-Japanese war has changed prognostications somewhat. India is afraid of Japan, and Congress loathes Fascism; many Indians realize that British imperialism is not so bad as Japanese or Fascist imperialism.

Chapter XXX

The Far Frontiers

〜〜〜〜〜〜〜〜〜〜〜〜〜〜〜〜〜〜〜〜〜〜〜〜〜〜〜

THE North West Frontier Province is *sui generis*. It is unique. It is the remote region separating India from Afghanistan and Turkestan, the barrier between India and the great world of the West, the chief bastion of India, the reef of rock over which conquerors have climbed from Alexander the Great to Genghis Khan and into modern times. It is the "best" part of India, the British say.

A series of rippling gray-brown crags and valleys; the winding road with one channel for camels, one for autobuses; loose and scrawny bullocks in the sparse fields; intolerable mud when it rains, intolerable dust when it doesn't; 120 in the shade for months on end, and bitter cold in winter; well-armed tribesmen coming to market, wearing multicolored turbans; the thick yellowish houses behind mud walls, and a sentry tower for each compound; men squatting in loose circles before the glassless shops of the bazaar—such are the villages on the Frontier, along the Khyber Pass, and in Waziristan.

The Frontier region is complex. The people are mostly Sunni Moslems by religion; they are Afghan by race, and speak a language known as Pushtu; they have a Congress government. The generic name for the tribesmen is "Pathan" (pronounced Pa-*tan*); subdivisions include Mohmands, Tirahs, Wazirs, and the warlike Afridis. The Pathans are not a fierce people unless provoked, but they are primitive, and they like to be let alone; the whole area is, as it were, in *purdah*, behind a curtain. As a whole it can muster perhaps 600,000 rifles.

Political consciousness among the tribes, especially the Afridis, is growing strongly. The young men don't like the basic conservatism of the *maliks*, their elders. Some tribal unions choose their own foreign ministers, finance ministers, and the like, after the manner of western states, though they may command only a few dozen scattered villages. Then there are the Red Shirts. These cut across tribal and feudal lines and belong to the Indian National Congress, under the leadership of Khan Abdul Gaffar Khan, the "Frontier Gandhi."

Like other mountain barriers—the Caucasus for instance—the Frontier region is a wonderful living museum of anthropological lore.

Many of the more primitive folk live by raiding. So the local proverb says, "A moonlight night is my daughter's dowry." Another legend is that, in the old days, a mother cut a hole in the wall of her mud hut when a son was born. Three times she would stick the infant's head through the hole, muttering three times the incantation "Be a thief." It was the only way to earn a decent living. Along the roads the greeting, as one villager encounters another, is "Be not wary." The second villager replies, "Be not poor."

The roads are the veins of the country. So along the roads a curious ritual is observed. They are considered neutral ground for all. It is considered tactless in the extreme to shoot anyone on the road. Public convenience demanded this amelioration. In the hills you may be anybody's victim; on the roads you are safe. Many villagers have as a result built tunnels from their central watchtower to the roads, so that they can cross the intervening fields safely. At sundown the pace quickens along the roads. All cattle, all women, must be indoors by dusk.

Near the town of Kohat in tribal territory is an arms factory, one of the most bizarre things I have ever seen. In open huts, squatting in the mud, giving power to rude machines by pedaling bicycle wheels, a group of perhaps forty workmen is busy manufacturing—rifles! The tribesmen smuggle the steel, bore the barrels, cast the bolts, whittle the woodwork, assemble the parts, and stamp the finished guns—with handsome counterfeit dies—with whatever British insignia is fashionable. The factory can turn out thirty rifles a month, which cost from 35 to 50 rupees each. The British are perfectly aware that this arms factory exists, but they wink at it, even though it makes weapons to shoot British troops. The catch is that the rifles aren't much good. They last only 150 or 200 rounds before they need reboring. And if the tribesmen were not allowed to make their own bad guns, they might buy good ones from Afghanistan. The factory does not produce machine guns. Perhaps it would be suppressed if it tried to. But the Pathans do not like machine guns, on the picturesque theory that they use too much ammunition.

· · · · · · ·

The most interesting thing about the Frontier is that there are two frontiers.

This is an essential as well as extraordinary point. The two frontiers are (a) the Durand Line, which is the political boundary between British India and Afghanistan, the only one shown on most maps, and (b) the line known as the "Administrative Boundary," which runs irregularly about thirty miles east of the political boundary, and which demarcates the zone actually administered by Britain. In other words there is a belt of land along the whole Frontier, varying in width, which is part of British India on the map (all maps except big-scale military maps), but which is not British India in fact. This belt, this buffer, a No-Man's Land, is known as "tribal" territory. It is like the princely states—a part of the Empire in which British authority does not rule by law. Neither the parliament in London nor the government of India legislates for this region, which is governed by the tribes themselves under their *jirgas* or tribal councils.

The reason for this anomaly is historical. Ever since the occupation of India by Britain the Frontier has been a special problem. For one thing, fear of Russia in the old days—the Walking Bear of Mr. Kipling—demanded a "strong" frontier policy. This gateway to India had to be protected. For another, the tribes themselves made trouble, marauding from their hills into the Indus plains. For fifty or sixty years, say from the Indian Mutiny to Lord Curzon, the tribesmen made repeated raids, and had regularly to be pushed back. The point was—how far to push them back?

There were two schools of British thought. One, the "Forward School," suggested cleaning up the tribes once for all right to the Afghan Frontier. This would have meant exhaustive and expensive military operations. The other, the "Close Border" school, suggested retiring altogether from the hills and making Britain's line of defense the river Indus. Neither school had its way. Lord Curzon invented a compromise, which has persisted with modifications to this day. The frontier region is divided into two spheres. In one, the British hold complete power in the ordinary way. In the other, the elastic belt between the two frontiers, the tribesmen remain in theory independent.

This compromise turned out to be particularly useful in relations between Britain and Afghanistan. Should Afghanistan be unfriendly—and there was an Afghan war as late as 1919—the tribal area provides a convenient buffer. If Afghanistan is friendly, as it is now, the British, acting against the tribes, are saved the embarrassment of pushing them into Afghan territory. The belt of tribal area permits the British to deal with the tribes without coming too close to Afghanistan. And the Afghans are among the most sensitive of the earth's people in regard to territorial infringements.

The British control their own territory by, of course, British law and British force of arms, under a Congress government. They control tribal territory largely by a system of subsidies—bribes. The tribes are divided into two categories, the "assured clans," and those not assured. The "assured clans" are those that get money. They are paid to keep quiet; in return the British "assure" them protection. All told, the annual "assurance" bill on the North West Frontier is probably half a million pounds.

The military complexion of the Frontier is picturesque. There are no British troops in tribal territory—with one exception to be noted presently below. In British territory there are, it goes without saying, troops of the Indian army and of the British Army in India; in tribal territory there are tribal levies called Khassadars.

These Khassadars wear almost any kind of costume, though a *puggeri* (turban) distinguishes them; they supply their own rifles and their own food; they are paid 25 rupees per month. It is a remarkable system. The men are volunteers, and many former raiders have given up warfare to join up. The Khassadars look fairly sloppy, but I was assured that they made good troops. They are a great convenience to the British, not only because many tribesmen are bought off from making trouble, but because—if the Khassadars should happen to join warring tribes or run away—the British lose no rifles, no officers, no prestige. The Khassadar system transmits to the tribesmen themselves the responsibility of maintaining order.

But in one tribal district the British have definitely undertaken military penetration and occupation. This is Waziristan. Here distinction between "administered" and "non-administered" areas loses its meaning; here the administrative boundary has been pushed almost to the actual Durand Line, or political Frontier. This happened when the British determined to clean up Waziristan after the Afghan war in 1919; they dotted the country with military posts, and began to build roads, in order to keep the Wazirs—a turbulent people—permanently subdued. This decision caused much woe.

Helen of Troy on the North West Frontier

Her name was Musamat Ram, and she came from a town named Bannu. At least that was her name in the beginning; now she is called "Islam Bibi," the Baby of Islam if you prefer. Her story happened to coincide with that of a tribal chieftain known as the Faqir of Ipi, and the combination of the two produced a war. This Baby of Islam, this modern Helen of Troy, was a contributory cause to setting more than 35,000 British and Indian troops in motion. Probably she never saw $100 in her life. So far she, plus circumstances, has cost the British and Indian taxpayer about $37,500 per day above normal military expenditure, or a total of roughly eleven million dollars to the end of 1937.

Helen of Troy, wife of Menelaus, ran off with the Trojan Paris some twenty-nine hundred years ago. So the legend goes. Musamat Ram, "Islam Bibi," ran off with a Moslem schoolmaster in 1936. The abduction of the first Helen of Troy set Greeks marching against the inhabitants of Asia Minor. The abduction of this contemporary Helen of Troy set Wazirs marching against British. The first Helen was carried off by an alien prince; her people rose to retrieve her. The second Helen went away with one of her own people, but against her people's will. The first Helen caused a war in which many gods played great part. The second performed her rôle because of a fierce religious crisis.

Musamat Ram was a girl of good Hindu family who—note well the approximate age—was "about" sixteen when she met a young Moslem named Nur Ali Shah. He was a schoolmaster in her native town. Also he was a Sayyed, or lineal descendant of the Prophet Mohammed, and thus a Moslem of a peculiarly Moslem sort. Of course Hindu-Moslem tension and bitterness is an old story on the Frontier. Musamat Ram ran off with the young Moslem of her own free will, she says; he abducted her, according to the story of her outraged parents.

They were so indignant not only because her abductor was a Moslem, but because she was under age and had married without her parents' consent. The Hindu family system is parsimoniously rigid; daughters are their parents' property and should bring a good price at matrimony. So the parents called in the police, who brought

Musamat Ram back, and jailed her young man. Then began a long
series of legal processes.

First Nur Ali Shah was sentenced to jail for two years for abduction. Later the sentence was reduced. Musamat Ram rose in court,
amid a tangle of lawyers and birth certificates, and denied she was a
Hindu any longer; she said that she had embraced Islam. The court
ruled that she must return to her parents anyway. The case was appealed, and again the parents won. Musamat Ram, still asserting that
she was now a Mohammedan, was dragged back to her parents' home.
They packed her off to exile, and betrothed her to a Hindu.

Now the affair entered politics. Some one called the Faqir of Ipi
took it up. He took it up by making war.

The Waziristan War

The war known as the Waziristan War, led on the Waziristan
side by the Faqir of Ipi, began in November 1936, fizzled out after
a year of serious fighting in December 1937, and cropped up in the
shape of minor rebellions again in 1938. The Faqir, a youthful
fanatic, was not well known in Waziristan before the war began.
British intelligence officers ticketed him No. 40 in their list of Waziri
chiefs. His brother was supposed to be a much more important fellow. The Faqir held a minor post in government service for some
years and had a reputation for fervent devotion to Mohammedanism
and little more.

What the Faqir did was to seize on the abduction case and make a
burning issue of it. He inflamed the countryside by harangues ex-
plaining the scandal and denouncing the *kafirs*, infidels, who had
brought ruin to this converted Moslem maiden. He gave her the
new name, Islam Bibi, and exhorted his followers to revenge themselves on the British and the Hindus. He preached a *jehad*, holy war.
The countryside became restive, and in November 1936 the British
decided to make a show of force in the region, by means of a "Flag
March" through the disaffected territory; they sent out a small detachment to impress the villagers. Then a curious incident occurred.
A stampede of mules took place and some 400 mules laden
with their burden, which happened to be military overcoats, scampered
into the hills of the Khaisora Valley. So a wonderful rumor spread—
that the British had been defeated in battle, and the 400 overcoats

were looted from the dead! A small item perhaps, but it increased tension. Hostilities began.

The British found that the Faqir of Ipi—he took this name from the Waziri villiage which was his headquarters—was a person of some quality. He had political ability and he was full of tricks. For instance, he knew that the British never bombed a locality without first sending down warning pamphlets. So, moving to a new encampment, he told his followers that he had the power to turn bombs into paper. The Royal Air Force squadrons duly turned up; they scattered their leaflets, as the Faqir knew they would; proudly he showed the village the bits of paper which he said had been bombs.

On another occasion the Faqir claimed that he could turn machine-gun bullets into paper too. Serious fighting had begun by this time. A mournful woman showed him the body of her son, fallen in battle, and demanded that the Faqir eat his boastful words. He imperturbably replied, "Ah, yes, your son is dead; it is because you did not believe in me enough."

The Faqir seized not only on the Islam Bibi affair but on other sources of Hindu-Moslem trouble, for instance the Shahidgunj Mosque case in Lahore—a complicated business in regard to rights of religious worship—and the old case of Rangila Rasul. A Hindu journalist named Rajpal wrote a book called *Licentious Prophet.* It purported to be a biography of Mohammed and it was furiously resented by the Moslem community. The author was arrested, and the High Court acquitted him after a lower court had given him five years on a criminal libel charge. Fierce controversy raged. There were three different attempts to assassinate Rajpal; finally a young Moslem got to him and did kill him. The Moslem assassin was then hanged. The Moslems in the north have considered this a bitter grievance ever since.

These were various items in the origin of the Waziristan War. The Faqir himself would add another. He denies that he ever encouraged the tribes to raid or loot; he asserts that he acted purely as a nationalist patriot. The basic cause of the war, he insists, was the occupation by Britain of the Waziri tribal areas: the British provoked the people of Waziristan to armed resistance by entering territory they had no "right" to enter, and the Waziris had to defend themselves.

The British technique in a highly difficult and expensive campaign was to advance slowly, establish posts ahead, build safe roads between them, and, above all, use the air. The air was indispensable. Yet all the time the British had to act with the utmost caution; they had to keep two contrary objectives in view, to wipe up the Wazirs and capture the Faqir; second, to do this as gently as possible, so that other tribesmen would not rise and join the enemy. They had to catch the Faqir, but they had to catch him inconspicuously. They had to conquer one enemy, but by means which would not give them more enemies in the same region.

The war ended in a draw. First, the Faqir was never caught. (Had he been caught, he would not have been hanged or even punished; instead, in their curious way, the British would have given him a good job somewhere.) He dodged back into the Madda Khel country, close to the Afghan border, and the British can't find him. Second, the other tribes did not rise. Had the fighting spread to the Mahsuds nearby, the war would have been thrice as difficult and costly. Midway through the war Musamat Ram, Islam Bibi, ceased to be an important issue. The court reversed the previous verdict. She was adjudged a Moslem after all, her lover got out of jail, and triumphantly she rejoined him.

. . . .

There are three schools of thought among the British as to means of permanent settlement of the Waziri problem and the Frontier area. The hardboiled school says to wipe the tribes out, disarm them completely, and end the paradox whereby there are two frontiers. But to put this policy into effect would cost millions of pounds, and might necessitate a ten years' campaign. Also it might bring complications with Afghanistan.

The second school suggests maintaining the present system, but improving it. That is, build barbed wire fences, build more forts, keep the tribes in better order by stricter military means. Third, other military experts and most of the civilians say let matters rest as they are, trust in the subsidy system and the Khassadars, and hope for the best. The easiest solution is to train the tribes to maintain order themselves.

A major constituent of the Frontier problem is economics. The tribes raid for booty. Give them enough to live on, and they will raid no more. But there are great difficulties in the way of economic improvement. The country is arid, irrigation is impracticable: the native Khans or landowners are jealous of their privileges. The best thing to do is build more roads. The roads add life to the land; they help to make the land safe, to bring security and gain.

Afghanistan

We have little space for Afghanistan, Tibet, Burma, and the other regions adjacent to India. Afghanistan, an independent kingdom, rugged and railroadless, is a kind of footnote to Persia, which I will deal with in the next chapter, but it is several generations behind Persia. The Afghans are incredibly sensitive. A London newspaper correspondent once inadvertently called the British Legation the "Residency," which it had recently been; the Afghans considered themselves so affronted that they refused him permission to reënter the country. Another journalist once aroused severe protests by mentioning that flies swarmed in the bazaars of Kabul, the remote capital.

Even educated Afghans have little experience of the West. It is said of the former king, Amanullah, that on his trip to Europe in 1927 he became convinced that the Russian navy was stronger than the British, because in Leningrad harbor he saw old fashioned cruisers with four tall funnels, whereas the up-to-the-minute British ships had only one short one! When an American diplomat presented his credentials some years ago, he was the third American citizen to arrive in Kabul. Amanullah asked him where he came from. The diplomat replied, "California." Amanullah commented that California must obviously be the most important American state, since the other two Americans who had been in Afghanistan had also—it happened—been Californians. One Afghan foreign minister was delighted to attend the Disarmament Conference at Geneva. He thought that, if disarmament came, it would provide a good chance for Afghanistan to buy arms cheaply. One Afghan ruler got tremendous pleasure out of Sears-Roebuck catalogues. He couldn't read them, but the pictures fascinated him.

Amanullah came to the throne in 1919, after his father, a powerful monarch, had reigned for twenty years. From about 1880 Great Britain had special "treaty relations" with Afghanistan, and paid the country a subsidy of £120,000 per year, in return for which it protected the Frontier and "superintended" its foreign relations. Amanullah, a stout person, resented this, and waged war on Britain.

The British slapped him back, and then—with that consummate shrewdness which distinguishes British imperialism—gave him what he wanted. They withdrew their control, and stopped the subsidy. Afghanistan became an independent state, poorer by £120,000 a year— and with Britain still unofficially holding the strings.

This Amanullah, worthy and well-meaning, was bitten deep with western virus. He wanted to modernize his primitive country, organize the wild tribesmen into a stable state. He was greatly influenced by his intelligent and able wife, Souriya, the daughter of a newspaper man who was descended from the old kings of Khandahar. But Amanullah had incessantly to beat down his own people, who, extremely backward Moslems, resented improvement. He wanted to reduce the power of the *mullahs*—priests—and to divide up the land. In 1923 civil war started because his government passed a law modifying the old right of a father to marry his daughter to whom he chose. In 1923 a girl did not like her father's choice of fiancé; she heard of the new law, and sought to have it invoked in her case. Her father promptly locked her up, consulted the village elders, shot her, and stirred up a revolution. In 1929 came another revolution, as a result of which Amanullah had to abdicate and flee. He had ordered deputies to the new parliament to wear western dress—shocking innovation!—and he had pushed other reforms too fast, especially those aimed at the priests. He wound the watch too tight; it sprang back at him. To-day, a royal exile, he lives in Rome.

The British hated to see Amanullah displaced. They liked him and worked well with him—even though he had been "too impressed" by Moscow. A confused period followed. For a week he was succeeded by a brother, whom the British had hopes of; the brother was in turn forced off the throne, and the R. A. F. flew him out of Kabul. Then came the king known as the "Water Boy," Bacha Saqao, an upstart of peasant blood, who lasted nine months and whose regime collapsed—in the stately words of the London *Times*—"in an orgy of licentiousness." Bacha was chased out by a cousin of Amanullah's known as Nadir, who became king as Nadir Shah. He had been Amanullah's best general, and was serving as Minister to Paris when the Water Boy seized power. Nadir gave promise of exceptionally enlightened rule, and might have become one of the great men of contemporary Asia, but in 1933 he was murdered by an inflamed student.

The King to-day is Nadir's youthful son, who was born in 1914.
But the real rulers are his three uncles, who are Nadir's surviving
brothers. The uncles form a powerful triumvirate, and the British
hope devoutly that nothing happens to them. One, Hashim Khan,
the strongest man in the country, is prime minister; another, Shah
Mahmud, is defense minister.

Afghanistan has twelve million people. Its 250,000 square miles
are a broad nugget between Persia, the U.S.S.R., the extreme western tip of Sinkiang (China), and British India. Were the country
more penetrable, more developed economically, the obvious strategic
importance of this position would be enhanced. As it is Kabul is the
scene of covert tension between Britain and the U.S.S.R.; Germany,
too, has been active diplomatically. Spies of several nations are attached to the remote consulates and listening posts. Even the Japanese
have entered the Afghan picture. They sell bicycles in Kabul for
$5.00, and hire secret agents. But it is said their tactics in espionage
are not good; they pick spies already hired by others.

Here—at long last—we can say good-by to the Japanese, with whom
indeed we have had little contact for some time. They play little
political rôle in Asia beyond Afghanistan.

Tibetan Topsyturvy

Here one must hold one's head. Tibet is without parallel. I have
written to the point of satiety about the interrelations of religion and
politics in Asia; in Tibet the admixture reaches its extreme form, for
it is a purely theocratic state. It is governed by Buddhist or Lamaist
priests who are considered almost literally divine, and who exert
their power by terms of an extraordinarily complex convention. The
rulers of the country are incarnations of the Heavenly Buddha—no
less.

There are two chief sources of spiritual (which means temporal)
authority, the Tashi Lama (lama = priest) and the Dalai Lama. They
are in theory of equal rank, and *both* are, as it were, the leader of
the country; it is as if England had two kings, or Vatican City two
popes. The Dalai Lama lives in Lhassa, the capital, and tends
to stress the temporal side of rule, while the Tashi Lama, more
spiritual, lives in Shigatse monastery. Often there is rivalry between the two, but in theory they complement each other. They are

like the Archbishops of Canterbury and York; depending on circumstances and personality, one may at the moment be more prominent than the other.[1] The Tibetans want two lamas, so that the elder may train the younger, and so that the younger may assist in the divination of the successor when the elder dies.

The lamas are chosen by reincarnation. Tibet is, it may be safely asserted, the only state in the world in which the heir is selected by inflexible rule *after* the ruler's death; until the ruler dies, no one can know who the successor will be, because the successor should be an infant born at approximately the moment that the lama dies. The principle is that of reincarnation: the soul of the departing lama who is a personification of Buddha, must enter a child born as nearly as possible at the same time, so that the progression is continuous; the life of Buddha never stops. The new lama, usually a child, is found by divination. Secret signs are discerned; initials of the previous lama may shimmer in his home. But the successor must be *searched for*, and found, among all the children in the realm.

Sometimes—in fact often—no reincarnation of the lama can be discovered for years. The Tibetans are very strict in following their ritual. Parties are sent out to look for the chosen infant, and may spend a decade in the search, with frequent false alarms. This means, obviously, that there are often long *regencies*; some have lasted twenty years. Thus developed, too, abuse of the ritual, because unscrupulous regents could attempt to retain power by frustrating the search, or even—as happened several times in the last century—by poisoning prospective candidates. Not merely the Tashi and Dalai lamas are reincarnated. So are hundreds of others, the chief dignitaries in the great monasteries and other personages of state.

The situation in 1939 is that Tibet has no Tashi Lama. The last one, a distinguished and pious old man, died in exile in China last year—he shocked Tibet greatly by fleeing for political reasons—and no reincarnation has been found. The present Dalai Lama is a boy of four, who is said to have been discovered in March, 1938, in a remote part of Tibet, after a five-year search. The former Dalai Lama died in 1933, a man of humble origin. He was the thirteenth of his line, the first Dalai Lama having been created in 1391 A.D.

[1] The double motif is conspicuous in Tibetan life; for instance there are two equal commanders-in-chief of the army—neither of whom incidentally may be a military man.

Government is dominated by the priestly class, which is not surprising since at least one son of every family becomes a monk; one-fifth of the total population are priests. Since only one lama exists at present, and since he is a small child, the contemporary power resides with a regency—in theory. The present regent, a priest named Thupten Jampel Yishey Gyantsen, was born in 1911, a poor boy. He was discovered to be the fifth incarnation of the head of the great Reting monastery, and took part in the search for the new Dalai Lama. On completion of his studies at the monastery of Sera in 1934 he became regent. For a special reason. There are complications in Tibet.

Behind the regent is a more potent figure, the prime minister. The present one is Yapshi Langdun Kung; he was born in 1906, and he became prime minister in 1926. He is not a priest, and he got his job from the then Dalai Lama, who deliberately wanted a very youthful (and hence weak) prime minister; when the Dalai Lama died, this young prime minister (who was not so weak) turned posthumous tables on him by appointing the regent, who is even younger (and weaker) than himself. So to-day we have a new Dalai Lama, a boy of four, for whom a 28-year-old regent reigns, who is in turn controlled by a 33-year-old prime minister. The prime minister is boss. However—just to make it simple—this is not the whole story. Behind all these dignitaries is the personage known as the "Official Oracle." Born in 1894, he is the Great Lama of Nechung monastery, and must be consulted by all in any crisis. In giving advice he goes into a trance, thus putting himself at the disposal of the deity.

The chief lamas are buried in Lhassa, the capital. They are given magnificent shrines. A new one, erected in memory of the last Dalai Lama, was recently built at Potala, on a hill crowning the city; it is roofed in solid gold worth one million pounds.

A word on temporal matters. Tibet, as we know, is technically part of China, and is shown to be Chinese territory on most maps. In plain fact the Chinese government plays no political rôle in Lhassa whatever. Ever since the British first forced their way into the country, through the Younghusband mission in 1902, Tibet has been predominantly under their influence—exerted largely by remote control. There is no British representative in Lhassa, where the Tibetans do not wish foreigners to live; a British agent is stationed at Gyantse, nearer the Frontier. Treaty relations between Britain and China over Tibet are obscure. Occasionally a British mission visits the country. The most recent one brought something that Tibet had never seen before—movies. The shrewd British chose a Rin-Tin-Tin dog film, an old Chaplin comedy, and a documentary of England's kings.

The British spearhead into Tibet is Sikkim, the most northward of the Indian princely states. Normally one assumes Tibet to be locked off from the world by some kind of special barrier; in fact the only barrier is the natural one of geography (the pass into the country is 14,000 feet high), and there is not even a gendarme at the Sikkim-Tibet boundary. The real frontier is that between British India and Sikkim, which is carefully controlled. Visitors to Sikkim are required to sign a pledge that they will not enter Tibet. Should a visitor do so, he probably would not be torn to pieces if he behaved sensibly; the Tibetans are pleasant if aloof people, and strangers—if they get in—are simply escorted back to the Frontier.

The Maharaja of Sikkim is a shy, smiling Buddhist in a yellow robe, whose hair is still braided, who listens to London on a huge new radio, and whose children ask wistfully about gangsters in Chicago.

Two Political Curiosities

Nepal is an extraordinarily interesting state in the Himalayas between Tibet and British India. Since 1923 it has been independent, though the British continue to give it an annual subsidy—1,000,000 rupees ($370,000) a year, which is not much—and to recruit from Nepal the Gurkhas who are among the best troops in the Indian army. Nepal, though flanked by Buddhist states, is a citadel of Hinduism in its most extreme form; the penalty of killing a cow is—still!—death. It is ruled by a king, known as the Golden Basilisk, a figurehead; by Nepalese tradition, power is vested in the Maharaja or prime minister, who holds his post by a semi-hereditary process. His relation to the king is almost precisely that of the Shogun to the Japanese Emperor before 1868.

Since 1934 Nepal has sent a minister to the Court of St. James. This flattered the Nepalese—who are enormously sensitive, like the Afghans—but it presented difficulties, since no Nepalese Brahman may cross water without losing caste. Eventually it was arranged that the Nepalese envoy should take the trip, duly lose caste, and then regain it when he returned to Nepal by a special and drastic purification ceremony.

The neighboring state of Bhutan is in a category of its own; it is neither completely independent, nor is it a princely state like other Indian native states. Like Nepal, it was originally part of China, and like Tibet, it is Buddhist in religion. The British control the foreign relations—if any—of Bhutan, and pay it a small subsidy. The ruling Maharaja, born in 1926, has the picturesque name of Jig-me Wang-chuk; the Chinese strain is very conspicuous in his features, and he wears his hair long. His prime minister is an engaging and intelligent personality, the Raja Dorji. Bhutan is probably the only state in the world in which elephants became a problem in policy. An "Elephant Convention" has been signed with British India, so that the Bhutanese get recompense for their elephants who migrate to Indian territory every spring, and get killed there.

The Pleasant Burmese

Burma is a big country. It covers 261,000 square miles, precisely the area of the old Austria-Hungary. It has conspicuous resources in silver, tin, teak, tungsten, and oil, and is the biggest rice exporting nation in the world; the British detached it from the dying body of the Manchu Empire in the 1860's, and have exploited it ever since. The Burmese, a pleasant people, still bear strong Chinese characteristics; they are Buddhists, and by and large are more animated than Indians, more cheerful. There is no caste in Burma, no purdah. The Englishman says that you can tell when you have entered Burma because the Burmese smile.

Burma was separated from India by the 1935 Act. At present, like Ceylon, it is administered by the colonial office, though later it will have a special status. The British, as always, are elastic. By cutting Burma off from India (Aden on the Arabian peninsula was cut off at the same time), Britain insures itself of footholds on both sides of India, should the almost inconceivable eventuality of successful Indian revolution occur. But the Indian National Congress is increasing its strength in Burma steadily.

The chief political issue in Burma is resentment by the underpossessed, who have now reached political consciousness through the "Thakins," or young radicals, against the privileges of the yellow-robed Buddhist priests. During 1938 there were intermittent serious riots between Moslems and Buddhists, especially in the capital, Rangoon. The prime minister, and the biggest man in the country, is a 45-year-old lawyer, Dr. Ba Maw. He is cautiously Leftist. The competent home minister, a chunky smiling man, whose wife is American, is U Paw Tun. In Burmese "U" is an honorific corresponding roughly to Mister.

So much for the vast complex of India and its periphery. We turn now to the new world of the Middle East.

Chapter XXXI
King of Kings: The Shah of Iran

∾∾∾∾∾∾∾∾∾∾∾∾∾∾∾∾∾∾∾

I have made my country young, and myself old.
—His Imperial Majesty Reza Shah Pahlevi

Entrance into Iran, which is the official name of Persia nowadays,
is explosive. Here is the real Asia, here is Asia naked. This is
the magnificent and impregnable inner fastness of the Moslem world.
For two days, three days, your car bounces and slithers, writhes and
groans, climbing the terrific passes between Bagdad and Teheran,
wallowing in stones and mud, leaping crevasses and landslips, pene-
trating villages which can have changed very little since the days of
Xerxes, and cutting across country the color of Gorgonzola cheese
and the consistency of pumice stone.

This country, which killed Alexander the Great and produced the
Ardebil carpet, exists in several dimensions. On the horizontal plane
it lies between the Caspian and the Persian Gulf and thus is a
buffer between the Soviet Union and British India. Considered verti-
cally, it is a crust of rock, like wax sealing a bottle of paste, on top
of some of the richest oil deposits in the world. From the point of
view of time, it is one of the most ancient of states—and until recently
one of the most dilapidated—brought by the energy and acumen of the
present Shah to the threshold of modern times.

Iran is a fastness not only because of its inflexible geography and
remoteness, but by reason of the primitive character of its people. There
are about 15,000,000 of them, living on a plateau three times as
big as France. They are villagers and nomads mostly. Iranians are
Aryan by race, not Semitic like the other peoples of the middle
East; their language, though it is written in roughly the same alphabet as Arabic, differs from Arabic as much, say, as English differs
from Portuguese. They are mostly Moslems of the Shia variety,
fanatically backward. All through his career the Shah has had to
fight the *mullahs*, priests. A foreigner will, literally, be torn to pieces
should he try to gain entrance to some of the more holy shrines.

499

Recently the Shah introduced a considerable reform: visitors may enter some mosques—provided they have police protection!

The villages, built mostly of mud, haven't changed much since Xerxes—but they do have filling stations. They are desolate with poverty and squalor—but the petrol pump has become the center of the community. The trucks, the camions, drink the gasoline, then plunge onward to Ispahan or Shiraz or Teheran. The trucks roar up and down the Iranian roads all day, all night, carrying cargoes of tea and opium, rugs and lubricating oil. The roads are dangerous. On the three-day trip to Teheran I counted five monsters demolished at the bottom of ravines.

As more cars, more trucks, lunge through the rocks and mud, as more roads are built, the life of the modern world comes to the villages. I saw children marching neatly to school—the girls wear a gray smock with white cuffs, a sort of uniform—and one proudly showed me her new geography textbook. The old restrictions on travel, which were incredibly onerous—the visitor had to pass a police examination entering *and* leaving every village, even if he were traveling direct from the frontier to Teheran—have been largely eliminated. There are movies in some of the towns. Along the road, the gendarmes try to be helpful; they are uniformed in blue, blue being the color of hope.

We slid into a camel caravan just outside Teheran. The road was asphalt at last, incredible and merciful relief.

My chauffeur, who spoke a little French, permitted himself an observation. The Shah, who believes in the modern world, will not admit camels into Teheran itself, the chauffeur said; in fact, he almost refuses to concede that camels still exist. So the caravans have to sleep outside the city gates. The chauffeur chuckled. Then he asked quite seriously: "Have you got rid of the camels yet in Paris and New York?"

Entrance into Teheran is exciting too. The city is one of the most beautiful I have ever seen, dominated by the 16,000 feet of snowy Mount Demevand. The new boulevards are spacious, the trees are nicely planted. But between street and sidewalk are the ditches, full of dogs, cats, and the drinking water. Teheran does things by sudden jumps. It is a mixture of primitiveness and sophistication. Splendid boulevards and dial telephones—but no sewage system!

At the end of one imposing, tree-lined street I came across a building that puzzled me. Architecturally it seemed familiar. It was handsomely built, severe in style, a sturdy cube of steel and concrete. Inside I saw what seemed to be a concourse, concrete ramps, broad steps leading somewhere, and oval windows guarded by shining rails. Then it dawned on me. The building was the new railway station. But my guide explained that, although the station was complete, there still were no trains.

A large area near the center of Teheran has been leveled. This is— if I may use the word "is"—the stock exchange or bourse. Several years ago the Shah decided that Teheran, like other great capitals, must have a bourse. An international architects' competition produced admirable plans. Then some one saw pictures of another stock exchange bigger than the winning blueprints. So the plans were scrapped. The Shah wanted the biggest bourse in the world. But financial stringency came to Iran, the building was never erected, and the site is still an empty ruin.

Recently the new and magnificent opera house was completed. But Iran has no opera!

Career of the Shah-in-Shah

Reza Shah Pahlevi, whose story is one of the greatest Horatio Alger episodes in history, was born in the district of Mazanderan, near the Caspian, about sixty-five years ago. No one knows the exact date or exact circumstances. The man who reached one of the most renowned thrones in the world, who became *Shah-in-Shah* (King of Kings), Shadow of the Almighty, Vice Regent of God, and Center of the Universe, is distinctly a man of the people, a kind of modern Cæsar or Cromwell, who lifted himself into history by his own bootstraps, who rose from humble origins by his own inherent qualities of courage and endurance. At forty he was an unknown officer. In his early fifties he was Shah of Persia.

Very little is known of his youth. He was certainly poor, though his family may have been well established in the region. He could have had only the briefest schooling, because when he first became prominent he was almost illiterate. Probably he tended flocks in Mazanderan, like the other peasant boys; probably he lived in a mud hut and ate bits of sheep for supper; possibly he had heard of Darius and Cyrus, whom he was to succeed. One story is that for a time he was a servant in a foreign legation in Teheran. It is more likely, however, that he may have been posted to duty there as a legation guard, after he joined the army. Teheran is full of apocryphal stories of the Shah's humble origins and early career.

We begin with a fact. As a boy Reza took to soldiering; he enlisted in the Cossack division of the Persian army, a Persian force officered by Russians. Weak Persia used foreign officers then; the old dynasty was crumbling, and the country was a battleground of mercenaries. In the north the Cossack division exerted a strong Russian influence; the South Persian Rifles, officered by British, dominated the south; a neutral Swedish gendarmerie kept order in Teheran. For twenty years Reza was a trooper in the Cossack division. He finally rose from the ranks to become an officer.

The War came and it seemed for a time that the old hungry enemies, Britain and Russia, would gobble Persia between them. Technically Persia remained neutral; nevertheless British troops occupied a zone in the south, and operated, first against the Turks, then against the Russians, in the north. Once again we cross the trail of Western imperialism and its ambitions. The Bolshevik revolution led to intervention by the Allies, and British and Soviet troops fought along the Caspian. Meantime the old Russian officers fled or were killed, and the Cossack division began to disintegrate.

A British colonel named Smythe was stationed at Kazvin, in northern Persia. This was in 1920, by which time the British had a virtual protectorate over the country. Smythe spotted Reza as an officer of courage, and put him in command of the Cossack division, hoping thus to save it. Later General Sir Edmund Ironside came to Kazvin to arrange withdrawal of British troops. Ironside confirmed Reza's appointment. Had it not been for the discerning eyes of these two British officers, Reza Khan (as he was then known) might have lived and died an obscure Cossack officer.

Intervention against the Bolsheviks failed; the British gave up their Persian foothold, and Lord Curzon saw his dream disappear, that of a roseate British bloc from Dardanelles to the Indus, through Turkey, Persia, and Afghanistan. At about the same time the Russians, for quite different reasons, dropped Persia too; Lenin offered to give up special rights there, and in 1921, a Russian-Persian treaty freed Persia from its obligations to the Czar. The Russians gave Persia joint command of the Caspian Sea, canceled about $20,000,000 indebtedness, and proclaimed the end of Czarist imperialism. On the other hand, the Russians maintained the right to send troops into Persia in case intervention began again.

It didn't. And an interesting thing happened. Persia had been so long a buffer between Britain and Russia that it had seemingly no will to live alone. Tension between the two great powers supported her; when the tension was withdrawn she collapsed. Corruption ruled Teheran, and banditry all but ruled the country. The foreign troops were gone, and the morale of government sank to an unbelievable level. Everything was toppling. The reigning sovereign, Sultan Ahmed Shah, last of the Kajar dynasty, a fat puppet, lived in Deauville and gave fortunes in rubies to chorus girls. He was called the Grocer-Boy Shah, when he wasn't called something even less complimentary, because he bought the entire grain crop of the country during a famine and then sold it to the starving people at fantastic prices.

In *Asia* Magazine Vincent Sheean has preserved a precious anecdote of this period. "Corruption was at its height in Teheran in those days, but it is yet to be proved that anyone got anything for his money. Rothstein, the Soviet Ambassador in Teheran at the time, told me long afterward in Moscow that he had come to the conclusion that Persia was 'fundamentally sound.' Asked to give the reasons for this view, he found an almost unanswerable one. 'They will take money from anyone,' he explained, 'from the British today and from the Russians tomorrow, or from the French or the Germans or anybody else. But they will never do anything for the money. You may buy their country from them six times over, but you will never get it. Therefore I say Persia can never go under. Persia is fundamentally sound.'"

But then something happened—something more significant than anything in Persian history since Genghis Khan and Tamurlane.

Reza Khan, the veteran Cossack trooper, now in command of his division, advanced into the picture.

A group of young men, led by a journalist, Sayyed Zia-ed-Din, decided to make a coup d'état. Their intention was not to change the dynasty but merely to install a reformed government and they chose Reza as their military arm. Reza picked 2,500 men from the Kazvin garrison and entered Teheran on the night of February 20, 1921. The plans were well made, and the coup was bloodless. Reza's troops simply occupied the government offices and a new cabinet was proclaimed, with Reza as commander-in-chief of the army.

Then events came quickly. Reza was obviously the power behind the government. He got rid of Zia-ed-Din, and made himself minister of war. In 1923, he took office as prime minister. He spent two years consolidating his position and bringing the remote provinces under his control. He began his reforms by importing an American financial commission, and he crushed the last powerful semi-autonomous chieftains in the south.

The Grocer-Boy Shah, Sultan Ahmed, returned from the ladies of Biarritz and Deauville to take one quick peek at his transformed country. He looked with approval, and apparently was not interested enough in Reza's growing strength to combat it. He went back to Paris, gave more rubies to chorus girls, and retired to the American hospital there, where he died after a fantastically expensive illness. Reza, meantime, unusually among Oriental figures, did not bother to revenge himself on the old dynasty, members of which still live peaceably in Teheran.

But he ended the old dynasty. He did not wait for Sultan Ahmed to die. In October, 1925, he forced a measure through the Majlis (parliament) unseating Ahmed and the Kajars; a few months later he was declared sovereign of Persia, the founder of the dynasty of Pahlevi, the name which he now adopted. For a time it seems that Reza flirted with the idea—like Kemal in Turkey—of making Persia a republic. But he could not risk further affronting the old *mullahs*, who were shocked enough at the displacement of the former royal line.

On April 25, 1926, Reza Shah Pahlevi was crowned. He had a new crown made, and, like Napoleon, put it on his own head.

Habits and Characteristics

"Now, O King, establish the decree, and sign the writing that it be not changed, according to the laws of the Medes and Persians, which altereth not."
—DANIEL vi. 8

The Shah to-day, in his middle or late sixties—no one knows exactly how old he is—is still a considerable figure of a man. From the earliest days his stature and physique marked him. The beaked nose (which is deeply scarred), the wide, pure white mustaches, the breadth of shoulder—these give him a regal presence. So do his formidable temper and the awe in which his people hold him. One revealing little anecdote is of the jockey who lost a big race in Teheran because he stopped to salute the Shah in the royal box.

His Imperial Majesty likes the races, and other stories seem to link his good hot trooper's temperament with racing. Once an unknown Turcoman tribesman beat a Persian officer, evidently a strong favorite, in a Teheran race. In full view of the diplomatic corps and the élite of Iranian society, the unfortunate winner was led to the Shah, who, in the words of the *London Times* (November 28, 1933), "delivered a short lecture and proceeded to kick the tribesman in the stomach."

It is recorded that the Queen, quite by accident, let part of her face be seen while worshiping some years ago in Kum, the burial place of Fatima, daughter of the prophet. She was rebuked by the priest in charge, and there was a demonstration against her. The Shah sent tanks and armored cars to Kum, walked into the mosque with his shoes on, and with his own hands administered a severe beating to the priest.

Teheran officialdom is full of nerves every autumn after the annual races on the Turkoman steppe, which the Shah particularly likes, partly because they are in his home province of Mazanderan. The Shah relaxes at the races and returns to his capital refreshed. Then the purge begins. Fur and feathers fly, jobs and careers disappear, the underlings whimper and whisper, until His Majesty's spirits calm down.

His nationalism is violent. For instance, only Persian characters may be used in street signs and the like. Nameplates of foreigners in Teheran will be torn from the doors unless they are in Persian. Even the kilometer posts along the roads are painted with Arabic numerals—which are quite different from the English numerals which we call "Arabic." When he is ill—which is seldom—he insists on Persian doctors.

His political sense, his shrewdness and cunning are highly developed. Once he was suspicious of the loyalty of a minister of war who was a representative of the powerful Bakhtiari tribe. So the Shah launched a ballon d'essai to the effect that he himself was ill. Duly the tribe became restive. Promptly the Shah "recovered," dismissed the minister of war, and broke the Bakhtiari power.

There is virtually no public debt in Persia, and the Persian budget is always in balance. The finance minister, since he would not conceivably dare face the Shah with a deficit, always *under*estimates the national revenue. Oil royalties and income from the monopolies and other state enterprises, which Reza controls, go for public works. Recently the Shah donated his private gold to the country, and those crown jewels which have no great historical interest are to be sold.

He works enormously hard, like almost all modern dictators; he rises usually at five, and any cabinet officer or other high official may expect a call at any time of day or night. No matter what the time is, the person summoned is supposed to be at the palace within fifteen minutes. At cabinet meetings he scourges his ministers, pumping them full of his own vitality, making them work, making them proud to work, making them proud of Iran. He works too hard to have any hobbies—except the precious railroad he is building. He likes French wine, and smokes a little opium occasionally. He always carries a short string of amber beads which he fingers while talking.

Rulers of eastern countries like to keep their ears close to the ground, and it is said that the first person the Shah sees every day is the head of the secret police of the army, second, the head of the civilian secret police, third, the head of the regular police. After these come the regular audiences. He receives a great many people, and tends to an infinity of details himself. When he receives the foreign diplomats he is courteous and almost easy-going; he stands instead of sitting on one of his thrones; he usually greets a newcomer by saying that he is merely a "simple soldier," which of course he is not.

He has two palaces in Teheran, one just outside Teheran at Saadabad, and several summer residences on the Caspian. The Gulistan (Rose Garden) Palace, traditionally the home of the king, is no longer used except for official functions. Part of it is now a museum, and part houses the ministry of foreign affairs. The Peacock Throne, which is incidentally not a throne at all, but a sort of divan, is in the Gulistan Palace. The town palace where the Shah actually lives is a much simpler and more modern building. It lies in the best residential quarter of Teheran, surrounded by heavy trees and a twenty-foot brick wall. No traffic is permitted on the streets surrounding this palace after eight at night.

The Shah is believed to be the largest individual landowner in

Asia, except possibly the Emperor of Japan. He owns vast properties throughout Iran, largely those confiscated from rebellious former owners. Early in his reign he set out to break the power of the feudal landlords; he did so by the simple and direct method of taking over their property. He has not yet attempted a land reform in the sense of giving property to the peasants, but all the revenues from his land are supposed to be turned into the state budget for the common welfare. His Imperial Majesty is, oddly enough, the only monarch in the world in the hotel business. Travel in Persia is a state monopoly; the Shah personally owns most of the hotels, especially those along the Caspian. His motive is to build up a tourist trade, and to be able to see that visitors are treated well.

He never entertains, even officially; this is the prime minister's job. He is not easily accessible. Only one foreign journalist, Eugene Lyons, then of the United Press, has ever interviewed him. He has few confidantes, few friends. He rotates people in power, and officials are not apt to be conspicuous for very long periods. No one dares to say No to him. Probably he is one of the loneliest men in the world.

When the Shah travels, and he travels incessantly, he puts up an impressive show. He likes to go out and see the country himself, to investigate conditions on the spot, to check local affairs with his own eyes. He generally uses a big, very old Rolls-Royce, bulletproof; his eldest son, the Crown Prince, usually rides with him. The cavalcade, what with guards and advisers, may number sixteen cars; they whip along fairly comfortably, because no traffic of any kind is permitted for a day in advance on any road that the Shah is using. The roads are put in order, and the whole route refurbished; houses must be whitewashed in the villages where Reza stops, and fences painted green. The school children get new uniforms, and are drilled for days to present themselves. They must stand rigid when he passes, with the exception that they are taught to shift their eyes gradually from left to right or vise versa, in order to keep him in their vision while remaining motionless. The contrast to procedure before the Emperor of Japan is interesting; the Japanese, as we know, are not allowed to lift their eyes to see the monarch. When the Shah travels the dogs are killed in any village where he spends the night. This is because he is a light sleeper, easily disturbed by noise.

It isn't as heartless as it sounds, because there are thousands of stray dogs in the country, most of them with rabies.

Simple things please him greatly—things simple to us, but perhaps complicated to him. Once he set out to administer wholesale rebukes in a province near Azerbaijan. (He is full of strong localisms, and he happened to have a grudge against this section of his country.) But entering it he saw a jackknife bridge erected by one of his engineers. He had never seen one before, and he was so pleased that he called off the purge.

Reza, the Shah's first name, is common in Persia; it is the name of a well-known Shia saint, the Imam Reza, who is buried in the sacred city of Meshed. Pahlevi, the name he adopted for his dynasty, is an old word for the Persian language. (Incidentally "Pahlevi" was the telegraphic address of the Imperial Bank of Persia until the Shah appropriated it. The bank changed its telegraphic address to "Bactria.") He has renamed towns all over the country, some with his own name. In Soviet Russia we have Stalinabad, Stalinsk, Stalingrad; in Iran, we have Rezaieh for Urumia, Pahlevi for Enzeli, and so on. And he has, as everyone knows, changed the name of the country itself. "Persia" gave way to "Iran" in 1935, because the word "Persia" derives merely from the province of Fars, a limited area, whereas Iran denotes a wider territory—the whole great plateau from Turkey to Afghanistan.

Very little is known about the Shah's family life. He has had several wives and several children. His first marriage, like Mussolini's, took place long before he became famous; then he married a lady, related to the governor of Teheran, who was also a member of the Kajar family, and who is now his queen. This shows how strongly Reza is interested in dynasticism; he wanted to link his succession to the previous reign. His eldest son, Mohammed Reza,[1] is being carefully trained in the duties of kingship. The Shah, very fond of him, has paid close attention to his education. This is in striking contrast to other Oriental monarchs, like Feisal of Iraq and Fuad of Egypt who, even though they knew they would have to hand the succession to their sons, neglected some aspects of their education shamefully. It is a curious thing that many men of the East, caring deeply for both their kingdoms and their families, forget that the two are one. But Reza is an exception. He is doing everything possible to

[1] In March, 1939, he married Princess Fawziya, sister of the King of Egypt.

train his boy for the enormous job that faces him. He sent him to an
excellent school in Gstaad, Switzerland, then put him through an intensive course of military training, and now takes him everywhere,
so that he may see the political wheels turning.

The boy, a handsome lad, is supposed to be very liberal. The
future of Iran is very much tied up with this youngster. The chief
demerit of dictatorship or personal government is that it starves the
roots of the future, and the Shah knows this well. He has perhaps
deliberately prevented any of his underlings from becoming too powerful, so that, when he dies, the way will be clear for his son. But
this policy has created resentments, and the boy may find his path
crossed by his father's secret enemies.

The Shah has two daughters, each of whom has made political
marriages. One, a twin sister of the crown prince, married an important tribal chieftain, who thereupon found good reason to be loyal
to the Pahlevi régime. The other married the son of the present prime
minister, who has the pleasant name Mohammed Jam.

Recently at the autumn maneuvers five young princes are said to
have appeared, all approximately the same age. Their existence had
hitherto been unknown. They wore court uniforms, and all were
named Reza. The presumption is that they are the sons of His Imperial Majesty by other marriages.

Enemies of the Shah say that he is cruel, secretive and domineer-
ing. Iran, they complain, is a vast prison ruled only by fear. No man
knows how long he will stay in favor; no man knows when he may
be disposed of. A person may simply disappear, as did Khan Timur-
tash, who for some years was Minister of Court and the second most
powerful man in the realm. The Shah is a despot, and his personal
word rules all.

A fortress near Teheran, once a home of the previous dynasty,
is supposed to house political prisoners. There is no trial, no sentence. Enemies are supposed to be removed, if removal for good is
deemed necessary, not by the headman's ax or firing squad but by the
more melodramatic method of poisoning. The disgruntled call it
cheerlessly the *inoculation Pahlevi*. A pellet in the breakfast coffee
one fine day—and then there aren't any more fine days. It may be
announced that the victim has died of a "stroke."

A less drastic criticism of the Shah is that he is capricious, and
lacks sense of balance. He builds a railway station before the tracks

are laid; he spends 2,000,000 tamans ($1,200,000) on the new offi-
cers' club in Teheran, a sum which might give the city a sewage
system. He, a dictator, says in effect "Let There Be Light," and
then expects the light to shine, whereas no technicians are on hand
to turn the switch or push the button. He has to do it all himself.
And he is inclined to defy the laws of nature. For instance, impatient recently that his medical service was progressing slowly, he
decreed simply that nurses should finish their training in two years
instead of three, quite refusing to recognize that three years were
necessary if the nurses were to be competent.

But most fair-minded people think that the Shah's merits of character far outweigh his defects, which are mostly the product of lack
of education and eastern environment. The Shah has courage, he has
vitality, he has vision. He ended the terrible debility of the old régime, he brought the breath of new life to a decaying country. Every
day of the week, every week of the year, he struggles manfully to
make the people cognizant of themselves, proud of their history. He
is a patriot, completely unselfish, and considerably in advance of his
own people. His only ambition is to put the country in working order, advance it to modern times, and turn it over to his son.

Reforms à la Turk

Beyond doubt the greatest personal and political influence on the
life of the Shah was Mustapha Kamal Ataturk, the dictator of Turkey,
whose career he has closely followed. In 1934, he visited Kamal in
Ankara—the only time he has ever been outside Iran. Both Kamal
and the Shah are military adventurers, upstarts, but it would be
grossly inaccurate to dismiss them as nothing else. Both have brought
new life, new dignity, to their peoples. And the careers of both are
dominated by a tremendous zest to westernize, to modernize, to
break the power of the old corrupt régime.

The first reforms the Shah undertook were in the realm of public
order, public security. He wiped out brigandage, which had defaced
whole provinces for generations; he gave the land the lifeblood of
new roads, new ports and harbors; he reorganized the army, which
had been a rabble, on the basis of conscription. He got rid of foreign officers, foreign advisers, and made the army a kind of school,
like the Japanese army, for the man power of the nation. This

was a most important step. Recently he has begun to develop an air force and even a small navy.

He decided early that Persians should have some national badge. So he devised what was called the Pahlevi cap, a peaked cap like a Pullman porter's cap, and every male in the kingdom had to wear it. This, like Kamal Ataturk's abolition of the fez, struck at the power of the Church, since a good Moslem cannot pray if he is wearing a hat with a brim. A few years later Reza abolished the Pahlevi cap as suddenly as he had introduced it, and decreed simply that every Persian must wear some kind of European headgear. Anything goes in Iran nowadays from a derby to a sailor straw.

Many of the reforms[2] he copied from Turkey. He abolished the régime of capitulations (foreign consular and judicial rights, like extraterritoriality in the Far East), and ended foreign control of the customs. He introduced coeducation in the schools, built more and more schools, and inaugurated a program for adult education. He introduced modern commercial and criminal law codes, thus depriving the religious courts of their former competence. He abolished titles and broke up the big estates. He permitted courses in human anatomy in the medical colleges, the first in the history of Persia, and decreed that marriage and divorce were civil as well as religious ceremonies. The *mullahs* fought these reforms furiously. They were beaten.

Women in the old Persia had about as many rights as cattle, and early in his reign Reza set about emancipating them. First, women were permitted to go to restaurants and other public places, something previously unheard of in Persia, and to accompany men in public. The minimum legal age for women to marry was raised from nine (the age authorized by the Koran) to fifteen, and women were given the right to divorce their husbands. The question of the veil was difficult. Not even the Shah dared outlaw the veil by decree. So, very cautiously, he set about discouraging its use. For instance, the Queen appeared in public without a veil, and school girls began to wear modern costumes. Then the Shah—subtle fellow!—set apart the most fashionable streets of Teheran, including the shopping center, and suggested that here, at least, women might dispense with

[2] Henry Filmer's *The Pageant of Persia* contains an authoritative account of these reforms.

the veil. Then came an officially inspired whispering campaign that only prostitutes still really cared for veils!

Iran is a difficult place. Not only the *mullahs* have opposed the Shah. Centuries of backwardness, of obscurantism, oppose him too. For instance, in an attempt to broaden the basis of government, he decreed that any citizen with a complaint might telegraph it to him personally without charge. But in practice the local police often interfere with such messages.

There are no political parties in Iran; the Majlis, founded after a revolution in 1906, is not even a debating society, and the Constitution means very little. Here too, Reza follows Kamal. There are no issues, except to obey the Shah; there are no Ins, no Outs, except by the criterion of royal favor. The chief domestic problem, as in Turkey, is money—money especially for the army, which absorbs forty-four percent of the budget—and the pinch of hard times.

Next to that of Turkey, the influence of the Soviet Union is most marked in Iran. As in the U.S.S.R., a considerable number of enterprises are state monopolies: tourism, for instance, sugar, tea, salt, opium, foreign trade, transport, petroleum. There is much Russian local color: people eat caviar (if they can afford it), call tea "chai," count on an abacus, wear belted blouses, and fear the secret police. Russia is by far Iran's chief provider of imports, and her third best customer. The best customer is Britain, but German economic influence has been growing.

The foreign policy of Reza Shah is simple and traditional: to play Russia and Britain against each other, to prevent the Russians from being too influential in the north, and the British in the south. He has been successful in both courses. Nor has he had much difficulty lately, since both the Russians and the British want a reasonably strong buffer state in Persia, and Reza gives it to them. Far better an autocratic and occasionally idiosyncratic Shah than Iran in chaos.

The other object of Reza's policy is peace, good relations with his smaller neighbors. He envisages a sort of middle Asian community of border states—Afghanistan, Iraq, and Turkey combined with Iran to hold off the great powers and work for their common good. To this end his government signed the pact of Saadabad in July, 1937, linking the border states in a non-aggression treaty. He is very careful to keep the prestige of his small neighbors high. For instance, both Turkey and Afghanistan, as well as the U.S.S.R., have ambassadors in Iran, whereas even Great Britain has only a minister, though the great compound of the British Legation maintains the glamour and tradition of former days.[3]

The Sensitive Plant

One thing everyone in Iran agrees about—the Shah's very pronounced sensitiveness, both in regard to his own career and the prestige of Iran. Sensitiveness, of course, is usually a sign that a man is not sure of himself.

The Persian minister to Washington was arrested in Maryland recently for speeding. Forthwith he was recalled to Iran, and diplomatic relations with the United States were all but severed. (The American government maintains a representative in Teheran, called a chargé d'affaires instead of minister, but till very recently there was no Iranian representation in the United States.)

A New York tabloid newspaper laughed at the Iranians for their touchiness. As retaliation, second class mail privileges of Americans in Iran were curtailed.

A French newspaper made a joke about the Shah. It was of the same variety as the old pun, *Dans la nuit les chats sont gris,* which means both "At night the cats are gray" and "At night the Shahs are tight." The Iranian minister of France was recalled, and diplomatic relations broken off.

The Shah, like Mr. Herbert Hoover, is supposed to take masochistic delight in his press clippings. He reads them all, and every Iranian diplomat is under standing orders to send to Teheran any reference about him printed anywhere.

Railway Worth Its Weight in Gold

The new railway is Reza's chief d'œuvre, his masterpiece, and his precious toy. Persia has never had a railway before, and the difficulties of construction were judged to be insuperable. The line traverses the plateau for a thousand miles from northeast to southwest, and crosses two mountain masses, one of which is 120 miles

[3] The British Legation—a minor point but perhaps one that shows again the wonderful British luck or skill in being in the right place at the right time— contains a well with the only good drinking water in Teheran. The whole town uses it. Another point—perhaps it indicates that the British aren't much interested in Iran any more—is that Teheran is the only capital between Cairo and Peking without an English daily newspaper.

wide, the other sixty, as well as a desert where communications have hitherto been impossible. There is one stretch of fourteen kilometers which cost $5,000,000. The cost as a whole will be $150,000,000, not including two new towns being built as termini. Every cent comes from within Persia, out of taxes or other revenue. No foreign loans for Reza Shah!

Linking Teheran with both the Caspian and the Persian Gulf, the railway has great strategic and political as well as commercial importance. The British wanted Persia to build an east-to-west railway, from Bagdad to the borders of India. The Russians wanted a railway up to their end of the Caspian. Very carefully the Shah contrived to defeat both British and Russian aims; his line is exclusively Persian, linking the two Persian coasts. The northern port, Bandar Shah (King's Harbor), is removed as far as possible from European Russia, and the egress at the south is not Mohammerah, which would have been the most convenient spot, but Bandar Shahpur (Harbor of the King's Son) which is further from the Iraq frontier. Bandar Shahpur is not ideal from one point of view; not only has an entirely new city had to be built, but it lies at a point where the tide rises twenty feet a day, making unloading of cargo difficult. But to the Shah strategy is more important than easy engineering.

An American company had the first concession for the railway. It lapsed, and a consortium of several nationalities, mostly Dutch and Swedish, took over the job. British engineers had the hardest sector of track to build—the climb to the great plateau. This is an ascent of almost 6,000 feet in about fifty miles. Practically all material, rails, ties, and so on, had to be imported, and most of the native labor never saw a railway line before, or handled modern tools.

Oil

The Shah takes a certain pleasure in playing cat-and-mouse with foreigners. For a time he allowed the German Lufthansa Company to run a domestic air service; than he canceled the arrangement. He refuses to let Imperial Airways, a British company, fly over Persian territory; therefore Imperial has to use the longer alternative route along the western shore of the Persian Gulf. The Dutch K.L.M. line, on the other hand, is permitted to fly along the eastern coast, over actual Persian soil, with a landing at Jask; but the Dutch are said to have to ask for an extension of this privilege every two months.

Persia is the third oil-producing country in the world, and its oil—fifty to sixty million barrels per year—is produced and marketed by the Anglo-Iranian Oil Company (more familiarly known as the Anglo-Persian), the controlling interest of which is owned by the British government. The concession dates from 1901, when William Knox D'Arcy paid a reputed $20,000 for the right to exploit 500,000 square miles of Persia (four-fifths of the country) for oil until 1961. In 1909 the Burma Oil Company bought the D'Arcy concession and formed the Anglo-Persian Company. The Persian government agreed to accept a royalty of sixteen percent of the net profits. In 1914, in order to assure supply of oil for the navy, the British government bought control of the Anglo-Persian.

Things went along fairly smoothly until 1932. The Anglo-Persian drilled wells, explored territory, paid Persia a sum running to £11,-000,000 in royalties, spent another £22,000,000 inside Persia on wages and so on, built the great plant at Amadan near the Persian Gulf, and was by far the largest enterprise in the country. On November 27, 1932, with hardly a hint of warning, the Shah suddenly canceled the concession.

What he wanted was, of course, a bigger share of the profits. He got it handily. For six months the British piously protested at the Shah's "confiscatory" tactics, denounced him vigorously, and put the case before the League of Nations. The Shah stood firm, and issued a long list of complaints, for instance, that the original concession was obtained under pressure, that the amount of royalty had been unfairly calculated, that the company had refused to pay income tax, and that the cost of oil in Persia was prohibitive. The company, backed by the British government, denied these charges. Finally a compromise was worked out. It was called a compromise, but in reality the Shah won hands down, by holding to his implied threat to close down the Anglo-Persian establishment. The British had to give in.

The new agreement, dated April 28, 1933, cut the area of the concession in half, with the proviso that it would be further limited to 100,000 square miles after 1938; it withdrew from the company the exclusive right to lay pipelines and made other arrangements beneficial to Iran; above all, it changed the royalty system from a share of net profits to a specific rate per ton of oil, with the proviso that it never fall below a certain figure (£750,000) per year. Also it was agreed that the Iranian government should get a further twenty percent of the profits of the company after the shareholders received a preliminary sum, and that after sixty years all the company's property should revert to Iran. The new agreement greatly increased Iran's income from the company. In 1931, for instance, the Persian government received £306,872 in royalties; in 1934 it received over two million pounds.

This achievement may seem less exciting than the railroad, but it is spectacular just the same. The Shah has done something almost unique. It isn't everybody who so successfully grabs Britain by the throat and shakes until the sterling flows.

Chapter XXXII
Arab World

〜〜〜〜〜〜〜〜〜〜〜〜〜〜〜〜〜〜〜〜〜〜〜〜〜〜〜

*And when ye meet those who misbelieve—then strike off
the heads until ye have massacred them, and bind fast the
bonds!*

—KORAN, xlvii, 15

G UESS about whom this was written:
"His earlier life was almost a blank. . . . It may be taken
as certain that he came of humble stock. If prophets are like poets,
then what made him a prophet will never be known. Whether we
regard it as a 'pathological case,' or a grand example of mystical.
ecstasy, the thing is essentially inexplicable, though at the outset of
his mission a dominating motive can be discerned. He was first and
foremost a revealer, who uttered by inspiration truths which lay behind the ken of his listeners. . . . His chief quality was *vision* rather
than logical power or learning. . . . His speaking was apparently
unpremeditated, a rapturous utterance, as though a power not himself
were using him as a vehicle of communication."

No, this is not a description of Adolf Hitler, to whom it almost
perfectly applies, but of the Prophet Mohammed, taken from the introduction to the Oxford edition of the Koran.

The temptation to include Mohammed in a gallery of living portraits
is almost irresistible. His career of conversion, incitation, and terrific
conquest is extraordinarily contemporary. Half a dozen times in
discussing his life and career one comes across modern analogies.
For instance, the Hegira, Mohammed's flight from Mecca to Medina,
is startlingly like the March on Rome. Like Mussolini, Mohammed
prepared the way well in advance, and did not travel himself until
his underlings had arranged and guaranteed a good reception. He
was—as Hitler is—a mystic, an anti-Semite, and an expansionist.

Mohammed,[1] known as "the Trusty," a holy man who had several

---

[1] There are at least a dozen ways of spelling this name, since English cannot reproduce Arabic sounds exactly. The most correct transliteration would
be "Muhammad." Other variants range from Mahomet to Mehmed. I am

wives, the founder of a great world religion who was an illiterate
merchant in his youth, was born posthumously in A.D. 570, in Mecca,
the holy city of Arabia. Islam is the youngest of the mass religions.
Mohammed was an unexceptional character until the age of forty.
Then he began to receive visions of peculiar intensity, and became
convinced that, like Abraham and Jesus, he was a prophet empowered
to convey the word of God. He converted his family, then his coterie
of friends; news of his mission spread, and in 622 came the Hegira
(correctly, *hijra*), the traditional date of the foundation of Islam. He
fled from Mecca to Medina to avoid arrest by the Meccans, who
considered his teaching dangerous. Mohammed himself was hardly
an exemplary personage; he was reputedly cruel, lustful, truculent,
and vain; but what he taught began at once to show extraordinary
vitality. In 628, he was bold enough to write to all the monarchs then
known in the world, communicating to them the substance of his
creed; in 629, he recaptured Mecca, began other conquests, and set
the stage for the subsequent unification of Arabia and the wonderful
Arab campaigns later in the century. In 632, he died, worn out by his
visionary labors.

Mohammed's first wife was the widow Kadija, to whom he had
previously been a servant. He lived with her happily for many years;
when she died he took other wives. One was a Copt, named Mary,
from Egypt; one was a Jewess, Safiya, whose husband he executed
the night before the wedding. (Incidentally, after one of his battles,
he ordered all his Jewish prisoners slain; his creed borrowed very
heavily from Judaism, for instance in the matter of the universality
and oneness of God, but he appears to have disliked individual
Jews—a characteristic which has a connotation in the present day.)
In addition he had several concubines. Yet, strangely enough, none of
his real sons survived him. His favorite daughter, Fatima, married
Ali, who was also his cousin and adopted son. Dissension between
multitudinous members of the family after his death led to sectarian
divergences and family squabbles which, believe it or not, persist to
this day.

Islam means literally "submission" or "resignation"—to the will
of God—a strange choice of name considering that it is the most

conforming to simplified American usage in saying Mohammed. Similarly I
am using "Moslem," though British usage tends to "Muslim." In India Moslems
are usually called "Mussulmans."

militant of all religions. Its gospel, the Koran (correctly, *Qur'an,*
which means "recitation"), is a "collection of manifestoes, diatribes,
harangues, edicts, discourses, sermons, and suchlike miscellaneous
pieces" which Mohammed took down from heaven as the words
reached his earthly ear. He is not considered to be God himself, but
merely the greatest prophet of God. The creed of Islam, as he developed it, borrowed partly from the savage and superstitious Arab
tribes; for instance, Mecca—the only city in the world, except perhaps
Lhasa in Tibet, utterly excluded to non-believers on religious grounds
—was a holy city to the Arabs long before Mohammed; the Prophet
had to perform some complex compromises in order to associate Islam,
which renounces idol-worship, with the traditional Arab veneration
of such objects as the Kaaba, a black stone in Mecca which is still
sacrosanct to orthodox Mohammedans. Mainly Mohammed's teaching
was a puritan and to some extent a cleansing and humanitarian appeal.
He preached against slavery, fornication, and cruelty to animals; he
attacked idolatry, blood feuds, and priestly privileges. He borrowed
the notion of hell-fire and Judgment Day from Christianity, and the
unity and righteousness of God from the Jews. And he invented the
principle that paradise, filled with wine and beautiful virgins, belonged only to the doughty believers, who were urged to kill as many
infidels as possible on earth.

Mohammedans, especially of the Sunni division, if they make
any pretense to orthodoxy at all, subscribe to five practices: (1) Re-
cite each day *There is no God but Allah, and Mohammed is the
prophet* (literally, "sent-one" or messenger) *of Allah.* (2) Pray five
times a day, with face toward Mecca. (3) Answer the call of the
Caliph for a *jihad* or holy war, if any. (4) Give alms to the poor up
to ten per cent of one's wealth. (5) Keep the holy month of Ramadan,
during which no food, water, or sexual intercourse is permitted between dawn and sunset. Additionally good Moslems should once in
their lives make the pilgrimage to Mecca.

For several generations the outstanding fact about Islam was its
inflammatory militancy. Consider the following passage from the
Koran, as quoted in Bertram Thomas's *The Arabs,* p. 44: "The sword
is the key of heaven and of hell; a drop of blood shed in the cause
of God, a night spent in arms, is of more avail than two months of
fasting and prayer: whosoever falls in battle, his sins are forgiven; at

the Day of Judgment his wounds shall be resplendent as vermilion and odoriferous as musk, and the loss of limbs shall be supplied by the wings of angels and cherubim." No wonder the Moslems fought— and still like to fight.

Mohammed himself set about temporal as well as spiritual conquest and rule. In this he is unique among the founders of religions. His great successors the Caliphs Abu Baqr (his father-in-law), Omar (brother-in-law), Othman, and Ali (cousin, son-in-law, and adopted son) and their highly competent generals began such a flood of conquest as the world had not seen since Alexander. In the space of one hundred years the terrific impact of Islam was felt from China to Spain. The Moslem warriors planted the flag of the green crescent along the entire Mediterranean shore, in Persia and Turkestan, in Sicily and Bagdad. In 732 Charles Martel beat them back from the gates of Paris, and the peak of religio-nationalist aggression diminished. The Moslems brought much of good in their wake, including a considerable attention to art, the use of paper, mathematics, and interest in exploration.

But the Moslems had then, as now, very little *political* sense. They invented a stable system of numerals, which we adopted; they did not invent stable governments. Their religion was strong enough to absorb future Asiatic conquerors like Genghis Khan, and to reach the uttermost parts of Asia, for instance the Philippines and Dutch East Indies as we have seen in this book; but it did not keep most of its converts from being destroyers rather than builders. The Great Moguls in India erected a beneficent dynasty. No other Moslems did.

The Arab world split at the time of Ali, the fourth Caliph; it has never been united since. Followers of Ali, the Shias, who consider him to be the true prophet, are still awaiting his proper successor. Rival dynasties scrambled for power, the Omayyids in Damascus, the Abbasids in Bagdad, the Fatimites in Egypt, and the Sherifians (descendants of Mohammed himself) in the Arabian peninsula. In the fifteenth century came the Turks, who took Constantinople and ended the Byzantine Empire, and then began to overrun the Arab dynasties and countries. From 1517, when the Turks conquered Egypt, until the aftermath of the Great War in 1918, there was no independent Arab state. Arab nationalism had perished.

Arab World To-day

First to define terms briefly. There are perhaps 250,000,000 Mohammedans, adherents of Islam, in the world at present, but only about 40,000,000 of them speak Arabic, and of these by no means all are Arabs. What happened was that Islam pushed forward, as it were, in a great wave that left three concentric loops. Religion went furthest, and language next; the Arab "race," if there is such a thing, the Arab "nation," made the smallest circle.

Nowadays when one says the "Near" East[2] one normally means Egypt, Palestine, Transjordan, Syria, Iraq, Saudi Arabia, Yemen, and the small states of the Arabian peninsula and the Persian Gulf. It is, in a word, the region between Persia and the Mediterranean, much of it desert inhabited by nomad peoples, and yet because of its strategic position a famous battleground of the great powers.

The chief common denominator is that it contains peoples who are basically Semitic in origin, whose predominant religion is Islam, and who speak varying shades of Arabic. The inhabitants of the southern Mediterranean littoral from Libya through Tunis and Algeria to Morocco would fit in this category, but they are outside the province of this book. Egypt, from the point of view of both power and population, considers itself the No. 1 Arab state (properly one should say Arab-*speaking* state, since Egyptians are not really Arabs), but Egypt is, after all, in Africa, not in Asia, and is likewise beyond the scope of the present work. Similarly I exclude Turkey, which I dealt with briefly in *Inside Europe*. The Turks are not Arabs but Turanians, and they do not speak Arabic, though for generations Islam was their religion. Nowadays the outlook of Turkey is essentially European.

I have said that the people of this Near Eastern area, inhabiting the eastern rim of the Mediterranean and the valleys of the Nile and the Tigris-Euphrates, together with the desert-*cum*-oasis peoples beyond—the whole region being strikingly analogous to that "Fertile Crescent" which H. G. Wells has described as the home of the first civilizations of mankind—are in the main Semites by race, Moslems by religion, and Arabic in language. Note the qualification "in the

[2] British usage calls the Balkans and Turkey the "Near East," and the rest the "Middle" East. American usage excludes the Balkans and European Turkey from the "Near" East, and calls Iraq and Iran the "Middle" East.

main." For Lebanon (a part of Syria) is largely Christian,[3] and in Iraq there are sun-worshipers, devil-worshipers, Yezidis, Kurds, and Assyrians. The educated Egyptian may speak roughly the same language as a tribesman from Transjordan, but the two differ as much as the Archbishop of Canterbury from the Scottsboro boys. As to race, the different admixtures are bewildering. Arabs intermarried with Greeks, Turks, Kurds, Cypriots, Armenians, and Egyptians to produce that disconcerting representative of centuries of fusion known as the Levantine. In the area are Sudanese as black as Mussolini's shirt, and white Circassians who evoke memories of the Russian steppes. The Near East—most distinctly—is not homogeneous.

The countries of the region are largely agricultural, and, Egypt perhaps excepted, their economy is primitive. All of them are poor. They live on the soil—when there is any soil. Yemen produces coffee, Egypt cotton, Iraq dates, Palestine oranges, and Syria trouble. Under the soil, in Iraq notably, is oil. The spectacle of great modern airplanes soaring between Jerusalem and Bagdad is infinitely challenging. They follow carefully an oil pipeline across the desert. Under the land, under the shadow of the plane, is the oil that feeds them. Figuratively as well as literally they pursue the oil across the sands.

The governments in the area differ widely. Libya is an Italian colony. Palestine and Transjordan are British mandated areas, and the states in Syria are under French mandate. Egypt and Iraq, technically at least, are independent nations, though the temptation to use quotation marks around "independent" is considerable. Yemen is a sort of sub-state. The most truly national of the group is Saudi Arabia, ruled by the greatest Arab of the Middle East, King Ibn Saud.

Pan-Arabism is to-day little more than a legend, a myth. As a political force of serious consequence it can hardly be said to exist.

For one thing, local jealousies are strong. Both Egypt and Iraq consider themselves "superior" to the other Arab countries. For many years Ibn Saud was the bitter enemy of the Sherifian family, represented in Transjordan by the Emir Abdullah and in Iraq by King Feisal and his son. This quarrel has been patched up—which is as if Stalin and the Pope should kiss—but there is little real community of interest. For another thing, Arab political development is

---

[3] There are many Christian Arabs, i.e., folk Arab by race and language who became converted to Christianity. There are even Jewish Arabs.

in general extremely backward. Schools, railways, commercial inter-course—almost all the incentives to unity—are lacking. As to educa-tion, for instance: Bagdad, capital of Iraq, is probably the only capital city in the world without a university. Again, there are re-ligious schisms. The Sunnis hate the Shias. There has been no Caliph, or supreme head of Islam, since the last Sultan was ejected from Constantinople after the War; the King of Egypt would like to become Caliph, but Ibn Saud—who can't be a candidate[4] himself—won't let him.

In the chapter on Persia I mentioned the non-aggression treaty which links Iraq, Iran, Turkey, and Afghanistan. But three of these four countries are not Arab countries; the identity of view binding them was common preoccupation with their great neighbor, the U.S.S.R., not Pan-Arabism. Recently a Treaty of Arab Brotherhood was signed between Iraq, Saudi Arabia, and Yemen, but it is only a beginning. In July, 1937, a conference met at Bludan, near Damas-cus, to outline a common program among Arab states against the partition of Palestine. It failed largely because Ibn Saud sent no representative.

The main reason why pan-Arabism is illusory is, however, some-thing beyond the control of the Arab states themselves, namely, western imperialism. The British control Iraq and Palestine, and are dominant in the foreign relations of Egypt and Iraq; the French control Syria; Italian influence is active everywhere. The western powers, jealous of each other, guarding their special spheres of in-fluence, play one Arab state against another. Thus Pan-Arabism is at best a function of Pan-Europeanism—which, in the good year of our Lord 1939, is not a hopeful augury. The western nations inhibit Arab unity.

The depredations of western imperialism are more pronounced in the Near and Middle East than in any other section of the world, even China not excluded. Once more, for the last time in this book, we confront the imperialist grab and scramble.

The Near East is the region where Kaiser Wilhelm dreamed about "Berlin-to-Bagdad," and from which to-day Hitler invites Arab guests to Nuremberg. It is the region where Disraeli pur-chased the Suez Canal for Britain, where Cromer built up modern Egypt, where Lawrence helped foment and lead an Arab nationalist

[4] Technically the Caliph must be a lineal descendant of the Prophet.

"revival." It is the region where France invaded Syria, flirted with the Turks, and cast longing eyes at the oil fields of Mosul. It is the region where the leopards keep old spots—where, in 1936, Russia asked for the right to push warships through the Dardanelles, where, in 1939, Italy was angling for a share in ownership of the Suez Canal.

Great Britain is, as everyone knows, the greatest Islamic power. The British appropriated Egypt from the Turks, sought to control Iran, bribed the Sherifians, set up new administrations in Palestine and Iraq after the War, and subsidized rising chieftains like Ibn Saud. Britain not only is—despite Mussolini's fulminations—the greatest Islamic power; it must continue to remain so, if the Empire as a whole is to remain intact. This is because the Near East is a crucial pivot in the world's communications. Both by air and sea, the Palestine-Suez area commands the route to India and the further east.

The British, cleverly flexible, have sponsored Egyptian and Iraqi independence, but with the retention of various special rights and privileges; they remain fixed in Transjordan, Palestine, Aden, the Hadramaut, and the Persian Gulf. But they are uneasy—especially since the Ethiopian war, the so-called Peace of Munich, and the cataclysmic explosions of early 1939. The world moves. Nowadays a comparatively new voice is being heard in Near Eastern matters. It is the voice of Italy, and it comes through—the ether.

Bari Broadcast

Seven-thirty P.M. in Bagdad. The streets are dark after the quick twilight of the Middle East, the cafés begin to fill up, and the Iraqis suck at their blazing coffee or the long, cool waterpipes. Here a tribesman, deep chocolate color, loaded with rags, from the marsh country. Here a Kurd, wrapped in twenty layers of cummerbund, aloof, dignified. Here a cultivated Effendi from the government offices, polishing his old-fashioned pince-nez. Seven-thirty P.M. The café proprietor turns to his radio, adjusts the loud speaker. Bari calling. Flash and splutter of bright monosyllables. And a sort of osmosis takes place; news spreads by absorption.

In Bari, on the heel of the Italian boot, the Italians have set up a broadcasting station which transmits news and propaganda—in Arabic—to the peoples of the Arab world. The voice of Bari is heard these days from the bazaars of Cairo to Bagdad's eight-mile-long main street, from the ocher lava-land of Transjordan to the swamps of the Euphrates. Arabs listen in groups and clusters. In the villages, even in the oases of the desert, the local sheik may have a radio—conveniently donated by Italian agents—and the tribesmen flock around to listen.

Of course the use of broadcasting as a political instrument is nothing new. In 1933, Hitler attacked Austria—through the air— when a powerful station in Munich set out to undermine the régime of Dr. Dollfuss. In Spain, from the broadcasting station at Seville, the redoubtable General Quiepo de Llano poured out a vituperative stream of calumny against the loyalists. Radio played a very considerable rôle in the Munich "Settlement" and the destruction of Czechoslovakia. It is an ideal weapon in the hands—or mouth—of a dictator with the gift of gab. It gives the technique of aggression a new and potent medium. (It also could—and should—be a superb instrument of peace.)

Broadcasting is, moreover, an especially effective instrument in undeveloped regions, such as the countries on the western flank of Asia. For its appeal may be so easily directed *to the submerged masses*—the illiterates. You don't have to know how to read or write in order to listen to the radio. The Bari broadcaster, however weak his programs may be in detail, crosses frontiers both in time and space. He jumps the Tigris; also he jumps the public school. The Arab-speaking countries of the Near and Middle East are approximately ninety per cent illiterate. Newspapers cannot reach them. But radio can.[5]

The Bari programs are assembled to include readings from the Koran, religious music (especially emphasized during the holy month of Ramadan), jazz, inspirational talks, and political information. The basic idea is to invade the area with pro-Italian, i.e., anti-British, propaganda, to tell the Arabs that the Italians, not the British, are their true friends. The Bari broadcaster—incidentally he is a Libyan who speaks with a strong Syrian accent—does not worship truth unduly; he peppers the Arab world with "facts" that are not remotely facts. He has described imaginary attacks on the Iraq petroleum

[5] On the other hand, comparatively few Arabs have individual sets capable of receiving short-wave transmission. There are supposed to be 150 such sets in Aden, 55,000 in Egypt, 4,000 in Iraq, 24,200 in Palestine, 6,000 in Syria, and 25 in Saudi Arabia.

pipeline, blown up imaginary bridges in Palestine, commented on imaginary battles in Transjordan, and invented wars in Arabia between the British and Ibn Saud.

For a time the British listened to Bari without retaliation except through corrections issued the next day over the government station in Jerusalem. Then annoyance came to Whitehall. Several times Mr. Eden appealed to the Italians to modify the Bari programs, and the matter was broached in the House of Commons; finally the British went into action with a comprehensive Arabic broadcast— from London—of their own. On the first program, which was ushered in with great ceremony, the Crown Prince of Yemen, who was visiting England at the time, sent a message to his father. The Arabs heard their own tongue, plus the chimes of Big Ben. Then promptly Italy retaliated. It was announced that Bari would be enlarged to send programs in Hindustani to the 39,720 receiving sets and 350,000,-000 people of India.

Bari is, of course, a symptom. It has no great immediate importance in itself. But it symbolizes the growth of Italian ambitions in the Near East, Italian power, Italian penetration. This phase of Italian activism dates from the Ethiopian war in 1935-36, as well as the sanctions crisis wherein Italy bluffed Britain to a standstill in the Mediterranean—which double victory still reverberates in eastern ears. The Italians are busy. They buy newspapers in Egypt, sell aircraft to Iraq and arms to Yemen, flirt with subversive groups in Syria, and flamboyantly encourage Arab terrorists in Palestine, even if they do not actively subsidize them.

Now, the Italians think, is a good time to fill the Near East with the heady water of Rome. For one thing, agitation in Egypt and especially Palestine is convenient blackmail. By promising to call off the Bari broadcasts, for instance, Mussolini was in a position to demand British recognition of the Ethiopian conquest as quid pro quo. Second, the European structure is so interlocked, and war seems so inevitable, that all the great powers are playing for position. Italian strength in the eastern Mediterranean serves to make Italy more dangerous elsewhere. If the Italians can pour troops from Libya into Egypt, while in the West they control the Balearics, the balance of power in the Mediterranean is considerably upset. Italian propaganda in Palestine is a part of the same process as Italian invasion of Spain. Finally, it is the obvious and corollary idea of the Duce to do all he can to weaken, to undermine, British prestige and power wherever he meets it.

A small item. Throughout Palestine to-day you hear Arabs say *"Taky Inglesi?"* as a slang equivalent for "Oh, yeah?" *"Taky Inglesi?"* means "You trust the British?" The question mark denotes derision.

Mussolini himself is quite explicit about his motives in the Near and Middle East. In Libya, in March, 1937, he was presented with a "Sword of Islam" and, accepting it, he announced that he was hereafter to be considered a protector of the entire Moslem world. "Fascist Italy," the Duce said, "means to ensure to the Moslem population of Libya peace, justice, well-being, and respect to the laws of the Prophet and wishes besides to show her sympathy to Islam and to the Moslems *of the whole world.* Very soon Rome, with her laws, will show you how much she interests herself in your developing destiny. You know I am a man sparing of promises, but what I have promised I maintain."

This alarmed the British, even though they understand that Italy is dangerous mostly for its nuisance value. The Anglo-Italian agreement finally put through by Mr. Chamberlain in 1938 was dictated partly by earnest British desire to keep the Near East tranquil, i.e., safe for itself.

Totalitarian Arabs?

The whole Near East is full of shirts. There are Green Shirts and Blue Shirts in Egypt, White Shirts and *Chemises-de-Fer* in Syria, and Blue Shirts in Palestine, who are the powerful labor party.[6] In Egypt the Blue Shirts are the private army of the Wafd, the Egyptian nationalist organization; they originated precisely as did the Storm Troops in Germany, as muscle-men to protect Wafd political meetings. The Green Shirts commonly are said to have been subsidized by Italy. When a young Green Shirt tried to assassinate Nahas Pasha, the Egyptian prime minister (Nahas had accused the organization of being in foreign pay), the Green Shirts were dissolved.

One may fairly ask if the Arab peoples are, by and large, sympathetic to Fascist and totalitarian ideas. We have seen how closely Mohammed resembles a modern Führer. The Arab states have very

---

[6] You tell nationalities apart by their headgear, however, not hats. Egyptians wear the tarboosh or fez, Arabs the *kufiya* or cloth held in place by cords, and Iraqis a black forage cap. Persians wear what they can get.

little experience of political democracy, no tradition of responsibility to the people. Several of the young rulers of Arab countries, like Farouk in Egypt, may find sweet the temptation of the strong hand. And most of the Arab states are profoundly anti-communist and suspicious of the Soviet Union. No Soviet citizens, for instance, are allowed in Egypt, and the Russians have no diplomatic relation with either Egypt or Iraq.

On the whole Arabs themselves deny hotly that they are food for totalitarianism. They point out, for instance, that they are individualists by innate conviction, and that their religion is democratic, without any clerical hierarchy. They say that they have no reverence even for national leaders. Ibn Saud greets his tribal chieftains democratically. Feisal, the late King of Iraq, was called, not King, but "Sidi," which means simply "Sir." A young Iraqi told me that any citizen could talk to Feisal with "his hands in his pockets." I asked about King Ghazi. Answer: "We didn't bother to talk to him at all."

Another point is that Italy, however ambitious it may be, impedes the growth of Fascism in Arab countries by its own policy in Libya. This Italian colony, the Arabs say, is not a good advertisement for Fascist ideals. The population of Libya has, for instance, decreased from 1,200,000 to 850,000 in ten years, a decrease caused not so much by casualties in the Senussi wars as by mass flight of Libyans from Fascist rule. The Libyan Arabs have been fleeing wholesale to oases on the Egyptian border. Now the Italians are building a fence around Libya—an actual barbed wire fence—to keep the loving Libyans in.

On the other hand, Hitler is tremendously popular with the Arabs. The reason is not far to seek—he is the enemy of the Jews, whom the Arabs consider their enemy in Palestine, and of Great Britain. Hitler pointedly invited Arabs to Germany as honored guests, and in the Nuremberg speech in 1938 he talked about the "defenseless Arabs in Palestine, left in the lurch." An Arab spokesman in Jerusalem replied promptly, "Now we are not without friends in Europe; our ultimate success as a nation lies in the hands of Hitler and Mussolini." The greatest contemporary Arab hero is—Adolf Hitler.

Near East Miscellany

I never knew till now that there are 129 holidays a year in Egypt, that you can fly over the desert from Palestine to Bagdad in a boat, and that Basra, in Iraq (where Mr. Wells established the new aërial civilization in his *Shape of Things To Come*), has already prepared itself by building the finest airport in the East. I always thought till now, English numerals being Arabic, that Arabic numerals were like English.

I never really believed till now that in Syria, if you don't tip the boy who parks your car, he puts the evil eye on it, which means filling it with dung. I never really believed till now that in Iraq they air-condition rooms *down* to 98° Fahrenheit.

I never knew till now that one of the chambermaids in the Hotel King David, Jerusalem, is a Ph.D. from the University of Lemberg, that homosexuality, which is astoundingly prevalent in the Near East, is considered "all right" under certain conditions, that Egyptian soldiers walk hand in hand, and that the barman in the Hotel Zia, Bagdad, is a Chaldean Christian named Jesus.

I still don't believe that the Yezedis near Mosul worship a holy peacock, that you can fly from Alexandria to Karachi in a day, that Jerusalem has three Sundays every week, and that two of the camels out by the Pyramids are named "Telephone Company" and "Baby New York City."

Chapter XXXIII
Kings of the Middle East

〜〜〜〜〜〜〜〜〜〜〜〜〜〜〜〜〜〜〜〜〜〜〜〜〜〜〜

*Kill them wherever ye find them, and drive them out
from whence they drive you out; for sedition is worse than
slaughter.* —KORAN, ii, 182

*Verily, for the pious is a blissful peace—gardens and vine-
yards, and girls with swelling breasts. . . . And God will
. . . cast on them brightness and joy; and their reward for
their patience shall be Paradise and silk! reclining therein
upon couches they shall neither see therein sun nor piercing
cold . . . and they shall be served round with vessels of
silver and goblets that are as flagons . . . and there shall go
round about them eternal boys; when thou seest them thou
wilt think them scattered pearls. . . . Verily this is a reward
for you, and your thanks are thanked.*

—KORAN, lxxvi, 5, and lxxviii, 32

DURING the Great War the Arabian peninsula, still subject to the
Turks and part of the Ottoman Empire, saw the growth to power
of two rival Arab potentates. One was Husein, Grand Sherif of
Mecca, a lineal descendant of the Prophet Mohammed, who held
the holy cities and the coastal strip known as the Hejaz. The other
was Ibn Saud, a reformist chieftain in the interior of the bleak, impenetrable peninsula. These two men became bitter enemies. The
course of Arabian history for many years was the feud between their
rival houses.

The British, fighting the Turks, sought to make use of both Husein
and Ibn Saud. Obviously an Arab group of armies, attacking Turkey
on its exposed flank, liberating the peninsula in the name of an
authentic national movement, would be of great tactical assistance.
So British agents prevailed upon Husein, a gross and perfidious old
man, to join the Allies, together with his sons, while at the same time
they secretly purchased support from Ibn Saud.

The Arabs subservient to Husein were, in effect, bribed to assist Britain by terms of the celebrated McMahon correspondence.[1] One of the letters from Sir Henry McMahon, then British High Commissioner to Egypt, to Husein, ends, "In token of our good faith . . . I am sending the sum of £20,000 with your trusted messenger." The Arabs have asserted consistently that the McMahon letters promised them national independence in a wide area including Syria and Palestine, as a reward for fighting the Turks. The point is important, because legally the Arab case in Palestine has no other basis. But on July 23, 1937, McMahon wrote a letter to the *London Times* categorically asserting that Palestine was *not* included in the projected Arab state, and that Husein himself "well understood" this. This seems completely to explode the Arab "case."

At any rate the British, with the ink hardly dry on the McMahon letters, proceeded—so the Arabs say—to betray their Arab allies, by negotiating with France and Russia the secret Sykes-Picot agreement. Of course this was during the period of the War when almost any territory, if it was helpless enough, was chopped up on paper; any kind of chicanery was "justified" if it encouraged the prosecution of the War and harmony among the allied powers. The Sykes-Picot agreement (1916) subdivided the Arab area into a French sphere in Syria and a British sphere in Iraq and Transjordan, with Palestine—note well—given a special status. Palestine was most distinctly not assigned to Arab hegemony. There have been many alterations in the frontiers, including the withdrawal of France from Mosul, since the Sykes-Picot document was signed, but in the main its provisions determine the political situation that exists to-day.

Husein, though he played a double game for a time by attempting to remain in the good graces of the Turks, became King of Arabia in 1917 with tacit British approval. (At the same time, however, the British continued to flirt with his deadly enemy, Ibn Saud.) Husein considered himself betrayed, as indeed he was, by the Sykes-Picot agreement and the Treaty of Versailles, and the British lost interest in him. Rashly he quarreled with Ibn Saud, who, a strong man, promptly squashed him. In 1924, Husein abdicated in favor of his eldest son, Ali, but Ibn Saud's armies advanced into the Hejaz and captured Mecca. Ali abdicated the next year. Husein fled to Cyprus

[1] Published in full for the first time in English in *The Arab Awakening*, by George Antonius.

and, a figure so pathetic he was almost comical, died soon after. Ibn Saud became master of the Arabian peninsula.

Husein had several sons. One, Feisal, was King of Syria for a brief time, and then the first King of Iraq. Another, Abdullah, is the present ruler of Transjordan. Husein's family still controls those quasi-independent Arab states which are not in the domain of Ibn Saud.

King of Saudi Arabia

Ibn Saud[2] is a terrific fellow. He is a full six foot four and correspondingly broad; he weighs 230 pounds, every ounce of it bone and muscle. He is a complete picture of the vigorous old-time Arab; the only western touch is his steel-rimmed spectacles. He has a magnificent voice, deep and plangent, and he likes to bellow. During one series of negotiations with the British, the interpreters were terrified by his interrupting shouts of the Arab equivalent of "What the hell!" They were measuring a new frontier in miles, and Ibn Saud wanted the distance explained in terms of the speed of fast or slow camels, the criterion he best understood.

He has married between one hundred and one hundred twenty wives; he has several score of sons and unnumbered daughters. The laws of the Prophet, and Ibn Saud is a very holy man, permit a husband only four wives, but the King of Arabia gets around this rule by marrying his wives seriatim. When he travels he takes three wives with him, so that there is always room for a fourth maiden who may catch his eye. Then he divorces one of the others. He is never married to more than four wives at the same time. After a wife bears a child, he ships her back to her native oasis or village, where she is a proud ornament to the community. Marriage, with Ibn Saud, is an instrumentality for the unification of Arabia. He said recently, "In my youth and manhood I made a nation. Now in my declining years I make men for its population."

[2] Correctly this doughty king's full name is 'Abdul 'Aziz Ibn 'Abdu'r-Rahman Al-Feisal Al Sa'ud. Shortened, it is correctly Ibn Sa'ud. Arabs have no family names; "ibn" means "son of"; Ibn Sa'ud means simply "Son of Sa'ud." Correctly Iraq is 'Iraq, Abdullah is 'Abdulla, Shia is Sh'ia, Maan is 'Ma'an, and so on. The apostrophe, known as a "glottal stop," represents the unpronounceable Arabic consonant 'Ain. I hope purists will not object, but I propose to leave these maddening apostrophes and the other diacritic symbols out.

Ibn Saud is a Wahabi. This means that he subscribes fervently to an extreme reformist subdivision of Islam; if the Sunnis, say, are the Low Church of the Moslem world, and the more severe Shias the High Church, then the Wahabis are the non-conformist fundamentalists. The Wahabis interpret the doctrines of Mohammed with great rigor, and add strictures of their own. No Wahabi may drink, smoke, or gamble. They wear no gold, silk, or ornaments, and they forbid prayer before images. Ibn Saud's men created a stir throughout the Moslem world, when, taking Mecca and Medina, they attempted to destroy some precious Moslem shrines; they even contemplated demolition of the tomb of the Prophet itself. Wahabis, believing in the untrammeled essence of Mohammedanism, do not even mention the Prophet's name in their prayers; they forbid the presence of women at funerals because the women, not Spartan enough, may weep. The main reason why Ibn Saud detested Husein and his Sherifian brood was that he considered them impious, soft, intolerably decadent, and corrupt.

Ibn Saud's career may be said to have begun with his great-great-great-grandfather, Mohammed Ibn Saud, who was converted to the Wahabite faith by a wandering mendicant, Abd-el Wahab, 150 years ago, and who set about imposing Wahabism on the Arabian peninsula. He was a fanatic puritan; he wanted to subdue and purify the entire Moslem world. And the campaigns of this long-forgotten Mohammed Ibn Saud in the early nineteenth century were considerable. He captured Mecca and Medina, like his great-great-great-grandson; he invaded Egypt and took Damascus; when he died in 1814, he was ready to attack Mesopotamia and Persia.

The contemporary Ibn Saud was born in Riad, the chief city of Nejd—which is the desolate and impregnable inner heart of Arabia—about sixty-five years ago. No one knows his exact age. His family had fallen on hard times. As a very young man he assisted his father in ousting a rival chieftain, Ibn Rashid, from power in Nejd; his father was so impressed by his prowess that he abdicated in his favor. This was as early as 1900, when Ibn Saud could not have been more than twenty-six or twenty-seven. He spent a quarter century then in subduing rival tribesmen and consolidating his power; in 1926, having taken Mecca and rid himself of the Sherifians, he proclaimed himself King of Arabia; in 1932, he gave the country a new name—his own.

Ibn Saud was shrewd enough to take money from the British when he needed it; he does so no longer. Saudi Arabia is an authentic, if primitive, national state, and Britain and the other powers recognize its sovereignty. The British respect Ibn Saud, and know his power; they are particularly appreciative that, during the Palestine crisis, he gave no overt or flamboyant support to the Palestine Arabs. He could have caused much trouble, so great is his prestige, had he done so. Ibn Saud may expect a quid pro quo for this, namely, rectification in his favor of the frontier between his country and Transjordan, which is still not finally demarcated. So the British are very, very polite to him.

Ibn Saud has a good robust sense of humor. He wanted to reward some Egyptian emissaries. So he gave them trophies that they themselves had once brought from Egypt for Husein, and which he had captured on taking Husein's capital.

His official car was for some years a battered Studebaker, which, when it went to meet a guest, carried six armed riders on the running boards who at intermittent junctures got out and pushed.

He eats, Arab fashion, with his fingers, from a colossal tray on which three or four entire sheep may repose; but he knows what knives and forks are, and keeps them for his occasional—very occasional—foreign guests. (A Christian foreigner could not, of course, enter Mecca to see him there, but might be received at some city, Jeddah for instance, not so holy.)

The ordinary people of the town and desert greet him without ceremony by addressing him with his first name, Abdul Aziz, and nothing else; but his courtiers, who are terrified of him, call him "Oh Thou Whose Name Is Law."

He prays three times a day, and obeys with scrupulous fidelity the Wahabite injunctions against liquor, tobacco, jewels, gambling, and fancy dress. Cigarettes are, however, kept in the royal palaces or camping sites for foreign guests. They are forbidden, of course, to the Wahabis themselves.

Once when a subordinate officer delayed giving food to a poverty-blanched and unknown nomad, who had stumbled into camp, Ibn Saud ordered the offending officer to be flogged, and after giving the nomad a regal feast, himself harnessed and led the nomad's camel— the highest honor that can be paid to anyone in Arabia.

He has almost supernatural knowledge of the terrain and climatology of Arabia. He can "smell" rain. He knows the intimate stigmata of every tribe. He is marvelously informed. Once in a raid he conquered a small force (when he was also facing a big force) by judging at a well how many enemies had drunk, thereupon determining which group of his enemies was the smaller.

He lives in the remote interior of Arabia by choice, and has never been outside the country, but when members of one British mission arrived to see him they found bottles of Evian water on their luncheon tray. Their first meal consisted of six courses, all mutton. Slaves outside the tent noiselessly answered any command.

He imposed a form of conscription on Arabia by means of his Ikhwan, or military colonies; he was the first Arab leader to make successful military use of the Bedouin Arabs (Bedouins are those without homes, vagrants who follow the grass) ; he created the first standing army in Arab history.

Ibn Saud's great accomplishment is the unification of the Arabian peninsula, a few peripheral states and Aden excluded. He belongs to the modern tradition of nationalist leaders, like Chiang Kai-shek, to whom national unity is overwhelmingly the first consideration. Other achievements have been marked, too. He tried to bring something of the modern world to Arabia in the form of radio and motor transport; he reformed the civil administration, attacked corruption, and punished raiders; he eased the way of pilgrims to Mecca, who formerly had been fleeced even for drinking water; he sought to lay the basis of a modern state. Which, in Arabia, is a job.

Ibn Saud has never received a foreign journalist, and indeed the number of white men he has seen in his life, mostly British emissaries, may be counted on the fingers of two hands. A great friend, however, is H. St. J. B. Philby, the English explorer and author, who has known him well for years. Ibn Saud has grown greatly since the time that he was a simple tribal warrior. He has come closer to western influence, even if indirectly, which has made him more cunning perhaps, less the simon-pure warrior chieftain.

His greatest personal tragedy was the death, from fever some years ago, of his favorite son, who was to have been his heir. Other sons are now being trained for kingship. But whether Ibn Saud's reforms can survive him, no man may know.

The State of Iraq

Iraq, the old Mesopotamia, with 2,800,000 people on 116,000 square miles, was created by two things: King Feisal and the British.

Feisal, son of old Husein, was an extraordinary personage. He is one of the very few men in history—Henry Pu-yi of Manchuria is another—who was king of two different countries in his lifetime, for Feisal reigned briefly in Syria until the French ejected him; then became first monarch of Iraq. There is an unforgettable portrait of Feisal in T. E. Lawrence's *Seven Pillars of Wisdom.* He was shrewd, restless, neurotic, a great player of cards, dangerous, and a superlative wire puller. He was a gentleman, and people liked him; but even as king he retained the characteristics of a tribal sheik. He could let nothing alone. He was like a boy taking a watch apart. Whenever he appointed a new cabinet, he began (Alfonso of Spain shared this attribute) surreptitiously to undermine it. He bargained shrewdly with the British, and got independence for Iraq partly by his attitude during the Palestine troubles of 1929, when he withheld overt support of the Palestine Arabs to win British favor. He pretended that he was above and beyond politics, but he was far and away the first politician of the land. He was, in his own person, the Wafd of Iraq, in other words the dominant expression of the independence movement. He would himself stimulate the extremists, then come to the British and say he had to be given something to give them! But he never had time to build up a solid basis of government, a healthy civil service, an administrative matrix. He detested his son, Ghazi, who succeeded him. He died in 1933, while on a trip to Europe, of a stroke suffered during emotional excitement. His death stranded Iraq, robbed it of an easy future.

Friends who accompanied Feisal on two important missions have described him to me vividly. He went to Iran to see the Shah. Feisal was gay, agile, handsome, with perfect manners. The Shah sat like stone. Once Feisal encountered Ibn Saud on the deck of a British sloop in the Persian Gulf, in a meeting designed to terminate the rivalry between Saud and the Sherifians. Each set out from shore to arrive on the ship at the same instant, so that precedence would not suffer; each paused, wary; then each rushed at the other. A salute of forty-two guns boomed forth; no one could hear a word. Ibn

Saud, in the subsequent talks, looked like a great big bear grasping at Feisal as if he were a leopard.

Iraq, an underpopulated and undeveloped country, poor except for the oil underneath its crust of sand, the most turbulent of the Arab states, became an independent nation and was admitted to the League of Nations in 1932. The British liquidated their mandate after a decade of tutelage, but England and Iraq remain bound by intimate treaty relations. A detachment of the Royal Air Force continues to be stationed in the country—though it is not permitted in the capital, Bagdad—to guard imperial communications and to defend Iraq against external attack. The British ambassador takes precedence over other foreign envoys, but it would be incorrect to call him the ruler of the country. The British are very careful not to mingle in internal affairs, and Iraq shows less foreign influence than any Arab state except Saudi Arabia.

The basic problem of Iraq is national integration. The country is riven with minorities.

The Arabs are mostly Shias, except in the towns; the government has been predominantly Sunni. In the Euphrates district are wild tribesmen who have never been completely pacified, and in the extreme south and west are primitive Marsh Arabs and Bedouins. But Arabs of various categories by no means comprise the entire population. There are over 40,000 Jews in Bagdad alone, and 70,000 in the whole country. There are Yezedis (devil worshipers),[3] Chaldean Catholics, Chaldean Christians, a very considerable body of Kurds (who are Aryans by race but Moslems by religion), Turks in the Mosul region, and a quantity of Assyrians, who were ruthlessly massacred after a violent outbreak in 1933.

When I first came to Bagdad, looking hopefully for traces of Babylon, Nineveh, and other departed glories of Mesopotamia in the sodden, shrunken streets, I noticed the Iraqi flag, and asked various Iraqis what it signified. It is indeed one of the most complex of modern flags, and few inhabitants of Bagdad could tell me all its meaning. The black stripe represents the Abbasid Caliphs, the white stripe the Ommayid Caliphs, the green stripe the Sherifians of Mecca. The red trapezoid stands for something else (no one is quite

---

[3] A friend in Iraq told me that the Yezedis, curious folk, are convinced that there is a good deal of evil in the world, and that it is more sensible to propitiate Satan, who is in charge of it, than the nicer deities.

sure what), and the two white stars originally represented the first two Arab states, Syria and Iraq. But Syria fell to the French. So the Iraqis redistributed the stars, assigning one to the Arab element of the population, the other to the Kurds. (The Kurds like to complain that they didn't get much else.) The flag was invented by an Englishman, Sir Gilbert Clayton.

The political structure of Iraq includes a king, cabinet, and parliament. This last is somewhat rudimentary, since there are no political parties; some seats are reserved to special communities, the Jews and Christians for instance, by means of a system like the Communal Award in India. As in most countries new to nationhood, the bureaucracy is powerful and inclined to be corrupt; many higher officials in Iraq are former Turkish officers. The chief political issue is that of the Ins trying to keep the Outs out, and of the Outs trying to get in.

One thing the Iraqis have discovered, which is that it is easier to clamor for independence than to rule an independent country efficiently. The responsibility of government has sobered and chastened Iraq. The extremists (as in Egypt) have tended to become more moderate now that they are in power—and are apt to run to the British Embassy for help, the same Embassy they once bitterly attacked, whenever they get in trouble. Iraq (again like Egypt) has become more and more pro-British since it became free—which is one reason why the astute British gave it freedom. Bygones are bygones. The present prime minister, a revolutionist in 1922, once had a price on his head. One Kurdish chieftain, Sheikh Mahmoud, known as the "King of Kurds," resisted the mandatory government for seven years, until a British officer "negotiated his surrender"—after a bit of bombing. Now he amicably takes tea at the British Embassy, and his son is studying economics at Columbia University.

The decisive way to play politics in Iraq is to make a coup d'état. The decisive way to make a revolution is to gain support from the restive Euphrates tribesmen, who can muster 50,000 rifles.

Iraq is the only Arab country which may be said to have had a Fascist interlude. In November, 1936, an ambitious officer Baqr Sidki Pasha, who had served in the Turkish army and who was of Kurdish origin (the Kurds are very strong in the Iraqi army), made a coup d'état. The Iraqi government appealed for British help, but the British ambassador, consulting with the cabinet and the opposition, considered that he had no right to intervene in an internal matter. Baqr Sidki's coup was successful—it is a pity to have to foreshorten a highly dramatic story—and the loyalist minister of defense, Jafar Pasha, was murdered as he brought a message to Sidki from the young King, Ghazi. Sidki set himself up as a dictator. He bought airplanes from Italy, which the British considered naughty, and planned a visit to Berlin. But he had caused the murder of Jafar, be it remembered, and a blood feud in an Arab country is a serious matter. Relatives of Jafar—even though after some months of office Sidki seemed to have gained the favor of the King—pursued Sidki, and in July, 1937, succeeded in murdering him. The King—like Carol of Rumania, who avoided the funeral of his murdered prime minister Duca—did not attend his obsequies.

Iraq lives on oil mostly, which is pumped from the Mosul fields to the Mediterranean in a double pipeline, one egress of which is under British control at Haifa, the other in French Syria. Revenue from oil royalties pays the bills; Iraq has no deficit, no public debt. The pipeline is an extraordinarily successful engineering feat, built against tremendous difficulties. The oil must be pumped—it does not flow—across 1,150 miles of the most onerous country imaginable. The oil concession is held 23¾ percent each by Royal Dutch-Shell, Anglo-Iranian, a French group, and a consortium of American companies. The five percent remaining is in the hands of a remarkable Armenian entrepreneur, C. S. Gulbeknian.

The most representative Iraq politician of the present day is Nuri Pasha al Said. He was educated in Bagdad and the military college in Constantinople; he fought with the Turks, then joined Feisal's Arab nationalists; he has been prime minister and foreign minister several times. His general policy, like Feisal's, is to stay close to Britain. He was a double brother-in-law of Jafar Pasha—he married Jafar's sister and Jafar married his sister—and when Jafar was murdered he thought it prudent to leave the country. The British flew him out, as they have similarly helped so many political refugees in many lands who may someday be useful.

Nuri is one of the fathers of the Round Table Conference idea to settle Jewish-Arab differences in Palestine. He is a pure Arab, with a talent for languages and negotiation, and remarkably liquid eyes.

King Ghazi

This somewhat ineffectual young man,[4] who appears to have inherited some of the less amiable characteristics of the Husein family, was born in 1913 in the Hejaz, and ascended the Iraq throne in 1933. He was educated, in a manner of speaking, at Harrow, where he did not stay long, and then by an English tutor. He was a grievous disappointment to Feisal, who, however, might have treated him with more consideration when he was a boy. Feisal, like Fuad in Egypt in relation to Farouk, seemed to be totally uninterested in his son, even though he knew he must pass the succession to him.

Young Ghazi married his first cousin, the daughter of Husein's son Ali, in 1933, and has an heir. The women of the royal family, like most women in Iraq, are in strict purdah. But Ghazi's sister, the Emirah Azza, fell in love with a Greek merchant from Rhodes, named Harolambos, and ran off with him. This was a stinging shock to the Moslem world—that a descendant of the Prophet should elope with a Christian infidel! Ghazi wanted to send emissaries to Rhodes for proper punishment of Azza and Harolambos, but was dissuaded. He wanted, in fact, to murder them, but was told that this would not be quite the thing to do.

Ghazi is not popular with all his subjects. He has a somewhat disconcerting sense of humor. For instance, young Nuri Pasha, son of the Nuri whom I have mentioned, became an aviator. He took Ghazi for a ride one day. Then Ghazi demanded that young Nuri take aloft one of his black slaves; he thought it would be good fun to terrify the slave, a favorite. The slave, overcome with fright, grasped the controls from Nuri's hands; the plane crashed, and young Nuri was paralyzed as a result of the accident. The slave was killed.

Ghazi is blamed by some observers for the brutal suppression of the Assyrians in 1933. It is more likely, however, that Baqr Sidki, the short-lived dictator, was responsible.

Yemen and the Persian Gulf

The sub-state of Yemen, like Bhutan and Nepal on the fringes of India (which it in no other way resembles), is a political curiosity. It is independent, but not a member of the League; for many years

[4] King Ghazi was tragically killed in an automobile accident in April, 1939, and was succeeded by his infant son Feisal II.

it was virtually closed to foreigners, and was very little known; its ruler, King Yahya Mohammed ed Din, is considered to be a *living* Imam (roughly, prophet) by his followers, who adhere to the Zaidi sub-sect of Islam. He is a fierce old man, now seventy-five, with nine fierce sons. The chief product of his hilly land is extraordinarily good coffee, exported from a town appropriately named Mokha.

Yemen is the Arab state most conspicuously under Italian influence to-day. In 1937, following some years of careful infiltration, Italy signed a twenty-five-year friendship treaty with Yemen; the Yemenese bought Italian arms in considerable quantity, and the Imam Yahya sent the King of Italy and Signor Mussolini gifts of Arab horses. Italian technical advisers are busy in Yemen, which was one of the first states to recognize the conquest of Ethiopia. The interest of Italy in Yemen is obvious, if one looks at the map; occupation of it would make the lower end of the Red Sea an Italian lake, since Yemen directly faces Italian East Africa.

Ibn Saud fought a war with Yemen in 1934, and won it. Freely this war was called a preliminary tussle between Britain and Italy, since the British supported Ibn Saud, and the Italians had armed the Yemenese. Ibn Saud, incidentally, showed his manifest qualities of statesmanship after this war; he won it hands down, but he imposed no punitive peace on the old Imam, demanded no territory, and sought a resumption of friendly relations as soon as possible.

On the other side of the Arabian peninsula, along the Persian Gulf, are a group of sub-states dominated by the British, operating largely through the India Office.[5] One is Kuweit, near the frontiers of Iraq and Iran; it has a certain strategic value, but little wealth. Further down the coast are the Bahrein Islands, notable until recently only for their pearl fisheries, but now believed to be possessed of fabulously rich deposits of petroleum. The Bahrein Oil Company is partly owned by Standard Oil of California. At the southern tip of the Persian Gulf is the Sultanate of Muscat and Oman. The Sultan, a young man of twenty-eight, named Sayyed [6] Said bin Timur, visited the United States in 1937. Interestingly enough Muscat was the

[5] It was the government of India which first thought, during the Great War, of sending an emissary to Ibn Saud. The influence of the Indian Civil Service is particularly strong among British in Iraq. Aden, on the southern tip of the Arabian peninsula, was administered by the India Office until 1935.

[6] He is thus another of the several thousand lineal descendants of the Prophet—or so they assert—scattered through the Middle East.

first country with which the United States of America ever negotiated a foreign treaty; it was designed to protect American sailors wrecked on the Oman coast. The Sultan was tremendously impressed in America by seeing a demonstration of a Thompson sub-machine gun. His country, which covers 82,000 squares miles, contains exactly thirty miles of road; his civil list is $225,000 per year. His rule, as the nice phrase has it, is dominated by the fact that his state is "in political relations" with the government of India.

Also on the Persian Gulf are a series of petty chieftains known as the "Trucial Sheikhs." There are six of these sheikhs, each with his tiny parcel of territory, whose forbears signed picturesque treaties with the old East India Company and then the government of India promising to abjure piracy and the slave trade. A chieftain known as Ahmed bin Rashid, the Umm ul Qawain, is the most important of them. They take their honors very seriously. Each receives his proper salute in guns according to the protocol of the government of India. The story is that the least of them, a minor personality indeed, gets only one gun—and fires it himself!

The Persian Gulf states are interesting strategically because the Shah of Iran forbids British airplanes to follow his shore; thus the British imperial air route depends on landing fields on the Arabian side. These incredibly remote and antediluvian principalities hear the swooping roar of four-motor planes, en route from England to India and Australia, almost every day of the year.

Abdullah of T. J.

"Why must the Moslem countries always quarrel? Why can't they live peacefully like the Christian nations?"

—EMIR ABDULLAH IBN HUSEIN

Transjordan is important. It looks like an ax, with the head chopping into Arabia. It is the British land and air bridge between Palestine and Bagdad, and even though its territory is mostly lava and desert, it is of paramount interest in British communications.

The origin of Transjordan as a separate state is curious, and its exact political status was for a long time obscure. In 1919, the British evacuated most of Transjordan, which was considered to be part of Syria; but friction came between France and Britain when Feisal was expelled from Damascus, and the British planted him in Bagdad. Then Abdullah, Feisal's brother, marched into Transjordan on the way to Damascus, where he intended to fight the French to avenge Feisal, and perhaps take the Syrian throne himself. The British were embarrassed at this incursion of Arab warriors. Quietly the Royal Air Force reoccupied Transjordan, and Abdullah halted in its capital, Amman. Winston Churchill and Sir Herbert Samuel put their heads together. They "invited" Abdullah to remain in Transjordan—partly as a threat to the French, partly to keep him from entering Palestine. And Abdullah has remained in Transjordan ever since—an amiable British puppet.

Abdullah, son of Husein, brother of Feisal, uncle of King Ghazi of Iraq, is a squat, humorous, rather sly, and very astute man in his late fifties, whose salary is $75,000 per year. He is not technically a king, because Transjordan has a special mandatory status, but merely an emir. In his youth he was the most politically active of Husein's sons: he first got in touch with Sir Henry McMahon during the War, and was a prominent figure in the Arab revolt, though Lawrence did not like him as well as Feisal. He was once chosen King of Iraq, but the job went to Feisal instead. Abdullah speaks no western language. He likes to laugh. Once he went to the movies in Jerusalem, and saw pretty girls unveiled; he rolled with laughter, muttering "God is great!" In the entrance hall of his palace in Amman I encountered the most extraordinary object I have ever seen outside an amusement park, a gigantic concave-convex mirror, which produces astoundingly distorted reflections of those who—as all must—look into it.

Transjordan was declared part of the British mandate for Palestine in 1922; but in 1923, it was decided that the articles in the mandate referring to Zionism—the creation of the Jewish National Home in Palestine—should not apply to Transjordan. The Zionists have resented this bitterly ever since. They consider it a serious injustice that the mandate should have such half-and-half application, especially since Transjordan is big enough and undeveloped enough—even though it is the poorest of all the Arab countries—to absorb a considerable Jewish immigration.

Since it is part of the Palestine Mandate—with Zionism omitted—Transjordan is ruled in effect by the British High Commissioner in Palestine (who is represented by a resident in Amman), that is to say, by the British colonial office in London. There is a vestigial legislative council; it has no power. Public security comes from the strong Royal Air Force station, and from two remarkable native armies, officered partly by British, the Transjordan Frontier Force and the Arab Legion.

The British do this sort of thing extremely well, as we have seen in India. Gold is much cheaper than gun-fire; don't shoot but buy. (This is a lesson, incidentally, that the Italians have not learned.) The Arab Legion, a superb body of men, which is technically responsible to the Emir, has exactly two British officers. One is the legendary Peake Pasha, who was an able assistant to Colonel Lawrence. The Transjordan Frontier Force, which is under the Palestine government, is officered by a handful of British. Not more than twenty or thirty admirably competent young Englishmen keep the peace all the way from Palestine to the Euphrates.

Syria and Lebanon

Iraq is complex, and so is Palestine, but Syria is most complex. The curse of Syria is sectarianism. Here religion becomes indistinguishable from nationality; it *is* nationality. And in Syria, which is only about as big as Illinois with 2,500,000 people, at least twenty different religions flourish. There are various categories of Moslems, including Malekites, Nusarii (in three sects), worshipers of the Caliph Ali, Metawali, and the Druses, who are a special sub-sect believing among other things in reincarnation. Among Christians there are Greek Orthodox, Greek Catholics, Maronites, Roman Catholics, Armenian Catholics, Armenian Protestants, Nestorians, Copts, and Chaldeans.

All are—in theory—Syrians. Which is why it is so difficult to tell what a Syrian is—not to mention the phenomenal admixture of races, which further complicates the problem.

At the beginning of 1939, Syria was divided into no fewer than five different states, each with its own administration, its own constitution, its own flag. This reductio ad absurdum of the theory of decentralization (which, as we have seen, is also practiced in Indo-China) was promoted by the French, who have the mandate for the whole country, first to satisfy Syrian sectarian aspirations, second to make the country easier to handle, by splitting and subdividing Arab nationalism. But the country has not been easy to handle. There have been six civil wars or revolutions since 1919.

The two chief states of "Syria" are Syria proper and the Lebanon.

Syria, with its capital at Damascus, is basically Arab and Moslem, and the seat of the most intense Syrian nationalism. Damascus, as everyone knows, is the oldest inhabited city in the world (though a town in Afghanistan, by name Balkh, claims the same honor); a beautiful city, the legend has it that Mohammed refused to enter it, saying that Paradise in heaven was enough. As at present demarcated the "Syrian" frontiers do not include any share of the Mediterranean coast, which the Syrians consider an outrageous attempt by France to keep the new country permanently weak.

The second state, the Lebanon, comprises most of the coastal strip, with capital at Beirut. The population is largely Levantine and Christian. Treaties have been drawn up by France with both Syria and the Lebanon, on the model of the British treaty with Iraq, and both states are to receive full national independence in 1940—if the French Chamber of Deputies ratifies the treaties. Native governments are already functioning. The two states, after 1940, will remain quite independent of each other. The treaties are, however, similar, except that whereas the French will keep a garrison in turbulent Syria for only five years, they will maintain armed forces in comparatively tranquil Lebanon for twenty-five. This seeming paradox is because the Lebanese Christians are afraid of attack by the Moslem Syrians and want French protection. The Moslems in Syria hate the Lebanese more deeply, if possible, than they hate the French.

The third subdivision of Syria at present is the "Republic" of Latakia, also under its own administration, which takes in the coastal strip above the town of Tripoli. The fourth is the region of the troublesome Druses in the Jebel-el-Druse, in the mountainous region below Damascus; it is "autonomous" under military control. The Druses rose in a bitter civil war in 1926. Finally there is the Sanjak of Alexandretta, adjacent to Turkey on the north, which in the autumn of 1938 became something quite new under the sun—a state ruled jointly by France and Turkey, though the population, which is roughly sixty percent Arab, forty percent Turkish, is promised autonomy as soon as Syria reaches independence. Turkey insisted on this new Alexandretta régime as protection for the Turkish minority later; Turks and Arabs are old enemies. The Turks have given a new name to the new Sanjak—Hatay. Thus one more new country, at least for collectors of postage stamps.

Chapter XXXIV
Land of Israel

〰〰〰〰〰〰〰〰〰〰〰〰〰〰〰〰〰〰〰

Once we had a country and we thought it fair;
Look in the atlas and you'll find it there.
We cannot go there now, my dear, we cannot go there now.
— W. H. AUDEN in *The New Yorker*

ZIONISM is, as everyone should know, as old as Moses. Even if Moses himself did not reach the Promised Land, he first emphasized the concrete political actuality of Jewish need to possess geographical borders, to have for themselves that most essential of all things—a homeland. Modern Zionism began in the late nineteenth century with the teaching of Theodore Herzl. He sought to save Jews from the pogroms of Russia and Central Europe, to counteract the assimilation of Jews in western countries, and to found in the Holy Land, the only possible place, a National Home for the Jewish people. Herzl organized the World Zionist Organization, and the first Zionist Congress was held in Basle in 1897.

During the Great War came the Balfour Declaration, of date November 2, 1917. This document, battered by events as it has been, remains Zionist scripture. The British promulgated it partly for humanitarian reasons, partly on account of the exigencies of the War, and partly because of the curious accident that Dr. Chaim Weizmann, the Zionist leader, was a celebrated chemist. For the chemistry episode we must await the next chapter. The British wanted profoundly to influence Jewish opinion, both in the United States and among the submerged Jewish populations of the Central Powers, to the side of the Allies. When the Balfour Declaration was issued, for instance, thousands of copies were smuggled into the enemy countries, so that Jewish peoples in Germany and Eastern Europe might see the Allies as their savior. The Balfour Declaration reads:

His Majesty's Government view with favor the establishment in Palestine of a National Home for the Jewish people, and will use their best endeavors to facilitate the achievement of this object, it being clearly understood that nothing shall be done which may prejudice the civil and religious rights[1] of existing non-Jewish communities in Palestine or the rights and political status enjoyed by Jews in any other country.

To-day the Jewish problem has far outdistanced anything even remotely envisaged in 1917. The events in Germany and Central Europe since the rise of Hitler have focused a blazing and savage spotlight on the intolerable plight of Jews. The refugee problem has become an enormously pressing and tragic contemporary phenomenon. Jews by the million, guilty of no crime except that they are Jews, are homeless, destitute, starving. What is left of civilization in the world recoils in successive shocks as new and pitiless outrages against Jews are perpetrated. The Jewish question, as it was said in London recently, has become a non-Jewish question. German and Italian policy makes it universal. The desperation of the Jewish position is, or should be, a preoccupation of all decent mankind.

This serves to make the Zionist experiment in Palestine a more cogent and intimate issue than it has ever been before. Zionism, if it could be made to work, might solve the Jewish problem. Let us explore.

Jews in Palestine

The basic facts of the Palestine deadlock are known to almost everyone. Very briefly we may recapitulate them. The Balfour Declaration did not install the Jewish National Home in a vacuum; it installed it in what was in effect an Arab country. It did not install the Jewish National Home in a territory remote from political contingencies like, say, Alaska; it installed it in a section of the world which for generations had been the focus of a fierce imperialist struggle.

(But Zionism could not have been installed anywhere else. Palestine *is* the Jewish National Home. I quote from *A Primer on Palestine*: "Even during the exile in Babylon the Jews said, 'How can we sing the Lord's song in a strange land?' For the last two thousand years every Jew has said at Passover, 'Next year in Jerusalem.'")

Legally the Arab case that Palestine is "their" country rests on the McMahon correspondence. It goes without saying that the Allies did play fast-and-loose with the Arabs. The Arabs were not the only people honored with such attention during the Great War. But, as

---

[1] Note that there is no mention of non-Jewish, i.e., Arab, *political* or *national* rights.

was pointed out in Chapter XXXIII, McMahon himself excludes Palestine from the territory promised to Arab sovereignty. Official British doctrine has never admitted that the McMahon pledge is valid in regard to Palestine.

The British thus whittled down their purported obligations to the Arabs; similarly they pared down their promises to the Jews. For twenty-one years the Balfour Declaration has been interpreted one way or other by various British governments. In 1922, Mr. Winston Churchill attempted to concentrate it in a White Paper which stated that Jews were to live in Palestine as of right, and not on sufferance, but that there should be no attempt to create an exclusive Jewish state in Palestine. In other words, the National Home for the Jewish people was to be a sort of island in a largely Arab country. Great Britain as the mandatory power was in charge of administration, empowered to inflict legislation on Jews and Arabs alike. So the experiment began.

Jewish brains, Jewish immigrants—and finally Jewish blood— began to irrigate the little country. But the Jews insist that they did not remove any rights from the Arabs, nor were they "taking" any land. They bought the land they settled on, at good prices, and even during the disturbances the Arabs were willing enough to sell. They did not dispossess any but an infinitesimal number of Arabs; at the beginning, at least, they scrupulously respected Arab religious and racial customs, and they did not "take" nearly as much of Palestine as is generally assumed. At present the Jews own about 300,000 acres of cultivable land, out of a total cultivable area estimated at 2,750,-000 acres.

The concrete achievements of Zionism have been considerable. An attempt to express spiritual homogeneity in geographical terms was unique; to many it was enthralling. I have watched the immigrants come in at Jaffa, on boats like troop ships, from the ghettos of Lemberg and Czernowitz and Prague. No, they were not handsome, vigorous young men. No, they were not lit by any apparent inward fire. Instead, they were wretchedly dressed and miserably poor, huddled in cantonments where brisk British officers shuffled and distributed them; they looked like refugees from slums. But a few years later I saw these same people tilling the soil, carving livelihoods out of the dusty rock of the Jordan hills and the plain of Esdraelon—upright, alert, self-sufficient, with pride in their work, pride in themselves. They were new men. The transformation was all but unbelievable.

In Palestine [wrote Sir Herbert Samuel, the first civilian High Commissioner] there are Oriental Jews from Bokhara and Persia and Iraq, and there are University men and women from New York and Chicago. There are Jews from the Yemen, of small stature and with gentle, refined features, good craftsmen in silver and ivory, or good laborers on the farms; and there are agricultural experts from the colleges of France, from Poland and Russia. There are students and writers, doctors and lawyers, architects and musicians, organizers and social workers, from Eastern Europe and Western, from Asia and America.

Zionism necessarily hand picks its colonists, since immigration is fixed by the Palestine (British) government; the quota has lately been severely cut down, after years of whittling. The immigration of *halutzim* (pioneers) is thus not fortuitous, but selective; the Zionist organization, represented by agents throughout Eastern Europe, chooses them man by man. Once in Palestine, the immigrants are organized into colonies and settled on the land. Some land is the property of the Jewish people as a whole, in perpetual lease to the Jewish National Fund; some may be privately bought and sold. The Jewish agricultural colonists are the heart of Zionism.

Accompanying Zionism came a Hebrew revival. The colonists learn Hebrew, and that tongue has been resuscitated as a living language. Hebrew theaters have been organized and a living literature in Hebrew has developed. Schools have been opened in considerable number; a great Hebrew university has been built on Mt. Scopus, near Jerusalem; a definite revivification of Jewish life has occurred, expressed in Hebrew terms.

Meantime the standard of living of the whole country was enormously increased. Jewish capital entered the country in large amounts. The remarkable town of Tel-Aviv arose on the Jaffa sands, the only exclusive Jewish municipality in the world. Swamps were drained; malaria controlled; irrigation and water power projects outlined; agriculture rationalized. The Jews built hospitals, welfare stations, libraries, clinics, laboratories for scientific research. They brought, in fact, the modern world to Palestine.

Immigration figures tell the story of rising Jewish strength and consequent Arab alarm. In 1920, 5,514 Jews came to Palestine; in

1925, 33,801. Then came a serious drop; but in 1933, immigration reached 30,000 again, and in 1934, it rose to 42,359, in 1935, to 61,854. In 1922, the total population of Palestine was about 750,000; it included 589,177 Moslems, 71,464 Christians, and 83,790 Jews. (Many Jews had settled in Palestine long before the War and the Balfour Declaration.) The Jews were, in other words, roughly eleven per cent of the total population. In 1936, the population of Palestine was 1,336,518, of whom 848,342 were Moslems, 106,474 Christians, and 370,483 Jews. The Moslems, one sees, increase very rapidly too. But the proportion of Jews to the total population rose in 1936 to roughly twenty-eight per cent.

It soon became clear that tension between Jew and Arab prevented any easy development of normal self-governing institutions. Indeed, the government of Palestine is unique. There is no constitution, no parliament, no president, no prime minister, no cabinet. The administration is purely colonial. New laws are posted simply by decree. The "government" is vested almost solely in the person of the British High Commissioner, who is responsible only to the colonial office in London, and, at an astronomical distance, to the Mandates Commission of the League of Nations. This has occurred because no legislative instrument could be devised satisfactory to Jew and Arab alike. Being outnumbered, the Jews refused any government based on proportionate representation, since it was Arab policy to abolish Jewish immigration altogether. And the Arabs refused anything else.

The Jewish accomplishment in Palestine came atop almost insuperable difficulties and obstacles. From the beginning Zionism faced not only political watering down of the mandate but deep-seated antipathy from anti-Semitic British officials. The Jews were violently discriminated against—in what was presumably to be their own country. William Ziff has outlined[2] some of the more outrageous details. Hitler's *Mein Kampf* was permitted in the Jerusalem bookshops; but not the *Brown Book of the Nazi Terror*. Alone among Arab states Palestine was asked to continue payments on the old Ottoman debt. The Jews were not allowed to build their own harbor at Tel-Aviv, or to equip it with a railway station. Palestine gets no revenue from the Iraq pipeline, though it goes through Palestine

[2] In *The Rape of Palestine*, a rip-roaring assault on Arabs, British and moderate Zionists alike.

territory. Jews were arrested for picketing German shops, and Jewish taxes paid for Arab schools—and to suppress Arab revolutions.

Not all Jews are active Zionists. In the United States, with some 4,000,000 Jews, only about 100,000 are members of the Zionist Organization. But in 1929, a new Jewish agency was created, including non-Zionists as well as Zionists, jointly pledged to support "Jewish" philanthropy and work in Palestine. This wisely broadened the base of Zionist activity. It seemed in 1929 that a new era in the development of the Jewish National Home might begin. But the optimists were wrong. The Arabs rose. A fierce religious crisis led to insurrection (Jerusalem is a holy city to Moslems as well as Jews), Jews were hideously massacred, and a period commenced of extreme difficulty and tension.

Arabs in Palestine

"Verily God loveth not the aggressors."

—MOHAMMED

Arab and Jew are astoundingly contradistinctive, considering that both are Semites. In religion, in language, in politics, in morals, in community ideals, in habit of mind they differ. As I heard it put: the Arab is a camel; the Jew is a motor-car, seeking new roads—and a place to put them.

The Arabs became alarmed early. Riots occurred as early as 1920 and 1921, though King Feisal and the Zionist leader, Dr. Weizmann, made a preliminary entente. What alarmed the Arabs most was realization of their own economic, political, and cultural inferiority. We have sketched enough of Arab background in preceding chapters to make this clear. Backward, nomadic, with no experience of western administration (they had been governed for centuries by Turks), largely illiterate, the Arabs were no match for the educated and hustling Jews.

The Arabs began to organize. A youthful leader, Haj Amin Effendi El Huseini, combined in his person the posts of president of the Supreme Moslem Council (a body founded by the British in 1921 to give the Arabs focus for political organization) and Mufti of Jerusalem. He is usually called the "Grand" Mufti,[3] but pedantically

---

[3] "Mufti" means priest, though technically there is no Moslem clergy. "Haj" is a name given to any Moslem who has made the pilgrimage to Mecca.

speaking there is no such title. Haj Amin was supposed to hold both jobs for life. He became the spearhead of the Arab nationalist movement.

In 1920, the Mufti had been condemned to five years' imprisonment by the British for complicity in the Jaffa riots; he fled, however, and was not captured. Then Sir Herbert Samuel, the High Commissioner, decided to pardon him; he announced the pardon at a public meeting in Amman, capital of Transjordan.

"Let Haj Amin come to Jerusalem; he will not be molested; we have pardoned him," Sir Herbert said.

There was a movement in the crowd and, to the amazement of the British, Haj Amin proceeded to appear, lifted on the shoulders of the Arabs. He had been hiding—in a good enough place!

Haj Amin—now in exile—was born in 1893 in Jerusalem, of the well-established and influential Huseini family. He was a student in Turkey when the Great War broke out; he became an officer in the Turkish army like so many Near Eastern personalities, and then was taken prisoner; on being released by the allied forces, he joined the Arab revolt, but he was never conspicuous in it. In character he is a flaming nationalist, in manner very cautious and slow-spoken.

He became Mufti of Jerusalem when he was only twenty-seven, in succession to his half-brother. The story is that he prepared himself for this important job by special studies at Al Azhar University in Cairo, but in fact he studied at Al Azhar only a few months. He was fourth in the list of candidates for Mufti. The other three were members of a rival family of Jerusalem Arabs, the Nashashibis. The Huseinis contrived anyway to procure the appointment for their man, Haj Amin. Presently he became president of the Supreme Moslem Council too and was in effect both religious and secular leader of the Arabs of Palestine.

His power did not reside in his personality. It resided in his position. By reason of his double job he was in control—until the British deprived him of his leadership of the Supreme Moslem Council—of the revenues of the *Waqf*, or Moslem religious foundations and endowments. These possess considerable property, mostly land; the *Waqf* revenues are supposed to amount to $300,000 per year, and—normally—are used to support schools, charities, and the like. But they helped finance the Mufti's revolution—so his enemies say. An additional point is that the Mufti, while president of the

Supreme Moslem Council, got a salary from the government. This salary continued to be paid—until his flight—even though he was overtly leading a revolt against the authorities who were paying him. The Mufti had for a time a third job, that of head of the supervisory board of the Moslem religious courts. He thus was in a position to nominate judges and the like, an important source of patronage.

There are no fewer than six different Arab parties in Palestine. The chief one is the Mufti's. For years the six vigorously opposed each other, but in 1936 they merged temporarily, under the leadership of the Mufti, to produce a joint executive, the Arab Higher Committee. When the Mufti fled, and when other important Arabs were arrested and deported, the Committee broke up and was outlawed. The National Defense Party, the next most important in Palestine, seceded from it. This party group, led by Ragheb Bey Nashashibi, has always taken a moderate line; Ragheb Bey was for fifteen years mayor of Jerusalem, and a bitter opponent of the Mufti.[4]

The moderate Arabs of the Nashashibi and similar varieties, though resenting Zionist power and penetration, have been appalled at the wave of terrorism and civil war that has inundated Palestine. In November, 1938, opposition to the Mufti came into the open. A member of the Defense Party, Fahkri Bey Nashashibi, a cousin of Ragheb Bey, sent a letter to the British High Commissioner stating:

1. That the anti-Mufti Arabs comprise seventy-five percent of the Arabs of Palestine, whom the Mufti has sought to crush through terrorism.

2. That the Mufti "used his official position and the funds collected for the national cause to exterminate or impoverish the leaders" opposed to him in Palestine.

3. That the British should realize that the Mufti does not alone represent the Arabs of Palestine, and that terrorism is encouraged by this assumption.

Response came quickly. An attempt was made to assassinate a member of the Nashashibi faction the next day. Five other members of the Nashashibi family were attacked or murdered shortly thereafter.

[4] He was born in Jerusalem in 1880, and was a member for Jerusalem in the Turkish parliament from 1914-19. In contrast to the Mufti he is widely traveled, well educated, a cosmopolitan with something of a western outlook. His wife is Christian.

The Mufti's men look far afield. In November, 1938, came a statement by the nationalist leader Arif Abdul Razik, threatening the United States with reprisals for "interfering in affairs which are none of its business," i.e., for expressing sympathy with Palestine Jews. The statement asserted that if such interference continued, the Arabs would (a) withdraw all Arab students from American schools, (b) boycott American goods, (c) destroy all American buildings in Palestine, and (d) seize all American property in Palestine.

The civil war began in effect in April, 1936, when a Jewish party was ambushed near Nablus and a Jewish immigrant killed. There were riots at his funeral, and agitation spread. The Arab Higher Committee declared a general strike, which for six months turned the country upside down. Imported guerrillas from Transjordan and Iraq did much of the Arab fighting. In the end the British had to pour almost 30,000 troops into the little country. Through it all, however, the Mufti himself, living in Jerusalem, was not arrested because the British High Commissioner still believed that a policy of "appeasement" and reconciliation would win the day.

The fighting was mopped up—temporarily—late in 1936; the general strike fizzled out; and a Royal Commission came to Palestine. This commission, led by Lord Peel, made its report in July, 1937. It did not waste much ink on the feelings of the Arabs. It found the Palestine mandate unworkable in its present form, and proposed the drastic surgical remedy of Partition. It envisaged creation of three separate states in Palestine (a country the size of Wales or New Jersey!), British, Jewish, Arab. The partition phase of Palestine history appeared about to begin.

It did not get very far. Again, furiously, the Arabs rose. They made another civil war, a much more serious one this time.

"What Thin Partitions Sense from Thought Divide!"

The attitude of the Jews to the idea of Partition was, at first, bitter. "Barbarous vivisection," said the Chief Rabbi of the British Empire. "An end of the great dream of a Jewish nation," complained Mr. Ussishkin of the Jewish National Fund. "A Palestine state without Jerusalem is a mockery," cried the *Palestine Post*, organ of the moderate Zionists. People said that a "new Jewish pale" was created actually in the national home. It was "Zionism without Zion."

Then leading Jews began to come round to sympathy with the idea when they explored its ramifications and discovered—a most important point—that the Arabs opposed it more vehemently than they did. Dr. Weizmann, the President of the World Zionist Organization, lent his formidable prestige to support the project. A stormy meeting of the Jewish Agency in Zurich, while reserving final judgment, opened the way to negotiation.

Few Jews, it may be said, liked Partition for its own sake, but they preferred it to intolerable unsettlement and tension. Moreover the "irresistible lure of sovereignty" began to win them. They talked of their new flag, their constitution-to-be, their new frontiers. They were going to have a state that really was their own—no matter how microscopically small.

Jewish grievances from 1919 to 1936 were summarized as follows in the Peel Report:

1. Obstruction in the establishment of the National Home owing to dilatory action by officials.
2. "Pro-Arab" proclivities by officials and their failure to carry out the Mandate.
3. Great delay in the decision of civil suits and inefficiency of criminal procedure. (For instance, eighty Jews were murdered in 1936 but no capital sentence against an Arab was carried out.)
4. Toleration by the Government (for a long time) of subversive activities, especially those of the Mufti of Jerusalem.
5. Failure to introduce a land system appropriate to the needs of the country.
6. Reluctance to facilitate immigration, and uncontrolled illegal Arab immigration.
7. Restriction of progress of Jewish municipalities by government regulations.
8. Failure of the British to ensure public security.

The Jewish "case" in Palestine, strongly underlined by the Royal Commission, is in essence simple. The Jews, a people without a homeland, have an inescapable moral, historical, and political right to one, and Palestine is the only one possible. They have as much "right" to Palestine as the Arabs; they mean no harm to Arabs, who have millions of square miles to live in if they find proximity to Jews uncomfortable. No Arabs have been asked to leave Palestine. Jewish "occupation" of Palestine has indeed greatly benefited the Arab community.

But the Arabs refused coöperation. In the words of the Peel Commission, "Not once since 1919 has any Arab leader said that coöperation with the Jews was even possible." (On the other hand, let it be repeated that all through the disturbances Arab landowners made money freely by selling Jews their land.) A modicum of hate of course accompanied these transactions; money counts, but blood counts too. "*The* underlying cause [of the unrest]," a Jewish witness told the Commission, "is that we exist."

Two questions put to the Mufti by the Royal Commission (the Arabs boycotted the Commission till the last possible moment and then gave evidence briefly) are of interest:

Q. Does Your Eminence think that this country can assimilate and digest the 400,000 Jews now in the country?

A. No.

Q. Some of them would have to be removed by a process kindly or painful as the case may be?

A. We must leave all this to the future.

Here was a new note of menace; not content with opposition to Jewish immigration, the Mufti was, in a guarded manner, indicating that Jews might in the "future" be expelled from the country if his party had its way. And in the civil wars from 1936 on, the Arabs were attacking, not only the Jews, but the British as well—an ominous sign.

Whereas the basic grievances of the Jews were in a sense mollified by the partition scheme, those of the Arabs were made more intense. This, in a nutshell, was the reason for renewed Arab clamor. The main Arab grievances, as outlined by the Royal Commission, were as follows:

1. Failure to develop self-governing institutions (i.e., Palestine has no parliament, prime minister, or the other paraphernalia of democracy, partly because the Jews fear what would be Arab numerical superiority in the legislature).

2. Acquisition of land by Jews. (But the Arabs sold it to them.)

3. Jewish immigration.

4. The use of Hebrew and English as official languages.

5. Employment of British and Jewish officers, and exclusion of Arabs from the higher posts.

6. Creation of a large class of landless Arabs, and the refusal of Jews to employ Arab laborers.

7. Inadequate funds for Arab education.

The Report says: "Whilst we believe that these grievances are sincerely felt, we are of the opinion that most of them cannot be regarded as legitimate under the terms of the mandate and we are therefore not called upon to make recommendations upon them."

Above and beyond the specific grievances is the major tenet of the Arabs, that Palestine is *their* country, and that the Jews are "taking it away." In the words of the Royal Commission:

The underlying causes of the disturbances, or (as we regard it) the rebellion of 1936 are, first, the desire of the Arabs for national independence; secondly, their antagonism to the establishment of the Jewish National Home in Palestine, quickened by their fear of Jewish immigration. Among contributory causes were the effect on Arab opinion of the attainment of national independence by Iraq, Transjordan, Egypt, Syria, and the Lebanon; the rush of Jewish immigrants escaping from Central Europe . . . ; the intensive character and the "modernism" of Jewish nationalism; and lastly the general uncertainty, accentuated by the ambiguity of certain phrases in the Mandate, as to the ultimate intentions of the Mandatory Power.

As to the Arab assertion that Palestine is exclusively their country, the Jews reply that they have the "right of prior occupation and historical connection." The Jews conquered Palestine in about 1200 B.C., and held it for thirteen centuries. Some Jews have been uninterruptedly in Nablus from 722 B.C. until the present day. The Arabs held the country from 637 A.D., when the Omayyid Caliphs began to rule in Damascus, until it was seized by the Ottoman Turks in 1516 A.D., who, with their descendants (and Turks are not Arabs, either linguistically or racially), held it till the Great War.

Palestine means more than race or language to the Arabs; it means religion. Jerusalem is holy to Moslem Arabs as well as to Christians and Jews. This is because of two sacred Moslem edifices there, one the Dome of the Rock, which was built on the site of Abraham's rock (the central point of the Temple of Solomon), the other the Mosque of Aqsa, which was originally a Christian church. The Mosque of Aqsa is supposed to mark the spot where Mohammed's winged horse was tethered before the flight to heaven; it is, after Mecca and Medina, the greatest shrine in Islam. But this same area is devoutly and correctly sacred to Jews too, because it contains the celebrated Wailing Wall[5] which was the site of Solomon's Temple, and which is as

---

[5] Effort by youthful Jews to extend their rights of worship at the Wailing Wall was a contributing factor of the 1929 disturbances.

Jewish as the Talmud. The sacredness was originally Jewish and Christian; the Moslems took it over because it *was* holy. Jewish and Arab religious monuments are inextricably conjoined.

Bloodshed Again

Terrorism came once more, and then war. The Arabs determined to fight the partition scheme to a finish. They did.

After sporadic disorder, with tension crackling, the British set out to arrest the Mufti. This was in July, 1937. But the Mufti with his Sudanese bodyguard escaped into the Temple Area, and the British did not dare follow him there, because invasion of such a hallowed Moslem sanctuary might have caused an unpredictable explosion. Until October the Mufti stayed inside the Temple, a priest in a cage; he was surrounded and helpless, and had no method of direct activity. On October 16 he fled to Syria, eluding the British police disguised as a beggar. Since that time he has resided in French territory.

Disorder continued to spread, and was probably encouraged by foreign interests who like to see the Palestine pot boiling. The Arabs became increasingly bold, and by the summer of 1938 all but paralyzed the country. British power seemingly collapsed in district after district. The Arab terrorists ran wild. The essence of terrorism is that it aims to disorganize the forces of authority by secret and subterranean means. And, by and large, it will continue to be successful so long as the bulk of the people are with the terrorists, and will conceal and assist them. The problem for the government is to make the people more afraid of the government than of the terrorists.

By the end of 1938 the Arabs had forced a stalemate. They were strong enough to invade and capture important towns. They were so successful, in fact, that the Jews firmly believe that the British never genuinely desired to beat them down. Otherwise such episodes as, for instance, the raids on police stations in big towns like Jaffa, or the virtual investment of Jericho, are almost inconceivable. "It would be ludicrous," said the Peel Report, "to suppose that it is beyond the resources of the British government to deal with a rebellion on so small a scale." Yet that is just what happened, though the Arab guerrillas probably never numbered more than 5,000 men.

On November 9, 1938, the British government withdrew the partition scheme, and announced that the whole Palestine problem would be reopened, with a Round Table Conference between Jews and Arabs as a preliminary step. Almost at once, the Arab revolt died down.

But the Round Table Conference, duly held in London, broke up in March, 1939. Not only did Jews and Arabs disagree; non-Mufti Arabs refused to sit with Mufti Arabs for a time. At the end the British issued proposals which both Arabs and Jews rejected, though presumably they will be the basis for subsequent discussion. The proposals suggested creation of an independent Palestine state after a transition period, with Jews in a permanent minority. It was believed that Jewish immigration would be permitted at 15,000 per year until the Jews became one-third of the population, when it was to stop. The Jews refused to consider this. So did the Arabs, who demanded cessation of Jewish immigration and an independent Arab state at once.

Immediately the conference failed resumption of trouble was threatened again in Palestine. So the tragic story winds itself along.

. . . .

Civilization is overwhelmingly on the side of the Jews; but civilization isn't always popular. Zionism is an emotional and practical necessity to countless Jews, and given intelligent statesmanship it should become the best single solution to the refugee problem. But it faces the bitterly fomented hostility of the Arab population. Arab hostility to Zionism is lamentable; but it is not going to be easy to erase. The British will not give up the Mandate, because Palestine is an essential item in the defense of the air route to India and of the Suez Canal; but to maintain the Mandate means almost intolerable disorder, tension, and dismay. Zionism rests on British bayonets—which have not been too glitteringly effective—and which seem in fact to be aiming at the Zionists.

Perhaps amelioration will come some day—amelioration to the refugee problem also—in the form of an exchange of populations. This is not practical politics yet; it could become practical politics any time the British believed in it. The Arabs might conceivably go into Transjordan or Iraq, where there is plenty of room; Jews from Europe could come then to Palestine. The idea may seem fantastic, but it worked when imposed by a strong hand on the Greeks and Turks. Something drastic must be done. The refugee issue forces new attention to Zionism as a way out.

Chapter XXXV
Dr. Chaim Weizmann

~~~~~~~~~~

*Yes, I am a Jew, and when the ancestors of the Right
Honorable Gentleman were brutal savages in an unknown
island, mine were priests in the Temple of Solomon.*

—DISRAELI

YEARS ago, when the late Lord Balfour was visiting Manchester
during an electoral campaign, he met a young Jewish chemist
named Chaim Weizmann. They liked each other at once, and Weizmann talked vividly of the great dream of his life—Zionism. Balfour
was moved and impressed. Already he was interested in the Zionist
project, and there had been talk of making Uganda, in Africa, a
Jewish colony. Balfour turned to Weizmann, as the young man, with
perfect poise, argued his point that only Palestine could be the proper
national home. "Tell me, Dr. Weizmann, are there many Zionists like
you?" Balfour asked. Weizmann smiled and replied, "Mr. Balfour,
the roads of Pinsk are paved with them."

Weizmann was referring to his birthplace. The Zionist leader, who
is one of the considerable men of the modern world, was born on
November 27, 1874, in the village of Motele, near Pinsk, Russia. He
was the third child of a family of fifteen, eleven of whom are alive
to-day. His father was a timber merchant of modest means, not rich;
his mother was an exceptionally devoted and courageous woman.
She managed, for instance, to send no fewer than nine of her children
to universities, though the family was poor, and the road to education for Jews in Russia in those days was arduous.

In that same early conversation with Balfour, Weizmann showed
his ingrown, innate, unshakable conviction that Zionism and Palestine were one. Weizmann asked Balfour, who was still thinking of
Uganda, "Would you give up London to live in Saskatchewan?"
"But we have always lived in London!" Balfour exclaimed. "Yes,"
Weizmann replied, "and we lived in Jerusalem when London was
still a marsh."

Not only has Weizmann, like most men of politics in the modern age, been dominated all his life by one idea; that idea—Zionism—was from his earliest years associated with the hope of British help. For instance, a letter exists to-day, which he wrote to a teacher when he was eleven years old, stating that the salvation of the Jews was Palestine, and that only the English could help get them there. Weizmann has been consistently pro-British all his career. This has not kept him from being a passionately good Jew, but it necessarily made him a master of political maneuver.

Young Weizmann went to the *cheder* (religious private school) in his village, then to the gymnasium in Pinsk. He was a brilliant student of science and mathematics, and his mother's favorite child.[1] He progressed to the University of Freiburg, supporting himself at odd jobs, and finally got his doctor's degree in science at the University of Berlin. He returned to Pinsk in the holidays, and was a devoted son. The family was spiritedly intellectual. The other sons became doctors or scientists, and the atmosphere at home was agitated with political and literary talk. Weizmann's father was an early Jewish nationalist.

Weizmann got a job as a lecturer's assistant in chemistry at Geneva, and lived there several years. He met a young woman, Vera (Veratchke) Chatzman, who was studying medicine and who became an M.D., fell in love with her, and married her. She has been his attractive and devoted companion ever since. They have two sons, Benjamin, a business man in London, and Michael, a science student at Cambridge. Weizmann left Geneva in 1903, when he was offered a lectureship at the University of Manchester, and England—plus Palestine—has been his home for thirty-five years. He still looks back with affection on his Geneva days. When he visits Geneva to-day he takes friends from the Hotel Beau Rivage, where he usually stays, to the laboratory in the basement of the University College building, near the Parc de la Reformation, and shows them where he got his start.

Weizmann probably met Lenin in those days. He is not sure. But Lenin lived in Geneva at the time, and most of the Russian students frequented the same cafés. More than once Weizmann sat in the

[1] Her maiden name was Rachel Tchemetinsky. She is alive to-day, and lives in a modest house Weizmann built for her in Haifa, at the foot of Mt. Carmel. He brought her out of Russia in 1926, when his father died. When he comes to Palestine he visits her at once, and the whole family celebrates Passover every year in the aged lady's house.

coffee house, unable to pay for the modest drink he had bought, waiting for some friend to come and bail him out. Most of his companions were scientists, not politicians. In any event, whether he met Lenin or not, one fact is extraordinary, if purely coincidental—and that is his facial resemblance to Lenin. He is darker than Lenin was, and his face is broader, but the similarity is exceptional. Once, when Weizmann happened to be at an international conference, the Russian delegates—this was in 1923 or thereabouts—kept staring at him as if he were a ghost, and the Swiss detectives set up a guard at his hotel door thinking that he *was* Lenin.

Long before the Manchester period Weizmann became a Zionist. He had—unlike most political leaders—two lives. He was a chemist by day, and a Zionist by night. Rather, since he is a genius, he was both a chemist and a Zionist twenty-four hours a day; he survived—and enjoyed—a compelling double activity. The only Zionist conference he ever failed to attend was the first one, in 1897. He was in Pinsk, and too poor to make the trip. He worked his way on a timber boat as far as Danzig, and then rushed overland to Basle, where the conference was held; but he got there two days late.

I cannot treat in any detail the complex inner history of Weizmann's relations with the Zionist movement from 1897 to the present. Suffice it to say that, from the beginning, he was marked for leadership; that as a youth of twenty-seven he dared to oppose Herzl, the founder of political Zionism, whom he considered to be too visionary; that from the outset he took a practical attitude, urging the training of Jews in colonization and agricultural work; that in his maiden speech to the biennial Zionist congress (1903), he conceived and put forward the project of a Hebrew University in Jerusalem; that for fifteen years he was the leader of the "Manchester Group" of British Zionists; that, finally, in 1921, he became president of the World Zionist Organization. Many trials, many crises and counter-crises, and many moments of elation and despair, are masked by this brief record.

In 1916 came the greatest moment of Weizmann's life. Chemistry and Zionism merged, though he did not know it then.

David Lloyd George was searching for technical assistance in the preparation of explosives. There was an acute shortage of acetone, a substance indispensable to cordite manufacture. This was in the darkest period of the war. Disaster loomed. Synthetic acetone—and much else—was an imperative necessity. Lloyd George called a conference, and asked the advice of C. P. Scott, the editor of the Manchester Guardian. Scott said to Lloyd George, "I know a remarkable professor of chemistry at Manchester University. He comes from somewhere near the Vistula; I don't know which side. I will ask him if he will place himself at the disposal of the state."

Weizmann went to London to see Lloyd George. He was then put in charge of the Admiralty laboratories.

Lloyd George said, "I need immediate action, immediate results."

Weizmann said, "How long can you give me? I'll work night and day."

Within some weeks Weizmann had discovered a method of synthesizing acetone. He studied the composition of cereals, and found a method of isolating organisms which permitted him to make acetone out of—horse chestnuts! The method was developed on a large scale. A sufficient supply of acetone, and thus cordite, was assured Great Britain. Lloyd George called for Weizmann again. He said in effect, "Dr. Weizmann, you have rendered great service to the state. I will recommend you to His Majesty for any honors you may wish."

"There is nothing I want for myself," Weizmann said.

Lloyd George hinted at a viscountcy, a monetary grant.

Weizmann shook his head. "There is only one thing I want," he said, "and that is a national home for my people."

A few months later came the Balfour Declaration, which—in theory—provided it. Zionism—it seemed then—was won. Of course, other factors contributed to the announcement of the Declaration, as we have seen. But Lloyd George himself says that the acetone incident led him to support the Zionist thesis, and that he brought Weizmann into contact with his old friend, Balfour, in order to open negotiations. When Balfour saw him, he said, "I need no introduction to Dr. Weizmann. He converted me to Zionism ten years ago." Lloyd George has stated that Weizmann will rank with Nehemiah "in the fascinating and inspiring story of the children of Israel."

The Zionist Colossus

Weizmann's home in Palestine is at Rehovoth, near Tel-Aviv. His house is surrounded by citrus groves, and is exquisitely appointed. Weizmann is a lover of life. He is a great host. He is something of a sybarite. He is not, like most nationalist leaders, arid in temperament, frugal in habit; he loves good food, good drink, good laughter. He is a resonant and capacious human being, with a delight in the life of the senses.

But he works hard. He works hard at Zionism, and at his chemistry still. The chief ornament of the colony at Rehovoth is not the glorious Ming porcelain inside his house, but his spare, squat laboratory across the grove. In this building, known as the Daniel Sieff Research Laboratory, his staff conducts various experiments, most of them of a practical nature associated with Palestinian agriculture. Weizmann guides them, and is himself working on the by-products of orange peel, in order to increase the value of Palestine's citrus crop.

In Rehovoth, two small but startling coincidences present themselves. The first concerns Dr. Friedrich Haber, the great German chemist who invented the fixation of nitrogen. Haber was a Jew who turned Christian; when the Nazis came to power he went to Weizmann and begged to be forgiven, and was enroute to Palestine, a Jew again, when he died in Basle. He left his chemical library to the Rehovoth establishment. Thus Weizmann, who helped win the war for Britain by synthesizing acetone, now works with the tools of another great chemist, Haber, who almost won the war for Germany by inventing another process of manufacturing explosives by new means.

Second, Weizmann's work on orange peel, which may have very important commercial developments, happens by an extraordinary coincidence to be a development of the same process he invented in regard to acetone twenty years before. Two decades ago, acetone produced Zionism. To-day, acetone may help Zionism live. It is as if some single-mindedness were pursuing Weizmann through the years, rigidly associating him with one line of development, one group of processes.

Weizmann adores Rehovoth. The land on which his house and laboratory were built belonged at one time—again a remarkable example of the unity of his life and career—to the first settler who left Pinsk, Weizmann's home town, for Palestine. When Weizmann was a boy of ten, he saw this settler off at the Pinsk railway station, not by any stretch of the imagination conceiving that forty years later he would chance to buy this same man's Palestine property.

When the partition scheme was being discussed, it was discovered that Rehovoth was on the very edge of the projected Arab state.

"Put it in the Palestine area at once," said the British boundary maker. "Palestine without Weizmann is impossible."

Once Weizmann was showing Rehovoth to Sir Arthur Wauchope, then the High Commissioner. Wauchope admired it. "You have a very beautiful place here, Dr. Weizmann," he said. "Yes," Weizmann replied, "and it wasn't built as a summer palace for the Grand Mufti, either."

Weizmann, a complex character—he is first of all a scientist, then a politician, but there is also a good deal of the artist in his nature—has some defects in temperament. He is moody. Occasionally he sulks. He is stubborn. For millions of Jews, he is Zionism, and Zionism is Weizmann, but he has a certain contempt—like Nehru in India—for the masses as a whole. He is not a good man in a crowd, though his wit, his elegance, his persuasive power in private conversation, are considerable.

He dislikes documents. He is sometimes slothful, and hates to get up early in the morning. He is apt to say, discussing administrative details, "If Shertok is agreed, let's go on from there." (Shertok is the "foreign secretary" of the Zionist movement.) He will stay up all night to read a scientific paper, but not a political paper. He hates to dictate letters. He writes everything in longhand, in tiny characters, in green ink on blue paper. He seldom keeps carbons of his correspondence, and it is said that a good many interesting records of his life have as a result been lost. When I saw him in Rehovoth in 1938 he talked a good deal about his forthcoming memoirs—they should be one of the great autobiographies of our time—but he couldn't for the life of him remember the name of his publisher.

The most serious charge against Weizmann is that, a prisoner of tradition and environment, he is too strongly pro-British. He is called timid, old-fashioned, and "too much a gentleman." Another is that he does not understand that it is not enough for Jews to be passive these days, that it is no longer any use fighting fire (the Arabs), with water, that they must be fought with fire. He does not, it is said, appreciate the modern activitist position of Jewry; he does not realize that very many youthful Jews are willing to fight—and die—for their homeland. In London recently Malcolm MacDonald, the colonial secretary, asked him in effect, "Are you willing that Zionism should rest indefinitely on Britain for support?" Weizmann said that he would have to consider the question before answering. But almost any modern Zionist would have replied instantly that, given a fair chance, the Zionists are perfectly capable of defending themselves, and would be delighted to have the opportunity. Give them the rights originally promised by the Mandate, give them unlimited immigration and arms, and they are more than willing to face the Arabs.

Many Jews think that the Arabs, in themselves, are no serious problem. It is only Arab-plus-England that is a problem.

The major point of forward-looking Zionists early in 1939, when Europe faced almost certain warfare in the Mediterranean, was that a securely established and numerous Zionist majority in Palestine— to put it bluntly, a really Jewish Palestine—would be an infinitely more valuable asset to Britain than Palestine in its present state of latent warfare. The Jews would bring stability to Palestine, plus essential and incontrovertible friendship for England, whereas the Arabs continually provoke trouble, and give the enemies of England —Hitler and Mussolini—incessant opportunity for fishing in a troubled desert. This is the point that activist Jews want Weizmann to make—no matter how often the British say that they must remember their responsibilities to the whole Moslem world, to the Mussulmans of India.

Many Zionists think that Dr. Weizmann does not emphasize sufficiently that the *Palestinian* Arabs made no effort to help Britain in the Great War, though the Jews did. This precedent is particularly relevant now.

Weizmann's positive qualities are many. He has, first of all, courage. Second, like Mr. Gandhi, he has considerable facility for compromise; he is a subtle and competent negotiator. He may be a bit of a prima donna, but his intellectual stature is undisputed. He reads, talks, and writes six languages with complete fluency, of which his favorite is Yiddish; he can perform wonderful tricks with the Yiddish tongue. A famous chemist once said that he would throw away his whole life's work to have written one page of Weizmann. Above all, he is a man of reason, a man of faith founded on rationality, and superbly honest; he never exaggerates, and always tends to understate rather than overstate a case. His eloquent voice is low. For emphasis, he lowers it. Some of his speeches are first-rate political literature. Finally, Weizmann is a man who has contributed so much to his cause that he has become indispensable. Movement and leader are, at the present juncture, one.

Jewish Organization and Other Leaders

At the top is the Jewish Agency, which includes non-Zionists. This is a world organization, represented in both Palestine and London by a Council, of which Dr. Weizmann is head, and an Executive, the chairman of which is David Ben-Gurion. Weizmann attends to policy and relations with the British; Ben-Gurion is the executive administrative officer. The most important branch of the Executive is the Political Department, headed by young Moshe Shertok. This is the liaison office between the Zionists and the Palestine government. If Palestine were ever to become an independent state, as envisaged in Partition, Dr. Weizmann would be President of Palestine, with Ben-Gurion as his first prime minister, and Shertok as minister of foreign affairs. The Jewish Agency is quite distinct from the World Zionist Organization, of which Dr. Weizmann is also president.

Ben-Gurion, the head of the Jewish Agency Executive, is short, compact, energetic, with a mane of white hair; he was born in Poland in 1886, the son of a lawyer, and came to Palestine in what they call the "second wave" of Jewish immigration, that is, in 1906; he worked in Galilee as a farm laborer for a time, and then became one of the first settlers in the Plain of Esdraelon. They say that Ben-Gurion doesn't know his own real name. His father, brought from Poland, lives now in Tel-Aviv; he is known simply as "the father of Ben-Gurion," though in Hebrew "ben" means "son of." Ben-Gurion is an emphatic labor party man, and indeed is the father of the labor movement in Palestine; also he is an author—in Hebrew—of distinction.

Moshe Shertok, the "foreign minister" and the most brilliant of the younger Zionists, was born in Kherson, in South Russia, in 1894. His father, a journalist, believed strongly in Zionism, and came to Palestine in 1906. He settled with his family near Nablus, where they lived in an Arab village, Ain Siniyah, for many years—the only Jews for miles around. Young Moshe learned Arabic in these years, and his intimate childhood knowledge of Arab customs has been very valuable to him. He is, incidentally, a dazzling linguist, speaking Russian, German, Hebrew, Yiddish, Turkish, Arabic,

French and English with equal ease. One of his good friends is Abdulla of Transjordan, with whom he likes to discuss Arabic poetry.

Shertok went to Constantinople to study law, and when the War broke out was conscripted for service in the Turkish army. His career in several curious respects parallels that of Haj Amin, the Arab Mufti; both are about the same age, both served as Turkish officers after training in Constantinople, both returned to Palestine— to become leaders of different sides. When the War ended Shertok gave himself up to the British. An intelligence officer questioned him— in German—and asked him if he knew Mustapha Kemal, later to become dictator of Turkey, and if he thought Kemal could be bought. Shertok said No. Then Shertok spent two years in an Arab village, studying the land, after which he went to England for several years at the London School of Economics. For some time he was a journalist. His future in Palestine is bound to be great. He is an exceedingly attractive personality. One of the greatest American jurists told me recently that he considered Shertok's state papers, reports on the political situation in Palestine and the like, to be unequaled by those of any contemporary government.

The Jewish Agency is, I have noted, composed partly of non-Zionists; the exclusive Zionist organization in Palestine is the celebrated Vaad Leumi, or National Council of Palestine Jews. The Vaad Leumi devotes itself in the main to local affairs, for instance public health, education, local finance, security. The head of the Vaad Leumi is another notable Zionist, Isaac Ben-Zvi.

Ben-Zvi and Ben-Gurion are called the twins. They have been closely associated for many years, and now they head the two parallel organizations which determine Jewish policy in Palestine. Ben-Zvi, an ardent laborite, joined Ben-Gurion to edit the newspaper *Haachdut* (Union) in 1910; they went together to study law in Turkey, and both were deported from Palestine, then under Turkish rule, for Zionist activity, after having received death sentences. They spent the early part of the war in America, and then returned to Palestine to enlist in the Jewish legion. Ben-Zvi and Ben-Gurion worked jointly to found the labor party in Palestine, and to initiate the trade union movement. Ben-Zvi lately has become passionately interested in archeology.

Within Zionism are several political parties. The most important by a considerable margin is the labor party, known usually as

"Mapai," which stands for the initials in Miflegeth Poalei Eretz-Israel (Labor Party of Palestine). The laborites, led by Ben-Gurion, Ben-Zvi, and Shertok, represent about fifty-five percent of the Zionists in the world, and control indisputably the Jewish Agency, the World Zionist Organization, and the Vaad Leumi. The complexion of the labor group is left-center; its trade union, the powerful Histadruth (Labor Federation), is affiliated with the Second Internationale, and has a membership close to 100,000. The members wear a uniform: blue shirts with a red emblem, and khaki shorts. The party is well organized, and draws most of its strength from the *halutzim* (pioneers) on the agricultural colonies; its system of coöperatives is growing. The labor party in Palestine, I heard it said in Jerusalem, differs from any labor movement elsewhere in the world in that (a) it perforce must encourage instead of opposing immigration and (b) it cannot countenance strikes, since Palestine depends for development on encouragement of new capitalist enterprise. Most Histadruth men are no more on the Left than Leon Blum or the British labor party. They detest the communists, who are illegal and underground in Palestine. One thing is quite clear; the labor party is so strong in Palestine that, if ever a Jewish state is set up, it will be a labor state. The laborites say that they built up the country, and that it will remain theirs.

Next come the Centrists, the old-line Zionist party, known as the General Zionists. The core was the old Hovevei Zion (Lovers of Zion) movement which began in the 1880's in Russia. The General Zionists exist in two forms, known as General Zionists A, led by Dr. Weizmann, and General Zionists B, led by the eminent patriot Menahem M. Ussishkin, who for many years was Weizmann's chief political opponent. The "A" group stand squarely in the center; the "B" group veers slightly to the right. There is also a group known as the "Progressives," led by Nahum Goldmann, the Zionist representative at Geneva, which flirts with labor.

Ussishkin is an interesting personality. A fanatic, a man of iron will, an inveterate hater of compromise, he is the "elder statesman" of Zionism; almost alone among eminent Zionists he was bold enough to oppose Partition in 1937-38. Ussishkin is seventy-five to-day. He established a Lovers of Zion movement in Russia in 1882, when he was only nineteen, more than a decade before the work of Herzl. A frugal man, with a tremendous iron obstinacy and almost intolerable stubbornness, he has been a rock of Zionist faith that no misfortune has ever shaken. For eighteen years he was head of the Jewish National Fund, the Karen Kayemeth, which helped settle colonists on the land.

To the right of the Centrists is the Misrachi party, composed of orthodox Jews. Next is the Jewish State party, an offshoot of the "Revisionists" of Vladimir Jabotinsky; they are a kind of "loyal opposition." Outside Zionism are the Agaduth Israel, the organization of fanatically religious orthodox Jews, and finally the Jabotinsky Revisionists, who wear Brown Shirts, who have been outlawed by the Zionist organization, and who are called by their enemies "Jewish Fascists." They stand for complete uncompromising independence. They want to kick the British out, abolish the Arabs somehow, and establish an unadulterated and undiluted Jewish state on both sides of the Jordan.

Jabotinsky, born in Poland about fifty-five years ago, is a man of excessive eloquence, excessive versatility, and explosive ideas. He is a magnetic personality, revered by his followers. Had he not taken an extreme line he would certainly have been Crown Prince of the movement under Weizmann. The British have barred him from Palestine, on account of the alleged incendiary nature of his utterances; he lives in exile, but in London. He likes to say that he devised the Brown Shirt uniform before Hitler did. He was a good officer in the Jewish legion, and probably the best orator that Palestine has produced. His career may develop very considerably if Weizmann should give up the leadership.

A Jewish Defense Force exists, but it has nothing to do with the Revisionists; it is, indeed, run largely—if secretly—by the labor party, who do not get on with the Revisionists at all. The defense force is called the Haganah. It arose out of the necessities of the moment; volunteers organized themselves to protect the lonely and isolated colonies, which were constantly subject to Arab attack. It is extra-legal and it drills secretly, but everyone admits that it exists, even the British. It even encourages secret immigration. The members are armed, but not uniformed. Probably the Haganah can muster 10,000 rifles.

Finally, one should mention a man technically outside politics, who fits into no party category, Dr. Judah Magnes, the rector of the Hebrew University on Mt. Scopus. A humanist, a pacifist, a liberal,

Dr. Magnes is one of the great modern Jews, though his opinions are not popular in Zionist circles, and at times his humanitarianism has made havoc of his judgment. Dr. Magnes, born in San Francisco in 1877, ordained as a rabbi in Cincinnati in 1900, is the great exponent in Palestine of a policy of complete conciliation with the Arabs. He thinks that a bi-national state is possible, and that the Arabs can be won over to friendly coöperation with the Jews. Like Ussishkin, he opposed Partition.

Chapter XXXVI
Circumnavigation Complete

~~~~~~

S O NOW, on the shores of the Mediterranean, within virtual sight—or gunshot—of Europe, our circumnavigation of the continent of Asia, which began some 10,000 miles away on the Sea of Japan, is complete.

This book is far too long to burden with a formal summary or conclusion. In any case, most of the chapters carry their own conclusions, implicitly if not explicitly. It remains, perhaps, to indicate a few specific trends, to adumbrate a final horizon view.

As to single countries, one might say the following:

Japan is on the march. The march is cruel and vigorous. Japan has the youthful obstreperousness, plus a unique sense of discipline, of an expanding state; it combines with the "legitimate" reasons for expansion a strong religious impulse, a kind of divine imperial mission, which makes it doubly formidable. Nothing will stop Japan except force—force stronger than Japan's—or, conceivably, social upheaval following grave military disaster.

And China, old as Japan is young, charming as Japan is crude, amiable as Japan is sinister, cultivated and gracious as Japan is dynamic and efficient, is in the grip of a convulsion partly of disintegration, partly of rebirth. The Chinese, surviving a terrific ordeal, are in a state of metamorphosis. There may be two Chinas, a Japanese China, a Chinese China. The old China, in more than a political sense, is gone.

In India, vastly numerous people are struggling for the sunlight of education, of freedom from religious shibboleth, of modern advance and political independence. It is not merely the British who govern India, who impede the growth of effective Indian nationalism. It is the Hindu religion, the strictures of mythology and of the caste system, and the ponderous decay of centuries of outworn tradition, which contribute to responsibility.

The Japanese push south, west, southwest. They will sooner or later encounter, first the Russians, who sit somberly and wait, second what is left of the British Empire—which is quite a lot. If they turn east, they may meet the United States.

The British control their incredible coagulation of territory not so much by Machiavellian shrewdness in diplomacy or power of arms, but by a subtle combination of luck, tenacity, intuition, and prestige. Several times we have mentioned those thirty or forty youngsters in dinner jackets who rule ten thousand square miles with a swagger stick. The British lose every battle, it has been said— except the last one.

And now to basic trends. What dominant chords do we find in the vast and complex Asiatic orchestra?

First and overwhelmingly, there is imperialism. Capitalize it. Imperialism. Because it was rich, because it was undeveloped, because it was comatose politically, Asia has been for generations the loot of Europe. The history of modern Asia has been that of predatory western powers struggling among themselves for the rich and prostrate body of the eastern continent. Geographically, Europe is an appendage of Asia. The appendage has wagged—and perhaps poisoned—the main body.

The Japanese, being good mimics, and being on the surface the most westernized of Asiatic peoples, promptly learned to imitate the west in this matter of imperialism. Hence the occupation of Manchukuo and Inner Mongolia, and the war in China.

Second, Asia is par excellence the continent of religious bondage and repression. Religion is an infinitely more powerful political force in Asia than in Europe. Asia is a serf to God. Japan is a prisoner of Shinto, and India of the Brahmans. The religious attitude leads to mysticism, as in Japan and India, to resignation, as in China, to a vicious degree of sectarian struggle, as in India, Iraq, Syria, and the Near East generally, and to murder, as in Palestine.

The Mohammedan religion, admirable in many of its qualities, has one dominant characteristic. It is the most militant of the great religions. The Koran (iii, 159) says, "Count not those who are killed in the way of God as dead, but living with their Lord," and (iv, 86), "If they (the disbelievers) turn their backs, then seize them and kill them wheresoever ye find them." There are about 250,000,000 Mohammedans in Asia. (This is not to say, of course, that in Islam there are not many thousands of splendid, peace-loving men.)

Religion in Asia produces, too, a sense of the past rather than of the present, a sense of looking backward, not forward. Much of Asia is possessed by demonology. Even westerners, T. E. Lawrence of instance, are viewed mystically. Much of Asia is ruined by its ruins.

Third, the poverty of Asia is unspeakably greater than any poverty known in the western world. A cause of this is the shockingly high birth-rate.

Fourth, the growth of Asiatic nationalism has been considerable despite these obstacles. China, the Mongolias, the Philippines, Siam, the Burmese, Persia, and all the Arab peoples have felt the sweet sting of national spirit, the surge and uplift of desire for authentic independence.

Fifth, and closely allied with nationalism, has been a slow, bitter, and tenacious struggle for democracy. This is particularly notable in India. Associated with the growth of democratic institutions has been a gradual—a very gradual—development of education. But illiteracy remains greater in China, in India, in the Middle East, than any comparable regions in the world.

Sixth, we must mention again the family system, and the fact that family groups are more cohesive in Asia than in the west, and play a far greater rôle in politics. In Europe domination of a country by a single family is unknown to the extent that the Soongs dominate China, or the Husein family the countries of the Middle East. Family feuds in the west seldom have the political significance that they have, for instance, in Jerusalem. No ruling caste in any European country has anything like the ramifying power of, say, the Fujiwaras in Japan.

Nevertheless, seventh, personality is almost as important in Asia as in Europe. Very nearly each country is dominated by a man. What would contemporary China be without Chiang Kai-shek, India without Gandhi, the Philippines without Quezon, Arabia without Ibn Saud, Iran without Reza Pahlevi? These men are—men.

Eighth, the social struggle that stimulates, provokes, or undermines so much of Europe is largely absent in Asia. The Japanese are experimenting with a form of state capitalism in Manchukuo. In China, a Red Army valiantly continues to conduct the guerrilla struggle, and in India Mr. Nehru is a socialist. But, by and large, partly because so much of Asia has been under the influence of imperialist tradition (and also because of the hampering factor of religious conservatism), very little consciousness of modern social forces exists.

Ninth, I believe—I hope my Asiatic friends will not think the less of me for saying so—that by and large Asiatics are less generally competent than Europeans. Of course, this generalization is crude. I do not mean that Asiatics are less intelligent than Europeans. The Chinese, I think, are the most intelligent people in the world; and in recent years India has had three Nobel prize winners. But, possibly because of generations of poverty and lack of education, Asiatics seem in general to have less stamina than westerners; they lack solidity, they lack shoulders.

Finally, Pan-Asia is an illusion. One can speak of Europe—even now—as a whole. But not Asia. One can speak of such a concept—at least till recently—as a "European mind." I do not think one would readily use such a phrase as an "Asiatic mind." A war in Spain can send tremors throughout Europe as far as the Baltic and beyond; a war in China is still only of remote, vestigial interest to the Asia of the Near East. Asia is not interlocked, intertwined, as Europe is, though it is interlocked *with* Europe. The Japanese are on the march—even in Teheran I saw a brand of Japanese canned goods known as Geisha sardines—but Asia is a long distance around. It is too big to be a unit. It is three continents in one.

THE END

Acknowledgments

~~~~~~

THIS book represents a long period of travel, research, and study. It would have been impossible to write but for the freely-given help by friends. In every country from Japan to Palestine I was the fortunate recipient of generous information, and a list of friends and acquaintances who helped me would run to several hundred names. Since it would be unwise in some cases to indicate the source of my material, I must, as in *Inside Europe*, content myself with a broad general acknowledgment.

Inside Europe had a wide sale in fourteen languages; it was reviewed comprehensively and I have received many letters about it and have listened to criticism in several countries. So far not more than a dozen or so errors of fact, mostly minor, have been detected among the many thousands of facts that book contained. I wonder if I can dare to hope that the same general level of accuracy is maintained in this book? Facts are evasive and elusive in Oriental lands. But I have arduously checked and double-checked every name, every date, every event, and parts of the manuscript have been checked by experts. I must cordially thank Mr. Stuart Chase, Mr. Walter Mallory, and Mr. Archibald MacLeish for reading the proofs in whole or in part.

Inside Europe was written fresh and as a whole, but I did incorporate in it some material I had gathered in previous work for the Chicago Daily News as well as several magazines. The case is different in this book. Every word in it is new. *Inside Asia* is fresh from top to bottom. Parts of it, however, were released for serial publication in magazines, and the North American Newspaper Alliance distributed some of my first impressions of China. As a rule, I took advantage of magazine publication to inspect my text anew, and in some cases I completely rewrote it. For permission to reprint serial material, I have the editors of the *Saturday Evening Post*, *Harper's Magazine*, *The Nation*, *Current History*, *Coronet*, *Asia*, the *Atlantic Monthly*, *Foreign Affairs*, and especially the *Reader's Digest* to thank.

I read widely in the preparation of this book. Among the periodicals I searched for background are the *Manchester Guardian*, the *New Statesman*, the *New York Times*, the *New York Herald Tri-*

bune, Foreign Affairs, the bulletins of both the Foreign Policy Association (New York) and the Royal Institute of International Affairs (London), *Asia,* the *London Times, The Hindu* (Madras), the *Palestine Post,* the *Japan Advertiser,* and the *China Weekly Review.* In some cases I read everything relevant for years back.

I read blue books until I was blue in the face. Among those especially valuable were the first volume of the Simon Report on India and the Peel Report on Palestine. Also of great value were the green-bound pamphlets of the Royal Institute of International Affairs, on China and Japan, Egypt, and Palestine.

Finally, I could not have written this book, any more than I could have written *Inside Europe,* without the patient—perhaps I should say impatient—encouragement and active collaboration of my wife, Frances Gunther, who accompanied me on the trip, and who assisted greatly in every aspect of the work.

J. G.

Bibliography

Abend, Hallett: "Tortured China," New York, 1932.
Abend, Hallett, and Billingham, Anthony J.: "Can China Survive?" New York, 1936.
Angell, Sir Norman: "This Have and Have Not Business," London, 1936.
Antonius, George: "The Arab Awakening," London, 1938.
Armstrong, H. C.: "Lord of Arabia," London, 1938.
Barton, Sir William: "The Princes of India," London, 1934.
Berkov, Robert: "Strong Man of China," Boston, 1938.
Bertram, James M.: "Crisis in China," London, 1937.
Bisson, T. A.: "Japan in China," New York, 1938.
Bose, Subhas C.: "The Indian Struggle," London, 1935.
Caballero, Isabelo P., and Concepción, M. de Gracía: "Quezon," Manila, 1935.
Causton, E. E. N.: "Militarism and Foreign Policy in Japan," London, 1936.
Chamberlain, Basil Hall: "Things Japanese," Kobe, 1927.
Chamberlin, William Henry: "Japan Over Asia," Boston, 1937.
Chatterjee, Lalitmohan and Mookerjee, Syamaprasad: "Representative Indians," Calcutta, 1936.
Chiang Kai-shek, General and Madame: "General Chiang Kai-shek," New York, 1937.
China Weekly Review: "Who's Who in China," Shanghai, 1936.
Colegrove, Kenneth W.: "Militarism in Japan," Boston, 1936.
"Congress Presidential Address," Madras, 1934.
Couling, Samuel: "The Encyclopaedia Sinica," Shanghai, 1917.
Crow, Carl: "Handbook for China," Shanghai, 1933.
Crow, Carl: "Four Hundred Million Customers," New York, 1937.
Crow, Carl: "Master Kung," London, 1937.
Cumming, Sir John (ed.): "Modern India," London, 1932.
Cumming, Sir John (ed.): "Political India," London, 1932.
Darling, Malcolm Lyall: "The Punjab Peasant in Prosperity and Debt," London, 1932.
Darling, Malcolm Lyall: "Wisdom and Waste in the Punjab Village," London, 1934.
Dubois, Abbe J. A., and Beauchamp, Henry K.: "Hindu Manners, Customs and Ceremonies," Oxford, 1936.
Eddy, J. P., and Lawton, F. H.: "India's New Constitution," London, 1935.

Filmer, Henry: "The Pageant of Persia," Indianapolis, 1936.

Fortune, Japanese Number (September, 1936), New York, 1936.

Fry, Varian: "War in China," New York, 1938.

Gandhi, M. K.: "The Story of My Experiments with Truth," Vols. I, II, Ahmedabad, 1929, 1933.

Gannett, Lewis S.: "Young China," New York, 1927.

Gauba, Kanhayalal: "H. H., or, The Pathology of Princes," Lahore, 1930.

Gibson, Ashley: "The Malay Peninsula and Archipelago," London, 1928.

Gilbert, Rodney: "What's Wrong with China," New York, 1932.

Hart, Henry H.: "Seven Hundred Chinese Proverbs. Stanford, 1937.

Hawkridge, Emma: "Indian Gods and Kings," Boston, 1935.

Hedges, Frank H.: "In Far Japan," Tokyo, 1935.

Herrmann, Albert: "Atlas of China," Cambridge, 1935.

Hsu, Shuhsi: "The North China Problem," Shanghai, 1937.

Hudson, G. F.: "The Far East in World Politics," Oxford, 1937.

Hutton, Graham: "Is It Peace?" New York, 1937.

The Indian Year Book, 1937-38, Bombay.

"Indictment of Patiala," Bombay, 1930.

Ireland, Philip Willard: "Iraq," London, 1937.

Jackson, J. Hampden: "The Post-war World," London, 1935.

The Japan Year Book, 1937, Tokyo.

The Japan-Manchukuo Year Book, 1938, Tokyo.

Johnston, Reginald F.: "Twilight in the Forbidden City," London, 1934.

Joüon, Rene: "Geographie Commerciale de la Chine," Shanghai, 1937.

Junior Hadassah: "A Primer on Palestine," New York, 1933.

Karlgren, Bernhard: "Sound and Symbol in Chinese," London, 1929.

Kastein, Josef: "History and Destiny of the Jews," New York, 1936.

Keir, David: "Guide to the Indian Problem," London, 1935.

Lamb, Gene: "A Tabloid History of China," Tientsin, 1936.

Lattimore, Owen: "Manchuria, Cradle of Conflict," New York, 1935.

Lin Yutang: "My Country and My People," London, 1936.

Lin Yutang (ed.): "The Wisdom of Confucius," New York, 1938.

Lo, R. Y.: "China's Revolution from the Inside," New York, 1930.

Lyall, L. A.: "China," New York, 1934.

Lynn, Jermyn Chi-hung: "Political Parties in China," Tientsin, 1930.

MacMunn, Lt. Gen. Sir George: "The Indian States and Princes," London, 1934.

Manshardt, Clifford: "The Hindu-Muslim Problem in India," London, 1936.

Margoliouth, D. S.: "Mohammedanism," London, 1936.

Mathews, Basil: "India Reveals Herself," London, 1937.

May, Henry John: "Little Yellow Gentlemen," London, 1937.

Mayo, Katherine: "Mother India," New York, 1934.

Millis, Walter: "The Future of Sea Power in the Pacific," New York, 1935.

Mitsui, The House of: "A Record of Three Centuries: Past History and Present Enterprises," Tokyo, 1937.

Mowrer, E. A.: "The Dragon Wakes," New York, 1939.

Nehru, Jawaharlal: "Glimpses of World History," Vols. I, II, Allahabad, 1934, 1935.

Nehru, Jawaharlal: "An Autobiography," London, 1936.

O'Malley, L. S. S.: "Indian Caste Customs," Cambridge, 1932.

Peffer, Nathaniel: "Must We Fight in Asia?" New York, 1935.

Popper, David H.: "The Puzzle of Palestine," New York, 1938.

Quirino, Carlos: "Quezon, Man of Destiny," Manila, 1935.

Redman, H. Vere: "Japan in Crisis," London, 1935.

Rolland, Romain: "Mahatma Gandhi," London, 1931.

Roosevelt, Nicholas: "The Restless Pacific," New York, 1928.

Royal Institute of International Affairs, The: "China and Japan," London, 1938.

Russell, Bertrand: "The Problem of China," London, 1922.

Sansom, G. B.: "Japan, a Short Cultural History," London, 1936.

Shah, K. T.: "Federal Structure," Bombay, 1937.

Shah, K. T.: "Provincial Autonomy," Bombay, 1937.

Shah, The Sirdar Ikbal Ali: "The Controlling Minds of Asia," London, 1937.

Sharman, Lyon: "Sun Yat-sen," New York, 1934.

Sheean, Vincent: "Personal History," New York, 1937.

Simonds, Frank H., and Emery, Brooks: "The Price of Peace," London, 1935.

Smedley, Agnes: "China Fights Back," New York, 1938.

Smith, Arthur H.: "Chinese Characteristics," New York, 1894.

Snow, Edgar: "Far Eastern Front," London, 1934.

Snow, Edgar: "Red Star Over China," New York, 1938.

Sokolsky, George E.: "The Tinder Box of Asia," London, 1933.

Stein, Guenther: "Made in Japan," London, 1935.

Stein, Guenther: "Far East in Ferment," London, 1936.

Stimson, Henry L.: "The Far Eastern Crisis," New York, 1936.

Strong, Anna Louise: "One Fifth of Mankind," New York, 1938.

Sun Yat-sen: "The Three Principles," Shanghai, 1927.

T'ang Leang-Li: "The Inner History of the Chinese Revolution," London, 1930.

Tanin, O., and Yohan, E.: "Militarism and Fascism in Japan," London, 1934.

Thomas, Bertram: "The Arabs," New York, 1937.

Tong, Hollington K.: "Chiang Kai-shek," Shanghai, 1937.

Torchiana, H. A. Van Coenen: "Tropical Holland," Chicago, 1921.

Trotsky, Leon: "Problems of the Chinese Revolution," New York, 1932.

Tyau, M. T. Z.: "Two Years of Nationalist China," Shanghai, 1930.

"The Union of Democratic Control: Eastern Menace," London, 1936.

Utley, Freda: "Japan's Feet of Clay," New York, 1937.

" 'Vigilantes': Inquest on Peace," London, 1935.

Vinacke, Harold: "A History of the Far East in Modern Times," New York, 1937.

Wang, Ching-wei: "China's Problems and Their Solution," Shanghai, 1934.

Ward, C. H. S.: "Outline of Buddhism," London, 1934.

Wells, H. G.: "The Outline of History," London, 1932.

Woodhead, H. G. W. (ed.): "China Year Book, 1938," Shanghai.

Young, Morgan A.: "Imperial Japan," New York, 1938.

Ziff, William B.: "The Rape of Palestine," New York, 1938.

Index

DATE DUE
